THE

ARMY LIST

2015

PART 1

Dandy Booksellers has sourced personnel entries from the Ministry of Defence Supplements of The London Gazette and compiled a dataset of personnel as of 1st March 2016. Details of major army and defence appointments have been sourced from governmental and army websites. Every precaution has been taken to make sure that the information contained in the Army List is correct at the time of publication. We cannot accept any liability for errors or omissions. Applications for reproduction should be made in writing to Dandy Booksellers Ltd, Units 3 & 4, 31-33 Priory Park Road, London NW6 7UP.

ISBN-13 978-1-78732-139-7

Dandy Booksellers Ltd

Published by Dandy Booksellers Ltd and available from:

Online

www.dandybooksellers.com

Mail, Telephone, Fax & Email

Dandy Booksellers Ltd

Units 3 & 4, 31-33 Priory Park Road, London NW6 7UP

Telephone orders / General enquiries: +44 (0)20 7624 2993

Fax orders: +44 (0)20 7624 5049

Email: enquiries@dandybooksellers.com

Published by Dandy Booksellers Limited

Typesetting by Dandy Booksellers Limited

Printed in the UK by Dandy Booksellers Limited

CONTENTS

NOTES

General

This publication of the Army List (Part1) is divided into four sections as follows:

a. *Section I* Contains military appointments and honorary ranks of Her Majesty The Queen and members of the Royal Family, appointments to the Queen, the Sovereign's Bodyguard and the Military Knights of Windsor.

b. *Section II* Contains details of major Defence and Army appointments, headquarters, establishments and agencies. This section also includes entries for affiliated institutions, military appointments of Commonwealth governments (including military reperesentives in the United Kingdom) and attachés & advisers of British Embassies in foreign countries.

c. *Section III* Contains regimental and corps lists of officers on the Active List of the Regular Army.

d. *Section IV* Contains regimental and corps lists of officers of the Army Reserve (formerly knwon as the Territorial Army) and the Army's Cadet Forces (Combined Cadet Force (Army) and the Army Cadet Force).

Part I

Editing

Every effort has been made to make this edition as accurate as possible. Personnel data has been sourced from the Ministry of Defence Supplements of The London Gazette and compiled to produce a dataset of personnel as of 1st March 2016. It is therefore possible that some detail will be incorrect as promotions, awards, etc. promulgated prior to this date may not have been included in the supplements. The Editor regrets any inaccuracy and difficulties this may cause, and will endeavour to ensure that corrections appear in the next edition.

This publication contains Sections I, II, III and IV. Section II is a *condensed* version of the 2005 official edition of this publication. This is due to unavailable or unconfirmed data.

The Senior Officer List

The Senior Officer List in Section III show Field Marshals and Former Chiefs of the General Staff classified by seniority date and date of appointment respectively. The listings of senior officers, in both Section III and Section IV, from Generals down to and including Colonels are shown under their substantive ranks and in alphabetical order by surname. Lieutenant Colonels and below are listed under their parent regimental or corps lists classified by suibstantive rank and in alphabetical order by surname. Honorary Colonel and Commandant appointments have been provided (date of appointment and date tenure expires) whereever possible.

Please note that the last official edition of this publication (2005) listed officers under their substantive rank and seniority date. This method of classification has been revised by Dandy Booksellers in all subsequent editions of the Army list aiming to promote easier referencing for readers. The term Graduation List has been rephrased in this edition as the Senior Officer List to reflect this change.

Amalgamated Regiments and Corps

Notes on amalgamated regiments and corps are shown at the beginning of respective entries.

Post Nominals

Post nominals are shown for all personnel, military or civilian where available.

Editorial Staff

Editor .... Miss Catherine Hooper

SYMBOLS AND ABBREVIATIONS

Symbol	*Short Title*
adp	Advanced Automatic Data Processing Course
ae	Long Aeronautical Engineering Course
aic	Long Armour/Infantry Course
ais	Advanced Information Systems Course
asq	Aerosystems Course
ato	Ammunition Technical Officer's Course
aws	Air Warfare Course
c	Long Civil Engineering Course
cafs	Combat Arms Fighting Systems Course
cl	Post-Graduate Personnel Management Course
df	Defence Fellow
dis	Design of Infonnation -Systems Course
dlm	Defence Logistic Management Course
dtc	Defence Technology Course
E	Long Electrical Engineering Course
ee	Long Electronic Engineering Course
ENG	Long Engineering Course
em	Long Electrical and Mechanical Course
eoe	Explosive Ordnance Engineer
fs	RAOC Officers Food Supply Course
g†	Instructor-in-Gunnery (AA)
g	Instructor-in-Gunnery (Field)
g(a)	In.structor-in-Gunnery (Air Defence)
g(gw)	Instructor-in-Gunnery (Guided Weapons)
g(s)	Instructor-in-Gunnery (Surface to Surface Guided Weapons)
g(ss)	Instructpr-in-Gunnery (Surface to Surface)
g(y)	Instructor-in-Gunnery (Locating)
gsd	Gun System Design Course
gw	Guided Weapons Course
hcsc	Higher Command and Staff Course
hp	Half Pay
I*	Interpreter First Class
I	Interpreter Second Class
idc	Imperial Defence College Course
ifp	International Fellows Programme
im	Industrial Administration Course
jsc	Graduate of WRAC Staff College
jsdc	Joint Services Defence College Course
jssc	Joint Services Staff College Course
lc	Long Civil Catering Course
lcc	LCL Command Certificate (Ocean Going)
M	Long Mechanical Course
mda	Master of Defence Administration Course
me	Long Mechanical Engineering Course
mese	Military Electronic Systems Engineering Course
mvt	Military Vehicles Technology Course
nadc	NATO Defence College Course
ndc	National Defence College Course
ocws(US)	US Air War College Course
ocds()	Overseas College of Defence Studies Course
odc()	Overseas Defence College Course
olpm	Officers Long Port and Maritime Course
o	Ordnance Officers Course
osc()	Overseas Staff College Course
owc	LCL Watch-Keeping Certificate (Ocean Going)
p	Officers Long Plant Course
pc	Postal & Courier Officer Course
pfc	Long Finance and Accountancy Course
ph	Rotary Wing Pilot
ph(i)	Rotary Wing BI Flying Instructor
ph(cfs)	Rotary Wing A2 Flying Instructor
ph(cfs*)	Rotary Wing AI Flying Instructor
pi	Long Petroleum Installation Course
pl	Fixed Wing Pilot
pl(i)	Fixed Wing BI Flying Instructor
pl(cfs)	Fixed Wing A2 Flying Instructor
pl(cfs*)	Fixed Wing AI Flying Instructor
psc(J)	Advanced Command and Staff Course at the Joint Services Command and Staff College
psc†	Army Staff Course (Division I or II at RMCS followed by Staff College Camberley)
psc()†	Army Staff Course (Division I or II at RMCS followed by Staff College in Australia, India or Pakistan)
psc	Army Staff Course (Division III at RMCS followed by Staff College Camberley)
psc()	Army Staff Course (Division III at RMCS followed by Staff College in Australia, India or Pakistan. Alternatively Staff College in Canada or Germany without attending RMCS)
psc(n)†	Naval Staff Course (preceded by Division I or II at RMCS)
psc(n)	Naval Staff Course (preceded by Division III at RMCS)
psc(a)†	Air Force Staff Course (preceded by Division I or II at RMCS)
psc(a)	Air ForceStaff Course (preceded by Division III at RMCS)
psm	Advanced Certificate of Royal Military School of Music
ptsc	Technical Staff Course
qs	Staff Course RAF Staff College
qtm	Joint Targetting Mission Support Course
rcds	Royal College of Defence Studies Course
rly	Railway Course
s	Food Technology Course
sowc	Senior Officers' War Course, Royal Naval College, Greenwich
sq	Staff qualified (other than at aStaff College)
sq(V)	Staff Qualified (TA)
sq(w)	Staff Qualified Weapons
svy	Army Survey Course
svy(cg)	Advanced Cartography Course
svy(gy)	Advanced Geodesy Course
svy(pg)	Advanced Photogrammetry Course
svy(pr)	Advanced Printing Course
t	Advanced Transport Course
t*	Advanced Transportation Course (US)
tacsc	TA Command and Staff Course
te	Telecommunicationns Engineering Course
tem	Telecommunication Engineering Management Course
tn	Long Transportation Course
tp	Empire Test Pilots' Course
tt	Tank Technology Course
wes	Weapons Effects Simulation Course
y	Instructor in Counter-Bombardment
+	Army Staff Course Div 1 or Div 2 RMCS
†	On probation (before entry)
††	University Medical or Dental Cadet (before entry)
Ø	Denotes a female officer (not QARANC)
¶	Non-regular Permanent Staff (AR only)

ORDERS, DECORATIONS AND MEDALS

VC ....Victoria Cross

GC ....George Cross

KG ....Knight of the Order of the Garter

KT ....Knight of the Order of the Thistle

OM ....Member of the Order of Merit

GCB ......Knight Grand Cross or Dame Grand Cross of the Order of the Bath

GCMG ...Knight Grand Cross of the Order of St Michael and St George

GCVO ...Knight Grand Cross or Dame Grand Cross of the Royal Victorian Order

GBE ....Knight Grand Cross or Dame Grand Cross of the Order of the British Empire

CH ....Member of the Order of the Companion of Honour

KCB ......Knight Commander of the Order of the Bath

KCMG ...Knight Commander of the Order of St Michael and St George

KCVO ...Knight Commander of the Royal Victorian Order

DCVO ...Dame Commander of the Royal Victorian Order

KBE ....Knight Commander of the Order of the British Empire

DBE ....Dame Commander of the Order of the British Empire

CB ....Companion of the Order of the Bath

CMG .....Companion of the Order of St Michael and St George

CVO ......Commander of the Royal Victorian Order

CBE ....Commander of the Order of the British Empire

DSO ....Companion of the Distinguished Service Order

LVO ....Lieutenant of the Royal Victorian Order

OBE ....Officer of the Order of the British Empire

MVO .....Member of the Royal Victorian Order

MBE ......Member of the Order of the British Empire

CGC ......Conspicuous Gallantry Cross

RRC ....Member of the Royal Red Cross

DSC ....Distinguished Service Cross

MC ....Military Cross

DFC ....Distinguished Flying Cross

AFC ....Air Force Cross

ARRC ....Associate of the Royal Red Cross

GM ....George Medal

QGM .....The Queen's Gallantry Medal

BEM ......British Empire Medal

RVM ......Royal Victoria Medal

TD ....Territorial Decoration or Efficiency Decoration (Obsolescent)

QVRM ...Queen's Volunteer Reserves Medal

QSO........Queen's Service Order

• ....Denotes the award of a bar to a decoration or medal for valour. The award of additional bars is indicated by the addition of a further similar symbol for each award.

REGIMENTAL AND CORPS ABBREVIATIONS

AAC.......................Army Air Corps
AGC.......................Adjutant General's Corps
AGC(ALS).............Adjutant General's Corps (Army Legal Services Branch)
AGC(ETS).............Adjutant General's Corps (Educational and Training Services Branch
AGC(MPS)............Adjutant General's Corps (Provost Branch)
AGC(RMP)............Adjutant General's Corps (Royal Military Police)
AGC(SPS)..............Adjutant General's Corps (Staff and Personnel Support Branch)
APTC.....................Army Physical Training Corps
CAMUS.................Corps of Army Music
COLDM GDS........Coldstream Guards - Guard's Division
GREN GDS...........Grenadier Guards - Guard's Division
GSC........................General Service Corps
HAC.......................Honourable Artillery Company (TA), Royal Artillery
HLDS.....................The Highlanders
IG...........................Irish Guards - Guard's Division
INT CORPS...........Intelligence Corps
KRH.......................The Kings's Royal Hussars - RAC
LANCS..................The Duke of Lancaster's Regiment - King's Division
LD..........................The Light Dragoons - RAC
LG..........................The Life Guards - Household Cavalry
LONDONS............The London Regiment (TA) - Guard's Division
MERCIAN.............The Mercian Regiment - Prince of Wales's Division
OTC........................Officer Training Corps
PARA.....................The Parachute Regiment
PWRR....................Princess of Wales's Royal Regiment - Queen's Division
QARANC...............Queen Alexandra's Royal Army Nursing Corps
QDG.......................1st The Queen's Dragoon Guards - RAC
QGE.......................The Queen's Gurkha Engineers - Brigade of Gurkha's
QG SIGNALS........The Queen's Gurkha Signals - Brigade of Gurkha's
QOGLR..................The Queen's Own Gurkha Logistic Regiment - Brigade of Gurkha's
QRH.......................The Queen's Royal Hussars - RAC
QRL........................The Queen's Royal Lancers - RAC
RA..........................Royal Regiment of Artillery
R ANGLIAN..........The Royal Anglian Regiment - Queen's Division
RAC.......................Royal Armoured Corps
RAChD..................Royal Army Chaplains' Department
RADC....................Royal Army Dental Corps
RAMC....................Royal Army Medical Corps
RAVC.....................Royal Army Veterinary Corps
RDG.......................The Royal Dragoon Guards - RAC
RE..........................Corps of Royal Engineers
REME....................Corps of Royal Electrical and Mechanical Engineers
RG..........................The Royal Gibraltar Regiment
RGR.......................The Royal Gurkha Rifle's - Brigade of Gurkha's
RHG/D...................The Blues And Royals - Household Cavalry
RIFLES..................The Rifles
R IRISH.................The Royal Irish Regiment
RL...........................The Royal Lancers - RAC
RLC........................Royal Logistics Corps
RRF........................The Royal Regiment of Fusiliers - Queen's Division
R SIGNALS...........Royal Corps of Signals
RTR........................The Royal Tank Regiment - RAC
R WELSH..............The Royal Welsh - Prince of Wales's Division
SAS........................Special Air Service Regiment
SASC......................Small Arms School Corps
SCOTS...................Royal Regiment of Scotland - Scottish Division
SCOTS DG............The Royal Scots Dragoon Guards - RAC
SG..........................Scots Guards - Guard's Division
WG.........................Welsh Guards - Guard's Division
YORKS..................The Yorkshire Regiment - King's Division
9/12L......................9th/12th Royal Lancers - RAC

ARMY RESERVE

UNIT TITLES WHICH DIFFER FROM THOSE OF REGULAR UNITS

HAC ....The Honourable Artillery Company

HIGHLAND ....51st Highland Regiment

KCR ....The King's and Cheshire Regiment

LONDONS ....The London Regiment

LOWLAND ....52nd Lowland Regiment

QOY ....The Queen's Own Yeomanry

RANGERS.............The Royal Irish Rangers

RMLY......................The Royal Mercian and Lancastrian Yeomanry

R MON RE(M) ......The Royal Monmouthshire Royal Engineers (Militia)

RIFLE VOL ....The Rifle Volunteers

RWR........................The Royal Welsh Regiment

R Wx Y...................The Royal Wessex Yeomanry

RY ....The Royal Yeomanry

SNIY ....Scottish and Northern Irish Yeomanry

PRECEDENCE OF REGIMENT AND CORPS, ETC

1. The Life Guards and The Blues and Royals (Royal Horse Guards and 1st Dragoons)
2. Royal Horse Artillery (a)
3. Royal Armoured Corps
4. Royal Regiment of Artillery (Royal Horse Artillery excepted)
5. Corps of Royal Engineers
6. Royal Corps of Signals
7. Regiments of Foot Guards
8. Regiments of Infantry (b) (c)
9. Special Air Service Regiment
10. Army Air Corps
11. Royal Army Chaplain's Department
12. The Royal Logistics Corps
13. Royal Army Medical Corps
14. Corps of Royal Electrical and Mechanical Engineers
15. Adjutant-General's Corps
16. Royal Army Veterinary Corps
17. Small Arms School Corps
18. Royal Army Dental Corps
19. Intelligence Corps
20. Army Physical Training Corps
21. General Service Corps
22. Queen Alexandra's Royal Army Nursing Corps
23. Corps of Army Music
24. The Royal Monmouthshire Royal Engineers (Militia) (Territorial Army)
25. The Honourable Artillery Company (Territorial Army)
26. Territorial Army (other than 24 and 25) (d)
27. The Royal Gibraltar Regiment
28. The Bermuda Regiment

(a) But on parade, with their guns, to take the right and march at the head of the Househld Cavalry.

(b) The precedence of the individual infantry regiments remains as it was before the grouping of infantry regiments was introduced.

(c) The Royal Marines are no longer in the Army order of precedence, but now assume precedence within the Royal Navy at all times.

(d) In order of arms as for the Regular Army.

PRECEDENCE OF ROYAL ARMOURED CORPS REGIMENTS

1st the Queen's Dragoon Guards
The Royal Scots Dragoon Guards (Carabiniers and Greys)
The Royal Dragoon Guards
The Queen's Royal Hussars (The Queen's Own and Royal Irish)
The Royal Lancers
The King's Royal Hussars
The Light Dragoons
Regiments of the Royal Tank Regiment

PRECEDENCE OF REGIMENTS OF FOOTGUARDS

Grenadier Guards
Coldstream Guards
Scots Guards
Irish Guards
Welsh Guards

PRECEDENCE OF REGULAR INFANTRY REGIMENTS

The Royal Regiment of Scotland
The Princess of Wales' Royal Regiment (Queen and Royal Hampshire's)
The Duke of Lancaster's Regiment (King's, Lancashire and Border)
The Royal Regiment of Fusiliers
The Royal Anglian Regiment
The Rifles
The Yorkshire Regiment
The Mercian Regiment
The Royal Welsh
The Royal Irish Regiment
The Parachute Regiment
The Royal Gurkha Rifles

PRECEDENCE WITHIN THE ADJUTANT GENERAL'S CORPS

AGC (Support and Personnel Support Branch)

AGC (Royal Military Police)

AGC (Military Provost Staff)

AGC (Educational and Training Services Branch)

AGC (Army Legal Services Branch)

PRECEDENCE OF YEOMANRY REGIMENTS

The Royal Yeomanry

The Royal Wessex Yeomanry

The Royal Mercian and Lancastrian Yeomanry (disbanding 2015)

The Queen's Own Yeomanry

Scottish and Northern Irish Yeomanry

PRECEDENCE OF ARMY RESERVE INFANTRY REGIMENTS

6 SCOTS ....6th (Volunteer) Battalion SCOTS

7 SCOTS ....7th (Volunteer) Battalion SCOTS

3 PWRR ....3rd (Volunteer) Battalion The Princess of Wales's Royal Regiment

LONDONS ....The London Regiment

4 LANCS ....4th (Volunteers) Battalion The Duke of Lancaster's Regiment

5 RRF ....5th (Volunteer) Battalion Royal Regiment of Fusiliers

3 R ANGLIAN.......3rd (Volunteer) Battalion The Royal Anglian Regiment

4 YORKS ....4th Battalion The Yorkshire Regiment

4 MERCIAN ....4th Battalion Mercian Regiment

3 R WELSH ....3rd Battalion The Royal Welsh

2 R IRISH ....2nd Battalion Royal Irish Regiment

4 PARA ....4th Battalion The Parachute Regiment

6 RIFLES ....6th (Volunteer) Battalion The Royal Rifles

7 RIFLES ....7th (Volunteer) Battalion The Royal Rifles

SECTION I

(as at 1st March 2016)

THE QUEEN

COLONEL IN CHIEF:- LG (060252), RHG/D (010469), SCOTS DG (020771), RL, RTR (020653), RE (060252), GREN GDS (060252), COLDM GDS (060252), SG (060252), IG (060252), WG (060252), SCOTS, LANCS, R WELSH, AGC (060492).

AFFILIATED COLONEL IN CHIEF: - QGE (070993)

CAPTAIN GENERAL:- RA (060252), HAC (060252), CCF (020653)

PATRON:- RAChD (060292), ACFA, CCFA

ROYAL COLONEL:- Balaklava Company 5 SCOTS

Commonwealth Forces

COLONEL IN CHIEF:- The Governor General's Horse Guards (of Canada), The King's Own Calgary Regiment (Royal Canadian Armoured Corps), Canadian Military Engineers Branch, Royal 22e Regiment (of Canada), Governor General's Foot Guards (of Canada), The Canadian Grenadier Guards, The Stormont, Dundas and Glengarry Highlanders, Le Regiment de la Chaudiere (of Canada), North Shore (New Brunswick) Regiment, The Royal New Brunswick Regiment, The 48th Highlanders of Canada, The Argyll and Sutherland Highlanders of Canada (Princess Louise's), The Calgary Highlanders, Royal Australian Engineers, Royal Australian Infantry Corps, Royal Australian Army Ordnance Corps, Royal Australian Army Nursing Corps, The Corps of Royal New Zealand Engineers, Royal New Zealand Infantry Regiment, The Malawi Rifles

CAPTAIN GENERAL:- Royal Regiment of Canadian Artillery, Royal Regiment of Australian Artillery, Royal Regiment of New Zealand Artillery, Royal New Zealand Armoured Corps

Private Secretary to HM The Queen
The Rt Hon Edward Young *CVO*
Office: Buckingham Palace, London SW1A 1AA Tel: 020 7930 4832

MEMBERS OF THE ROYAL FAMILY

Field Marshal His Royal Highness The Prince Philip Duke of Edinburgh KG KT OM GBE ONZ QSO AK GCL CC CMM ADC(P)

FIELD MARSHAL (150153)

COLONEL IN CHIEF:- QRH (100402), RIFLES (010207), REME (010769), INT CORPS (110677), ACF (150153)

COLONEL:- GREN GDS (010375)

ROYAL COLONEL:- The Highlanders 4 SCOTS (280306)

MEMBER: Honourable Artillery Company (1957), ACF Association (Jan 1962)

Commonwealth Forces

FIELD MARSHAL:- Australian Military Forces (010454), New Zealand Army (110677)

GENERAL:- Royal Canadian Army

COLONEL IN CHIEF:- The Royal Canadian Regiment (1953), The Royal Hamilton Light Infantry (Wentworth Regiment of Canada) (1978), Duke of Edinburgh's Own Cameron Highlanders of Ottawa (1967), The Queen's Own Cameron Highlanders of Canada (1967), The Seaforth Highlanders of Canada (1967),The Royal Canadian Army Cadets (1953), The Royal Australian Corps of Electrical and Mechanical Engineers (1959), The Australian Army Cadet Corps (1963)

GENERAL:- Royal Canadian Army (Jun 2011)

HONORARY COLONEL:- The Trinidad and Tobago Regiment (1964)

Field Marshal His Royal Highness The Prince of Wales KG KT GCB OM AK QSO ADC(P)

FIELD MARSHAL (160612)

COLONEL IN CHIEF:- QDG (010703), MERCIAN (010907), RDG (310792), PARA (110677), RGR (110677),AAC (010392)

COLONEL:- WG (010375)

ROYAL COLONEL:- Black Watch 3 SCOTS (280306), 51st Highland 7 SCOTS (TA) (280306)

ROYAL HONORARY COLONEL:- QOY (230500)

Commonwealth Forces

FIELD MARSHAL: - New Zealand Army (030815)

COLONEL IN CHIEF:- The Royal Canadian Dragoons, Lord Strathcona's Horse (Royal Canadians), Royal Regiment of Canada, Royal Winnipeg Rifles, Royal Australian Armoured Corps, The Royal Pacific Islands Regiment, Black Watch (Royal Highland Regiment) of Canada, Toronto Scottish Regiment, 2nd Battalion Irish Regiment of Canada (090515).

Her Royal Highness The Duchess of Cornwall GCVO

ROYAL COLONEL:- 4th Battalion RIFLES (010206)

Commonwealth Forces

COLONEL IN CHIEF:- The Queen's Own Rifles of Canada, Royal Australian Corps of Military Police

Major His Royal Highness The Duke of Cambridge KG KT ADC(P)

ROYAL COLONEL:- IG (100211)

Capt His Royal Highness Prince Henry of Wales

CAPTAIN:- RHG/D

His Royal Highness The Duke of York KG GCVO ADC(P)

COLONEL IN CHIEF:- YORKS, R IRISH (010692), SASC (010703)

ROYAL COLONEL:- The Royal Highland Fusiliers 2 SCOTS

DEPUTY COLONEL IN CHIEF:- The Royal Lancers

Commonwealth Forces

COLONEL IN CHIEF:- The Queen's York Rangers (1st American Regiment), Royal New Zealand Army Logistics Regiment, The Royal Highland Fusiliers of Canada; The Princess Louise Fusiliers (Canada)

His Royal Highness The Earl of Wessex KG GCVO ADC(P)

ROYAL COLONEL:- 2nd Battalion RIFLES (010207)

ROYAL HONORARY COLONEL:- R Wx Y (010703), LONDONS (010511)

Commonwealth Forces

COLONEL IN CHIEF:- The Hastings and Prince Edward Regiment (041002), Saskatchewan Dragoon (120603), The Prince Edward Island Regiment (310505)

Her Royal Highness The Countess of Wessex GCVO

COLONEL IN CHIEF:- QARANC (010703), CAMUS (010907)

ROYAL COLONEL:- 5th Battalion RIFLES (010207)

Commonwealth Forces

COLONEL IN CHIEF:- The Lincoln and Welland Regiment (131004), The South Alberta Light Horse Regiment (280205)

Her Royal Highness The Princess Royal KG KT GCVO QSO

COLONEL IN CHIEF:- KRH (041292), R SIGNALS (110677), RLC (050493), RAVC (010703)

AFFILIATED COLONEL IN CHIEF:- QGS (070993), QOGTR (070993)

COLONEL:- RHG/D (010998)

ROYAL COLONEL:- The Royal Scots Borderers 1 SCOTS, 52nd Lowland 6 SCOTS

ROYAL HONORARY COLONEL:- University of London OTC (210489), City of Edinburgh Universities OTC (210715)

COMMANDANT-IN-CHIEF:- First Aid Nursing Yeomanry (Princess Royal's Volunteer Corps) (180881)

Commonwealth Forces

COLONEL IN CHIEF:- 8th Canadian Hussars (Princess Louise's), The Grey and Simcoe Foresters (Royal Canadian Armoured Corps), Canadian Forces Communications and Electronics Branch, The Royal Regina Rifle Regiment, Canadian Forces Medical Service, Royal Australian Corps of Signals, Royal Australian Corps of Transport; Royal New Zealand Corps of Signals, Royal New Zealand Nursing Corps, Royal Newfoundland Regiment

His Royal Highness The Duke of Gloucester KG GCVO

COLONEL IN CHIEF:- R ANGLIAN, RAMC (010703)

DEPUTY COLONEL IN CHIEF:- RLC (050493)

ROYAL COLONEL:- 6th Battalion RIFLES

ROYAL HONORARY COLONEL:- R MON RE(M) (110677)

Commonwealth Forces

COLONEL IN CHIEF:- Royal New Zealand Army Medical Corps

Her Royal Highness The Duchess of Gloucester GCVO

COLONEL IN CHIEF:- RADC (170600), The Royal Bermuda Regiment

DEPUTY COLONEL IN CHIEF:- AGC (060492)

ROYAL COLONEL:- 7th Battalion RIFLES

VICE-PATRON:- Adjutant General's Corps Regimental Association

PATRON:- Royal Army Educational Corps Association, Army Families Federation

Commonwealth Forces

COLONEL IN CHIEF:- Royal Australian Army Educational Corps, Royal New Zealand Army Educational Corps, Royal Canadian Dental Corps

Field Marshal His Royal Highness The Duke of Kent KG GCMG GCVO ADC(P)

FIELD MARSHAL (110693)

COLONEL IN CHIEF:- RRF (010769);

DEPUTY COLONEL IN CHIEF:- SCOTS DG (021293)

ROYAL COLONEL:- 1st Battalion RIFLES

COLONEL:- SG (090974)

Commonwealth Forces

COLONEL IN CHIEF:- Lorne Scots (Peel, Dufferin and Hamilton Regiment)

Her Royal Highness The Duchess of Kent GCVO

HONORARY MAJOR GENERAL (280267)

DEPUTY COLONEL IN CHIEF:- RLC (050493), AGC (060492), RDG (310792)

His Royal Highness Prince Michael of Kent GCVO

HONORARY COLONEL (091110)

ROYAL HONORARY COLONEL:- HAC (2012)

SENIOR COLONEL: - KRH (101110)

Commonwealth Forces

COLONEL IN CHIEF:- Essex and Kent Scottish Regiment (Ontario)

Her Royal Highness Princess Alexandra, the Hon Lady Ogilvy KG GCVO

DEPUTY COLONEL IN CHIEF: RL (250693)

ROYAL COLONEL:- 3rd Battalion RIFLES

ROYAL HONORARY COLONEL: RY (100402)

Commonwealth Forces

COLONEL IN CHIEF: The Canadian Scottish Regiment (Princess Mary's)

APPOINTMENTS TO THE QUEEN

PERSONAL AIDES DE CAMP TO THE QUEEN

FM *HRH The Duke of* Edinburgh *KG KT OM GBE ONZ QSO AK GCL CC CMM ADC(P)*
FM *HRH The Prince of* Wales *KG KT GCB OM AK QSO ADC(P)*
FM *HRH The Duke of* Kent *KG GCMG GCVO ADC(P)*
Cdr *HRH The Duke of* York *KCVO ADC(P)*
Maj *HRH The Duke of* Cambridge *KG KT PC ADC(P)*
HRH The Earl of Wessex *KG GCVO ADC(P)*
V Adm *Sir* Timothy James Hamilton Laurence *KCVO CB ADC(P)*
Capt Mark AP Phillips *CVO ADC(P) (retired)*

AIDES DE CAMP GENERAL TO THE QUEEN

Gen *Sir* Richard Lawson Barrons *KBE CBE ADC Gen* (*late* RA) *(until 5 Apr 16)* 190413
Gen Sir Nicholas Patrick Carter *KCB CBE DSO ADC Gen* 050914

AIDES DE CAMP TO THE QUEEN

Col D G Scott *ADC* (*late* REME) *(until 18 Sept 16)* 010713
Col T J Murray *ADC* (*late* INT CORPS) *(until 10 Oct 16)* 160913
Col A N King *ADC* (*late* AGC (ETS)) *(until 1 Nov 16)* 010714
Col J R Collinge *ADC* (Late RA) *(until 11 Aug 17)* 120115
Col H J Deacon *OBE ADC* (late QDG) 190615
Col D L D Bigger *ADC* (*late* RE) 010815
Col S G Hutchinson *MBE ADC* (*late* R SIGNALS) 010815
Col R M Green *ADC* (*late* AAC) 080515
Col G H J Deacon *OBE ADC* (*late* QDG) 190615

Aide de Camp (Reserve)

Brig J P Mooney *QVRM TD ADC* (Late LONDONS) 050115
Brig A B R Bruce of Crionaich *OBE ADC DL* (*late* Gen List (AR)) 120115
Brig C A Coull *ADC* (late SCOTS (AR)) 050115

EQUERRIES TO THE QUEEN

Crown Equerry

Col Toby Browne *LVO*

Equerry

Lt Col A C Richards *CVO (Deputy Master of the Household)*

Equerry in Waiting to the Queen

Cdre Andrew Canale *RN*

Extra Equerries

V Adm *Sir* Tom Blackburn *KCVO CB*
Maj *Sir* Shane Blewitt *GCVO*
Lt Col Robert Cartwright *LVO*
Maj Gen *Sir* Simon Cooper *GCVO*
Air Cdre *the Hon Sir* Timothy Elworthy *KCVO CBE*
The Lord Fellowes *GCB GCVO QSO*
Lt Col *Sir* Andrew Ford *KCVO*
R Adm *Sir* John Garnier *KCVO CBE*
Lt Col *Sir* Seymour Gilbart-Denham *KCVO*
Malcolm Hazell Esq. *CVO AM*
The Rt Hon Sir William Heseltine *GCB GCVO AC QSO*
Grp Capt Tim Hewlett *LVO OBE*
V Adm Tony Johnstone-Burt *CB OBE*
Lt Col Anthony Mather *CVO OBE*
Lt Col *Sir* Alexander Matheson of Matheson *Bt LVO*
Cdre Anthony Morrow *CVO*
Sir John Parsons *KCVO*
Lt Col *Sir* Malcolm Ross *GCVO OBE*
Sir Kenneth Scott *KCVO CMG*
AM *Sir* David Walker *KCVO OBE*
V Adm *Sir* James Weatherall *KCVO KBE*
Lt Col George West *CVO*
R Adm *Sir* Robert Woodard *KCVO*
Charles Curwen *CVO OBE*
Lt Col Michael Vernon

HONORARY CHAPLAINS TO THE QUEEN

The Rev Dr D G Coulter *CB QHC CF* (RAChD)....181007
The Rev J Woodhouse (RAChD)....010808
The Rev W G Ashton (RAChD)....290711
The Venerable P A Eagles *QHC CF* (RAChD)....171013
The Rev I A Evans (RAChD)....150615
The Rev A J Totten *MBE* (RAChD)....160216

HONORARY PHYSICIANS TO THE QUEEN

Col P W Gilbert *TD DL* (*late* RAMC (AR))....010414
Col R C Owers (*late* RAMC)....010614
Col D A Ross (*late* RAMC)....010114
Brig K C Beaton *OBE* (*late* RAMC)....010114
Col D A F H Parkhouse (*late* RAMC)....070314

HONORARY SURGEONS TO THE QUEEN

Maj Gen J F Rowan *CB OBE QHS* (*late* RAMC) *(until 6 Jun 16)*....011110
Lt Col A I M MacMillan (RAMC (Volunteers))....011110
Brig R H B Williamson (*late* RAMC)....011012
Lt Col N R M Tai (*late* RAMC)....010314
Col P F Mahoney *CBE TD* (*late* RAMC)....151214

HONORARY NURSE TO THE QUEEN

Col K J Irvine *RRC*....310116

Honorary Nurse (Army Reserve)

Col S E McDowell *TD* (*late* QARANC (AR)) *(until 01 Jul 16)*....010514

HONORARY DENTAL SURGEONS TO THE QUEEN

Col S J Creasey (*late* RADC)....120115
Col P D Jackson *TD* (*late* RADC(AR))....210915

HONORARY VETERINARY SURGEON TO THE QUEEN

Col D A MacDonald (*late* RAVC)....180714

HER MAJESTY'S BODY GUARD OF THE HONOURABLE CORPS OF GENTLEMEN AT ARMS

(ESTABLISHED IN THE YEAR 1509)

Uniform - Scarlet Facings - Blue Velvet

Agents - Lloyds Bank plc, Cox's & King's Branch

Captain

Lord Taylor of Holbeach *CBE*

Lieutenant

Col T C R B Purdon *OBE* (*late* WG)....040900

Standard Bearer

Lt Col P D Browne *MBE* (*late* RGJ)....150103

Clerk of the Cheque and Adjutant

Col CD MacKenzie-Beevor *CBE* (*late* QDG)....301102

Harbinger

Maj J D Kennard (*late* IG)....220403

Gentlemen-at-Arms

Maj O C Howard (*late* RH)....050600
Maj W G Peto (*late* 13/18 H)....021100
Lt Col J R D Kaye (*late* KRH)....021103
Col P R C Flach *MBE* (*late* KRH)....270806
Maj Charles Macfarlane (*late* COLDM GDS)....241106
Lt Col R Ingleby-Mackenzie *MBE* (*late* SG)....250307
Col E Bolitho *OBE* (*late* GREN GDS)....150208
Lt Col R Traherne (*late* WG)....260308
Maj J A N Russell (*late* RGJ)....090409
Maj R C D Lendrum (*late* RHG/D)....200909
Maj G W Maclean (*late* COLDM GDS)....040510
Col E G Cameron *TD* (*late* 13/18 H)....230610
Lt Col A C T Blackmore (*late* QRH)....130710
Maj T H Breitmeyer (*Late* GREN GDS)....041210
Lt Col S S Milne *MBE* (*late* RM)....180711
Maj C McGrath *MBE* (*late* IG)....120812
Col T R Wilson *OBE* (*late* QDG)....080713
Col R A Charrington (*late* 9/12L)....240614
Col B R E Butler *OBE* (*late* AAC)....110814
Gp Capt M Driver (*late* RAF Regt)....021214
Brig J R H Stopford (*late* IG)....151215
Lt Col C W N Crewdson *OBE* (*late* 9/12L)....310316
Maj Sir Hugh Robertson *KCMG* (*late* LG)....110716
Brig P M L Napier *OBE MSM* (*late* R Welsh)....030117
Maj T R Easby (*late* QRH)....250517

HM TOWER OF LONDON

Constable

Gen *Sir* Nicholas Houghton *GCB CBE ADC Gen* 310716

Resident Governor and Keeper of the Jewel House

Col Richard Harrold *OBE* 2011

THE QUEEN'S BODY GUARD OF THE YEOMAN OF THE GUARD

(INSTITUTED 1485)

Uniform - Scarlet *Facings* - Blue Velvet

Agents - Lloyds Bank plc, Cox's & King's Branch

Captain

The Lord Gardiner of Kimble *(2015 - 2016)*
The Earl of Courtown *(2016 -)*

Lieutenant

Col M Kingscote (*late* 17th/21st L)

Clerk of the Cheque and Adjutant

Maj H Robertson (*late* 9/12 L)

Ensign

Maj C Cox (*late* COLDM GDS)

Exons

Col J Schute *OBE* (*late* RGJ)
Maj S Treadgold (*late* WG)

WINDSOR CASTLE

Constable and Governor

Adm *Sir* James Perowne *KBE* .... Aug 2014

MILITARY KNIGHTS OF WINDSOR

(INSTITUTED 1348)

Badges - (i) A Shield charged with Cross of St George
(ii) The Star of the Order of the Garter

Uniform - Scarlet *Facings* - Blue

(as at 17 October 2017)

Governor

Lt Gen P T C Pearson *CB CBE* (*late* RGR)

Royal Foundation

Lt Col R R Giles *MVO* (*late* RHG/D)
Col D R Axson (*late* REME)
Lt Col C I P Webb (*late* RSDG)
Lt Col S A Watts *OBE* (*late* CAMUS)
Col R B Watson (*late* RLC)
Lt Col W J Willans (*late* RRF)
Col D K P Steele *MBE* (*late* A&SH)
Col B J Fairman *OBE* (*late* RA)
Lt Col F R J Maclean (*late* R SCOTS)
Lt Col M A Harding (*late* RHG/D)
Col S J Durnford (*late* RAMC)
Lt Col J M W Moody *OBE*

THE QUEEN'S BODY GUARD FOR SCOTLAND
ROYAL COMPANY OF ARCHERS

ORGANISED IN THE YEAR 1676 (RECONSTITUTED 1703)

Uniform - Green *Facings* - Black with Red Velvet

Captain-General and Gold Stick for Scotland

The Duke of Buccleuch and Queensberry *KBE (HM Lord-Lieutenant Roxburgh, Ettrick and Lauderdale)* 010911

Captains

The Earl of Dalhousie 180412
Maj Gen *The Hon* S H R H Monro *CBE LVO* 160414
Maj *Sir* Michael Strang Steel Bt *CBE* 130416
R Adm A M Gregory *OBE (HM Lord-Lieutenant Dunbartonshire)* 270417

Lieutenants

Lt Col *Sir* Malcolm Ross *GCVO OBE (HM Lord-Lieutenant Kirkcudbright)* 130416
Brig M S Jameson *CBE (HM Lord-Lieutenant Perth & Kinross)* 270417
Capt D J Bowes-Lyon 270417
Capt M E Tennant 270417

Ensigns

Maj Gen M J Strudwick *CBE* 130416
Sir Robert Clerk of Penicuik *Bt OBE (HM Lord-Lieutenant Midlothian)* 270417
Lt Gen *Sir* Alistair Irwin *KCB CBE* 270417
Col N J F Dalrymple-Hamilton *OBE TD* 270417

Brigadiers

A G Simpson *Esq* 180407
Prof *Sir* Hew Strachan *MA PhD FRSE FRHistS (HM Lord-Lieutenant Tweeddale)* 230408
Lt Col J C Stewart *(HM Lord-Lieutenant Clackmannanshire)* 150409
The Duke of Roxburgh 310310
Lt Gen A J N Graham *CB CBE* 180412
Brig *The Hon* H B H E Monro *CBE* 230413
Lt Col R Callander *OBE TD* 160414
Col A D Mathewson *OBE* 150415
Col A K M Miller *CBE* 150415
Maj Gen J H Gordon *CB CBE* 130416
Col A P W Campbell 270417
Mr R W Balfour *(HM Lord-Lieutenant Fife)* 270417

Adjutant

Lt Col J C Stewart 191109

Secretary

Lt Col R Callander *OBE TD* 180407

Surgeon

Major A W Orr *FRCGP* 120400

Chaplain

The Very Rev Dr John B Cairns *LTh LLB DD LLD* 180407

FOREIGN SOVEREIGNS AND MEMBERS OF FOREIGN ROYAL FAMILIES

who are Colonels in Chief or hold Honorary Rank in the Army

His Majesty KING HARALD V OF NORWAY *KG GCVO*
Honorary General (050794)

His Majesty KING ABDULLAH OF JORDAN *KCVO*
Colonel in Chief LD (010703)

Her Majesty QUEEN MARGRETHE II OF DENMARK *KG*
Colonel in Chief PWRR (250297)

His Majesty Sultan
HAJI HASSANAL BOLKIAH MU'IZZADDIN WADDAULAH SULTAN AND YANG DI-PERTUAN OF BRUNEI DARUSSALAM *GCB GCMG*
Honorary General (230284)

His Royal Highness Prince Mohammed Bolkiah of Brunei *CVO*
Honorary Lieutenant IG (151171)

His Royal Highness The Grand Duke Jean of Luxembourg *KG*
Honorary General (170395)

His Royal Highness The Grand Duke of Luxembourg *GCVO*
Honorary Major PARA (190789)

DISBANDED REGIMENTS

ROYAL MILITARYACADEMY BAND CORPS

(Disbanded 1985)

The Royal Cypher within a circlet bearing the words ROYAL MILITARY ACADEMY SANDHURST surmounted by The Crown, below the circlet a scroll bearing the words SERVE TO LEAD

THE CAMERONIANS (SCOTTISH RIFLES)

THE YORK AND LANCASTER REGIMENT

(Both Regimental Headquarters were disbanded in 1987)

THE TYNE TEES REGIMENT (TA)

(Disbanded 2004)

19 LIGHT BRIGADE

(Disbanded 2013)

SECTION II

(as at 1st March 2016)

DEFENCE COUNCIL

The Right Honourable Sir MICHAEL FALLON *MP*
Secretary of State for Defence (Chairman of the Defence Council)

The Right Honourable EARL HOWE
Minister of State for Defence and Deputy Leader of the House of Lords

Ms HARRIET BALDWIN *MP*
Parliamentary Under Secretary of State and Minister of State for Defence Procurement

Mr MARK LANCASTER *TD MP*
Minister of State for the Armed Forces

The Right Honourable Mr TOBAIS ELLWOOD *MP*
Parliamentary Under Secretary of State and Minister for Defence People and Veterans

Mr JULIAN BRAZIER *MP (until 2016)*
Parliamentary Under Secretary of State and Minister for Reserves

Air Chief Marshal Sir STUART PEACH *KCB CBE ADC BA MPhil DTech DLitt FRAeS RAF* (from Jul 2016)
Chief of the Defence Staff

Mr STEPHEN LOVEGROVE
Permanent Secretary of State

Admiral Sir PHILIP JONES *KCB ADC*
First Sea Lord and Chief of Naval Staff

General Sir NICHOLAS PATRICK CARTER *KCB CBE DSO ADC Gen*
Chief of the General Staff

Air Chief Marshal Sir ANDREW PULFORD *KCB CBE ADC RAF (until 10 Jul 2016)*
(**Air Chief Marshal Sir STEPHEN HILLIER** *KCB CBE DFC ADC MA RAF (from 11 Jul 2016)*)
Chief of the Air Staff

General Sir GORDON MESSENGER *KCB DSO* OBE ADC*
Vice Chief of the Defence Staff

General Sir RICHARD BARRONS *KCB CBE ADC Gen (until Apr 2016)*
(**General Sir CHRIS DEVERELL** *KCB MBE Gen (from Apr 2016)*)
Commander of Joint Forces Command

Professor HUGH DURRANT-WHYTE
MOD Chief Scientific Adviser

Mr TONY DOUGLAS
Chief Executive Officer of Defence Equipment and Support

Ms CAT LITTLE
Director General Finance

ARMY BOARD OF THE DEFENCE COUNCIL

Civilian

The Right Honourable Sir MICHAEL FALLON *MP*
Secretary of State for Defence
(Chairman of the Defence Council and Chairman of the Army Board of the Defence Council)

Mr MARK LANCASTER *TD MP*
Minister of State for the Armed Forces

Ms HARRIET BALDWIN *MP*
Minister of State for Defence Procurement

The Right Honourable Mr TOBAIS ELLWOOD *MP*
Parliamentary Under Secretary of State and Minister for Defence People and Veterans

British Army

General Sir NICHOLAS PATRICK CARTER *KCB CBE DSO ADC*
Chief of the General Staff

Major General NICK WELCH *OBE*
Assistant Chief of the General Staff

Lieutenant General Sir JAMES BASHALL *CBE*
Commander Home Command (previously Commander Personnel and Support Command)

Lieutenant General Sir CHRIS DEVERELL *KCB MBE (until 2016)*
Lieutenant General PAUL JAQUES *CBE (from 2016)*
Quartermaster General to the Forces (QMG) / Chief of Materiel (Land)

Lieutenant General Sir JAMES EVERARD *CBE (until Dec 16)*
Lieutenant General PATRICK SANDERS *CBE DSO (from Dec 16)*
Commander Field Army

Warrant Officer Class One GLENN HAUGHTON
Army Sergeant Major

EXECUTIVE COMMITTEE OF THE ARMY BOARD (ECAB)

Chairman ....Permanent Secretary (Chair)
Members ....Chief of the Defence Staff (co-chair)
Vice Chief of the Defence Staff (co-chair)
Chief of Defence People
Chief Scientific Adviser
Deputy Chief of the Defence Staff (Military Capability)
Deputy Chief of the Defence Staff (Military Strategy and Operations)
Director General Finance
Director General Head Office and Commissioning Services
Director General Nuclear
Director General Security Policy

MINITRY OF DEFENCE

SECRETARY OF STATE FOR DEFENCE

SECRETARY OF STATE FOR DEFENCE .... *The Right Honourable* MICHAEL FALLON *MP*

MINISTER OF STATE FOR DEFENCE PROCUREMENT .... Ms HARRIET BALDWIN *MP*

MINISTER OF STATE FOR THE ARMED FORCES .... Mr MARK LANCASTER *TD MP*

MINISTER OF STATE AND
DEPUTY LEADER OF THE HOUSE OF LORDS .... *The Right Honourable* EARL HOWE

PARLIAMENTARY UNDER SECRETARY OF STATE AND
MINISTER FOR DEFENCE PEOPLE AND VETERANS .... Mr TOBAIS ELLWOOD *MP*

PARLIAMENTARY UNDER SECRETARY OF STATE AND
MINISTER FOR RESERVES .... Mr JULIAN BRAZIER *MP*

CHIEF OF THE DEFENCE STAFF .... ACM *Sir* STUART PEACH *KCB CBE ADC BA MPhil DTech DLitt FRAeS RAF*

VICE CHIEF OF THE DEFENCE STAFF .... Gen *Sir* GORDON MESSENGER *KCB DSO* OBE ADC*

CHIEF OF THE NAVAL STAFF AND FIRST SEA LORD .... Adm *Sir* PHILIP JONES *KCB ADC*

CHIEF OF THE GENERAL STAFF .... Gen *Sir* NICHOLAS PATRICK CARTER *KCB CBE DSO ADC Gen*

CHIEF OF THE AIR STAFF .... ACM *Sir* ANDREW PULFORD *KCB CBE ADC RAF (until 10/07/16)*
(ACM *Sir* STEPHEN HILLIER *KCB CBE DFC ADC MA RAF (from 11/07/16)*)

COMMANDER OF JOINT FORCES COMMAND .... Gen *Sir* RICHARD BARRONS *KCB CBE ADC Gen (until 04/04/16)*
(Gen *Sir* CHRIS DEVERELL *KCB MBE Gen (from 05/04/16)*)

HEAD OFFICE AND CORPOATE SERVICES

(as of 31st March 2016)

CHIEF OF DEFENCE STAFF

Chief of the Defence Staff .... Gen *Sir* Nicholas R Houghton *GBE CBE ADC Gen (until Jul 16)*

Chief of the Defence Staff Principal Staff Officer .... Cdre William N Entwisle *OBE MVO (until Sep 16)*

Vice Chief of the Defence Staff .... ACM *Sir* Stuart Peach *KCB CBE ADC BA MPhil DTech DLitt FRAeS RAF (until May 16)*

Defence Senior Adviser Middle East .... Lt Gen Tom Beckett *CBE (late PARA)* 060115

Director General MOD Saudi Armed Forces Projects .... AM Ian Morrison *CBE*

Service Complaints Ombudsman .... Nicola Williams

MILITARY STRATEGIC OPERATIONS

Deputy Chief of Defence Staff (Military Strategic Operations) .... Lt Gen Gordon Messenger *DSO* OBE CB ADC*

Assistant Chief of Defence Staff (Operations) .... AVM Edward Stringer *CBE (until Jan 18)*

Assistant Chief of Defence Staff (Defence Engagement) .... RAdm Simon J Ancona *(until Apr 17)*

Head Defence Engagement Strategy .... Air Cdre James Linter *OBE*

Head of International Policy & Planning (Military) .... Air Cdre Nicholas Bray *CBE (until April 2016)*

.... Brig Stephen McMahon *CBE (from April 2016)*

Head of International Policy & Planning (Civilian) .... N/D

Head of Defence Operational Capability .... Cdre Monty Long

Director Operational Policy .... Dominic Wilson

Head Military Strategic Effects .... Air Cdre Jonathan Burr *CBE DFC*

Head Ops Policy .... N/D

Head Afghanistan, Pakistan, Iraq and Syria Policy .... N/D

Head Special Forces & Legal Policy .... N/D

Head of Ops Military .... *N/D*

BRITISH DEFENCE STAFF - UNITED STATES (BDS-US)

British Embassy Washington, 3100 Massachusetts Avenue NW, Washington DC 20008, USA
(Tel: +1 202 588 6500   Email: BDSUS-COMMUNICATIONS@mod.uk)

Head of BDS-US/Defence Attaché .... Maj Gen Richard Cripwell *CB CBE*

Minister (Defence Materiel) .... Steve McCarthy

Deputy Director Commonwealth Integration, Washington .... AVM Sean Corbett *MBE*

Senior British Military Advisor to United States Central Command, Tampa .... Maj Gen Neil Marshall *OBE*

Naval Attaché .... Cdre Richard Allen

Military Attaché .... Brig James Illingworth *OBE*

Air Attaché .... Air Cdre Richard Powell *CBE*

Councellor Defence Acquistion and Technology .... Simon Gadd

Counsellor Defence Policy and Nuclear .... Richard Berthon *OBE*

Chief of the Defence Staff's Liaison Officer to the Chairman of the US Joint Chiefs of Staff .... Air Cdre Steve Shell *OBE*

J2 Deputy Director Mission,
Headquarters US Central Command, Tampa ....Air Cdre Steve Thornber

Royal Marine Attaché...Col Al Lister *RM*

Assistant Military Attaché ....Col Nick Lock

Assistant Air Attaché ....Grp Capt Colin Da'Silva

MILITARY CAPABILITY

Deputy Chief of Defence Staff (Military Capability) ....Lt Gen Mark Poffley *OBE (from Jan 16)*

Assistant Chief of Defence Staff (Capability & Force Design)....RAdm Tim Fraser *(until Jan 17)*

Head of Fin Mil Capability Plans ....Brig Jeremy Bennett

Head of Fin Mil Capability Joint Plans....................................Air Cdre Andrew Wallis *OBE*

Head of FMC Strategy ....Robert Shopland-Reed

Director Carrier Strike..RAdm Graeme MacKay

Head Carrier Strike...Air Cdre John Prescott *OBE*

Head of Strategic Programmes..Ian Forber

Head of Nuclear Capablility ....Cdre Tim Hodgson

Head of Nuclear Enterprise Strategy..N/D

Head of Weapons, Evaluation & Capability Assurance............Dr I D (Dai) Morris

DEFENCE PERSONNEL

Deputy Chief of Defence Staff (People) ....Lt Gen *Sir* Andrew R Gregory *KGB CB (until Apr 16)*

Assistant Chief of Defence Staff (Personnel Capability) /
Defence Services Secretary..Lt Gen Richard Nugee *CVO CBE (until May 16)*

Head Training Education Skills, Recruitment
and Resettlement ....Air Cdre Warren James *CBE (until Aug 16)*

Head Service Personnel Support...Helen Helliwell

Assistant Chief Defence Staff (Reserves & Cadets) ....Maj Gen John Crackett *CB TD VR*

Head Reserve Forces and Cadets ....Brig Mark van der Lande *CBE*

Head Capability and Cadets ....Cdre Jonathan Fry

Director Service Personnel Policy...Heather McNaughton / Caroline Pusey

Head Strategy & NEM Programme Manager...........................Brig Fiona Gardner

Armed Forces Remuneration...Air Cdre Gary Tunnicliffe

Head People Secretariat ....Paula Hothersall

Service Policy Assurance Adviser ....Vacant

Head Armed Forces Bill..David Howarth

Director Service Prosecutions...Andrew Cayley

Deputy Director Service Prosecutions ....Brig Stuart Lythgoe

Director Civilian Human Resources ....Esther Wallington

SECURITY POLICY

Director General Security Policy & Operations ....Peter Watkins *CBE*

Assistant Chief of Defence Staff (Nuclear and Chemical and Biological)..R Adm Mark Beverstock

Head Chemical, Biological, Radiological & Nuclear Policy ...Cdre John R MacDonald *(until 2016)*

Head Export Policy...N/D

Head Arms Control & Counter Proliferation............................Vacant

Head Cyber and Space Policy...Nick Ayling

Director International Security Policy...Nick Gurr

Head NATO & Europe Policy...Giles Ahern

Head Wider Europe Policy..Nigel Phillips *CBE*

Director Strategic Planning...Will Jessett

Head Defence Strategy and Priorities ....Paul Wyatt

Director Judicial Engagement Policy..Peter Ryan

Head Public Enquiries..N/D

Head Policy and Dsiclosure and Defence Inquests Unit..........N/D

DEFENCE SAFETY AUTHORITY

Defence Safety Authority, 1st Floor, Zone 6-L, Main Building, Whitehall, London SW1A 2HB
(Email: DSA-Enquiries@mod.uk)

Director General Defence Safety Authority......................................AM Richard Garwood *CB CBE DFC RAF*

Director Defence Safety Authority..Vacant

Defence Nuclear Safety Regulator..N/D

Director Military Aviation Authority (MAA)................................R Adm Paul Chivers *OBE*

Head Analysis & Plans MAA..N/D

Director Technical Military Aviation Authority and Chief Technical Officer..AVM Martin Clark

Head Oversight & Approvals MAA...Air Cdre David Cooper

Head Regulation and Certification MAA..................................N/D

PERMANENT UNDER SECRETARY OF STATE (PUS)

(as of 31st March 2016)

Permanent Under Secretary of State .... Jon Thompson

Secretary of State Chief of Staff .... Graeme Biggar

Permanent Under Secretary Chief of Staff .... N/D

Chief Scientific Adviser .... Prof Vernon Gibson

Defence Science & Technology Strategy Director .... Dr Paul Hollinshead

Chief Executive of Defence Electronics and Components Agency ... Geraint Spearing

FINANCE

Director General Finance .... Louise Tulett *CBE*

Director Performance and Analysis .... Jonathon Nancekivell-Smith

Head Corporate Strategy and Governance .... *N/D*

Head Defence Statistics .... *N/D*

Head Defence Economics .... *N/D*

Director Finance Strategy .... Heather Tayler

Head Financial Management, Policy and Accounting .... N/D

Head Contracting, Purchasing & Finance .... N/D

Director Financial Planning and Scrutiny .... Richard Jones

Head of Defence Resources .... N/D

Head of Scrutiny .... Lois Nicholson

Head of Defence Portfolio Approvals and Scrutiny .... Annette Matton

Director of Audit, Risk and Assurance .... Amarjit Atkar

Head of Fraud Defence .... Stephen Newman

Head of Internal Audit .... N/D

Head of Risk and Assurance .... Simon King

HEAD OFFICE AND COMMISSIONING SERVICES

Director General Head Office & Commissioning Services .... Mark Preston

Director Central Legal Services .... Frances Nash

Head of Operational International Humanitarian Law Division .... John Swords

Head of Corporate Strategy Law Division .... Vacant

Chief Executive Officer Defence Business Services .... Kathy Barnes

Head of Veteran Services .... Jon Parkin

Head of DBS National Security Vetting .... Caroline Rumming

Head of DBS Military Personnel .... Cdre Ian Bisson

Head of DBS Civilian Personnel .... Andrew Stafford

Head of DBS Finance .... Andy Dowds

Head of DBS Resources .... Georgina Benzies

MINISTRY OF DEFENCE POLICE (MDP)
MDP HQ, Wethersfield, Braintree, Essex CM7 4AZ
Email: MDP-FOI-DP@mod.uk Tel: 01371 854000)

Chief Constable of the Minsitry of Defence Police .... Alfred Hitchcock

Deputy Chief Constable MOD Police .... Andy Adams

Head of Corporate Services MOD Police .... Justin Oliver

Assistant Chief Constable Operations .... Paul McLaughlin

T/Assistant Chief Constable Organisational Development and Crime .... David Long

Divisional Commander Nuclear Division .... Chief Supt Beth Disher

Director Head Office .... Alison Stevenson

Head of Resources .... N/D

Head HOCS Security, Safety and Business Resilience .... N/D

Head Defence Reform Unit .... Robin Riley

Director Business Resilience .... Vacant

Head Defence Security Policy .... *N/D*

Head Corporate Services Transformation Team .... N/D

Director Commercial .... Steven Morgan

Head Commercial HOCS .... Rachel Pearson

Head Commercial Army .... Fiona Phillips

Head Commercial Assurance, Scrutiny & Due Diligence .... Jenny Giblett

Head Commercial Contract Management .... Morag Stewart

Head Policy, Process & Procedures .... Richard Marwood

Head Commercial JFC .... Ian Burton

Director Commissiong Services .... David Marsh

Head Defence Infrastructure Governing Authority .... Liesl Neale

Head Business Strategy and Governance .... N/D

Head Acquisition System Authority .... N/D

CSTT-FDBS Transaction Lead .... N/D

DEFENCE COMMUNICATIONS

Director Defence Communications .... Carl Newns

Head of Defence Public Relations .... James Shelley

Head of Stategy .... Cdre Mike Beardall

Head of Secretariat, Business Management & Contents Services .... Vacant

Head of Defence Communications Capability Programme .... Charlie McBride

ARMY HEADQUARTERS

Secretariat IDL 24, Marlborough Lines, Monxton Road ANDOVER SP11 8HJ
(Website: www.army.mod.uk)

THE GENERAL STAFF

Chief of the General Staff .... Gen Sir Nicholas Carter *KCB CBE DSO ADC* 050914

Deputy Chief of the General Staff .... Lt Gen Nickolas Pope *CBE* 041215

Chaplain General .... Rev Dr David G Coulter *CB QHC CF*

Deputy Chaplain General .... Ven Peter Eagles *QHC CF (until 2017)*

Director General Army Medical Services (DGAMS) .... Maj Gen Jeremy F Rowan *CB OBE QHS (until Jun 16)*

Director Medical Capability (Army) .... Brig Martin Nadin *OBE (until Jul 16)*

Director Army Basing and Infrastructure .... Maj Gen Alastair Dickinson *CBE*

Director Infrastructure .... Brig Stephen Vickery

Brigadier Army Staff .... N/D

Director Capability .... Maj Gen Robert Bruce *CBE DSO*

Capability Director Combat .... Brig Ian Gibb

Capability Director Combat Suppport .... Brig Simon Humphrey *OBE*

Capability Director Information .... N/D

Director Force Development .... Brig Iain Harrison

Capability Director Combat Service Support .... Brig Martin Moore *CBE*

Director Strategy .... Maj Gen James Swift *OBE* 240316

Head of Strategy .... Brig Roland Walker

Director Information .... Maj Gen Richard Semple *CBE*

Head of Information Superiority .... Brig Jon Cole

Head of Cyber and Security .... N/D

Director Support .... Maj Gen Mark Gaunt *CEng FIMechE MRAeS* 070415

Director Logistics .... Brig Crispin Walker *MBE*

Assistant Chief of the General Staff .... Maj Gen Nicholas Welch *OBE*

Director Army Reform .... Paul Kett

Brigadier General Staff .... Brig Felix Gedney *OBE*

Deputy Director J5 CENTCOM .... Brig Timothy Lai

Provost Marshal (Army) .... Brig Bill Warren *MBE*

Senior British Officer to the US Security Coordinator .... Brig Alistair Deas *MBE*

Head of Information Exploitation .... Brig Timothy Carmichael

Director Resources .... David Stephens

Head of Finance .... N/D

Head of Army Aecretariat & Civilian Workforce .... Damian Paterson

Director Iraq Historic Allegations Team .... Mark Warwick

COMMANDER HOME COMMAND

Commander Home Command ....Lt Gen James I Bashall *CBE*

Chief of Staff Home Command..Brig Mark Abraham *OBE*

Head Arms & Services HQ Home Command...............................Vacant

Director Equipment..Brig Colin McClean

Director Personnel Capability ....Brig Christopher Ghika *OBE*

Director Personnel Operations ....Brig Matthew Lowe

GOC London District and Maj Gen The Household Division...........Maj Gen *Sir* Edward Smyth-Osbourne *KCVO CBE*

Deputy Commander London District..Brig Michael McGovern

Director Army Recruiting and Training...Maj Gen Christopher Tickell *CBE*

Commandant Royal School of Military Engineering (RSME) ......Brig David Southall *OBE*

Commander Collective Training Group..Brig Tim Hyams *OBE*

Director Recruit Training (Operations).......................................Brig Nick Fitzgerald *MBE*

Head of Programmes Army Recruiting & Training Division........*N/D*

Commander Initial Training Group ....Brig Alexander Potts

Director Education Capability..Vacant

Commandant School of Infantry ....Brig Andrew Williams *OBE (until May 16)*
Col Peter Stitt *(after May 16)*

Commander Defence College of Logistics
& Personnel Administration..Brig Stephen Shirley *MBE*

Director Training ....Brig James Woodham *CBE MC*

Command Secretary (Secretariat) ....Vacant

Director Children and Young People ....Mike Cooper

Commandant Royal Military Academy Sandhurst ....Maj Gen Paul A E Nanson *CBE*.......................... 030915

Director General Army Legal Services...Maj Gen Susan K Ridge

Brigadier Operational Law...Brig Juliet Bartlett

OTHER DEFENCE TRAINING ESTABLISHMENTS

ARMOUR CENTRE

HQ Armour Centre, Allenby Barracks, Bovington, Wareham, Dorset BH20 6JA

Commander...Col J M Williams

ARMY AVIATION CENTRE

AACEN, Middle Wallop, Stockbridge, Hampshire, SO20 8DY

Commandant...Col J D Bryant *OBE (Late AAC)*

11 (ROYAL SCHOOL OF SIGNALS) SIGNAL REGIMENT

Regimental Headquarters, 11th Signal Regiment, Blandford Camp, Dorset DT11 8RH

Garrison Commander...Col Andrew Percival

Assistant Commander ....Col C Edwards *TD*

Officer Commanding 2(Catterick Squadron)...Maj L Kelly

Officer Commanding 3(Harrogate) Squadron..Maj D Galey

Officer Commanding 4(Military Training) Squadron...Maj G L M Dunn

THE ROYAL SCHOOL OF MILITARY ENGINEERING (RSME) GROUP

Brompton Barracks, Chatham, Kent ME4 4UG (Tel: 01634 822277)
Gibraltar Barracks, Blackwater, Surrey GU17 9LP

Commandant HQ RSME Group...Brig David Southall *OBE*

1 Royal School of Military Engineering Regiment (1 RSME)

Professional Engineer Wing, Brompton Barracks, Chatham, Kent ME4 4UG

Commanding Officer 1 RSME..Lt Col Sean Cunniff

3 Royal School of Military Engineering Regiment

Royal Engineers Warfare Wing, Gibraltar Barracks, Blackwater, Surrey GU17 9LP

Defence Animal Centre (DAC)

Welby Lane, Melton Mowbray, Leicester LE13 0HX

Commanding Officer ....Lt Col Mark Morrison

Defence Explosive, Ordnance Disposal, Munitions and Search (DEMS) Training Regiment

DEMS Trg Regt, St. George's Barracks, Arncott Wood Road, Bicester, Oxfordshire OX25 1PP

Commanding Officer ....N/A

Royal Military School of Music (RMSM)

Kneller Hall, Twickenham TW2 7DU

Commandant...Col B W Jenkins .... Jan 12

DEFENCE SCHOOL OF ELECTRONIC AND MECHANICAL ENGINEERING (DSEME)

DSEME, 8 Training Battalion REME, DSEME,
MOD Lyneham, Chippenham, Wiltshire SN15 4XX

Commandant...Col Ed Heal *OBE*.................. Sep 16

INFANTRY BATTLE SCHOOL (IBS)

IBS, Dering Lines, Brecon, Powys LD3 7RA

Commanding Officer ....Lt Col Alex Rennie *MBE*

INFANTRY TRAINING CENTRE (ITC) CATTERICK

Scotton Road, Catterick Garrison, North Yorkshire DL9 3PS

Garrison Commander..Brig Oliver Stokes *MBE*

Army School of Bagpipe Music & Highland Drumming

Inchdrewer House, 299 Colinton Road, Edinburgh EH13 0LA

Director..Capt Gordon Rowan ....Oct 16

Army School of Ceremonial

Scotton Road, Catterick Garrison, North Yorkshire DL9 3PS

Commanding Officer .... Capt Graham White *MCGI*

Parachute Training Support Unit (PTSU)

PTSU, RAF Brize Norton, Oxfordshire OX18 3LX

SPECIALIST WEAPONS SCHOOL (SWS), WARMINSTER

SP WPNS SCH, Waterloo Lines, Imber Road, Warminster, Wiltshire BA12 0DJ

Commanding Officer ....Lt Col Adam Clark

DEFENCE SCHOOL OF TRANSPORT (DST)

DST, Normandy Barracks, Leconfield, Beverley, East Yorkshire HU17 7LX

Commandant.. Col Rob Peacock

COMMANDER FIELD ARMY (CFA)

Commander Field Army .... Lt Gen *Sir* James R Everard *CBE* 070814

Deputy Commander Land Forces (Reserves) .... Maj Gen Simon Brooks-Ward *CVO OBE TD VR*

Military Secretary and General Officer Scotland .... Maj Gen Nick Ashmore *CB OBE*

Deputy Military Secretary .... Brig Peter Dennis

Chief of Staff Land Forces .... Maj Gen Tim P Robinson *CBE*

Chief of Staff Field Army .... Maj Gen Ivan Jones

Assistant Chief of Staff Operations .... Brig Rupert Jones *CBE (until 2016)*

Assistant Chief of Staff Land Forces .... N/D

Director Land Warfare .... Brig Richard Toomey

Director Personnel .... Maj Gen Robert Nitsch *CBE*

Director Manning (Army) .... Vacant

Director Personnel Services (Army) .... Brig John Donnelly *CBE*

Head of Individual Develpoment .... Brig Suzanne Anderson

Deputy Commanding General (Readiness) (US) 1st Infantry Div..... Vacant

Deputy Commanding General (Interoperability) (US)
82nd Airborne Division .... Brig James Learmont *CBE (until Aug 17)*

REGIONAL COMMAND

General Officer Commanding Regional Command .... Maj Gen Richard J A Stanford *MBE*

Chief of Staff Regional Command .... Brig Simon Banton *OBE*

Deputy Commander Cadets .... Brig Matthew Lowe

BRITISH FORCES GERMANY

JHQ, Rheindahlen (BFPO 140)

Commander British Forces Germany .... Brig Ian Bell

Director British Forces Germany Health Service .... Brig Charlie Beardmore

JOINT HELICOPER COMMAND (JHC)

HQ JHC, Army Headquarters, Marlborough Lines, Monxton Road, Andover SP11 8HJ

Commander Joint Helicopter Command .... Maj Gen Richard F P Felton *CBE (until Apr 17)*

Deputy Commander .... Brig Andrew T G Cash *(until Jul 17)*

Capability Director .... Vacant

16 AIR ASSAULT BRIGADE

Merville Barracks, Colchester, Essex CO2 7UT

Commander .... Brig Colin Weir *DSO MBE (until 2017)*

Brigade Units:

7th Parachute Regiment Royal Horse Artillery, 23 Engineer Regiment (Air Assault)
2nd Battalion The Parachute Regiment, 3rd Battalion The Parachute Regiment
2nd Battalion The Royal Gurkha Rifles
13 Air Assault Support Regiment The Royal Logistic Corps
16 Medical Regiment, 216 (Parachute) Signal Squadron
Pathfinder Platooon, 4th Battalion The Parachute Regiment (Army Reserve)

DIVISIONS AND BRIGADES

Brigade constituent units are based on the Army 2020 Report v2 and unit rotation as at 1 Sep 2016
(AR) indicates Army Reserve unit, (Hy) indicates hybrid unit

1st (UNITED KINGDOM) DIVISION

Impahl Barracks, Fulford Road, York YO10 4HD

General Officer Commanding 1 (UK) Division....................................Maj Gen Giles P Hill *CBE*
Deputy Commander..Brig James Illingworth
Army Inspector..Brig Andrew Hughes *MBE*

4 INFANTRY BRIGADE AND HQ NORTH EAST

Peronne Lines, Catterick Garrison

Commander...Brig Gerald Strickland *DSO MBE (Apr 15 - Dec 16)*
Brig Oliver Stokes *MBE (from Jan 17)*

Deputy Commander...Col Mike Butterwick *(until May 16)*
Col Andy Hadfield *(after May 16)*

Deputy Commander (Reserves)..Col David Middleton *MBE TD*

Light Cavalry:
The Light Dragoons (*Catterick*)
Reserve Light Cavalry:
The Queen's Own Yeomanry (AR) (*Newcastle*)
Light Protected Mobility:
2nd Battalion The Duke of Lancaster's Regiment (*Catterick*)
Reserve Light Infantry Role:
4th Battalion The Yorkshire Regiment (AR) (*York*)

7 INFANTRY BRIGADE AND HQ EAST

Chetwynd Barracks, Chilwell, Nottingham NG9 5HA
(Tel: 0115 957 2845 (media enquiries) Email: 7X-0HQMailbox@mod.uk)

Commander...Brig Jonny Bourne *OBE*

Deputy Commander...Col Stuart Williams

Light Cavalry:
1st The Queen's Dragoon Guards (*Swanton Morley*)
Reserve Light Cavalry
The Royal Yeomanry (AR) (*London*)
Light Protected Mobility
2nd Battalion The Royal Anglian Regiment (*Cottesmore*)
Light Role Infantry
1st Battalion The Royal Irish Regiment (*Woolwich*)
Reserve Light Role Infantry
3rd Battalion The Royal Anglian Regiment (AR) (*Bury St Edmunds*)
Reserve Light Role Infantry
3rd Battalion The Princess of Wales's Royal Regiment (AR) (*Canterbury*)

11 INFANTRY BRIGADE AND HQ SOUTH EAST

Roebuck House, Aldershot Garrison
(Tel: 01252 347 970 Email: 11X-CE-0GroupMailbox@mod.uk)

Commander...Brig Phil W C Kimber *OBE*.................................. Jan 16

Deputy Commander...Col Andy Barr *OBE (until Sep 17)*
Col Simon J R Browne *OBE (from Sept 17)*

Light Protected Mobility
1st Battalion Welsh Guards (*Pirbright*)
Light Role Infantry
1st Battalion Grenadier Guards (*Aldershot*)
1st Battalion The Royal Gurkha Rifles (*Shorncliffe*)
Reserve Light Role Infantry
3rd Battalion The Royal Welsh (*Cardiff*)
The London Regiment (*Westminster*)

38 (IRISH) BRIGADE
Thiepval Barracks, Lisburn

Commander........Brig Ralph Wooddisse *MBE MC*

Deputy Commander........Col Jamie Piggott

Light Role Infantry
1st Battalion The Royal Regiment of Scotland (*Belfast*)
2nd Battalion The Rifles (*Ballykinler*)
Reserve Light Role Infantry
7th Battalion The Rifles (AR) (*Reading*)

42 INFANTRY (NORTH WEST) BRIGADE
(renamed HQ NORTH WEST as of 1st Jan 17)
Fulwood Barracks, Preston

Commander........Brig Chris Coles *(until Dec 16)*
Col Philip Harrison *(from Jan 17)*

Deputy Commander........Col Philip Harrison *(until Jan 17)*

Light Role Infantry
2nd Battalion The Duke of Lancaster's Regiment (*Weeton*)
2nd Battalion The Mercian Regiment (*Chester*)
Reserve Light Role Infantry
4th Battalion The Mercian Regiment (AR) (*Wolverhampton*)
4th Battalion The Duke of Lancaster's Regiment (*Preston*)

51 INFANTRY BRIGADE AND HQ SCOTLAND
Forthside, Stirling

Commander........Brig Gary Deakin *CBE*

Deputy Commander........Col Rob Jeffries *CBE (until Sep 2016)*
Col Charlie Wallace *(from Sep 2016)*

Deputy Commander (Reserves)........Col Stephanie Jackman *MBE TD (from Apr 16)*

Light Cavalry
The Royal Scots Dragoon Guards (Carabiniers and Greys) (*Leuchars*)
Reserve Light Cavalry
Scottish and North Irish Yeomanry (AR) (*Edinburgh*)
Light Protected Mobility
3rd Battalion The Rifles (*Edinburgh*)
3rd Battalion The Royal Regiment of Scotland (*Fort George*)
Light Role Infantry
2nd Battalion The Royal Regiment of Scotland (*Edinburgh*)
Reserve Light Role Infantry
5th Battalion The Royal Regiment of Fusiliers (AR) (*Newcastle*)
6th Battalion The Royal Regiment of Scotland (AR) (*Glasgow*)
7th Battalion The Royal Regiment of Scotland (AR) (*Perth*)

160 INFANTRY BRIGADE AND HQ WALES
The Barracks, Brecon

Commander........Brig Martyn Gamble

Deputy Commander........Col Lance Patterson

Light Role Infantry
1st Battalion The Rifles (*Chepstow*)
Light Protected Mobility
1st Battalion The Royal Irish Regiment (*Tern Hill*)
Reserve Light Role Infantry
6th Battalion The Rifles (AR) (*Exeter*)
2nd Battalion The Royal Irish Regiment (AR) (*Lisburn*)

102 LOGISTIC BRIGADE
102 Log Bde,Prince Wm of Glos Barracks, 1 Belvoir Ave, Granthan, NG31 7TA

Commander........Brig David Eastman *MBE*

Deputy Commander........Col Paul Fish

Deputy Commander (Medical)........Col Phil Carter

Force Logistic Regiments
6 Regiment The Royal Logistic Corps (*Dishforth*)
7 Regiment The Royal Logistic Corps (*Cottesmore*)
Close Support
1 Close Support Battalion Royal Electrical and Mechanical Engineers (*Catterick*)
2 Close Support Battalion Royal Electrical and Mechanical Engineers (*Leuchars*)
Medical Regiments
2 Medical Regiment (Hy) (*North Luffenham*)
3 Medical Regiment (Hy) (*Preston*)
Reserve Transport Regiments
150 Transport Regiment The Royal Logistic Corps (AR) (*Hull*)
158 Transport Regiment The Royal Logistic Corps (AR) (*Peterborough*)
Reserve Supply Regiment
159 Supply Regiment The Royal Logistic Corps (AR) (*Coventry*)
Reserve Medical Regiments
225 (Scottish) Medical Regiment (AR) (*Dundee*)
253 (North Irish) Medical Regiment (AR) (*Belfast*)
254 (East of England) Medical Regiment (AR) (*Cambridge*)
Reserve Equipment Support
101 Battalion Royal Electrical and Mechanical Engineers (AR) (*Wrexham*)
102 Battalion Royal Electrical and Mechanical Engineers (AR) (*Newton Aycliffe*)
104 Battalion Royal Electrical and Mechanical Engineers (AR) (*Northampton*)
106 Battalion Royal Electrical and Mechanical Engineers (AR) (*Glasgow*)

3rd (UNITED KINGDOM) DIVISION

Picton Barracks, Bulford Camp, Salisbury, Wilts SP4 9NY
(Tel: 01980 672420 Mil: 94321 2420)

General Officer Commanding....................Maj Gen Patrick N Y Sanders *CBE DSO (late RIFLES)*.................... 110515

Deputy Commander....................U.S. Brig Gen Michael J Tarsa *(from Sep 15)*

1 ARMOURED INFANTRY BRIGADE

Tidworth, Wiltshire

Commander....................Brig Bill Wright *OBE*

Armoured Cavalry
The Household Cavalry Regiment (*Windsor*)
Armour
The Royal Tank Regiment (*Tidworth*)
Armoured Infantry
1st Battalion The Royal Regiment of Fusiliers (*Tidworth*)
1st Battalion The Mercian Regiment (*Bulford*)
Heavy Protected Mobility
4th Battalion The Rifles (*Aldershot*)
Reserve
The Royal Wessex Yeomanry (AR) (*Bovington*)

12 ARMOURED INFANTRY BRIGADE

Ward Barracks, Bulford Camp, Wiltshire

Commander....................Brig Rob Sergeant

Armoured Cavalry
The Royal Lancers (*Catterick*)
Armour
The King's Royal Hussars (*Tidworth*)
Armoured Infantry
1st Battalion The Yorkshire Regiment (*Warminster*)
1st Battalion The Royal Welsh
Heavy Protected Mobility
1st Battalion Scots Guards
Reserve *(under operational command of 1 Armoured Infantry Brigade)*
The Royal Wessex Yeomanry (AR) (*Bovington*)

20 ARMOURED INFANTRY BRIGADE
Sennelager, Paderborn, Germany

Commander .... Brig Ian Mortimer

Armoured Cavalry
The Royal Dragoon Guards (*Catterick*)
Armour
The Queen's Royal Hussars (Queen's Own and Royal Irish) (*Tidworth*)
Armoured Infantry
1st Battalion The Princess of Wales's Royal Regiment (*Bulford*)
5th Battalion The Rifles (*Bulford*)
Heavy Protected Mobility
4th Battalion The Royal Regiment of Scotland (*Catterick*)
Reserve *(under operational command of 1 Armoured Infantry Brigade)*
The Royal Wessex Yeomanry (AR) (*Bovington*)

101 LOGISTIC BRIGADE
Aldershot

Commander .... Brig Simon Hamilton *OBE*

Close Support Logistic Regiments
1 Logistic Support Regiment The Royal Logistic Corps, (*Bicester*)
3 Logistic Support Regiment The Royal Logistic Corps (*Aldershot*)
4 Logistic Support Regiment The Royal Logistic Corps (*Abingdon*)
Theatre Logistic Regiments
10 The Queen's Own Gurkha Logistic Regiment (*Aldershot*)
9 Theatre Logistic Regiment The Royal Logistic Corps (*Hullavington*)
27 Regiment The Royal Logistic Corps (*Abingdon*)
Armoured Medical Regiment
1 Armoured Medical Regiment (*Tidworth*)
4 Armoured Medical Regiment (*Aldershot*)
5 Armoured Medical Regiment (*Tidworth*)
Armoured Close Support
3 Armoured Close Support Battalion Royal Electrical and Mechanical Engineers (*Tidworth*)
4 Armoured Close Support Battalion Royal Electrical and Mechanical Engineers (*Tidworth*)
6 Armoured Close Support Battalion Royal Electrical and Mechanical Engineers (*Tidworth*)
Force Support
5 Force Support Battalion Royal Electrical and Mechanical Engineers (*Cottesmore*)
Reserve Transport Regiments
151 Transport Regiment The Royal Logistics Corps (AR) (*Croydon*)
154 (Scottish) Transport Regiment The Royal Logistics Corps (AR) (*Dunfermline*)
157 (Welsh) Transport Regiment The Royal Logistics Corps (AR) (*Cardiff*)
Reserve Supply Regiment
156 Supply Regiment The Royal Logistics Corps (AR) (*Liverpool*)
Reserve Equipment Support
103 Battalion Royal Electrical and Mechanical Engineers (AR) (*Crawley*)
105 Battalion Royal Electrical and Mechanical Engineers (AR) (*Bristol*)

FORCE TROOPS COMMAND

Upavon, Wiltshire

General Officer Commanding .... Maj Gen Tyrone R Urch *CBE (late RE)* 270215

1 ARTILLERY BRIGADE AND HQ SOUTH-WEST
Jellalabad Barracks, Tidworth Camp

Commander .... Vacant

Close Support
1st Regiment Royal Horse Artillery (*Larkhill*)
3rd Regiment Royal Horse Artillery (*Harlow Hill*)
4th Regiment Royal Artillery (*Topcliffe*)
19th Regiment Royal Artillery (*Larkhill*)
26th Regiment Royal Artillery (*Larkhill*)

Reserves Artillery
101st (Northumbrian) Regiment Royal Artilley (AR) (*Gateshead*)
103rd (Lancashire) Regiment Royal Artilley (AR) (*St Helens*)
105th Regiment Royal Artilley (AR) (*Edinburgh*)

8 ENGINEER BRIGADE
Gibraltar Barracks, Minley

Commander..Brig John Ridge

Deputy Commander..Col Andrew Bellingall

Deputy Commander (Reserves)..Col David Jones

25 (CLOSE SUPPORT) ENGINEER GROUP (*Minley*)
21 Engineer Regiment (Hy) (*Catterick)*
22 Engineer Regiment (*Perham Down*)
26 Engineer Regiment (*Perham Down*)
32 Engineer Regiment (Hy) (*Catterick)*
35 Engineer Regiment (*Perham Down*)

12 (FORCE SUPPORT) ENGINEER GROUP (*Wittering*)
36 Engineer Regiment (*Maidstone*)
39 Engineer Regiment (*Kinloss*)
71 Engineer Regiment (AR) (*Leuchars)*
75 Engineer Regiment (AR) (*Warrington*)
The Royal Monmouthshire Royal Engineers (Militia) (AR) (*Monmouth*)
20 Works Group Royal Engineers (Air Support) (*Wittering*)

170 (INFRASTRUCTURE SUPPORT) ENGINEER GROUP (*Chilwell*)
62 Works Group Royal Engineers (Hy) (*Chilwell*)
63 Works Group Royal Engineers (Hy) (*Chilwell*)
64 Works Group Royal Engineers (Hy) (*Chilwell*)
65 Works Group Royal Engineers (AR) (*Chilwell*)
66 Works Group Royal Engineers (Hy) (*Chilwell*)

29 EXPLOSIVE ORDNANCE DISPOSAL AND SEARCH GROUP (*Aldershot*)
11 Explosive Ordnance Disposal Regiment The Royal Logistic Corps (*Didcot*)
33 Engineer Regiment (Explosive Ordnance Disposal) (Hy) (*Wimbish*)
101 (City of London) Engineer Regiment (Explosive Ordnance Disposal) (Hy) (*Wimbish*)
1 Military Working Dogs Regiment (Royal Army Veterinary Corps) (Hy) (*North Luffenham*)

11 SIGNALS AND WEST MIDLAND BRIGADE
Venning Barracks, Donnington, Telford TF2 8AF

Commander..Brig Robin Anderton-Brown

Deputy Commander..Col Richard Mayberry

7 SIGNAL GROUP (*Stafford*)
Close Support
1st Signal Regiment (*Stafford*)
16th Signal Regiment (*Stafford*)
21st Signal Regiment (*Colerne*)
General Support
2 Signal Regiment (*York*)
3 Signal Regiment (*Bulford*)

2 SIGNAL GROUP (*Donnington*)
Reserve Signal Regiments
32nd Signal Regiment (AR) (*Glasgow*)
37th Signal Regiment (AR) (*Redditch*)
39th Signal Regiment (AR) (*Bristol)*
71st (City of London) Yeomanry Signal Regiment (AR) (*Bexleyheath*)
Specialist Technical Support Regiments
10 Signal Regiment (Hy) (*Corsham*)
15 Signal Regiment (Information Systems) (Hy) (*Blandford*)

104 LOGISTIC SUPPORT BRIGADE
Duke of Gloucester Barracks, South Cerney

Commander...Brig Simon Hutchings *OBE*

Assistant Commander...Col Simon Dixon *TD*

Port & Maritime Regiments
17 Port & Maritime Regiment The Royal Logistic Corps (*Marchwood*)
165 (Wessex) Port and Enabling Regiment The Royal Logistic Corps (AR) (*Plymouth*)
Postal, Courier & Movement Regiments
29 Regiment The Royal Logistic Corps (*South Cerney*)
162 Postal Courier and Movement Regiment The Royal Logistics Corps (AR) (*Nottingham*)
Reserve
152 Fuel Support Regiment The Royal Logistic Corps (AR) (*Belfast*)
167 Catering Support Regiment The Royal Logistics Corps (AR) (*Grantham*)
2 Operational Support Group The Royal Logistics Corps (AR) (*Grantham*)

2 MEDICAL BRIGADE
HQ 2 MED BDE, Queen Elizabeth Barracks, Strensall, York, YO32 5SW

Commander...Brig Kevin Beaton *OBE QHP*

Field Hospitals
22 Field Hospital (*Aldershot*)
33 Field Hospital (*Gosport*)
34 Field Hospital (*Strensall*)
Reserve Field Hospitals
201 (Northern) Field Hospital (AR) (*Newcastle-upon-Tyne*)
202 (Midlands) Field Hospital (AR) (*Birmingham*)
203 (Welsh) Field Hospital (AR) (*Cardiff*)
204 (North Irish) Field Hospital (AR) (*Belfast*)
205 (Scottish) Field Hospital (AR) (*Glasgow*)
207 (Manchester) Field Hospital (AR) (*Manchester*)
208 (Liverpool) Field Hospital (AR) (*Liverpool*)
212 (Yorkshire) Field Hospital (AR) (*Sheffield)*
243 (Wessex) Field Hospital (AR) (*Bristol*)
256 (City of London) Field Hospital (AR) (*Walworth*)
Reserve Support
306 Hospital Support Regiment (AR) (*Strensall*)
335 Medical Evacuation Regiment (AR) (*Strensall*)
Operational HQ Support Group (AR) (*Strensall*)

1 INTELLIGENCE, SURVEILLANCE AND RECONNAISSANCE BRIGADE
Upavon

Commander...Brig James Bowder *(from Jun 2016)*

Surveillance & Target Acquisition
The Honorable Artillery Company (AR) (*City of London*)
5th Regiment Royal Artillery (*Catterick*)
Unmanned Aerial System
32nd Regiment Royal Artillery (*Larkhill*)
47th Regiment Royal Artillery (*Larkhill*)
104th Regiment Royal Artillery (MUAS) (AR) (*Newport*)
Electronic Warfare
14th Signal Regiment (Electronic Warfare) Royal Corps of Signals (*St Athan*)
Military Intelligence
1 Military Intelligence Battalion (*Catterick*)
2 Military Intelligence Battalion (*Upavon*)
3 Military Intelligence Battalion (AR) (*Hackney*)
4 Military Intelligence Battalion (*Bulford*)
5 Military Intelligence Battallion (AR) (*Edinburgh*)
6 Military Intelligence Battallion (AR) (*Manchester*)
7 Military Intelligence Battallion (AR) (*Bristol*)
Land Intelligence Fusion Centre (*Hermitage*)
Defence Cultural Specialist Unit (*Hermitage*)
Specialist Group Military Intelligence (AR) (*Hermitage*)

77 BRIGADE
Denison Barracks, Hermitage, Thatcham, Berks RG18 9TP

Commander .... Brig Alastair Aitken

Brigade Units:
No.1 Column - Planning Support, No.2 Column - Detail Synchronisation and Delivery of Effect
No.3 Column - Deployable Specialists to Armed Forces and Other Government Organisations
No.4 Column - Professional Specialists in Security Capacity Building in Defence
No. 5 Column - Media Operations and Civil Affairs, No.7 Column - The Engineer and Logistics Staff Corps

1 MILITARY POLICE BRIGADE
Marlborough Lines, Andover

Provost Marshal (Army) .... Brig David Neal *(from Jul 2016)*

Military Police Regiments
1st Regiment Royal Military Police (Hy) (*Catterick*)
3rd Regiment Royal Military Police (Hy) (*Bulford*)
4th Regiment Royal Military Police (Hy) (*Aldershot*)
Specialist Units
Special Investigation Branch Regiment Royal Military Police (Hy) (*Bulford*)
Special Operations Unit Royal Military Police (*Longmoor*)
Military Corrective Training Centre (Hy) (*Colchester*)

JOINT GROUND-BASED AIR DEFENCE COMMAND
RAF High Wycombe, Naphill, Buckinghamshire HP14 4UE

Command Units:
12 Regiment Royal Artillery, 16 Regiment Royal Artillery
106 (Yeomanry) Regiment Royal Artillery (Army Reserve)

OVERSEAS DEPLOYED UNITS

Cyprus: 1st Battalion The Duke of Lancaster's Regiment,
2nd Battalion The Princess of Wales's Royal Regiment

Brunei: 1st Battalion The Royal Gurkha Rifles

UNITS ATTACHED TO JOINT FORCES COMMAND

Attached Units: 42 Engineer Regiment (Geographic), Defence Human Intelligence Unit

LONDON DISTRICT

Reporting to Home Command
Horse Guards, Whitehall, London, SWIA 2AX
(Tel: 020 7414 2332)
The City of London, the London Metropolitan Police Area, and the Royal Borough of Windsor

General Officer Commanding London District and
Major General The Household Division .... Maj Gen *Sir* Edward Smyth-Osbourne *KCVO CBE*

Deputy Commander London District .... Brig Michael McGovern

Chief of Staff .... Col Crispin Lockhart *MBE*

Deputy Chief of Staff .... Col John Grinstead

Brigade Units:
The Household Cavalry Mounted Regiment (*Knightsbridge*)
The King's Troop Royal Horse Artillery (*Woolwich*)
1st Battalion Coldstream Guards (*Windsor*)
1st Battalion Irish Guards (*Hounslow)*
Nijmegen Company Grenadier Guards
No 7 Company Coldstream Guards, F Company Scots Guards

HQ ALLIED RAPID REACTION CORPS (ARRC)

HQ ARRC, Public Affairs Office, Imjin Barracks, Innsworth, Gloucester GL3 1HW
(Tel: +44(0)1452 718007 Fax: +44(0)1452 718875 Email: pao.admin@arrc.nato.int Website: www.arrc.nato.int)

Commander (COMARRC) ....Lt Gen Tim P Evans *CBE DSO (until 250716)*......................................300813
Lt Gen Tim B Radford *CB DSO OBE (from 250716)*

Chief of Staff (COSARRC) ....Maj Gen Richard Wardlaw *OBE*

Chief Joint Fires & Influence Branch ARRC ....Brig Paul Tennant

Chief Engineer ARRC...Brig Ben Hughes *OBE*

Deputy Chief of Staff Combat Service Support............................Brig Allan McLeod

Chief G2 ARRC ....Brig Joe O'Sullivan

Chief G6 ARRC ....Brig Sharon Nesmith

Chief G7 Training & Development ARRC ....Brig Andrew Jackson

1 (UK) SIGNAL BRIGADE

Imjin Barracks, Innsworth, Gloucester

Commander..Brig Sharon Nesmith

Brigade Units:

22nd Signal Regiment, 30th Signal Regiment
ARRC Support Battalion, 299 Signal Squadron (Special Communications)

JOINT FORCES COMMAND (JFC)

JFC HQ, Joint Headquarters Building 410, Northwood Headquarters,
Sandy Lane, Northwood, Middlesex HA6 3HP

Commander JFC .... Gen *Sir* Richard L Barrons *KCB CBE ADC Gen*

Chief of Staff JFC .... RAdm Tony Radakin *(from Jan 16)*

Assistant Chief Defence Staff (Logistics Operations) .... Maj Gen Angus S J Fay

Head Defence Logistic Operations and Capability .... Cdre Andy Kyte

Head Defence Logistic Policy .... Air Cdre Damian Alexander

Director Joint Warfare .... Maj Gen Craig Lawrence *CBE (until May 16)*

Commander Joint Air Land Organisation .... Brig Henry Nickerson

Deputy Director Joint Warfare .... Brig Peter S Cameron *(until Jun 16)*

Director Capability JFC .... Maj Gen John Patterson

Head of Capability C4ISR .... Air Cdre Nicholas Hay *OBE*

Head of Capability Joint Plans .... Air Cdre Andrew Wallis *OBE*

Director Resources and Policy .... Andy Helliwell

Deputy Director Poilicy .... N/D

Deputy Director Resources .... N/D

PERMANENT JOINT HEADQUARTERS (PJHQ)

PJHQ, Sandy Lane, Northwood, Middlesex HA6 3AP

Chief of Joint Operations .... Lt Gen *Sir* John Lorimer *KCB DSO MBE (until Jun 17)*

Chief of Staff (Operations) .... AVM Stuart Atha *DSO CB ADC (until May 16)*

Assistant Chief of Staff Personnel/Admin & Logistics (J1/J4) .. Cdre Richard A Murrison

Assistant Chief of Staff Intelligence (J2) .... Air Cdre Stephen R Thornber *(until Mar 16)*

Assistant Chief of Staff Operations (J3) .... Brig Ralph W Wooddisse *(until Ap 17)*

Assistant Chief of Staff Policy & Plans (J5) .... Cdre Andrew Betton *(until Sep 16)*

Assistant Chief of Staff Communications (J6) .... Brig Frederick E Hargreaves *OBE (until Dec 16)*

Chief of Staff (Policy & Finance) .... Damian Parmenter

Assistant Chief of Staff Policy, Legal & Media Ops (J9) .... Vacant

Assistant Chief of Finance & Civilian Support to Operations (J8) .... N/D

PERMANENT JOINT OPERATING BASES (PJOBs)

Joint Commands and Overseas Support, Joint Forces Command,
Sandy Lane, Northwood, Middlesex HA6 3AP

BRITISH FORCES CYPRUS

HQ British Forces Cyprus, BFPO 53

Commander .... AVM Mike Wigston *(until Feb 17)*

Chief of Staff British Forces Cyprus .... Brig Nick Orr

Joint Commands and Overseas Support Chief of Staff .... N/D

Chief Officer of the Sovereign Base Area (SBA) Admin .... Dr Philip Rushbrook

Chief Constable of SBA .... Chris Eyre

Attorney General and Legal Adviser SBA .... Stuart Howard

Head of Operations SBA Customs .... Andy Reed

BRITISH FORCES GIBRALTAR
HQ British Forces Gibraltar, BFPO 52

Commander........Cdre Ian McGhie

BRITISH FORCES SOUTH ATLANTIC ISLANDS
HQ British Forces South Atlantic Islands, BFPO 655

Commander........Cdre Darren Bone *(until Apr 17)*

BRITISH FORCES BRITISH INDIAN OCEAN TERRITORIES
HQ British Forces British Indian Ocean Territories, BFPO 485

STANDING JOINT FORCE HQ (SJFHQ)

Commander........Maj Gen Stuart Skeates *CBE*

Chief of Joint Force Operations........Brig Charles R Stickland *(unti Sep 17)*

Commander Joint Force Logistics Component........N/D

DEFENCE ACADEMY OF THE UNITED KINGDOM (DEFAC)

Shrivenham, Wiltshire SN6 8LA
(Tel: 01793 314828 Website: www.da.mod.uk)

Director General........V Adm Duncan Potts *CB*

Operations Director........Mark Alexander

ROYAL COLLEGE OF DEFENCE STUDIES (RCDS)
Seaford House, 37 Belgrave Square, London SW1X 8NS

Commandant........*Sir* Tom Phillips *KCMG*

Deputy Commandant........Maj Gen Alexander J S Storrie *CB CBE (until Apr 16)*

JOINT SERVICES COMMAND AND STAFF COLLEGE (JSCSC)
Faringdon Road, Shrivenham, Swindon SN6 8TS

Commandant........Maj Gen Julian R Free *CBE (until Feb 17)*

Deputy Commandant........Air Cdre Alistair Byford *(until Jun 16)*

Assistant Commandant (Maritime)........Cdre Jeremy J F Blunden

Assistant Commandant (Land)........Brig Chalres L G Herbert *(until Jun 17)*

Assistant Commandant (Air)........Air Cdre Alistair J Byford *(until Nov 16)*

Director Army Division........Brig Edward J R Chamberlain

WELBECK DEFENCE SIXTH FORM COLLEGE
Forest Road, Woodhouse, Loughborough, Leicetershire, LE12 8WD
(Tel: 01509 891700 Email: helpdesk@dsfc.ac.uk)

Principal........Mr J Peter Middleton *MA*

Director of Operations........Lt Col (Retd) Richard Spiby *MA, BA*

Vice Principal Military........Maj Jules Swindells *MSc, BEng*

ARMED FORCES CHAPLAINCY CENTRE
Amport House, Amport, Andover, Hampshire SP11 8BG

DEFENCE CENTRE OF TRAINING SUPPORT
Kermode Hall, RAF Halton, Aylesbury, Buckinghamshire HP22 5PG

SURGEON GENERAL

HQ Surgeon General, Coltman House, DMS Whittington, Lichfield Barracks,
Whittington, Lichfield, Staffordshire WS14 9PY

Surgeon General..Surg RAdm Alasdair Walker *OBE QHS*

Director Healthcare Delivery and Training..AVM *The Hon* Richard Broadbridge *QHS*

Commander - Defence Medical Group..Surg Cdre Andrew Hughes

Commander - Defence Primary Healthcare..................................Surg Cdre Paul Hughes

Head of Healthcare Education and Training................................Brig Robin Simpson

Head of Future Healthcare...Air Cdre Maria Byford

Director Medical Policy and Operational Capability..........................Maj Gen Martin C M Bricknell *QHP* 141215

Head of Medical Strategy and Policy...Air Cdre Alastair Reid *QHP*

Medical Director..Brig Tim Hodgetts *CBE*

Head of Medical Operational Capability......................................N/D

Inspector General..Cdre Inga Kennedy *QHNS QARNN*

Head Strategy Planning & Business Finance....................................N/D

Head of Secretariat & Finance..N/D

DEFENCE INTELLIGENCE

Chief of Defence Intelligence...AM Philip Osborn *CBE*

Deputy Chief of Defence Intelligence..Paul Rimmer

Head of Defence Intelligence Strategic Assessments...............N/D

Head of Defence Intelligence Capability Assessments............N/D

Head of Defence intelligence Resources..................................N/D

Head of Defence Intelligence Counter Proliferation...............N/D

Head of Defence Intelligence Operations.................................Air Cdre Mike Hart

Director Cyber, Intelligence and Intformation Integration...........Maj Gen James Hockenhull *OBE*

Deputy Director JFC GCO...N/D

Head of C4ISR Joint User...Air Cdre John Philliban

Commander Joint Cyber and Electromagnet Activity Group....Air Cdre Ian Vallely *OBE*

Deputy Director Military Support, JSSU Cheltenham..............Air Cdre Nigel Colman *OBE*

JOINT FORCES INTELLIGENCE GROUP (JFIG)
RAF Wyton, Wyton Airfield, Huntingdon, Cambridgeshire PE28 2EA (Tel: 01480 52451)

Commander JF Intelligence Group..Brig Robert Magowan *CBE*
Deputy Comander...Col David Kelly *OBE*

Defence Geographic Centre (DGC)
Bomford Building, Elmwood Avenue, Feltham, Middlesex TW13 7AH (Tel: 020 8818 2180)

Director..Mr Ian Spencer

Defence Intelligence Fusion Centre (DIFC)
RAF Wyton, Wyton Airfield, Huntingdon, Cambridgeshire PE28 2EA

Director..Gp Capt Jonathan Rolf

Joint Services Signals Organisation (JSSO)
RAF Digby, Lincoln, Lincolnshire LN4 3LH

Commander...Gp Capt Tim Neal-Hopes

DEVELOPMENT CONCEPTS AND DOCTRINE CENTRE

(Tel: 01793 314347 Email: dcdc-coordso2@mod.uk)

Director .... RAdm John Kingwell *(until April 16)*

Head of Doctrine, Air and Space .... Air Cdre Nicholas W G Laird *CBE*

Head of Future and Maritime .... Cdre Michael J Wainhouse *(until Aug 16)*

Head of Land and Research .... Brig Darrell P Amison *CBE*

INFORMATION SYTEMS AND SERVICES (ISS)

Chief Digital and Information Officer (CDIO - DG) .... Mike Stone

ISS Chief Operating Officer .... Richard Holroyd

Head of Finance .... N/D

Head of Transformation .... N/D

ISS Director Service Development .... David Lynam *MBE*

ISS Battlefield and Tactical Communication and Information Systems (BATCIS) Head .... Brig Richard Spencer

ISS SANGCOM Project Director .... Brig Peter Drew

ISS Head of Deployed Platform Services .... Cdre Jamie Hay

ISS Head of Networks .... Brig Michael Griffiths

ISS Director Service Design .... AVM Mark Neal *OBE*

ISS MOD Information Head of Profession .... Claire Fry

ISS Director Service Operations .... Maj Gen Ivan Hooper

ISS Head of Service Performance .... N/D

ISS Head of Operate and Defend .... Air Cdre Chris Moore

ISS Head of Customer Services .... N/D

ISS Director Commercial .... Rob Lees

ISS People Change Deputy Director .... Vacant

DEFENCE INFRASTRUCTURE ORGANISATION (DIO)

DIO Headquarters, Kingston Road, Sutton Coldfield, West Midlands B75 7RL
(Tel: 0121 311 2140 Email: DIOSEC-GroupMailbox@mod.uk
Website: www.gov.uk/government/organisations/defence-infrastructure-organisation)

Chief Executive .... David Mitchard *(until Oct 16)*

Chief of Staff .... N/D

Director Commmercial .... Sean Balmer

Head Strategic Stakeholder Engagement & Comms .... N/D

Chief Operating Officer .... Colin Wood

Director Service Delivery .... Richard McKinney

Director Projects & Programme .... Leo O'Shea

Director Asset Strategy & Portfolio .... Geoff Robson

Director Finance .... Marcus Leek

Director Data Analytics & Insight .... Tony Gosling

Director Transformation & Change .... Nik Doyle

Director Human Resources .... David Billingham

DEFENCE EQUIPMENT AND SUPPORT (DE&S)

Ministry of Defence, DE&S Secretariat, Maple 0a, #2043,
MOD Abbey Wood, Bristol BS34 8JH
Tel: 030 679 32222 Email: DESSec-Internet@mod.uk
Website: www.gov.uk/government/organisations/defence-equipment-and-support
Tel: 030 679 30206 Email: DESSec-ParliamentaryBusiness@mod.uk

(as of May 2106)

Non-Executive Chair .... Paul Skinner *CBE*

Chief Executive .... Tony Douglas
Chief of Staff .... Dawn Cunningham-Martin
PSO .... Col Gavin Thompson
Private Secretary .... Thomas Tiner

Chief of Materiel Fleet .... VAdm Simon Lister *CB OBE*
Military Assistant .... Cdr Mark Grenfell-Shaw *RN*

Chief of Materiel Land .... Lt Gen Paul Jaques *CBE*
Military Assistant .... Lt Col Paul Cummings

Chief of Materiel Air .... AM Julian Young *CB OBE*
Military Assistant .... Wg Cdr Ben Trapnell

Chief of Materiel Joint Enablers .... Pete Worrall
Military Assistant .... Maj Simon Burkill
Private Secretary .... Teresa Ashman

Director General Resources .... Michael Bradley
Private Secretary .... Lesley Richardson

Director General Commercial .... Nick Elliott
Chief of Staff .... Ann Williams
Private Secretary .... Beth Hope

Director Corporate Affairs .... Barry Burton

Director Commercial Operations .... Alan Peter

Director Technical .... AVM Michael Quigley

Director Learning & Talent .... David Ball

Director Human Resources .... Shirley Spencer

MATERIEL LAND

Chief of Materiel Land .... Lt Gen Paul Jaques *CBE*

Head Land Domain and Army Customer Team .... Brig Doug Gibson

Chief Finance Officer (Land) .... Mark Binnersley

Chief Operating Officer (Land) .... Dan Wood

LAND EQUIPMENT

Director Land Equipment .... Maj Gen Robert Talbot-Rice *CBE*

Military Assistant .... Maj Phil Pascoe

Head LE Armoured Vehicle Programmes .... Dr Allan Paterson

Head LE Portfolio & Programme Support .... Huw Cable

Head LE Equipment Commerical .... Anna-Marie Barrow

Head LE Soldier Training and Special Programmes .... Brig James Daniel

Head LE Operational Support Programme .... Roddy Malone

WEAPONS

Director Weapons....................Richard Smart
Military Assistant....................Lt Cdr Stuart Lowe RN
Head Weapons Engineering....................Hugh Bellars
Head Weapons Team Complex Weapons....................Jonathan Barratt
Head of Weapons Commercial....................Kim Woodward
Head Weapons Munitions International & Torpedoes....................Nick Hunt
Head Weapons Support....................Neil Rixon

SUPPORT ENABLERS OPERATING CENTRE

Director Support Enablers Operating Centre....................Andrew Cannon-Brookes
Chief of Staff....................Col Colin Francis
Military Assistant....................Lt Cdr Tim Grimley *RN*
Head Support Chain Processes....................Tony Doherty
Head Support Chain Information Services....................Steve Glass
Head Support Chain Engagement....................Brig Justin Stanhope-White
Head Support Chain Professional Development....................Ingrid Morris
Head Support Chain Finance....................Mike Turner
Head Commercial....................Alan Richardson

LOGISTICS DELIVERY

Director Logistics Delivery....................Roger West
Chief of Staff....................Col Matthew Wilkinson
Military Assitant....................Sqn Ldr Georgina Mews
Head Commissioning Managing Organisation....................Richard Parkinson
Head Operations Commissioning and Managing Organisation....................Anthony Roberts
Head Progamme Management....................Mark Snell
Head Defence Supply Chain Operations & Movements....................Brig Duncan Capps
Head LCS, Joint Support Chain Finance....................Victoria Charles-Jones

DISPOSALS SERVICES AUTHORITY

Disposals Services Authority, Defence Equipment & Support (DE&S), Building H9, Ploughley Road, Lower Arncott, Bicester, Oxon OX25 2LD
(Tel: 030 6770 2911 Email: DESLCSLS-eDisposals@mod.uk)

Head Disposal Services Authority (DSA)....................Lee Nicholls
Commmerical Disposals TL (Bichester)....................Richard Norris
Captial Equipment Sales TL....................Dave Bruce

BRITISH FORCES POST OFFICE

HQ BFPO, West End Road, Ruislip, Middlesex HA4 6DQ
(Tel: +44 (0)345 769 7978 Email: DESBFPO-enquiries@mod.uk
Website: www.gov.uk/bfpo)

Head of BFPO....................Col Tim Blackmore *OBE*

OFFICE OF THE JUDGE ADVOCATE GENERAL (OJAG)

9th Floor, Thomas More Building, The Royal Courts of Justice, The Strand, London WC2A 2LL
(Tel: 020 7013 1618 Fax: 0870 3240044 Email: Ben.Yallop@judiciary.gsi.gov.uk)

Judge Advocate General ....His Honour Judge Blackett..................281004

Vice-Judge Advocate General....................Judge Michael Hunter..................010184

Assistant Judge Advocate General....................Judge Camp..................180488

Judge McGrigor..................031005

Judge Hill..................101005

Judge Large..................010110

THE MILITARY COURT SERVICE

Building 398, Trenchard Lines, Upavon, Pewsey, Wilts SN9 6BE
(Tel: 01980 618058 Fax: 01980 618060 Email: mcs-group@mod.uk)

Military Court Centres:

Bulford (Wilts)
Catterick (Yorks)
Colchester (Essex)
Sennelager (Germany)
Portsmouth (Hants)

THE COLLEGE OF ARMS

130 Queen Victoria Street, London, EC4V 4BT
(Tel: 020 7248 2762 Fax: 020 7248 6448)

Inspector of Regimental Colours
(Garter King of Arms)....................Thomas Woodcock *CVO BA LLB DL FSA*

Deputy Inspector of Regimental Colours
(Norfolk Herald Extraordinary)....................Maj David Rankin-Hunt *CVO MBE KCN TD*

NATO AND EU FORMATIONS

NATO HEADQUARTERS

Boulevard Leopold III, 1110 Brussels, Belgium
(Nato HQ, Brussels, Belgium BFPO 49)
(as of March 16 unless otherwise stated)

Assistant Secretary General for Operations .... Mr Patrick Turner .... Oct 15

INTERNATIONAL MILITARY STAFF

Executive Co-ordinator .... Cdre S P Hardern *RN (until 170916)* 2012
Air Cdre D J Toriati *OBE (from* 170916)

MILITARY COMMITTEE

NATO Chief of Staff, UK .... Gen *Sir* Nicholas Houghton *GCB CBE ADC Gen*... 2013

UK Military Representative to NATO .... VAdm Ian Corder *CB (until May 16)*
Lt Gen *Sir* George Norton *KCVO CBE (from May 16)*

Director General International Military Staff .... AM *Sir* Christopher Harper *KBE*
(until 27 Jul 16) 300713

UK JOINT DELEGATION TO NATO

UKDel NATO, Boulevard Leopold III, 1110 Brussels, Belgium
(Tel: +32 2 707 7501 Fax: +32 2 707 7596 Email: UKDEL.NATOGeneralEnquiries@fco.gsi.gov.uk)

UK Permanent Representative to the North Atlantic Council .... *Sir* Adam Thomson *KCMG*

UK Military Representative to NATO .... VAdm Ian Corder *CB* 150513

ALLIED COMMAND OPERATIONS (ACO)

Strategic Level Command:

SUPREME HEADQUARTERS ALLIED POWERS EUROPE (SHAPE)

Public Affairs Office, B-7010 SHAPE (Mons), Belgium, BFPO 26
(SHAPE, MONS, Belgium, BFPO 26)
(Tel: +32 (0) 65-44-4154 Fax: +32 (0) 65-44-3100 Email: shapepao@shape.nato.in)

Deputy Supreme Allied Commander Europe (DSACEUR) .... Gen *Sir* Adrian Bradshaw *KCB OBE (until Mar 17)*

United Kingdom National Military Representative .... Brig William N Aldridge *CBE (until Aug 16)*
Air Cdre W J Millington *(from Aug 16)*

Operational Level Commands:

JOINT FORCE COMMAND HEADQUARTERS (JFC BRUSSNUM)

HQ Allied JFC BRUNSSUM, Public Affairs Office, Box 270, 6440 AG Brunssum, The Netherlands
(NATO JFC, Holland, BFPO 28)
(Email: pao@jfcbs.nato.int)

Deputy Chief of Staff Plans .... Acting RAdm S P Hardern *RN (until Nov 17)* .... Nov 16

Resolute Support Headquarters (Afghanistan)
(Tel: +93 (0)70-013-2114 / +93 (0)70-013-2928 Website: www.rs.nato.int)

Resolute Support Mission Deputy Commander .... Lt Gen Tim B Radford *CB DSO OBE (until Oct 17)*.... Jul 15
Lt Gen Richard Cripwell *CB CBE (from Oct 17)*

JOINT FORCE COMMAND HEADQUARTERS (JFC NAPLES)

Allied Joint Force Command Naples, Via Madonna del Pantano, 80014 Lago Patria,
Giugliana in Campania, Naples, Italy
(NATO JFC, NAPLES, Italy, BFPO 8)
(Tel: 081-721-2752 / 081-721-3838 Email: http:JFCNPPAOGROUP@jfcnp.nato.int)

Deputy Chief of Staff Plans .... Maj Gen Ian Cave

Tactical Level Commands

ALLIED AIR COMMAND (HQ AIRCOM)

HQ AIRCOM, Public Affairs Office - Büro für Öffentlichkeitsarbeit, Building/Gebäude 313, Flugplatz Ramstein, D-66877 Ramstein-Miesenbach, Germany (BFPO 109)
(Email: airn.pao@airn.nato.int Website: www.airn.nato.int)

Deputy Chief of Staff Support HQ .... Air Cdre Wendy Millington (Designate) *(until Aug 16)*
Deputy Commander - Afghanistan .... Air Cdre S E Reeves *(until Apr 16)* .... Oct 15
Acting Air Cdre J M Dixon *AFC (until Oct 16)*... Apr 16
Acting Air Cdre A P T Smith *(until Apr 17)*........ Oct 16

ALLIED LAND COMMAND (HQ LANDCOM)

NATO Land Command, General Vecihi Akin Garrison 35148 Izmir / TURKEY
(Email: lc.registry@lc.nato.int Website: www.lc.nato.int)

Deputy Commander .... Lt Gen Edward Davis *CB CBE KStJ (until Mar 16)*

ALLIED MARITIME COMMAND (HQ MARCOM)

Atlantic Building, Northwood Headquarters, Sandy Lane, Northwood, Middlesex, HA6 3HP
(Tel: 01923 956 763 (Public Affairs Office) Email: publicaffairs@mc.nato.int Website: www.mc.nato.int)

Commander .... VAdm Clive Johnstone *CB CBE*

Tactical Air C2 Elements:

NATO CIS GROUP (NCISG)

(Based in Mons. Belgium)

NAVAL STRIKING AND SUPPORT FORCES NATO (STRIKFORNATO)

Reduto Gomes Freire, Estrada Da Medrosa, 2780 - 070 Oeiras, Portugal
(Tel: +351 21 440 4116 (Public Affairs Office) E-mail: pao@sfn.nato.int Website: hwww.sfn.nato.int)

Deputy Commander .... RAdm Paddy McAlpine *CBE*

NATO AIRBORNE EARLY WARNING AND CONTROL FORCE COMMAND (NAEW&CF)

NATO AEW and CF, P.O. Box 40800, Lilienthalallee 100, 52511 Geilenkirchen, Germany
(Tel: +49 (0) 2451 63 2485 (Public Affairs Office) Fax: +49 (0) 2451 7936 (Public Affairs Office)
Email: ofc-hqfhp@naew.nato.int Website: www.e3a.nato.int)

E-3D Component, RAF Waddington, Lincoln LN5 9NB

Deputy Commander and Chief of Staff (HQ) .... Air Cdre Andrew T Martin
Deputy Commander E3A Component .... Air Cdre I D Teakle *DSO OBE* 210714
Commander E-3D Component .... Wg Cdr Jez Batt

RAPIDLY DEPLOYABLE CORPS HEADQUATERS

Headquarters Allied Command Europe Rapid Reaction Corps (ARRC)

HQ ARRC, Public Affairs Office, Imjin Barracks, Innsworth, Gloucester GL3 1HW
(Tel: +44(0)1452 718007 Fax: +44(0)1452 718875
Email: pao.admin@arrc.nato.int Website: www.arrc.nato.int)

Commander (COMARRC) ....Lt Gen Tim P Evans *CBE DSO (until 250716)*....................300813
Lt Gen Tim B Radford *CB DSO OBE (from 250716)*

Headquarters Rapid Deployable Corps Italy (NRDC-ITA)

Via per Busto Arsizio, 20, 21058 Solbiate Olona (VA), Italy
(Tel: +39 0331 34 5111 (Switchboard) Email: nrdcitapaoweb@gmail.com Website: www.nrdc-ita.nato.int)

Deputy Commander ....Lt Gen *Sir* George Norton *KCVO CBE*

ALLIED COMMAND TRANSFORMATION (ACT)

HQ SUPREME ALLIED COMMAND TRANSFORMATION (HQ SACT)

Public Affairs Office, 7857 Blandy Road, Suite 100, Norfolk, VA23551-2490, USA, BFPO493
(Tel: +1 (757) 747-3600 Fax: +1 (757) 747-3234 E-mail: pao@act.nato.int
Website: www.act.nato.int Email: pao@act.nato.int)

Chief of Staff to Supreme Allied Commander ....AM *Sir* Graham Stacey *KBE CB MA BSc CCMI*

Joint Warfare Centre (JWC)

Joint Warfare Centre, PO Box 8080, Eikesetveien, 4068 Stavanger, Norway
(Tel: + (47) 52 87 9130/9131/9132 Email: pao@act.nato.int)

Joint Force Training Centre (JFTC)

Joint Force Training Centre, Central Registry , ul. Szubinska 2, 85-915 Bydgoszcz, Poland
(Tel: +48 261 41 9777 Fax: +48 261 41 1579 Email: JFTC@jftc.nato.int Website: www.jftc.nato.int)

Joint Analysis and Lessons Learned Centre

Avenida Tenente Martins, Monsanto, 1500-589 Lisboa, Portugal
(Tel: + 351 21 771 7007/8/ 9 Email: jallc@jallc.nato.int Website: www.jallc.nato.int)

ORGANISATIONS AND AGENCIES

Nato Eurofighter & Tornadeo Management Agency

General Manager ....AVM Graham Farnell *OBE*

Combined Joint Operations from the Sea Centre of Excellence (CJOS COE)

1562 Mitscher Ave., Suite 250, Norfolk, VA 23551-2487
(Website: www.cjoscoe.org)

Deputy Director, Combined Joint Operations ....Cdre Phillip Titterton *OBE*

EUROPEAN UNION MILITARY COMMITTEE

European External Action Service , 9A Rond Point Schuman, 1046 Brussels, Belgium
(Tel: +32 2 584 11 11 Website: /eeas.europa.eu)

UK Military Representative to NATO ....VAdm Ian Corder *CB (until May 16)*
Lt Gen *Sir* George Norton *KCVO CBE (from May 16)*

EUROPEAN DEFENCE AGENCY

Rue des Drapiers, 17-23, B-1050 Ixelles, Belgium
(Tel: +32 25042800 Fax: +32 25042815 Email: info@eda.europa.eu Website: www.eda.europa.eu)

Director Capability, Armament & Technology ....Air Cdre Pete Round *(until Mar 17)*....................Jul 12

DEFENCE EXECUTIVE AGENCIES

DEFENCE ELECTRONICS AND COMPONENTS AGENCY

Welsh Road, Deeside, Flintshire CH5 2LS (Tel: 01244 847745 Email: decainfo@deca.mod.uk
Website: www.gov.uk/government/organisations/defence-electronics-and-components-agency)
(as of March 16)

Chief Executive..Geraint Spearing

Finance Director..Lin Longman

Support Services Director..Ian Doughty

Operations Director..Wayne Baker

Commercial & Contracts Director...Keith Pavett

Business Development Director..Ian Cole

Head of Strategy, Governance & Secretariat............................Jason Leeks

DEFENCE SCIENCE AND TECHNOLOGY LABORATORY (DSTL)

DSTL Headquarters, Porton Down, Salisbury, Wilts SP4 0JQ
(Tel: 01980 613121 (central enquiries) Tel: 01980 613000 (Switchboard) Email: centralenquiries@dstl.gov.uk
Website: www.gov.uk/government/organisations/defence-science-and-technology-laboratory)

Chairman..*Sir* David Pepper *KCMG*

Chief Executive..Jonathan Lyle

Non-Executive Directors..Elisabeth Astall
Gerard Connell
David English
Dr David Grant *CBE*
Prof Dame Wendy Hall
David Marsh

Director for Technology...Dr Bryn Hughes

Finance Director..David English

Infrastructure Director...Graham Balmer

People and Business Services Director....................................Joanne Peel

Transformation Director..Jennifer Henderson / Alexander Lambert

CENTRE FOR DEFENCE ENTERPRISE

Building R103, Fermi Avenue, Harwell, Oxford OX11 0QX (Tel: 030 6770 4236 / 4237 Email: cde@dstl.gov.uk)

Head of Operations...Jim Pennycook

UK HYDROGRAPHIC OFFICE (UKHO)

UKHO, Admiralty Way, Taunton, Somerset TA1 2DN
(Tel: 01823 337 900 Email: customerservices@ukho.gov.uk Website: www.gov.uk/ukho)

Non-Executive Chair...Adam Singer

Chief Executive..John Humphrey

UK Hydrographer and Deputy Chief Executive........................R Adm Tim Lowe

Non-Executive Directors..Barry Wooton
Marion Leslie
Heather Tayler (MOD Non-Executive Director)
Capt David Robertson *RN* (Hydrographer of the Navy)

HER MAJESTY'S NAUTICAL ALMANAC OFFICE

UK Hydrographic Office, Admiralty Way, Taunton TA1 2DN
(Tel: +44 (0)1823 4844444 Email: hmnao@ukho.gov.uk)

Head ....Dr Steve Bell

MISCELLANEOUS INSTITUTIONS AND ORGANISATIONS

(as of Nov 17)

THE NAVY, ARMY AND AIR FORCE INSTITUTES (NAAFI)

NAAFI Building 1/150, Room 103, Murrays Lane (PP19B),
HM Naval Base Portsmouth, Portsmouth Hampshire, PO1 3NH (Website: www.naafi.co.uk)

PATRON .... HER MAJESTY THE QUEEN

Council

NAAFI Chairman .... *Sir* Ian Prosser

Chief of Defence .... Gen *Sir* Nicholas R Houghton *GBE CBE ADC Gen*

Commander Home Command .... Lt Gen James I Bashall *CBE*

Second Sea Lord (2SL) .... VAdm Jonathan Woodcock *OBE*

Air Member for Personnel & Capability .... AM Baz North *OBE MA RAF*

Chief of Joint Operations (CJO), PJHQ .... Lt Gen *Sir* John Lorimer *KCB DSO MBE (until Jun 17)*

Defence Infrastructure Organisation Operations .... N/A

Board of Directors

Managing Director .... Steve Marshall *(from May 16)*

NAAFI Chairman .... *Sir* Ian Prosser

Non-Executive Directors .... Reg Curtis
Alan Smith *BA FRAeS*
Gen *Sir* Redmond Watt *KCB KCVO CBE*

ABF THE SOLDIERS' CHARITY

Mountbarrow House, 12 Elizabeth Street, London SW1W 9RB
(Tel: 0207 901 8900 Fax: 0207 901 8901
Email: supportercare@soldierscharity.org Website: www.soldierscharity.org/)

PATRON .... HER MAJESTY THE QUEEN

President .... Gen *Sir* Mike Jackson *GCB CBE DSO DL*

Chairman of the Board of Trustees .... Lt Gen Philip Jones *CB CBE*

Vice Chairman of the Board of Trustees .... Simon Martin

Trustees .... Peter Baynham *BA(Hons) FCA AMCT*
Mary Fagan
Damien Francis
WO1 Glenn Haughton
Paul Hearn
Maj Gen (Retd) Malcolm Wood *CBE*
Maj Gen Robert Nitsch *CBE*
James Rouse

Chief Executive .... Maj Gen Martin Rutledge *CB OBE*

Chief of Staff and Secretary to the Board of Trustees .... Brig Robin Bacon

NATIONAL ARMY MUSEUM

Royal Hospital Road, London SW3 4HT
(Tel: 020 7730 0717 Email: info@nam.ac.uk Website: www.nam.ac.uk)

Patron .... FM *HRH The Duke of* Kent *KG GCMB GCVO ARC(P)*

Chairman of the Council .... Gen *Sir* Richard Shirreff *KCB CBE*

Council .... Mr Patrick Aylmer
Mr Keith Baldwin
Brig Douglas Erskine Crum
The Rt Hon The Lord Hamilton of Epsom *PC*
Ms Jessica Spungin
Mr William Wells

Director General .... Mrs Janice Murray

Museum Director .... Mr Mike O'Connor

Assistant Director (Collections) .... Mr Ian Maine

Assistant Director (Commercial and Visitor Experience) .... Ms Dawn Watkins

Assistant Director (Human Resources) .... Ms Teresa Scott

DUKE OF YORK'S ROYAL MILITARY SCHOOL (DYRMS)

Dover, Kent CT15 5EQ
(Tel: 01304 245023 Fax: 01304 245019
Email: admin.office@doyrms.com Website: www.doyrms.com)

Patron .... FM *HRH The Duke of* Kent *KG CGMC GCVO ADC(P)*

Principal and Commandant .... Mr A Foreman *BA PGCE*

Vice Principal (Recruitment and Military) .... Mr S S Saunderson *BA PGCE*

Vice Principal (Curriculum and Progress) .... Mr S P Haslehurst *MA (Oxon) PGCE*

Vice Principal (Boarding, Health & Welfare) .... Mrs A Kehaya *MA*

Director of Finance and Operations .... Mr Kent

Chaplain .... Mr S Saunderson

Contingent Commander (CCF) .... Lt Col S Saunderson *(CCF)*

Director of Military Music .... Maj (Retd) D W Cresswell *BBCM psm*

Chair of Governors .... Mrs Georgina Martin

Governors .... Mr Alex Foreman
Brig Matt Bazeley
Mr Nigel Bryant
Mr Russell Collier
Revd Dr David Coulter *CB QHC CF*
Lt Gen *Sir* Gary Coward *KBE CB CGIA*
Mr Daren Gregg
Lt Col Alan Jones
Ms Jenny Lycett Chartered *FCIPD*
Mr Andrew Nunn
Mr Damian Pinel
Mr Leyland B Ridings *MBE JP*
Col Philip Smith *BA (Hons) MBA FCMI*
ColAndy Thorne
Mrs Daniela Vandepeer *MSc MA CMathTeach TEFL Cert*
Mr Christopher Wacher *BSc (Soc Sci)*

Clerk to the Governors .... Mrs T Elkins
Chair of Trustees .... Lt Gen James Bashall *CBE*

ROYAL HOSPITAL CHELSEA

Royal Hospital Road, London SW3 4SR
(Tel: 020 7881 5200 (Switchboard) Email: claire.nott@chelsea-pensioners.org.uk (enquiries)
Website: www.chelsea-pensioners.co.uk)

(as of 31 March 16)

Board of Commisioners

Ex-Officio Commissioners

HM Paymaster General.................*Rt Hon* Matthew Hancock *MP (Chairman)*

Minister of State for the Armed Forces.................Penny Mordaunt *MP*

Minister for Defence Personnel, Welfare and Veterans.................Mark Lancaster *TD MP*

Director Resources & Command Secretary(Army).................Mr David Stephens *Esq*

Director General Army Medical Services.................Maj Gen Jeremy Rowan *CB OBE QHS*

Assistant Chief of the General Staff.................Maj Gen N Welch *OBE*

Governor, Royal Hospital Chelsea.................Gen *Sir* Redmond Watt *KCB KCVO CBE DL*

Specially Apointed Commissioners
M Waterson *Esq OBE*
Stuart Corbyn *Esq*
A Titchmarsh *Esq MBE VMH DL*
Justin Fenwick *Esq QC (Deputy Chairman)*
Prof *the Lord* Kakkar *PC*
David Rosier *Esq*
Mrs Angela Gillibrand
Dame Barbara Monroe *DBE*
Mark Gallagher *Esq*
Charles Lewington *Esq OBE*
Ms Jo Cleary
Dr Roger Bowdler

Chief Executive Officer and Accounting Officer
Gary Lashko *(from 1 Feb 16)*

Secretary
PWD Hatt *Esq*

Senior Management

The Governor.................Gen *Sir* Redmond Watt *KCB KCVO CBE DL*

Physician & Surgeon.................Dr Fergus Keating *MBBS MRCGP*

Director of Health and Wellbeing.................Prof Deborah Sturdy *OBE*

Quartermaster and Director of Facilities.................Lt Col Andy Hickling *MBE*

Chaplain.................*The Revd* Steven Brookes

Human Resources Director.................Celia Kowalkowski

Finance Director.................Nick Cattermole

QUEEN VICTORIA SCHOOL

Dunblane, Perthshire FK15 0JY
(Tel: 01786 822288 (Switchboard) Email: enquiries@qvs.org.uk Website: www.qvs.org.uk)
Motto: "In Defens"

(as of March 16)

Patron .... *HRH The Prince* Philip Duke of Edinburgh *KG KT OM GBE ONZ QSO AK GCL CC CMM ADC(P)*

Head .... Wendy A Bellars *MA(Hons)DipEdMA(Ed Man) PGCE*

Senior Deputy Head .... Donald J Shaw *BSc(Hons) PGCE*

FIRST AID NURSING YEOMANRY (PRINCESS ROYAL'S VOLUNTEER CORPS) (FANY (PRVC))

FANY (PRVC), PO Box 68218, London SW1P 9UP
(Tel: 020 7976 5459 Email:hq@fany.org.uk Website: www.fany.org.uk)

Commandant-in-Chief .... *HRH The Princess Royal KG KT GCVO QSO*

Commanding Officer .... Commandant Kim McCutcheon

ST JOHN AND RED CROSS DEFENCE MEDICAL WELFARE SERVICE (DMWS)

Headquaters, The Old Stables, Redenham Park, Redenham, Nr Andover SP11 9AQ
(Tel: 01264 774 000 Email: info@dmws.org.uk Website: www.dmws.org.uk)

Champions .... *Baroness* Audrey Emerton *DBE DL*
The Lord Smith of Kelvin *KT CH*
Gen *Sir* Gordon Messenger KCB *DSO* OBE ADC*
Lt Gen (Retd) *Sir* Alistair Irwin *KCB CBE*
Lt Gen (Retd) *Sir* Mark Mans *KCB CBE DL*
Prof *Sir* Cary Cooper *CBE*
Maj Gen R T I Munro *CBE TD VR (Late PARA)*
Maj Gen (Retd) S M Andrews *CBE*
Maj Gen (Retd) John Stokoe *CB CBE*
Dr Rosemary Kennedy *CBE OStJ TD*
Dr Gordon Paterson *OBE*
Christine Atkinson
Simon Brown
Nigel Jackson
Sue Liburd *MBE*
Kevin Mackie
Sally Scott
Andrew Stewart-Roberts

Trustees

Chairman of Trustees .... Maryanna Burton *JP*

Deputy Chairman .... Steve Cowden

Trustees .... David Keenan *OBE*
James Plastow *CBE*
Andrew Buckham (Partner with Irwin Mitchell)
Barbara Cooper *CBE*
Paul Taylor

Leadership Team

Chief Executive .... Nicky Murdoch *MBE*

Chief Operating Officer .... Paul Gaffney

THE BRITISH RED CROSS SOCIETY

UK Office, 44 Moorfields London EC2Y 9AL
(Tel: 0344 871 11 11 (switchboard) Tel: +44 (0)2071 3879 00 (overseas) Fax: 020 7562 2000
Email: information@redcross.org.uk Website: www.redcross.org.uk)

(as of 2016 - British Red Cross Trustees Report and Accounts 2016)

PATRON .... HER MAJESTY THE QUEEN

President .... FM *HRH The Prince of* Wales *KG KT GCB OM AK QSO ADC(P)*

Deputy Presidents .... *HRH Princess* Alexandra, *the Hon Lady* Ogilvy *KG GCVO*
The Countess Mountbatten *of Burma CBE CD JP DL*

Honorary vice-presidents .... *Lord* Barnard *TD*
The Rt Hon Baroness Chalker *of Wallasey*
Sylvia, *Countess of* Limerick *CBE*
Prof John McClure *OBE*
Mrs Elspeth Thomas *CBE DL*
Sir Nicholas Young

Vice-presidents .... Mr Anthony Andrews
Ms Angela Rippon *OBE*
Mrs Maria Shammas *MBE*

Board of Trustees

Chairman of Trustees .... Mr David Bernstein *CBE*

Vice-Chair of Trustees .... Mr John Dauth *AO LVO*
Mrs Hilary Douglas *CB*
Mr Paul Taylor

Treasurer .... Mr David Howell *(until 28 Mar 16)*

Trustees .... Mrs Fionnuala Cook *DL OBE*
Mr Robert Dewar *CMG*
Mrs Uzo Iwobi *OBE*
Mr Steve John
Mr Gordon Low
Mrs Gill Moffat
Mrs Amanda Nicholson
Dr Daniel Sedgewick
Mr Keith Shipman

External Adviser .... Vicky Wright

Executive Leadership Team

Chief Executive .... Michael Adamson

Executive Director of UK Operations .... Norman McKinley

Executive Director of People, Learning and Strategic Change .... Roger Smith *OBE FCIPD*

Executive Director of Fundraising .... Mark Astarita *OBE*

Executive Director of International .... David Peppiatt

Interim Executive Director of Finance, Planning and Resources .... Phil Hughes

Chief Information Officer .... Rosie Slater

Executive Director of Communications and Engagement .... Zoe Abrams

COMMONWEALTH WAR GRAVES COMMISSION (CWGC)

2 Marlow Road, Maidenhead, Berkshire SL6 7DX
(Tel: +44 (0)1628 634221 (English Enquiries) Tel: +32 (0) 57224750 (French, Dutch and German Enquiries)
Email: enquiries@cwgc.org Website: www.cwgc.org)

(as of 2016 - CWGC Annual Report 2015-2106)

Commissioners

President..*HRH The Duke of* Kent *KG GCMG GCVO ADC(P)*

Chairman..*The Rt Hon Sir* Michael Fallon MP
(The Secretary of State for Defence (UK))

Vice Chairman..V Adm *Sir* Tim Laurence *KCVO CB ADC(P)*

Representatives of Member Governments..*HE The Rt Hon Sir* Lockwoood Smith *KNZM PhD*
High Commissioner for New Zealand
HE the Hon Alexander Downer *AC*
High Commissioner for Australia
HE Mr Obed Mlaba
High Commissioner for the Republic of South Africa
HE Mr Gordon Campbell
High Commissioner for Canada
HE Ranjan Mathai
High Commissioner for the Republic of India

Members..Prof *Sir* Hew Strachan *PhD FRSE*
The Rt Hon Keith Simpson *MP*
Mr Kevan Jones *MP*
Mr Edward Chaplin *CMG OBE*
The Hon Mrs Ros Kelly *AO*
Mr Robert Fox *MBE*
Lt Gen *Sir* William Rollo *KCB CBE*
AM Daivd Walker *CB CBE AFC*

Principle Officers at Head Office

Director General (Secretary of the Commission)..Victoria Wallace

Director of Human Resources..Stephen Luckhurst

Director of Operations..Barry Murphy

Director of Legal Services..Gillian Stedman

Director of External Relations..Colin Kerr

Director of Resources..Judith O'Connell

United Kingdom & Northern Area

CWGC, 2 Marlow Road, Maidenhead, Berkshire SL6 7DX
Tel: +44 (0) 1628 634221 Fax: +44 (0) 1628 771208 E-mail: enquiries@cwgc.org

Head..Chris Lee

Western Europe Area

Elverdingestraat 82 , B-8900 Ieper , Belgium
Tel: +32 (0) 57 22 36 36 Fax: +32 (0) 57 21 80 14 E-mail: contact.wea@cwgc.org

Director..Richard Nichol

France

5 -7 Rue Angèle Richard CS1019, 62217 Beaurains, France
Tel: +33 (0) 3 21 21 77 00 Fax: +33 (0) 3 21 21 77 10 E-mail: contact.wea@cwgc.org

Mediterranean Area

CWGC, PO Box 40970, TT 6308, Cyprus

Tel: +357 24819460 Fax: +357 24661969 E-mail: maoffice@cwgc.org

Director .... Ian Hussein

Africa & Asia Pacific Area

CWGC, 2 Marlow Road, Maidenhead, Berkshire SL6 7DX

Tel: +44 (0) 1628 634221 Fax: +44 (0) 1628 771643 E-mail: aapaoffice@cwgc.org

Director .... Richard Hills

Australia

Office of Australian War Graves Department of Veterans' Affairs GPO Box 9998

Canberra ACT 2601, Australia

Tel: +61 (0) 2 6289 6477 Fax: +61 (0) 2 6289 4861 E-mail: wargraves@dva.gov.au

Canada

Canadian Agency, CWGC, 66 Slater Street, Suite 1412

Ottawa, Ontario K1A 0P4 , Canada

Tel: +1 613 992 3224 Fax: +1 613 995 0431

E-mail: enquiries@cwgc.org Web Site: www.cwgc-canadianagency.ca

Secretary-General .... Brig Gen (Retd) David Kettle

New Zealand

Heritage Operations, Ministry for Culture and Heritage PO Box 5364,

Wellington, New Zealand

Tel: +64 (0) 4 499 4229 Fax: +64 (0) 4 499 4490 E-mail: info@mch.govt.nz

South Africa

South African Agency

c/o Africa, Asia and Pacific Area CWGC Head Office

2 Marlow Road , Maidenhead, Berkshire, SL6 7DX

Director .... Juan Maree

ARMY COMMANDS OF COMMONWEALTH COUNTRIES

(Defence appointments of listed countries are correct as of Nov 2017 unless otherwise stated.
Diplomatic Staff of Commonwealth states in London are sourced from the London Diplomatic List as of 6th Oct 17)

Commonwealth Secretariat
Marlborough House, Pall Mall, London SW1Y 5HX
(Tel: +44 (0) 20 7747 6500 Fax: +44 (0) 20 7930 0827
Email: info@commonwealth.int Website: www.thecommonwealth.org)

Head........ *HM* Queen Elizabeth II
Secretary-General........ *Rt Hon* Patricia Scotland *QC*........010416
Deputy Secretary-General........ Dr Josephine Ojiambo (2015-)
Chair-in-Office........ *Hon* Dr Joseph Muscat *MP KUOM* (Prime Minister, Malta)
Commonwealth Ministerial Action Group (CMAG)
(Rotatation of foreign ministers from 8 member states
plus the foreign minister of the Chair-in-Office)........ Cyprus (Chair), Guyana, India, Kenya, Malta, Namibia, New Zealand, Pakistan and Solomon Island

COMMONWEALTH COUNTRIES OF THE CARIBBEAN AND AMERICAS

ANTIGUA AND BARBUDA

(Joined Commonwealth: 1981)

Governor General........ *HE Sir* Rodney Errey Lawrence Williams *KGN GCMG KStJ MBBS*
Prime Minister........ *Hon* Mr Gaston Alfonso Brown

Royal Antigua and Barbuda Defence Force
(1st Antigua and Barbuda Regiment (1ABR), Service and Support Battalion (SSB), Coast Guard (ABCG) and Cadet Corps (ABNCC))

Chief of Defence........ Col *Sir* Trevor Thomas
Commanding Officer Coast Guard........ Lt Cdr Auden Nigel Nicholas

Office of the High Commission of Antigua and Barbuda in the United Kingdom
2nd Floor 45 Crawford Place, London W1H 4LP
(Tel: 020 7258 0070 Fax: 020 7258 7486
Email: highcommission@antigua-barbuda.com Website: www.antigua-barbuda.com)

High Commissioner........ *HE* Ms Karen-Mae Hill........100116
Minister-Counsellor (Administration & Consular Affairs) ...Mrs Althea Allison Vandepoole Banahene

BAHAMAS, THE

(Joined Commonwealth: 1973)

Governor General........ *HE Dame* Marguerite Pindling........080714
Prime Minister........ *The Rt Hon* Perry Gladstone Christie *PC MP*
Minister of National Security........ *The Hon* Marvin Hanlon Dames........150517
Permanent Secretary........ Carl F Smith

Royal Bahamas Defence Force (RBDF)
(Land Force, Navy and Air Wing)

CommanderDefence Force........ Capt Tellis A Bethel *MALIC*........150315
Captain Coral Harbour........ Capt Clyde Sawyer........Nov 06

Office of the High Commission of The Bahamas in the United Kingdom
10 Chesterfield Street, London W1J 5JL
(Tel: 020 7408 4488 Fax: 020 7499 9937
Email: information@bahamashclondon.net Website: www.bahamashclondon.net)

High Commissioner........ Vacant
Deputy High Commissioner........ Ms Allison Paulette Booker
2nd Secretary & Vice Consul........ Mr Wilfred Timothy Adderley
3rd Secretarys & Vice Consuls........ Mr Marchea Alexander Mackey
Ms Aklia Melissa Ingraham

BARBADOS

(Joined Commonwealth: 1966)

Governor General .... *Sir* Philip Marlowe Greaves *KA QC* .... Feb 17
Prime Minister .... *Hon* Mr Freundel Stuart

Barbados Defence Force (BDF)
(including Barbados Coast Guard)

Chief of Staff .... Col Glyne S Grannum
Deputy Chief of Staff .... Cdr Aquinas Clarke

Commander, Barbados Regiment .... Maj Wendy Yearwood
Commander (Acting), Barbados Coast Guard .... Lt Cdr Mark Peterson
Commander, Barbados Cadet Corp .... Lt Col Errol Braithwaite

Office of the High Commission of Barbados in the United Kingdom
1 Great Russell Street, London WC1B 3ND
(Tel: 020 7299 7150 Fax: 020 7323 6872 Email:london@foreign.gov.bb)

High Commissioner .... *HE* Mr Guy Arlington Hewitt
Deputy High Commissioner .... Ms Alphea Wiggins
Minister - Counsellor .... Mr Euclid Goodman

BELIZE

(Joined Commonwealth: 1981)

Governor General .... *Sir* Colville Norbert Young *GCMG MBE*
Prime Minister .... *Hon* Dean Oliver Barrow 080208
Minister of Police and National Security .... *Hon* John B Saldivar

Belize Defence Force
(Army, BDF Air Wing, Belize Coast Guard and Belize Police Department)

Commander .... Brig Gen David Nejemiah Jones 010213
Deputy Commander .... Col Steven Ortega 010213
Force Sergeant Major .... WO1 Roberto Pop
Commander, Belize National Coastguard .... Adm John Borland
Commissioner of Police .... Mr Allen Whylie

Office of the Belize High Commission in the United Kingdom
Third Floor, 45 Crawford Place W1H 4LP
(Tel: 020 7723 3603 Email: info@belizehighcommission.co.uk
Website: www.belizehighcommission.co.uk)

High Commissioner .... *HE* Ms Perla Maria Perdomo
Minister - Counsellor .... Mrs Laura Frampton
1st Secretaries .... Ms Jolene Kidd
Ms Karen Dawn Simplis

CANADA

(Joined Commonwealth: 1931 (Statute of Westminster))
Canadian Forces: Canadian Army, Royal Canadian Navy, Royal Canadian Air Force and
Canadian Joint Operations Command)

Governor General and
and Commander-in-Chief .... *HE the Rt Hon* David Johnston *CC CMM COM CD*
Minister National Defence .... *Hon* Harjit Sajjan *OMM MSM CD MP*
Associate Minister Defence.. Mr Kert Hehr
Deputy Minister DND.. Mr John Forster

Chief of the Defence Staff

Chief of the Defence Staff... Gen Jonathan Holbert Vance *CMM (OMM) MSC* CD (MID)*
Judge Advocate General... Cdre Genevieve Bernatchez *CD*
Vice Chief of the Defence Staff.. Lt Gen Alain J Parent *CMM CD*
Commander of the Royal Canadian Navy .... V Adm R Lloyd *CMM CD*
Commander Canadian Army .... Lt Gen P F Wynnyk *CMM MSM CD*
Commander of the Royal Canadian Air Force .... Lt Gen M J Hood *CMM CD*
Commander Canadian Joint Operations Command......... Lt Gen Stephen Joseph Bowes *CMM MSC MSM CD*
Chief of Military Personnel Command............................ Lt Gen C A Lamarre *CMM MSC CD*
Surgeon General /Commander Canadian Forces
Health Services Group.. Brig Gen A M T Downes *CD*
Chairman Committee of Chief Military Medical
Services in NATO (COMEDS) .... Maj Gen J J -R S Bernier *OMM CD QHP BA MD*
MPH DEH DSc(Hon) FRCPC(Hon)
Honorary Captain (Navy) for Military Personnel
Command... *HE* Sharon Johnston *CC*
Chief of Defence Intelligence Command.......................... R Adm Scott E G Bishop *CMM CD*
Chief of Canadian Special Operations Forces Command.. *N/D*
North American Aerospace Defence Command (NORAD) .. Gen Lori J Robinson

Canadian Army

Commander .... Lt Gen P F Wynnyk *CMM MSM CD*
Deputy Commander Canadian Army................................ Maj Gen C J Turenne *OMM MSC CD*
Chief of Staff Army Operations... Brig Gen M A J Carignan *OMM MSM CD*
Chief of Staff Army Strategy.. Brig Gen S Kelsey *CD*
Chief of Staff Army Reserve .... Brig Gen Rob Roy Everett MacKenzie *OMM CD*
Commander Canadian Army Doctrine and Training
Centre Headquarters... Maj Gen S C Hetherington *OM MSC CD*
Commander 1st Canadian Division.......................................Maj Gen Dean J Milner *OMM CD*
Commander 2nd Canadian Division and
Joint Task Force East... Brig Gen J P H H Gosselin *OMM MSM CD*
Commander 3rd Canadian Division.................................... Brig Gen Trevor John Cadieu *MSM CD*
Commander 4th Canadian Division and
Joint Task Force Central.. Brig Gen S M Cadden *CD*
Commander 5th Canadian Division .... Brig Gen D A Macaulay *CD*
Command Warrant Officer.. CWO A Guimond *MMM CD*

Office of the Canadian High Commission in the United Kingdom

Canada House, Trafalgar Square SW1Y 5BJ
(Tel: 0207 004 6000 Fax: 0207 004 6050
Email: ldn@international.gc.ca Website: www.UnitedKingdom.gc.ca)

High Commissioner .... *HE* Mrs Janice Charette
Deputy High Commissioner.. Mr Alan Kessel
Counsellor (Defence Research & Development).................. Mr Christopher Michael Allan
Commander & Defence Adviser .... Brig Gen Lowell Thomas
Army Adviser... Col Rory Radford
Naval Adviser.. Capt (N) Maurice Aucoin
Air Force Adviser.. Col Joseph Bigaouette
Assistant Army Adviser .... Lt Col Simon Rushen
Assistant Naval Adviser .... Cdr Lawrence Trim
Assistant Air Force Adviser... Lt Col Tressa Home

DOMINICA, COMMONWEALTH OF

(Joined Commonwealth: 1978)
(Dominica has no regular military forces Defence is the responsibility of the Commonwealth of Dominica Police Force (includes Coast Guard))

President .... *HE* Charles Savarin *DAH*
Prime Minister .... *Hon* Roosevelt Skerrit
Minister of Justice, Imigratin & National Security .... *Hon* Rayburn Blackmoore
Attorney General .... *Hon* Levi A Peter
Permanent Secretary .... Ms Jo-Anne Commodore

Chief of Police .... Mr Daniel Carbon
Deputy Chief of Police .... Mr Hobbs Jno Baptiste

Office of the Commonwealth of Dominica High Commission in the United Kingdom
1 Collingham Gardens SW5 0HW
(Tel: 020 7370 5194 Fax 020 7373 8743
Email: info@dominicahighcommission.co.uk Website: www.dominicahighcommission.co.uk)

Acting High Commissioner .... Mrs Janet Charles
3rd Secretary .... Ms Nakinda Daniel

GRENADA

(Joined Commonwealth: 1974)
(Grenada has no regular military forces. Defence is the responsibility of the Royal Grenada Police Force (RGPF) (includes Coast Guard))

Governor General .... *Dame* Dr Cecile La Grenade *GCMG OBE PhD*

Prime Minister and Minister of National Security .... *Rt Hon* Dr Keith C Mitchell
Commissioner of Police (Acting) .... Mr Winston James
Division Headquarters Commander .... Supt Floyd Dragon
Northern Division Commander .... Supt Sebastian Mitchell
Eastern Divsion Commander .... Supt Reuben Maitland
Western Divsion Commander .... Supt Arthur Renaud
Commanding Officer Coast Guard .... Cutter Heriberto Hernández

Office of the Grenada High Commission in the United Kingdom
The Chapel, Archel Road, West Kensington, London, W14 9QH
(Tel: (020) 7385 4415 Fax: (020) 7381 4807
Email: office@grenada-highcommission.co.uk Website: www.grenadahclon.co.uk)

High Commissioner .... *HE* Mr Ignatius Joachim Karl Hood 080116
Consular Officer .... Mr Samuel Sandy
Diplomatic Attaché .... Ms Xiaowei Chen

GUYANA

(Joined Commonwealth: 1966)

President and Commander in Chief...................................... *HE* Brig (Retd) David Arthur Granger
Prime Minister.. *Hon* Moses Veerasammy Nagamootoo
Minister of State and Defence... Mr Joseph Harmon

Guyana Defence Force (GDF)

(Army includes Air Command and Coast Guard)

Chief of Staff.. Brig George Lewis
Chief of Staff.. Brig Patrick West
Deputyy Chief of Staff/ Colonel General Staff.................. Col Nazrul Hussain
Quatermaster General (QMG).. Col Paul Arthur
Adjutant General.. Col Beaton
Commander Guyana Coast Guard.................................... Col Orin Porter
Commander Air Command.. Lt Col Courtney Byrne

Office of the Guyana High Commission in the United Kingdom

3 Palace Court, Bayswater Road, London W2 4LP
(Tel: 020 7229 7684 Fax: 020 7727 9809
Email: guyanahc1@btconnect.com Website: www.guyanahclondon.co.uk)

High Commissioner.. *HE* Mr Frederick Hamley Case...130416
Counsellor... Mrs Pegy McLennan

JAMAICA

(Joined Commonwealth: 1962)

Governor-General... *Most Hon Sir* Patrick Linton Allen *ON GCMG CD KSt J*..260209
Prime Minister and Minister of Defence............................. *Hon* Andrew Michael Holness *ON MP*
Minister of National Security.. *Hon* Robert Montague...250216

Jamaica Defence Force

(includes Ground Forces, Coast Guard and Air Wing)

Chief of Defence Staff... Maj Gen Rocky R Meade *OD JP PhD MMAS MA BA(Hons) psc*..011216
Deputy Chief of Defence... Brig David Cummings
Colonel General Staff... Col D G Pryce
Colonel Adjutant Quartermaster.. Col Roderick A Williams
Inspector General.. Cdre D P Chin Fong
Principal Staff Officer - Personnel and Administration......... Lt Col R A Tyndale
Principal Staff Officer - Intelligence, Operations & Training. Lt Col R F Johnston
Principal Staff Officer - Legal.. Lt Col P A Cole
Principal Staff Officer - Strategy, Plans & Policy................ Lt Col K P Johnson
Commanding Officer - 1st Battn Jamaica Regt..................... Lt Col M G Pryce
Commanding Officer - 2nd Battn Jamaica Regt................... Lt Col G O Sterling
Commanding Officer - Support and Services Battn.............. Lt Col D N Smalling
Commanding Officer - JDF Air Wing.................................. Lt Col R M Rowe
Commanding Officer - JDF Coast Guard............................. Cdr A S Wemyss-Gorman
Commanding Officer - 1 Engineer Regiment (JDF)............. Lt Col D I Creary
Commanding Officer - Combat Support Battn...................... Lt Col M A Matthews
Commanding Officer - 3rd Battn Jamaica Regt (Reserve).... Lt Col W W Walcott

Office of the Jamaican High Commission in the United Kingdom

1–2 Prince Consort Road, London SW7 2BZ
(Tel: 020 7823 9911 Fax: 020 7589 5154
Email: jamhigh@jhcuk.com Website: www.jhcuk.com)

High Commissioner.. *HE* Mr Seth George Ramocan 221216
Deputy High Commissioner.. Mrs Angella Rose-Howell
Counsellors.. Miss Carol Lee-Lea
Mrs Renee Lloyd

SAINT LUCIA

(Joined Commonwealth: 1979)
(Saint Lucia has no regular military forces.
Defence is the responsibility of the Royal Saint Lucia Police Force (RSLPF)
(includes Special Service Unit and Marine Unit))

Governor-General ... *HE Dame* Calliopa Pearlette Louisy *GCSL GCMG*
Prime Minister ... *Hon* Allen M Chastanet ... 2016
Minister of Home Affairs, Justice & National Security ... *Sen Hon* Hermangild Francis
Permanent Secretary ... Dr Cadelia Lane Ambrose

Commissioner of Police ... Severin Moncherry ... 010416
Deputy Commissioner of Police ... Frances Henry
Commander RSLOF Marine Unit ... Supt John Preville

Office of the High Commission of Saint Lucia in the United Kingdom
1 Collingham Gardens, London SW5 0HW
Tel: 020 7370 7123 Fax: 020 7370 1905 Email: enquiries@stluciahcuk.org)

High Commissioner ... Mr Guy Mayers ... 171216
1st Secretary ... Mrs Rose-Anne Evelyn-Bates
Vice Consul ... Mr Verne Augustin

ST KITTS AND NEVIS

(Joined Commonwealth: 1983)

Governor-General ... *HE Sir* Samuel Weymouth Tapley Seaton *GCMG CVO QC JP*
Deputy Governor-General ... *HE His* D Michael Arthur Morton *JP*
Prime Minister and Minister of National Security ... *Hon* Dr Timothy Harris ... 160215
Permanemt Secretary, National Security ... Mr Osmond Petty

Saint Kitts and Nevis Defence Force (SKNDF)
(includes Coast Guard and Royal St Kitts & Nevis Police Force)

Commander ... Lt Col Patrick Wallace
Commissioner of Police ... Mr Ian Queeley
Officer Commanding Coast Guard ... Maj Anthony J Comrie

Office of the High Commission of Saint Kitts (Christopher) & Nevis in the United Kingdom
10 Kensington Court, London W8 5DL
lTel: 020 7937 9718 Fax: 020 937 7484
Email: mission@sknhc.co.uk Website: www.stkittsnevisuk.com)

High Commissioner ... *HE* Dr Kevin M Isaac ... 120111

ST VINCENT AND THE GRENADINES

(Joined Commonwealth: 1979)
(Saint Vincent and the Grenadines has no regular military forces.
Defence is the responsibility of the Royal Saint Vincent and the Grenadines Police Force (RSVGPF))

Governor-General ... *HE Sir* Frederick Nathaniel Ballantyne *GCMG*
Prime Minister and Minister of National Security ... *Hon* Dr Ralph Everard Gonsalves
Permanent Secretary ... Mr Godfred Pompey
Commissioner of Police ... Mr Renold Harvey
Deputy Commissioner of Police ... Mr Colin John

Office of the High Commission of Saint Vincent and the Grenadines in the United Kingdom
10 Kensington Court, London W8 5DL
Tel: 020 7460 1256 / 020 7565 2874 Fax: 020 7937 6040
Email: info@svghighcom.co.uk Website: www.svghighcom.co.uk

High Commissioner ... *HE* Mr Cenio E Lewis ... 240401
Minister-Counsellor ... Mrs Doris Charles
Counsellor ... Ms Carolin de Freitas-Sawh

TRINIDAD AND TOBAGO, REPUBLIC OF

(Joined Commonwealth: 1962)

President and Commander in Chief of the Armed forces	*HE* Anthony Thomas Aquinas Carmona	
Prime Minister	Dr *the Hon* Keith Christopher Rowley *MP*	
Minister of National Security	Maj Gen (Retd) Edmund Dillion	090915

Trinidad and Tobago Defence Force (TTDF)

(Trinidad and Tobago Army, Coast Guard, Air Guard and Defence Forces Reserves)

Chief of Defence Staff	Cdre Hayden Pritchard	090817
Vice Chief of Defence Staff	Brig Gen Archilus L N Phillips	260717
Deputy Inspector General	Lt Cdr Dexter Baptiste *BSc MSc*	Feb 15
Deputy Director Intelligence Operations	Lt Col Claude Bridgewater	
Acting Commanding Officer, Trinidad and Tobago Regiment	Lt Col Ronald Jeffery	
Command Sergeant Major Trinidad and Tobago Army	WO1 Dereck McClean	
Commanding Officer, Trinidad and Tobago Reserves	Capt (N) Kent Moore *(until Sep 15)*	
Commanding Officer, Air Guard	Grp Capt Darryl Daniel	Aug 14
Acting Commanding Officer, Coast Guard	Cdr Wayne Armour *ED psc Attorney at Law*	Oct 16

Office of the High Commission the Republic of Trinidad and Tobago in the United Kingdom

42 Belgrave Square, London SW1X 8NT
(Tel: 020 7245 9351 Fax: 020 7823 1065
Email: hclondon@foreign.gov.tt Website: foreign.gov.tt/hclondon)

High Commissioner	*HE* Mr Orville London	130517
2nd Secretary	Ms Darcyl Legall	
Defence Attaché	Mr Hiram Mohammed	

COMMONWEALTH COUNTRIES OF THE PACIFIC

AUSTRALIA

(Joined Commonwealth: 1931 (Statute of Westminster))
(as at 26 Sept 2017)

Governor-General of the Commonwealth and Commander-in-Chief .... *HE* General *the Hon Sir* Peter Cosgrove *AK MC (Retd)*
Minister for Defence .... *Senator The Hon* Marise Payne
Assistant Minister for Defence .... *The Hon* Darren Chester *MP*
Minister for Defence Industry .... *Hon* Christopher Pyne
Minister for Defence Personnel .... *Hon* Dan Tehan
Minister for Defence Materiel and Science .... Mr Michael McCormack

Secretary Defence .... Mr Greg Moriarty
Associate Secretary .... Mr Brendan Sargeant
Acting Chief Information Officer .... Mr Aiyaswami Mohan
Deputy Secretary Defence People .... Ms Roxanne Kelley
Deputy Secretary Estate & Infrastructure .... Mr Steve Grzeskowiak
Chief Finance Officer .... Mr Phillip Prior
Deputy Secretary Strategic Policy and Intelligence .... Mr Mark Ablong
Deputy Secretary Capability Acquisition & Sustainment. Mr Kim Gillis
Chief Defence Scientist .... Dr Alex Zelinsky

Australian Defence Force (ADF)
(Australian Army, Royal Australian Navy (includes Naval Aviation Force),
Royal Australian Air Force, Joint Operations Command (JOC)

Chief of Defence Force .... ACM Mark Binskin *AC*
Vice Chief of Defence Force .... VAdm Ray Griggs *AO CSC*
Chief of Navy .... VAdm Tim Barrett *AO CSC*
Chief of Joint Operations .... VAdm David Johnston *AM*
Chief of Joint Capabilities .... AVM Warren McDonald
Chief of Air Force .... AM Leo Davies *AO CSC*
Chief of Army .... Lt Gen Angus J Campbell *DSC AM*
Deputy Chief of Army .... Maj Gen Rick Burr *DSC AM MVO*
Commander Forces Command .... Maj Gen Fergus McLachlan *AM*
Commander 1st Division .... Maj Gen Paul McLachlan *AM CSC*
Commander 2nd Division .... Maj Gen Stephen Porter *AM*
Commander Special Operations Command .... Maj Gen A G Findlay *AM*
Head Land Capability .... Maj Gen Kathryn Toohey *AM CSC*

Regimental Sergeant Majors

Army .... WO Don Spinks *OAM*
Forces Command .... WO David Galloway
1st Division & Deployable Joint Force HQ .... WO Craig David Allen
Special Operations Command .... WO Paul Dunbavin
2nd Division .... WO Leane Iseppi

Office of the Australian High Commission in the United Kingdom
Australia House, Strand, London WC2B 4LA
(Tel: (020) 7379 4334 Fax: (020) 7240 5333 Website: www.uk.embassy.gov.au)

High Commissioner .... *HE* Mr Alexander Downer 190514
Deputy High Commissioner .... Mr Matthew Anderson
Head of Australian Defence Staff .... Air Cdre Brian Edwards
Army Adviser .... Col Richard Parker
Naval Adviser .... Capt Shane Craig
Air Force Adviser .... Grp Capt Anthony Martin
Counsellor (Defence) .... Mr Ky Blackman
Counsellor (Defence Science) .... Dr Yi Yue
Counsellor (Defence Material) .... Mr Michael Garrety
Assistant Defence Adviser (Strategy) .... Wg Cdr Ruth Elsley
Assistant Defence Adviser .... Lt Col Graham Price
Assistant Army Adviser .... Lt Col Brendan Hogan
Assistant Naval Adviser .... Cdr Geoffrey Fiedler

FIJI, REPUBLIC OF

(Joined Commonwealth: 1970 (rejoined in 1997 after ten-year lapse))

President and Commander in Chief.. *HE* Jioji Konusi (George) Konrote *OF MC*
Prime Minister.. *Hon* R Adm JosaiaVoreqe (Frank) Bainimarama *CF MSD OStJ*
Minister for Defence and National Security.. *Hon* Ratu Inoke Kubuabola
Permanent Secretary.. Mr Osea N Cawaru
Deputy Secretary.. Mr Ilai Moceica

Republic of Fiji Military Forces (RFMF)
(Land Forces and Naval Forces)

Commander, HQ RFMF.. Cdre Viliame Naupoto *OF(Mil) MSD psc*
Deputy Commander, HQ RFMF.. Brig (Dr) Gen Mohammed Aziz *OF(Mil) MSD LLB LLM SID*
Chief of Staff, HQ RFMF.. Col Litea Vulakoro Seruiratu *MSD MBA psc*
Director Finance/Logistics/Accounts.. Cdr Lepani Vaniqi
Director Human Resources.. Lt Col Samuela Vuetaki
Director Coordination.. Lt Col Isoa Loanakadavu
Director Force Development.. Lt Col Maika Baleinaloto
Director Army Legal Services.. Lt Col Kitione Tuinaosara
Director Peasce Support Organisation.. Lt Col Pacolo Luveni

Chief of Navy.. Cdr Humphrey Biu Tawake
Commander Land Force Command.. Col Onisivoro Niumataiwalu Covunisaqa
Chief of Staff Land Force Command.. Lt Col Jofiliti Talemaibau

Office of the High Commission of the Republic of Fiji in the United Kingdom
34 Hyde Park Gate, London SW7 5DN
(Tel: 020 7584 3661 Fax: 020 7584 2838
Email: mail@fijihighcommission.org.uk Website: www.fijihighcommission.org.uk)

High Commissioner.. *HE* Mr Jitoko Cakacakabalavu Tikolevu 300116
1st Secretary.. Mrs Paulini Tala Tokaduadua Cakacaka

KIRIBATI, REPUBLIC OF

(Joined Commonwealth: 1979)
(Kiribati has no regular military forces (establishment prevent by the constitution).
Defence Assistance provided by Australia and New Zealand for defence.
Law enforcement is the responsibility of the Kiribati Police Service and Prison (KPSP))

President and Head of State and Government.. *HE* Taneti Maamau
Commissioner of Police.. Ioeru Tokantetaake

Office of the High Commission of the Republic of Kiribati in the United Kingdom
c/o Office of the President, P.O. Box 68, Bairiki, Tarawa, Kiribati

Acting High Commissioner.. Mrs Makurita Baaro

Honorary Consular Representative
The Great House Llanddewi Rydderch Monmouthshire NP7 9UY
Tel: 01873 840 375 / 01873 840 152 Fax: Fax 01873 840 375
Email: mravellwalsh@btopenworld.com

Honorary Consul.. Mr Michael Ravell Walsh

NAURU, REPUBLIC OF

(Joined Commonwealth: 1968)

(Nauru has no regular military forces.
Law enforcement is the responsibility of the Nauru Police Force.
Australia is responsible for Nauru's defence under an informal agreement between the two countries.)

President and Head of State & Government and Minister for Police and Emergency Services .... *HE* Baron Waqa *MP* 110613
Chief Justice .... Judge Mohammed Shafiullah Khan
Police Commissioner .... Mr Corey Caleb
Deputy Police Commissioner .... Ms Kalinda Blake

Honorary Consular Representative

Romshed Courtyard, Underriver, Nr Sevenoaks, Kent TN15 0SD
(Tel: 01732 746 061 Fax: 01732 746062 Email: nauru@weald.co.uk)

Honorary Consul .... Mr Martin W L Weston

NEW ZEALAND

(Joined Commonwealth: 1931 (Statute of Westminster))

Governor General and and Commander-in-Chief .... *Dame* Patsy Reddy *GNZM QSO DStJ* 280916
Minister of Defence .... *Hon* Mark Mitchell
Secretary of Defence and Chief Executive MOD .... Helene Quilter .... Dec 12
Deputy Secretary of Defence .... Tony Lynch .... Jun 14

New Zealand Defence Force

(New Zealand Army, Royal New Zealand Navy, Royal New Zealand Air Force)

Chief of Defence Force .... Lt Gen Tim Keating *MNZM* .... Jan 14
Chief of Staff .... Brig C J Parsons *MNZM DSD* .... Jun 15
Warrant Officer of the Defence Force .... WO1 Danny Broughton 310114
Vice Chief of Defence Force .... AVM Kevin Short 310314
Chief Defence Strategy and Governance .... N/A
Chief People Officer .... Ms Debbie Francis 2015
Chief Financial Officer .... Ms Jo Devine .... Nov 12
Chief Joint Defence Services .... Brig Charles Lott .... Mar 15
Chief of Army .... Maj Gen Peter Kelly *MNZM* 100915
Chief of Navy .... RAdm John Martin *ONZM* 301115
Chief of Air Force .... AVM Tony Davies *MNZM* 230316
Commander Joint Forces .... Maj Gen Tim Gall 310314

New Zealand Army

Chief of Army .... Maj Gen Peter Kelly *MNZM* 100915
Deputy Chief of Army .... Brig C J Parsons *MNZM DSD* .... Jun 15
Sergeant Major of Army .... WO1 Clive Douglas
Land Component Commander .... Brig Michael Shapland
Director Army Reserve .... Col Christopher James Faulls

Office of the New Zealand High Commission in the United Kingdom

2nd Floor New Zealand House, 80 Haymarket, London SW1Y 4TQ
(Defence Staff and Defence Purchasing Office Tel: (020) 7930 8400 Fax: (020) 7930 8401
Email: aboutnz@newzealandhc.org.uk Email: consular@newzealandhc.org.uk Website: www.mfat.govt.nz/uk)

High Commissioner .... *HE The Rt Hon Sir* Jerry Mateparae 270317
Deputy High Commissioner .... Mr David Evans
Defence Adviser & Head New Zealand Defence Staff .... Brig Evan Williams
Military Adviser .... Lt Col Katherine Lee
Naval Adviser .... Cdre Christopher David Crossman
Air Adviser .... Wg Cdr Lisa D'Oliveira
Logistics Adviser .... Lt Cdr Ian Andrew *RNZN*
Business Manager .... WO Stephen Clarke

PAPUA NEW GUINEA

(Joined Commonwealth: 1975)

President and Commander in Chief........ *Grand Chief Sir* Robert Bofeng Dadae *GCL GCMG KStJ*
Prime Minister........ *Rt Hon* Peter Charles Paire O'Neill *CMG MP*
Minister for Defence........ *Hon* Solan Mirisim *MP*
Secretary of Defence........ Mr Fredrick M Punangi

Papua New Guinea Defense Force (PNGDF)
(includes Maritime Operations Element, Air Operations Element)

Commander........ Brig Gen Gilbert Toropo *CBE*

Office of the High Commission of Papua New Guinea in the United Kingdom
14 Waterloo Place, London SW1Y 4AR
Tel: 020 7930 0922 Fax: 020 7930 0828
Email: kunduldn3@btconnect.com Website: www.pnghighcomm.org.uk

High Commissioner........ *HE* Ms Winnie Anna Kiap........240811

SAMOA

(Joined Commonwealth: 1970)
(Samoa has no regular military forces.
Law enforcement is the responsibility of the Samoa Police Force.)

Head of State........ *His Highness* Tuimalealiifano Vaaletoa Sualauvi II
Prime Minister........ *Hon* Susuga Tuilaepa Sailele Malielegaoi
Deputy Prime Minister........ Afioga Fiame Naomi Mataafa
Minister of Police........ *Hon* Sala Fata Pinati

Commissioner of Police........ Fuiavailili Egon Keil

Honorary Consular Representative
Church Cottage, Pedlinge, Nr Hythe, Kent CT12 5JL
Tel: 01303 260 541 Fax 01303 238 058

Honorary Consul........ Mrs Prunella Scarlett *LVO*

SOLOMON ISLANDS

(Joined Commonwealth: 1978)
(The Solomon Islands has no regular military forces.
Law enforcement is the responsibility of the Royal Solomon Islands Police Force.)

Governor-General........ *HE Sir* Frank Kabui
Prime Minister........ *Hon* Manasseh Damukana Sogavare........191114
Minister for Police, National Security & Correctional Services........ *Hon* Peter Shanel Agovaka

Commissioner of Police........ Mr Matthew Varley

Office of the High Commission for the Solomon Islands in the United Kingdom
10 Greycoat Place, London SW1P 1SB

High Commissioner (Non-Resident)........ *HE* Mr Moses Kouni Mose........110215
Deputy High Commissioner........ Mr Trevor Unusu

TONGA

(Joined Commonwealth: 1970)

Head of State .... *His Majesty* King Tupou VI 180312
Prime Minister .... *Hon* Samuela'Akilisi Pohiva 180114
Deputy Prime Minister .... *Hon* Siaosi 'Ofakivahafolau Sovaleni

Tonga Defense Services (TDS)

(Land Force (Royal Guard), Maritime Force (includes Royal Marines, Air Wing))

Commander .... *Crown Prince* (Col) Tupouto'a 'Ulukalala

Office of the High Commission of Tonga in the United Kingdom

36 Molyneux Street, London W1H 5BQ
(Tel: 020 7724 5828 Fax: 020 7723 9074)

Acting High Commissioner .... Mr Sione Sonata Tupou 131212

TUVALU

(Joined Commonwealth: 1978)
(Tuvalu has no regular military forces.
Law enforcement is the responsibility of the Tuvalu Police Force.)

Governor-General .... *HE Sir* Iakoba Taeia Italeli *GCMG* 160410
Prime Minister .... *Rt Hon* Enele Sopoaga 100415
Commissioner of Police .... Mr Luka Falefou

Honorary Consular Representative

Tuvalu House, 230 Worple Road, SW20 8RH
Tel: 020 8879 0985 Fax: 020 8879 0985 Email: Tuvaluconsulate@netscape.net

Honorary Consul .... *Sir* Iftikhar A Ayaz *KBE*

VANUATU

(Joined Commonwealth: 1980)
(Vanuatu has no regular military forces.
Law enforcement is the responsibility of the Vanuatu Police Force (VPF)
(includes Vanuatu Mobile Force (VMF) and Police Maritime Wing (PMW)))

President .... *HE* Tallis Obed Moses 060717
Prime Minister .... *Hon* Charlot Salawi 110216
Commissioner of Police .... *Mr* Albert Nalpini 110517

Office of the High Commission of Tonga in Belgium

Avenue de Tervueren 380, Chemin de Ronde, 1150, Brussels, BELGIUM
Tel/Fax: 0032 2 771 74 94 Email: info@vanuatuembassy.be

High Commissioner .... *HE* Mr Roy Mickey Joy 110411

COMMONWEALTH COUNTRIES OF AFRICA

BOTSWANA, REPUBLIC OF

(Joined Commonwealth: 1966)

President and Commander in Chief...................................... *HE* Lt Gen Dr Seretse Khama Ian Khama
Vice President.. *His Hon* Dr Ponatshego Honorius Kefhaeng Kedikilwe
Minister of Defence, Justice and Security (MDJS)............... *Hon* Mr Shaw Kgathi
Liaison Officer.. Brig Sianang Sianang

Botswana Defence Force (BDF)

(Ground Forces Command, Air Arm Command, Defense Logistics Command)

Commander... Lt Gen Placid Segokgo 020916
Deputy Commander... Maj Gen Gotsileene Morake...020916
Commander (Ground Forces Command)............................... Maj Gen Molefi Seikano...010615
Chief of Staff Ground Force Commander.......................... Brig Mbakiso Mukokomani..010615
Commander (Defence Logistics Command).......................... Brig George Tlhalerwa
Air Arm Commander... Maj Gen Seleka Phatshwane...010615
Deputy Air Arm Commander... Brig Mukani Mokobi 010615

Office of the High Commission of the Republic of Botswana in the United Kingdom

6 Stratford Place, London W1C 1AY
(Tel: 020 7499 0031 / 020 7647 1000 Fax: 020 7495 8595 / 020 7409 7382
Email: bohico@govbw.com)

High Commissioner.. *HE* Mr Roy Warren Blackbeard..291298
Defence Adviser... Brig Gabriel Addanes

CAMEROON, REPUBLIC OF

(Joined Commonwealth: 1995)

President... *HE* Mr Paul Biya..061182
Prime Minister.. *Hon* Mr Philémon Yunji Yang...300609
Minister of Defence.. *Hon* Mr Joseph Beti Assomo
Secretary of State for Defence (Gendarmerie)....................... Mr Jean Baptiste Bokam
Secretary of State for Defence (Veterans & War Victims)...... Mr Issa Koumpa

Cameroon Armed Forces

(Army, Navy (includes naval infantry), Air Force,
National Gendarmerie and Presidential Guard)

Chief of Joint Chiefs of Staff.. Maj Gen Nkoa Atenga
Chief of Army Staff.. Lt Gen Rene Claude Meka
Chief of Air Force.. Brig Gen Jean Calvin Momha
Chief of Navy.. R Adm Jean Mendoua

Office of the High Commission of the Republic of Cameroon in the United Kingdom

84 Holland Park, London W11 3SB
(Tel: 020 7727 0771 Fax: 020 7792 9353
Email: info@cameroonhighcommission.co.uk Website: www.cameroonhighcommission.co.uk)

High Commissioner.. *HE* Mr Nkwelle Ekaney..031008
Minister Counsellor.. Mrs Anna Baninla Tasha Mbur
Defence Adviser... Col Gilbert Fondufe Banka

Assistant Defence Adviser... Lt Col Guy-Roger Oyono
Naval Attaché... Lt Col Marthe Tsogo
Attachés.. Lt Col Gaskreo Reyang
Maj René Dieudonné Mezang Oyono
Capt Alain Nagmou Pene
Lt Casimir Augustin Menye Melingui

GHANA, REPUBLIC OF

(Joined Commonwealth: 1957)

President and Commander-in-Chief .... *HE* Mr Nana Dankwa Akufo-Addo .... Jan 17
Minister for Defence .... *Hon* Mr Dominic Nitiwul

Ghana Defence Force
(Army, Navy and Air Force)

Chief of the Defence Staff .... Maj Gen Obed Akwa
Chief of Army Staff .... Maj Gen Azure Ayamdo
Chief of Naval Staff .... R Adm Faidoo
Chief of Air Staff .... AVM Maxwell Mantserbi-tei Nagai

Office of the Republic of Ghana High Commission in the United Kingdom
13 Belgrave Square, London SW1X 8PN
(Tel: 020 7201 5900 Fax: 020 7245 9552 Email: gh.lonlon@gmail.com; ghmfa31@ghc-uk.org
Website:www.ghanahighcommissionuk.com)

High Commissioner .... *HE* Mr Papa Owusu-Ankomah 130617
Defence Adviser .... Brig Gen Isaac Mensah Tetteh
Deputy Defence Adviser .... Gp Capt Eric Agyen-Frempong

KENYA, REPUBLIC OF

(Joined Commonwealth: 1963)

President and Commander in Chief of the Armed forces .... *HE Hon* Uhuru Muigai Kenyatta *CGH*
Cabinet Secretary for Defence .... *Amb* Raychelle Omamo *SC*
Principal Secretary .... Torome Saitoti

Kenya Defence Forces Services
(Army, Navy and Air Force)

Chief of Defence Forces .... Gen Samson Mwathethe E*GH MBS DCO ndc (K) psc (UK)*
Vice Chief of Defence Forces .... Lt Gen Joseph K Kasaon *MGH CBS DCO ndc (K) cgsc (USA)*
Head of Personnel, Defence HQ .... Brig Martin Kizito Onyango Ong'oyi
Chief of Operations, Defence HQ .... Brig George Odhiambo Walwa
Chief of Operations, Plans & Training, Army HQ .... Brig Godfrey Aumah Buluma
Assistant Chief of Defence Forces (Operations, Training and Doctrine) .... Maj Gen Adan Mulata

Rapid Deployment Capability Commander .... Brig Daniel Kimutai Pyaban
Force Commander UN Mission, South Sudan (UNMISS Commander) .... Lt Gen Johnson Ondiek
Director International Peace Support Training Centre .... Brig Muta Nderitu
Commandant National Defence College (NDC) .... Lt Gen Leonard Ngondi
Commandant Defence Staff College (DSC) .... Maj Gen Ngewa Mukala
Deputy Commandant .... Maj Gen Simon Mureithi Wachira
Commandant Kenya Military Academy (KMA) and General Officer Commanding Westcom .... Maj Gen George Owino

Commander Kenya Air Force .... Maj Gen Samuel N Thuita *MGH EBS OGW ndc psc (K)*
Deputy Commander, Kenya Air Force .... Brig Francis Omondi Ogolla
Commander Kenya Navy .... Maj Gen Levi Franklin Mghalu *MGH MBS ndc (K) psn (RSA)*
Deputy Commander, Kenyasn Navy .... Brig Gen Charles M Kahariri

Kenya Army

Commander Kenya Army .... Lt Gen Robert Kibochi MHG CBS ndc (K) psc (UK) 280716
Deputy Commander Kenya Army .... Maj Gen Walter Koipaton
Commander - Eastern .... Maj Gen Benjamin Biwott
Commander - Kahawa .... Maj Gen Henry Noah Ofulah
Commander - Montgwe Base .... Maj Gen Vincent Naisho Loonena
Sergeant Major Kenya Army .... WOI William Ogutu
Chief of Logistics, Kenya Army .... Brig James Magige Gitiba

Office of the Kenyan High Commission in the United Kingdom
45 Portland Place, London W1B 1AS
(Tel: 020 7636 2371 FAz: 020 7323 1932 Website: www.kenyahighcom.org.uk)

High Commissioner .... *HE* Mr Lazarus Ombai Amayo 171114
Defence Adviser .... Col Peter Muteti

LESOTHO, THE KINGDOM OF

(Joined Commonwealth: 1966)

Head of State .... *His Majesty King* Letsie III
Prime Minister .... *Rt Hon* Bethuel Pakalitha Mosisili
Minister of Defence and National Security .... *Hon* Sentje Lebona
Principal Secretary .... Col Tanki Mothae

Lesotho Defence Force (LDF)
Army (includes Air Wing and Paramilitary Wing)

Acting Commander .... Maj Gen Lineo Poopa
Acting Commander Air Wing .... Maj Gen Mojalefa Letsoela

Office of the High Commission of the Kingdom of Lesotho in the United Kingdom
7 Chesham Place, Belgravia, London SW1 8HN
(Tel: 020 7235 5686 Fax: 020 7235 5023 Email: hicom@lesotholondon.org.uk
Website: www.lesotholondon.org.uk)

High Commissioner .... *HE* Dr Jhn Naazi Oliphant 160517
Counsellor .... Mrs Mosele Majoro
1st Secretary .... Mr Potjo Peter Ptojo

MALAWI, REPUBLIC OF

(Joined Commonwealth: 1964)

President, Minister of Defence and Commander in Chief of the Malawi Defence Force .... *HE* Prof Arthur Peter Mutharika
Deputy Minister of Defence .... *Hon* Everton Chimulirenji .... Jul 17

Malawi Defence Force (MDF)
(includes Air Wing and Naval Detachment)

Army Commander, Malawi Defence Force (MDF) .... Lt Gen Griffin Supuni
Deputy Commander (Operations & Training) .... Maj Gen Clement Namangale
Commandant Malawi Armed Forces College .... Brig Gen Swithun Mchungula

Office of the High Commission of the Republic of Malawi in the United Kingdom
36 John Street, London WC1N 2AT
(Tel: 020 7421 6010 Fax: 020 7831 9273
Email: malawihighcommission@btconnect.com Website: www.malawihighcommission.co.uk)

High Commissioner .... *HE* Mr Kenna Alewa Mphonda 180615
Deputy High Commissioner .... Mrs Quent Madalo Kalichero
Defence Attaché .... Col Sydney Crispen Linyama

MAURITIUS, REPUBLIC OF

(Joined Commonwealth: 1968)

President................................ *HE Dr* Ameenah Gurib-Fakim *GCSK CSK PhD DSc*
Prime Minister / Minister of Defence................................ *Rt Hon Sir* Anerood Jugnauth *KCMG QC GCSK PC*
Senior Chief Executive................................ Mr Premhans Jhugroo
Permanent Secretary................................ Mr Medha Gunputh

Mauritius Police Force (MPF)

(Mauritius has no regular military forces.
Defence is the responsibility of the Mauritius Police Force,
Paramilitary Special Force and National Coast Guard)

Commissioner of Police (CP)................................ Mr Karl Mario Nobin *PMSM*................................200315
Commandant National Coast Guard................................ Capt Saurabh Thakur

Office of the Mauritius High Commission in the United Kingdom

32-33 Elvaston Place, London SW7 5NW
(Tel: 020 7581 0294/5 Fax: 020 7823 8437 / 020 7584 9859 Email: londonhc@govmu.org
Email: londonconsul@govmu.org (consular matters only))

High Commissioner................................ *HE* Mr Girish Nunkoo................................090815
1st Secretary................................ Mr Khemraj Jingree

MOZAMBIQUE, REPUBLIC OF

(Joined Commonwealth: 1995)

President and Commander-in-Chief of the Defence & Security Forces................................ *HE* Filipe Jacinto Nyusi................................150115
Prime Minister................................ *HE* Carlos Agostinho Do Rosario................................170115
Minister of National Defence................................ Mr Atanásio Salvador Ntumuke
Deputy Minister of National Defence................................ Mr Patrício José

Mozambique Armed Defense Forces (FADM)

(Army, Navy, Air Force and Logistics Command)

Chief of General Staff................................ Gen Lazaro Menete
Deputy Chief of Staff................................ Maj-Gen Raul Dique
Chief of Army................................ *tbc*
Chief of Navy................................ Adm Sunil Lanba
Chief of Air Force................................ Maj Gen André Niposso

Office of the Republic of Mozambique High Commission in the United Kingdom

21 Fitzroy Square, London W1T 6EL
Tel: 020 7383 3800 Website: www.mozambiquehighcommission.org.uk

High Commissioner................................ *HE* Mr Filipe Chidumo................................Nov 15
Minister-Counsellor................................ Mr Omar Remane

NAMIBIA, REPUBLIC OF

(Joined Commonwealth: 1990)

President & Commander-in-Chief Namibian Defence Force.... *HE* Dr Hage Gottfried Geingob................................210315
Prime Minister................................ *Rt Hon* Saara Kuugongelwa................................210315
Minister of Defence................................ *Hon* Penda Ya Ndakolo................................210315
Permanent Secretary of the Ministry of Defence................................ R Adm Peter Hafeni Vilho................................010917

Namibian Defense Force (NDF)

(Army, Navy and Air Force)

Chief of the Defence Force................................ Lt Gen John Mutwa
Commander Army................................ Maj Gen Nestor Shali Shalauda
Commander Navy................................ R Adm Sinsy Ndeshi Bamba Nghipandua
Commander Air Force................................ AVM Martin Pinehas

Office for the Republic of Namibia High Commission in the United Kingdom
6 Chandos Street, London W1G 9LU
Tel: 020 7636 6244 Fax: 020 7637 5694 Email:info@namibiahc.org.uk

High Commissioner .... *HE* Mr Steve V Katjiuanjo 211013
Minister-Counsellor .... Mr Michael Ndivayele

NIGERIA, FEDERAL REPUBLIC OF

(Joined Commonwealth: 1960 (suspended 1995–99))

President, Commander-in-Chief .... *HE* Muhammadu Buhari GCFR
Minister of Defence .... Brig Gen (Retd) Mansur Mohammed Dan Ali

Nigerian Armed Forces
(Army, Navy and Air Force)

Chief of Defence Staff .... Gen Abayomi Gabriel Olonishakin *GSS CMH psc+ fwc*
Director of Defence Information .... Maj Gen John Enenche
Chief of Defence Intelligence .... AVM Mohammed Saliu Usman
Chief of Army Staff .... Lt Gen Tukur Yusaf Buratai *NAM OMM(BR) psc+ ndc*
Chief of Air Staff .... AM Sadique Baba Abubakar
Chief of Naval Staff .... V Adm Ibok-Ete Ekwe Ibas *GSS AM psc+ ndc*
National Security Adviser .... Maj Gen Mohammed Babagana Monguno

Office for the Federal Republic of Nigeria High Commission in the United Kingdom
Nigeria House, 9 Northumberland Avenue, London, WC2N 5BX
(Tel: 020 7839 1244 Fax: 020 7839 8746 Email:information@nigeriahc.org.uk
Email: chancery@nigeriahc.org Website: www.nigeriahc.org.uk)

High Commissioner .... Vacant
Deputy High Commissioner .... Mr Kabiru Bala
Defence Adviser .... Maj Gen Gbolahan Oyefesobi Ogidi
Deputy Defence Advisers (Navy) .... Capt J Ojone Ajodo
Deputy Defence Adviser (Air) .... Wg Cdr Eyo Benson
Deputy Defence Adviser (Finance) .... Col Y H Musa
Deputy Defence Adviser (Library) .... Maj O A Sanni

RWANDA

(Joined Commonwealth: 2009)

President .... *HE* Paul Kagame 240300
Prime Minister .... *Hon* Mr Edouard Ngirente 180817
Minister of Defence and National Security .... Gen James Kabarebe

Rwanda Defense Force (RDF)
(Army and Air Force)

Chief of Defence Staff .... Lt Gen Patrick Nyamvumba 120713
Chief of Staff of Army .... Maj Gen Jacques Musemakweli
Chief of Staff of the Air Force .... Brig General Joseph Demali
Commander of the Republican Guard .... Maj Gen Alex Kagame

Office for the Rwanda High Commission in the United Kingdom
120-122 Seymour Place, London W1H 1NR
(Tel: 020 7224 9832 Fax: 020 7724 8642
Email: uk@rwandahc.org Website: www.rwandahc.org)

High Commissioner .... *HE* Ms Yamina Claris Karitanyi 090116
1st Counsellor .... Mr Fidelis Mironko
1st Secretary .... Mr James Wizeye

SEYCHELLES , REPUBLIC OF

(Joined Commonwealth: 1976)

President and Commander in Chief.. *HE* Mr Danny Antoine Rollen Faure
Vice-President.. *Hon* Mr Vincent Meriton
Spokesperson Seychelles People's Defence Force (SPDF) .. Maj Jean Attala

Seychelles People's Defense Forces (SPDF)

(Army (includes infantry, Special Forces (Tazar)),
Coast Guard (includes Naval Wing, Air Wing))

Chief of Defence Forces.. Brig Leopold Payet
Deputy Chief of Defence Forces.. Col Clifford Rosline
Commanding Officer Naval Wing.. Maj Fernand Laporte
Commanding Officer Air Force.. Lt Col Michael Pouponneau
Commanding Officer Coast Guard.. Lt Col Leslie Benoiton

Office of the Republic of Seychelles High Commission in the United Kingdom

130-132 Buckingham Palace Road, London SW1W 9SA
(Tel: 020 7730 2046 Fax 020 7730 0087
Email: seyhc.london@btconnect.com Website: www.seychelleshc.org)

High Commissioner.. *HE* Mr Derick Ally..250117
Princial Counsellor.. Mrs Lalatiana Accouche

SIERRA LEONE, REPUBLIC OF

(Joined Commonwealth: 1961)

President and Commander in Chief.. *HE* Dr Ernest Bai Koroma
Minister of Defence.. Maj (Retd) Alfred Paolo Conteh
Deputy Minister of Defence.. Capt (Retd) Abdul R Kamara
The Defence Spokesman.. Brig Gen Usman Turay

Chief of Defence Staff.. Lt Gen John E Milton *psw fwc MSc*......................................180416
Deputy Chief of Defence Staff.. Maj Gen M M Keita
Assitant Chiefs of Defence Staff (ACDS): -
Training & Doctrine .... Brig Gen M M Samura
Operations & Plans .... Brig Gen D T O Taluva
Support & Logistics .... Brig Gen T R Alieu
Gender & Equal Opportunity .... Brig Gen K O Kabia

Director General of Defence .... Mr Sanah Marrah
Civilian Adviser.. Mr Craig Henderson
Deputy Secretary of Policy and Procurement .... Mr James Freeman
Deputy Secretary of Finance and Adminstration .... Mr Digger Sydney Macfoy
Director of Organisation Management and Audit .... Mr Samuel Bangura

Republic of Sierra Leone Armed Forces (RSLAF)

Army (includes Maritime Wing and Air Wing)

Commander Joint Force (CJF).. Maj Gen Mohamed Mamadi Keita
Head, Joint Force Command .... Maj Gen Brima Sesay
Surgeon General Joint Medical Unit - RSLAF.................. Brig Gen Foday Sahr

Office of the Republic of Sierra Leone High Commission in the United Kingdom

41 Eagle Street, London WC1R 4TL
(Tel: 020 7404 0140 Fax: 020 7430 9862
Email: info@slhc-uk.org.uk Website: www.slhc-uk.org.uk)

High Commissioner.. *HE* Mr Edward Mohamed Turay 090110
Deputy High Commissioner .... Mr Tamba Mansa Ngegba
Head of Chancery.. Mr Allan Logan
Counsellor.. Mr Obai Taylor-Kamara

SOUTH AFRICA, REPUBLIC OF

(Joined Commonwealth: 1931 (Statute of Westminster; left in 1961, rejoined in 1994))

President and Commander-in-Chief	President Jacob Zuma	181207
Minister of Defence and Military Veterans	Ms Nosiviwe Noluthando Mapisa-Nqakula	120612
Deputy Minister of Defence and Military Veterans	*The Hon* Mr Kebby Maphatsoe	260514
Secretary for Defence and Military Veterans	Dr Sam Makhudu Gulube	Dec 11

South Africa National Defence Force (SANDF)

(Army, Navy, Air Force and Military Health Services)

Chief of South African National Defence Force	Gen Solly Zacharia Shoke	
Chief of South African Air Force	Lt Gen Fabian Zimpande Msimang	
Chief of South African Navy	VAdm M S Hlongwane *MMS MMB*	
Chief of South African Military Health Service	Lt Gen A P Sedibe *DMG MMS MMB OStJ*	010413
Provost Marshal General	R Adm Mokgadi Alpheus Maphoto	270717

Army

Chief of the South African Army	Lt Gen L Yam *MMS CLS RCDS ENSP*	010216
Warrant Officer of the South African Army	*SCWO* Ncedakele Elliot Mtshatsheni	050916
Defence Intelligence Division - Chief Director Collection	Maj Gen B Ngcobo	010917
Defence Legal Services Division - Adjutant General	Maj Gen E Z Mnisi	010617
Chief of Command Management Information Systems Division (CMIS)	Maj Gen S Sipika	010217

Joint Operations

Deputy Chief of Joint Operations	Maj Gen E F Drost	010317
Chief of Staff of Joint Operations	Maj Gen A M Sibango	010617
General Officer Commanding Joint Operations HQ	Maj Gen T C Mokhosi	010717
Human Resources Division - Chief Joint Training	Maj Gen L K Mbatha	010317

Office of the Republic of South Africa High Commission in the United Kingdom

South Africa House, Trafalgar Square, London WC2N 5DP

(Tel: (020) 7451 7299 Fax: (020) 7839 5670)

High Commissioner	*HE* Mr Thembinkosi Obed Mlaba
Deputy High Commissioner	Mr Azwitamisi Golden Neswiswi
Defence & Air Advisor	Brig Gen Sithabiso Mahlobo
Deputy Defence & Air Advisor	Col Daisy Nompumelelo Tshiloane
Defence Office Chief Clerk	WO1 Rodney Thomas Marks

SWAZILAND, KINGDOM OF

(Joined Commonwealth: 1968)

Head of State and Commander in Chief	*His Majesty King* Mswati III
Prime Minister	*The Hon* Dr Barnabas Sibusiso Dlamini
Principal Secretary	Mr Victor Nxumalo

Umbutfo Swaziland Defence Force (USDF)

(Ground Force (includes Air Wing))

Commander	Maj Gen Sobantu Stanley Dlamini
Deputy Commander	Brig Gen Patrick Motsa
Formation Commander	Brig Gen Jeffrey S Tshabalala

Office of the High Commission of the Kingdom of Swaziland in the United Kingdom

20 Buckingham Gate, London SW1E 6LB

(Tel: 020 7630 6611 Fax: 020 7630 6564

Email: enquiries@swaziland.org.uk)

High Commissioner	*HE* Mr Christian Muzie Nkambule
Counsellor	Ms Temnotfo L C Nkambule
1st Secretary (Information)	Mr Themba Simelane

UGANDA, REPUBLIC OF

(Joined Commonwealth: 1962)

President and Commander in-Chief .... *HE* Yoweri Kaguta Museveni
Vice President.. *HE* Edward Kiwanuka Ssekandi
Minister of State for Defence and Veteran Affairs .... *Hon* Mwesige Adolf 060616
Deputy Minister for Defence and Veteran Affairs.................. Col Chalres Engola Okello
Senior Presidential Advisor for Special Operations............. Maj Gen Muhoozi Kainerugaba
Senior Presidential Advisor on Air Force Matters .... Maj Gen Sam Turyagenda

Uganda Peoples Defence Force (UPDF)
(Land Forces (includes Marine Unit) and Air Force)
(as of 10 Jan 17)

Chief of Defence Forces... Maj Gen David Muhoozi 090117
Deputy Chief of Defence Forces.. Maj Gen Wilson Mbadi
Deputy Commander Operation Wealth Creation.................. Lt Gen Charles Angina
Commander Land Forces .... Maj Gen Peter Elwelu
Commander Field Artillery Division .... Maj Gen Sam Okiding
Commander Air Forces... Maj Gen Lwanga Lutaaya
Commander Air Defence Division.................................... Brig Gavas Mugyenyi
Acting Commander Special Forces (SFC) .... Col Don Nabaasa
General Officer Commanding Reserves................................ Maj Gen Chalres Otema
Chief of Logistics and Engineering....................................... Brig Chalres Bakahumura
Chief of Military Intelligence.. Lt Col Abel Kandoho

Office of the Uganda High Commission in the United Kingdom
Uganda House, 58-59 Trafalgar Square, London WC2N 5DX
(Tel: 020 7839 5783 Fax: 020 7839 8925
Email: info@ugandahighcomission.co.uk Website: www.ugandahighcommission.co.uk)

High Commissioner ....*HE* Mr Julius Peter Moto 300817
Counsellor (Head of Consular) .... Mrs Juliet Namiiro Mugerwa
Defence Advisor... Brig Matthew James Murari Gureme

TANZANIA, UNITED REPUBLIC OF

(Joined Commonwealth: 1961)

President of the United Republic and
Commander in Chief of the Armed Forces .... President John Pombe Magufuli 051115

Minister for Defence and National Service .... *The Hon* Dr Hussein Mwinyi

Tanzania People's Defense Force (TPDF)
(Army, Naval Wing (includes Coast Guard), Air Defence Command
(includes Air Wing), National Service)

Chief of Defence .... Gen Venance Salvatory Mabeyo
Chief of Staff.. Lt Gen James Mwakibolwa
Commander Land Forces.. Vacant
Commander Naval Forces .... R Adm Rogastian S Laswai
Commander Air Forces.. Brig Gen William Ingram
Chief of National Service.. Brig gen M W Isamuhyo

Office of the United Republic of Tanzania High Commission in the United Kingdom
3 Stratford Place, London W1C 1AS
(Tel: 020 7569 1470 Fax: 020 7491 3710
Email: ubalozi@tzhc.uk Website: www.tzhc.uk)

High Commissioner ....*HE Dr Asha-Rse Migiro*...140616
Defence Adviser ....Col Jackson Mwaseba

ZAMBIA, REPUBLIC OF

(Joined Commonwealth: 1964)

President and Commander in Chief...................................... *HE* Mr Edgar Chagwa Lunga
Vice President.. *Her Honour* Inonge Mutukwa Wina
Minister of Defence.. *Hon* Mr Chama Davies
Deputy Minister of Defence... *Hon* Mr Christopher Mulenga

Zambain Defence Force (ZDF)

(Army, Air Force and National Service)

Commander, Zambia Army... Lt Gen Paul Mihova
Deputy Commander & Chief of Staff, Zambia Army........ Maj Gen Jackson Miti
Commander, Zambia Air Force (ZAF)................................... Lt Gen Eric Mwaba Chimese
Deputy Commander ZAF... Maj Gen David Muma
Commander Zambia National Service (ZNS)........................ Lt Gen Nathan Mulenga
Deputy Commander ZNS.. Maj Gen Alick Kamiji

Office of the High Commission of the Republic of Zambia in the United Kingdom

Zambia House, 2 Palace Gate, Kensington, London W8 5NG

(Tel: 020 7581 2142 Email: info@zambiahc.org.uk Website: www.zambiahc.org.uk)

High Commissioner... *HE Mr Muyeba Shichapwa Chikonde*.................................*070815*
Deputy High Commissioner... Ms Patricia Sikaala
Defence Attaché... Gen Blackson Nyoni

COMMONWEALTH COUNTRIES OF ASIA

BANGLADESH, THE PEOPLE'S REPUBLIC OF

(Joined Commonwealth: 1972)

President and Supreme Commander of the People's Republic of Bangladesh .... *HE* Mr Abdul Hamid
Prime Minister and Minister of Defence .... *Hon* Sheikh Hasina

Armed Forces of Bangladeesh
(Army, Navy and Air Force)

Chief of Army Staff .... Gen Abu Belal Muhammad Shafiul Huq *ndc psc* 260615
Chief of Naval Staff .... V Adm Nizamuddin Ahmed *OSP BCGM ndc psc* 270116
Chief of Air Staff .... AM Abu Esrar *BBP ndc acsc* 120615

Principal Staff Officer .... Lt Gen Md Mahfuzur Rahman rcds ndc afwc psc PhD
Director General (Operations and Plans) .... Brig Gen Azazul Bar Chowdhury, ndu, psc
Director General (Intelligence) .... Brig Gen Monirul Islam Akhand, ndc, psc
Director General (Training) .... Air Cdre Mohammad Kamrul Islam, GUP, nswc, afwc,psc
Director General (Administration and Logistics) .... Brig Gen Md Ahsanul Kabir, afwc, psc
Director General (Civil Military Relations) .... Cdre Sheikh Mohammad Abul Kalam Azad (G) NGP, ndc, psc,BN

Office of the High Commission of The People's Republic of Bangladesh in the United Kingdom
28 Queen's Gate, London SW7 5JA
(Tel: 020 7584 0081 Fax: 020 7581 7477
Email: info@bhclondon.org.uk Website: www.bhclondon.org.uk)

High Commissioener .... *HE* Mr Mohammed Nazmul Quaunine 281016
Deputy High Commissioner .... Mr Khondker M Talha
Minister (Consular) .... Mr T M Jobaer
Defence Adviser .... Brig Gen A K M Aminul Haque

BRUNEI DARUSSALAM

(Joined Commonwealth: 1984)

Prime Minister, Minister of Defence and Supreme Commander of the Royal Bruneu Armed Forces .... *His Majesty Sultan* Haji Hassanal Bolkiah Mu'izzaddin Waddaulah Ibni Al-Marhum Sultan Haji Omar 'Ali Saifuddien Sa'Adul Khairi Waddien
Deputy Minister of Defence .... 1st Adm (Retd) Dato Seri Pahlawan Haji Abdul Aziz bin Haji Mohd Tamit 221015
Permanent Secretary of Defence .... Capt (Retd) Dato Paduka Abd Rahman bin Begawan Mudim Dato Paduka Haji Bakar 201116

Royal Brunei Armed Forces
(Land Forces, Navy and Air Force)

Commander .... Yang Dimuliakan Pehin Datu Pererma Jaya Maj Gen Dato Paduka Seri Mohd Tawih Bin Abdullah 300114
Commander Land Force .... Brig Gen Pg Dato Seri Pahlawan Aminan bin Pg Haji Mahmud
Commander Navy .... 1st Adm Pg Dato Seri Pahlawan Norazmi Bin Pg Haji Muhammad *PSPNB PJG (Tent) AFDC MSc psc pwo* 130315
Commander Air Force .... Brig Gen (U) Dato Seri Pahlawan Shahril Anwar bin Haji Ma'awiah 260915
Joint Force Commander .... Brig Gen (U) Dato Seri Pahlawan Haji Hamzah bin Haji Sahat 191214

Office of the High Commission of Brunei Darussalam in the United Kingdom
19–20 Belgrave Square, London, SW1X 8PG
(Tel: 020 7581 0521 Fax: 020 7235 9717 Email: info@bdhcl.co.uk)

High Commissioener .... *HE* Maj Gen (Retd) Dato Paduka Seri Haji Aminuddin Ihsan Bin Pehin Orang Kaya Saiful Mulok Dato Seri Paduka Haji Abidin 290514
Counsellor .... Mr Pg Dato Yusof Sepiuddin

INDIA, REPUBLIC OF

(Joined Commonwealth: 1947)

President of the Republic of India.......... Ram Nath Kovind..........250717
Minister of Defence.......... Smt. Nirmala Sitharaman..........030917

India Armed Forces

(Army, Navy (includes naval air arm), Air Force and Coast Guard)

Chief of the Army Staff.......... Lt Gen Bipin Rawat..........311216
Chief of the Naval Staff.......... Adm Sunil Lanba *PVSM AVSM ADC*..........310516
Chief of the Air Staff.......... ACM Birender Singh Dhanoa PVSM AVSM YSM VM ADC..........311216
Director General of the Coast Guard.......... Mr Rajendra Singh..........010316

Office of the India High Commission in the United Kingdom

India House, Aldwych, London WC2B 4NA
(Tel: (020) 7836 8484 Fax: (020) 7836 4331
Email: administration@hcilondon.in Website: www.hcilondon.in)

High Commissioner.......... *HE* Mr Yashvardhan Kumar Sinha..........051216
Military Adviser.......... Brig Rajesh Kumar Jha
Naval Adviser.......... Cdre Sameer Saxena
Air Adviser.......... Air Cdre Anil Sabharwal

MALAYSIA

(Joined Commonwealth: 1957)

Supreme Head of State and Commander of the Malaysian Armed Forces.......... *Sultan* Muhammad V..........131216
Deputy Supreme Commander and First Deputy Prime Minister.......... *HRH Prince* Salman bin Hamad Al Khalifa
Minister of Defence.......... Y.B. Dato' Seri Hishammuddin Tun Hussein
Deputy Minister of Defence.......... Dato' Wira Mohd Johari Bin Bararum
Secretary-General of Defence Ministry.......... Y. Bhg. Dato' Sri Abdul Rahim Mohamad Radzi

Malaysian Armed Forces (MAF)

(Army, Navy and Air Force)

Chief of the Defence Force.......... Gen Tan Sri Raja Mohamed Affandi Bin Raja Mohamed Noor
Chief of Staff MAF.......... Lt Gen Dato' Abdul Halim Bin Hj Jalal
Chief of Army.......... YM Jen Tan Sri Raja Mohamed Affandi bin Raja Mohamed Noor..........161216
Deputy Chief of Army.......... Lt Gen Dato' Seri Panglima Hj Ahmad Has Hasbullah Bin Hj Mohd Nawai..........010811
Chief of Navy.......... Adm Tan Sri Ahmad Kamarulzaman Bin Haji Ahmad Badaruddin..........181115
Deputy Chief of Navy.......... V Adm Dato' Anuwi Bin Hassan..........181115
Chief of Air Force.......... Gen Dato' Sri Hj Affendi Bin Buang..........211216
Deputy Chief of Air Force.......... Lt Gen Dato' Sri Ackbal Bin Hj Abdul Samad
Chief Judge Advocate.......... Mazelan Bin Jamaluddin

Office of the Malaysian High Commission in the United Kingdom

45 Belgrave Square, London SW1X 8QT
(Tel: 020 7919 0274 *(Defence)* Email: mwlon@btconnect.com)

High Commissioner.......... *HE* Dato Ahmad Rasidi Hazizi..........240114
Defence Adviser.......... Brig Gen Dato Hj Kamarol Fauzi Mohd Said
Assistant Defence Adviser.......... Lt Col Ahmad Rashidi Ithnin

ISLAMIC REPUBLIC OF PAKISTAN

(Joined Commonwealth: 1947 (left in 1972, rejoined in 1989)

President / Chief of Army Staff... *Hon* Mr Mamnoon Hussain
Minister of Defence... Engr Kurram Dastgir Khan...040817
Secretary of Defence... Lt Gen (Retd) Zamir Ul Hassan Shah HI(M) 250816

Pakistan Armed Forces

(Army (includes National Guard), Navy (includes Maritime Security Agency) and Air Force)

Chairman Joint Chiefs of Staff Committee............................ Gen Zubair Mahmood Hayat *NI(M) Arty*
Chief of Naval Staff... Adm Zafar Mahmood Abbasi *HI(M)*..................................071017
Director General, Pakistan Maritime Security Agency..... R Adm Jamil Akhtar *HI(M)*
Chief of Air Staff... ACM Sohail Aman *NI(M)*..190315

Chief of Army Staff... Gen Qamar Javed Bajwa *NI(M) Baloch*.............................291116
Chief of General Staff... Lt Gen Bilal Akbar *HI(M) Arty*
Vice Chief of the General Staff.................................. Maj Gen Syed Muhammad Adnan *Punjab*
Commander Army Air Defence Command........................ Lt Gen Muhammad Zahid Latif Mirza *HI(M) AD*
Commander Army Strategic Force Command.................. Lt Gen Mian Muhammad Hilal Hussain *HI(M) Arty*
GOC Special Service Group.................................... Maj Gen Tahir Masood Bhutta
Adjutant General... Lt Gen Anwar Ali Hyder *HI(M) FF*
Surgeon General... Lt Gen Zahid Hamid
Inspector General Arms... Lt Gen Sadiq Ali *HI(M) AC*
Inspector General, Training and Evaluation.................. Lt Gen Hidayat Ur Rehman *HI(M) AK*
Director General Inter-Services Intelligence (ISI)........... Lt Gen Naveed Mukhtar *HI(M) AC*
DG (Analysis)... Maj Gen Nauman Mahmood *Baloch*
DG (Counter-Intelligence).. Maj Gen Faiz Hamid *Baloch*
DG (Planning)... Maj Gen Muhammad Abdul Aziz *HI(M) Arty*
Director General, Strategic Plans Division...................... Lt Gen Sarfraz Sattar *HI(M) AC*
Director General, Inter Service Public Relations (ISPR).. Maj Gen Asif Ghafoor ....Dec 16
Director General, Frontier Works Organisation (FWO)... Lt Gen Muhammad Afzal
Deputy General FWO... Maj Gen Saeed Akhtar
Pakistan Military Academy.. Maj Gen Abdullah Dogar
Commandant, Command and Staff College...................... Lt Gen Aamir Abbasi *afwc rcds (UK) psc (L) qsl*
Chairman, National Disaster Management Authority (NDMA)..Lt Gen Omar Mahmood Hayat *HI(M) Ord*

Office of the High Commission for The Islamic Republic of Pakistan in the United Kingdom

35-36 Lowndes Square, London SW1X 9JN
(Tel : 020 7664 9276 Fax: 020 7664 9224 Email: phclondon@phclondon.org
Website: www.phclondon.org)

High Commissioner... *HE* Mr Syed Ibne Abbas..041014
Deputy High Commissioner.. Dr Israr Hussain
Defence & Naval Adviser.. Cdre Raja Rab Nawaz
Army & Air Adviser... Col Sardar Nadeem Iqbal Khan
Counsellor PATLO-I... Col Jaffer Sultan
1st Secretary *PATLO-II*... Maj Umer Shaukat Ali
Defence Procurement Adviser.................................... Capt Abdus Sami

SINGAPORE, REPUBLIC OF

(Joined Commonwealth: 1965)

President	*The Hon* Halimah Yacob *MP*
Prime Minister	*Hon* Lee Hsien Loong
Minister for Defence	*HE* Dr Ng Eng Hen
Second Minister for Defence	Mr Ong Ye Kung
Senior Minister for Defence	Dr Mohamad Maliki Bin Osman
Permanent Secretary Defence	Mr Chan Yeng Kit
Permanent Secretary (Defence Devlopment)	Mr Neo Kian Hong
Senior Advisor	Mr Chnag Chie Foo
Chief Defence Scientist	Mr Quek Gim Pew

Singapore Armed Forces (SAF)

(Army, Navy and Air Force)

Chief of Defence Force, SAF	Lt Gen Perry Lim
Sergeant Major, SAF SM	CWO Ng Siak Ping
Chief of Staff - Joint Staff	Brig Gen Lim Tuang Liang
Chief of Navy	R Adm Lew Chuen Hong
Chief of Air Force	Maj Gen Mervyn Tan

Singapore Army

Chief of Army	Brig Gen Melvyn Ong
Chief of Staff - General Staff	Brig Gen Siew Kum Wong
ACGS (Personnel)	Col Tan Tiong Keat
ACGS (Intelligence)	Col Leung Shing Tai
ACGS (Operations)	Brig Gen Ng Ying Thong
ACGS (Plans)	Col Lee Yi-Jin
ACGS (Training)	Col Chua Jin Kiat
Head NS Affairs Department	Col Clifford Keong
Head Army Safety Inspectorate	Col Tong Yi Chuen
Chief Systems Integration Officer	Col Lim Wei Lian
Head Army Information Centre	SLTC Cheong Yunn Shaur

Army Formations

Commander, TRADOC	Brig Gen Kenneth Liow
Commander CSSCOM	Brig Gen Lam Sheau Kai
Commander, 3rd Division	Brig Gen Alfred Fox
Commander, 6th Division	Brig Gen Goh Si Hou
Commander, 9th Division/Chief Infantry Officer	Col Andrew Lim
Commander, 21st Division/Chief Guards Officer	Col Seet Uei Lim
Commander, 25th Division/Chief Armour Officer	Col Yew Chee Leung
Commander, 2nd People's Defence Force	Col Dinesh Vasu Dash
Chief Commando Officer	Col Nicholas Ang
Chief Artillery Officer	Col Michael Ma
Chief Army Medical Officer	Col (DR) Lo Hong Yee
Chief Maintenance & Engineering Officer	ME6 Tan Mu Yen
Chief Signal Officer	Col Rajagopal
Chief Army Intelligence Officer	Col Paul Cheak
Chief Engineer Officer	Col Melvin Ong
Commander, PERSCOM	Col Lee Yem Choo
Chief Supply Officer	Col Terry Tan
Chief Transport Officer	Col James Liew

Office of the High Commission for the Republic of Singapore in the United Kingdom

9 Wilton Crescent, London SW1X 8SP

(Tel: 020 7235 8315 Fax: 020 7245 6583

Email: singhc_lon@mfa.sg Website: mfa.gov.sg/london)

High Commissioner	*HE* Ms Foo Chi Hsia	010914
Deputy High Commissioner and Counsellor	Ms Rozana Binte Abdul Majid	
1st Secretary (Admin & Consular)	Mr Philip Paul Peters	

SRI LANKA, DEMOCRATIC SOCIALIST REPUBLIC OF

(Joined Commonwealth: 1948)

President of Sri Lanka and Minister of Defence.................... *HE* Maithripala Sirisena
Prime Minister and Deputy Minister of Defence.................. *Hon* Ranil Wickremesinghe *MP*
State Minister of Defence.. *Hon* Ruwan Wijewardene *MP*
Secretary - Defence.. Kapila Waidyarante *PC*
Secretary - State Ministry of Defence.................................... Mr Sunil Samaraweera
Additional Secretary - Defence.. Mr R M S Sarath Kumara
Chief Financial Officer.. W D R Weerasundara
Militiary Liasion Officer.. Maj Gen DAR Ranawaka *RSP ndu IG*

Sri Lanka Armed Forces

(Army, Navy (includes Marine Corps), Air Force and Coast Guard)

Chief of Defence Staff.. Adm Ravindra C Wijegunaratne *WV RWP& Bar RSP VSV USP ndc psn*
Commander of the Army.. Lt Gen N U M M W Senanayake *RWP RSP USP psc*..........270617
Commander of the Navy... V Adm Sirimevan Ranasinghe *WWV RWP USP ndc psc AOWC*..261017
Commander of the Air Force... AM Kapila Jayampathy *WWV RWP RSP (3 bars) MSc (Int Rel) MIM (SL) qhi fndu(China)*
Director General of the Coast Guard.................................... R Adm Samantha Wimalathunge *RWP USP MSc (DS) Mgt MA (SSS) MSc (NS & WS)*

Office of the High Commission of The Democratic Socialist Republic of Sri Lanka in the United Kingdom

13 Hyde Park Gardens, London W2 2LU
(Tel: 020 7262 1841 Fax: 020 7262 7970
Email: mail@slhc-london.co.uk Website: www.srilankahighcommission.co.uk)

High Commissioner.. *HE* Ms Amari Mandika Wijewardine 060816
Deputy High Commissioner.. Mr Pahala Rallage Sanathana Sugeeshwara Gunaratna m
Minister-Counsellor (Defence)... Brig Andige Priyanka Indunil Fernando
Counsellor.. Mr Manoj Asela Warnapala

COMMONWEALTH COUNTRIES OF EUROPE

CYPRUS, REPUBLIC OF

(Joined Commonwealth: 1961)

President, Commander-in-Chief .... Mr Nicos Anastasiades
Minister of Defence .... Dr Christoforos Fokaides

Cypriot National Guard

(includes naval and air elements)

Commander Cypriot National Guard .... Lt Gen Elias Leontaris
Deputy Commander .... Lt Gen Andreas Markides
Chief of Staff .... Brig Gen Georgios Karagiannis

Office of the High Commission of the Republic of Cyprus in the United Kingdom
13 St James's Square, London SW1Y 4LB
(Tel: 020 7321 4100 Fax: 020 7321 4164/5 Email: CyprusinUK@mfa.gov.cy)

High Commissioner .... *HE* Mr Euripides L Evriviades 041113
Deputy High Commissioner .... Mr Solon Savva
Counsellor .... Mr Andreas Eliades
Consul General .... Mr Ioannis Koukoularides
Defence Attaché .... Lt Col Eleftherios Hadjistefanou

MALTA

(Joined Commonwealth: 1964)

President .... *HE* Marie Lousie Coleiro Preca
Prime Minister .... *Hon* Dr Joseph Muscat *MP KUOM*
Minister for Home Affairs and National Security .... Dr Michael Farrugia *MD MP*
Prinicipal Permanent Secretary .... Mr Kevin Mahoney

Armed Forces of Malta (AFM)

(includes land, maritime and air elements)

Commander of the Armed Forces of Malta (AFM) .... Brig Jeffrey Curmi
Deputy Commander .... Col Mark Mallia
Commander - 1st Regiment, AFM .... Lt Col Edric Zahra
Commander - 3rd Regiment, AFM .... Lt Col Claudio Terribile
Commander - 4th Regiment, AFM .... Lt Col Wallace Camilleri
Commander - Air Wing, AFM .... Lt Col James Thomas Grech
Commander - Maritime Squadron, AFM .... Lt Col Etienne Scicluna

Office of the Malta High Commission in the United Kingdom
Malta House, 36-38 Piccadilly, London W1J 0LE
(Tel: 020 7292 4800 Fax: 020 7734 1831
Email: maltahighcommission.london@gov.mt Website: www.foreign.gov.mt)

High Commissioner .... *HE* Mr Norman Hamilton 310813
Senior Counsellor, Deputy Head of Mission .... Mr Mario Buttigieg
Counsellor .... *Ms Chantal Sciberras*
Maritime Attaché .... Dr Michaela Muscat

ATTACHES AND ADVISERS TO BRITISH EMBASSIES IN FOREIGN COUNTRIES

UK MOD Attaché Corps based at Defence Sections in British Embassies.
Includes non residential accreditations (NRCs). Listings correct as of March 2016.

ABU DHABI (UAE)

Defence Attaché .... Col Tim Kingsberry .... Sep 14 / Sep 17
Air Attaché .... Wg Cdr Mike Wood .... Jul 12 / Jul 18

ABUJA (NIGERIA)

Defence Adviser .... Col S D (Dom) Fletcher .... Dec 13 / Dec 16

ACCRA (GHANA)

Defence section resident in Accra with NRAs to Cote D'Ivoire (Abidjan), Mali (Bamako) and Togo (Lome).

Defence Attaché .... Lt Col Ben Richards .... Apr 13 / Apr 16

ADDIS ABABA (ETHIOPIA)

Defence section resident in Addis Ababa with NRAs to Djibouti (Djibouti), Somaliland, and African Union.

Defence Attaché .... Col Mike Scott .... Jun 13 / Sep 17

ALGIERS (ALGERIA)

Defence section resident in Algiers with NRA to Tunisia (Tunis)

Defence Attaché .... Lt Col Alistair J Bryant .... Jul 14 / Jul 17

ASTANA (KAZAKHSTAN)

Defence section resident in Astana with NRAs to Kyrgyzstan (Bishkek) and Tajikistan (Dushanbe).

Defence Attaché .... Lt Col Jonny Dart .... Sep 15 / Aug 17

AMMAN (JORDAN)

Defence and Military Attaché .... Col H E (Ted) Shields *MBE* .... Sep 13 / Sep 16
Naval and Air Attaché .... Wg Cdr Jock Cochrane *RAF* .... Apr 13 / Apr 17

ANKARA (TURKEY)

Defence and Military Attaché .... Col Christopher (Toffer) Beattie .... Jul 15 / Jul 18
Naval and Air Attaché .... WCdr Bryan Hunt .... Jun 15 / Jun 18

ATHENS (GREECE)

Defence section resident in Athens with NRA to Bulgaria (Sofia).

Defence and Military Attaché .... Capt Richard Blackwell *RN* .... Feb 15 / Feb 18

BAGHDAD (IRAQ)

Defence Attaché .... Brig Gareth Collett *CBE* .... Mar 16 / Mar 18
Deputy Defence Attaché .... Lt Col Paul Meldon .... Nov 13 / Sep 16

BANDAR SERI BEGAWAN (BRUNEI)

Defence section resident in Bandar Seri Begawan with NRA to Philippines (Manila).

Defence Adviser .... Col Mike Page *RM* .... Jan 15 / Jan 18

BANGKOK (THAILAND)

Defence Attaché ......Col Chris Luckham *OBE* ......Dec 13 / Dec 16

BEIJING (CHINA)

Defence section resident in Beijing with NRA to Mongolia (Ulaanbaatar) and North Korea.

Defence and Military Attaché ......Brig Simon Levey *LD* ......Oct 13 / Oct 16

Deputy Defence, Naval and Air Attaché ......Mike Lavender *OBE RAF* ......Nov 15 / Jun 19

Assistant Military Attaché ......Maj Matt Hayward ......Jul 15 / Jul 18

BEIRUT (LEBANON)

Defence Attaché ......Lt Col Chris Gunning ......Apr 15/ Apr 18

Assistant Defence Attaché ......WO Dave Elder *RAF* ......Sep 14 / Sep 17

Assistant Defence Attaché, Damascus ......Sgt Paul Lowthian ......Mar 15 / Mar 17

BELGRADE (SERBIA)

Defence section resident in Belgrade with NRA to Montenegro (Podgorica).

Defence Attaché ......Lt Col Simon P (Fitz) Fitzgibbon ......Mar 15 / Apr 18

BERLIN (GERMANY)

Defence Attaché ......Col Rob Rider *CBE* ......Feb 15 / Feb 20

Naval Attaché ......Capt Dan Howard *RN* ......Feb 15 / Apr 18

Military Attaché ......Col Richard J Wakefield ......Apr 13 / May 17

Air Attaché ......Gp Capt Roland Smith ......Jul 12 / Aug 18

BOGOTA (COLOMBIA)

Defence section resident in Bogota with NRAs to Peru (Lima), Venezuela (Caracas).

Defence Attaché ......Col Jonathan P S Wright ......Jul 14 / Jul 17

Deputy Defence Attaché ......Lt Cdr Lee Davies *RN* ......Nov 15 / Jan 19

BRASILIA (BRAZIL)

Defence Attaché ......Gp Capt Simon Hindmarsh ......Sep 13 / Sep 16

BUCHAREST (ROMANIA)

Defence Attaché ......Lt Col Tim D Bakewell *RM* ......Apr 13 / Dec 16

BUENOS AIRES (ARGENTINA)

Defence section resident in Buenos Aires with NRAs to Uruguay (Montevideo), Paraguay (Ascuncion).

Defence Attaché ......Capt Andy Hancock *RN* ......Apr 13 / Apr 17

Deputy Defence Attaché ......Sqn Ldr Ian S Clements ......Feb 13 / Feb17

CAIRO (EGYPT)

Defence and Military Attaché ......Capt Simon Ahlgren *RN* ......Nov 15 / Nov 18

Deputy Defence Attaché ......Lt Col Ed Sandry ......Mar 15 / Mar 18

CANBERRA (AUSTRALIA)

Defence section resident in Canberra with NRA to Papua New Guinea (Port Moresby)

Defence and Naval Adviser ......Cdre Richard L Powell *OBE MA MSc RN* ......Feb 14 / Feb 17

Military and Air Adviser ......Wg Cdr Jonathan Hough *BA MSc RAF* ......Jan 15 / Jan 18

COPENHAGEN (DENMARK)

Defence Attaché ....Col Sarah Johansen .... Jan 13 / Jan 16

DHAKA (BANGLADESH)

Defence Adviser ....Lt Col Dom D Spencer .... Nov 15 / Jan 19

DOHA (QATAR)

Defence Attaché ....Wg Cdr Graeme Davis .... Apr 13 / Apr 16

DUBLIN (IRELAND)

Defence Attaché ....Col Max Walker .... Sep 15 / Sep 18

Non Resident Naval Attaché (London)....................Cdr Tim Henry

Non Resident Military Attaché (London) ....Lt Col Adrian Jones

Non Resident Air Attaché (London) ....Wg Cdr Archie McCallum *RAF*

FREETOWN (SIERRA LEONE)

Defence section resident in Freetown with NRAs to Guinea (Conakry) and Liberia (Monrovia).

Defence Adviser ....Cdr Derek S Deighton *RN*.................... Aug 13 / Aug 16

HANOI (SOCIALIST REPUBLIC OF VIETNAM)

Defence Attaché ....Grp Capt Tim Below .... Nov 13 / Nov 16

HARARE (ZIMBABWE)

Defence section resident in Harare with NRAs Defence Adviser to Malawi (Lilongwe), Botswana (Gaborone) and Zambia (Lusaka).

Defence Attaché ....Col Ian Mills .... Jun 14 / Jun 17

ISLAMABAD (PAKISTAN)

Defence and Military Adviser ....Brig Murray Whiteside .... Sep 15 / Sep 17

Deputy Defence Adviser....................Gp Capt John Alexander .... an 15 / Jan 17

Military Adviser ....Lt Col Paul Ryalls .... Oct 14 / Oct 17

Assistant Military Adviser....................Maj Luke Davey .... Jan 16 / Jan 18

JAKARTA (INDONESIA)

Defence section resident in Jakarta with NRA to Timor Leste (East Timor).

Defence Attaché ....Col Adrian Campbell-Black.................... Jun 14 / Jun 17

Deputy Defence Attaché....................Maj Mike J Lynskey .... Dec 14 / Dec 17

JUBA (SOUTH SUDAN)

Defence Attaché ....Lt Col Jonnie Williamson .... Aug 15 / Aug 16

KAMPALA (UGANDA)

Defence section resident in Kampala with NRAs to Burundi (Bujumbura) and Rwanda (Kigali).

Defence Adviser ....Lt Col Mike N Nicholls .... Aug 14 / Aug 17

KABUL (AFGHANISTAN)

Defence Attaché ....Col Stuart Barnard *GCLI MA* .... Jul 14 / Jul 17

KATHMANDU (NEPAL)

Defence Attaché is Commander British Gurkhas Nepal and Director Gurkha Welfare Scheme.

Assistant Military Attaché is MLO British Gurkhas Nepal.

Defence Attaché ....Col Ian Logan ....Sept 15 / Jul 18

Assistant Military Attaché..Maj. Dhan Bahadur Gurung....................................Sep 15 / Sep 18

KHARTOUM (SUDAN)

Defence Attaché ....Lt Col Edward J V F Melotte *MBE IG* ....May 13 / Sep 16

KINGSTON (JAMAICA)

Defence section resident in Kingston with NRAs - Defence Attaché to Cuba, Dominican Republic and Haiti; Defence Adviser to Bahamas (Nassau), Belize, Guyana, British Dependent Territories (Cayman Islands, Turks & Caicos) and British Overseas Territories (Anguilla, British Virgin Islands & Montserrat).

Defence Adviser ....Lt Col Patrick Brown .... Aug 13 / Mar 17

KUALA LUMPAR (MALAYSIA)

Defence Adviser ....Col Stephen J Hall ....Mar 15 / Mar 18

KUWAIT CITY (KUWAIT)

Defense Attaché...Col David C Pardy *MBE*..Nov 12 / Apr 16

KYIV (UKRAINE)

Defence section resident in Kyiv with NRA to Republic of Moldova (Chisanau).

Defence Attaché ....Capt Karen McTear *RN*.. Aug 14 / Aug 17

Deputy Defence Attaché...Lt Cdr Dan Hallett *RN* ....Oct 15 / May 18

MADRID (SPAIN)

Defence Attaché ....Capt Paul Lemkes *RN*..Dec 12 / Nov 16

MEXICO CITY (MEXICO)

Defence Attaché ....Col David Strawbridge *MBE* ....Jul 14 / Jul 17

Assistant Defence Attaché..CPO Sally Franks... Nov 14 / Nov 17

MANAMA (BAHRAIN)

Defence Attaché ....Lt Col Andrew Price *RM*...Sep 14 / Sep 17

MOGADISHU (SOMALIA)

The defence section is lodged in Mogadishu but their support is lodged in Nairobi, Kenya.

Defence Adviser.. Lt Col Steve Kilmartin RM.................................. Apr 15 / Apr 17

MOSCOW (RUSSIA)

Defence section resident in Moscow with NRAs to Turkmenistan (Ashkabat) and Belarus (Minsk)

Defence and Air Attaché ....Air Cdre Carl Scott ....Sep 11 / Sep 17

Naval Attaché..Post Vacant

Assistant Naval Attaché ....Lt Cdr Ryan Coatalen-Hogdson.............................Sep 15 / Oct 18

Assistant Military Attaché..Post vacant

Head of Defence Support (HDS)...CPOLogs(Pers) Chris Donkin................................ Oct 14 / Sep 18

Defence Operations Support (DOS) ....WO2 Sara Plant.. Oct 14 / Mar 18

MUSCAT (OMAN)

Defence and Military Attaché .... Brig Peter G D Taylor *OBE RM* .... Oct 14 / Oct 17

Naval and Air Attaché .... Cdr Kevin Broadley *RN* .... Aug 15 / Aug 18

NAIROBI (KENYA)

Defence section resident in Nairobi with NRAs Defence Adviser to Tanzania (Dar-es-Salaam) and Sychelles (Mahe) .

Defence Adviser .... Brig Mark Christie .... Oct 15 / Oct 18

Military Adviser (British Loan Officer) .... Lt Col Alastair Kern *RM* .... Mar 15 / Mar 18

NEW DELHI (INDIA)

Defence and Military Adviser .... Brig Mark Goldsack .... May 15 / May 18

Naval and Air Adviser .... Capt Stuart A Borland *RN* .... May 14 / May 17

Assistant Defence and Military Adviser .... Lt Col Simon De Labilliere .... May 15 / May 18

NICOSIA (CYPRUS)

Defence Adviser .... Col Seb T Pollington .... Jun 14 / Jun 17

OSLO (NORWAY)

Defence section resident in Oslo with NRAs to Iceland (Reykjavik).

Defence Attaché .... Lt Col Matt Skuse *RM* .... Sept 12 / Jul 16

OTTAWA (CANADA)

Defence and Military Adviser .... Brig Jonathan D Calder-Smith .... Feb 14 / Feb 17

Naval and Air Adviser .... Wg Cdr Simon Hulme .... Jul 15 / Jul 18

Staff Officer British Defence Liaison Staff .... Lt Cdr (Retd) Andy Arnold .... Oct 09 /

PARIS (FRANCE)

Defence section resident in Paris with NRA to Monaco

Defence Attaché .... Air Cdre Paul Lyall *OBE RAF* .... Sep 14 / Sep 17

Deputy Defence Attachés .... Capt Chris Clough *RN* .... Aug 13 / Aug 16

Col Geoff S Wright .... Sep 13 / Sep 16

Gp Capt Chris Stockill *RAF* .... Jul 15 / Jul 18

PRAGUE (CZECH REPUBLIC)

Defence section resident in Prague with NRA to Slovakia (Bratislava)

Defence Attaché .... Gp Capt Mike Longstaff *OBE* .... Mar 16 / Mar 19

PRETORIA (SOUTH AFRICA)

Defence section resident in Pretoria with NRAs to Angola. Naval and Air Adviser is Defence Adviser to Namibia (Windhoek) and Mozambique (Maputo).

Defence and Military Adviser .... Col John A McCardle *RM* .... Nov 12 / Jul 16

Naval and Air Adviser .... Wg Cdr Nigel Cookson .... May 13 / May 16

RABAT (MOROCCO)

Defence section resident in Rabat with NRAs Defence Attaché to Senegal (Dakar), The Gambia (Banjul) and Mauritania (Nouakchott).

Defence Attaché .... Lt Col Charlie Warner .... Dec 14 / Feb 18

RANGOON (BURMA)

Defence Adviser .... Col Anthony Stern .... Oct 13 / Oct 16

RIYADH (SAUDI ARABIA)

Defence and Military Attaché ....Brig David Russell-Parsons .... Oct 15 / Oct 18
Naval and Air Attaché ....Cdr Robert M C Bruford .... Aug 13 / Aug 16

ROME (ITALY)

Defence section resident in Rome with NRA to Malta.
Defence and Military Attaché ....Col Lindsay MacDuff .... Nov 12 / Apr 16
Naval / Air Attaché and Defence Adviser to Malta ....Cdr Neil Thompson *OBE* .... Apr 15 / Apr 18

SANA'S (YEMEN)

Defence section lodged in Saudi Arabia at this time. NRA to Eritrea (Asmara).
Defence Attaché ....Col J (Iain) Maybery *RM* .... Sep 15 / Sep 17

SANTIAGO (CHILE)

Defence Attaché ....Gp Capt Paul Warwick .... Mar 16 / Mar 19

SARAJEVO (BOSNIA AND HERZEGOVINA)

Defence Attaché ....Lt Col Paul Marshall *MBE* .... Sep 14 / Sep 17

SEOUL (KOREA)

Defence and Military Attaché ....Brig Andrew M Cliffe .... Dec 13 / Jun 16

SINGAPORE (SINGAPORE)

Defence Adviser ....Cdr Andy G Lamb *OBE RN* .... July 14 / Jul 17

SKOPJE (MACEDONIA)

Defence section resident in Skopje with NRAs to Albania (Tirana) and Kosovo (Pristina).
Defence Attaché ....Lt Col Richard Parry .... Sep 13 / Sep 16

STOCKHOLM (SWEDEN)

Defence section resident in Stockholm with NRA Defence Attaché to Finland (Helsinki).
Defence Attaché ....Wg Cdr Mike R K Palmer .... Nov 13 / Nov 17

TALLINN (BALTIC STATES)

Defence section resident in Tallinn with NRAs to Latvia (Riga), Lithuania (Vilnius). Following closure of Finhad (Helsinki) attache post in 2009, all related matters are refered to this defence section.
Defence Attaché ....Cdr Gary Brooks *RN* .... Nov 15 / Nov 18
Assistant Defence Attaché ....CPO Darren Taylor .... Nov 15 / Nov 18

TASHKENT (UZBEKISTAN)

Defence Attaché ....Sqn Ldr Andrew Strefford .... Nov 14 / Nov 17

TBILISI (GEORGIA)

Defence section resident in Tbilisi with NRAs to Armenia (Yerevan) and Azerbaijan (Baku).
Defence Attaché ....Lt Col Nick C B Wilkes .... Sep 13 / Sep 16

TEL AVIV (ISRAEL)

Defence and Military Attaché ....Col Ronnie Westerman .... Jan 16 / Jan 19
Deputy Defence Attaché ....Wg Cdr Tim Yates .... Sep 15 / Sep 18

THE HAGUE (NETHERLANDS)

Defence section resident in The Hague with NRAs Defence Attaché to Belgium (Brussels) and Luxembourg.

Defence Attaché .... Col James I R Phillips .... Jan 16 / Jan 19

TOKYO (JAPAN)

Defence section resident in Tokyo with NRA to Korea.

Defence Attaché .... Capt Charles Ashcroft *RN* .... Aug 13 / Aug 16

Deputy Defence Attaché .... Maj Tosh Suzuki .... Aug 14 / Aug 16

TRIPOLI (LIBYA)

Defence section removed to Tunis, Tunisia

Defence Attaché .... Col Dougie Hay .... Nov 15 / Nov 17

Assistant Defence Attaché .... SSgt Gary Chapman .... Apr 15 / Apr 17

UNITED NATIONS, UK Mission (New York)

Military Attaché .... Col Mark Maddick .... Oct 13 / Oct 16

Assitant Military Attaché .... Lt Col Andrew Norris *MBE* .... Jul 14 /Jun 17

VIENNA (AUSTRIA)

Defence section resident in Vienna with NRA to Slovenia (Ljubljana) and Senior Military Adviser to OSCE.

Defence Attaché .... Lt Col Andrew F R James *MBE* .... Apr 14 / Apr 17

WARSAW (POLAND)

Defence, Naval and Military Attaché .... Gp Capt Simon J Blake *RAF* .... Feb 15 / Feb 18

WASHINGTON DC (UNITED STATES OF AMERICA)

Defence section resident in Washington DC with NRA to Bermuda (Hamilton).

Defence Attaché .... Maj Gen Richard Cripwell *CB CBE* .... Mar 15 / Mar 17

Minister (Defence Materiel) .... Mr Steve McCarthy .... Sep 14 / Sep 17

Naval Attaché .... Cdre Richard Allen *RN* .... Sep 13 / Sep 16

Military Attaché .... Brig James T E Illingworth *OBE* .... Sep 13 / Sep 16

Air Attaché .... Air Cdre Richard J C Powell *CBE* .... Sep 14 / Sep 17

Assistant Naval Attaché / Royal Marine Attaché .... Col Al Litster *RM* .... Jul 13 / Jul 16

Assistant Military Attaché .... Col Nick Lock .... Jul 14 / Jul 17

Assistant Air Attaché .... Gp Capt Colin Da'Silva *RAF* .... Jun 15 / Apr 16

Counsellor Defence Acquisition and Technology .... Mr Simon Gadd .... Aug 15 /

Counsellor Defence Policy and Nuclear .... Mr Richard Berthon *OBE* .... Dec 12 /

Head British Defence Liaison Service (North America) .... Col Chris Collett .... May 14 / May 17

WELLINGTON (NEW ZEALAND)

Defence section resident in Wellington with NRAs to Fiji (Suva), Tonga (Nuku'alofa) and Vanuata (Port Vila).

Defence Adviser .... Cdr Guy Haywood .... Apr 16 /

ZAGREB (CROATIA)

Defence section resident in Zagreb with NRA to Hungary (Budapest).

Defence Attaché .... Lt Col Tony A Bramwell .... Jan 15 / Feb 17

BRITISH LOAN SERVICE TEAMS & SPECIAL DEFENCE ADVISORY TEAMS

BRUNEI

British Military Advisory Training Team

Senior British Loan Service Officer .... Cdr Simon Martin

CZECH REPUBLIC

British Military Advisory Training Team Central and Eastern Europe

Commander .... Col David A Cutmur

Chief of Staff .... Maj Colin McInroy

JORDAN

British Military Mission

Commander .... Col Alex Macintosh

KENYA

British Peace Support Team

Commander .... Col Richard A Leakey

Chief of Staff .... Maj Gee Jenner

Deputy Chief of Staff .... Maj Ed Watters

KUWAIT

British Military Mission

Commander .... Brig Piers D Hankinson

Director of Studies KJCSC .... Col Timothey N J Wordsworth

MALAYSIA

Headquarters Integrated Area Defence System

Director of Development .... Wg Cdr Colin Would

NIGERIA

Command British Military Advisory Training Team Nigeria

Commander .... Col P Hugh Baker

Chief of Staff / SO2 Air .... Sqn Ldr Ian Partridge

OMAN

Loan Service Oman

Senior British Loan Service Officer (Oman) .... Maj Gen Charlie Fattorini

Senior British Loan Service Officer (RN) .... Capt Gary Pettit RN

Senior British Loan Service Officer (Army) .... Col Ben P Edwards

Senior British Loan Service Officer (RAF) .... Gp Capt A W D (Toby) Craig

QATAR

Loan Service Qatar

SO2 Course Design .... Maj Guy D Gatenby

Qatar JCSC Divisional Colonel .... Col David M Bennett

SAUDI ARABIA

British Military Mission to the Saudi Arabian National Guard

Commander.. Brig Hugh Blackman

Chief of Staff.. Lt Col Ian C Laver

Royal Naval Liaison Team

Officer Commanding.. Lt Cdr Mark P Stannard *RN*

Saudi Arabia National Guard Communications Project (SANGCOM)

Project Director.. Brig Peter E J Drew

SO1 OM&T... Lt Col Stuart T Gillespie

Ministry of Defence Saudi Armed Forces Projects (MODSAP)

SO2 Support... Sqn Ldr Derek H Heffernan

SIERRA LEONE

International Military Advisory Training Team

MOD Adviser.. Lt Col Gary R Wolfenden

SOUTH AFRICA

British Peace Support Team

Commander.. Col Simon R West

SO2 Co-ord... Maj Steve Bowerbank

UNITED ARAB EMIRATES

British Loan Service Team Abu Dhabi

Senior British Loan Service Officer...................................... Col Tim Kingberry

Signals Adviser... Lt Col Keith E Emmerson

SO1 EW & INT... Lt Col George Hume

SECTION III

(as at 1st March 2016)

SENIOR OFFICER LIST

SENIOR OFFICERS OF THE ARMY ON THE ACTIVE LIST

(as at March 2016)

FIELD MARSHALS

HRH The Prince PHILIP *Duke of* EDINBURGH *KG KT OM GBE ONZ QSO AK GCL CC CMM ADC(P) psc(n)*..........150153

BRAMALL of Bushfield *Baron* Edwin *KG GCB OBE MC JP DL idc psc*..........010882

VINCENT of Coleshill *Baron* Richard *GBE KCB DSO rcds psct psc ptsc g(a)*..........020491

CHAPPLE *Sir* John *GCB CBE MA dfjssc psc*..........140292

HRH The Duke of KENT *KG GCMG GCVO ADC(P) psc*..........110693

INGE of Richmond *Baron* Peter *KG GCB PC DL jssc psc*..........150394

HRH The Prince of Wales *KG KT GCB OM AK QSO ADC(P)*..........160612

GUTHRIE of Craigiebank *Baron* Charles *GCB LVO OBE DL*..........160612

WALKER of Aldringham B*aron* Michael *GCB CMG CBE DL*..........130614

CHIEF OF THE DEFENCE STAFF (CDS)

Houghton Gen *Sir* Nicholas *GCB CBE ADC Gen (until Jul 16)*..........180713

Peach ACM *Sir* Stuart *KCB CBE ADC BA MPhil DTech DLitt FRAeS RAF (from Jul 16)*

FORMER CHIEFS OF THE GENERAL STAFF (CGS)

Wheeler Gen *Sir* Roger *GCB CBE*..........030297

Jackson Gen *Sir* Mike *GCB CBE DSO DL*..........010203

Dannatt Gen *the Lord* Richard *GCB CBE MC DL*..........290806

Richards of Herstmonceux *Baron* David *GCB CBE DSO DL*..........280809

Wall Gen *Sir* Peter *GCB CBE DL FREng*..........150910

GENERALS

Barrons *Sir* RL *KCB CBE ADC Gen (Late RA)(Cdr Joint Forces Command)*..........190413

Bradshaw *Sir* AJ *CB KCB OBE (late KRH)(Deputy Supreme Allied Cdr Europe)*..........280314

Carter *Sir* NP *KCB CBE DSO ADC Gen (Late RGJ) (Chief of the General Staff)*..........050914

LIEUTENANT GENERALS

Bashall *Sir* JI *KBE CB (Late PARA) (Cdr Personnel & Support Training)*..........290615

Beckett TA *CBE (Late PARA) (Senior Defence Advisor to the Middle East)*..........060115

Deverell *Sir* CM *KCB MBE (Late RTR) (QMG / Chief of Materiel (Land))*..........100712

Evans TP *CB CBE DSO (Late LI) (Cdr ARRC)*..........300813

Everard *Sir* JR *KCB CBE (Late QRL) (Cdr Field Army)*...010313

Gregory *Sir* AR *CB (Late RA) (Deputy CDS (People))*....040413

Jaques PW *CBE (Late REME) (Chief of Materiel Land, DE&S)*..........080316

Jones PD *CB CBE (Late R ANGLIAN)*..........041013

Lorimer *Sir* JG *KCB DSO MBE (Late PARA) (Chief of Joint Operations)*..........090713

Poffley MW *OBE (Late RLC) (Deputy Chief of Defence Staff (Military Capability))*..........280214

Pope NAW *CBE (Late R SIGNALS) (Deputy Chief of the General Staff)*..........041215

Radford TB *CB DSO OBE (Late LI) (Deputy Cdr Resolute Support Mission)*..........200715

ARMY STAFF

ARMY HEADQUARTERS, ANDOVER

MAJOR GENERALS

Ashmore ND *CB OBE (Late RA) (General Officer Scotland and Military Secretary)* 220811
Bathurst BJ *CBE (Late WG)* 080614
Bramble WJF *CBE (Late RA)* 100615
Bricknell MCM *QHP (Late RAMC)* 141215
Bruce RB *CBE DSO (Late SCOTS) (Colonel SCOTS)*...241114
Carleton-Smith MAP *CBE (Late IG)* 200212
Cave IJ *(Late MERCIAN)* 310715
Chalmers DM *DSO OBE (Late PWRR)* 130715
Chiswell JR *CBE MC (Late PARA)*.............................. 011012
Cripwell RJ *CB CBE (Late RE)* 080113
Cullen DM *CB OBE (Late RA)* 201011
Dickinson AS *CBE (Late RE)* 160614
Fattorini CS *(Late QRL)*... 040814
Fay ASJ *(Late RLC)* 141114
Felton RFP *CBE (Late AAC)*.. 280314
Foster AJ *CMG MBE (Late RA)*.................................. 110609
Free JR *CBE (Late RA)* 290312
Gaunt MJ *CEng FIMechE MRAeS (Late REME) (Director Supply Army HQ)* 040415
Hill GP *CBE (Late PARA)* 070415
Hockenhull JR *OBE (Late INT CORPS)*...................... 110613
Hooper I *(Late R SIGNALS)* 220914
Jones IBL *(Late RE)*... 271115
Lawrence JC *CBE (Late RGR)* 271014
Marshall N *OBE (Late RA)* 270116
Nanson PAE *CBE (Late RRF) (Commandant RMA Sandhurst)*...030915
Nitsch RMB *CBE (Late REME)* 300813
Norton *Sir* GPR *KCVO CBE (Late GREN GDS)*......... 080711
Nugee RE *CVO CBE (Late RA)* 080612
Patterson JR *(Late RTR)*... 201014
Ridge SK *(Late AGC(ALS)) (Director Army Legal Services)*...300915
Robinson TP *CBE (Late 9/12L)* 250515
Rowan JF *CB OBE QHS (Late RAMC)* 301111
Sanders PNY *CBE DSO (Late RIFLES)* 130313
Semple RJ *CBE (Late RE) (Director Information Army HQ)* 251113
Skeates SR *CBE (Late RA) Standing Force Jt Cdr*......300813
Smyth-Osbourne *Sir* EA *KCVO CBE (Late LG)* 091012
Stanford RJA *MBE (Late WG) (GOC Support Command)*... 040615
Storrie AJS *CB CBE (Late D and D)* 151011
Swift JFP *OBE (Late R Welsh)* 240316
Talbot-Rice RH *CBE (Late WG)*.................................. 110414
Tickell CL *CBE (Late RE)* 310813
Urch TR *CBE (Late RE)* 081112
Wardlaw R *OBE (Late RE)* 040915
Welch N *OBE (Late RGBW)* 030714

CHAPLAIN GENERAL

Coulter DG *CB QHC CF (Late RAChD)* 170914

DEPUTY CHAPLAIN GENERAL

Eagles PA *QHC CF (RAChD)*.. 300614

BRIGADIERS

Abraham CM *OBE (Late RLC)*.................................. 300613
Aitken AJ *OBE (Late SCOTS)*.................................. 300614
Amison DP *CBE (Late RLC)*.................................. 300613
Anderson S *(Late AGC(ETS))*.................................. 300615
Baker NA *OBE (Late INT CORPS)*.................................. 300615
Bartlett JK *(Late AGC(ALS))*.................................. 300614
Beardmore CE *(Late RAMC)*.................................. 300614
Beaton KC *OBE QHP (Late RAMC)*.................................. 300614
Bell IR *(Late RA)*.................................. 300615
Bennett JMJ *CBE (Late RA)*.................................. 300614
Blackman HH *CBE (Late SCOTS DG)*.................................. 300614
Borton NRM *DSO MBE (Late SCOTS)*.................................. 300613
Bourne AJP *OBE (Late RGR)*.................................. 300612
Burns PR *(Late AGC(SPS))*.................................. 300612
Cain PA *QHS MBChB MMedSc MSc DAvnMed M*
(Late RAMC).................................. 300612
Calder-Smith JD *(Late RA)*....300614
Capps DF *CBE MA CGCI psc(J) (Late RLC)*.................................. 300610
Carmichael TJ *BEng (Hons) MSc MIET ACIL*
(Late R SIGNALS).................................. 300613
Carr-Smith JSA *(Late RDG)*.................................. 300615
Cartwright PAS *OBE (Late RHF)*.................................. 300613
Cash ATG *(Late AAC)*.................................. 300615
Cavanagh NJ *(Late RE)*.................................. 300609
Chamberlain EJR *(Late RIFLES)*.................................. 300612
Christie MP *MBE OBE (Late PARA)*.................................. 300615
Cliffe AM *BSc MSc MBA (Late RE)*.................................. 300613
Cole JJ *OBE (Late R SIGNALS)*.................................. 300612
Coles CMB *(Late QRH)*.................................. 300614
Copinger-Symes TR *OBE (Late RIFLES)*.................................. 300614
Dalton NJ *OBE (Late AAC)*.................................. 300615
Daniel JD *(Late RIFLES)*.................................. 300614
Deakin GC *CBE (Late LANCS)*.................................. 300613
Deas AJ *(Late RLC)*.................................. 300609
Dennis P *(Late WFR)*.................................. 300611
Donnelly JPS *CBE (Late CHESHIRE)*.................................. 300610
Drew PEJ *(Late R SIGNALS)*.................................. 300615
Duncan AP *(Late RLC)*.................................. 300614
Eastman DJ *MBE (Late REME)*.................................. 300615
Fitzgerald NO *MBE (Late RA)*.................................. 300611
Fletcher GW *(Late R SIGNALS)*.................................. 300615
Ford LK *(Late RA)*.................................. 300613
Francis DRK *(Late RA)*.................................. 300610
Gamble MJ *(Late RA)*.................................. 300614
Gardner FH *CBE (Late RLC)*.................................. 300615
Gedney FG *OBE (Late SCOTS DG)*.................................. 300612
Ghika CJ *CBE (Late IG)*.................................. 300614
Gibb IJ *MA (Late RTR)*.................................. 300613
Gibson DCR *(Late RE)*.................................. 300615
Goldsack MR *CBE (Late RIFLES)*.................................. 300612
Griffiths M *(Late R SIGNALS)*.................................. 300614
Hamilton SP *OBE (Late REME)*.................................. 300615
Hankinson PDP *MBE (Late RTR)*.................................. 300608
Hargreaves FE *OBE (Late R SIGNALS)*.................................. 300615
Harkness PK *MBE MTheol (Hons) MA*
(Late SCOTS).................................. 300613
Harrison ASD *DSO MBE (Late PARA)*.................................. 300614
Harrison IG *OBE (Late RA)*.................................. 300608
Herbert CLG *OBE (Late SCOTS)*.................................. 300613
Hill AG *BEng(Hons) MSc CEng FIET*
(Late R SIGNALS).................................. 300609
Hodgetts TJ *CBE PhD MMEd MBA FRCP FRCSEd*
(Late RAMC).................................. 300614
Hughes AG *CBE (Late QRL)*.................................. 300613
Hughes BJ *OBE (Late RE)*.................................. 300615
Humphrey SL *(Late RA)*.................................. 300612
Hyams TD *OBE (Late RDG)*.................................. 300611
Illingworth JTE *OBE (Late AAC)*.................................. 300610
Jackson AT *(Late YORKS)*.................................. 300612
Jones RTH *CBE (Late RIFLES)*.................................. 300613
Kingdon WJF *(Late RA)*.................................. 300605
Lai TJ *(Late SCOTS)*.................................. 300609
Lawrence FM *OBE (Late LANCS)*.................................. 300615
Learmont JJ *CBE (Late RA)*.................................. 300615
Levey SR *(Late LD)*.................................. 300607
Lowe MP *MBE (Late PARA)*.................................. 300610
Lowth RG *(Late RE)*.................................. 300614
Lythgoe SGS *(Late AGC(ALS))*.................................. 300612
McClean CT *MBE (Late REME)*.................................. 300614
McGovern MAJ *(Late R IRISH)*.................................. 300614
McKend IG *CBE (Late RLC)*.................................. 300614
McLeod AB *MA (Late RLC)*.................................. 300608
McMahon SC *CBE (Late RLC)*.................................. 300614
Mitchell GI *MBE (Late REME)*.................................. 300609
Moore MP *CBE (Late RLC)*.................................. 300613
Mortimer IS *(Late QRH)*.................................. 300615

BRIGADIERS (contd.)

Nadin MN *OBE MA DipHSM FIHM (Late RAMC)*.....300613
Nesmith SPM *(Late R SIGNALS)* 300615
Nickerson GHF *(Late SG)* 300612
Nixon-Eckersall RB *(Late QRL)* 300614
Noble FR *(Late RE)* 300612
Orr JNN *(Late KRH)* 300613
O'Sullivan JSS *(Late PARA)* 300613
Page CST *MBE (Late SG)* 311214
Parkinson RE *(Late RLC)* 300612
Rider RJ *CBE (Late RE)* 300615
Rigden IA *(Late RGR)* 300613
Robson DG *CBE (Late R SIGNALS)* 300610
Russell BWO *MBE (Late SCOTS)* 300613
Russell-Parsons DJC *OBE (Late GREN GDS)* 300615
Sexton ND *(Late AAC)* 300613
Shirley SJ *MBE (Late RLC)* 300612
Simpson RG *MBCHB FRCGP MFFP DRCOG DOCC ME (Late RAMC)* 300615
Smith RR *CBE (Late LI)* 300607
Southall DW *OBE (Late RE)* 300614
Spencer RJB *(Late R SIGNALS)* 300614
Stevenson JIS *MBE (Late RS)* 300609
Strickland GM *DSO MBE (Late RGR)* 300615
Thomas INA *OBE (Late RGR)* 300612
Thomson RJ *DSO CBE DSO (Late RIFLES)* 300612
Toomey RHD *CBE (Late D and D)* 300604
Van Der Lande MC *CBE (Late LG)* 300609
Vickery SJ *(Late R SIGNALS)* 300610
Walker CPJ *MBE (Late RLC)* 300612
Walker CRV *DSO (Late GREN GDS)* 300614
Walton-Knight RJ *CBE (Late RE)* 300614
Warne DB *(Late R SIGNALS)* 300613
Warren RW *MBE (Late AGC(RMP))* 300613
Watson HA *MBE (Late LD)* 300613
Weir CRJ *DSO MBE (Late R IRISH)* 300615
Wheeler GH *CBE (Late R Welsh)* 300612
Whiteside MC *OBE (Late AAC)* 300615
Wild AJC *MBE MBA MSc MA (Late R ANGLIAN)*......300611
Williams AP *OBE (Late STAFFORDS)* 300610
Williamson RHB *QHS (Late RAMC)* 300611
Wilson GW *(Late R SIGNALS)* 300614
Wooddisse RW *MBE MC (Late R Anglian)* 300614
Woodham JM *CBE MC psc(j)+ (Late R ANGLIAN)*....300613
Workman SR *(Late R SIGNALS)* 300613
Wright WSC *OBE (Late RIFLES)* 300615

COLONELS

Acornley JD *(Late RE)*....... 300612
Adam SR *OBE (Late AGC(SPS))*....... 300610
Adams JS *(Late R SIGNALS)*....... 311213
Adams MS *(Late RAMC)*....... 300613
Adams OJ *OBE (Late RA)*....... 300612
Addley GN *CEng (Late R SIGNALS)*....... 300614
Alers-Hankey RR *MA psc(j) (Late SCOTS DG)*....... 300615
Allison NC *(Late RLC)*....... 300613
Anderson JFM *(Late AAC)*....... 300613
Ansell DNT *BSc(Eng) MSc MA CEng FIMECHE (Late REME)*....... 300611
Archer S *ARRC psc(j) (Late QARANC)*....... 300614
Armstrong PJ *(Late REME)*....... 300608
Aspray RJ *(Late REME)*....... 300609
Aston MP *DSO MC (Late R ANGLIAN)*....... 300615
Ayers RJ *(Late RAMC)*....... 300613
Baker BC *(Late RAMC)*....... 300608
Baker PHS *(Late RA)*....... 300614
Banton SJ *OBE (Late MERCIAN)*....... 300611
Barnard S *(Late AAC)*....... 300611
Barnett CMJ *(Late AGC(ALS))*....... 300612
Barr AJP *OBE (Late RE)*....... 300609
Barrington DG *(Late AGC(SPS))*....... 300612
Barry CBK *OBE (Late R Welsh)*....... 300614
Bartholomew JGE *OBE (Late SCOTS DG)*....... 300614
Batty RJ *(Late AGC(ALS))*....... 300610
Bazeley MTG *(Late RE)*....... 300613
Beattie CJ *(Late RIFLES)*....... 300612
Bedding DP *BEng CEng MA MSc FIMechE (Late REME)*....... 300614
Bell CJ *OBE* (Late SG)....... 310715
Bellingall AD *(Late RE)*....... 300608
Bennett BW *OBE (Late RA)*....... 300613
Bennett DM (Late 9/12L)....... 300609
Bennett MJ *(Late RLC)*....... 300609
Bennett RNH *MVO (Late REME)*....... 300607
Bex AG *OBE (Late RLC)*....... 300611
Bhabutta RK *OBE FRCP MFPH MSc MBChB L/RAM (Late RAMC)*....... 300608
Biddick DSJ *MBE MC (Late R ANGLIAN)*....... 310715
Biggart JU *(Late SCOTS DG)*....... 300612
Bigger DLD *ADC (Late RE)*....... 300606
Bird CB *(Late INT CORPS)*....... 300611
Bisset RJ *(Late RAMC)*....... 300604
Blackmore TR *OBE (Late RLC)*....... 300614
Blair-Tidewell JT *(Late RLC)*....... 300615
Bodington RHW *LVO MBE (Late WG)*....... 300610
Boreham AC *(Late RAMC)*....... 300609
Borneman CA *(Late RDG)*....... 300613
Bowder JMH *OBE (Late GREN GDS)*....... 300615
Bowron JH *DSO OBE (Late RIFLES)*....... 300610
Boyd J *OBE (Late PARA)*....... 300615
Boyd RJ *OBE (Late LANCS)*....... 300612
Brand AG *(Late R SIGNALS)*....... 300612
Bridge STW *MB (Late KRH)*....... 300615
Brown RC *(Late RE)*....... 300615
Browne SJR *OBE (Late R ANGLIAN)*....... 300610
Browse SJ *(Late RE)*....... 300613
Bryant DG *(Late RADC)*....... 300607
Bryant JD *OBE (Late AAC)*....... 300613
Buck VW *(Late AGC(RMP))*....... 300613
Bullard MJA *MBE MBA MSc BSc Eng CEng (Late REME)*....... 300615
Burke SM *MBE (Late R IRISH)*....... 300614
Burley RMW *BSc MBChB AFRCS DRCOG FRCGP (Late RAMC)*....... 311215
Butterwick MR *(Late RRF)*....... 300613
Buttery PA *(Late RE)*....... 300610
Byers M *OBE (Late RAMC)*....... 300611
Calder CS *OBE (Late RRF)*....... 300612
Caldicott MEG *MBE (Late RLC)*....... 300615
Caldwell RB *(Late RA)*....... 300606
Campbell JC *(Late RA)*....... 300607
Campbell SW *(Late RAMC)*....... 300607
Campbell-Black AH *(Late R SIGNALS)*....... 300609
Cantelo RAR *FRCA (Late RAMC)*....... 300611
Carter PA *(Late RAMC)*....... 310715
Carter RJ *(Late R SIGNALS)*....... 300614
Cartwright SJ *OBE (Late SCOTS)*....... 300612
Casey DD *OBE (Late RE)*....... 300612
Castle FE *(Late AGC(SPS))*....... 300613
Channer NHD *(Late SCOTS)*....... 300612
Clark PJ *(Late INT CORPS)*....... 300615
Clasper JC *(Late RAMC)*....... 300610

COLONELS (contd.)

Claydon MN *OBE (Late MERCIAN)* 300608
Clements RM *(Late RA)* 300615
Cole TAR *Rev MA BD MTh (RAChD)* 300412
Collett C *(Late AAC)* 300603
Collett GP *CBE (Late RLC)* 300611
Collinge JR *ADC OBE (Late RA)* 300615
Collins CS *DSO MBE (Late RIFLES)* 300614
Colthup ED *(Late YORKS)* 300612
Connelly JC *(Late RLC)* 300614
Connor P *FRCP AGAF MCGI (Late RAMC)* 300612
Cook JA *(Late QARANC)* 300613
Cooper JW *(Late R SIGNALS)* 300614
Coote JC *DSO OBE (Late PWRR)* 300614
Copsey KM *OBE (Late RE)* 300614
Corrie DN *MBE (Late RLC)* 300615
Corrigan EA *(Late RLC)* 300613
Cosgrove RP *(Late REME)* 300614
Craft DA *(Late R SIGNALS)* 300612
Crawford J *(Late RE)* 300613
Creasey SJ *(Late RADC)* 300610
Crook AW *(Late RE (SVY))* 300614
Crook DH *CEng MIET (Late REME)* 300613
Crossfield SB *MSc BEng CEng CMgr psc(j) dis (Late REME)* 300615
Curnow AL *BA (Hons) (Late RLC)* 310715
Dalal SR *MRCGP (Late RAMC)* 300613
Dawes APL *(Late RA)* 300614
Dawes EJM *(Late RA)* 300614
De Quincey-Adams JJ *OBE (Late QDG)* 300614
Deacon GHJ *OBE (Late QDG)* 300607
Deans AJ *MBE (Late AGC(ETS))* 300613
Den-Mckay NA *OBE (Late SCOTS)* 300615
Dennis A *OBE (Late LANCS)* 300608
Dick GH *(Late AAC)* 300612
Dickinson R *(Late R WELSH)* 300615
Dooley MS *MBE (Late R SIGNALS)* 300613
Eagles PA *Rev QHC CF (RAChD)* 270108
Earnshaw NM *(Late QARANC)* 300615
Eble KJ *(Late AGC (ALS))* 300615
Edmunds AJ *MA psc (Late PWRR)* 300613
Edwards BP *OBE (Late SCOTS DG)* 300607
Edwards PJ *MBE (Late RLC)* 300613
Eggett TJ *(Late REME)* 300614
Elviss MR *MBE (Late RA)* 300614
English SN *(Late RLC)* 300608
English WPO *(Late QRL)* 300611
Etherington J *OBE (Late RAMC)* 300609
Etherington JS *(Late AAC)* 300614
Evans IA *Rev (RAChD)* 160712
Evans MH *(Late RTR)* 300614
Ewart-Brookes G *(Late RLC)* 300613
Facer JM *(Late AAC)* 300614
Falconer GP *(Late AAC)* 300610
Fallows AM *(Late R SIGNALS)* 300612
Fensom MJ *MA (Late R SIGNALS)* 300612
Field JM *(Late RAMC)* 300611
Finch GJ *(Late RE)* 300613
Finn AP *(Late RAMC)* 300613
Fish PL *(Late RLC)* 300615
Fitzgibbon SP *(Late REME)* 300615
Fletcher SD *(Late RLC)* 300613
Folkes SEF *(Late RAMC)* 300612
Forgrave MW *OBE QGM (Late MERCIAN)* 300613
Forrest JD *CEng CITP CMgr (Late R SIGNALS)* 300614
Fox DP *MBE MSc psc(j) MA (Late RA)* 300613
Fraser-Hitchen A *(Late REME)* 300612
Frazer RS *(Late RAMC)* 300613
Freely EBM *(Late R IRISH)* 300613
Germain PS *(Late YORKS)* 300613
Gibb IE *FRCS ED MB CH B FRCR (Late RAMC)* 300615
Gibson IP *(Late REME)* 300611
Gill RMF *(Late RAMC)* 300604
Goodman RT *(Late AGC(SPS))* 300610
Goshai H *(Late RAMC)* 300607
Greaves I *QHS (Late RAMC)* 300610
Green FJ *(Late RE)* 300612
Green RM *(Late AAC)* 300612
Griffiths AD *OBE (Late RAMC)* 300614
Griffiths AWA *OBE (Late SCOTS)* 300613
Griffiths PR *(Late R SIGNALS)* 310715
Griffiths TY *CBE (Late AAC)* 300613
Grinstead JS *MBE ADC (Late RLC)* 300607
Hadfield AN *(Late MERCIAN)* 300614
Hair JC *MSc MIHM psc(j) (Late RAMC)* 300612
Hall LP *MSc BSc (Hons) (Late RLC)* 300611
Hall SJ *(Late RTR)* 300613

COLONELS (contd.)

Hardy JB *(Late AGC(ALS))* 300614
Harrison P *(Late RAMC)* 300607
Hartington K *(Late RAMC)* 300613
Hassell AC *FCIPD (Late AGC(SPS))* 300614
Hay DW *(Late SCOTS)* 300614
Hayhurst RM *(Late RA)* 300614
Head RA *MC (Late RIFLES)* 300615
Heal ERB *OBE FIMechE (Late REME)* 300615
Heath GC *(Late RADC)* 300608
Heath SG *OBE (Late RA)* 300613
Heatlie RJ *psc(j) (Late RAMC)* 300613
Henning JDR *FRCA (Late RAMC)* 300613
Heron SD *(Late RLC)* 300612
Hickman KC *MC (Late RIFLES)* 300615
Hill JG *(Late R SIGNALS)* 300615
Hill PF *(Late RAMC)* 300614
Himbury SJE *(Late AAC)* 310715
Hoare JCG *(Late RLC)* 300614
Hodges JM *(Late R SIGNALS)* 300610
Holden LG *(Late RAMC)* 300611
Holford SW *(Late REME)* 300614
Holmes SJ *(Late AGC(ETS))* 300614
Hones JA *(Late RE)* 300615
Horrocks CL *(Late RAMC)* 300610
House TW *(Late RIFLES)* 300613
Howard JR *(Late QRH)* 300615
Howieson RM (Late SG) 300614
Hudson DJ *OBE (Late RA)* 300609
Hunter NW *(Late KRH)* 300613
Hutchings ST *OBE (Late RLC)* 300612
Hutchinson SG *MBE ADC (Late R SIGNALS)* 300611
Ilic N *MBE QGM* 300615
Ingram M *(Late RAMC)* 300615
Irvine KJ *(Late QARANC)* 300612
Jackson ATD *(Late PARA)* 300612
Jackson CJ *(Late RAMC)* 300605
Jackson MCF *(Late RE)* 300614
Jagdish S *(Late RAMC)* 110510
James DRH *(Late R WELSH)* 300613
Jefferies R *CBE (Late SCOTS)* 300610
Jefferson NT *(Late RA)* 300605
Jenkins BW *(Late RA)* 300609
John PF *(Late RAMC)* 300607
Johnston DP *MSc MGDS FFGDP BDS (Late RADC)* 300610
Johnston JAE *(Late AGC(ALS))* 300612
Jones NF *(Late AGC(ALS))* 300607
Jones TJ *(Late RAMC)* 300608
Jose AM *OBE (Late RAMC)* 300608
Joy MHW *OBE CEng FIMechE (Late REME)* 300613
Judd GA *(Late LD)* 300612
Kay AR *(Late RAMC)* 300612
Keating MR *(Late AAC)* 300615
Kelly DA *OBE (Late RLC)* 300607
Kelly MJ *(Late RA)* 300612
Kennedy AP *(Late LANCS)* 300615
Kenyon MP *OBE (Late LANCS)* 300613
Kerr AD *(Late RAMC)* 300611
Kerr JR *OBE (Late RE)* 300615
Kimber AE *(Late RLC)* 300613
King AN *(Late AGC(ETS))* 300611
Kingsberry TL *(Late R IRISH)* 300610
Kite BDA *OBE (Late INT CORPS)* 300612
Knaggs CPH *OBE (Late IG)* 300606
Lambert AN *(Late AAC)* 300614
Lambert CF *(Late SCOTS DG)* 300614
Lammiman SA *(Late RLC)* 300614
Landon J *MBE (Late RRF)* 300612
Lane IBF *MBE (Late RADC)* 300607
Langston CM *Rev (RAChD)* 300614
Law TF *(Late RA)* 300613
Lawrence SA *OBE (Late RE)* 300614
Lawton SPW *(Late RLC)* 300613
Leakey RA *(Late AAC)* 300608
Lee RM *ADC (Late RA)* 300610
Lewis AJ *RRC (Late QARANC)* 300615
Lewis RG *(Late RE)* 300611
Little PM *OBE (Late SCOTS)* 300615
Livingstone GR *(Late PARA)* 300615
Llewellyn N *(Late RLC)* 300614
Lloyd-Jones RH *MBE (Late R WELSH)* 300610
Lock NJ *OBE (Late R WELSH)* 300612
Logan ISC *(Late RGR)* 310715
Long A *(Late R SIGNALS)* 300615
Luck NA *OBE (Late RLC)* 300613

COLONELS (contd.)

Luckham CA *OBE (Late PWRR)* 300614
Luedicke AC *OBE (Late RLC)* 300612
Lynch WR *(Late RA)* 300615
Lyne RFL *(Late R ANGLIAN)* 300613
Maber-Jones AS *PhD MBA PG Dip PGCE KLJ (Late RLC)* 300615
MacDonald DA *(Late RAVC)* 300602
MacDuff LR *(Late SCOTS)* 300611
MacIntosh GAJ *OBE (Late WG)* 300614
Mack DNM *(Late SCOTS)* 300615
Macleod A *(Late RTR)* 300611
MacOnochie CS *(Late RIFLES)* 300613
MacRostie SK *MBE (Late R SIGNALS)* 300605
Madden DAG *MBE (Late QRH)* 300614
Mahan JK *(Late RAMC)* 300615
Mahoney PF *OBE TD MBBS FRCA OSTJ FIMC MSc (Late RAMC)* 300609
Makin NS *OBE (Late RA)* 300614
Marshall D *(Late RLC)* 300614
Matthews JA *OBE (Late RRF)* 300614
Maybery RL *QGM (Late RLC)* 300611
McBride HGM *MSc FCMI MIHM psc(j) sq (Late RAMC)* 300610
McCall PJ *BA LHCIMA (Late RLC)* 300607
McConnell SJ *MA psc(j) CISM (Late R SIGNALS)* 300614
McCulloch JR *(Late QARANC)* 300614
McDonald AM *(Late RADC)* 300615
McKeown D *MBE (Late RE)* 300613
McRae AD *MBE (Late RLC)* 300614
Mead JR *OBE (Late RA)* 300615
Mills AS *(Late RAMC)* 300608
Mills IP *MBE (Late RLC)* 300614
Mistlin A *(Late RAMC)* 300612
Mitchell PG *(Late REME)* 300606
Moffat AD *OBE (Late RLC)* 300614
Monteith DP *MBE (Late YORKS)* 300614
Moore CA *BSc MBBS MRCGP (Late RAMC MO)* 300614
Moreton DA *MBE psc(j)(G) (Late RE)* 300614
Morgan DC *OBE (Late RLC)* 300615
Morris RH *(Late AGC(RMP))* 300615
Murray TJ *ADC (Late INT CORPS)* 300614
Musgrave JB *(Late RA)* 300612
Neal DS *(Late AGC(RMP))* 300612
Nicol AM *(Late RAMC MO)* 300614
Norris DWH *OBE (Late QDG)* 300605
Norton GR *ADC (Late R SIGNALS)* 300607
Nottingham NFC *OBE (Late R IRISH)* 300612
Ogden JW *(Late LD)* 300606
Orr JCM *MBE (Late AAC)* 300614
Orr SA *OBE (Late RAMC)* 300613
Owers RC *(Late RAMC)* 300609
Page NA *MA psc+ (Late RE)* 300612
Palmer JV *(Late RAMC MO)* 310715
Pardy DC *(Late RE)* 300609
Parker PJ *(Late RAMC)* 300611
Parkes NM *MBE (Late AGC(RMP))* 300615
Parkhouse DAF *OBE QHP (Late RAMC)* 300612
Patterson L *(Late AGC(SPS))* 300611
Peacock R *(Late RLC)* 300605
Pearce AL *(Late INT CORPS)* 300614
Pendlington MA *CEng FIMechE (Late REME)* 300611
Perry NCL *DSO MBE* 300615
Phillips AW *(Late RE)* 300608
Pittman AJ *(Late QDG)* 300609
Plummer SP *OBE (Late RIFLES)* 300612
Pointing WJ *(Late RIFLES)* 300608
Pollington ST *(Late RTR)* 300614
Pomroy MA *(Late AGC(SPS))* 300615
Poneskis DA *(Late AGC(RMP))* 300613
Porter DS *(Late RAMC)* 310715
Potts ATL *(Late KRH)* 300613
Potts DH *(Late REME)* 300613
Proctor MC *OBE (Late INT CORPS)* 300615
Pullan M *MBE (Late RA)* 300615
Pullman RW *(Late RE (SVY))* 300615
Purnell MJ *OBE (Late REME)* 300613
Pyle SD *(Late AGC(SPS))* 300613
Quare M *MBE CEng CMgr FCMI FInstRE (Late RE)* 300615
Ralph JK *(Late RAMC)* 300614
Ramage SL *(Late RADC DO)* 300615
Rea FJ *(Late RGR)* 300615
Reynolds AMH *(Late RA)* 300613
Rhodes JC *(Late RE)* 300613
Richardson KM *(Late RADC)* 300612
Richardson NJ *(Late RE)* 300611
Richmond AS *OBE (Late QDG)* 300611

COLONELS (contd.)

Ricketts HTS *OBE (Late RE)* 300615
Ridge JH *(Late RE)* 300614
Ridgway TRD *MBE (Late RA)* 300614
Robinson AK *(Late RLC)* 300609
Robinson AT *(Late REME)* 300613
Robinson JG (Late RGR) 300614
Robson HJ *CEng FIMechE (Late REME)* 300613
Roe AM *(Late YORKS)* 300614
Rogers AMC 300615
Roohan MF *(Late RAVC)* 300614
Ropel MA *(Late RE)* 300615
Rose CJS *(Late RLC)* 300612
Ross DA *MSc MRCGP FRCPCH FFPHM (Late RAMC)* 300609
Ross FJ *(Late RE)* 300613
Rowland TL *(Late RAMC)* 300610
Rumsey RDW *(Late R SIGNALS)* 300614
Russell RJ *(Late RAMC)* 300613
Sandiford TA *OBE (Late STAFFORDS)* 300608
Scott DG *ADC (Late REME)* 300613
Scott MG *(Late PWRR)* 300608
Sergeant RCN *(Late COLDM GDS)* 300614
Sharifi KD *(Late QRL)* 300613
Sharkey SL *(Late R SIGNALS)* 300613
Shaw MD *(Late AGC(SPS))* 300615
Shepherd AJ *(Late RA)* 300608
Shervington MW *OBE (Late PARA)* 300615
Shields HE *MBE (Late RIFLES)* 300609
Simpson MA *TD VR (Late REME)* 110416
Simson TML *(Late RTR)* 300612
Smith AG *(Late PWRR)* 300613
Smith MJV *OBE (Late AAC)* 300611
Smith NC *(Late RAVC)* 300609
Smith PG *QGM (Late RLC)* 300610
Smith RM *(Late RA)* 300612
Standley DM *(Late RAMC)* 300613
Stanhope-White JP *(Late RLC)* 300608
Stenning ZR *OBE (Late YORKS)* 300614
Stern AD *(Late INT CORPS)* 300613
Stewart DM *OBE (Late AGC(ALS))* 300610
Stockley SP *OBE (Late RE)* 300615
Stokes OW *MBE (Late PWRR)* 300615
Stone JM *(Late RAMC)* 300605
Story CRM *BEng MSc MCGI MInstRE psc(j) (Late RE)* 300615
Strawbridge DL *(Late RE)* 300609
Stuart AJW *MBE (Late REME)* 300612
Sturgeon MJM *(Late RE)* 300614
Sturrock AJW *(Late RE)* 300613
Swift J *OBE (Late RRF)* 300615
Swinyard LFM *(Late AGC(ETS))* 300612
Sykes FC *(Late PWRR)* 300612
Sykes MP *(Late AGC(SPS))* 300614
Tai NRM *(Late RAMC)* 300614
Targett BF *(Late RLC)* 300611
Taylor A *(Late AGC(ALS))* 300613
Taylor RC *DSO (Late LG)* 300613
Tennant PP *(Late AAC)* 300614
Terrell AG *(Late RAMC)* 300613
Theakston NST *BEng CEng FIMechE MBA (Late REME)* 300615
Thompson GJ *(Late RTR)* 300612
Thomsett SC *MBE MA psc(j) (Late PWRR)* 300615
Thornhill MJ *CBE (Late RA)* 300610
Thorpe NB *OBE (Late REME)* 300614
Thorpe PJ *(Late RLC)* 300605
Thurgood AM *(Late RLC)* 300612
Thurlow RD *(Late RE (SVY))* 300610
Timmis JRH *(Late RLC)* 300614
Timothy JR *(Late RAMC)* 300608
Tingey L *(Late RE)* 300614
Todd M *MBE (Late QRL)* 300614
Tomes SC *(Late RHG/D)* 300614
Toney MA 300615
Totten AJ *Rev MBE (RAChD)* 300612
Tuck JJH *CBE (Late RAMC)* 300606
Tucker AV *(Late AAC)* 300606
Unsworth N *OBE (Late LANCS)* 300615
Vallings TG *(Late YORKS)* 300613
Vassallo DJ *(Late RAMC)* 061210
Veitch AB *(Late RE)* 300614
Venn DF *(Late AAC)* 300606
Vignaux PA *(Late RLC)* 300611
Waddington ST *(Late REME)* 300612
Wakefield DC *OBE (Late AGC(ALS))* 300611
Wakefield RJ *(Late RA)* 300610

COLONELS (contd.)

Walker PAJ *(Late R IRISH)* 300614
Wallace CP *(Late SCOTS)* 300612
Warner DM *(Late PARA)* 300612
Watkin SJ *(Late RLC)* 300606
Watts RJ *(Late R SIGNALS)* 300613
Waymouth MR *(Late RA)* 300612
West SR *(Late SCOTS)* 300613
Westerman LC *(Late R SIGNALS)* 310715
Wheeler DM *(Late R WELSH)* 300614
Wheelton SP *(Late RLC)* 300610
White DS *(Late RAVC)* 300607
White PJ *MBE (Late SCOTS)* 300615
Whitwham C *(Late AGC(ALS))* 300610
Wilby AR *(Late RE (SVY))* 300614
Wildish TCL *(Late RE)* 300612
Williams LH *(Late RE)* 300613
Williams MD *(Late RAMC)* 131210
Williams SC *(Late RA)* 300613
Williamson S *(Late REME)* 300605
Wills MR *MBE ADC (Late PARA)* 300615
Wilson AJI *(Late QRH)* 300613
Wilson DR *MBChB MD FRCP (Late RAMC)* 300612
Wilson GC *OBE (Late SCOTS)* 300612
Wilson NA *(Late RA)* 300610
Woodhouse S *OBE (Late QARANC)* 300615
Worden DC *(Late R SIGNALS)* 300614
Wordsworth TNJ *(Late RA)* 300610
Wrench BMA *(Late SCOTS)* 300614
Wright GS *EurIng CEng FIET (Late REME)* 300608
Wright JK *(Late YORKS)* 300613
Wright JPS *(Late PWRR)* 300610
Yates JT *(Late RAMC)* 300607
Young JJ *(Late RAMC)* 300607

HOUSEHOLD CAVALRY
AND
ROYAL ARMOURED CORPS

Household Cavalry

Comprises:

Household Cavalry Regiment (*The Life Guards and The Blue and Royals)*

Household Cavalry Mounted Regiment (*The Life Guards and The Blue and Royals)*

Lieutenant Colonel Commanding .... Maj Gen *Sir* Edward A Smyth-Osbourne *KCVO CBE* 290514

Royal Armoured Corps

Heavy Cavalry .... 1st The Queen's Dragoon Guards
Royal Scots Dragoon Guards *(Carabiniers and Greys)*
Royal Dragoon Guards

Light Cavalry .... The Queen's Royal Hussars (The Queen's Own and Royal Irish)
The King's Royal Hussars
The Light Dragoons
The Royal Lancers (formed on 020515 from amalgamation of:
9th/12th Royal Lancers (Prince of Wales's)
The Queen's Royal Lancers)

The Royal Tank Regiment ....The Royal Tank Regiment

HOUSEHOLD CAVALRY

THE LIFE GUARDS

April 1922
1st Life Guards and
2nd Life Guards amalgamated to form
Life Guards (1st and 2nd)

June 1928
Redesignated The Life Guards

The Royal Arms

Dettingen, Peninsula, Waterloo, Tel el Kebir, Egypt 1882, Relief of Kimberley, Paardeberg, South Africa 1899-1900

The Great War: **Mons, Le Cateau,** Retreat from Mons, **Marne 1914, Aisne 1914, Messines 1914,** Armentieres 1914, **Ypres 1914, 15, 17,** Langemarck 1914, Gheluvelt, Nonne Bosschen, St Julien, Frezenberg, **Somme 1916, 18,** Albert 1916, **Arras 1917, 18,** Scarpe 1917, 18, Broodseinde, Poelcappelle, Passchendaele, Bapaume 1918, **Hindenburg Line,** Epehy, St Quentin Canal, Beaurevoir, Cambrai 1918, Selle, **France and Flanders 1914-18**

The Second World War: Mont Pincon, **Souleuvre,** Noireau Crossing, Amiens 1944, **Brussels,** Neerpelt, **Nederrijn,** Nijmegen, Lingen, Bentheim, **North-West Europe 1944-45,** Baghdad 1941, **Iraq 1941, Palmyra, Syria 1941, El Alamein, North Africa 1942-43**, Arezzo, Advance to Florence, Gothic Line, **Italy 1944**

Wadi al Batin, **Gulf 1991,** Al Basrah, **Iraq 2003**

Regimental Marches

Quick Marches....................................... (i) Milanollo (ii) Men of Harlech
Slow Marches... (i) The Life Guards Slow March (ii) Men of Harlech

Agents... Lloyds Bank plc Cox's & King's Branch
Headquarters Household Cavalry......... Horse Guards, Whitehall, London SW1A 2AX
(Tel: 0207 414 2392 Email: LONDIST-HQHCavRegtAdjt@mod.uk)

Allied Regiment of the Pakistan Army

The President's Bodyguard

Colonel in Chief..................................... HER MAJESTY THE QUEEN
Colonel... FM (Retd) *the Lord Guthrie* of Craigiebank *GCB LVO OBE*.............................010199
Lieutenant Colonel Commanding.......... Maj Gen *Sir* Edward A Smyth-Osbourne *KCVO CBE* 290514

Lieutenant Colonels

Gaselee JDA	300613
Griffin RRD *MA psc(j)*	300606
James D	300613
Kingston MEW *MBE MSc*	061214
Kitching MR *MBE*	260216

Majors

Armitage TJ	310709
Douglas W	310713
Giffard TAH	310708
Howell JEM	310708
Long TMR	310714
Rogers BE	310715
Stewart NM	310715

Captains

Ashby GR	130611
Boyt HBH	311213
Campbell JC	130214
Carefoot J	280314
Chambers RI	160309
Chishick PJR	120612
Fry SK	010413
Galvin AJ	020410
Gibson BK	020415
Harbord JHS	170614
Hitchings DJ	020412
Holliday EJH	200614
Horne AGF	310713
Jordan HJB	180613
Payne DJ	050710
Taylor SB	010411
Whiting TAR	080212
Woolf BF	110211

Lieutenants

Bond RE	120415
De Ritter TGA	110813
Lewis CE	130414
McAllister KRE	050115
Mulholland WA	120415
Penrose ST	050115
Pile JE	100814
Seccombe TL	140413

2nd Lieutenants

Kjellgren JAF	110415
Marlow-Thomas CMA	121215
Stewart TMW	121215
Van Der Lande EMB	090814
Vaughan HMH	090814

Officer Cadet

Pagden-Ratcliffe FAX	040514

THE BLUES AND ROYALS
(ROYAL HORSE GUARDS AND 1st DRAGOONS)

On 29 March 1969

Royal Horse Guards (The Blues) and
Royal Horse Dragoons (1st Dragoons) amalgamated to form:
The Blues and Royals (Royal Horse Guards and 1st Dragoons)

The Royal Arms

Tangier 1662-80, Dettingen, Warburg, Beaumont, Willems, Fuentes D'onor, Peninsula, Waterloo, Balaklava, Sevastopol, Tel el Kebir, Egypt 1882, Relief of Kimberley, Paardeberg, Relief of Ladysmith, South Africa 1899-1902

The Great War: Mons, **Le Cateau,** Retreat from Mons, **Marne 1914,** Aisne 1914, **Messines 1914,** Armentieres 1914, **Ypres 1914, 15, 17,** Langemarck 1914, **Gheluvelt,** Nonne Bosschen, St Julien, **Frezenberg, Loos, Arras 1917,** Scarpe 1917, Broodseinde, Poelcappelle, Passchendaele, **Somme 1918,** St Quentin, Avre, **Amiens, Hindenburg Line,** Beaurevoir, **Cambrai 1918, Sambre, Pursuit to Mons, France and Flanders 1914-18**

The Second World War: Mont Pincon, **Souleuvre,** Noireau Crossing, Amiens 1944, **Brussels,** Neerpelt, **Nederrijn,** Nijmegen, Veghel, **Rhine,** Lingen, Bentheim, **North-West Europe 1944-45,** Baghdad 1941, **Iraq 1941, Palmyra, Syria 1941,** Msus, Gazala, **Knightsbridge,** Defence of Alamein Line, **El Alamein,** El Agheila, **Advance on Tripoli, North Africa 1941-43, Sicily 1943,** Arezzo, Advance to Florence, Gothic Line, **Italy 1943-44**

Falkland Islands 1982, Al Basrah, **Iraq 2003**

Regimental Marches

Quick Marches....................................... Grand March from Aida and The Royals
Slow Marches... Slow March of The Blues and Royals

Agents.. Lloyds Bank plc Cox's & King's Branch
Headquarters Household Cavalry......... Horse Guards, Whitehall, London SW1A 2AX
(Tel: 0207 414 2392 Email: LONDIST-HQHCavRegtAdjt@mod.uk)

Alliances

Canadian Armed Forces......................... The Royal Canadian Dragoons
The Governor General's Horse Guards

Colonel in Chief.................................... HER MAJESTY THE QUEEN
Colonel.. *HRH The Princess Royal KG KT GCVO QSO* 011098
Lieutenant Colonel Commanding.......... Maj Gen *Sir* Edward A Smyth-Osbourne *KCVO CBE* 290514

Lieutenant Colonels

Bedford PA	300612
Evetts RS	300615
Goodwin-Hudson MP	311213
Lockhart CA *MBE*	300606
Maher VP	010113
Miller SSM	300610
Philipson-Stow RR	300614
Woyka GVD	300604

Majors

Archer-Burton TJ *BA(Hons) MA MSc*	310709
De St John-Pryce JEA	310709
Deverell SP	310714
Gorman RIL	310714
Lewis RHA	310707
Lukas SS	310715
Mackie EP	310715
Pass J	310714
Spiller RJ	310713
Twumasi-Ankrah NK	310712
Williams PJ *MC*	310708

Captains

Bacon CMI	110815
Barnes JB	130214
Boyd-Thomas WE	310713
Churcher JMM	191214
Clive JFM	171012
Dingsdale SA	140415
Gardner AC	020410
Gore Langton CJB	180613
Horgan RW	080212
Mawson JA	171012
Mountain TDE	130814
Nicholls SRA	020415
Owen AGR	121010
Owens DM	020412
Robson DH	010414
Sudlow JG	311213
Thomas HJ	200614
Turnor WMF	161013
Wilmot MDD	180613

Lieutenants

Cochrane-Dyet JI	120415
Faire JRG	100814
Fitzgerald JR	110813
Huda NZB	100814
Hunt-Grubbe RB	050115
Mapples TL	110813

Murphy CJP	151213
Nicole ETG	050115
Soames AC	050115

2nd Lieutenants

Comyn EJF	090814
Crosthwaite-Eyre O	110415
Flay PRM	110415
Perera REC	131214
Titman BR	080815

ROYAL ARMOURED CORPS

In front of two concentric circles broken and barbed at the top, a gauntlet, clenched, charged with a billet. Inscribed with the letters RAC the whle ensigned with The Crown

Alliances

Canadian Armed Forces........................Royal Canadian Armoured Corps
Australian Military Forces....................Royal Australian Armoured Corps
New Zealand Armed Forces..................Royal New Zealand Armoured Corps

Colonel Commandant ....Lt Gen *Sir* James R Everard *KCB CBE* 051211
Gen *Sir* Christopher Deverell *KCB MBE ADC Gen* 010117

The origins of amalgmated Regiments now included in The Royal Armoured Corps are as follows:

1st THE QUEEN'S DRAGOON GUARDS

On 1st January 1959
1st King's Dragoon Guards and
The Queen's Bays (2nd Dragoon Guards) amalgamated to form:
1st The Queen's Dragoon Guards

THE ROYAL SCOTS DRAGOON GUARDS (CARABINIERS AND GREYS)

On 11 April 1922
3rd Dragoon Guards (Prince of Wales's) and
The Carabiniers (6th Dragoon Guards) amalgamated to form:
3rd/6th Dragoon Guards

On 31 December 1928 the Regiment was redesignated
3rd Carabiniers (Prince of Wales's Dragoon Guards)

On 2 July 1971
3rd Carabiniers (Prince of Wales's Dragoon Guards) and
The Royal Scots Greys (2nd Dragoons) amalgamated to form:
The Royal Scots Dragoon Guards (Carabiniers and Greys)

THE ROYAL DRAGOON GUARDS

On 11 April 1922
4th Royal Irish Dragoon Guards and
7th Dragoon Guards (Princess Royal's) amalgamated to form:
4th/7th Dragoon Guards

On 31 October 1936 the Regiment was redesignated
4th/7th Royal Dragoon Guards

On 11 April 1922
5th Dragoon Guards (Princess Charlotte of Wales's) and
The Inniskillings (6th Dragoons) amalgamated to form:
5th/6th Dragoons

On 31 May 1927 the Regiment was redesignated
5th Inniskilling Dragoon Guards
On 30 June 1935 the Regiment was redesignated
5th Royal Inniskilling Dragoon Guards

On 1 August 1992
4th/7th Royal Dragoon Guards and
5th Royal Inniskilling Dragoon Guards amalgamated to form:
The Royal Dragoon Guards

THE QUEEN'S ROYAL HUSSARS (THE QUEEN'S OWN AND ROYAL IRISH)

On 3 November 1958
3rd The King's Own Hussars and
7th Queen's Own Hussars amalgamated to form:
The Queen's Own Hussars

On 24 October 1958
4th Queen's Own Hussars and
8th King's Royal Irish Hussars amalgamated to form:
The Queen's Royal Irish Hussars

On 1 September 1993
The Queen's Own Hussars and
The Queen's Royal Irish Hussars amalgamated to form:
The Queen's Royal Hussars (The Queen's Own and Royal Irish)

9TH/12TH ROYAL LANCERS (PRINCE OF WALES'S)

On 11 September 1960
9th Queen's Royal Lancers and
12th Royal Lancers (Prince of Wales's) amalgamated to form:
9th/12th Royal Lancers (Prince of Wales's)

On 2 May 2015
Amalgamation of 9th/12th Royal Lancers with the Queen's Royal Lancers
to form The Royal Lancers as part of the Army 2020 reformation.

THE KING'S ROYAL HUSSARS

On 25 October 1969
10th Royal Hussars (Prince of Wales's Own) and
11th Hussars (Prince Albert's Own) amalgamated to form:
The Royal Hussars (Prince of Wales's Own)

On 11 April 1922
14th King's Hussars and
20th Hussars amalgamated to form:
14th/20th Hussars

On 31 December 1936 the Regiment was redesignated
14th/20th King's Hussars

On 4 December 1992
The Royal Hussars (Prince of Wales's Own) and
14th/20th King's Hussars amalgamated to form:
The King's Royal Hussars

THE LIGHT DRAGOONS

On 11 April 1922
13th Hussars and
18th Royal Hussars (Queen Mary's Own) amalgamated to form:
13th/18th Hussars

On 31 December 1935 the Regiment was redesignated
13th/18th Royal Hussars (Queen Mary's Own)

On 11 April 1922
15th The King's Hussars and
19th Royal Hussars (Queen Alexandria's Own) amalgamated to form:
15th/19th Hussars

On 31 October 1932 the Regiment was redesignated
15th The King's Royal Hussars
On 31 December 1933 the Regiment was redesignated
15th/19th The King's Royal Hussars

On 1 December 1992
13th/18th Royal Hussars (Queen Mary's Own) and
15th/19th The King's Royal Hussars amalgamated to form:
The Light Dragoons

THE QUEEN'S ROYAL LANCERS

On 11 April 1922
16th The Queen's Lancers and
5th Royal Irish Lancers amalgamated to form:
16th/5th Lancers

On 16 June 1954 the Regiment was redesignated
16th/5th The Queen's Royal Lancers

On 11 April 1922
17th (Duke of Cambridge's Own) Lancers and
21st (Empress of India's) Lancers amalgamated to form:
17th/21st Lancers

On 25 June 1993
16th/5th The Queen's Royal Lancers and
17th/21st Lancers amalgamated to form:
The Queen's Royal Lancers

On 2 May 2015
Amalgamation of The Queen's Royal Lancers with the 9th/12th Royal Lancers to form The Royal Lancers as part of the Army 2020 reformation.

ROYAL TANK REGIMENT

On 28 July 1917
The Tank Corps was formed from the Heavy Branch of the Machine Gun Corps

On 18 October 1923
The Corps was redesignated Royal Tank Corps

On 4 April 1939
The Corps was redesignated the Royal Tank Regiment

On 1 August 2014
Amalgamation of 1st Royal Tank Regiment (1RTR) and 2nd Royal Tank Regiment (2RTR) to form a single regiment, The Royal Tank Regiment.

HEAVY CAVALRY

1ST THE QUEEN'S DRAGOON GUARDS

The Imperial Eagle
Pro Rege et Patria

Blenheim, Ramillies, Oudenarde, Malplaquet, Dettingen, Warburg, Beaumont, Willems, Waterloo, Sevastopol, Lucknow, Taku Forts, Pekin 1860, South Africa 1879, South Africa 1901-02

The Great War: **Mons, Le Cateau,** Retreat from Mons, **Marne 1914**, Aisne 1914, **Messines 1914,** Armentieres 1914, **Ypres 1914, 15,** Frezenberg, Bellewaarde, **Somme 1916, 18,** Flers-Courcelette, **Morval,** Arras 1917, **Scarpe 1917, Cambrai 1917, 18,** St Quentin, Baupaume 1918, Rosieres, **Amiens,** Albert 1918, Hindenburg Line, St Quentin Canal, Beaurevoir, **Pursuit to Mons, France and Flanders 1914-18, Afghanistan 1919**

The Second World War: **Somme 1940,** Withdrawal to Seine, North-West Europe 1940, **Beda Fomm, Defence of Tobruk,** Tobruk 1941, Tobruk Sortie 1941, Relief of Tobruk, Msus, **Gazala,** Bir el Aslagh, Bir Hacheim, Cauldron, Knightsbridge, Via Balbia, Mersa Matruh, **Defence of Alamein Line,** Alam el Halfa, **El Alamain,** El Agheila, **Advance on Tripoli, Tebaga Gap,** Point 201 (Roman Wall), **El Hamma,** Akarit, El Kourzia, Djebel Kournine, **Tunis,** Creteville Pass, **North Africa 1941-43,** Capture of Naples, Scarfati Bridge, **Monte Camino,** Garigliano Crossing, Capture of Perugia, Arezzo, **Gothic Line, Coriano, Rimini Line,** Ceriano Ridge, Carpineta, Cesena, **Lamone Crossing,** Defence of Lamone Bridgehead, **Argenta Gap, Italy 1943-45,** Athens, Greece 1944-45

Wadi al Batin, **Gulf 1991,** Al Basrah, Iraq 2003

Regimental Marches

Quick March ....Regimental March of 1st The Queen's Dragoon Guards
(Radetsky March and Rusty Buckles)
Slow March ....(i) 1st Dragoon Guards Slow March (ii) 2nd Dragoon Guards Slow March

Agents ....Lloyds Bank plc Cox's & King's Branch
Home Headquarters ....1st The Queen's Dragoon Guards, Maindy Barracks,
Whitchurch Road, Cardiff, CF14 3YE
(Tel: 02920 781213 Fax: 02920 781384
Email: adminofficer@qdg.org.uk Website: www.qdg.org.uk)

Alliances

Canadian Armed Forces ....The Governor General's Horse Guards
Australian Military Forces ....1st/15th Royal New South Wales Lancers
Pakistan Army.......................................11th Cavalry (Frontier Force)
Sri Lanka Army ....1st Reconnaissance Regiment
South African Defence Forces ....1st Special Service Battalion

Colonel in Chief ....FM *HRH The Prince of* Wales *KG KT GCB OM AK QSO ADC* 010703
Colonel ....Lt Gen (Retd) *Sir* Simon V Mayall *KBE CB* 191207
Regimental Secretary...........................Mr Mark L Hawtin

Lieutenant Colonels		*Majors*			
Botsford MWL *MBE*	300611	Alford AJ	310707	Nicholas BR	310713
Davies WHL *MBE*	300612	Beaver CWC	310715	Parkyn B	310713
Fenton NJ	300608	Bond PLC	310707	Pilcher HJ	310714
Parry RJ	300606	Coles I	310715	Ruggles-Brise CE	310715
Stenhouse JGE *DSO*	300615	Corfield P	310710	Staveley DGO	310711
Smith KP	210313	Farebrother STB *MC*	310709	Sudlow AM	310715
Thomas N	300615	Hoey DCM	310715	Tyson GE	310715
		Lloyd HT	310710		
		Moore T	310715		

Captains

Dunne JO	010412
Findlay REM	110815
Garland NS	121010
Jackson JAF *PhD*	140415
John S	130709
Jones PD	010413
Jones DS	020415
Jones MJ	010414
Lough JCF	060712
Machale MD	170614
Mansel RC	020415
Martel CGL	170614
Matthews BCJ	050610
Mossop HEH	180613
Roberts CJ	130611
Robinson RG	120612
Thomas SR	010414
Wiggins DM	130214
Williams B	080212

Lieutenants

Barcroft HWL	141214
Carter CE	151213
Cowen JP	190414
Dumont AA	240812
McKechnie MAJ	130414
McKellar RW	100814
Paine HDG	110813
Poppleton CR	100814
Wilks EP	151213
Woodhart JGH	130610
Woolland FCL	130414

2nd Lieutenants

Campbell AD	121215
Carter CE	110415
Carter MJ	110415
Fraser HJH	090814
Jackson GES	131214
Owen ETP	090814
Simpson WLT	121215

THE ROYAL SCOTS DRAGOON GUARDS (CARABINIERS AND GREYS)

The Napoleonic Eagle superimposed upon two carbines in saltire upon plinth inscribed WATERLOO, over a scroll bearing ROYAL SCOTS DRAGOON GUARDS

Second to None

In the centre, a thistle within a circlet bearing the motto NEMO ME IMPUNE LACESSIT enfiled by a wreath of roses, thistles and shamrocks, ensigned with The Royal Crown. Below, the honorary distinction, The Napoleonic Eagle. In the first corner, the White Horse of Hanover within a scroll. In the second, the Plume of The Prince of Wales bearing the motto ICH DIEN and in the third, SCOTS DG in gold, each corner upon a yellow ground within a wreath of roses, thistles and shamrocks. In the fourth corner, the Red Dragon of Wales within a scroll

Blenheim, Ramillies, Oudenarde, Malplaquet, Dettingen, Warburg, Beaumont, Willems, Talavera, Albuhera, Vittoria, Peninsula, Waterloo, Balaklava, Sevastopol, Delhi 1857, Abyssinia, Afghanistan 1879-80, Relief of Kimberley, Paardeberg, **South Africa 1899-1902**

The Great War: Mons, Le Cateau, **Retreat from Mons, Marne 1914, Aisne 1914, Messines 1914,** Armentieres 1914, **Ypres 1914, 15,** Gheluvelt, Nonne Bosschen, Neuve Chapelle, St Julien, Frezenberg, Bellewaarde, Loos, **Arras 1917,** Scarpe 1917, **Cambrai 1917, 18, Somme 1918,** St Quentin, Avre, Lys, Hazebrouck, **Amiens,** Albert 1918, Bapaume 1918, Hindenburg Line, Canal du Nord, St Quentin Canal, Beaurevoir, Selle, Sambre, **Pursuit to Mons,** France and Flanders 1914-18

The Second World War: Caen, **Hill 112, Falaise,** Venlo Pocket, **Hochwald, Aller,** Bremen, North-West Europe 1944-45, **Merjayun,** Syria 1941, **Alam el Halfa, El Alamein,** El Agheila, **Nofilia,** Advance on Tripoli, North Africa 1942-43, **Salerno,** Battipaglia, Volturno Crossing, Italy 1943, **Imphal,** Tamu Road, **Nunshigum, Bishenpur, Kanglatongbi, Kennedy Peak,** Shwebo, **Sagaing, Mandalay, Ava, Irrawaddy,** Yenangyaung 1945, Burma 1944-45.

Wadi al Batin, **Gulf 1991,** Al Basrah, **Iraq 2003**

Regimental Marches

Military Band

Quick March ....“3 DG’s”
Slow March..The Garb of Old Gaul

Pipes and Drums

Quick March ....Heilan’ Laddie
Slow March ....My Home

Agents ....Holt’s Branch , Royal Bank of Scotland plc, Lawrie House, Farnborough, Hants GU14 7NR
Home Headquarters ....The Castle, Edinburgh, EH1 2YT
(Tel: 0131 310 5100 Fax: 0131 310 5101 Email: HHQScotsDG-RegtSec@mod.uk)

Alliances

Canadian Armed Forces ....The Windsor Regiment
Australian Military Forces.....................12th/16th Hunter River Lancers
New Zealand Army................................The New Zealand Scottish
South African Defence Force.................The Natal Carbineers

Colonel in Chief....................................HER MAJESTY THE QUEEN
Deputy Colonel in Chief.........................FM *HRH The Duke of* Kent *KG GCMG GCVO ADC (P)* 031293
Colonel...Brig (Retd) H D (David) Allfrey *MBE* 011015

Lieutenant Colonels		*Majors*			
				Erskine-Naylor BG	310712
Cattermole BJ *MBE*	300612	Ambrose JS	310705	Foulerton NG	310708
Coombes DCD	300615	Anderson RHG	310715	Halford-MacLeod JPA	310707
Williamson JMW	300615	Anderson RM	310712	Hanlon JM	310708
		Bishop JWH	310708	Hayward ME	310708
		Brotherton BH	310713	Irwin JSG	310714
		Craig GG	310710	Jackson AW	310715

Landon DGA	310715
Leek WRG	310708
Lillie MM	310714
Marjoribanks AD	310713
McDowell KG	310713
McLeman JFS	310708
O'Brien ED	310710
Ongaro RJ	310709
Ridge BDA	310702
Soulsby DB	310708
Spenlove-Brown TP	310705
Stone JE	310709
Turpin AC	310704
Walters SJ	310709

Captains

Baillie JD	011015
Ballard-Whyte LO	161211
Erskine-Naylor MS	121011
Gardiner J	171210
Graham TJ	130214
Jackson RJH	121010
Lamb I	010413
Lee DP	161013
MacLaurin AJB	170614
Majcher CPS	090211
McNeil BA	090211
O'Connor WD	210614
Probst SJA	180613
Pyman CG	131210
Reith AJS	150612
Taylor B	010413
Von Der Heyde OHS	140415
Woodhams NGB	090211

Lieutenants

Bradford C	110813
Brazier WPH	100814
Dawson JC	130414
Knox HES	151213
Mitchell EW	120415
Nurick RJ	130414
Rider FGR	110813
Sheehan RMS	100814
Stewart ADJ	120415
Thornton EH	151213

2nd Lieutenants

Blackhall JJH	121215
Cairns F	131214
Dent-Pooley BPF	121215
Houstoun MP	131214
MacFarlane GKR	110415
Moore DGF	110415

THE ROYAL DRAGOON GUARDS

The eight-pointed Star of St Patrick in silver, surmounted by a Garter blue circle inscribed ROYAL DRAGOON GUARDS above MCMXCII in gold. Within the circle, The Red Cross of St George upon a white field surmounted by Inniskilling Castle above a scroll bearing the name INNISKILLING in gold

The badge of the Royal Dragoon Guards within a circle inscribed ROYAL DRAGOON GUARDS all within the Union Wreath, the whole ensigned with St Edward's Crown. The motto QUIS SEPARABIT inscribed within a scroll upon the tie of the Wreath. In the first corner, the White Horse of Hanover and in the second corner, the Coronet of Her Late Majesty the Empress and Queen Frederick of Germany and Prussia as Princess Royal of Great Britain and Ireland. In the third corner, the Star of the Order of St Patrick and in the fourth corner, the Castle of Inniskilling

Blenheim, Ramillies, Oudenarde, Malplaquet, Laffeldt, Dettingen, Warburg, Beaumont, Willems, Salamanca, Vittorio, Toulouse, Peninsula, Waterloo, South Africa 1846-47, Balaklava, Sevastopol, Tel el Kebir, Egypt 1882, Elandslaagte, Defence of Ladysmith, South Africa 1899-1902

The Great War: Mons, Le Cateau, Retreat from Mons, Marne 1914, Aisne 1914, La Bassee 1914, Messines 1914, Armentieres 1914, Ypres 1914, 15, Givenchy 1914, St Julien, Frezenberg, Bellewaarde, Somme 1916, 18, Bazentin, Flers-Courcellette, Morval, Arras 1917, Scarpe 1917, Cambrai 1917, 18, St Quentin, Rosieres, Avre, Lys, Hazebrouck, Amiens, Albert 1918, Hindenburg Line, St Quentin Canal, Beaurevoir, Pursuit to Mons, France and Flanders 1914-18

The Second World War: Dyle, Withdrawal to Escaut, St Omer - La Bassee, Dunkirk 1940, Normandy Landing, Odon, Mont Pincon, St Pierre la Vielle, Lisieux, Risle Crossing, Seine 1944, Nederrijn, Lower Maas, Geilenkirchen, Roer, Rhineland, Cleve, Rhine, Ibbenburen, Bremen, North-West Europe 1940, 44-45 The Hook 1952, Korea 1951-52

Regimental Marches

Quick March ....Fare Thee Well Inniskilling
Slow March..4th Dragoon Guards Slow March and
....7th Dragoon Guards Slow Match combined

Agents...Holt's Branch, Royal Bank of Scotland plc, Lawrie House, Farnborough, Hants GU14 7NR
Home Headquarters...............................3 Tower Street, York, YO1 9SB
(Tel: 01904 642036 Fax: 01904 642036 Mil: 94777 8129
Email: RAC HQ-RDG-HHQ-RegtSec@mod.uk)

Alliances

Canadian Armed Forces.........................The British Colombia Dragoons
The Fort Garry Horse
Australian Military Forces.....................4th/19th Prince of Wales's Light Horse
3rd/9th Light Horse (South Australian Mounted Rifles)
New Zealand Army ....Queen Alexandra's Mounted Rifles
Indian Army ....The Deccan Horse
Pakistan Army..15th Lancers

Colonel in Chief ....*HRH The Prince of* Wales *KG KT OM GCB AK QSO ADC*
Duchess Colonel ....Hon Maj Gen *HRH The Duchess of* Kent *GCVO* 310792
Colonel..Col (Retd) Nick C T Millen *OBE* 261114
Regimental Secretary............................Maj (Retd) G M Green

Lieutenant Colonels

Bateman TJ *MBE* 300610
Baxter JWL 300605
Brooking JG 300607
Brown ANR 300604
Campbell-Smith H *MBE* 300610
Lane JJS *MBE* 300613
Mallory HP 300615
Piggott FAJ *OBE MSc GCGI* 300610
Rawlins DJ 300613
Rowan JR 230415
Rynehart MA 300615
Young V 020615

Majors

Brooks DT 310715
Coker TF 310714
Davey DRT 310711
Hey M 310715
Inkester MRJ 310709
Kace RPJ 310705
Kirkman S 310711
Mackain-Bremner CJA *MA (Oxon)* 310714
Mawby EE 310712
Nicholl JT 310713
Pearce Gould H 310709
Searle YN 310708
Smith RJA 310706
Taneborne P 310711

Tanner DJ	310714
Tory LHW	310715
Townrow JN	310710
Walker RD	310714
Watts BK	310709
Wright TE	310710

Captains

Bell DJ	010414
Clover CJ	140213
Clover JC	130214
Emmerson RJ	150610
Hann JEM	130810
Heath JG	161013
Hollas JD	101011
Kelly WJ	081010
Mackey SW	120612
McConkey RJS *BSc(Hons)*	130214
McGann A	080612
McGinn JP	010612
Moncrieff AD	161013
Morris CWJ	110815
O'Shea RA	120612
Ramage SAO	140415
Roome WO	120612
Shorland Ball TA	140213
Smith AM	140213
Torrens-Spence DJ	140213
Vine SJ	161013
Walton-Rees LW	080711
Williams PAN	140213
Yiend FH	121010

Lieutenants

Anderson TJ	141214
Chapman MP	151213
Evans CJ	151213
Jack AKN	100814
Kerr AG	141214
Moag BG	130414
Ritchie COT	130414
Sanders TD	130414
Solway WCA	120415
Torrens-Spence JP	151213

2nd Lieutenants

Calvert PE	121217
Davey OC	131214
Duncan CP	080815
Fuller TJ	121215
Hennings-Haahr GH	131214
Skinner PJ	090814
Slinger WJN	090814
Stephenson MSD	080815
Wood EFW	090814

LIGHT CAVALRY

THE QUEEN'S ROYAL HUSSARS
(THE QUEEN'S OWN AND ROYAL IRISH)

The Angel Harp of The Queen's Royal Irish Hussars superimposed on the Regimental Cypher of The Queen's Own Hussars surmounted by The Queen's Crown, with a scroll underneath giving the Regiment's title in blue and gold

Mente et Manu

Dettingen, Warburg, Beaumont, Willems, **Leswarree, Hindoostan,** Talavera, **Albuhera, Salamanca,** Vittoria, **Orthes, Toulouse, Peninsula, Waterloo,** Ghuznee 1839, **Afghanistan 1839,** Cabool 1842, **Moodkee, Ferozeshah,** Sobraon, **Chillianwallah,** Goojerat, Punjaub, Alma, **Balaklava,** Inkerman, **Sevastopol, Central India, Lucknow,** Afghanistan 1879-80, **South Africa 1900-02**

The Great War: **Mons,** Retreat from Mons, Le Cateau, **Marne 1914,** Aisne 1914, Messines 1914, Armentieres 1914, **Ypres 1914, 15,** Langemark 1914, Gheluvelt, **Givenchy 1914,** St Julien, Bellewaarde, **Somme 1916, 18,** Bazentin, Flers-Courcelette, Arras 1917, Scarpe 1917, **Cambrai 1917, 18,** St Quentin, Bapaume 1918, Rosieres, Lys, Hazebrouck, **Amiens,** Albert 1918, Hindenburg Line, Canal du Nord, St Quentin Canal, Beaurevoir, Selle, Sambre, Pursuit to Mons, France and Flanders 1914-18, **Khan Baghdadi,** Sharqat, Mesopotamia 1917-18

The Second World War: **Villers Bocage,** Mont Pincon, Dives Crossing, Nederrijn, Best, Lower Maas, Roer, **Rhine,** North West Europe 1944-45, Egyptian Frontier 1940, Sidi Barrani, **Buq Buq, Beda Fomm,** Sidi Suleiman, **Sidi Rezegh 1941,** Relief of Tobruk, Gazala, Bir el Igela, Mersa Matruh, Defence of Alamein Line, Ruweisat, **Alam el Halfa, El Alamein,** North Africa 1940-42, **Citta della Pieve, Ancona,** Citta di Castello, **Coriano,** San Clemente, Rimini Line, Conventello-Comacchio, Senio Pocket, Senio, Santerno Crossing, Argenta Gap, **Italy 1944-45,** Proasteion, Corinth Canal, **Greece 1941, Crete,** Pegu, Paungde, **Burma 1942**

Seoul, Hill 327, **Imjin,** Kowang-san, **Korea 1950-51,** Wadi al Batin, **Gulf 1991**

Honorary Distinction: Canadian Forces Unit Commendation

Regimental Marches

Quick March ....The Regimental Quick March of The Queen's Royal Hussars
Slow Marches..(i) The 3rd Hussars Slow March
(ii) Litany of Loretto – Slow March of the 4th Hussars
(iii) The Garb of Old Gaul – Slow March of the 7th Hussars
(iv) March of the Scottish Archers – Slow March of the 8th Hussars

Agents ....Lloyds Bank plc Cox's & King's Branch
Home Headquarters................................Regent's Park Barracks, Albany Street, London NW1 4AL
(Tel: 0207 756 2275 Fax: 0207 756 2276 Email: regsec@qrhussars.co.uk)

Alliances

Canadian Armed Forces ....The Sherbrooke Hussars
The Royal Canadian Hussars (Montreal)
8th Canadian Hussars (Princess Louise's)
Australian Military Forces......................2nd/14th Light Horse (Queensland Mounted Infantry)
3rd/9th Light Horse (South Australian Mounted Rifles)
3rd Battalion The Royal Australian Regiment
Victorian Mounted Rifles Squadron, 4th/19th Prince of Wales Light Horse
New Zealand Army.................................Queen Alexandra's Mounted Rifles
South African Defence Force.................Natal Mounted Rifles
Umvoti Mounted Rifles
Light Horse Regiment

Colonel in Chief....................................FM *HRH The Prince Philip Duke of* Edinburgh *KG KT OM GBE ONZ QSO AK GCL CC CMM ADC(P)*
Colonel ....Lt Gen Tom A Beckett *CBE (Late PARA)* 301114

Lieutenant Colonels					
		Ormerod JC	300605	Strickland WJ *OBE*	300611
Greenwood RNH	300614	Porter JDH	300613		

Majors

Burgess MP	310712
Cameron CA	310712
Cox PM	310706
Cubitt M	310714
Davies JR	310707
Forsyth AV	310708
Guyatt M	310715
Haines CJ	310709
Jefford TE	310708
Johnston EM	310711
Kearse GW *MBE*	310714
Lerwill OWD	310714
Maggs SP	310706
McIlwaine TLU	310711
Mercer DN	310708
Moody BCW	310710
Paterson MJ	310715
Shann JT	310710
Tims DF	310715
Vines RE	310708

Captains

Algate FJG	180613
Atchison RC	170614
Beer JCN	140415
Bishop AJW	311213
Campbell-Wild MP	010114
Cronian LS	020415
Davidson C	010213
Freeland HO	140415
Gray TB	010609
Leeming OAJ	180613
Meneer JS	020412
Mossop JON	080212
Pennington MJ	110815
Rudd N	010815
Thorne RLP	261012
Trypanis GAF	140213

Lieutenants

Dudley TE	151213
Durrant SJ	130414
Field AJ	120415
Fyfe BJ	100814
Glasspool TAK	110813
Graham DJ	130414
Kemp WJ	141214
Nicholas GH	110813
North AE	130414
Roberts LDP	110813
Ross DAM	120415
Wood EH	141214

2nd Lieutenants

Barter TLJ	090814
Morant MGV	090814
Nice J	121215
Pass RA	121215
Pattison ATT	080815
Pawson G	121215
Spink BFJ	131214

THE ROYAL LANCERS

A pair of thigh bones surmounted by a silver Death's Head. A scroll across the lower portion of the bones inscribed OR GLORY

The Regimental Badge known as The Motto ('Death or Glory') with crossed lances behind.

The Regiment was formed following the amalgamation of the 9th/12th Royal Lancers (Prince of Wales's) and The Queen's Royal Lancers on the 2nd May 2015.

Regimental Marches

Quick March ....Wellington
Slow March...Coburg

Home Headquarters...............................Lancer House, Prince William of Gloucester Barracks, Grantham, Lincs NG31 7TJ
(Tel: 0115 957 3195 Fax: 0115 957 3361 Email: m.pocock@theroyallancers.org)

Alliances

Canadian Armed Forces.........................Lord Strathcoma's Horse (Royal Canadians)
Pakistan Army..12th Cavalry (Frontier Force)

Colonel in Chief ....HER MAJESTY THE QUEEN
Deputy Colonels in Chief.......................HRH *The Duke of* York KG G*CVO ADC (P)*
HRH Princess Alexandra *the Hon Lady* Ogilvy *KG GCVO*
Colonel ....Brig A G Hughes *CBE* 010515

Lieutenant Colonels

Best NJ *OBE*	300610
Brodey AC	300608
Buczacki JNE	300612
Campbell-Barnard JR *MBE*	300614
Farrer JA	300614
Goggs DM	300613
Lyle TSD	300614
Mudd MJ *DSO*	300614
Simpson AEB *BA (Hons)*	300615
Slack RO *OBE*	300611
Walker JAK	300612
Watson RGJ	300608
Woolgar NRE *MA psc(j)*	300614
Woolley MMR	300613

Majors

Badcock C	310707
Bam DSR	310715
Bannister KL MA MSc psc(j) sq(w) cafs	300901
Barnett LJ	310711
Barrington Barnes DT	310705
Bigg JBT	310708
Blakey CJ	310703
Bowie ADG	310714
Clark JE *MSc*	300901
Clitheroe SJ	310712
Cossens BMJ	310707
Dart JF	300997
Doherty SP	310706
Duffield GJN	310715
Evans PC	310711
Farmer RJT	310714
Foden ANB *DSO*	310708
Foot-Tapping NA	310713
Fox A	310715
Greig WNC	310715
Hampson RW	310710
Hatton CS	310715
Howard JR	310709
Kierstead CS	310711
Knight CJ	310714
Lance JE	310709
Mack ERJ	310702
Minards WJ	310711
Morrissey MP	310713
Prideaux TE	310710
Priestley DK	310715
Rathbone JA	310715
Richmond WJR	310711
Scattergood JW	310714
Simpson HG	310710
Welborn ML	310714
Woodward MHJ	310714

Captains

Aitken RES	120612
Beuttell LA	240114
Burwell TJ	180613
Champion AJ	130611
Claughton RM	161013
Davis JET	101011
Dieppe FI	140415
Faulkner EGA	140213
Fowler HH	101011
Grant AJ	130611
Gray CPW	130214
Guest CM	140415
Hewitt MA	020415
Horsfall AJ	130611
Jones MA	020413

Jones TR	050111
Minards EJ	080212
Monckton EGC	130214
Moon GEG	170614
Mossop TCH	180613
Newman AW	010310
O'Shea CGP	200614
Poole J	310308
Pritchard TCI	130214
Purbrick AJ	140213
Richardson HA	161013
Rickett J	150111
Ryan JND	020415
Seccombe SO	200614
Semken HR	090211
Styles JA	010411
Swain LJ	010414
Taylor-Dickson FWH	171012
Theakston WMF	080212
Whitehead CR	020412
Willcox JJ	170614
Wythe T	311213
Yapp CJ	140415

Lieutenants

Barnes MV	110813
Cowie JP	100814
Goodenough RH	151213
Gouldstone RF	120415
Harnett WPM	141214
Humphreys AR	100814
Jibb JN	120415
Meeke AJ	110813
Nickell-Lean ETB	151213
Parker JRG	141214
Randle CA	130414
Robertson SJ	100814
Vowles MJ	151213
White S	141214

2nd Lieutenants

Anani-Isaac JA	090814
Clarkson DJ	131214
Gardner RJ	080815
Henson CNG	110415
Kellard WAO	090814
Luke ER	110415
Marriott HSD	121215
Paterson JE	080815

THE KING'S ROYAL HUSSARS

A Prussian Eagle Sable royally crowned Or grasping in the dexter claw a Sceptre and in the sinister an Orb both gold and on the Eagle's breast the Cipher FR also gold

A Universal Wreath containing a circle inscribed THE KING'S ROYAL HUSSARS. The circle, surmounted by a crown. Inside the circle, a Prussian Eagle Sable royally crowned Or grasping in the dexter claw a Sceptre and in the sinister an Orb both gold and on the Eagle's breast the Cipher FR also gold. In the first corner, the White Horse of Hanover; in the second, the Royal Cipher within the Garter; in the third, the Arms and Motto of the House of Saxe-Coburg-Gotha; in the fourth, the Plume and Motto of The Prince of Wales. Centrally, beneath the badge, the Spinx superscribed EGYPT

Warburg, Beaumont, Willems, Vimiera, Douro, Talavera, Fuentes D'Onor, Salamanca, Vittoria, Pyrenees, Orthes, Peninsula, **Waterloo, Bhurtpore, Chillianwallah, Goojerat,** Punjaub, **Alma, Balaklava, Inkerman, Sevastopol, Persia, Central India, Ali Masjid,** Afghanistan 1878-79, **Egypt 1884, Suakin 1885, Relief of Kimberley, Paardeberg, Relief of Ladysmith,** South Africa 1899-1902

The Great War: **Mons,** Retreat from Mons, Le Cateau, **Marne 1914, Aisne 1914, Messines 1914,** Armentieres 1914, **Ypres 1914, 15,** Langemarck 1914, Gheluvelt, Nonne Bosschen, Neuve Chapelle, St Julien, Frezenberg, Bellewaarde, Loos, **Somme 1916, 18,** Flers-Courcelette, **Arras 1917, 18,** Scarpe 1917, **Cambrai 1917, 18,** St Quentin, Bapaume 1918, Rosieres, Avre, Lys, Hazebrouck, **Amiens,** Albert 1918, Drocourt-Queant, Hindenburg Line, St Quentin Canal, Beaurevoir, Selle, **Sambre,** Pursuit to Mons, France and Flanders 1914-18, **Tigris 1916, Kut al Amara 1917, Baghdad,** Mesopotamia 1915-18, **Persia 1918**

The Second World War: Somme 1940, **Villers Bocage,** Bourguebus Ridge, Mont Pincon, Jurques, Dives Crossing, La Vie Crossing, Lisieux, La Toques Crossing, Risle Crossing, Roer, **Rhine,** Ibbenburen, Aller, North West Europe 1940, 44-45, **Egyptian Frontier 1940,** Withdrawal to Matruh, Bir Enba, Sidi Barrani, Buq Buq, Bardia 1941, Capture of Tobruk, **Beda Fomm,** Halfaya 1941, Sidi Suleiman, Tobruk 1941, Gubi I, II, Gabr Saleh, **Sidi Rezegh 1941,** Taieb el Essem, Relief of Tobruk, **Saunnu,** Msus, **Gazala,** Bir el Aslagh, Defence of Alamein Line, Alam el Halfa, **El Alamein,** Advance on Tripoli, El Hamma, Enfidaville, El Kourzia, Djebel Kournine, **Tunis,** North Africa 1940-43, Capture of Naples, Volturno Crossing, Coriano, Santarcangelo, Cesena, Cosina Canal Crossing, Senio Pocket, Valli di Commacchio, **Argenta Gap, Bologna, Medicina,** Italy 1943-45

Wadi al Batin, **Gulf 1991**

Regimental Marches

Quick March ....The King's Royal Hussars
Slow March ....Coburg

Agents ....Lloyds Bank plc Cox's & King's Branch
Home Headquarters ....North – Fullwood Barracks, Preston, Lancs PR2 8AA
(Tel: 01772 260480)
South – Peninsula Barracks, Winchester, Hants, SO23 8TS
(Tel: 01962 828540)
Email: RACHQ-KRH-HHQ-S-RegtSec@mod.uk /
regimental-secretary@krh.army.mod.uk

Affiliated Regiment
The Royal Gurkha Rifles

Bond of Friendship
HMS Dauntless

Alliances

Canadian Armed Forces ....1st Hussars
Australian Military Forces.....................10th Light Horse
2nd/14th Light Horse (Queensland Mounted Infantry)
New Zealand Army................................Queen Alexandra's Mounted Rifles
Pakistan Army..The Guides Cavalry (Frontier Force)
Zambia Army...The Zambian Armoured Car Regiment

Colonel in Chief....................................*HRH The Princess Royal KG KT GCVO QSO*
Senior Colonel.......................................*HRH The Prince* Michael *of Kent GCVO*
Colonel..Gen (Retd) *Sir* Richard Shirreff *KCB CBE*..051212

Lieutenant Colonels

Berchem NPF *BSc psc(US)*	300610
Harman AC *MA psc(j)*	300615
Holloway TM	300613
Kingsford JNJ	300612
MacGregor CS	300612
Mallinson TG	300615
Porter AJH	300614
Simpson I *MBE*	031015
Smith JRL	300615
Valdes-Scott CAJ	300615
Wilkinson MN	300615

Majors

Carey-Hughes JEM	310704
Cullinan RJ	310706
Denning JCV	300998
Gibbs TJ	310715
Hay JC	310709
Hodgkinson WD	310710
Hood JR	310715
Hope-Hawkins RM	310709
Jackson RM	310705
Jacques-Grey BNA	310709
Kvesic MG	310710
Michael AHL	310708
Perowne PJ	310711
Ponde AT	070202
Preston GRO	300901
Sharman AE	310709
Sloan KC	150814
Smith CDW	310708
Tilney AMA *MC MEng MMAS psc (US)*	310710
Tyson JDJ	310715
Wills GD	310712
Witham MA	310715

Captains

Astley Birtwistle EMT	140213
Barclay DS	020411
Barrow GJ	030414
Bird RW	101011
Brearley GW	110815
Dunn CJ	020415
Fleming JE	170614
Foster HGS	130214
Gillespie JE	011014
Higton CJ	170614
Kennedy RJ	120109
Lambert MRS	310713
Mawby EGK	170614
Padgett TH	110815
Price WE	020410
Scott JD	121010
Sherbrooke LLP	140213
Stephens GHS	160414
Taylor NJ	230413
Wade WPG	110815
Walker GM	161013
Walsh-Woolcott MJD *BSc*	130214
Welford DTM	090211
Westlake-Toms NSJ	180613
Williamson JSP	310713
Wilson RO	311213

Lieutenants

Bartles HB	151213
Churton OV	100814
Cowell De Gruchy W	100814
Gornall PA	100814
Gregory DJ	130414
Hatchley KJ	120415
Kirkham TW	151213
Nicholls RD	151213
Pryor S	141214

2nd Lieutenants

Burnet FET	080815
Kula-Przezwanski AC	080815
Lynch-Staunton GHC	090814
Nicholson AAJ	110415
Pollard-Jones JL	121215
Rutter SPJ	090814
Selfe PGA	131214
Unwin BAH	121215
Walch AJ	090814

THE LIGHT DRAGOONS

The monogram LD within a circle inscribed with the mottoes VIRET IN AETERNUM and MEREBIMUR within a wreath of laurel surmounted by the Crest of England, all upon a Cross Patee

The monogram LD within a circle inscribed THE LIGHT DRAGOONS above MCMXCII all within a wreath of roses and thistles surmounted by The Crown; on two scrolls at the tie of the wreath the Regiment's mottoes. Beneath the wreath the distinction, the Elephant, superscribed ASSAYE. In the first and fourth corners, the White Horse of Hanover. In the second corner, XIII XVIII RH within a wreath of roses and thistles upon a white ground. In the third corner, XV XIX KRH within a wreath of roses and thistles upon a white ground

Distinction: The distinction is also worn in uniform by all ranks

Emsdorf, Mysore, Villers-en-Cauchies, Willems, Seringapatam, Egmont-op-Zee, Sahagun, Albuhera, Vittoria, Orthes, Toulouse, Peninsula, Niagara, Waterloo, Alma, Balaklava, Inkerman, Sevastopol, Afghanistan 1878-80, Tel el Kebir, Egypt 1882-84, Nile 1884-85, Abu Klea, Defence of Ladysmith, Relief of Ladysmith, South Africa 1899-1902

The Great War: **Mons, Le Cateau, Retreat from Mons, Marne 1914, Aisne 1914,** La Bassee 1914, Messines 1914, **Armentieres 1914, Ypres 1914, 15,** Langemark 1914, Gheluvelt, Nonne Bosschen, Gravenstafel, St Julien, Frezenberg, **Bellewaarde, Somme 1916, 18,** Flers-Courcelette, Arras 1917, Scarpe 1917, **Cambrai 1917, 18,** St Quentin, **Rosieres, Amiens,** Albert 1918, Bapaume 1918, **Hindenburg Line,** St Quentin Canal, Beaurevoir, **Pursuit to Mons, France and Flanders 1914-18, Kut al Amara 1917, Baghdad, Sharqat, Mesopotamia 1916-18**

The Second World War: Dyle, **Withdrawal to Escaut, Ypres-Comines Canal, Normandy Landing,** Breville, **Caen,** Bourguebus Ridge, **Mont Pincon,** St Pierre la Vielle, **Seine 1944,** Hechtel, Nederrijn, Venraji, **Geilenkirchen,** Roer, **Rhineland,** Waal Flats, **Goch, Hochwald,** Rhine, **Ibbenburen, Aller,** Bremen, **North-West Europe 1940, 44-45**

Regimental Marches

Quick March ....Balaklava
Slow March..Denmark – 19th Hussars Slow March

Agents ....Lloyds Bank plc Cox's & King's Branch
Home Headquarters..............................Fenham Barracks, Newcastle-upon-Tyne NE2 4NP
(Tel: 0191 239 3138/3140/3141 Fax: 0191 239 3139
Email: roberta.goldwater@twmuseums.org.uk / HHQLD-AsstRegtlSec@mod.uk)

Alliances

Canadian Armed Forces.........................The Royal Canadian Hussars (Montreal)
The South Alberta Light Horse
Australian Military Forces.....................1st/15th Royal New South Wales Lancers
Indian Army ....1 HORSE (Skinner's)
Pakistan Army.......................................6th Lancers
19th Lancers
Malaysian Army....................................The 2nd Royal Reconnaissance Regiment, Malaysian Armed Forces

Colonel in Chief...................................*His Majesty King Abdullah II* of the Hashemite Kingdom of Jordan
Colonel...Maj Gen (Retd) David J Rutherford-Jones *CB*..130513

Lieutenant Colonels		*Majors*		Quicke EJ *BSc (Hons)*	310715
Chitty ROM	300607	Bartholomew A	310709	Robinson TRM	310711
Deakin GA	300609	Black JCB	310715	Sapwell JR	310703
Godfrey J	300614	Chandler JE	310705	Scott RD	310709
Nurton OJF	070811	Claydon-Swales NC	310713	Ward SJA	310707
Plant SJ *MBE*	300611	Colbeck CT	310707		
Senior JM	300613	Durrans NM	310713	*Captains*	
Smith JK	250314	Jordan S	310710	Bartholomew G	020410
Wiles RE	280715	Moon TEG	300901	Cuthbertson GL	020415
Wiles SP	180214	Pearce ACB	310704	Dodington LC	090211
		Pery AP	300999	Dunn CWL	121010

Freeman HC	261012
Glover RP	161013
Harle J	140213
Luckyn-Malone RGS	310713
McManners WJ	311213
Paske DFE	120612
Pullinger JMH	200614
Ruddock AV	010411
Stott SC	050811
Taylor PA	011012
Thirlaway AC	010414
Tod WMC	080212
Werner ALR	130214

Lieutenants

Barkes BR	151213
Davies WRV	120415
Everard JWS	151213
Geaves H	100814
Gray JR	141214
Gubbins CGM	151213
Holford-Walker EFA	130414
Nicholson SD	151213
Rutherford-Jones GA	151213
Scrope ERW	110813
Tibbitts GWS	141214

2nd Lieutenants

Batterbury QC	080815
Bernard PAF	121215
Johnson AAA	080815
Quicke JA	121215
Rose HTC	131214
Smith NE	131214
Stewart GHR	090814

THE ROYAL TANK REGIMENT

A tank encircled by a wreath of laurel and surmounted by The Crown

Fear Naught

The Great War: **Somme 1916, 18, Arras 1917, 18, Messines 1917, Ypres 1917, Cambrai 1917,** St Quentin 1918, **Villers Bretonneux, Amiens, Bapaume 1918, Hindenburg Line,** Epehy, Selle, **France and Flanders 1916-18,** Gaza

The Second World War: Arras counter attack, Calais 1940, St Omer-La Bassee, Somme 1940, Odon, Caen, Bourguebus Ridge, Mont Pincon, Falaise, Nederrijn, Scheldt, Venlo Pocket, Rhineland, **Rhine,** Bremen, **North-West Europe 1940, 44-45, Abyssinia 1940,** Sidi Barrani, Beda Fomm, Sidi Suleiman, **Tobruk 1941,** Sidi Rezegh 1941, Belhamed, Gazala, Cauldron, Knightsbridge, Defence of Alamein Line, Alam el Halfa, **El Alamein,** Mareth, Akarit, Fondouk, El Kourzia, Medjez Plain, Tunis, **North Africa 1940-43,** Primosole Bridge, Gerbini, Adrano, **Sicily 1943,** Sangro, Salerno, Volturno Crossing, Garigliano Crossing, Anzio, Advance to Florence, Gothic Line, Coriano, Lamone Crossing, Rimini Line, Argenta Gap, **Italy 1943-45, Greece 1941, Burma 1942**

Korea 1951-53, Al Basrah, Iraq 2003

Regimental Marches

Quick March ....Regimental March of the Royal Tank Regiment – My Boy Willie
Slow March..Royal Tank Regiment Slow March

Agents ....Holt's Branch, Royal Bank of Scotland plc, Lawrie House, Farnborough, Hants GU14 7NR
Home Headquarters.............................Stanley Barracks, Bovington Camp, Wareham, Dorset BH20 6JB
(Tel: 01929 403331 Fax: 01929 403488 Email: regtlsec@royaltankregiment.org)

Alliances

Canadian Armed Forces.........................12e Régiment Blindé du Canada
Australian Military Forces.....................1st Armoured Regiment
New Zealand Army ....Royal New Zealand Armoured Corps
Queen Alexandra's Mounted Rifles
Indian Army ....2nd Lancers/Gardner's Horse
Pakistan Army.......................................13th Lancers (Baloch Regiment)

Colonel in Chief ....HER MAJESTY THE QUEEN
Colonel Comandant..............................Maj Gen John R Patterson 270615
Deputy Colonels Commandant.............Brig Ian J Gibb..........220315
Col Gavin J Thompson 060315
Regimental Secretary...........................Maj (Retd) Colin Hepburn

Lieutenant Colonels	
Billings JD *MBE*	300611
Bird GE	300813
Briggs TA *psc(j)*	300612
Britton AM *MBE*	300610
Clooney IG	300612
Cowey NJ *MBE*	300612
Fake IC	300615
Fisher CJ *MBE*	300615
Gash AS *OBE*	300605
Hall CJ	300609
Heywood ACR	300613
How TD	300610
Laver IC	300607
Longman MJL	300614
Macro PJW *psc(j) MSc MA*	300612
Mason KJS	300608
McAfee AJM	300609
Medhurst-Cocksworth CR	300614
Metcalf SJ	010713
Miles JP	300615
Phipps AS	300611
Ridgway SA *MBE*	300614
Sheffield J	300614
Smith MJT	300613
Spicer PG	300606
Steven PP	240615
Waugh WJL *MBE*	300614
Williams JM	300609
Woodward RJR	300611

Majors	
Bagshaw CEI	310710
Bonner MPN	310715
Brennan WC	310715
Chuter CS	310711
Clarke SF	310709
Coetzee H	061114
Davies MP	310715
Ferman JDL	310713
Fielder MT	310708
Forde KJ	310711
Gilham AE	310713
Gillett SP	310712
Green JR	310712
Grimditch A	310712
Holloway AT	310715

Howard AC	310715
Hunt JCA	300996
Livingstone R	310711
Lloyd-Jukes T	310715
Luson MNH	310714
Morris GA	310711
Moseley RJ	310712
Page RJ	310709
Ridgway NP	310708
Rimmer CP	310710
Rimmer JSC	310713
Shearer LT	310713
Taylor AP	310714
Tillotson S	310715
Whitmarsh MLG	310713
Wight-Boycott TA	310711
Wilkinson GCH	310715
Williams SJ	310710
Worth SP	310711

Captains

Barker TR	311212
Bee SR	080212
Berry DJE	130611
Bishop TRG	171012
Blakey R	010411
Bridges NM	141009
Burgess PW	030414
Bullock AS	180613
Curry JOM	080212
Davison HL	170614
Dunlop R	010414
Eadon PR	080212
Eaton JD	101011
Emery JDC	261012
Ewing CD	140415
Ford JF	171214
Goodall JA	130214
Green J *BSc (Hons) MSc PhD*	090213
Halkerston CM	020415
Harding JCB	191214
Hartley PSA	161211
Herbert MPA	110114
Heslop MR	020412
Hollis RM	160414
Holloway WFJ	090211
Jeal GR	161013
Kaulback AF	171210
Maggs AW	101011
McCullough RLJ	010213
Millen CJ	121010
Morgan RP	130214
Noone ML	010413
Pilsworth AJ *BA (Hons)*	101011
Rodrigues Bernet M	130611
Rooney PD	010411
Ross AR	180613
Sandeman JC	120612
Scott TJ	311213
Simmons BWR	090211
Skivington R	020415
Stafford NJ	140213
Stanton JWF	171214
Stork JP	070610
Wood AJ	100314

Lieutenants

Chesnais MA	140413
Chisholm WN	130414
Hague MR	110813
Hall EFJ *BSc (Hons)*	151213
Hall WB	151213
Halls KA	151213
Hughes ME	151213
Last P	130414
McIlroy KB	141214
Morgan TA	110813
Murray DC	110813
Peters GED	120415
Robertson AJE	151213
Smith MJ	110813

2nd Lieutenants

Benn J	121215
Boland KR	131214
Carter RJ	110415
Chandler B	080815
Miller CA	090814
Nye TP	090814
Vincent RO	090814
Walton SAB	080415
Winters MB	080815

INFANTRY

Infantry Colonel Commandant ....Lt Gen (Retd) Andrew J N Graham *CB CBE* 010713

THE GUARDS DIVISION

(5 regiments of Foot Guards, with three representing Northern Ireland, Wales and Scotland)

Grenadier Guards

Coldstream Guards

Scots Guards

Irish Guards

Welsh Guards

THE SCOTTISH DIVISION

(1 remaining infantry regiment from Scotland)

Royal Regiment of Scotland

THE KING'S DIVISION

(regiments from the north of England)

The Duke of Lancaster's Regiment (King's Lancashire and Border)

The Yorkshire Regiment (14th/15th, 19th and 33rd/76th Foot)

THE QUEEN'S DIVISION

Princess of Wales's Royal Regiment (Queen's and Royal Hampshire)

The Royal Regiment of Fusiliers

The Royal Anglian Regiment

THE PRINCE OF WALES' DIVISION

(regiments from the west of England and Wales)

The Mercian Regiment

The Royal Welsh

The Royal Irish Regiment

The Parachute Regiment

The Brigade of Gurkha's

The Royal Gurkha Rifles

The Queen's Gurkha Engineers

The Queen's Gurkha Signals

The Queen's Own Gurkha Logistic Regiment

Band of The Brigade of Gurkha's

The Gurkha Staff and Personnel Support Company (GSPS)

The Rifles

The Royal Gibraltar Regiment

THE GUARDS DIVISION
GRENADIER GUARDS

Honi Soit Qui Mal Y Pense

The Queen's Colours:

1st Battalion – Gules (crimson): In the centre The Imperial Crown; in base a Grenade fired proper

2nd Battalion – Gules (crimson): In the centre the Royal Cypher reversed and interlaced, or ensigned with The Imperial Crown. In base a Grenade fired proper; in the dexter canton the Union (Suspended animation. Colours now carried by Nijmegen Company, Grenadier Guards)

3rd Battalion – As for the 2nd Battalion, with, for difference, issuing from the Union in bend a pile wavy or (Suspended Animation)

The Regimental Colours:

The Union: In the centre a company badge ensigned with The Imperial Crown; in base a Grenade fired proper. The 30 company badges are borne in rotation, one on the Regimental Colour of each of the Battalions

The Battle Honours shown in heavy type below are borne upon the Queen's and Regimental Colours:

Tangier 1680, Namur 1695, Gibraltar 1704-5, Blenheim, Ramillies, Oudenarde, Malplaquet, Dettingen, Lincelles, Egmont-op-Zee, Corunna, Barrosa, Nive, Peninsula, Waterloo, Alma, Inkerman, Sevastopol, Tel-el-Kabir, Egypt 1882, Suakin 1885, Khartoum, Modder River, South Africa 1889-1902

The Great War: Mons, Retreat from Mons, **Marne 1914, Aisne 1914, Ypres 1914-17,** Langemark 1914, Gheluvelt, Nonne Bosschen, Neuve Chapelle, Aubers, Festubert 1915, **Loos, Somme 1916, 18,** Ginchy, Flers-Courcelette, Morval, Pilckem, Menin Road, Poelcappelle, Passchendaele, **Cambrai 1917, 18,** St Quentin, Bapaume 1918, **Arras 1918,** Lys, **Hazebrouck,** Albert 1918, Scarpe 1918, **Hindenburg Line,** Havrincourt, Canal du Nord, Selle, Sambre, **France and Flanders 1914-18**

The Second World War: Dyle, **Dunkirk 1940,** North Africa 1942-43, **Mareth, Medjez Plain, Salerno,** Volturno Crossing, **Monte Camino, Anzio,** Cagny, **Mont Pincon, Gothic Line, Nijmegen,** Battaglia, Reichswald, **Rhine,** Italy 1943-45, North-West Europe 1940, 44-45.

Wadi al Batin, **Gulf 1991**

Regimental Marches

Quick March .... (i) The British Grenadiers (ii) The Grenadiers' March
Slow March .... (i) Scipio (ii) The Duke of York's March (iii) The Grenadiers' March

Agents .... Lloyds Bank plc Cox's & King's Branch
Regimental Headquarters .... Wellington Barracks, Birdcage Walk, London SW1E 6HQ
(Tel: 0207 414 3271 Fax: 0207 414 3443)

Alliances

Canadian Armed Forces .... The Canadian Grenadier Guards
Australian Military Forces .... 1st Battalion The Royal Australian Regiment
Trinidad and Tobago Defence Force .... Trinidad and Tobago Regiment
Royal Navy .... HMS Queen Elizabeth

Colonel in Chief .... HER MAJESTY THE QUEEN
Colonel .... FM *HRH The Prince Philip Duke of* Edinburgh *KG KT OM GBE ONZ QSO AK GCL CC CMM ADC(P)* 010375
Regimental Lieutenant Colonel .... Lt Gen *Sir* George P R Norton *KCVO CBE* 100612
Deputy Regimental Lieutenant Colonel. Col (Retd) Richard D Winstanley *OBE* 010812

Lieutenant Colonels

Broughton CL	300612
David MP MC	300613
Denison-Smith GR	300609
Gaunt M	010116
Green RJH	300615
James AFR *MBE*	300612
Maundrell RT *MVO*	300610
Mckay AR *MBE*	300615
Soskin SG	300613

Majors

England NA *MBE*	310713
Gask G *MBE*	090706
Gordon-Lennox SC	310712
Greaves JCM	310710
Green JR	310711
Harries WHL	310715
Jesty BJR	310712
Keeley JA *MBE*	190508
King-Evans RE	310713
Paintin EJ	070202
Seddon JA	310710
Shaw JEN	310712
Strachan NA	310715

Captains

Bayliss AWE	090211
Budge AHM	180613
Butcher A *MBE*	120408
Cartwright HC	180613
Conway BG	110815
Da-Gama RC	101011
Dobson MWS	130214
Farrell IM	020411
Garton JAL	130214
Hardy HRW	160414
Harris WLR	311213
Hathaway-White JJ	180613
Haughton GJ	091213
Hendriksen TR	080212
Moynan FCB	130214
Munro SC	130412
Rice PJ	090211
Sanford CHP	280714
Shirreff AJP	110815
Stevenson CJD	310713
Stonor AJP	180613
Taylor JR	311212
Waterfield HR	110815
Welham DR	110815
Wellesley-Wood AA	311212
Westlake DR	160614
Wills NPH	301112

Lieutenants

Barnes G	131215
Hargreaves THR	100814
Laing RDS	131215
Naughton CJ	090815
Parkes TR	141214
Phillips REL	090815
Silver J	131215
Tracey BRN	141214
Varmuza KMD	141214
Wace OM	141214
Williams CAG	151213
Wright CLJ	130414

2nd Lieutenants

Bolitho TA	080815
Harding R	080815
Harmer ER	080815
Staunton OSB	110415
Thompson RE	110415

COLDSTREAM GUARDS

The *State Colours:*

First State Colour – Gules (crimson); in the centre the Star of the Order of the Garter proper, within the Union Wreath or, ensigned with the Crown, in each of the four corners a Sphinx argent, between two branches of laurel fructed and tied with a riband or. In the centre below the Star of the Order of the Garter, on a scroll azure, the word "Egypt" or, with the following honorary distinctions:- Lincelles, Talavera, Barrosa, Peninsula, Waterloo.

Second State Colour – Gules (crimson); in the centre the Star of the Order of the Garter proper within the Union Wreath or, ensigned with the Crown, in each of the four corners a Sphinx argent, between two branches of laurel fructed and tied with a riband or, superscribed "Egypt" also or, with the following distinctions in addition to those borne on the First State Colour:- Alma, Inkerman, Sevastapol.

The Queen's Colours:

1st Battalion – Gules (crimson): In the centre the Star of the Order of the Garter proper, ensigned with The Imperial Crown; in the base a Sphinx, argent between two branches of laurel and tied with a riband vert; above a scroll or, the word "Egypt" in black letters.

2nd Battalion – Gules (crimson): In the centre a Star of eight points argent, within the Garter proper, ensigned with The Imperial Crown; in the base the Sphinx superscribed "Egypt" as for the 1st Battalion, in the dexter canton the Union (suspended animation but now carried by Number 7 Company Coldstream Guards)

3rd Battalion – (now in safekeeping): As for the 1st Battalion, and for difference, in the dexter canton, the Union, and issuing there from in bend dexter a pile wavy or. (Suspended Animation).

The Regimental Colours:

The Union: In the centre a company badge ensigned with The Crown; in base the Sphinx superscribed EGYPT. The 24 company badges are borne in rotation, two at a time, one on the Regimental Colour of both the 1st Battalion and Number 7 Company

The Battle Honours shown in heavy type below are borne upon the Queen's and Regimental Colours:

Tangier 1680, Namur 1695, Gibraltar 1704-5, Oudenarde, Malplaquet, Dettingen, Lincelles, Talavera, Barrosa, Fuentes d'Onor, Salamanca, Nive, Peninsula, Waterloo, Alma, Inkerman, Sevastopol, Tel-el-Kab, Egypt 1882, Suakin 1885, Modder River, South Africa 1899-1902

The Great War: Mons, **Retreat from Mons, Marne 1914, Aisne 1914, Ypres 1914, 1917,** Langemark 1914, Gheluvelt, Nonne Bosschen, Givenchy 1914, Neuve Chapelle, Aubers, Festubert 1915, **Loos,** Mount Sorrel, **Somme 1916, 1918,** Flers-Courcelette, Morval, Pilckem, Menin Road, Poelcappelle, Passchendaele, **Cambrai 1917, 18,** St Quentin, Bapaume 1918, **Arras 1918,** Lys, **Hazebrouck,** Albert 1918, Scarpe 1918, Drocourt-Queant, **Hindenburg Line,** Havrincourt, Canal du Nord, Selle, Sambre, France and Flanders 1914-18

The Second World War: Dyle, Defence of Escaut, **Dunkirk 1940,** Cagny, **Mont Pincon,** Quarry Hill, Estry, Heppen, Nederrijn, Venraij, Meijel, Roer, **Rhineland,** Reichswald, Cleve, Goch, Moyland, Hochwald, Rhine, Lingen, Uelzen, **North-West Europe 1940, 1944-45,** Egyptian Frontier 1940, **Sidi Barrani,** Halfaya 1941, **Tobruk 1941, 1942,** Msus, Knightsbridge, Defence of Alamein Line, Medenine, Mareth, Longstop Hill 1942, Sbiba, Steamroller Farm, **Tunis,** Hammam Lif, North Africa 1940-43, **Salerno,** Battipaglia, Cappezano, Volturno Crossing, Monte Camino, Calabritto, Garigliano Crossing, **Monte Ornito,** Monte Piccolo, Capture of Perugia, Arezzo, Advance Florence, Monte Domini, Catarelto Ridge, Argenta Gap, **Italy 1943-45**

Gulf 1991

Regimental Marches

Quick March .... 'Milanollo'
Slow March .... 'Figaro'
Agents .... Lloyds Bank plc Cox's & King's Branch
Regimental Headquarters .... Wellington Barracks, Birdcage Walk, London SW1E 6HQ
(Tel: 0207 414 3263 (Mil: 94631 3263) Fax: 0207 414 3444 (Mil: 94631 3444)
Email: INFHQ-FTGDS-CG-RegtAdjt@mod.uk)

Alliances

Royal Navy .... HMS Ocean
Canadian Armed Forces .... Governor General's Foot Guards
Australian Military Forces .... 2nd Battalion The Royal Australian Regiment

Colonel in Chief.................................... HER MAJESTY THE QUEEN
Colonel of the Regiment......................... Lt Gen (Retd) *Sir* James Bucknall *KCB CBE*..251009
Regimental Lieutenant Colonel .... Brig Rob C N Sergeant 110515
Assistant Regimental Adjutant............... Capt (Retd) R W C Matthews

Lieutenant Colonels

Bagshaw JD	300608
Clarke GJ	010113
Overton NJ *MBE*	010116
Short NP	300608
Thurstan JHF	300614
Till TPO *MBE*	300612

Majors

Bailey TR	310710
Biggs OJ	310711
Brinn JD	310708
Bysshe ME	310712
Coleby JW	310713
Foinette CMJ	310711
Green SW	310715
Johnston FGC	310714
Kendall BM	310715
Lock GWJ *MBE*	310712
Radcliffe TPY	310714
Rutt JB	310715
Tower WJ	300995
Watkins RJM	310715
Wells FOB	310713

Captains

Allan NR	020915
Bragger JEJ	161013
Codrington HC	170614
Cuccio DJF	080212
Downes PF	020409
Evans DKH	180613
Fleck M	060415
Gambarini PN	170614
Hanking-Evans RP	121010
Hannan DJ	020309
Howlin JR	080212
Jones PA	020712
Jones S	170110
Mills FJC	170614
Monckton JT	140415
Morley OJH	130611
Morrell DTP	210413
Olley JC	110815
Philp RAH	310712
Ritchie AHS	110815
Rossiter TB	161013
Russell FNG	270415
Spencer J	120612
Starkey CE	120612
Stokes AJ	020412
Taylor S	220615
Tollemache TAH	140213
Townsend MS	140415
Wills NJN	180610
Wright RJ	020411

Lieutenants

Barttelot HR	141214
Brown JE	100814
Bucknall HCC	130414
Bucknall JC	130414
Cazalet GO	130414
Deering RMF	120415
Dickinson AJ	251214
Dutton HRM	141214
McCaul IH	090815
McLean CWM	120415
Stinton WE	100814
Young JM	120415

2nd Lieutenants

Bird WJC	110415
Bowman-Shaw RAR	110415
Tennant-Bell AJ	110415
Potter JEC	080815
Shirley MPS	121215
Woodbridge TG	121215

SCOTS GUARDS

The Queen's Colours:

1st Battalion – Gules (crimson): In the centre Royal Arms of Scotland, ensigned with The Crown. Motto EN FERUS HOSTIS in base the Sphinx superscribed EGYPT

2nd Battalion – Gules (crimson): In the centre the Thistle and the Red and White Roses conjoined, issuant from the same stalk all proper, ensigned with The Crown. Motto UNITA FORTIOR; in base the Sphinx superscribed EGYPT; in the dexter canton the Union (Suspended Animation, but now carried by F Company Scots Guards)

The Regimental Colours:

The Union: In the centre a company badge ensigned with The Crown; in base the Sphinx superscribed EGYPT. The 24 company badges are borne in rotation, two at a time, one on the Regimental Colour of each of the two Battalions

The Battle Honours shown in heavy type below are bourne upon the Queen's and Regimental Colours:

Namur 1695, Dettingen, Lincelles, Talavera, Barrosa, Fuentes d'Onor, Salamanca, Nive, Peninsula, Waterloo, Alma, Inkerman, Sevastopol, Tel-el-Kabir, Egypt 1882, Suakin 1885, Modder River, South Africa 1889-1902

The Great War: **Retreat from Mons, Marne 1914, Aisne 1914, Ypres 1914-17,** Langemark 1914, Gheluvelt, Nonne Bosschen, Givenchy 1914, Neuve Chapelle, Aubers, **Festubert 1915, Loos, Somme 1916, 18,** Flers-Courcelette, Morval, Pilckem, Poelcappelle, Passchendaele, **Cambrai 1917, 1918,** St Quentin, Albert 1918, Bapaume 1918, Arras 1918, Drocourt-Queant, **Hindenburg Line,** Havrincourt, Canal du Nord, Selle, Sambre, **France and Flanders 1914-18**

The Second World War: Stien, Norway 1940, Halfaya 1941, Sidi Suleiman, Tobruk 1941, **Gazala,** Knightsbridge, Defence of Alamein Line, **Medenine,** Tadjera Khir, Medjez Plain, Grich el Oued, **Djebel Bou Aoukaz 1943, I, North Africa 1941-3,** Salerno, Battipaglia, Volturno Crossing, Rocchetta e Croce, **Monte Camino, Anzio,** Campoleone, Carroceto, Trasimene Line, Advance to Florence, Monte San Michele, Catarelto Ridge, Argenta Gap, **Italy 1943-45,** Mont Pincon, **Quarry Hills,** Estry, Venlo Pocket, **Rhineland,** Reichswald, Cleve, Moyland, Hochwald, Rhine, Lingen, Uelzen, **North-West Europe 1944-45.**

Tumbledown Mountain, **Falkland Islands 1982, Gulf 1991**

Regimental Marches

Pipes and Drums
Quick March .... Heilan' Laddie
Slow March .... The Garb of Old Gaul

Regimental Band
Quick March .... Heilan' Laddie
Slow March .... The Garb of Old Gaul

Agents .... Lloyds Bank plc Cox's & King's Branch
Regimental Headquarters .... Wellington Barracks, Birdcage Walk, London SW1E 6HQ
(Tel: 0207 414 3271 Fax: 0207 414 3445 Email: hqscotguards@dial.pipex.com)

Alliances

Royal Navy .... HMS Sceptre
Australian Military Forces .... 3rd Battalion The Royal Australian Regiment

Colonel in Chief .... HER MAJESTY THE QUEEN
Colonel .... FM *HRH The Duke of* Kent *KG GCMG GCVO ADC(P)* 090974
Regimental Lieutenant Colonel .... Brig G H F S (Harry) Nickerson 110711

Lieutenant Colonels		*Majors*			
French MA	300615	Alderman JP	310714	Kerr L *MBE*	310711
Hancock JHT *SG BA (Hons) MA*	300604	Anderson GGF	310711	Middlemiss PJ	310710
Kitching REC *MBE*	300614	Cape MA	310713	Parsons TM	310709
Lindsay RH	300610	Dunn JH	310708	Rowe SG	310713
Shannon RMT	300615	Hayward JR	300991	Turner CRG	130208
Speed AP *MBE*	300611	Hickie MDJ	310708	Viscount Marsham DC	310709
		Holling KB	300998		
		Hutchison TMO	310702		

Captains

Brown J	130715
Bull J	100411
Connolly CG	110815
Craven CA	200614
Dalrymple- Hamilton EJR	080212
Dunning G	130409
Dyson JH	180613
Edwards HAM	200614
Greenly SJH	110815
Greeves RHC	311212
Grierson NR	010412
Holloway M	110815
Jackson AEM	170614
Kershaw SE	130611
Lavington TPT	071113
MacLaren LJD	140415
MacPhee DS	011014
Manassie JD	020415
Maxwell-Scott A	130214
McCallum JB	020409
McClelland NA	140613
McLaughlan P	080908
McLay MTW	171012
Mortensen TFW	170614
O'Gilvy TAW	120612
Proudfoot CT	140610
Prys-Roberts PM	110815
Tulloch WJL	080212
White GS	030513

Lieutenants

Arbuthnott MMJ	120415
Carmichael OGO	131215
Carpenter GCF	120415
Curtis J	141214
Fleming JEG	090815
Forrest AEJ	141214
Martin HAT	120415
Pawson CE	141214
Tillard OJB	130414
Wesley SJS	141214
Wilson TWA	120415

2nd Lieutenants

Hogarth-Jones WAB	080815
Joly De Lotbiniere T	080815
Lowden SP	121215
Potter AD	080815
Stuckes D	121215
Warren-Smith SK	121215

IRISH GUARDS

The Queen's Colours:

1st Battalion – Gules (crimson): In the centre the Royal Cypher or, within the Collar of the Order of St Patrick with badge appendant proper, ensigned with The Crown

2nd Battalion – Gules (crimson): In the centre the Star of the Order of St Patrick ensigned with The Crown; in the dexter canton the Union (Suspended Animation)

The Regimental Colours:

The Union, in the centre a company badge ensigned with The Crown. The 22 company badges are borne in rotation
The Battle Honours shown in heavy type below are bourne upon the Queen's and Regimental Colours:

The Great War: Mons, **Retreat from Mons, Marne 1914, Aisne 1914, Ypres 1914, 17,** Langemark 1914, Gheluvelt, Nonne Bosschen, **Festubert 1915, Loos, Somme 1916, 18,** Flers-Courcelette, Morval, Pilckem, Poelcappelle, Passchendaele, **Cambrai 1917, 18,** St Quentin, Lys, **Hazebrouck,** Albert 1918, Bapaume 1918, Arras 1918, Scarpe 1918, Drocourt-Queant, **Hindenburg Line,** Canal du Nord, Selle, Sambre, France and Flanders 1914-18

The Second World War: Pothus, **Norway 1940, Boulogne 1940,** Cagny, **Mont Pincon, Neerpelt, Nijmegen,** Aam, **Rhineland,** Hochwald, Rhine, Bentheim, **North-West Europe 1944-45,** Medjez Plain, **Djebel Bou Aoukaz 1943, North Africa 1943, Anzio,** Aprilla, Carroceto, Italy 1943-44.

Al Basrah, Iraq 2003

Regimental Marches

Quick March .... St Patrick's Day
Slow March.. Let Erin Remember

Agents .... Lloyds Bank plc Cox's & King's Branch
Regimental Headquarters .... Wellington Barracks, Birdcage Walk, London SW1E 6HQ
(Tel: 0207 414 3271 Fax: 0207 414 3446 Email: igwebmaster@btconnect.com)

Alliances

Australian Military Forces..................... 4th Battalion The Royal Australian Regiment (Suspended)
Montserrat Royal .... Montserrat Defence Force

Colonel in Chief.................................... HER MAJESTY THE QUEEN
Colonel of the Regiment......................... Maj *HRH The Duke of* Cambridge *KG KT ADC(P)* 100211
Regimental Lieutenant Colonel............. Lt Gen Mark AP Carleton-Smith *CBE* (*Late* IG)..180312

Lieutenant Colonels		Oakley TDH	310714	Sprake GC	130611
Craig-Harvey CA	300608	Rogers TPT	310714	Taylor BR	311215
Hannah DM *MBE*	310807				
MacMullen PCA *MBE*	300608	*Captains*		*Lieutenants*	
Melotte EJF *MBE*	300606	Brettle DR	110814	Bell CEL	120415
Owen SP	300699	Butler MI	020414	Connolly JM	090815
Palmer JAE *MBE*	300615	Dooher MF	280312	Grant RG	141214
Segrave SO	300608	Fletcher K	090414	Hamilton MCW	140115
Stewart MRN	300615	Foggin EPM	110815	Jerram DA	090815
Turner IAJ *DSO*	300613	Gore RSt JE	171012	Moore WMC	120415
		Johnston DD	020412	Nunn HC	120415
Majors		Larkin HGR	110815	Ronan JJG	100814
Duggan WJ	310710	Leigh CFA	141014	Stodel DJC	100814
Fagin PA	310715	McMichael SA	020414		
Fox KTD	310710	Mulira CWE	121010	*2nd Lieutenants*	
Howell FW	310715	Parke JG	020414	Craig Harvey C	110415
Irwin-Clark BJ	310715	Pumphrey DL	110815	Jones FM	110415
Light GC	310706	Rostron OG	110815	Knight JJ	110415
Money RP	310711	Simpson FJJ	161013	McGrath RC	121215
Nichols SM *MBE*	310712	Sixsmith R	180515	Orchard T	080815

WELSH GUARDS

The Queen's Colours:

1st Battalion – Gules (crimson): In the centre a Dragon passant or, underneath a scroll with motto CYMRU AM BYTH, the whole ensigned with The Imperial Crown

2nd Battalion – Gules (crimson): In the centre a leek Or within the Garter, ensigned with The Imperial Crown, in the dexter canton the Union (Suspended animation)

The Regimental Colours:

The Union. In the centre a company badge ensigned with The Imperial Crown. The fifteen Company Badges are borne in rotation.

The Battle Honours shown in heavy type below are borne upon the Queen's and Regimental Colours:

The Great War: **Loos,** Somme 1916, 18, **Ginchy, Flers-Courcelette, Morval,** Ypres 1917, **Pilckem, Poelcappelle,** Passchendaele, **Cambrai 1917, 18, Bapaume 1918,** Arras 1918, Albert 1918, Drocourt-Queant, Hindenburg Line, Havrincourt, **Canal du Nord,** Selle, **Sambre,** France and Flanders 1915-18

The Second World War: **Defence of Arras, Boulogne 1940,** St Omer-La Bassee, Bourguebus Ridge, Cagny, **Mont Pincon, Brussels, Hechtel,** Nederrijn, Rhineland, Lingen, North-West Europe 1940, 44-45, **Foundouk,** Djebel el Rhorab, Tunis, **Hammam Lif,** North Africa 1943, **Monte Ornito,** Liri Valley, Monte Piccolo, Capture of Perugia, Arezzo, Advance to Florence, Gothic Line, **Battaglia,** Italy 1944-45.

Falkland Islands 1982

Regimental Marches

Quick March .... Rising of the Lark
Slow March .... Men of Harlech

Agents .... Lloyds Bank plc Cox's & King's Branch
Regimental Headquarters .... Wellington Barracks, Birdcage Walk, London SW1E 6HQ
(Tel: 0207 414 3288 Fax: 0207 414 3447 Email: infhq-ftgds-wg-regtadjt@mod.uk)

Alliances

Royal Navy .... HMS THE PRINCE OF WALES
Australian Military Forces .... 5th Battalion The Royal Australian Regiment
French Military Forces .... Regiment de Marche du Tchad

Colonel in Chief .... HER MAJESTY THE QUEEN
Colonel .... FM *HRH The Prince of* Wales *KG KT GCB OM AK QSO ADC(P)* 010375
Regimental Lieutenant Colonel .... Maj Gen Richard J A Stanford *MBE* 070715

Lieutenant Colonels

Bevan DWN	300615
Cooling M	060314
Harris GR *DSO MBE*	300612
Mott NP *MBE*	200515
Ramsay BPN *OBE*	300613
Stone GCG	300615

Majors

Aldridge JW	310711
Badham TJ	310711
Bettinson HGC	310706
Bowen AF	020407
Davies CJP	310715
Dawson K *MBE*	310714
Lewis ML	310708
Llewelyn-Usher HS	310709
Moukarzel NRK	170608
Salusbury AJ	310710
Salusbury JD	310708
Sargent CT *MBE*	310707
Smith TA	310708
Spencer Smith TC	131008

Captains

Beare CHL	130611
Birrell ECS	200614
Budge AW	130214
Campbell A	020414
Charles-Jones GCF	130411
Dinwiddie JO	110815
Dunlop AJH	090211
Emlyn-Williams ER	310713
Evans TAG	110815
Fenton CSN	121010
Figgures-Wilson BJ	120612
Hughes AJ	130611
Hutton TWJ	130214
Luther-Davies D	170614
Major AL	120612
Marsden JP	140415
Pollard MS	020413
Pridmore DW	020408
Smith AJN	110815
Wright MJ	191213
Young JM	130611

Lieutenants

Alsop OFA	120415
Campbell-Schofield TR	131215
Clarke EJ	141214
Evans TWJ	131215
Farmelo JR	141214
Gill JP	131215

Martin JFZ	090815
McNeill Love MRC	131215
Webster JWB	100814

2nd Lieutenants

Elletson GF	080815
Lewis JJC	110415
Razzall PDE	080815
Ross C	080815

THE SCOTTISH DIVISION

As of 2006, the Scottish Division is seven infantry battalions in a single large regiment, the Royal Regiment of Scotland. This also involved the amalgamation of the Royal Scots and The King's Own Scottish Borderers to form the Royal Scots Borderers.

Comprising.. The Royal Scots Borderers, 1st Battalion The Royal Regiment of Scotland
The Royal Highland Fusiliers, 2nd Battalion The Royal Regiment of Scotland
The Black Watch, 3rd Battalion The Royal Regiment of Scotland
The Highlanders, 4th Battalion The Royal Regiment of Scotland
The Argyll and Sutherland Highlanders, 5th Battalion
The Royal Regiment of Scotland
52nd Lowland, 6th Battalion The Royal Regiment of Scotland
51st Highland, 7th Battalion The Royal Regiment of Scotland
The Royal Regiment of Scotland (5 Regular Battalions and 2 Reserve)

Regimental Headquarters .... RHQ SCOTS, The Castle, Edinburgh, EH1 2YT Scotland

The origins of amalgamated Regiments now included in the Scottish Division are as follows:

THE ROYAL REGIMENT OF SCOTLAND

On 20 January 1959

The Royal Scots Fusiliers (21) and

The Highland Light Infantry (City of Glasgow Regiment) (71 and 74) amalgamated to form:

The Royal Highland Fusiliers (Princess Margaret's Own Glasgow and Ayrshire Regiment) (21, 71 and 74)

On 7 February 1961

Seaforth Highlanders (Ross-shire Buffs, The Duke ofAlbany's) (72 and 78) and

The Queen's Own Cameron Highlanders (79) amalgamated to form:

Queen's Own Highlanders (Seaforth and Camerons) (72, 78 and 79)

On 17 September 1994

Queen's Own Highlanders (Seaforth and Camerons) (72, 78 and 79) and

The Gordon Highlanders (75 and 92) amalgamated to form:

The Highlanders (Seaforth, Gordons and Camerons) (72, 75, 78, 79 and 92)

On 28 March 2006

The Royal Scots Borderers and

The Royal Highland Fusiliers and

The Black Watch, 3rd Battalion and

The Highlanders (Seaforth, Gordons and Camerons) and

The Argyll and Sutherland Highlanders amalgamated to form:

The Royal Regiment of Scotland

THE ROYAL REGIMENT OF SCOTLAND

A saltire Argent surmounted of a Lion rampant ensigned in chief by a representation of the Crown of Scotland Or and in base on an Escrol Argent the Motto NEMO ME IMPUNE LACESSIT in letters Sable

Tangier 1680, Namur 1695, Blenheim, Ramillies, Oudenarde, Malplaquet, Dettingen, Louisburg, **Minden, Guadaloupe 1759,** Belleisle, **Martinique 1762,** Havannah, North America 1763-64, **Carnatic,** Hindoostan, Sholinghur, Mangalore, Mysore, Martinique 1794, **Seringapatam, Egmont-op-Zee,** Mandora, Egypt, St Lucia 1803, Assaye, **Cape of Good Hope 1806,** Maida, Rolica, Vimiera, Corunna, Martinique 1809, Busaco, Fuentes d'Onor, Java, Almarez, Cuidad Rodrigo, **Badajoz, Salamanca, Vittoria,** Pyrenees, **St Sebastian,** Nivelle, **Nive,** Orthes, Toulouse, **Peninsula, Niagara,** Bladensburg, **Waterloo, Nagpore,** Maheidpoor, Ava, South Africa 1835, South Africa 1846-47, 1851-52-53, Alma, Balaklava, Inkerman, **Sevastopol,** Koosh-ab, Persia, Delhi 1857, Lucknow, Central India, Taku Forts, Pekin 1860, **Ashantee 1873-4,** Peiwar Kotal, Charasiah, **Kabul 1879, South Africa 1879,** Kandahar 1880, **Afghanistan 1878-80, Tel-el-Kebir,** Egypt 1882,'84, Kirbekan, Nile 1884-85, Burma 1885-87, **Chitral, Tirah, Atbara,** Khartoum, **Defence of Ladysmith, Modder River, Relief of Ladysmith, Paardeberg, South Africa 1899-1902**

The Great War: **Mons, Le Cateau,** Retreat from Mons, **Marne 1914, 18, Aisne 1914,** La Bassee 1914, Messines 1914,18, Armentieres 1914, **Ypres 1914, 15, 17, 18,** Langemark 1914,17, Gheluvelt, Nonne Boschen, Festubert 1914,15, Givenchy 1914, Neuve Chapelle, Hill 60, Gravenstafel, St Julien, Frezenburg, Bellewaarde, Aubers, Hooge 1915, **Loos, Somme 1916,18,** Albert 1916,18, Bazentin, Delville Wood, Pozieres, Guillemont, Flers-Courcelette, Morval, Thiepval, Le Transloy, Ancre Heights, Ancre 1916,18, **Arras 1917,18,** Vimy 1917, Scarpe 1917,18, Arleux, Bullecourt, Messines 1917,18, Pilckem, Langemarck 1917, Menin Road, Polygon Wood, Broodseinde, Poelcappelle, Passchendaele, **Cambrai 1917,18,** St Quentin, Bapaume 1918, Rosieres, **Lys,** Estaires, Hazebrouck, Bailleul, Kemmel, Bethune, Scherpenberg, Soissonnais-Ourcq, Tardenois, Amiens, Drocourt-Queant, **Hindenburg Line,** Havrincourt, Epehy, Canal du Nord, St Quentin Canal, Beaurevoir, Courtrai, Selle, Valenciennes, Sambre, France and Flanders 1914-18, Piave, Vittoria Veneto, Italy 1917-18, **Struma, Doiran 1917,18, Macedonia 1915-18,** Helles, Landing at Helles, Krithia, Suvla, Scimitar Hill, **Gallipoli 1915-16,** Rumani, Egypt 1915-17, **Gaza,** El Mughar, Nebi Samwil, Jaffa, Jerusalem, Tell'Asur, Megiddo, Sharon, Damascus, **Palestine 1917-18,** Tigris 1916, **Kut al Amara 1917,** Baghdad, Sharqat, **Mesopotamia 1915-18,** Archangel 1918-19

The Second World War: Dyle, Withdrawal to Escaut, **Defence of Escaut,** Defence of Arras, St Omer-La-Bassee, Ypres-Comines Canal, **Dunkirk 1940,** Somme 1940, Withdrawal to Seine, Withdrawal to Cherbourg, St Valery-en-Caux, Saar, Cambes, Breville, Tourmauville Bridge, **Odon,** Fontenay Le Pesnil, Cheux, Defence of Rauray, **Caen,** Esquay, Troarn, Mont Pincon, Quarry Hill, Estry, Falaise, Falaise Road, Dives Crossing, La Vie Crossing, Lisieux, La Touques Crossing, Seine 1944, Aart, **Arnhem 1944,** Nederrijn, Best, Le Havre, Antwerp-Turnhout Canal, Scheldt, South Beveland, Walcheren, **Flushing,** Venraij, Lower Maas, Meijel, Venlo Pocket, Ourthe, Roer, Rhineland, **Reichswald,** Cleve, Goch, Moyland, Moyland Wood, Weeze, **Rhine,** Ibbenburen, Lingen, Dreirwalde, Aller, Uelzen, **Bremen,** Artlenburg, **North-West Europe 1940, 44-45,** Jebel Shiba, Agordat, Barentu, **Keren,** Massawa, Abyssinia 1941, Barkasan, British Somaliland 1940, **Sidi Barrani, Tobruk 1941,42,** Tobruk Sortie, Gubi II, Carmusa, Gazala, **Cauldron,** Mersa Matruh, Fuka, **El Alamein,** Advance on Tripoli, Medenine, Zemlet el Lebene, Mareth, Wadi Zigzaou, **Akarit,** Wadi Akarit East, Djebel Roumana, Djebel Azzag 1942, Kef Ouiba Pass, Mine de Sedjenane, Medjez Plain, **Longstop Hill 1943,** Sidi Mediene, Tunis, North Africa 1940-43, Landing in Sicily, Vizzini, Augusta, Francofonte, Sferro, Gerbini, Adrano. Sferro Hills, Centuripe, **Sicily 1943,** Termoli, Sangro, Garigliano Crossing, Minturno, Anzio, Cassino, Liri Valley, Aquino, Rome, Advance to Tiber, Advance to Florence, Monte Scalari, Poggio del Grillo, **Gothic Line,** Travoleto, Coriano, Pian di Castello, Casa Fortis, Rimini Line, Casa Fabbri Ridge, San Marino, Monte Reggiano, Savio Bridgehead, Marradi, Monte Gamberaldi, Monte Casalino, Monte Spaduro, Monte Grande, Senio, Santerno Crossing, Argenta Gap, Italy 1943-45, Athens, Greece 1944-45, **Crete,** Heraklion, Madagascar, Adriatic, Middle East 1941,42,44, North Malaya, Grik Road, Central Malaya, Ipoh, Slim River, Singapore Island, **Malaya 1941-42,** South East Asia 1941, Donbaik, North Arakan, Buthidaung, Razibil, Ngakyedauk Pass, **Imphal,** Kanglatongbi, Ukhrul, Shenam Pass, Litan, **Kohima,** Aradura, Relief of Kohima, Naga Village, Tengnoupal, Pinwe, Shwebo, Shweli, Mandalay, Meiktila, Ava, Irrawaddy, Mt Popa, Kama, Chindits 1944, **Burma 1942-45**

Pakchon, Kowang-San, Maryang-San, **The Hook 1952, Korea 1950-53,** Wadi Al Batin, Gulf 1991, Al Basrah, **Iraq 2003**

Regimental Marches

Quick March .... Scotland the Brave
Slow March .... The Slow March of The Royal Regiment of Scotland
(My Home, Mist Covered Mountain and the Highland Cradle Song)

Agents .... The Bank of Scotland, St Andrew's Square Branch
Regimental Headquarters .... The Castle, Edinburgh EH1 2YT
(Tel: 0131 310 5001 Fax: 0131 310 5075
Email: RHQSCOTS-RegtSec-SO1@mod.uk)

Alliances

1st Battalion

Canadian Armed Forces........................ The Canadian Scottish Regiment (Princess Mary's)
The Royal Newfoundland Regiment
1st Battalion The Royal New Brunswick Regiment (Carleton and York)
Australian Military Forces.................... 25th/49th Battalion The Royal Queensland Regiment
South African Army.............................. Witwatersrand Rifles
Malaysian Army.................................... 5th Battalion Royal Malay Regiment

2nd Battalion

Canadian Armed Forces........................ The Royal Highland Fusiliers of Canada
New Zealand Army............................... 1st Battalion The Royal New Zealand Infantry Regiment
South African Army.............................. Prince Alfred's Guard
Pakistan Army...................................... 11th Battalion Baloch Regiment

3rd Battalion

Canadian Armed Forces........................ The Prince Edward Island Regiment (RCAC)
1st Air Defence Regiment (Lanark and Renfrew Scottish)
Royal Canadian Artillery
The Black Watch (Royal Highland Regiment of Canada)
Australian Military Forces.................... The Royal New South Wales Regiment
The Royal Queensland Regiment
New Zealand Army............................... The New Zealand Scottish (RNZAC)
South African Army.............................. Transvaal Scottish

4th Battalion

Canadian Armed Forces........................ The Cameron Highlanders of Ottawa
48th Highlanders of Canada
The Queen's Own Cameron Highlanders of Canada
The Seaforth Highlanders of Canada
The Toronto Scottish Regiment (Queen Elizabeth The Queen Mother's Own)
Australian Military Forces.................... 5th Battalion The Royal Australian Regiment
7th Battalion The Royal Australian Regiment
5th / 6th Battalion The Royal Victoria Regiment
16th Battalion The Royal Western Australia Regiment
10th/27th Battalion The Royal South Australia Regiment
New Zealand Army............................... 4th Battalion (Otago and Southland) The Royal New Zealand Infantry Regiment
7th Battalion (Wellington {City of Wellington's Own} and Hawkes Bay) The Royal New Zealand Infantry Regiment
South African Army.............................. Cape Town Highlanders

5th Battalion

Canadian Armed Forces........................ The Argyll and Sutherland Highlanders of Canada (Princess Louise's)
The Calgary Highlanders
Australian Military Forces.................... The Royal New South Wales Regiment
The Royal Queensland Regiment
Pakistan Army...................................... 1st Battalion (Scinde) Frontier Force Regiment

Colonel in Chief.................................... HER MAJESTY THE QUEEN
Royal Colonels
1st Battalion.. *HRH The Princess Royal KG KT GCVO QSO*
2nd Battalion... *HRH The Duke of* York *KG GCVO ADC(P)*
3rd Battalion.. FM *HRH The Prince of* Wales *KG KT GCB OM AK QSO ADC(P)*
4th Battalion.. FM *HRH The Prince Philip Duke of* Edinburgh *KG KT OM GBE ONZ QSO AK GCL CC CMM ADC(P)*
5th Battalion.. HER MAJESTY THE QUEEN
6th Battalion.. *HRH The Princess Royal KG KT GCVO QSO*
7th Battalion.. FM *HRH The Prince of* Wales *KG KT GCB OM AK QSO ADC(P)*

Colonel	Maj Gen (Retd) J M Cowan *CBE DSO (until 020716)*	280214
	Maj Gen Robert B Bruce *CBE DSO (from 020716)*	
Deputy Colonels	Maj Gen Robert B Bruce *CBE DSO*	010912
	Brig (Retd) George E Lowder *MBE*	010912
	Brig P K Harkness *MBE*	011113
	Brig P aul A S Cartwright *OBE*	300914
	Brig Alastair J Aitken *OBE*	310315
Honorary Colonels	*His Grace The Duke of* Buccleuch and Queensbury	010111
	Brig C S Grant *OBE*	010909

Lieutenant Colonels

Aitchison A *MBE*	060415
Barry JF	300615
Cave-Gibbs TJ	300614
Clark HIM *MBE*	300614
Cochran DJS	300613
Connolly RJ	300614
Drummond LJ *MBE*	300613
Ewing MJF	300608
Fitzpatrick AJ	300611
Forsyth AR	300614
Haughie JJ *MBE*	031213
Hill TAS *MBE*	300608
Ingram TAW *MBE*	300609
Jack DT	300615
Lane CAM	300614
Lindsay RRE	300611
Macgregor NC	210915
Mackay AJ *MBE*	270614
Mckay J *MBE*	010213
Onslow MPD	300608
Perkins TGS *MBE*	300615
Philp AM	300613
Platt CE	300607
Potts KM *MBE MA GCGI psc(j)*	300606
Reilly AP	300612
Rennie AM *MBE*	300614
Scott JA	300609
Sheldrick DM	300615
Shirras JD	300605
Steel DG	300607
Steele AFL	300614
Strudwick PGB	300614
Tait AG	300615
Tink JD	300610
Tomlin NKG	300614
Wearmouth GC *OBE*	300613
Wemyss SG *MBE*	010114
Wight-Boycott NM	300615
Wood K	010913
Wright NAP	300611

Majors

Adamson GK	310709
Adamson RAG	310710
Bailey JRP	310710
Bayne AB	310711
Bridle NP	310711
Bridle OW	310714
Broadbent CMB	310709
Brocklehurst GR *MC*	310709
Brookfield RA	310709
Cameron JA	310712
Campbell LI	310714
Cargill NK	310714
Christie JM	310705
Christie TSB	310706
Close DC	310708
Cochrane SG	310715
Colquhoun RJ	310715
Colquhoun WA	310709
Colville AJ	310712
Cooper B	310714
Curren IR *MC*	310715
Curson LJ	310713
Cuthbertson AJ	310715
Dallard SP *MBE*	310709
Dobson OPB	310709
Draper TJJ	310709
Dunn JB	310711
Espie G	310712
Frazer CD	300900
French JA	310709
Garmory SJ	310710
Giles JF	310708
Gilmour VT	310712
Grant AT *MBE*	020404
Harvey DM	270103
Havelock AJ	310715
Hayton MC	310712
Hedderwick RSJ	310708
Henderson GA	310714
Hogg GR	310715
Hood D	310715
House JD	310715
Howe J	310712
Hunter WG	310714
Hutton AGS	310704
Jordan-Barber NG *MSc*	310706
Kerr MD	310712
Law CK	310715
Law JK	310712
Lumley AD	310708
Mackinnon DDJ	310710
MacNair FJC	310714
McAleney AG	310714
McAuley WC	310715
McCallum JD	020404
McClure RRD	310710
McCutcheon D	310715
McGown GA *MBE DipSM*	310707
McInroy C	310709
Moffat NJ	310712
Morgan PJ	130407
Muir GW	310713
Muir RKS	310710
O'Neill BA *BSc (Hons)*	310712
Petransky TJ	310708
Petrie BE	310706
Phillips AJ *MC*	310715
Ramsay GAC	200797

Reed DE 310714
Reid JA 310709
Richards AP 310708
Robb MSP 310714
Robertson DM 310715
Rodger MJ 310712
Sefton GJ 310708
Small SG 310712
Smith RA 310713
Steele AD 310715
Stewart RJ 310714
Stuart RJ *MBE MSc* 310713
Sweet AM 310713
Tait G MBE 310708
Thompson JA 310715
Whitelegge RSB 300900
Williams RAD 310707
Wilson IG 310711
Wood CM 310713

Captains

Alder MTH 171012
Allen-Perry NW 180613
Altenhoven MD 140213
Anderson FA 180613
Badger J 151215
Ballantyne GC 151215
Barron AD 160712
Blair TH 180613
Borthwick PP 240609
Bowler NR 161013
Broumley Young C 161013
Brownjohn PA 161013
Buchan SA 110815
Campbell AM 101011
Carson JK 121010
Challis EP *MBE* 140213
Coats NPJ 161013
Colville PD 160714
Cummings TB 311212
Cunningham AH 010714
Cunningham SG 080212
Davey BSE 161211
Deck AH 110815
Dickson JJ 020415
Dobson MA 130411
Donkin JE 161013
Douglas HJ 170614
Dowds MC 180211
Draper NJ 150811
Dunlop DAJ 170614
Falconer A 020415
Falconer DC 151215
Fish JE 151215
Flannigan M 151215
Garrick W 091213
Gorrie EB 150610
Gourd OCJ 110815
Grant CM 121010
Griffiths NT 160414
Hamilton DF 161013
Hawke LW 140415
Hesketh CJ 140412
Hill CJC 110815
Hold RM 140213
Hold RR 170614
Houston IJ 110612
Howell EJ 150612
Illing RA 130214
James M 010710
Law G 020411
Lennox RWJ 130814
Lindsay TM 070414
Lipowski AG 010414
Loudon RL 080615
MacGregor GC 150610
MacKenzie S 130810
MacKinnon JN 310713
MacLachlan IA 240615
MacLeod AM 160609
MacLeod RN 130214
Magee AJ 161211
Malpass LJ 150712
Marshall P 110612
Martin RM 161013
McCauley SDA 110815
McConnell RW 090211
McDonagh LS 080212
McDougall L 010510
McLaren WMG 290413
McQuillin SI 080615
McRobbie CG 180613
Mulliner BJ 280314
Ogilvie JG 170614
Oliver A 140415
Park DWM 130812
Pearson MJ 190408
Pearson RM 110815
Pemberton MI 311213
Philbin EG *MBE* 010713
Pullen WRK 140415
Rae SA 030308
Rivington MH 101011
Ronaldson AD 140814
Rowan GM 030412
Russell AW 010815
Russell SW 110209
Shaw S 090614
Simpson SG 120710
Stanning MP 090211
Stark FM 130214
Stewart RJ 080212
Tait D 010710
Tait JR 311213
Taylor SR 080212
Torrance JRE 110815
Towler TJH 140213
Treasure CM 311213
Voce-Russell CG 161013
Walker IK 170614
Wallace G 080609
Waring HR 080212
Weir RC 180613
Wright ST 161013
Wright WAB 160410

Lieutenants

Atterbury AEF 120415
Bickerton CM 141214
Buchanan GAC 140413
Bullen AFH 090815
Christie AJN 141214
Coles NJT 130414
Collister AG 090815
Crook RLM 151213
Cumming JR 131215
Forbes JPO 100814
Gibson RH 120415
Graham JP 100814
Hughes CJ 131215
Kelly WR 090815
Knott KC 120415
Lungmuss HD 090815
Melgaard NG 090815

Moffett JP	120415
Pearson ADS	100814
Porro CD	120415
Ramsay JII	100814
Roberts MAR	100814
Robinson KIS	141214
Ross GJD	130414
Rupasinha MC	100814
Sarfraz MA	141214
Smyth ZW	110813
Walsh A	120415
Whelan A	100814
Wilkinson CJP	130414
Wotherspoon LEL	131215
Young JA	130414

2nd Lieutenants

Bond WRR	090814
Callard TW	110415
Chalk GWM	110415
Clarke RH	080815
Colthurst RC	080815
Duncan CP	080815
Gardner CF	110415
Gibson AW	110415
Hannay ND	080815
Hill RJ	131214
Holmes NR	100813
Mitchell JE	121215
Phillips MEL	110415
Punter AG	120414
Spencer DJ	121215
Swinhoe A	110415
Topping MG	121215

THE QUEEN'S DIVISION

Comprising..The Princess of Wales's Royal Regiment (2 Regular Battalions, 1 TA Battalion)
The Royal Regiment of Fusiliers (2 Regular Battalions, 1 TA Battalion)
The Royal Anglian Regiment (2 Regular Battalions, 1 TA Battalion)

Divisional Headquarters..Headquarters Infantry, Warminster, Wilts BA12 ODJ
(Tel: 01985-222466)

Colonel Commandant..Lt Gen (Retd) *Sir* Paul Newton *KBE*..010610

The origins of amalgamated Regiments now included in The Queen's Division are as follows:

THE PRINCESS OF WALES'S ROYAL REGIMENT (QUEEN'S AND ROYAL HAMPSHIRES)

On 14 October 1959

The Queen's Royal Regiment (West Surrey)(2) and
The East Surrey Regiment (31 and 70) amalgamated to form:
The Queen's Royal Surrey Regiment

On 1 March 1961

The Buffs (Royal East Kent Regiment) (3) and
The Queen's Own Royal West Kent Regiment (50 and 97) amalgamated to form:
The Queen's Own Buffs, The Royal Kent Regiment

On 31 December 1966

The Queen's Royal Surrey Regiment
The Queen's Own Buffs, The Royal Kent Regiment
The Royal Sussex Regiment (35 and 107) and
The Middlesex Regiment (Duke of Cambridge's Own) (57 and 77) amalgamated to form:
The Queen's Regiment

On 9 September 1992

The Queen's Regiment (2, 3, 35, 50, 57, 70, 77, 97 and 107) and
The Royal Hampshire Regiment (37 and 67) amalgamated to form:
The Princess of Wales's Royal Regiment (Queen's and Royal Hampshires)

THE ROYAL REGIMENT OF FUSILIERS

On 23 April 1968

The Royal Northumberland Fusiliers (5)
The Royal Warwickshire Fusiliers (6)
The Royal Fusiliers (City of London Regiment) (7) and
The Lancashire Fusiliers (20) amalgamated to form:
The Royal Regiment of Fusiliers

THE ROYAL ANGLIAN REGIMENT

On 2 June 1958

The Bedfordshire and Hertfordshire Regiment (16) and

The Essex Regiment (44 and 56) amalgamated to form:

The 3rd East Anglian Regiment (16th/44th Foot)

On 29 August 1959

The Royal Norfolk Regiment (9) and

The Suffolk Regiment (12) amalgamated to form:

The 1st East Anglian Regiment (Royal Norfolk and Suffolk)

On 1 June 1960

The Royal Lincolnshire Regiment (10) and

The Northamptonshire Regiment (48 and 58) amalgamated 'to form:

The 2nd East Anglian Regiment (Duchess of Gloucester's Own Royal Lincolnshire and Northamptonshire)

On 1 September 1964

1st East Anglian Regiment (Royal Norfolk and Suffolk)

2nd East Anglian Regiment (Duchess of Gloucester's Own Royal Lincolnshire and Northamptonshire)

3rd East Anglian Regiment (16th/44th Foot) and

The Royal Leicestershire Regiment (17) amalgamated to form:

The Royal Anglian Regiment

PRINCESS OF WALES'S ROYAL REGIMENT

A Dragon upon a mount with a double red rose fimbriated gold below within the Garter. Above the Dragon and superimposed on the Garter the Plume of The Prince of Wales

Unconquered I Serve

A Paschal Lamb upon an eight pointed Star ensigned with The Crown. A White Horse rampant above a scroll inscribed INVICTA. The Star of the Order of the Garter over the Roussillon Plume. A Naval Crown superscribed 1ST JUNE 1794. The Sphinx superscribed EGYPT. The Royal Tiger, superscribed INDIA.
The Cypher of Queen Catherine of Braganza

Tangier 1662-80, Namur 1695, Gibraltar 1704-5, Blenheim, Ramillies, Oudenarde, Malplaquet, Dettingen, Minden, Louisburg, Guadaloupe 1759, Quebec 1759, Belleisle, Tournay, Barrosa, Martinique 1762, Havannah, St Lucia 1778, Mysore, Martinique 1794, **Seringapatam, Maida,** Vimiera, **Corunna,** Douro, **Talavera,** Guadaloupe 1810, **Allbuhera, Almaraz,** Cuidad Rodrigo, Badajoz, Salamanca, **Vittoria,** Pyrenees, Nivelle Nive, Orthes, Toulouse, **Peninsula,** Ghuznee 1839, Khelat, Afghanistan 1839, Cabool 1842, **Punniar, Moodkee,** Ferezoshah, Aliwal, **Sobraon,** South Africa 1851-53, Alma, **Inkerman, Sevastopol, Lucknow, Taku Forts, Pekin 1860, New Zealand,** Charasiah, **Afghanistan 1879-80,** South Africa 1879, Kabul 1879, Egypt 1882, Abu Klea, **Nile 1884-85,** Suakin 1885, **Burma 1885-87,** Chitral, Tirah, **Relief of Ladysmith,** Relief of Kimberley, **Paardeberg, South Africa 1899-1902.**

The Great War: **Mons,** Le Cateau, **Retreat from Mons,** Marne 1914, 18, **Aisne** 1914, La Bassee 1914, Messines 1914, 17, 18, Armentieres 1914, **Ypres 1914, 15, 17, 18,** Langemarck 1914, 17, Gheluvelt, Nonne Boschen, Givenchy 1914, Neuve Chappelle, Hill 60, Gravenstafel, St Julien, Frezenberg, Bellewaarde, Aubers, Festubert 1915, Hooge 1915, Loos, **Somme 1916, 18,** Albert 1916, 18, Bazentine, Delville Wood, Pozieres, Guillemont, Ginchy, Flers-Courcelette, Morval, Thiepval, Le Transloy, Ancre Heights, Ancre 1916, 18, Bapaume 1917, 18, **Arras 1917,** 18, Vimy 1917, Scarpe 1917, 18, Messines 1917, Langemark 1917, Arleux, Oppy, Bullecourt, Pilcken, Menin Road, Polygon Wood, Broodseinde, Poelcappelle, Passchendaele, **Cambrai 1917,** 18, St Quentin, Bapaume 1918, Rosieres, Avre, Villers Bretonneux, Lys, Estaires, Hazelbrouck, Bailleul, Kemmel, Bethune, Tardenois, Scherpenberg, Soissonnais-Ourcq, Amiens, Drocourt-Queant, **Hindenburg Line,** Havrincourt, Epehy, Canal du Nord, St Quentin Canal, Beaurevoir, Courtrai, Selle, Valenciennes, Sambre, France and Flanders 1914-18, Piave, Vittorio Venito, **Italy 1917-18,** Kosturino, Struma, **Doiran 1917-1918,** Macedonia 1915-18, Helles, **Landing at Helles,** Krithia, **Suvla,** Landing at Suvla, Sari Bair, Scimitar Hill, Gallipoli 1915-16, Rumani, Egypt 1915-17, **Gaza,** El Mughar, Nebi Samwil, **Jerusalem,** Jaffa, Jericho, Jordan, Tell' Asur, Megiddo, Sharon, **Palestine 1917-18,** Aden, Shaiba, Defence of Kut al Amara, **Kut al Amara 1915,** 17, Tigris 1916, Bagdad, Khan Baghdadi, Sharqat, **Mesopotamia 1915-18, North-West Frontier India 1915, 1916-17,** Murman 1918-19, Dukhovskaya, Siberia 1918-19, Persia 1918-19, Archangel 1919, Afghanistan 1919.

The Second World War: Dyle, Defence of Escaut, Amiens 1940, St Omer-La-Bassee, Foret de Nieppe Ypres-Comines Canal, **Dunkirk 1940,** Withdrawal to Seine, **Normandy Landing,** Tilly sur Seulles, Cambes, Breville, Villers Bocage, Odon, **Caen,** Orne Hill 112, Bourgebus Ridge, Troarn, Mont Pincon, Jurques, St Pierre, Falaise, Seine 1944, Nederrijn, Le Havre, Lower Maas, Venraij, Meijel, Geilenkirchen, Venlo Pocket, Roer, Rhineland, Reichswald, Goch, **Rhine,** Lingen, Brinkum, Bremen, **North-West Europe 1940, 44-45,** Karora-Marsa Tacai, Cubcub, Mescelit Pass, Keren, Mt Englehat Massawa, **Abyssinia 1941,** Syria 1941, Sidi Barrani, Sidi Suleiman, Tobruk 1941, Tobruk Sortie, Omars, Alem Hamza Benghazi, Alem el Halfa, Deir El Munassib, **El Alamein,** El Aghelia, Advance on Tripoli, Medenine, Mareth, Tebaga Gap, El Hamma, Akarit, Djebel el Meida, Djebel Roumana, Djebel Abiod, Tebourba, **Tebourba Gap,** Sidi Nsir, **Hunt's Gap,** Montagne Farm, Fondouk, Pichon, El Kourzia, Ber Rabal, Djebel Assag 1942, 43 Robas Valley, Fort McGregor, Oued Zarga, Djjebel Bech Chekaoui, Djebel Ang, Heidous, Djebel Diaffa Pass, Medjez Plain, **Longstop Hill 1943,** Si Abdallah, Tunis, Montarnaud, **North Africa 1940-43,** Francofonte, Sferro, Adrano, Sferro Hills, Centuripe, Monte Rivoglia, Landing in Sicily, Regalbuto, **Sicily 1943,** Termoli, Trigno, San Salvo, Landing at Porto san Venere, Sangro Romagnoli, Impossible Bridge, Villa Grande, **Salerno,** Monte Stella, Salerno Hills, Battipaglia, Cava di Tirreni, Scafati Bridge, Volurno Crossing, Monte Camino, Garigliano Crossing, Damiano, Monte Ornito, Cerasola, Anzio, Carroceto, **Cassino,** Monastery Hill, Castle Hill, Cassino II, Liri Valley, Aquino, Piedimonte Hill, Rome, Massa Vertecchi, Trasimene Line, Arezzo, Advance to Florence, Monte Scalari, **Gothic Line,** Monte Gridolfo, Montegaudio, Coriano, Montigallo, Pian di Castello, Gemmano Ridge, Monte Reggiano, Capture of Forli, Cosina Canal Crossing, Lamone Crossing, Pideura, Cassa Fortis, Senio Pocket, Senio Floodbank, Rimini Line, Casa Fabbri Ridge, Savio Bridgehead, Monte Pianoereno, Monte Spaduro, Monte Grande, Senio, Menate, Filo, Argenta Gap, Montescudo, Frisoni, **Italy 1943-45,** Athens, Greece 1944-45, Leros, Middle East 1943, **Malta 1940-42,** Kampar, **Malaya 1941-42, Hong Kong,** South East Asia 1941, North Arakan, Razabil, Mayu Tunnels, Kohima, **Defence of Kohima,** Pinwe, Pinwe, Shweli, Myitson, Taungtha, Yenangyaung 1945, Sittang 1945, Chindits 1944, **Burma 1943-45.**

Naktong Bridgehead, Chongiu, Chongchon II, Chaum-Ni, Kapyong-chon,
Kapyong, **Korea 1950-51**

Regimental Marches

Quick March	The Farmers Boy, leading into The Soldiers of the Queen
Slow March	The Minden Rose

Agents	Holt's Branch, Royal Bank of Scotland plc, Lawrie House, Farnborough, Hants, GU14 7NR
Area Headquarters	AHQ PWRR, Howe Barracks, Canterbury, Kent CT1 1JY (Tel: 01227 818056 Fax: 01227 818057 Email: RHQPWRR-AREAHQ-AA@mod.uk)
Regimental Headquarters	RHG PWRR, HM Tower of London, EC3 4AB (Tel: 0203 1666 902 Email: giles.clapp473@mod.uk)

Alliances

Canadian Armed Forces	The Queen's York Rangers (1st American Regiment) (RCAC)
	The South Alberta Light Horse (RCAC)
	49th (Salt Ste Marie) Field Artillery Regiment Royal Canadian Artillery
	The Queen's Own Rifles of Canada
	The Hastings and Prince Edward Regiment
	The Essex and Kent Scottish
	1st Battalion The Royal New Brunswick Regiment (Carleton and York)
Australian Military Forces	The Royal New South Wales Regiment
	The Royal Western Australia Regiment
	The University of New South Wales Regiment
New Zealand Army	2nd (Canterbury, Nelson, Marlborough and West Coast) Battalion Group
	5th (Wellington, West Coast and Taranaki) Battalion Group
Pakistan Army	12th, 14th, 15th and 17th Battalions The Punjab Regiment

Colonel in Chief	*Her Majesty* Queen Margrethe II of Denmark	
Colonel	Maj Gen Douglas M Chalmers *DSO OBE*	100216
Deputy Colonels	Col (Retd) Patrick T Crowley	010108
	Col Oli W Stokes *MBE*	011215
	Col James C Coote *DSO OBE*	010815

Lieutenant Colonels

Baynham JL	300612
Betts AFJ	300614
Cornwell MD	300613
Crawley AJ	300609
Davies CD *MBE MBA MA*	300613
Flay AJ	300613
Fotheringham GI	300610
Jones GP Sq	300612
Long HB	300609
Minton GE *MBE psc(j)*	300610
Nooney MAP *MC*	300615
Saunders GDM	300612
Scott LM *MBE*	300610
Taylor SJ *MBE*	300612
Wall S	311215

Majors

Baker BG	310704
Barley ND	310708
Brooks S *MBE*	310710
Burgess AJ *MC*	310715
Burley NSM	310715
Cherry AJG	310715
Deane RG *MC*	100807
Dobson RJ	310711
Doyle SJ *MBE*	310707
Elsey DP	120506
Hickman ME	310705
Hollis MD	310712
Houghton SP	310703
Hughes MJ	010901
Hunter ER	310715
Jose CDR	310714
King GR	310715
Mans DR	310714
Moore M *BSc*	310712
Moorhouse BD	310714
Panayi AAT	310715
Pennells IO	310714
Rands JE	310711
Reed DS	310715
Rendall AJ	310713
Reynolds ET	310714
Singleton CK	310715
Skelton JS *MBE*	310709
Smith JC	310714
Stapley AM	310714
Stoffberg CJ	310713
Taylor RM	300997
Thomas DP	310714
Volker TB	310715
Wells RJ *MBE*	310709
Wood MAJ	310715

Captains

Anderson MJ	020408
Barker JW	140415
Beckett JM	171012
Benton AW	200414
Borwick AM	170614
Buckley MJ	200614
Bullen OJD	311213
Charlesworth PM	090812
Cole DBL	140415
Davey LA	311213

Eaton CAP	130814
Farren EC	140213
Flynn LM	130214
Forster SJT	100314
Frampton JC	080212
Gibbs SD	261012
Gray SSA	080212
Horder SA	040410
Hunt SJ	101011
Hunter FG	090211
Jackson GD	020415
Jordan KH	020413
Keith OS	140213
Kelly BL MC	050413
Lancashire NE	020410
Lee CD	130611
O'Brien MA	020613
Phillips RS	020408
Reynolds GA	140213
Richardson AW	310712
Shotter PAC	110612
Simpson LPT	140415
Swales HE	110815
Thomas JMD	140213
Thornton IJ	161013
Trezise CH	130214
Vail J	080212
Walsh JA	300911

Lieutenants

Black JA	151213
Bowden JR	090815
Evans MB	120415
Ferguson RMF	090815
Griffiths CJ	151213
Happel WC	141214
Hare SE	141214
Heads DJ	100814
Jefferies SBJ	141214
Knowles TEN	110813
Lauder DA	141214
Lockey HJN	120415
Machnicki PJ	140413
Mangion AJ	120415
Pomroy WJ	120415
Praill LD	120415
Scriven Baker TE	130414
Smith RJ	141214
Weir RJ	120415
Willis CJ	151213
Wilson TC	100814

2nd Lieutenants

Dagger R	121215
Hopla J	121215
King RAF	110415
Noakes C	121215
Spires L	110415
Sutton O	110415
Weller PM	080815

THE ROYAL REGIMENT OF FUSILIERS

St George and the Dragon within the Garter

Honi Soit Qui Mal Y Pense

The United Red and White Rose slipped ensigned with the Royal Crest. An Antelope, gorged with a ducal coronet with rope reflexed over back. The White Horse of Hanover. The Red Rose of Lancaster. The Sphinx superscribed EGYPT

Namur 1695, Dettingen, Minden, Wilhelmstahl, St Lucia 1778, Martinique 1794, 1809, Egmont-op-Zee, Maida, Rolica, Vimiera, Corunna, Talavera, Busaco, Ciudad Rodrigo, Badajoz, Albuhera, Salamanca, Vittoria, Pyrenees, Nivelle, Orthes, Toulouse, Peninsula, Niagara, South Africa 1846-47, 1851, 2, 3, Alma, Inkerman, Sevastopol, Lucknow, Kandahar 1880, Afghanistan 1878-80, Atbara, Khartoum, Modder River, Relief of Ladysmith, South Africa 1899-1902.

The Great War: **Mons,** Le Cateau, Retreat from Mons, **Marne 1914, Aisne 1914, 18,** La Bassee 1914, Messines 1914, 17, 18 Armentieres 1914, **Ypres 1914, 15, 17, 18,** Langemarck 1914, 17, Gheluvelt, Nonne Bosschen, Neuve Chapelle, Gravenstafel, **St Julien,** Frezenburg, Bellewaarde, Hooge 1915, Aubers, Festubert 1915, Loos, **Somme 1916, 18,** Albert 1916, 18, Bazentin, Delville Wood, Pozieres, Guillemont, Ginchy, Flers-Courcelette, Morval, Thiepval, Le Transloy, Ancre Heights, Ancre 1916, 18, **Arras 1917, 18,** Vimy 1917, Scarpe 1917, 18, Arleux, Bullecourt, Oppy, Pilckem, Menin Road, Polygon Wood, Broodseinde, Poelcappelle, **Passchendaele, Cambrai 1917, 18,** St Quentin, Bepaume 1918, Rosieres, Avre, Villers Bretonneux, Lys, Estaires, Hazebrouck, Bailleul, Kemmel, Bethune, Scherpenberg, Amiens, Drocourt-Queant, **Hindenburg Line,** Havrincourt, Epehy, Canal du Nord, St Quentin Canal, Beaurevoir, Courtrai, Selle, Valenciennes, Sambre, France and Flanders 1914-18, **Piave,** Vittorio Veneto, Italy 1917-18, **Struma,** Doiran 1917, **Macedonia 1915-18,** Helles, **Landing at Helles,** Krithia, **Suvla, Sari Bair,** Landing at Suvla, Scimitar Hill, **Gallipoli 1915-16,** Rumani, **Egypt 1915-17,** Megiddo, Nablus, Palestine 1918, Tigris 1916, Kut al Amara 1917, **Baghdad,** Mesopotamia 1916-18, Baku, Persia 1918, Troitsa, Archangel 1919, Kilimanjaro, Behobeho, Nyangao, East Africa 1915-17.

The Second World War: **Defence of Escaut,** Arras counter attack, St Omer-La Bassee, Wormhoudt, Ypres-Comines Canal, **Dunkirk 1940, Normandy Landing,** Odon, Caen, Bourgebus Ridge, Cagny, Mount Pincon, Falaise, Nederrijn, Venraji, **Rhineland,** Lingen, Brinkum, **Bremen, North-West Europe 1940, 44-45,** Agordat, **Keren,** Syria 1941, Sidi Barrani, **Defence of Tobruk,** Tobruk 1941, Belhamed, Cauldron, Ruweisat Ridge, El Alamein, Advance on Tripoli, Medenine, Djebel Tebaga, **Medjez el Bab,** Oued Zarga, Peter's Corner, **North Africa 1940-43,** Adrano, Sicily 1943, Termoli, Trigno, **Sangro, Mozzagrogna,** Caldari, **Salerno,** St Lucia, Battipaglia, Teano, Volturno Crossing, Monte Camino, Garigliano Crossing, Damiano, **Anzio, Cassino II,** Ripa Ridge, Trasimene Line, Gabbiano, Advance to Florence, Monte Scalari, **Gothic Line,** Coriano, Croce, Monte Ceco, Casa Fortis, Monte Spaduro, Savio Bridgehead, Vali di Comacchio, Senio, Argenta Gap, Italy 1943-45, Athens, Greece 1944-45, **Malta 1941-42,** Singapore Island, Rathedaung, Htizwe, **Kohima,** Naga Village, Chindits 1944, **Burma 1943-45.**

Seoul, **Imjin,** Kowang-San, **Korea 1950-53,** Wadi al Batin, **Gulf 1991,** Al Basrah, Iraq 2003

Regimental Marches

Quick March .... The British Grenadiers
Slow March .... Rule Britannia, De Normandie
(i) St George (Northumberland)
(ii) Macbean's Slow March (Warwickshire)
(iii) De Normandie (London)
(iv) The former Lancashire Fusiliers' Slow March

Agents .... Lloyds TSB, 72 Fenchurch Street
Regimental Headquarters .... HM Tower of London, Tower Hill, London EC3N 4AB
(Tel: 0203 166 6909 Fax: 0203 166 6920
Email: INFHQ-QUEENS-RRF-RegtSec@mod.uk)

Alliances

Canadian Armed Forces .... 31 Combat Engineer Regiment (The Elgins)
The Royal Canadian Regiment
The Lorne Scots (Peel, Dufferin and Halton Regiment)
Les Fusiliers du St Laurent
The Royal Westminster Regiment
Australian Military Forces .... 5th/6th Battalion The Royal Victoria Regiment
New Zealand Army .... 6th Hauraki Regiment

Colonel in Chief .... FM *HRH The Duke of* Kent *KG GCMG GCVO ADC(P)*
Colonel .... Maj Gen Paul A E Nanson *CBE* 011015

Deputy (Area) Colonels .... Northumberland: .... Col Mike R Butterwick *CBE* 010115
Warwickshire: .... Col Peter B Stitt 141016
London: .... Col James W Taylor *MBE* 010216
Lancashire: .... Brig Jon Swift *OBE* 010715

Lieutenant Colonels

Butterfill J *MC*	300612
Coates RM *MBE*	300614
Cooke MJ *MBE*	300615
Evans HS	300604
Gawthorpe AS	300613
Kippen IR	300607
Lamb J *MC*	300614
Mace KN *BSc (Hons) MSc*	300612
Robinson JPC	300611
Samways DA	281015
Stitt PB	300611
Stott JR	300612
Taylor JW *MBE*	300612
Travers MPM	300608

Majors

Anabtawi N	310708
Austin JS *psc(j) (US)*	310707
Baines CJ *MBE*	310710
Bird JM	310709
Boyd GJ *MBE*	310707
Broadbent DM	310711
Campbell CO	310709
Carter SR	310714
Charnock CA	310709
Clarke ME	310714
Cleeveley HGP	310714
Dear JJ *MBE*	310715
Falconer DM	310711
Fern JN	310712
Gammon JG	310713
Hall AJ	020407
Head CA *MC*	310709
Hedley MJI *MBE*	310712
Higgs ARA	310703
Howe DJ	310714
Jackson RS	310715
Kelly SA	310710
Kennedy DP	310715
Kibble TJ	310710
Mills AJ	310711
Milne MH	310714
Musson CE	310715
Oliver T	310714
Ralphs MJ	310712
Renyard K	310715
Ridgway JD	310711
Rowbottom L	310715
Smith RD	310711
Snowden DJ	310714
Strachan-Heyes GT	310715
Sutthery EP	310707
Swann AC	310710
Walters B	310708
Webster MR	070108
Williams CM	310715
Williamson AD	310715
Wilson DR	310705
Wilson LP	310709

Captains

Ashton JEC	200614
Atkinson TM	
Boardman G	080612
Bowkett WH	140415
Bryant AD	130611
Chacksfield JR	310713
Cooper SA	080212
Cotton HGS	140415
Cox ST	161013
Danby CMR *BSc*	121010
Edwards ROM	110815
Everson BF	110612
Frost NA	020411
Gilbert JRM	160414
Gilbert SMR	311213
Grant L	020411
Greaves RP *MBE*	030411
Halloran RAG	020415
Hicks GF	200614
Jackson DP	020415
Jonas MD	180613
King MS	080212
Marriott GE	180613
Miller N	020613
Mitchinson S	290515
Murray JT	110815
O'Hara PE	130214
Pearce SJ	090211
Phillips TL	150610
Piper JA	310712
Pugh J	010710
Purvis AJ	121010
Ranger JS	121010
Roberts EC	140415
Russell JP	110815
Selby MA	010711
Smith RM	200712
Snelling D	030412
Taylor TDA	140213
Walters ML	080212
Wilkinson D	020415

Lieutenants

Bennett TJH	120415
Blaszkowski JR	090815
Booth ST	100814
Cox J	130414
Fairhall GS	100814
Glanvill JRA	090815
Parker B	120415
Peatman JG	151213
Roberts PW	100814
Sweetman GE	100814
Ward DC	120415
Ward PA	151213
West CW	151213

2nd Lieutenants

Davies DA	110415
Dutney JS	080815
Edmund AWG	050114
Heseltine WR	080815
Hutcheson LG	110415
Rolfe MJ	080815

THE ROYAL ANGLIAN REGIMENT

The Castle and Key of Gibraltar upon an eight pointed Star

The figure of Britannia. The Sphinx superscribed EGYPT. The Castle and Key superscribed GIBRALTAR, 1779-83 and with the motto MONTIS INSIGNIA CALPE underneath. The Royal Tiger superscribed HINDOOSTAN. An Eagle within the Garter

Namur 1695, Blenheim, Ramillies, Oudenarde, Malplaquet, Dettingen, Louisburg, Minden, Quebec 1759, Belleisle, Martinique 1762, 1794, Moro, **Havannah,** India, **Seringapatam,** Surinam, Maida, Rolica, Vimiera, **Peninsula, Corunna,** Douro, **Talavera,** Busaca, **Albuhera, Badajoz, Salamanca, Vittoria,** Pyrenees, St Sebastian, Nivelle, Nive, Orthes, Toulouse, **Bladensburg, Waterloo, Ava,** Afghanistan 1839, **Ghuznee 1839, Khelat, Cabool 1842, 79, Moodkee, Ferozeshah, Sobraon, New Zealand,** Mooltan, **Goojerat, Punjaub, South Africa 1851-53,** Alma, **Inkerman, Sevastopol, Lucknow, Taku Forts,** South Africa 1879, **Afghanistan 1878-80,** Ali Masjid, **Nile 1884-85,** Chitral, **Tirah, Atbara, Khartoum, South Africa 1899-1902.** Modder River, Relief of Kimberley, **Paardeburg, Defence of Ladysmith.**

The Great War: **Mons, Le Cateau,** Retreat from Mons, **Marne 1914, Aisne 1914, 18,** La Bassee 1914, Messines 1914, 17, 18, Armentieres 1914, Givenchy 1914, **Ypres 1914, 15, 17, 18,** Langemarck 14, 17, Gheluvelt, Nonne Bosschen, Festubert 1914, 15, Neuve Chapelle, Hill 60, Gravenstafel, St Julien, Frezenberg, Bellewaarde, Aubers, Hooge 1915, **Loos, Somme 1916, 18,** Albert 1916, 18, Bazentin, Delville Wood, Pozieres, Guillemont, Flers-Courcelette, Morval, Thiepval, Le Transloy, Ancre Heights, Ancre 1916, 18, Bapaume 1917, 18, **Arras 1917, 18,** Vimy 1917, Scarpe 1917, 18, Arleux, Oppy, Pilckem, Menin Road, Polygon Wood, Broodseinde, Poelcappelle, Passchendaele, **Cambrai 1917, 18,** St Quentin, Rosieres, Avre, Villers Bretonneux, Lys, Estaires, Hazebrouck, Bailleul, Kemmel, Bethune, Scherpenberg, Amiens, Drocourt-Queant, Hindenbu Line, Havrincourt, Epehy, Canal du Nord, St Quentin Canal, Beaurevoir, Courtrai, Selle, Valenciennes, Sambre, **France and Flanders 1914-18,** Italy 1917-18, Helles, Landing at Helles, Struma, Doiran 1918, **Macedonia 1915-18,** Krithia, Suvla, Landing at Suvla, Scimitar Hill, **Gallipoli 1915-16,** Rumani, Egypt 1915-17, **Gaza,** El Mughar, Nebi Samwil, Jerusalem, **Jaffa,** Tell' Asur, Megiddo, Sharon, Damascus, **Palestine 1917-18,** Tigris 1916, **Shaiba,** Kut al Amara 1915, 17, Ctesiphon, Defence of Kut al Amara, Baghdad, **Mesopotamia 1914-18.**

The Second World War: Vist, Norway 1940, Defence of Escaut, **St Omar-la Basse,** Defence of Arras, Ypres-Comines Canal, **Dunkirk 1940,** St Valery-en-Caux, **Normandy Landing,** Cambes, Tilly sur Seulles, Fontenay Pesnil, Odon, Defence of Rauray, Caen, Orne, Bourguebus Ridge, Troarn, Le Perier Ridge, **Brieux Bridgehead,** Falaise, Nederrijn, Le Havre, Antwerp-Turnhout Canal, Scheldt, Venraij, Venlo Pocket, Zetten, Rhineland Hochwald, Lingen, Brinkum, Bremen, Arnhem 1945, **North-West Europe 1940, 44-45,** Abyssinia 1940, Falluja, Tobruk Sortie, Belhamed, Baghdad 1941, Iraq 1941, Palmyra, Jebel Mazar, Syria 1941, Sidi Barrani, **Tobruk 1941,** Tobruk Sortie, Belhamed, Mersa Matruh, **Defence of Alamein Line,** Deir El Shein, Ruweisat, Ruweisat Ridge, El Alamein, Matmata Hills, Akarit, Enfidaville, Djebel Garci, Djedeida, Djebel Djaffa, Montagne Farm, Sedjenane 1, Mine de Sedjenane, Oued Zargo, Djebel Tanngoucha, Argoub Tanngoucha, Argoub Sellah, Sidi Ahmed, Tunis, Ragoubet Souissi, **North Africa 1940-43,** Landing in Sicily, Adrano, Sicily 1943, Trigno, Sangro, **Villa Grande, Salerno,** Vietri Pass, Capture of Naples, Cava di Tirreni, Volturno Crossing, Calabritto, Garigliano Crossing, Monte Tuga, **Anzio, Cassino i-ii,** Castle Hill, Hangman's Hill, Monte Gaddione, Trasimene Line, Montorsoli, **Gothic Line,** Monte Gamberaldi, Monte Gridolfo, Monte Ceco, Gemmano Ridge, Lamone Crossing, Monte Columbo, Monte Grande, San Marino, Monte La Pieve, Argenta Gap, **Italy 1943-45,** Athens, Greece 1944-45, **Crete, H**eraklion, Madagascar, Kampar, Johore, Muar, Batu Pahat, **Singapore Island, Malaya 1941-42,** Donbaik, Point 201 (Arakan), **Yu,** North Arakan, Buthidaung, **Ngakyedauk Pass, Imphal,** Tamu Road, Bishenpur, **Kohima,** Aradura, Monywa 1945, Mandalay, Myinmu Bridgehead, Irrawaddy, Ramree, **Chindits 1944, Burma 1943-45.**

Maryang-San, **Korea 1951-53**

Regimental Marches

Quick March .... Rule Britannia and Speed the Plough
Slow March .... The Slow March of The Northamptonshire Regiment

Agents .... Holt's Branch, Royal Bank of Scotland plc, Lawrie House, Farnborough, Hants.
Regimental Headquarters .... The Keep, Gibraltar Barracks, Bury St Edmunds, Suffolk, IP33 3RN
(Tel: 01284 752394 Fax: 01284 752026
Email: RHQRANGLIAN-RegSec@mod.uk)

Alliances

Canadian Armed Forces .... Sherbrooke Hussars (RCAC)
The Lincoln and Welland Regiment
The Essex and Kent Scottish
The Lake Superior Scottish Regiment
Australian Military Forces .... The Royal Tasmania Regiment
New Zealand Army .... 3rd Battalion (Auckland (Countess of Ranfurly's Own) and Northland) Royal New Zealand Infantry Regiment
South Africa Army .... Regiment de la Rey
First City Regiment

Pakistan Army .... 5th Battalion Frontier Force Regiment
Malaysian Armed Forces .... 1st Battalion Royal Malay Regiment
Barbados .... The Barbados Regiment
Gibraltar .... The Royal Gibraltar Regiment
Bermuda .... The Bermuda Regiment
Belize .... The Belize Defence Force

Colonel in Chief .... *HRH The Duke of* Gloucester *KG GCVO*
Colonel .... Lt Gen Philip D Jones *CB CBE* 070912
Deputy Colonels .... Brig A J C Wild *MBE (until 210317)* 010412
Col Simon J R Browne *OBE (from 210317)*
Col James M Woodham *CBE MC* 070912
Maj Gen Simon L Porter *CBE* 051014

Lieutenant Colonels

Andrews STH	300607
Brown OCC	300612
Foden GB	300615
Johnson NA	300609
Mackness D	031014
Morris TPD	300613
Wright JCJ	300614
Wylie AM	300605
York JA	300608

Majors

Allen BM	310707
Bennett-Madge JW	310713
Biggs A	310708
Birch PM	300901
Blanchfield PN	260403
Bredin RJ *MBE*	020505
Broomfield DN	310713
Broomfield SM	310715
Buxton AJ	170813
Coleman TGB	310711
Cook MR	310709
Dart AK	310711
Goodey GJ	310713
Grinonneau AG	310705
Grounds FJR	310703
Haggar DJ	310712
Hawes BT	091006
Hudson GJR	310712
Jones T	020404
Lanham JM	310714
MacLay AI	310711
McGinley NJP	310714
Meddings WJ	310711
Melia MC	310708
Mellar TB	310706
Messenger PJ	310705
Moxey PC *MBE*	310708
Muncey PA	310706
Ormiston OB	310712
Otridge WS	310715
Roberts SF	310710
Robinson DJ	310710
Robinson IJ *MBE*	150908
Smith SR	310705
Stefanetti DJ *MBE*	310705
Weston BD	310708
Wicks RA	310715
Wilde APT	310710
Wolfe AP *MBE*	310707

Captains

Allnutt OE	161013
Atkins FK	121010
Barron ND	080212
Crosbie DT	121010
David MJ	020414
Duncalfe CJ	090211
Eaton FA	110815
Emerson AR	080212
Faupel ARC *MBE*	010914
French BS	020411
Garner MR	110612
Goodman MP	171012
Granfield DT	010810
Green TJW	171012
Grice DA	020415
Harris WN	110815
Hearne TG	090211
Heugh JRP	161013
Hopkin C	250515
Hoy WR	110612
Jay LW	010610
Lenthall PRA	311212
Luff AK	160410
MacKness AD	150610
Main K	020412
Marsden G	160414
Monk CC	130814
Payne ST	140415
Penn AJ	020409
Perring JA	130208
Peters AC	130214
Powell JE	110612
Revell M	140415
Roden TC	090211
Ryan JG	140415
Shaw D	020412
Smith AJE	130214
Thomas S	180610
Thompson BRB	010213
Tomlinson DM	140213
Vazquez N	220713
Waghorn LA	010610
Walters JM	171012
Weston RL	110612
Willies HJ	140412
Winterman CM	180613
Wright SP	180613

Lieutenants				*2nd Lieutenants*	
Arnold OM	151213	Pugh JSD	151213	Humphreys B	121215
Basey-Fisher AJ	151213	Raschen JF	120415	Johnston HFJ	131214
Brunsdon MJ	141214	Rowden JSJ	141214	King SR	080815
Durkin MC	090815	Shea TM	141214	Mattin JA	121215
Durrant SJ	090815	Sheaf LJ	100814	McCurley J	131214
Forse SAC	100814	Snoddon JR	110813	Pickering WG	131214
Gordon JH	100814	Tovey MN	130414	Reid T	080815
Leese CE	120415			Taylor J	080815
Miles CL	130414			Tracey JR	110415
Morgan DR	120415			Watkins NTB	050114

THE KING'S DIVISION

Comprising..The Duke of Lancaster's Regiment (2 Regular Battalions, 1 AR Battalion)
The Yorkshire Regiment (3 Regular Army Battalions, 1 AR Battalion)

Divisional Office ....Headquarters Infantry, Warminster, Wilts BA12 ODJ
(Tel: 01985 222681)

Colonel Commandant ....Brig Andrew T Jackson 010215

The origins of amalgamated Regiments now included in The King's Division are as follows:

THE DUKE OF LANCASTER'S REGIMENT (KING'S, LANCASHIRE AND BORDER)

On 1 July 1958

The East Lancashire Regiment (30 and 59) and

The South Lancashire Regiment (The Prince of Wales's Volunteers) (40 and 82) amalgamated to form:

The Lancashire Regiment (Prince of Wales's Volunteers)

On 1 September 1958

The King's Regiment (Liverpool) (8) and

The Manchester Regiment (63 and 96) amalgamated to form:

The King's Regiment (Manchester and Liverpool) (8, 63 and 96)

On 13 December 1968 the Regiment was redesignated

The King's Regiment

On 1 October 1959

The King's Own Royal Regiment (Lancaster) and

The Border Regiment (34 and 55) amalgamated to form:

The King's Own Royal Border Regiment

On 25 March 1970

The Lancashire Regiment (Prince of Wales's Volunteers) (30,40, 59 and 82) and

The Loyal Regiment (North Lancashire) (47 and 81) amalgamated to form:

The Queen's Lancashire Regiment

On 1 July 2006

The King's Own Royal Border Regiment and

The King's Regiment and

The Queen's Lancashire Regiment, together with their respective companies of

The Lancastrian and Cumbrian Volunteers and The King's and Cheshire Regiment amalgamated to form:

The Duke of Lancaster's Regiment (King's, Lancashire and Border)

THE YORKSHIRE REGIMENT

On 24 April 1958

The West Yorkshire Regiment (The Prince of Wales's Own) (14) and

The East Yorkshire Regiment (Duke of York's Own) (15) amalgamated to form:

The Prince of Wales's Own Regiment of Yorkshire

On 6 June 2006

The Prince of Wales's Own Regiment of Yorkshire (14th/15th Foot) and

The Green Howards (Alexandra, Princess of Wales's Own Yorkshire Regiment) (19th Foot) and

The Duke of Wellington's Regiment (West Riding) (33rd/76th Foot) and their

associated Territorial Army units amalgamated to form:

The Yorkshire Regiment

THE DUKE OF LANCASTER'S REGIMENT (KING'S, LANCASHIRE AND BORDER)

Nec Aspera Terrent

The Red Rose of Lancaster charged with the Royal Crown, with the motto 'Nec Aspera Terrent' on a scroll beneath the Rose, all within a gold 'Fontenoy' Laurel Wreath

The Regiment was formed on 1st July 2006, by the amalgamation of the King's Own Royal Border Regiment, the King's Regiment and the Queen's Lancashire Regiment together with their respective companies of The Lancastrian and Cumbrian Volunteers and The King's and Cheshire Regiment.

The Great War: **Mons,** Le Cateau, **Retreat from Mons, Marne 1914**, **Aisne 1914, 18,** La Bassee 1914, **Messines 1914, 17, 18,** Armentières 1914, **Ypres 1914, 15, 17, 18,** Langemarck 1914, Gheluvelt, Nonne Bosschen, Givenchy 1914, **Neuve Chapelle,** Gravenstafel, St Julien, Frezenberg, Bellewaarde, Aubers, Festubert 1915, **Loos, Somme 1916, 18,** Albert 1916, Bazentin, Delville Wood, Pozières, Guillemont, Ginchy, Flers-Courcelette, Morval, Thiepval, Le Transloy, Ancre Heights, Ancre 1916, Bapaume 1917, **Arras 1917, 18,** Vimy 1917, **Scarpe 1917, 18,** Arleux, Oppy, Bullecourt, Messines 1917, Ypres 1917, Pilckem, Langemarck 1917, Menin Road, Polygon Wood, Broodseinde, Poelcappelle, Passchendaele, **Cambrai 1917, 18,** St Quentin, Bapaume 1918, Rosieres, Arras 1918, Avre, Ancre 1918, Villers-Bretonneux, **Lys,** Estaires, Hazebrouck, Bailleul, Kemmel, Béthune, Scherpenberg, Marne 1918, Soissonais-Ourcq, Amiens, Albert 1918, Drocourt-Queant, **Hindenburg Line,** Epéhy, Canal du Nord, St Quentin Canal, Beaurevoir, Courtrai, Selle, Valenciennes, Sambre, France & Flanders 1914-18, Piave, **Vittorio Veneto,** Italy 1917-18, Kosturino, Struma, Doiran 1917, Doiran 1918, **Macedonia 1915-18,** Helles, Landing at Helles, Krithia, Suvla, **Sari Bair,** Landing at Suvla, Scimitar Hill, **Gallipoli 1915-16,** Rumani, Egypt 1915-17, Gaza, Nebi Samwil, Jerusalem, Jaffa, Tell'Asur, **Megiddo,** Sharon, Palestine 1917-18, Tigris 1916, **Kut al Amara 1917, Baghdad,** Mesopotamia 1916-18, **Kilimanjaro,** East Africa 1914-16, North-West Frontier 1915-17, Baluchistan 1918, Archangel 1918-19, **Afghanistan 1919**

The Second World War: Dyle, Withdrawal to Escaut, Defence of Escaut, Defence of Arras, St Omer-La BasseeOwn Ypres-Comines Canal, **Dunkirk 1940,** Somme 1940, North-West Europe 1940, **Normandy Landing,** Odon, Caen, Esquay, Borguebus Ridge, Troarn, **Falaise,** Nederrijn, **Arnhem 1944,** Scheldt, Walcheren Causeway, Flushing, **Lower Maas, Ourthe,** Venraij, Venlo Pocket, Roer, The Rhineland, **Reichswald,** Goch, Weeze, Hochwald, Rhine, Ibbenburen, Dreirwalde, Aller, Bremen, North-West Europe 1944-45, **Defence of Habbaniya,** Falluja, Iraq 1941, Merjayun, Jebel Mazar, Syria 1941, **Tobruk 1941**, Tobruk Sortie 1941, **Madagascar,** Middle East 1942, Banana Ridge, Djebel Kesskiss, Medjez Plain, **Gueriat el Atach Ridge,** Gab Gab Gap, Djebel Bou Aoukaz 1943, I, North Africa 1940-4, **Landing in Sicily, Anzio, Cassino II,** Rome, Trasimene Line, Tuori, Montone, Citta di Castello, Fiesole, Gothic Line, Monte Gridolfo,Coriano, San Clemente, Gemmano Ridge, Rimini Line, Montescudo, Monte Gamberaldi, San Martino Sogliano, Montilgallo, Cesena, Monte Ceco, Capture of Forli, Monte Grande, Lamone Crossing, Bridgehead, Italy 1944-45, **Malta 1940-42,** Athens, Greece 1944-45, Johore, Batu Pahat, **Singapore Island,** Malaya 1941-42, **Chindits 1943, North Arakan,** Mayu Tunnels, **Chindits 1944, Imphal,** Sakawng, Tamu Road, Shenam Pass, **Kohima,** Ukhrul, Pinwe, Schwebo, Mandalay, Myinmu Bridgehead, Meiktila, **Nyaungu Bridgehead,** Letse, Irrawaddy, Rangoon Road, Pyawbwe, Sittang 1945, **Burma 1943-45**

Korea 1952-53, The Hook 1953

Regimental Marches

Quick March .... Arrangement of 'Corn Riggs are Bonnie' and 'John Peel' and 'The Lass o' Gowrie'
Slow March .... The Red Rose

Regimental Headquarters .... Fulwood Barracks, Preston, PR2 8AA
(Tel: 01772 260426 Fax: 01772 260583
Email: rhqlancs-regsec@mod.uk)

Affiliated Regiments

Italy: The Julia Brigade
France: 126e Regiment, Brive

Alliances

Canadian Armed Forces......................... The Royal Regiment of Canada.
The Princess of Wales's Own Regiment
The West Nova Scotia Regiment
The King's Own Calgary Regiment
The Loyal Edmonton Regiment
Australian Military Forces..................... 10th/27th Battalion, The Royal South Australia Regiment

	The Royal Queensland Regiment
	The Royal Tasmania Regiment
New Zealand Army	The Otago and Southland Regiment
	7th Battalion (Wellington (City of Wellington's Own) and Hawkes Bay), The Royal New Zealand Infantry Regiment.
Indian Army	5th Battalion The Sikh Regiment
Malaysian Armed Forces	2nd Battalion Royal Malay Regiment
Pakistan Army	8th Battalion, The Punjab Regiment
	14th Battalion, The Punjab Regiment
	1st Battalion (Scinde), The Frontier Force Regiment
	15th Battalion, The Frontier Force Regiment
South Africa Army	The Kimberley Regiment

Colonel in Chief .... HER MAJESTY THE QUEEN
Colonel .... Brig (Retd) Peter S Rafferty *MBE* 061213

Lieutenant Colonels

Barnett SN *MBE*	300604
Blakesley PJ *MBE*	300611
Bostock SE *OBE*	300603
Cheetham NJ	300610
Cormack HGG *MBE*	300613
Driver PR	300615
Griffin CM *OBE*	300601
Hemesley EJ	300613
Hewitt GM	300607
MacKenzie NP	300615
Maskell AJ	300612
Maund GA *OBE*	300612
Metcalf IP	300612
Reeves ID	300614
Routledge SJ	300613
Royce AAD	300612
Russell JS	300615
Serle N	300614
Thorpe DM *OBE*	300609
Tingey PJ	300614
Wood NI *OBE*	300609

Majors

Adams AJM	310715
Arrandale N	310712
Caldwell SE	310713
Calunniato AE	310710
Carter CP	310713
Claydon DRG	310711
Clayton APT	310713
Conran DMC	310712
Davison RH	310711
Donohue AJ	310709
Downey A	310713
Edmonds RS	310713
Flynn JM	310708
Fraser EA *BA (Hons)*	310709
Gardner JA	300995
Gilbody JL	310712
Higgins NF	310712
Hill RAL	310712
Howard CA *MBE*	010806
Howard MA	310710
Jones DI	310710
Latimer DA	310715
Locke AN	310710
Lockwood AG	310714
Main ISJ	310713
McEwen DA	310713
McGrory CF	310708
McKenny A	310715
McNeil PW	310709
Metcalfe S	310712
Michell EGM	310714
Muspratt J	310711
Nathan PR	310704
Peel MP	151206
Pinchen GM	310703
Pino B	310715
Poole TRM	310713
Rawsthorne JPI	310707
Small RJ	130606
Stephen CA *MBE*	310712
Sweeney AK	310707
Tortoishell D	310713
Walker MPM	310705
Walton SK	310710
Whitting CEG	310713
Witherell AN	310710

Captains

Athanassiadis PW	151215
Berry PD	160614
Boreham WJC *MC*	311213
Borthwick JA	140214
Bowen S	140410
Brooks AM	030411
Clarkson G	161013
Coleman FP	101011
Collier BA	311212
Crompton AG	171012
Cronin MT	151215
Dale AE	020414
Davies TWW	130611
Dodd AJH	130611
Eastham AR	140415
Gardner CH	160412
Garnett BJ	140415
Glover JAS	310713
Hamilton SFX	140213
Hayward MA	080212
Heywood PJ	130611
Hodgson PA	150610
Holden WE	310712
Holland JO	140214
Hoy JPA	080212
Ivinson SJ *MA (Hons) Geog*	180613
Jones BE	140213

Jones JP	120411
Julian SM	151215
Liladhar N	140412
Marlowe J	020412
McAulay L	310713
McKone LM	140415
McWilliam JJ	161013
Miller A	310713
Millns TD	130611
Morris LMJ	110815
Neilson KF	130611
Poots MA	310712
Porter S	080613
Postles AR	140415
Pyper KS	170614
Reid AD	130415
Reynolds TC	140214
Roberts-Morgan P	310712
Robinson MN	110815
Rowlandson CT	020412
Russell-Blackburn HJ	130411
Saunders MC	160410
Sawyer A	311212
Small CR	130408
Stones MA	040708
Sweeney PJ	020407
Szymanski DM	030413
Thorogood MD	120612
Tickle SJ	300712
Walker DJ	120612
Watt JD	131010
Whishaw MT	310712
Wiejak DA	170614
Wragg COL	141009

Lieutenants

Ainsworth LEJ	160614
Bush TJM	090815
Campbell RFJ	130414
Cleave GPR	130414
Coates P	090815
Day LM	090815
Farrell-Southin LS	090814
Holder-Williams CHM	120415
Martin LAD	120415
Pettitt RJ	120415
Sanders JM	090814
Voigt JR	090815
Webb AHJ	141214

2nd Lieutenants

Baines P	131214
Clark GO	141213
Clarke JG	080815
Heller L	121215
Johnston WO	121215
Meller CA	121215
Moore WJ	080815
Steele GA	110415

THE YORKSHIRE REGIMENT

(Battle honours - including those inherited from preceding units)

The Great War: **Mons,** Le Cateau, Retreat from Mons, **Marne 1914 and 1918, Aisne 1914 and 1918, Armentières 1914,** La Bassée 1914, **Ypres 1914, 15, 17, 18,** Langemarck 1914 and 1917, Gheluvelt, Nonne Bosschen, Neuve Chapelle, **Hill 60,** Gravenstafel, St. Julien, Frezenberg, Bellewaarde, Aubers, Festubert, Hooge 1915, **Loos, Somme 1916, 18,** Albert 1916, 18, Bazentin, Delville Wood, Pozières, Flers-Courcelette, Morval, Thiepval, Le Transloy, Ancre Heights, Ancre 1916, **Arras** 1916, **17, 18,** Scarpe 1917, 18, Arleux, Oppy, Bullecourt, Hill 70, Messines 1917, 18, Pilckem, Langemarck 1917, Menin Road, Polygon Wood, Broodseinde, Poelcappelle, Passchendaele, **Cambrai 1917, 18,** St Quentin, Bapaume 1918, Rosieres, Ancre 1918, Villiers Bretonneux, **Lys,** Estaires, Hazebrouck, Bailleul, Kemmel, Bethune, Scherpenberg, Marne 1918, **Tardenois,** Amiens, Drocourt-Quéant, Hindenburg Line, Havrincourt, Epéhy, Canal du Nord, St Quentin Canal, Beaurevoir, **Selle, Valenciennes,** Sambre, France and Flanders 1914-18, **Piave, Vittorio Veneto,** Italy 1917-18, Struma, **Doiran 1917,** Macedonia 1915-18, **Suvla,** Landing at Suvla, Scimitar Hill, Gallipoli 1915, Egypt 1915–16, Archangel 1918, **Afghanistan 1919**

The Second World War: Otta, **Norway 1940,** Withdrawal to Escaut, Defence of Escaut, Defence of Arras, French Frontier 1940, Ypres-Comines Canal, **Dunkirk 1940, St. Valery-en-Caux, Normandy Landing,** Tilly sur Seulles, **Odon, Fontenay Le Pesnil,** Caen, Bourguebus Ridge, Troarn, Mont Pincon, St Pierre La Vielle, Gheel, Nederrijn, Aam, Venraij, Rhineland, **Schaddenhof,** Brinkum, Bremen, **North-West Europe 1940, 44–45,** Jebel Defeis, **Keren,** Ad Teclescan, Abyssinia 1940–41, **Gazala,** Cauldron, Mersa Matruh, Defence of Alamein Line, **El Alamein, Mareth,** Wadi Zigzaou, **Akarit,** North Africa 1940–42, North Africa (before 1942–43), Banana Ridge, Medjez Plain, Gueriat el Atach Ridge, Tunis, **Djebel Bou Aoukaz 1943,** North Africa 1943, Primasole Bridge, Landing in Sicily, Lentini, **Sicily 1943, Minturno, Anzio,** Campoleone, Rome, **Monte Ceco,** Italy 1943–44 and 43–45, **Sittang 1942, 45, Pegu 1942,** Paungde, Yenangyaung 1942, North Arakan, Maungdaw, **Defence of Sinzweya, Imphal,** Bishenpur, Kanglantonbi, Kohima, **Meiktila,** Capture of Meiktila, Defence of Meiktila, Rangoon Road, Pyawbwe, Arakan beaches, Chindits 1944, **Burma 1942-45**

The Hook 1953, Korean War 1952–53, Iraq 2003

Regimental Marches

Quick March .... 'Ca Ira'
Slow March .... 'The Duke of York'

Regimental Headquarters .... The Yorkshire Regiment, 3 Tower Street, YORK, YO1 9SB
(Tel: 01904 461012 Mil: 947778112 Fax: 01904 461021)

Alliances

The Rocky Mountain Rangers
The Queen's York Rangers (1st American Regiment)
The Royal Montreal Regiment
1st Battalion the Royal New Brunswick Regiment (Carlton and York)
Les Voltigeurs de Quebec
10th Battalion the Baloch Regiment of the Pakistan Army
Falkland Islands Defence Force

Bonds of Friendship

HMS Iron Duke
HMS Richmond

Other Affiliations

The Company of Merchant Adventurers of York
HM Kongens Guard (The King's Guard) of Norway

Colonel in Chief .... *HRH The Duke of* York *KG GCVO ADC(P)*
Colonel of the Regiment .... Maj Gen (Retd) GJ Binns *CBE DSO MC*
Deputy Colonel .... Brig Andrew T Jackson 180616
Regimental Secretary .... Lt Col (Retd) David RE O'Kelly

Lieutenant Colonels					
		Garner AS *MBE*	300613	McNicholas P	300614
Astley IWK	300609	Hall RJ	300615	Newson H	300609
Bassingham-Searle PJ	300612	Hancock DS	300606	O'Connor AT	010114
Bower MW *MBE QGM*	300609	Humphris SL *MBE*	300614	O'Connor RC	300613
Cowell PMJ	300615	Johnson AT	300615	Palmer MCA	300615
Crowley IG *MC*	300610	Kennedy JA	300615	Rhodes NP	300610
Fox PR	300610	Marshall MI	300613	Robinson M *MBE*	300612

Thom NGD	300615
Wagstaff TE	300609
Wolfenden GR	300615
Wood NMB	300611

Majors

Armitage CD	310710
Ashworth JE	310712
Awad SAJ	310710
Ayre JJ	310711
Bibby F	310707
Birkett MP *MBE*	060606
Bowden HCR	310712
Breach A	310715
Bulmer N	060605
Caine S	020405
Carman RJP	310712
Carr RM	310709
Clough MD	121005
Colver ERH *MBE*	310708
Davies SR	310715
Day SG	310715
Dwyer SP	310713
England GA	310714
Exton T	310710
Faithfull BJT *BA(Hons) psc(j)*	300999
Farley S	310714
Glossop JA	310707
Grieve RW	310708
Holloway DP	310714
James TP	310705
Lyons EAR	310714
Mathieson ES	310712
Mclellan MG *MBE*	310708
Metcalfe-Tarren JA	310713
Miller TJ	310709
Ness M	310711
Pearce JL	310711
Pledger AW	310708
Powers CPA	310707
Prew DM	310710
Redshaw BGT	310713
Richardson S	300901
Robinson P *MBE*	310710
Saunby JM	310712
Smith EWM	310710
Stear MMD	310704
Terry BFS	310707
Townend AAR	300707
Tucker RJ	310711
Wade RT	310709
Whitaker AD	310714
Willis ME *MBE*	310710
Wilson NS *MBE*	310713

Captains

Allison WL	161211
Appleyard TM	140214
Arnold D	311213
Athow-Frost JA	110210
Atkins IG	130611
Bambrick OJC	110815
Barraclough JW	140214
Bates HM	130611
Beaumont CJ	180613
Becher CR	140213
Berry WR	110815
Binns TJ	151215
Boggs JA	310713
Bosher DJ	161013
Brindley CR	311212
Burnham TG	140415
Cameron CM	160614
Clarke MD	030714
Cocker SP	020414
Coltman DL	011013
Cookman TJ	110815
Crowther JD	140213
Flanagan TP	180614
Flecchia TH	080212
Fletcher DCM	151215
Gayfer RA	180613
Gill TSB	311212
Glover TC	160614
Hammond AP	090211
Hinchliffe INF	010615
Hugill AM	140214
Jenkins JR *BEng*	151215
Kesterton SA	090410
Kume-Davy JN	180613
Ledger AM	170614
Lucas AM	140415
Lunn CW *MC*	140412
MacKenzie A	020712
Mason SM	100413
Maxwell WJ	110815
Merchant RK	311013
Pendlebury AGF	160614
Quraishy KS	160614
Ross NA	101011
Ryan TP	140213
Rylands TPG	311213
Scott M	280711
Simms PW	130415
Sparks OCJ	080212
Stannard MD	160608
Stanton JG	101011
Stow HJ	171210
Thompson PL	010813
Townsend RC	120612
Waters ETM	101011
Watts EC	110815
White DJ	161013
White SG	120612
Wildey LD *MBE*	020411

Lieutenants

Beck CD *BSc(Hons)*	120415
Borley JS	141214
Crichton ATM	271212
Harrison NC	141214
Hodgson IR	090814
Loxton WHJ	120415
Marshall SJ	120415
Mcclement AW	161213
Odlum PR	090815
Redshaw AGS	151213
Saunders MI	141214
Smith MA	130414
Strachan FM	090815

2nd Lieutenants

Charlesworth PRM	120414
Cross SJ	110415
Farquhar DCE	080815
Holder-Williams GD	110415
Lech RM	110415
Millar SJ	120414
Morgan DJ	080815
Narey MJ	080815
Slight JI	121215
Sturley DT	131214
Taylor HM	131214
Williams RG	131214

THE PRINCE OF WALES'S DIVISION

Comprising...The Mercian Regiment (3 Regular Battalions, 1 AR Battalion)
The Royal Welsh (2 Regular Battalions, 1 AR Battalion)

Divisional Headquarters..Headquarters Infantry, Land Warfare Centre, Warminster, Wilts BA12 ODJ
(Tel: 01985 222235)

Colonel Commandant..Lt Gen *Sir* James Everard *KCB CBE*..230413

The origins of amalgamated Regiments now included in The Prince of Wales's Division are as follows:

THE MERCIAN REGIMENT

On 31 January 1959
The South Staffordshire Regiment (38 and 80) and
The North Staffordshire Regiment (The Prince of Wales's) (64 and 98) amalganlated to form:
The Staffordshire Regiment (The Prince of Wales's)

On 28 February 1970
The Worcestershire Regiment (29 and 36) and
The Sherwood Foresters (Nottinghamshire and Derbyshire Regiment) (45 and 95) amalgamated to form:
The Worcestershire and Shelwood Foresters Regiment (29th/45th Foot)

On 1 September 2007
The Cheshire Regiment and
The Worcestershire & Sherwood Foresters Regiment and
The Staffordshire and West Midlands
and Kings Cheshire Regiments amalgmated to form:
The Mercian Regiment

THE ROYAL WELSH

On 11 June 1969
The South Wales Borderers (24) and
The Welch Regiment (41 and 69) amalgamated to form:
The Royal Regiment of Wales (24th/41st Foot)

On 1 March 2006
The Royal Welch Fusiliers
The Royal Regiment of Wales
The Royal Welsh Regiment (TA) amalgamated to form:
The Royal Welsh

THE MERCIAN REGIMENT

Double headed Mercian Eagle with Saxon crown

Formed on 1 September 2007 by amalgamation of the 1st Battalion, 22nd (Cheshire) Regiment, 1st Battalion, Worcestershire and Sherwood Foresters Regiment (29th/45th Foot), 1st Battalion, Staffordshire Regiment (The Prince of Wales's) and the West Midlands Regiment.

Regimental Marches

Quick March .... Under the Double Eagle

Slow March.. Stand Firm and Strike Hard

Regimental Headquarters .... The Mercian Regiment, Heath Avenue, Lichfield, Staffordshire WS14 9TJ
(Tel: 01543 434390 Email: RHQMERCIAN-AOWelfare@mod.uk)

Alliances

Canadian Armed Forces......................... 2nd Battalion The Nova Scotia Highlanders (Cape Breton)
The Grey and Simcoe Foresters
4e Battalion Royal 22e Regiment (Chateauguay)
Australian Military Forces..................... 8th/7th Battalion The Royal Victoria Regiment
Jamaica.. Jamaica Defence Force
Leeward Isles .... The Antigua and Barbuda Defence Force
Pakistan Army... 13th Battalion The Punjab Regiment
7th The Baloch Regiment
Royal Navy .... HMS Albion (out of service)
HMS Nottingham

Colonel in Chief..................................... FM *HRH The Prince of* Wales , *Earl of Chester, KG KT GCB OM AK QSO ADC(P)*
Colonel of the Regiment......................... Brig Andrew P Williams *OBE* 060613
Deputy Colonels...................................... Brig Peter Dennis 010907
Maj Gen Ian J Cave..........010912

Lieutenant Colonels		*Majors*			
Balls JB *MBE*	300608	Agnew RJ	310712	Green SR	131004
Bayliss GJ	300614	Atherton RG	310708	Grover RCO *MBE*	310710
Boath DW	300609	Bailey DJS	310711	Hallam DA	080107
Bryant OJH	300614	Ballard JF	310714	Hayes SR	310711
Butt SWD	300609	Baxter MC	310707	Hickmott ML	310714
Casey SA *MBE*	300614	Bell AJ	310715	Hoy RAJ	310707
Chynoweth M	300608	Blackhurst WH	310711	Jerome FJE	310709
Cox AD *MBE*	300613	Boudet-Fenouillet SN	310713	Kelly NA *OBE*	310709
Davies C	300610	Bourne AJ	310713	Lawrence SW	310714
Ellwood MCP *MBE*	300613	Breen NH	020406	Lincoln KA	310715
Ginn CRP	300614	Brown GA	310714	Lygo NJE	310713
Grant Mc ND	300615	Brown NJ	310710	Mclannahan ATG	310709
Holden MA	300606	Burton SP *MBE*	310708	Moore DIS	310709
Layton AP *MBE*	300609	Canham DD	310708	Moorhouse RS	310704
Parrott IS	240315	Charlesworth EL	310711	Mulira JJS	310713
Richards BL	300605	Cooper PS PhD	310714	Nowell JP	310704
Richardson NS	300614	Cotterill GD	310707	Paul CJ	310714
Robinson SPU	300606	Cresswell NP	020408	Paul MRH	310711
Smallbone AT	300608	Davis MT	310708	Pollitt SM	310715
Steed M	300608	Garrett AR	310708	Porteous HF	310710
Turner JF	300611	Gatenby GD	310703	Powell BME	310714
Wilde BM *MBE*	300614	Godsiff PS	310715	Prentice RA *MA MSc*	310706
				Sanchez R	310711

Sernberg RAJ	310707
Shergold PJD *BSc (Hons)*	310715
Skillen JH	310708
Slaney R	090503
Snell AP	310713
Somers CJ	310710
Stanier JP	310708
Strong IJ	300901
Thompson AR *MBE*	310712
Westwood JC	310708
Woodward CM	310711

Captains

Bagguley GM	270409
Bard MJ	140308
Bell DJ	110815
Bermingham CNJ	140415
Blackshaw TM	060513
Broadhurst SJ	160614
Burgess MJ	310713
Burridge JJK	110815
Clark JT	171012
Clayton J	010809
Coutts JN	310712
Crow TW	140415
Davis JR	140213
Dermott NM	040208
Fisher TJ	140213
Flackett OE	121010
Fulford MJ	080212
Graves VP	110612
Groves CA	060611
Harrison JD	110815
Hudson N	110815
Kersey ARD	120808
Kimberlin GC	010410
Lambert TD	160614
Lewis PA	200511
Lowe SM	171214
Maddock DSH	310713
McNeil JD	140415
Mears RJ	140714
Middleton TPP	140213
Mitchell B	040711
Moffat DL	110612
Muckle PS	020415
Nicholls GJ	160414
O'Dell MA	160410
Onion TP	180613
Page RG	020415
Pope SA	180613
Priggs FT	161013
Proctor RJ	171210
Sawyer RT	090211
Sharland OW	110815
Silbermann TL	160414
Smith DC	160614
Smyth BP	120811
Spoors D	190410
Teasdale M	160614
Travis D	020412
Trehane JM	311213
Triandafilou D	020412
Vause SJ	140415
Viveash SL	270415
Webber W	140415
Whatling EC	140415
Wheeler MJ	150610
Whillock MR	020411
Williams TJ	010912
Wilson HA	281012

Lieutenants

Anderson P	151213
Brown DD	141214
Cartwright JDN	100813
Elliott OJA	130413
Ellison MJ	130413
England JWD	131215
Lloyd CJM	141214
Parry CJA	130413
Peacock RB	151213
Price PT	131215
Randall SG	130413
Russell JJ	100813
Sones MB	141214
Stewart DJH	130413
Zeal AN	131215

2nd Lieutenants

Berridge JA *BA(Hons)*	090814
Brannon NMR	121215
Cole AP	120414
Courtney RG	090814
England JWD	131215
Gledhill MP	090814
Greenway T	121215
Ireland EA	110415
Johl AP	080815
Mead LB	110415
O'Connell LWJ	121215
Prettyjohn TE	110415
Skelding TA	120414

THE ROYAL WELSH
(23, 24, 41, 69)

Gwell Angau Na Chywilydd

Comprising.. 1st Battalion The Royal Welsh (The Royal Welch Fusiliers)
2nd Battalion The Royal Welsh (The Royal Regiment of Wales)
3rd (AR) Battalion The Royal Welsh

Queen's Colour

A Silver Wreath of Immortelles borne around the Colour pike

Regimental Colour

The Badge of the Heir Apparent within a circlet inscribed THE ROYAL WELSH within the Union Wreath surmounted by The Crown, across the tie of the Wreath a scroll inscribed with the motto GWELL ANGAU NA CHYWILYDD; the Battle Honours of the Regiment with a Naval Crown superscribed 12 APRIL 1782 subscribed ST VINCENT 1797. In the first quarter The Royal Cypher. In the second quarter the Red Dragon Rampant. In the third quarter the White Horse of Hanover with the motto NEC ASPERA TERRENT. In the fourth quarter the Rising Sun. The Sphinx superscribed EGYPT above a Laurel Wreath at the base.

Cap Badge

The Badge of the Heir Apparent with a scroll below inscribed THE ROYAL WELSH

Battle Honours

Those below in bold are borne on the Colours

(The Honours for Egypt(1801), The Saints (1782) and St Vincent (1797) do not have separate scrolls as they are incorporated as part of the distinctive Badges emblazoned on the Regimental Colour)

Namur 1695, Blenheim, Ramillies, Oudenarde, Malplaquet, Dettingen, Minden, Belleisle, Martinique 1762, 1809, India, Cape of Good Hope 1806, Corunna, Talavera, Bourbon, Busaco, Fuentes d'Onor, Albuhera, Java, Badajoz, Salamanca, Detroit, Queenstown, Miami, Vittoria, Pyrenees, Nivelle, Orthes, Toulouse, Niagara, Peninsula, Waterloo, Ava, Candahar 1842, Ghuznee 1842, Cabool 1842, Chilianwallah, Goojerat, Punjaub, **Alma, Inkerman, Sevastopol, Lucknow, Ashantee 1873-74, South Africa 1877-8-9, Burma 1885-87,** Relief of Kimberley, Paardeberg, Relief of Ladysmith, **South Africa 1899-1902, Pekin 1900.**

The Great War: **Mons,** Le Cateau, Retreat from Mons, **Marne 1914, Aisne 1914, 18,** La Bassee 1914, Messines 1914, 17, 18, Armentieres 1914, **Ypres 1914, 15, 17, 18,** Langemarck 1914, 17, **Gheluvelt,** Noone Bosschen, Givenchy 1914, Neuve Chapelle, Gravenstafel, St Julien, Frezenberg, Bellewaarde, Aubers, Festubert 1915, **Loos, Somme 1916, 18,** Albert 1916, 18, Bazentin, Delville Wood, Pozieres, Guillemot, Flers-Courcelette, Morval, Le Transloy, Ancre Heights, Ancre 1916, 18, Arras 1917, 18, Scarpe 1917, Arleux, Bullecourt, **Pilckem,** Menin Road, Polygon Wood, Broodseinde, Poelcappelle, Passchendaele, **Cambrai 1917, 18,** St Quentin, Bapaume 1918, Lys, Estaires, Hazebrouck, Baileul, Kemmel, Bethune, Scherpenberg, Drocourt-Queant, **Hindenburg Line,** Havrincourt, Epehy, St Quentin Canal, Beaurevoir, Courtrai, Selle, Valenciennes, Sambre, France and Flanders 1914-18, Piave, **Vittorio Veneto,** Italy 1917-18, Struma, **Doiran 1917, 18,** Macedonia 1915-18, Helles, **Landing at Helles,** Krithia, Sulva, Sari Bair, Landing at Sulva, Scimitar Hill, **Gallipoli 1915-16,** Rumani, **Egypt 1915-17, Gaza,** El Mughar, Jerusalem, Jericho, Tell 'Asur, Megiddo, Nablus, Palestine 1917-18, Aden, Tigris 1916, Kut al Amara 1917, **Baghdad,** Mesopotamia 1916-18, **Tsingtao.**

The Second World War: **Norway 1940,** Dyle, Defence of Escaut, **St Omer-La Bassee, Normandy Landing, Sully,** Odon, **Caen,** Esquay, Bourguebus Ridge, Mont Pincon, Souleuvre, Le Perier Ridge, Falaise, Risle Crossing, Antwerp, **Le Havre,** Nederrijn, Antwerp-Turnhout Canal, Scheldt, **Lower Maas,** Venlo Pocket, Zetten, Ourthe, Rhineland, **Reichswald,** Goch, **Weeze,** Hochwald, **Rhine,** Ibbenburen, Aller, Arnhem 1945, North-West Europe 1940, 44-45, Benghazi, Gazala, **North Africa 1940-1942,** Sicily 1943, Coriano, **Croce,** Rimini Line, Ceriano Ridge, Argenta Gap, **Italy 1943-45, Crete, Canea,** Withdrawal to Sphakia, **Madagascar,** Middle East 1941-42, **Donbaik, North Arakan, Mayu Tunnels, Kohima, Pinwe, Kyaukmyaung Bridgehead,** Shweli, Mandalay, Myitson, Ava, Maymyo, Rangoon Road, **Sittang 1945, Burma 1943-45.**

Korea 1951-52

Regimental Marches

Quick March .... Men of Harlech

Slow March... The War Song of the Men of Glamorgan

Agents... Holt's Branch, Royal Bank of Scotland plc, Lawrie House,
Farnborough, Hants GU14 7NR

Regimental Headquarters .... RHQ The Royal Welsh, (23rd, 24th, 41st and 69th Foot), Maindy Barracks Cardiff, CF14 3YE (Tel: 029 20781202 Fax: 029 20641281 Email: RHQRWELSH-RegtlSec@mod.uk / RHQRWELSH-AsstRegtlSec1@mod.uk Website: www.royalwelsh.org.uk)

Alliances

Canadian Armed Forces........................ Le Royal 22e Regiment
The Ontario Regiment RCAC
Australian Military Forces.................... The Royal New South Wales Regiment
South African Defence Forces.. .... 121 South African Infantry Battalion
The Pretoria Regiment
Pakistan Army....................................... 4th Battalion The Baluch Regiment
3rd Battalion The Frontier Force Regiment
Malaysian Armed Forces .... 4th Battalion The Royal Malay Regiment

Bonds of Friendship
HMS Trenchant
The Royal Regiment of Fusiliers
The United States Marine Corps
The Royal Welch Fusiliers in America
SAS Isandlwana

Colonel in Chief.................................... HER MAJESTY THE QUEEN
Colonel of the Regiment........................ Maj Gen James F P Swift *OBE* 150116

Lieutenant Colonels

Beynon MRG	300615
Boyle SC	300615
Brown CTB	300604
Cannon MK	300613
Clarke AW	300614
Clayton PJ *MBE*	300613
Crewe-Read NO	300614
Davies GM	300615
Dixon PA	120613
Hackney SRD	300612
McGregor RJA	300605
Moss RG	300614
Palmer M	300614
Pughe-Morgan JED	300608
Slay JP *MSc*	300607
Spencer DD	300614

Majors

Adams MD	310714
Beard OGW	310714
Bedford-Smith SJ	310714
Carver CMB	310707
Cookson CR	310715
Crimmins DJ	310714
Davies LK	310714
Davies RD	310714
Fraser JAR	310715
Gavin CC	310713
Greswell WJG	310712
Harris ECN	310705
Hughes DL	310708
Kent AG	310713
Lewis MGT *BScECON MLitt*	310709
Luke OD *MBE*	310708
Maclachlan SR	310711
Major OER	310706
Matthews JP	310707
McCarthy P *MBE*	310709
McDougall AW	310715
Moynihan J	310715
Osborne IJ	020405
Page KA	121005
Pritchard RO	310708
Rabbitt AJ	310715
Rees RK	310715
Rose WKC	310712
Shields MA	310710
Spencer JEB	310714
Stone DE	310714
Stone GJ	310712
Taaffe KD	310707
Tagg OJ	310715
Thomas MR	310714
Waters JR	110803
Willcox EMG	310714
Williams GG	111201
Woodfine JR	310715
Zorab NEJ	310713

Captains

Aroskin AA	130214
Bexon AE	111011
Black J	161013
Booth C	140415
Chronik NR	130611
Clarke APH	110612
Cooper P	010609
Dale D	160614
Davies DE	190410
Davies GG	131015
Davies JGP	110612
Douglas DJ	161007
Elias TR	140213
Ellis SJ	140415
Ellison MO	180613
Goodall PA	080212
Gray DMJ	020412
Groves JAE	290414
Harris WG	161013
Hewitt AS	010610
Hoare RJ	161013
Jones N	150612
Kretzschmar M	020413

Large BP	101011
Lavercombe R	140414
Lewis MC	130611
Leyshon MA	110515
Marden JS	130611
Matthews DM	140714
McAndrew DJC	161012
Morrell DJ	221013
Murgatroyd JP	130814
Murphy JA	101212
Phillips BC	080212
Pooley GA	140415
Pope OM	060211
Reeves B	130814
Roberts W	010610
Rumming PJ	140415
Sobik TWJ	171214
Stockdale CJ	280412
Walker RP	161013
Wall DA	090211
Wickham OL	180613

Lieutenants

Baxter RAM	140412
Edis JJ	100813
Hanson PJ	151212
Jones WR	130413
Nicholls PJ	151213
Richards AJ	081115
Williams TC	220313

2nd Lieutenants

Craig WA	120414
Davey CB	080815
Hughes DAJ	090814
Ixer MJ	110415
Large SJ	110415
Lee L	110415
Parry TD	090814
Willetts MJ	131214

THE ROYAL IRISH REGIMENT

An Irish Harp and Crown surrounded by a wreath of shamrock with the Regiment Title inscribed

Martinique 1762, Havannah, St Lucia 1778, 1796, India, Cape of Good Hope 1806, Maida, Monte Video, Talavera, Bourbon, Busaco, Barrosa, Fuentes d'Onor, Java, Tarifa, Ciudad Rodrigo, Badajoz, Salamanca,Vittoria, Pyrenees, Nivelle, Niagara, Orthes, Toulouse, Peninsula, Waterloo, Ava, South Africa 1835, 1846-7, Sevastopol, Central India, Tel-el-Kebir, Egypt 1882, 1884, Relief of Ladysmith, South Africa 1899-1902.

The Great War: **Mons, Le Cateau,** Retreat from Mons, **Marne 1914,** Aisne 1914, La Bassee 1914, **Messines 1914, 17, 18,** Armentieres 1914, **Ypres 1914, 15, 17, 18,** Nonne Bosschen, **Neuve Chapelle, Loos,** Frezenberg, Aubers, Festubert 1915, Gravenstafel, St Julien, Bellewaarde, **Somme 1916, 18, Albert 1916,** Bazentin, Pozieres, Guillemont, Ginchy, Le Transloy, Ancre, Ancre Heights, **Arras 1917,** Scarpe 1917, Pilckem, Langemarck 1917, Polygon Wood, Broodseinde, Poelcappelle, **Cambrai 1917, 18, St Quentin,** Rosieres, **Hindenburg Line,** Lys, Bailleul, Beaurevoir, Kemmel, Courtrai, Selle, Sambre, **France and Flanders 1914-18,** Kosturino, Struma, **Macedonia 1915-17,** Helles, Landing at Helles, Krithia, **Suvla,** Sari Bair, Landing at Suvla, Scimitar Hill, **Gallipoli 1915-16,** Egypt 1916, **Gaza, Jerusalem,** Tell'Asur, Megiddo, Nablus, **Palestine 1917-18.**

The Second World War: **Dyle,** Withdrawal to Escaut, Defence of Arras, **St Omer-La Bassee,** Ypres-Comines Canal, **Dunkirk 1940, Normandy Landing,** Cambes, **Caen,** Troarn, Venlo Pocket, **Rhine, Bremen,** North-West Europe 1940, 44-45, Two Tree Hill, **Bou Arada,** Stuka Farm, Oued Zarga, Djebel Bel Mahdi, Djebel Ang, Djebel Tanngoucha, **North Africa 1942-43,** Landing in Sicily, Solarino, Simeto Bridgehead, Adrano, **Centuripe,** Salso Crossing, Simento Crossing, Malleto, Pursuit to Messina, **Sicily 1943,** Termoli, Trigno, San Salvo, **Sangro,** Fossacesia, **Garigliano Crossing,** Monte Grande, **Argenta Gap,** San Nicolo Canal, **Italy 1943-45,** Leros, Middle East 1942, **Malta 1940, Yenangyaung 1942,** Donbaik, **Burma 1942-43.**

Seoul, **Imjin, Korea 1950-51, Iraq 2003**

Regimental Marches

Quick March .... Regimental March of the Royal Irish Regiment 'Killaloe'
Slow March .... 'Eileen Alannah'

Regimental Headquarters .... Palace Barracks, Holywood, Belfast. British Forces Post Office 806
(Tel: 028 9042 0629 Fax: 028 9042 0627
Email: RHQRIRISH-Mailbox@mod.uk)

Alliances

Canadian Armed Forces .... The Princess Louise Fusiliers
2nd Battalion The Irish Regiment of Canada (Sudbury)
The Irish Fusiliers of Canada (Vancouver Regiment) (ceased)
Australian Military Forces .... Adelaide University Regiment
New Zealand Army .... 2nd Battalion (Canterbury, Nelson, Marlborough and West Coast)
Royal New Zealand Infantry Regiment
Pakistan Army .... 1st Battalion The Punjab Regiment
9th Battalion (Wilde's) The Frontier Force Regiment
South African Defence Force .... South African Irish Regiment
Gibraltar .... The Royal Gibraltar Regiment
HMS Bulwark

Colonel in Chief .... *HRH The Duke of* York *KG GCVO ADC(P)*
Colonel .... Brig Joe S S O'Sullivan 010713
Deputy Colonel .... Col Michael B Murdoch *MBE ADC* 110213

Lieutenant Colonels

Barron JB *MBE*	300615
Bell RSC *psc(j) (US)*	300614
Doherty DP	300608
Goodwin RN *MA(CANTAB) DTC(MA) psc(j)*	300605
Hargreaves HG	300615
Hart AM *OBE*	300606
Hyland GMS *MA*	300613
Kenny DB *OBE*	300613
L'Estrange PJ	300615
Mann DJ	300615
Morphew RER *OBE*	300610
O'Cock SP	300607
Pritchard HW *MBE*	300603
Robinson RA *OBE*	300602

Majors

Andrews EJ	310715
Bradley NJ	310713
Campbell NR	310714
Cox BN	310715
Crow VRT	310706
Davis BJ	310715
Dixon AC	310711

Forrest TA	010311
Gillespie RM *MBE*	310715
Herbert JJ	310714
Hobbs RJ	310707
Holden SC	310708
Humphreys JA *MBE*	310707
Hutchison G	310713
Johnston BD	310711
Martin PJ	310714
McCleery DK	310708
McGroarty M	310715
Miller J	310715
Murphy GJ	310707
Nellins IC *QGM BEM*	310708
Potter MLF	310708
Rainey GDB *MC*	310712
Shannahan LK	310711
Wright CJN	310713

Captains

Barrow MC	130611
Brown WH	140213
Clarke DJ	030415
Coulson WSJ	140415
Cronin JPD	020412
Everett SW	121010
Goatly RPA	130214
Kirkham AJ	140415
Maguire SRD	130214
McConville JM	161013
McFarland PD *MC*	120612
Muir GT MA	130611
O'Connor FPJ	030412
Potter SA	011215
Pratt PJ	120612
Reid NR	171012
Roy W *MBE*	010514
Ryan DP	110815
Smyth GI	160614
Somerville A	010610
Spence RA	040414
Stevenson TJ	311213
Walker JWR	120612
Watts GA	010609
Whitmarsh T	130211

Lieutenants

Cushnie TG	151213
Gamble JC	130413
McCulloch RJA	130414
Riley MD	130413
Sawford PT	130414
Smee RJ	141214

2nd Lieutenants

Crowe AW	080815
Hazlett MJ	090814
Hynes AMP	120414
Maggs DE	120414
McCracken CD	090814
O'Neill DD	080815
Thame SEW	110415
Whitley GA	080815

THE PARACHUTE REGIMENT

Upon a spread of wings, an open parachute; above the Royal Crest

Utrinque Paratus
(Ready for Anything)

The Second World War: **Bruneval, Normandy Landing,** Pegasus Bridge, Merville Battery, **Breville,** Dives Crossing, La Touques Crossing, **Arnhem 1944,** Ourthe, **Rhine, Southern France,** North-West Europe 1942, 44-45, Soudia, **Oudna,** Djebel Azzag 1943, Djebel Alliliga, El Hadjeba, **Tamera,** Djebel Dahra, Kef el Debna, North Africa 1942-43, **Primosole Bridge,** Sicily 1943, Taranto, Orsogna, Italy 1943-44, **Athens,** Greece 1944-45

Goose Green, Mount Longdon, Wireless Ridge, **Falkland Islands 1982, Iraq 2003,** Al Basrah

Regimental Marches

Quick March .... Ride of the Valkyries
Slow March .... Pomp and Circumstance No 4

Agents.......... Holt's Branch, Royal Bank of Scotland plc, Lawrie House, Farnborough, Hants GU14 7NR
Regimental Headquarters .... RHQ PARA. Merville Barracks, Colchester, Essex. CO2 7UT (Tel: 01206 817073 Mil: 94660 7073 Email: secretary@prahq.com)

Alliances

Australian Military Forces.......... 8th/9th Battalion (Disbanded), The Royal Australian Regiment
Canadian Military Forces.......... The Canadian Airborne Regiment (Disbanded)

Colonel in Chief.......... *HRH The Prince of* Wales *KG KT GCB OM AK QSO ADC(P)*
Colonel Commandant.......... Lt Gen *Sir* John G Lorimer *KCB DSO MBE* 030914
Deputy Colonels.......... Lt Gen James I Bashall *CBE*..........010116
Lt Gen Tom A Beckett *CBE*..........010116
National Secretary, The Parachute Regimental Association.......... Maj (Retd) Paul A Raison

Lieutenant Colonels

Baldwin BL *OBE*	300605
Cansdale MT *MBE*	300614
Cradden LPB *MBE*	300615
Gargan FJ *MBE*	270415
Halse TH *CMgr CMI ACIPD*	300613
Hanley NP *MBE*	011114
Jackson AB	300608
Kingsbury OJ *OBE*	300611
Lee DO	180114
Loudoun JD	300614
McLeod-Jones MI *MBE*	300611
Pott JM MBE	100814
Radbourne BA	300615
Townend AH *MBE*	270715
Truett AJE *MBE*	300613
Walton-Prince SJ *MBE MC*	091215

Majors

Billings PJ	310715
Brennan MO	310709
Burn DH	310714
Chalmers PM	310713
Chetty JR	310705
Chiswell JPR	310715
Coogan AF	310704
Davidson SRM *MC*	310715
Fox AM	310715
Harrop BM	310711
Haywood GA	310705
Hendry DJ	310711
Hickey SM	310715
Hitchins CF	310711
Howard AJP	310715
Hunt WTH	310711
Hursthouse PM	310715
Ireland CR	310714
Jackson BA *BA (Hons)*	310709
Killick SJ	310715
McVitie SA	310715
Mikulskis OM	310715
Mort P	310709
Muirhead DC *MBE*	140108
Phillips ST	310715
Prior CJ	310708
Raison PA	310712
Redding AR *MBE*	310706
Robertson G *MBE*	310709
Rowlatt IM	310715
Rutsch NE	310709
Slater AJ *MBE QGM*	310715
Swann MA	310710
Thwaite MJ	310715
Vines CW	310715
Wareing AM	150306
Wilson AJ	310710
Wright SM	310715

Captains

Armstrong A	030412
Beard ACW	140415
Bennett NPS	170614
Bennie MD	020415
Berger ER	120612
Bowden CMA	150515
Bowen JE	171012

Bridge MD	020410
Bryning JD	140415
Buff DE	270409
Cendrowski MA	070408
Child SR	010615
Clarke SC	080212
Collier CG	121010
Cruse J	311213
Devlin MJ	140213
Evans GJ	140213
Ewen MA	030414
Fitton TP	170614
Getty SP	220615
Gillum HJ	130214
Greenwood JLC	171012
Gurney PJR	030414
Hahndiek R	180613
Ham TC	110815
Kearse PG	101011
Lapham R	140415
Leitch DB	040615
Macey RDM	171012
Main OJ	020415
McCarthy WPD	120612
McComb P	020415
McDougall M *MC*	020415
McGrane AJ	020415
McMahon IM	020310
Monk JWF	091011
Neary BF	080212
Neve AM	130214
Palmer JFD	080212
Perlaki NF	030414
Ramsey JT	180613
Ratcliff SC	161013
Ruston AJ	161013
Scrivener JD	020413
Shackleton ME	180613
Shephard CA *MC*	090211
Smith CJ	130214
Squires RG	290615
Stone MA	170614
Suzuki TA	110210
Swarbrick DA	140415
Taylor SL	161013
Thompson IS	130814
Thomson LFS	130214
Thorburn RWJ	180613
Timlett TJ	110915
Turner SK *MBE*	010610
Wakefield MA	020415
Wetherall ICD	091011
Whitlam SJ	130611
Willetts MA	020411
Wright IA	230412

Lieutenants

Austin CMS	141214
Balch BL	100814
Barnes M	141214
Braithwaite CR	120415
Brecht EM	090815
Buitenhuis J	110813
Busby JHL	090815
Cameron ADM	090815
Clark T	141214
Common AP	051110
Courtney JL	141214
Evans JNG	241112
Gant DJ	110813
Glinn TC	110813
Hand TW	110813
Hirons EJ	151213
Johnston MDM	120415
Lee SJ	141214
Lewis AC	120415
Mackarness HOC	100813
Marshall MAJ	141214
McCool KO	090815
McMullan AA	151213
Meadows R	090815
Metcalfe JPG	100813
Mitchell HW	100813
Nunkoosing AMS	060512
Shaw LJJ	100813
Spencer-Chapman SF	090815
Tibble PD	100814
Whamond JAB	110813
Whittle RS	010214
Whittle TGR	130414
Wood DP	151213
Wright MH	161213
Young AJ	130413
Zownir RJ	120415

2nd Lieutenants

Austin FA	080815
Aymard MS	131214
Bairstow DH	110415
Camozzi MG	080815
Drew DF	080815
Evershed RM	121215
Griffiths THW	121215
Hibbert RO	131214
Jefferson TD	110415
Lovegrove DG	080815
Maughan JWP	110415
Newnham JR	131214
Robson JN	121215
Shaw TD	121215

THE BRIGADE OF GURKHAS

Two Kukris pointing upwards the blades crossed in saltire their cutting edges outwards

Comprising	The Royal Gurkha Rifles (2 Regular Battalions, 1st and 2nd) The Queen's Gurkha Engineers The Queen's Gurkha Signals The Queen's Own Gurkha Logistic Regiment The Band of The Brigade of Gurkhas Gurkha Staff and Personnel Support Company (GSPS)
Brigade Headquarters	Headquarters The Brigade of Gurkhas Robertson House (FASC), RMA Sandhurst, Camberley, Surrey, GU15 4PQ
Colonel Commandant	Lt Gen Nicholas W A Pope *CBE* 010916

Brigade March

Quick March .... Yo Nepali

Alliances

Canadian Armed Forces	The Queen's Own Rifles of Canada
Australian Military Forces	The Royal Australian Regiment
The New Zealand Army	2nd/1st Battalion, The Royal New Zealand Infantry Regiment
Brunei Armed Forces	The Royal Brunei Land Forces

The origins of amalgamated Regiments now included in the Brigade of Gurkhas are as follows:

THE ROYAL GURKHA RIFLES

On 1 July 1994

The 2nd King Edward VII's Own Gurkha Rifles (The Sirmoor Rifles)

The 6th Queen Elizabeth's Own Gurkha Rifles

The 7th Duke of Edinburgh's Own Gurkha Rifles and

The 10th Princess Mary's Own Gurkha Rifles amalgamated to form:

The Royal Gurkha Rifles

THE QUEEN'S OWN GURKA LOGISTIC REGIMENT

On July 2001

The Queen's Own Gurkha Transport Regiment was redesignated:

The Queen's Own Gurkha Logistic Regiment

On 30 Jun 2011

The Gurkha Staff and Personnel Services

THE ROYAL GURKHA RIFLES

Two Kukris pointing upwards, the blades crossed left over right, cutting edges outwards, ensigned with a crown, all in silver

Authorised to carry the Queen's Truncheon granted for distinguished Service at Delhi in 1857

Amboor, Carnatic, Mysore, Assaye, Ava, Bhurtpore, Aliwal, Sobraon, Delhi 1857, Kabul 1879, Kandahar 1880, Afghanistan 1878-80, Burma 1885-87, Tirah, Punjab Frontier.

The Great War: **La Bassee 1914, Festubert 1914-15, Givenchy 1914, Neuve Chapelle, Aubers, Loos,** France and Flanders 1914-15, **Helles, Krithia, Suvla, Sari Bair, Gallipoli 1915, Suez Canal, Megiddo, Egypt 1915-16, Sharon, Palestine 1918,** Shaiba, **Kut al Amara 1915,17, Ctesiphon, Defence of Kut al Amara, Tigris 1916, Baghdad, Khan Baghdadi, Sharqat, Mesopotamia 1915-18, Persia 1918, North West Frontier India 1915,** Baluchistan 1918.

Afghanistan 1919

The Second World War: Iraq 1941, Dei res Zor, Syria 1941, **Tobruk 1942, El Alamein,** Mareth, **Akarit,** Djebel el Meida, Enfidaville, **Tunis,** North Africa 1942-43, **Cassino I,** Monastery Hill, Pian di Maggio, Campriano, **Poggio Del Grillo, Gothic Line, Tavoleto, Coriano,** Poggio San Giovanni, Montebello-Scorticata Ridge, **Santarcangelo,** Monte Reggiano, **Monte Chicco,** Lamone Crossing, Senio Floodbank, **Bologna,** Sillaro Crossing, **Medicina,** Gaiana Crossing, **Italy 1944-45,** Greece 1944-45, North Malaya, **Jitra,** Central Malaya, Kampar, **Slim River,** Johore, Singapore Island, Malaya 1941-42, **Sittang 1942, 1945,** Pegu 1942, 1945, **Kyaukse 1942, 1945,** Monywa 1942, Shwegyin, **North Arakan, Imphal, Tuitum,** Tamu Road, Shenam Pass, Litan, **Bishenpur, Tengnoupal,** Shwebo, **Kyaukmyaung Bridgehead, Mandalay, Myinmu Bridgehead, Fort Dufferin,** Maymo, **Meiktila,** Capture of Meiktila, Defence of Meiktila, **Irrawaddy,** Magwe, **Rangoon Road,** Pyabwe, Toungoo, Point 1433, Arakan Beaches, Myebon, Tamandu, Chindits 1943, 1945, Burma 1942-45.

Falkland Islands 1982

Regimental Marches

Quick March .... Bravest of the Brave
Double March .... The Keel Row
Slow March.. (Band) God Bless The Prince of Wales
Slow March.. (Pipes) The Garb of Old Gaul

Affiliated Regiments

The King's Royal Hussars
The Royal Regiment of Scotland
The Rifles

Agents... Holt's Branch, Royal Bank of Scotland plc, Lawrie House, Victoria Road, Farnborough, Hants, GU14 7NR
Regimental Headquarters...................... Headquarters The Brigade of Gurkhas, Robertson House (FASC), RMA Sandhurst, Camberley, Surrey GU15 4PQ
(Email: GurkhasBde-RegtSec@mod.uk)

Colonel in Chief.................................... *HRH The Prince of* Wales *KG KT GCB OM AK QSO ADC(P)*
Colonel of the Regiment......................... Brig Gerald M Strickland *DSO MBE*..010216
Regimental Secretary............................. Maj (Retd) B McKay *MBE*

Lieutenant Colonels		*Majors*			
				Gurung R	310714
Birch JNB	300611	Anderson RT	310714	Hellier AMS	310709
Crowe CNA	300614	Angdembe G	310715	Houlton-Hart PA	120209
Davies JP *MBE*	300613	Aucott NJ	310708	James MJ	310710
Forbes AWA	300610	Bairsto CPA	310715	Jeffcoat JAE	310714
Jones AG	300610	Birkbeck BG	310711	Lloyd NR	310713
Marcandonatos SC	300615	Boryer CR *MBE*	310706	Mathers ARC	310712
Murray JC *RGR*	300614	Burton SS	310709	Mohara M	310712
O'Keeffe GM	300606	Chaganis G	310709	Morford RE *MEng*	310715
Reedman MH	300612	Conroy CPL	310709	Oldfield EP	310712
Rex DM *MVO*	300612	Gurung P	310714	Pack DT *MBE*	310709
Robinson DJ	300612	Gurung P	310715	Pun C	310713

Pun R	310712
Rana Y	010404
Roberts LM	310709
Tamang H	310714
Thapa C *MVO*	310712
Todd AP	310710

Captains

Armstrong JK	130214
Arney JE	130611
Badgami R	010713
Brown AS	130611
Buckley JW	090211
Burrows BC	070614
Chungbang J	240610
Connolly AC	010914
Cork BA	130713
Devall J	161013
Dhenga G	050711
Dura R	020415
England JJ *MMath*	130214
Evans RCE	120612
Ghale D	010913
Genillard AE	140213
Gurung B	170714
Gurung D	210708
Gurung D	010709
Gurung G	280613
Gurung K	200611
Gurung L	130711
Gurung M	311010
Gurung M	020412
Gurung P	020415
Kerung B	020415
Khatri Chhetri D	170611
Latham TEB	170614
Lawson JA	140213
Limbu K *MC*	170611
Limbu S	070909
Limbu T	140709
Locksam K	030615
Meadows ST	121010
Nightingale SR	130214
Norfield BE	120612
Phagami M	020412
Plumley WA	170614
Pun J	020412
Pun K	160614
Rai B	110412
Rai B	020415
Rai D	020412
Rai G	020413
Rai L	100814
Rai M	020412
Rai M	180609
Rai R	220908
Rai R	170611
Rai S	020414
Reardon MB	170614
Roberts RI	130611
Rose A	130214
Roylance RWA	141009
Russell CEF	080212
Schroeder CJ	141014
Thapa S *MVO*	300608
Withey ER	121010

Lieutenants

Addison-Black MQ	100813
Barney MF	090815
Boote CR	141214
Cassini RA	141214
Christy JP	120415
Collins CLJ	110813
Diamond CF	151213
Gardner-Clarke HH	110813
Gurung S	120415
Hunter TWC	090815
Jones CR	130414
Lambert POM	140413
Louw WA	141214
Millar JA	130414
Patrick WJD	100813
Reeve WP	090815

2nd Lieutenants

Adamson JG	110415
Carter DR	080815
Dick JR	110415
Gardner TP	080815
Goldfinger OCH	110415
Sears S	121215
Smith LP	110415

THE QUEEN'S GURKHA ENGINEERS

Two kukris points upwards the blades crossed in saltire, their cutting edge outwards, surmounted by the Royal Engineers' grenade, over the handles a scroll with the motto UBIQUE. The whole is surrounded by a wreath of laurel surmounted by a Queen's crown issuant thereon from the wreath a scroll; THE QUEEN'S GURKHA ENGINEERS

Regimental Marches

Quick March(Pipes) .... Far O'er the Sea
Quick March (Band) .... Wings

Regimental Headquarters .... RHQ QGE, 36 Engineer Regiment, Invicta Park Barracks, Maidstone, Kent ME14 2NA
(Tel: 01622 767 231 Mil: 94663 3231 Email: 36ENGR-RHQ-GM@MOD.UK)

Affiliated Corps

The Corps of Royal Engineers

Affiliated Colonel in Chief .... HER MAJESTY THE QUEEN
Colonel .... Maj Gen T R Urch *CBE (until 061016)* 311013
Maj Gen Richard Wardlaw *OBE (from 021016)*

Gurkha Major .... Maj B B Bhandari *MVO*

Majors		*Captains*			
Ghale BB	310713	Bhandari B	130608	Gurung M	110909
Gurung D *MVO*	310712	Gurung A	160410	Kc D	160410
Gurung E	310709	Gurung B	100415	Khapung Limbu K	270810
		Gurung G	270412	Rai B	080411
		Gurung K	220515	Rana G	190615
				Tamang P	080411

THE QUEEN'S GURKHA SIGNALS

Two Kukris point upwards, the handles crossed in saltire, the cutting edges of the blades inwards, between the blades the figure of Mercury, holding a Caduceus in the left hand, on a globe, the latter supported by a scroll bearing the motto "CERTA CITO" and below by nine laurel leaves all in silver, the whole surmounted by Saint Edward's Crown

Regimental Marches

Quick March .... Scotland The Brave

Regimental Headquarters .... 30 Signal Regiment, Gamecock Barrack, Bramcote, Nuneaton, Warwickshire, CV11 6QN

Affiliated Corps

Royal Corps of Signals

Affiliated Regiment

32 Signal Regiment (Volunteers)

Affiliated Colonel-in-Chief.................... *HRH The Princess Royal KG KT GCVO QSO*
Colonel.. Brig Jon J Cole *OBE* 011215

Lieutenant Colonels

Rana Y	200915

Majors

Ale P	310712
Bhandari N MVO	310711
Gurung B	310710
Gurung D MVO	310707
Gurung G	310714
Gurung L	310715
Gurung P	310713
Khamcha T	310710
Pun OP	310714

Captains

Garbuja Pun N	300312
Gurung A	011007
Gurung A	250409
Gurung K	160614
Gurung R	260413
Gurung S	260210
Gurung S	300312
Khokaja Pun D	160710
Pun H	011007
Pun K	170415
Pun V	260413
Rai D	170415
Rai K	011007
Shrestha A	040414
Shrestha B	040610
Shrestha R	030408

THE QUEEN'S OWN GURKHA LOGISTIC REGIMENT

An eight-pointed star in silver, thereon a scroll inscribed "QUEEN'S OWN GURKHA LOGISTIC REGIMENT", issuant therefrom a wreath of laurel all in gold, over all two kukris in saltire, the blades silver, the hilts gold, ensigned with the Royal Cypher in gold.

Regimental Marches

Quick March .... Wait for the Wagon

Regimental Headquarters .... Gale Barracks, Alison Road, Aldershot, Hampshire, GU11 2BX

Affiliated Corps
The Royal Logistic Corps

Affiliated Colonel-in-Chief..................... *HRH The Princess Royal KG KT GCVO QSO*
Colonel... Maj Gen Angus S J Fay 010109

Majors		*Captains*			
Ale D	310713	Chhantyal R	210610	Rai R	160614
Gurung K *MVO*	310714	Gurung D	050115	Shahi B	010414
Khatri CB	310715	Gurung G	040411	Tamang B	010408
		Gurung R	011007	Tamang G	040411
		Kala N	120710	Tamang I	010908
		Rai D	010415	Tamang P	011007
		Rai H	010908		

THE BAND OF THE BRIGADE OF GURKHAS

Band Headquarters................................ Building 9, Sir John Moore Barracks, Shorncliffe, FOLKSTONE, Kent CT20 3HJ
Telephone: 01303 225790 / 225212 Fax: 01303 225791
Email: BandGURKHA-AdminOffr@mod.uk

Director of Music................................... Maj P W Norley
Assistant Director of Music.................... Capt B D Gurung 150914

Captain	
Gurung B	150914

THE GURKHA STAFF AND PERSONNEL SUPPORT COMPANY (GSPS)

Crossed kukris surmounted by the Royal Crest superimposed on a laurel wreath and resting on a scroll inscribed "ANIMO ET FIDE" ***(with resolution and fidelity).***

(Formed on 30 Jun 2011)

GSPS Company Headquarters............... Headquarters of the Brigade of Gukhas,
FASC, RMAS, Camberley, GU15 4PQ
Telephone: 01412 242578 Email:
Website: http://www.army.mod.uk/GSPS

Colonel (Informal Appointment)............Col Andrew D Griffiths *OBE*...251116
Commanding Officer..............................Maj N K Gurung

Majors		*Captains*			
Rai SK	310715	Gurung A	030815	Hamal J	010612
Sherchan B	250407	Gurung N	020409	Rana A	020409
				Rana K	020409

THE RIFLES

The bugle horn surmounted by The Crown

Comprising.. 1st Battalion The Rifles (1st Battalion Devonshire and Dorset Light Infantry)
2nd Battalion The Rifles (1st Battalion The Royal Green Jackets)
3rd Battalion The Rifles (2nd Battalion The Light Infantry)
4th Battalion The Rifles (2nd Battalion The Royal Green Jackets)
5th Battalion The Rifles (1st Battalion The Light Infantry)
6th Battalion The Rifles (Army Reserve)
7th Battalion The Rifles (Army Reserve)

Regimental Headquarters .... Short Block, Peninsula Barracks, Romsey Rd, Winchester, Hants SO23 8TS
(Tel: 01962 828527 Email: rhq@the-rifles.co.uk)

Colonel in Chief.. FM *HRH The Prince Philip Duke of* Edinburgh *KG KT OM GBE ONZ QSO AK GCL CC CMM ADC(P)* 010207

Royal Colonels .... FM *HRH The Duke of* Kent *KG GCMG GCVO ADC(P)* 010207
HRH The Earl of Wessex *KG GCVO ADC(P)*....................................010207
HRH Princess Alexandra *The Hon Lady* Ogilvy *KG GCVO*...............010207
HRH The Duchess of Cornwall *GCVO* 010207
HRH The Countess of Wessex *GCVO*..010207
HRH The Duke of Gloucester *KG GCVO* 010207
HRH The Duchess of Gloucester *GCVO*..010207

Colonel Commandant .... Gen *Sir* Nicholas Carter *KCB CBE DSO ADC Gen* 010213

Assistant Colonel Commandant............................. Lt Gen T P Evans *CB CBE DSO (until 311016)* 010614
Lt Gen Tim B Radford *CB DSO OBE (from 311016)*

Deputy Colonels... Maj Gen Rupert T H Jones *CBE*..010614
Maj Gen Nick Welch *OBE*...150509
Brig Robert J Thomson *CBE DSO*...011114

THE RIFLES

On 1 February 2007

The Devonshire and Dorset Light Infantry

The Light Infantry

The Royal Gloucestershire, Berkshire and Wiltshire Light Infantry and

The Royal Green Jackets amalgamated to form:

The Rifles

Gibraltar, Dettingen, Plassey, Minden, Quebec, Martinique, Marabout, Peninsula, Waterloo, Afghanistan, Jellalabad, Ferozeshah, Delhi, Lucknow, New Zealand, Pekin, South Africa, Inkerman

The Great War: Nonne Boschen, Ypres, Somme, Vittorio Veneto, Megiddo

The Second World War: Calais, El Alamein, Kohima, Pegasus Bridge, Normandy, Italy 1943-45, Anzio

Imjin, Korea, Iraq 2003

Regimental Marches

Quick March ....Mechanised Infantry
Slow March ....Old Salamanca

Alliances

Canadian Armed Forces......................... The Royal Canadian Regiment
Princess Patricia's Canadian Light Infantry
The Queen's Own Rifles of Canada
Australian Military Forces..................... The Royal New South Wales Regiment
South African Army .... The Cape Town Rifles
Pakistan Army.. 1st Battalion, The Sind Regiment

Lieutenant Colonels

Baker MR	300615
Balls PJA *OBE*	300606
Bedford SER	300606
Bellamy ND	300613
Bewick TH *OBE*	300611
Bryant JEF	300613
Bull SH	300611
Davies SM	300615
Denning DJ	300612
Edkins MJ *MBE*	300605
Faux JA	300615
Field DCE	300607
Foster-Brown ME	300613
Gray SD	300604
Grist CED *MBE*	300613
Harper TA *MBE*	300613
Hartley JI	300610
Holmes NR *MBE*	300611
Hudson RJ	300608
Kitson JF	300612
Lane S	300612
McDade GA	300614
Moodie IRJ	300615
Ovey RJD	300608
Ridland A	300615
Smith RP *BSc*	300614
Tomkins BJH	300611
Turner EGE *OBE*	300607
Wakelin JC	300612
Wilson MCP *MBE*	300613

Majors

Anning JE	310708
Baines PW *MBE*	310709
Basset RWF	310710
Bates JE	310709
Boardman ANL	310711
Braithwaite JRO	150405
Bray PRG	310709
Brown DB	310715
Bryan REG	310708
Buchan-Smith KMA	310714
Burkill SD	310715
Cairncross TAW	240513
Campbell GI	310715
Carson EJM	310710
Casson BE *MBE*	310712
Cates SEA	310709
Cave RJD	310713
Child AJ	310709
Clayden MWM	310714
Coltart HJ	310714
Cousen JS	310709
Coward BIH	310715
Cutler RP *MBE*	040405
Dadd CD	310712
Davies GN	310708
Donovan AM	310711
Eden WL	310706
Edwards JAB	310714
Endersby MC	310715
Field AN *MBE*	310705
Forde MH *BSc*	310708
Foster Vander Elst MDJ	310715
Gayner JRH *MBE*	310707
Godfrey DR	310711
Greenman SM	310713
Hadfield JA *MBE*	310711
Hammond ESC	310715
Hastings ID	310706
Helsby MC	310712
Hignett WJA *MC*	310715
Hosegood MD	310712
Humphries R	060206
Husband AJ	310708
Jeffrey R	310713
Jellard HP	310708
Jones RT	010207
King CL	310715
King NCY	310706
Lamb CG *MBE*	040405
Mabb JD	310712
Macklin DR	310713
McBurney CA *MBE*	310715
Melhorn MU	310710
Melia BR *MBE*	310710
Mills JPG	310713
Muller MS	310715
Murch DR *MBE*	310714
Oliver CM *MBE MSc*	310711
O'Neil Roe RHD	310702
Pauncefort GTG	310714
Pearce AD	310710
Peltor WS	310711
Pemberton A *MBE*	310715
Pengilly SC	310713
Price ABL	310712
Redon TRJ	310715
Rowley RD	310708
Salt BM	310711
Sawyer GT *MBE*	310709
Sayer RA	310714
Scrase WG	310709
Streatfeild RC	310711
Teale NA	310706
Thatcher RS	310714
Watson N	310715
Wells WJD	310710
West AJ	310714
White JM	310708
White NF	310711
White RC	310715
Whitehouse ME	310712
Williams IR	310715
Wills MC	310711
Wilson ACD	310711
Wilson JAB	310715
Wood AA	310708

Captains

Atherden RTM	090211
Axford J	130214
Bailey WH	170614
Barrett CJ	170614
Barton PA	130214
Bewley JCC	030806
Boddam-Whetham AJ	161013
Bowerman V	050415
Boxall PJ	141009
Brown TJC	120612
Brown TM	180613
Case G	120413
Cripps MA	121010
Crossley GH	151209
Cullen IR	140415
Daniell PFA	140213
Darby MM	070610
Davies CA	090211
Dawnay NM	140415
Deakin DM	
Dickson SN	020415
Dishman AG	140415
Dunkeld IAN	161013

Eamer SF	020414
Egan PM	101011
Elliott MG	110210
Evans DO	070413
Fellows RG	090211
Fitz-Gerald TLP	180613
Flood CS	180613
Foster JEH	110815
Foster TC	110815
Foulkes-Arnold TH	130611
Francis P	070610
Francis TD	080313
Gage WP	140415
Gibson C	070610
Graves KP	090211
Hamblin TP	180613
Hancock JT	161013
Harris SJ *MBE*	020409
Harrison RW	070610
Hartley JEC	311213
Heal JWA	130214
Hedges NJ	020511
Hogg AL	020415
Howe NG	130214
Hunt RJ	140409
Hursey GPJ	080212
Hyde P *MC*	020415
James CER	130814
Jarvis TEC	130611
Jenner HJ	140415
Jones R	170614
Keating PFB	110815
Kennon SJA	140213
Kuss AD	140414
Legge TJ	140415
Lennon SG	080615
Lindley N	020411
Little OCS	101011
Lower CMB	090211
Maxwell CNH *QCB*	311212
McCarthy JEM	110210
McFarlane MG	310712
Mears VP	060409
Melia WNC	121010
Morley AC	080212
Murray JD	120612
North P	060715
Norton AM	130214
Pastouna JDA	121010
Pearson DR	170614
Perry AIG	130214
Poulter RA	050710
Raw A	270411
Reaney JW	161013
Redgwell DA	240415
Richardson EH	080212
Roberts LR	150411
Robinson GA	010611
Ross TM	101011
Rowntree JL	180613
Sawers HML	110815
Sawers RJO	080212
Sharp D	010611
Sharpe SA	130214
Simpson S	260414
Stevens CJ	150615
Stirling DJB	260914
Strutt MJ	060812
Sutherland JGO	140213
Thompson SN *MC*	040414
Thomson HSC	180613
Tisbury SJ	080413
Walker GJ	170614
Wallace RS	130214
Watts SP	020415
Whiskerd I	110815
White A	010613
Wilkinson BJ	101011
Wilson SAE	140415
Winstanley CER	090211
Wootton OM	130214
Yates BA	130214

Lieutenants

Ara KJ	140415
Ashurst CT	100814
Baggott La Velle RAJ	110813
Barron ALI	110813
Bossom TDA	130414
Brown JF	110813
Cantrell JE	130414
Carrow AE	140415
Cathcart CR	120415
Coltart FW	100814
Coombs DR	100814
Eaves JR	120415
Flye N	120415
Geddes JF	110813
Hewetson GW	110813
Jamison TI	141214
Jelly T	120415
Jenkinson AR	130414
Joyce TG	100814
Leccia JM	141214
Lister JA	110813
Makepeace RAA	100814
Marshall TW	130414
Massey NS	100814
McColl JAJ	151213
Miers JW	141214
O'Connor MJ	100814
Prince RMG	091114
Reed SJG	141214
Reynolds NJ	120415
Reynolds TS	100814
Swindells SFC	120415
Watson DJF	100814

2nd Lieutenants

Aitken ARC	131214
Baldwin JTI	121215
Bishop BJ	110415
Blackmore TA	080815
Brash TR	121215
Burton SJR	090814
Court TH	080815
Creed AWN	090814
Davis CTJ	121215
Dryburgh MA	121215
D'Souza F	110415
Evans RAL	131214
Fellows JWB	090814
Gillard GDE	080815
Gillies A	131214
Groombridge WR	090814
Henriques PJQ	110415
Jackson WFP	131214
Lane TJO	121215
Lee JEJ	110415
Loxton N	110415
Macbeth M	121215
Maddan JH	090814
Miller AR	090814
Murphy NJ	080815

Nattriss M	131214
Newman TA	080815
O’Brien ASR	110415
Poole DR	080815
Raymond AJ	080815
Robertson JC	080815
Scully LJ	131214
Smart RG	131214
Topham ME	090814
Udy BJD	121215
Walker ETE	131214

THE ROYAL GIBRALTAR REGIMENT

(Formerly The Gibraltar Defence Force 1939-1958 & The Gibraltar Regiment 1959 - 1999)

A Shield bearing the Castle and Key of Gibraltar superimposed on a decorative backing depicting the blue sky of The Mediterranean together with its sea and a three part scroll below inscribed with the motto NULLI EXPUGNABILIS HOSTI, the whole surmounted by The Crown

Commissions & Warrants

Granted by the Governor of Gibraltar on behalf of Her Majesty the Queen

Regimental Office ....Royal Gibraltar Regiment HQ, Devils Tower Camp, Gibraltar, BFPO 52
(Tel: 200 (5) 3056 Fax: 200 (5) 3613 Email: GIB-RG-CCLK@mod.uk
Website: www.royalgibraltarregiment.gi)

Commander in Chief..The Governor of Gibraltar
Commanding Officer..Lt Col Ivor Lopez
Honorary Colonel..The *Hon* Lt Col (Retd) Ernest M Britto *OBE TD*..................................310514

Authorised Abbreviation RG

Alliances

The Royal Anglian Regiment - 13 August 1968
The Royal Regiment of Artillery - 16 October 1973
Corps of Royal Engineers - 22 June 1996
The Royal Irish Regiment - 03 July 1999

Affiliations

HMS Calpe - 24 September 1988
19 (Gibraltar 1779 - 83) Battery Royal Artillery
21 (Gibraltar 1779 - 83) Battery Royal Artillery

Civic Honours

The Freedom of the City of Gibraltar - 25 September 1971

SPECIAL FORCES

22 SPECIAL AIR SERVICE REGIMENT (SAS)

A representation of King Arthur's Sword Excalibur surmounted by flames striking downwards woven on a shield with the motto WHO DARES WINS

The Second World War: North-West Europe 1944-45, Tobruk 1941, Benghazi Raid, North Africa 1940-43, Landing in Sicily, Sicily 1943, Termoli, Valli Di Comacchio, Italy 1943-45, Greece 1944-45, Adriatic, Middle East 1943-44

Falkland Islands 1982, Gulf 1991, Western Iraq

Regimental March

Quick March .... Marche des Parachutistes Belges
Slow March.. Lilli Marlene

Regimental Contact................................(Email: info@sasregiment.org.uk Website: www.sasregiment.org.uk)

Alliances

Australian Military Forces..................... Special Air Service Regiment
New Zealand Army .... 1st New Zealand Special Air Service Group

Colonel Commandant .... N/D
Commander.. N/D

SPECIAL RECONNAISSANCE REGIMENT (SRR)

(formed April 2005)

Colonel in Chief.....................................*HRH The Duchess of* Cornwall *GCVO*
Commander.. N/D

SPECIAL FORCES SUPPORT GROUP (SFSP)

(formed 3rd April 2006)

Commander.. N/D

COMBAT SUPPORT ARMS

Royal Regiment of Artillery

Corps of Royal Engineers

Royal Corps of Signals

Army Air Corps

Intelligence Corps

COMBAT SUPPORT SERVICES

Royal Army Chaplains Department

Royal Logistic Corps

Royal Army Medical Corps

Corps of Royal Electrical and Mechanical Engineers

Adjutant General's Corps

Royal Army Veterinary Corps

Small Arms School Corps

Royal Army Dental Corps

Royal Army Physical Training Corps

General Service Corps

Queen Alexandra's Royal Army Nursing Corps

Corps of Army Music

ROYAL REGIMENT OF ARTILLERY

A gun between two scrolls, that above inscribed UBIQUE, that beneath inscribed QUO FAS ET GLORIA DUCUNT; the whole ensigned with The Crown all gold

Regimental Marches

Quick Marches....................................... The Royal Artillery Quick March
Slow Marches... The Royal Artillery Slow March

Agents .... Lloyds Bank plc Cox's & King's Branch
Regimental Headquarters .... Artillery House, Royal Artillery Barracks, Larkhill, Salisbury, Wiltshire SP4 8QT
(Tel: 01980 845528 Fax: 01980 845210 Email: RARHQ-RegtSec@mod.uk)

Alliances

Canadian Armed Forces......................... Royal Regiment of Canadian Artillery
Australian Military Forces..................... Royal Regiment of Australian Artillery
New Zealand Army................................ Royal Regiment of New Zealand Artillery
South African Army............................... South African Artillery
Fiji .... Republic of Fiji Military Forces
Indian Army... Regiment of Artillery
Pakistan Army....................................... Regiment of Artillery
Sri Lanka Army..................................... Sri Lanka Artillery
Malaysian Army.................................... Royal Artillery Regiment
Singapore Army.................................... Singapore Artillery
Malta .... Armed Forces Of Malta
Gibraltar... The Royal Gibraltar Regiment

Captain-General.................................... HER MAJESTY THE QUEEN
Master Gunner, St James's Park........... Gen (Retd) *Sir* Timothy Granville-Chapman *GBE KCB* 210708
Colonels Commandant .... Gen (Retd) *Sir* Timothy Granville-Chapman *GBE KCB*.....................................140408
Lt Gen *Sir* Andrew R Gregory *KGB CB*...010312
Maj Gen Nick D Ashmore *OBE* 010312
Maj Gen (Retd) B Brealey *CB (until 010317)*...010312
Maj Gen Neil Marshall *OBE (from 010317)*
Maj Gen D M Cullen *CB OBE (until 010317)* 010312
Maj Gen (Retd) Rob P M Weighill *CBE (from 010317)*
Maj Gen (Retd) N H Eeles *CBE (until 010317)* 010312
Brig Iain G Harrison *OBE (from 010317)*
Maj Gen Julian R Free *CBE*..010412
Lt Gen Richard E Nugee *CVO CBE* 080612
Col Barry W Jenkins...010317

Lieutenant Colonels

Alston RN *MBE*	300615
Andrew NP	300614
Armitage PA *MBE*	300610
Badman SJG	300608
Baker R *OBE*	300611
Barker CH	300609
Bates PR	300611
Bengtsson EJ *MBE*	300613
Birch MJ	300613
Bolam W	300613
Bolton RB	300607
Bowman KP	300615
Bridge EL	300614
Broadfoot C *MBE MBA*	230514
Brockman EGS	300608
Canning SJ	300609
Carter EHJ	300609
Carter RJ	300611
Catto WJ	300612
Christopher RJ *MBE*	300612
Clarke DS *MBE*	300614
Cole NJ *MBE*	290813
Colyer SPD	300612
Comber IM	300613
Cook JP	300612
Cotterill JWS	300613
Cresswell JP	300613
Crisp MJ	300607
Crisp SG	040515
Day CG	300611
Dunk SP	300614
Dupuy PM *MBE*	300614
Edwards MKG	300614
Fitchett KD *MBE*	111214
Forster RA	300614
Foy RD	300615
Freeborn AM	300610
Gammon MCB	300606
Gee NM	300615
Gent C	300615
Grant SG	300614
Gunning CP	300606
Haines SR	300608
Harden TP	300607

Harris KR	300613
Harrison P *MBE*	300610
Hart RP	300613
Hercus DJ	300612
Hewitt CA	300613
Hill JD	300614
Hodgson JF	300611
Hodkinson AF *MBE*	300613
Hunt C	010514
Huthwaite CS	300609
Ingham BMD *MBE*	300615
Johnson AR	300615
Jones G	090714
Kernohan DA	300607
Kettler CCR	300613
Lawrence MA	010115
Lee AP	300610
Long SR	300607
Mackay DJ MA	300607
Malec GH	300613
Mardlin JE	300614
Martin M *MBE*	150216
Mawdsley JCW *MBE*	300615
McCaffrey PS	300615
McCarthy MP	070113
Murphy MJP	300612
Napier GR	300604
Neylan AJM	300615
Oates AG	300613
O'Gorman SJ	300603
Oldroyd JEK	300611
Osmond GIP	300608
Palmer C	300610
Palmer JGK	300615
Parkinson CEA *MBE*	300612
Parrott JM	300614
Peek NM *MBE*	300605
Penniall DP *MBE BEM*	190915
Phillips AB	300613
Phillips JIR	300608
Philpott AH	300614
Purvis CA	210313
Rafferty KP	300615
Rosier SD	300610
Sawyer NT	300610
Searle JMD	300615
Sempala-Ntege NM	300612
Servaes MJP	300607
Sharpe JEG MBE	300611
Shepheard-Walwyn P *MBE*	300609
Shepherd RCG	300610
Shepherd SJ *MBE*	300615
Sherrard DW	300612
Simpson CL	300614
Southby AM	300615
Spence NA	300613
Storey DN	300614
Stroud-Turp JR	300603
Taylor G	300614
Thompson PRC	300609
Thornton TG	120216
Tolley PK	291015
Tombleson P *OBE*	300607
Tyson EJ	300604
Ventham TJ *BA (Hons) PG CertBusAd*	300615
Vigne JEH	300611
Warner CR	300608
Welch EJ *OBE*	300608
Welsh AC	300606
Wentworth MD	300602
West CR	300612
West SR	300603
Whatmough GJ *RA MA*	300609
White MP	300613
Whiting FWG	300612
Whittle MHG *MBE*	300614
Wilkinson HJP	300611
Williams A	091015
Wood MW *MBE*	300614
Wood TM *BA (Hons)*	300604
Woods PD	300615
Wright PHD	300606

Majors

Abayomi S	310715
Ackroyd P	310710
Acton BJP	310715
Ainsworth CM	310715
Alder JJ	310712
Alderson EJ	310714
Allen JE	310711
Anderson CPM	310706
Andrews SP	310711
Arnold TG	310715
Axcell JP	310711
Bailey WGR	310714
Baker JA	310709
Baldwinson BM	310712
Barrett KR	310715
Beaumont P	310707
Beech MJ	310714
Beechey JV	310715
Belam DMC *MBE*	310713
Bell S	310714
Bersin JMJ	310712
Billups CW	310714
Birch MJ	310707
Bleakley VE	280412
Botterill EBJ	310704
Brett MW *MBE*	310703
Briant MI	310707
Briggs SI	310710
Brigstocke DMO	310712
Britton PNB *MC*	310710
Brocklesby ME	310710
Brooks NCR	310711
Brotherton AC	310708
Brumwell AA	300901
Budd NJM *MBE*	310709
Bulmer CM	310715
Burdick NW	310715
Burnett JS	310714
Burwell OD	310715
Butt DA	310710
Buxton JH	310709
Byrne CDM	310704
Cameron AC	310707
Cammack KC	310713
Campbell DJ	310712
Candy OAR *BSc (Hons) MSc*	310713
Carter AJ	310714
Chalker SC	310714
Chapman DJ	310709
Chapman LR	150814
Cheesman JA	310705
Coe JAC	310715
Constantine IF	310715
Cook KM	310715
Cooney DJ	310714
Cornes EN	310706
Coton CL	310708
Coulson IT	310710
Craven JFA	310706

Crawford RH	310708	Hakes CJ	310708	Kennedy CC *BSc*	310713
Crookes BDF	310708	Hall MP	310715	Kenny N	310715
Cross N	310705	Harding JAH	310704	Kerbey AJ	310709
Culver SCD *MBE*	310703	Harmer RC	310709	Kerr C	310714
Davie OM	310712	Harris SE	310711	Kerry-Williams CP	180203
Davies D	310715	Harris SJ	310715	Kirby R	310715
Davies TMD	310707	Harrop IJ	310707	Kirby SRJ	010197
Day CB	310702	Harvey AE *MBE*	310713	Knight O	310710
Deakin SNJ	310714	Harvey S	310712	Lackey AJ	310712
Deakin VE	310711	Haskell TDE	310714	Laing RA	310715
Deakin-Main KJ	310713	Haws DJ	300999	Lamb SC *MBE*	310706
Deane RJ	310715	Hay RJ	310711	Lane CM	310709
Diamond JFF	310708	Hay SI	310711	Layden AJ	310705
Dobson JP *MEng*	310714	Hayes DL	310714	Lee CRB	310714
Dornan MAA	310706	Heath AL	300901	Leister P	170813
Draper RD	310714	Heckles A	310715	Lenherr DC	310713
Dridge SP	110812	Henderson NDR	310708	Lewis JG	310713
Edward MG	310708	Henry WC	310713	Linsdell JP	310711
Edwards AS	310711	Herbert LJ	310714	Littler PWJ	310715
Ellis JG	310707	Herberts DC	310710	Logan DC	310709
Ellis MR	310709	Hewett KJ	310709	Lovick C	300901
Entwisle MIJ	310709	Hewitt CSH	310714	Luck JHA	310713
Evans LG *MVO*	310709	Higgins MR	310715	Luker TE	310704
Eze KLA	310715	Hill JRP	310715	Lynn TP	310709
Farrell PJ	310713	Hinds SS	310703	Lynskey MJ	310702
Felton AFG	310713	Hocking RM	310714	MacPherson AR	310713
Felton AJ	310713	Holland TC	310708	Magee MJK	310715
Ferguson DW	310713	Hollinrake RF	310703	Magill PD	310715
Fewster AM	310715	Hollis A	040513	Mann FD	310707
Field J	310709	Hooper JM *LLB (Hons)*	310712	Masheder CD	310715
Fittock SP	310715	Horne PD	310712	Mason TN	310703
Fletcher MD	310713	Hough A	310713	Masters DR	310707
Forrester-Addie DJ	310714	Howe SJ	310712	McCaffery JM	310710
Foss-Smith TP	310708	Hunt NDA	310715	McCallum RO	310711
Fox KM	310706	Hutchinson RAM	310714	McCauley SP *BSc (Hons)*	310703
Fox S	310714	Iddon TJ *MBE*	310712	McCleery JW	310704
Fraser CL	310711	Ireland AR	310712	McDermott A	310712
Gamp NJ	310709	Jackson A	310711	McMahon AJ	310713
Ganuszko PJ	310711	Jacques PJ *MBE*	040513	McNiff BS	310713
Gentles PL	310713	Jagger WHG	310708	McPherson PR	310715
George WB	310715	Jamieson TR	310715	Meagor AS	310710
Gillen JN	300901	Jenkins MA	310715	Mellor NM	310710
Glendenning DC	310710	Jenner GEJ *BSc (Hons) MA*	310705	Milton PD *MBE*	310714
Grant NC	310713	Joyce DS	310712	Montgomery GCM	310708
Greenfield AJ	310710	Joyce PD	310709	Mooney PN	300999
Grieve G	310713	Judd DJ	310713	Moore CT	310712
Grimsdell JP	310714	Keir S	310713	Moore JE	310712
Haines RE	310708	Kemp EMC	310705	Morton NI *MBE*	310707

Murray EA	310711
Nelson EM	310709
Newnham RM	310714
Newton CD	310715
Oakes TW	310713
Oates JR *MBE*	310712
O'Halloran CDD	310709
O'Keeffe JA	310713
O'Leary GJ	310707
Orvis RJ	310707
Osman TR	310708
Pack AR *MBE*	310709
Palastanga KV	310713
Palmer TG	310712
Papenfus JR	300997
Parrott JD	010606
Payne RB	310707
Peek K *MBE*	310711
Perris EJ	310709
Phillips KJ	310709
Phillips RDT	310715
Philp KJ	310711
Piggott PA	310712
Pitt AR	310702
Potter JJ	310710
Potter SH	140806
Pritchett JCR	300900
Punter OD	170608
Purser AGC	310714
Pusinelli RT	310715
Quigley PM	310712
Quin EM	310711
Radwell KD	300999
Rawcliffe DR	310715
Reay TV	310712
Reid ASW	310714
Reilly T	310710
Richardson AM	310714
Richardson BL	310707
Rigby MJ *BSc (Hons)*	310708
Riley RHG	310703
Roberts AAC	310715
Roberts AJ *BA (Hons)*	310709
Ronz RA	310714
Ross WJ	310702
Routh CA	231101
Rushmere TPW *QGM*	310712
Rushworth SH	310712

Salt-Forster IA	310713
Sargent MJ	310705
Searle AJ	310711
Sefton VM	310708
Shanklyn EM	310707
Shapland GD	300994
Sharnock DR	310715
Sharp LM	310715
Sharples AJ	310702
Sheldon KA	310707
Shipman GE	310714
Skeggs RA	310711
Skiffington AMV	310712
Smith DK	310707
Smith ER	310708
Smith LJ	310710
Smith MA	300901
Snodgrass PA	310705
Southall JE	310708
Spelling JA	310713
Squires WF	310712
Steel RJ	080710
Stickley MA	310710
Stuart OPL	310713
Sutherland RD	310710
Swan-Ingrey LTY	310710
Swannell AD	310707
Szczerbiuk A	310715
Talbot-King PF	300906
Taylor ALA	310713
Taylor AR	310707
Taylor ET	100510
Taylor RI	190510
Taylor TDK	300900
Thatcher DR	310714
Thomson SR	310709
Tickner DFW *CMgr MCMI MCGI NDipM*	310715
Turner SJ	310714
Turrell LW	310714
Tyler NG	310714
Vincent JD	310713
Vincent JH	310709
Wade RA	310707
Wade TE	310710
Walker DIB	310706
Waller HD	310712
Walsh CNP	300992

Walters JD *MBE*	310709
Wane CM	310715
Ward S	310708
Watson BJ	310711
Watt VA	310710
Way AM	310714
Webber NC *MBE*	310704
Webster DAC	310712
Webster P	310712
Weir-Ansell SD	280412
Westbrook PE	310715
White AB	310711
Whitham RH	250807
Wild CJ	310710
Williams G	310715
Wilman NA *MA BA(Hons)*	300998
Wilson A *MBE*	310710
Wing SC	310715
Wood AW	310705
Wood DG	310715
Wood GM	310703
Wood TA	310714
Woodhams EW	310713
Worley BJ	310715
Worsley VA	310715
Yank DM	310714
Young AP	310708
Young CA	310711
Young CR	310707

Captains

Adamson WF	010214
Allen JD	030414
Allnutt AJ	170614
Anderson RE	130214
Anthony PJ *BSc*	250915
Armitage B	140213
Armstrong PM	280512
Askham SJ	140415
Baileff JE	130214
Bailey EJ	150610
Baker GWJ	171012
Bale JBD	290615
Ball DJ	130611
Barge PJ	170614
Battersby IW	020410
Bayram WPE	130814
Beaton GDS	311213

Beebe MJ	121010
Bell CJ	121010
Bellinger LR	110815
Bennett AJG	130214
Bentley CO	020413
Biddulph AB	121010
Birtwistle AJ	171012
Blakiston C	120612
Blowers AJ	161013
Bociek RP	280414
Bogie EM	161013
Booth AJ	110815
Booth SH	130411
Boutle JJ	160410
Brackley J	130214
Bradley SL	170614
Brady CR	170614
Bramall RM	020414
Brennan KT	070111
Breslin HK	180613
Briers AP	060409
Brimacombe JG	110815
Burdis P	140415
Burnett R	110411
Burns IW	140415
Burton MJ	140213
Butcher BJ	020414
Butler RGW	261113
Button PB	090211
Calcutt A	140213
Campbell SA	080413
Cann AGR	170614
Carr SJ	101011
Chalmers AJ	311212
Chapman HV	120612
Charlton AM	170614
Charlton-Weedy EC	171210
Cheyne NC	130611
Childerley TS	060409
Clark MJN	170614
Clarke ALG	310713
Clarke EF	130611
Clayton AL	311212
Cobham EH	140412
Coffey AJL	310713
Cole AM	140415
Collett DP	130214
Collette LV	140213
Collins GM	020413
Compton PAC	141014
Cook RJA	150510
Corbett RSJ	101011
Cormier J	101011
Couchman DJ	140213
Crawford D	090112
Crosby TWH	140415
Crudge SS	180613
Cunningham LRP	020415
Dadd CJ	170614
Daniels BJ	010415
Davies ML	150713
Davies R	300411
Davis AR	140213
Davis MAC	190510
Denby-Hollis L	161013
Denton ES	161013
Dew DD	180613
Docherty AM	101011
Downing HA	170614
Drenon AJ	151215
Dulson AB	020515
Durant AG	180613
Durling RE	130611
Eachus C	151215
Eames JP	310713
Edens GW	140213
Edwards N	220413
Egan ME	310713
Ellison ME	130611
Felton DW	020414
Fenton AP *BA (Hons)*	020411
Fidler J	110112
Fidler RDB	180314
Finlay AJ	161013
Finlay RGC	130214
Fleming TMK	180613
Fleming WJ	020413
Flood VML	171012
Forsey JS	120612
Forster G	161214
Foster AD	121010
Fouracre SJ	171214
Fox DN	020412
Fry EJ	180613
Futcher JM	140415
Garmory JP	310713
Gascoigne J	050513
Gascoyne DC *MBE*	060409
Gerald AE	140213
Girling SAJ	101011
Glover TP	140213
Goldsmith MRD	311213
Goodall MJ	110210
Gorsuch CW	140415
Gould N	040612
Graham MW	150514
Gray SJ	080513
Grigg GS	020413
Grimsdell RP	130611
Gritton L	200410
Grocock DJ	140213
Guo S *BEng Arch*	171012
Hainsworth DJ	161013
Hall EF	020415
Hallam CM	120612
Hamlet CA	250511
Hardy AA	170614
Hargraves THG	110210
Harpham TM	140415
Hart AD	090109
Hart NSG	151215
Harvard JS	020411
Harvey TG *I Eng*	030407
Hawke SP	010615
Hawkesworth JPT	140415
Hayes MJ	020415
Hayzen-Smith SM	160412
Head JM	171012
Healy NTH	180613
Hellmers BL	180613
Helmrich CA	310713
Hine MJ	130214
Hoggard CW	171012
Hollyoak AC	171012
Hopewell LC *BA (Hons)*	020414
Hopper PV	100406
Hore TS	151215
Hothersall I	020409
Houston AS *BA MA*	161013
Hoyle TAV	140213
Hudson JM	311213
Hughes CJ	170614
Humphrey GW	070408
Hyslop HDG	310713

James SC	161013	McComb BW	110815	Price RHE	310712
Jarrett TE	170614	Medlycott FLS	141009	Prichard TLN	161013
Jee CRA	151215	Mellis CJT	120612	Prout ST	020413
Jeeves PI	020414	Middleton HGV	140213	Pugh DK	140213
Jepp RD	311213	Millar JJA	020116	Quarmby BJ	170614
Johnston BN	180613	Miller DG	090412	Radford NG	020411
Jones DA	120612	Moffitt DW	020414	Ramage AL	311212
Jones HS	121010	Molyneaux CE	090211	Ray KJ	180612
Jones SL	130814	Moodie RG	020413	Rea M RHA	171012
Jones T	090112	Moore LC	170614	Richards AN	100113
Joyce SR	101011	Morris RJ	151215	Richards PK	101011
Jump JA	140412	Mortimer D	020414	Rider JM	040511
Karadia RJ	150612	Mortimer DEJ	010611	Robbins PNB	161013
Kaye RH	180613	Mowbray GA	130611	Robinson AM	151215
Kennedy TP	121010	Mudd NI	020410	Robinson DK	020415
Kirkpatrick LD	121010	Murphy BP	151215	Robinson KM	290610
Lambden JW	140415	Musgrove JR	310713	Robinson LA	110815
Lauwerys TFD	101011	Nash GLM	120612	Roebuck OD	130611
Lavin KA	171214	Navarro JK	140213	Rose TOJ	080212
Leadbitter G	020410	Nelson TMS	060515	Rowland GL	130214
Ledward JC	170614	Newton FHE	170614	Roy JC	140415
Lennox SMB	120811	Newton SM	280515	Rutherford IJV	090211
Lewis MP	161013	Nicol EL	080212	Rydings EG	110815
Lilley BR	110815	O'Grady LM	011213	Sarchet SCX	130611
Litchfield REA *BSc (Hons)*	140213	O'Grady SP	140415	Scammell DN	060409
Litster W	020412	Oie JDB	130415	Scoullar MJ	290410
Lloyd Butler A	190410	Oldfield ME	140415	Searle JTG	300513
Lowes AE	180612	O'Neill AC	161013	Seath DB	140213
Ludlow TW	151215	O'Neill TJ	180613	Sharp NF	141009
MacDonald NG *MBE*	020413	Parker JCS	140415	Shaw MT	170614
MacNeill RT	130214	Parkinson JW	020415	Shears CJ	240510
MacPherson FDC *MA*	141009	Partridge JW	140415	Shellard MJ	110815
Mahoney W	120411	Paterson MJ	140414	Sheridan DE	121010
Male RD	110815	Patt JM	010615	Sheridan EA	151215
Mallett JH	130611	Paulus ND	140515	Shipley PP *MBE*	170912
Manning SA	171012	Payne DF	240613	Sillett SK	110515
Margolis RDW	120612	Pearce DM	020415	Silson JG	180613
Marsh DAN	121010	Pepper PW	120612	Simmons JHK	020411
Martin MJ	171012	Phillips BJ	171012	Siswick CP	140415
Martin S	101011	Phillips MS	190410	Smeddle SE	151215
Marwaha JS	160414	Phillips SJ	180613	Smith AC	161013
Mason LC	121010	Philpott A	101011	Smith BJ	130214
Mather SI	091114	Picken W	020510	Smith JM	160511
Mathers AJ	200315	Pitcher TME	170614	Smith PA	080212
Matheson AC	171012	Poskitt AIE	180613	Smith RL	270514
Maynard RL	280414	Powell JD	020412	Smyth GM	010711
McArthur RJL	151215	Preston CG	171012	Spencer PJ	190210
McClure I	010713	Price JAB	151215	Sprigge TW	180613

Stamp JL	140213
Stanley R	151215
Stanning HM *MBE*	300911
Stiven RKP	101011
Stoddart LM	110815
Stokes ID	020412
Storton NR	101011
Street NA	080212
Sturgess JP	110815
Sykes FL	311213
Szkoda JKT	130214
Tacey LA	010415
Taylor AM	101011
Taylor DB *GCGI*	050514
Thomson MJG	130214
Thorne BF *MBE*	040515
Thorne GI	020411
Tidman DG	020715
Tilley JA	080212
Touton AM	110815
Towes RJW	110815
Trafford D	160414
Treasure GJ	140212
Trevis RJ	120612
Tulett AG	080212
Tyler DJ	130214
Varley RJ	080212
Vincent CJR	140415
Vipond AR	310713
Wade GLE	151215
Wade MV	110815
Wadman LJ	170614
Wadsworth A	020411
Wakeham JL	121010
Walcott JC	190314
Walker-McClimens JS	310713
Walsh JP	170614
Wardall EL	180613
Wardle DP	140412
Warner RH	140415
Warner SJ	020413
Waterfield JC	170614
Watson MR	020413
Watson NCA	180613
Wells JT	121010
Wells MN	310714
West RD	120612
White DB	121010
Whiteley GE	110815
Whiting AD	110815
Whittaker HM	151215
Whitton O	140415
Wiggins CA	140213
Wilkinson SR	130212
Willey JS	110815
Williams DD	030912
Williams PT	130611
Willoughby JL	020414
Wills RD	140415
Wilson OAR	110815
Wood AF	130214
Wood DJ	170614
Woods MBR	151215
Woodsend JK	120612
Wooldridge JP	270314
Woosey PD	151215
Worboys JA	161013
Wraith SA	110211
Wright AG	080212
Wright DJ	080515
Wright N	010415
Youdan SD	130611
Young L	020415

Lieutenants

Ambler CJ	120415
Ashford CTA	100814
Ayles TJ	130414
Baker RIJ	090815
Barton JW	120415
Baslington JA	090815
Bate JRC	120415
Bird ATN	090815
Blanshard H	131215
Bonella SM	130414
Brame DWR	130414
Broe IHM	120415
Bryan PLG	131215
Budd BJR	100814
Burns-Hill S	090815
Chanter IWS	130414
Clark R	100814
Corliss AR	120415
Cox OG	141214
Davies OJ	100814
Daw TE	130414
Dimmer JA	141214
Donnelly JL	120415
Duncan RAJ	100814
Eldridge CJ	130414
Flanagan JJ	090815
Flynn G	120415
Foster GA	130414
Fountain TAG	120415
Geering SJG	120415
Goffin R	130414
Goring JG	141214
Harvey JN	090815
Hawkes-Rossi WD	141214
Hill WT	100814
Holliday HE	120415
Hollywell EJ	090815
Hook JA	130414
Hughes BJ	100814
Hunt LJ	151213
Ingram BW	130414
Ireland MG	130414
Irving HTJ	130414
Jameson WHD	090815
Johnston AJ	131215
Jones M	090815
Kavanagh Williamson F	090815
Kennedy SE	130414
Keracher SL	131215
Kilpatrick SA	120415
Knowles RL	100814
Lewis AH	090815
Lower CE	130414
Mason AR	141214
May R	100814
McCarthy RD	131215
McGuinness EJ	100814
Mills EC	151213
Moreman AJ	090815
Morrow R	120415
Mousley HJE	090815
Moxley J	141214
Moyle JD	141214
Murray TJ	141214
Nickless ARK	130414
Nolan TPJ	100814
Ojelade OF	120415
O'Neill CJ	090815
Parsons SC	130414

Potts C	141214
Richardson HK	131215
Ripley WR	120415
Robinson JRT	131215
Rogers BJ	100814
Sayer TM	100814
See H	100814
Smith ES	141214
Smith WM	100814
Stanley PJ	100814
Thomas RG	131215
Thompson S	100814
Thomson RL	131215
Tooze JP	120415
Usher VC	120415
Wade JR	131215
Walley JF	100814
Warner SM	151213
Watson-Campbell NK	131215
West SM	120415
White RA	240714
Whittington HJO	090815
Wiegman TC	090815
Wilson CC	130414
Wilson DI	090815
Winter JD	131215
Wise SA	131215
Wolf AP	090815
Wood JM	130414
Woosey ST	130414
Worley DJ	131215
Wright PM	141214
Yuldasheva N	130414

2nd Lieutenants

Athawes FJ	110415
Ayre-Smith JJC	080815
Bales R	110415
Basir SS	080815
Boucher WJC	110415
Cadbury JE	121215
Clarke DG	110415
Clarke PE	080815
Collin KJ	080815
Couch WDT	080815
Croucher WPJ	110415
Dalgarno MF	080815
Denyer LM	121215
Dixon P	121215
Dorey EC	110415
Douglas BS	110415
Dyson JFA	110415
Etienne S	080913
Evans PJS	121215
Fincham OW	121215
Forrester AW	080815
Goodman RD	080815
Griffiths BN	121215
Harrison JA	121215
Hicks JM	110415
Hinton PMJ	080815
Hudson LPC	121215
James HSR	080815
Jones DA	080815
Landers JE	121215
Lawson TRS	110415
Manley BG	121215
Mountford EG	080815
Petty WJ	080815
Purdy MJ	080815
Redshaw HJM	110415
Robinson TA	080815
Scouller CJC	060215
Shaw M	110415
Steel JE	110415
Steer AD	110415
Stephenson JEL	110415
Stoddart TE	110415
Thomas AP	121215
Thornton RT	110415
Tigwell PJ	121215
Valle C	121215
Watson LNH	080815
Zeal FA	110415

THE CORPS OF ROYAL ENGINEERS

The Garter and Motto surmounted by The Crown. Within the Garter the Royal Cypher; without the Garter a wreath of laurel; on a scroll at the bottom of the wreath ROYAL ENGINEERS. The Garter, Motto, Royal Cypher, Crown and scroll in gold raised above the laurel wreath in silver

The London Gazette of 10th July 1832 announced that King William IV had "been pleased to grant the Royal Regiment of Artillery and Corps of Royal Engineers, His Majesty's permission to wear on their appointments the Royal Arms and supporters, together with a cannon and the motto "Ubique quo fas et Gloria ducunt." This is traditionally translated as "Everywhere Where right and Glory Lead." The motto is sometimes shortened to "Ubique" (Everywhere) for some regimental purposes. The cannon was removed in 1868.

Regimental Marches

Quick Marches .... Wings
The British Grenadiers

Agents .... Lloyds Bank plc Cox's & King's Branch
Corps Headquarters .... Brompton Barracks, Chatham, Kent ME4 4UG
(Tel: 94661-2121 Email: corps.secretary@rhqre.co.uk)

Alliances

Canadian Armed Forces .... Canadian Military Engineers
Australian Military Forces .... Australian Engineers
New Zealand Army .... Corps of Royal New Zealand Engineers
South African Army .... South African Engineer Corps
Indian Army .... Corps of Engineers
Pakistan Army .... Corps of Engineers
Sri Lanka Army .... Sri Lanka Engineers
Malaysian Army .... Royal Engineer Regiment
Zambian Army .... Zambia Corps of Engineers
Gibraltar .... The Royal Gibraltar Regiment

Affiliated Regiment

The Queen's Gurkha Engineers

Colonel in Chief .... HER MAJESTY THE QUEEN
Chief Royal Engineer .... Lt Gen (Retd) *Sir* Mark F N Mans *KCB CBE DL* 140913
Colonels Commandant .... Maj Gen (Retd) Keith H Cima *CB* 010903
Maj Gen (Retd) R R Davis *CB CBE* 010311
Maj Gen (Retd) Shaun A Burley *CB MBE* 010511
Maj Gen (Retd) C L Wilks *CB CBE (until 201016)* 010811
Maj Gen Nick J Cavanagh *(from 201016)*
Maj Gen Tyrone R Urch *CBE* 010313
Maj Gen Chris L Tickell *CBE* 161013
Maj Gen Richard J Semple *CBE* 251113
Maj Gen Richard J Cripwell *CB CBE* 010814
Maj Gen Alastair S Dickinson *CBE* 141014
Maj Gen Richard Wardlow *OBE* 011015
Maj Gen Ivan B L Jones 011115

Corps Colonel .... Col Don Bigger *ADC*

Lieutenant Colonels

Abbott RJ	300604	Benn AEC *MBE*	300615	Brown IC	300615
Ainley J	300614	Bennett NAJ	300614	Brown PLO	300610
Balgarnie AD	300607	Bickers DJ *MBE*	300614	Brown SC	300615
Ballans A	100614	Blunt RM	300611	Browning SC	311213
Bartlam AI	210314	Boxall GJ *MBE*	300614	Burnet RJD	300609
Beddoe K	070514	Bradley SN	300613	Campbell-Colquhoun BHG	300612
Bell LN	300612	Brooks PJ	130814	Cannons SR *EurIng CEng MICE*	300605
		Brown AD	300615	Cartmill PB *MSc MICE CE*	300611

Carvel SJ 300615
Chapman NJ 110316
Chapman T 300607
Christie AJ *MBE* 300314
Church IJ 300615
Clark JL *MBE* 300613
Cockwell DR *MBE* 300610
Cottee TR 300609
Croall DM 300615
Cunniff SE 311212
Davidson PA 030413
Davies SW 300611
Denham PJ 280415
Devey AR *MBE* 300611
Douglas RA 300610
Doyle SPM 300615
Dzisiewska IK 300615
Easingwood AM *MInstRE MSc* 010713
Ellisdon CL *CEng MICE* 300614
Ellison DBE 300614
Endean GR *IEng MIET MInstRE* 260614
Farr S MBE 090815
Fawcett SAM *MSOE MIPlantE MInstRE* 300608
Fawcus RCD *MBE* 300613
Foley AJ *BEng MSc CEng MICE MInstRE* 300612
Forrest SJ 300615
Fortey C 300614
Fossey JE 300613
Fox JS *CEng* 300614
Fuller PT *MSc MA MCMI MInstRE* 300608
Garner DC 300609
Garrow AA *OBE* 300615
Gifford BRJ *BSc MSc* 300615
Gladen AP 300606
Gladwin RJ 300614
Goodman SC 170216
Gossage JPR *BEng (Hons) MInstRE* 300615
Grantham KJ *MBE QGM* 060713
Hatcher GP *OBE BEng MSc CEng MICE MInstRE* 300612
Hawkins RB *MBE* 300614
Hilton AC 300606
Honnor AMF *BEng (Hons) MSc CEng MICE MInstRE* 300609
Houlston PE 300612
Hourahane RS 300608
Hunter CW 300611
Jackson AJ 300609
Jackson LC 010115
Johnson-Ferguson ME *MA CEng MICE* 300608
Johnston BJR *psc(j) BEng (Hons) MSc MA* 300614
Kirmond JL 030815
Leach JE 250114
Lewis MD 300614
Livesey GM 300608
Lumley SR *BEng (Hons) MSc CEng MIMechE* 300615
MacDonald RJ *CEng MICE* 300615
MacDonald WR 271014
MacMillan HJB 300614
Marsden TGJ 300611
Mason AJ 300613
Massetti SM 300610
Masson CP 300615
McCulloch MM 010114
McMonagle LM 300615
Mifsud ND 300611
Millar ENS *MBE* 300612
Millar SD *MSc* 300614
Millard JR *MSc* 300613
Mogford MC *MBE* 040913
Moore AM *MSc CMILT MInstRE* 300608
Morgan SD 300606
Morton RS 300610
Neely JS 300612
Nicholls SO *GCGI* 070316
Nichols IES 300611
Nicholson PB *OBE* 300611
Noble PR 300609
Page AG 300605
Parfitt KD *TD* 300615
Parker HJ 300606
Piper RA *BSc MA MBA MInstRE* 300605
Quaite PT BEng(Hons) *MSc MA CEng MICE* 300612
Quinn LT *MBE MSc BEng CEng MICE RE* 300606
Roberts JK *MBE RE* 061215
Roberts VJ 300614
Robinson WH *B Engr(Hons) MCMI MCGI* 300615
Roose JJ 300615
Rowell PJ *MBE* 300612
Salberg TJ *MBE* 300615
Saunders CS 280414
Scott JH *MBE* 300614
Scrivens IH *MBE* 040813
Seabrook DY 300614
Sealy-Thompson NJ 300605
Simonds JD 300605
Smallwood WN *BEng (Hons)* 300613
Springett B 300613
Stevens AT *CEng FInstRE MIET MAPM* 300607
Stuthridge SR 300614
Swain AW 300614
Szabo AN *BEng MA CEng FIMechE MInstRE* 300607
Tait A 300609
Teeton AJ 300613
Thomas IM 300602
Thornley MT 300609
Tomlinson RK 300605
Walker RG 300612
Wallace PJ *MEng MSc CEng MICE* 300613
Warhurst CI 300613
Webster JD 300615
Wellard BP 300612
West JR 300613
White JV 300608
Whitlock SJ 300610
Whitticase SM 300614
Wilkinson MR *MBE* 300612
Wilson LM 090815
Witcombe ND 300613
Woods DL *psc(Pak)* 300615
Young NA *BEng (Hons) MBA MSc CEng* 300614
Youngman PB 300611

Majors

Adams CB *BEng MSc CEng MICE* 310707
Ahmed SI 310715
Allardice DN 310709
Allen GW 310714
Ankers CR *MBE* 310708
Anselme PT 310712

Auld JP	310714
Axford CD	310711
Baker MAS	310709
Barker NS	310715
Barnard CJ	310706
Barry PN	300999
Barter JC	310715
Barton AP	310713
Battey CW	310707
Baxter JE	310709
Beard AD	310714
Bennett MSR	310711
Beszant RE	310712
Birley AC	310712
Bishop P	310713
Black SJ	310709
Blencowe NJ *MBE*	310715
Blow DB *MSc BArch BA CEng RIBA MICE*	310706
Blunden GPJ	310705
Bond GS	310710
Boorman TD	310714
Bowen W	310713
Boyce TD *BSc MSc FCMI*	310707
Boyter BA	170813
Brazier PE	310714
Bremner AJ	310703
Brown CDT	310712
Brown D	310707
Brown MJ	310715
Buchanan JJ	310713
Buglass MA	310715
	310715
Cackett JA	310709
Calder DRJ	310712
Cameron KM	310714
Campbell R	310713
Campey D	310711
Carnochan AW	310710
Castro RP	310714
Cheales AJ *MEng (Oxon) MIMechE RE*	310711
Cheesman GS	310713
Chestnutt EM	310713
Clifford CR *MEng MSc*	310712
Colvin NJL	310715
Conn PW	310709
Cooney AP	310715
Cormack GH	310708
Cornell MJ	310712
Cox LB	310705
Cresswell IM *CMgr MCMI IEng MIET MInstRE*	310713
Crosbie DS	310714
Cross S	310711
Crossley JBA	310713
Cudlipp CR	310709
Cunane SC	310712
Darke CT	310713
Darvill NJ	310714
Davies AR	310713
Dawson GBJ	310712
Delaney TM	010515
Dias DJA	310713
Dollimore SB	310713
Donaghy OPR	310712
Donoghue SK	310713
Donohoe TA	290408
Douglas SJH	310715
Downham DW	310715
Drew J	310715
Drysdale GW	310713
Duff BD	310711
Duggan PCR	310710
Duke RM	310713
Duncan WM	310709
Edwards B *BEng (Hons) CMgr MCMI MCGI*	310709
Edwards JM	310711
Elliott RV	310715
Elsegood CJ	310709
Elson SJ	310713
Elworthy CC *MBE*	310711
Everett MA	310715
Eyre CA	310706
Fairnington SJ	310709
Farmer SA	310715
Featherstone SR	310714
Fell MA *CMgr MCMI MCGI*	310709
Fielding NT	310714
Finch SM *BSc (Hons) MRICS FAAV*	310707
Fisher G	310714
Fitzsimons NE	310710
Fleming LC *BEng(Hon) CEng MIMechE MInstRE*	310711
Fletcher GA	310711
Frost RB *MBE*	310706
Fry MJ	310715
Gale RH	310715
Garcia M	310711
Garrard CS	310714
Garthwaite RM	310715
Gauci APM	310713
Giannandrea R *IEng MInstRE*	310711
Gichuke JRC *BEng MSc CEng MIMechE*	310711
Gilbert TP	310712
Girling BM	310715
Golding PW *MBE*	310714
Gooch AA	310708
Graham SJ	310711
Granger SIJ	310714
Grant RD	310713
Greensmith JE	310712
Gregory AJ	310713
Griffin MJ	300996
Griffiths SS	310715
Hain VM	310709
Hales MC	310715
Hall SJ	310711
Hamilton A	310712
Hamilton RG	310713
Hammett PM	310709
Handford RJ	310713
Hardwick BC	310711
Harris AJ	310710
Harrison MA	310711
Hart SJ	310713
Hastings AE	310710
Hawkins AE	310708
Hawkins BJ *BEng (Hons) MSc IEng MIET*	310710
Hawkins HM	310712
Hawkins JW	310706
Hayakawa MJ	310710
Hebard KM	310710
Hedgeley NF	310712
Hembery DD *MBE*	010515
Hemns SM *CEng MICE*	310706
Hendry MD	310710
Henson GA	310713
Hewitt RA	310715
Higginbotham IJ	310714
Hill AJ	310708

Hill AR 040513
Hill RJA 310708
Hirst DJ 310713
Hislop KB 310707
Hobson-Smith SPM 310712
Hodgson R 010701
Hoey RA 310713
Holgate MN 310714
Homer MF 310710
Hone S *MBE IEng* 310708
Hooper HR 310713
Hopwood DA 310714
Hoult CGP 310710
Howard AJ 300999
Howells DG 140814
Hughes SD 310707
Hughes SP 170813
Hulme CA 310712
Hunt SDW 131004
Hunter DK 310709
Hyde NI 310709
Ives TE 310710
James CL 310709
James ER *MBE* 310708
Jarvis ARG 310705
Jenkins IG 310709
Jennings JA 310713
Jervis JJ 310714
Johnson NC 310712
Jones AC 310710
Jones DE 310708
Jones MS 310710
Judge JPJ *BA* 310715
Kelly JAG 310714
Kerr GJ 310707
Kerr J 310706
Kirkin AE 310715
Knowles DDB 310713
Kriehn AW 310711
Kurzeja AP 310715
Lakin NPH 310710
Lamont I 310710
Lawes AC 310710
Lea A 310712
Lilleyman TC 310712
Llewelyn JA 310706
Lord DS 300901
Loxley LJ 310715
MacKenzie AP 310711
MacKintosh IG 310715
Mangan AJ 310715
Marsh RG 310713
Marshall CJ 310704
Mather RB *MBE* 310712
Matten SD *MBE* 310703
Mayes AG 310709
Mayes SOL 310707
McCallion SEJ *BEng (Hons) MSc CEng MCGI* 310706
McCran AJ 270412
McCrea GR 310715
McGourty B 310714
McGrath A 310713
McGuirk RP 310714
McKay GA 310712
McKechnie ARI *MA MEng* 310703
McLean LJ 310710
McLenaghan CJ 310711
Meakins RDS 310715
Meek WR 310709
Merrett SJO 310712
Millbank RG 310709
Miller HT 310714
Mitchell CJ 310712
Monaghan JL 310714
Monger RLJ 310714
Montague JS 310715
Montgomery CGP 310713
Montgomery MD 310715
Moore PE 010314
Morley AM 310715
Moxham PD 100812
Myatt TGP 310715
Neild AJ 310712
Neville SM 310709
Nixon KJ 310714
Normile MJ 310710
Oakes RS 310712
Oats S *MBE* 310713
O'Connor JA 310715
O'Grady TF 310711
O'Neill CN 310713
Ord LP 310710
Oxley SJ *MBE* 310714
Palmer FN 310713
Peel AD 310713
Phillips RO 310714
Pilbeam IH 310715
Plackett AK 310712
Plimmer CLK 310709
Pogson-Hughes-Emanuel RG 310715
Porter RJ 310713
Price CJP 310710
Raper MD 310715
Rees RM 310711
Richardson MC 310714
Richardson PA 310705
Ridley R *MSc CEng MICE MInstRE* 310713
Rigby JD 310714
Riley DJ 310714
Robbins DJ 310709
Robbins RE 310709
Roberts HM 310715
Roberts RW 310714
Robertson LJ *MSc BSc (Hons) CEng MIMechE* 310711
Robinson AJ 310710
Robinson JGJ 310710
Robinson S 310704
Rogers KD 310708
Rollinson A 310715
Rudd AD 310713
Rudd DJ 310712
Rushworth PN 310712
Schofield MDW *MBE* 300901
Schreiber RT 310715
Scott AC 310715
Scott AJ 310711
Scotter FJ MBE 310706
Scrivener JM 310714
Scullion SF 310711
Seller C 310713
Serevena RK *BEng (Hons) MSc CEng MICE GCGI* 310714
Seymour EJ 310703
Shepperson SD 310710
Siemieniuch SK 310714
Simister GE 310715
Simister MJ 310715
Sinclair DG 300901
Sklenar CA 310710
Smith JR 310715
Smith MJ 310712

Smith MJE 310707
Smith MT 310710
Spencer NG 310709
Stamp HMM 310715
Stead DJ 310711
Stephenson MW 310711
Stewart MJ 140815
Stork RD 310715
Stroud-Caules TD 310708
Stuart JD 310708
Tearle R 310714
Teeling MR 310715
Teeton MW *MSc CEng MICE MInstRE* 310711
Thomas SJ *MSc CEng MICE* 310702
Thompson AG 310713
Thompson EJD 310715
Thompson EP 310711
Thoms CF 310711
Tomkinson DM 310714
Treffry-Kingdom MJ 310709
Turner WS *MBE* 310710
Underhill CN *MBE MSc* 310714
Vaughan AJE 310713
Viney J 310715
Waddington G 310715
Walker GJ 310708
Walker JWC 310714
Walker MA *MSc* 310715
Walker MP 310713
Walsh EW 310710
Walsh VJ 310711
Warner CM *MEng MSc CEng MIMechE MInstRE* 310714
Warner EF 310715
Warrington RE 310714
Warrington VBM *BSc (Hons) MinstRE* 310711
Wasilewski CTJ *MSc* 310711
Wendover RS 310712
Wernick BB *BEng CEng MICE MInstRE* 310714
West CJ 310715
West NJ 310715
Whishaw BWD *BEng (Hons) CEng MICE* 310704
Whishaw EAH 310705
White J 310704
White MAS 310711
Whiteman HD 310705
Wicks AJ 310715
Wilks NE 310714
Williams AD *BEng (Hons) MSc CEng FIMechE* 310705
Wilson AG 310714
Wilson JM *BEng (Hons) MSc CEng MIET* 310709
Witko MJ 310713
Wood JFC 310715
Woodings SJ 310714
Wright SM *MBE* 310715
York AM *MSc* 310712
Young PA 310708

Captains

Allchorn HT 170614
Allen CAA 311212
Anderson AS 161013
Andrew DM 310715
Andrews GS 140213
Andrews S 270412
Andrews SN 270712
Annear JT 131008
Antcliffe ER 121010
Anthony JR 161013
Ash JM 180613
Ashley MR 290814
Aspey PP 171012
Attrell BSC 101011
Babbington JM 131208
Bagshaw RD 170715
Bainger JM 131008
Baldry CB *RE* 170614
Barclay RM 060608
Barnes NDW 180613
Barry MDJ 141009
Bartlett AM 110210
Bartlett AS 170614
Bartram KS *MSc BEng (Hons) BSc (Hons)* 010814
Batley PJ 240415
Batty TS *BSc* 130214
Baxter SA 121010
Bayley A 130611
Beeforth CA 110211
Beeton AP 230410
Beresford BJ 170614
Berman JME 170614
Beveridge IJ 130214
Bird TW 101011
Birtwistle M 171012
Bland PG 140415
Blaylock J 120511
Bone AJ 040708
Borley MC *RE* 180613
Bostock AH 110210
Botha CM 171214
Bougourd TR *BEng (Hons)* 130214
Brain DHG 150610
Bramson AE 161013
Brand DR 110210
Brett AJ 130611
Brett F 101011
Britton AJ 120612
Brixton KG 030409
Brookfield M 310715
Broom AN 270712
Brown AA 310712
Brown EC *MEng MInstRE* 080212
Brunton S 250408
Bruton DJ 170614
Buckley JJ 250211
Buckley SP 310713
Bullock FM 101011
Burgess MW 040610
Burt WA 170614
Butterfield RJ 161013
Button CJ 040714
Byrne RJ 200209
Cadogan AR 311213
Caldwell AL 010515
Carroll G 130412
Cartwright J 120612
Castle DA 310715
Caulfield AP 130611
Chalkley PR 310715
Chalmers NT 310715
Chambers JG 170614
Charlton JH 090211
Cheesbrough TE 170614
Child OJ 060215
Clark OB 120612
Clifton LD 120612
Coates PD 240715
Cochrane TK 140213

Cole AR 120612
Coles CF 010313
Collins LJG 120612
Collins R 160710
Condon ST 171210
Conway JE 180613
Crago SP 260413
Crosby HH 121010
Crosby-Jones SD 160609
Crossen JA 040116
Crowther ON 090211
Curle CL 121010
Daniels RA 280815
Davidson CM 010814
Davies AA 210111
Davies PEB 121010
Davies SP 171012
De Silva TL 130214
Dickins EA 161013
Dixon D 171014
Dobinson PTA 130214
Docker TRB 090211
Dow AK 120612
Dudley MS 120612
Dullaghan JM 171012
Eadie JT 130214
Easton AEH 121010
Ellis DC 101011
Engelbrecht H 180912
Evans JE 130412
Evitts GO 161013
Exelby TL 120612
Fallon OG 160414
Farminer JEJ 101011
Fetters MH 130214
Fleming RS 161013
Flowers TI 140213
Foote TE 311213
Foster BA 170608
Foster JE 230410
Fowler A 290515
Francis MS 121010
Fraser DC 120612
Fullerton WR *BSc (Hons)* 031014
Gallagher RF 090211
Gallimore PT 120713
Gardiner M 120612
Garland RW *MSc CMgr FCMI MInstRE CertOSH* 070510
Garner J 010808
Gaskell SPA 180613
Gent ZC 130214
Gibson DJ *BSc (Hons) BEng (Hons)* 111111
Gibson PCR 140412
Giles RP 150610
Glazebrook BJ 180613
Gleave AMW 110210
Gledhill M 121010
Gostling LJW 110210
Graham RT 180613
Granger DG 130814
Grant JS 101011
Green AE 140213
Green BW 100709
Greenwood AA 090211
Greig AK 090211
Griffiths RF 230612
Griffiths TPA 161013
Grubb DJ 170409
Gunnell NR 160411
Haikney GK 130214
Hall RRO 150610
Hamilton AM 040714
Hamilton LI *MBE MInstRE MIET BEng CGCI* 030812
Hancock BA 150610
Hands DN 130611
Hardaker CE 120612
Hardman JR 150610
Harris ELT 090211
Hassall ML 130814
Hastings MLW 141009
Hawken SJ *MInstRE* 120811
Hawkes JM 110815
Hearn TR 170614
Heaton AJ 171012
Hebblethwaite DM 151010
Henson SM 280613
Hicketts DJ 140213
Higgins AR 100513
Hill G *EngTech MInstRE MCGI* 290612
Hindson AA *MBE* 210510
Holtham CC 161013
Horrocks MD 060511
Houston SC 180613
Howourth NS 080212
Hunt AS 050609
Hunt IJ 180613
Hurst PA *BSc MSc* 020514
Hutt TWJ 120612
Ingram PR 010808
Iwasaki ETW 041111
Jackson GEL 101011
Jackson GS 150610
Jackson P 080711
Jackson SM 170614
Jarvis GL 020710
Jinks SL 310513
Jobling MD 250512
Johnson MJ 111013
Johnson RPT *MC* 260609
Johnston-Smith LS 291211
Jones DA 140213
Jones IJ 140412
Kehoe JAC 120612
Kellgren-Parker L 140213
Kennedy NA 110915
Kennedy PS 180613
Kerr AJ 040610
Khanal AK 070510
Kiddie FPG 130214
Kukielka AP 130214
Ladd HK 150610
Lafferty JF 040411
Larsen M 180613
Lawrence LPD 140213
Lawrence RM 090211
Lawrenson MD 240415
Laws A 120612
Lawson CS 060415
Laycock AM 160609
Lee SJ 240812
Leggat CL 170614
Limbu Khim C 301015
Linares JC 130611
Lishman G 240611
Lloyd-Davies GW 101011
Locke QS 141011
Lodwick GW 161013
Loots AR 130611
Low HR 120612
Lowrie CI 101011

Lupke AF	311213
Luttig DW	230313
MacGill WJ *MSc DipCons AssocRICS MCIOB*	270209
MacKenzie PG	140415
MacKintosh PS *MEng MInstRE*	080212
MacPherson SA	090410
Marchant MJ	130809
Marsden MR	150711
Marsh BJ	090211
Marsh PE	050413
Martin EOG	101011
Martin GDH *BSc (Hons)*	291113
Mason AD	161013
Mason JE *MBE*	070313
Mayers SC	090813
Mayland SA	020710
McCloud P	070108
McCracken NT	110210
McLean AAI	170614
McLennan C	260615
Meadows R	120612
Melloy G	260615
Middleton SE	030415
Millar AJ	120612
Miller JJ	130611
Mitchell M	100709
Mitton R	240611
Moran KL	161013
Morris DG	010814
Morrison A	301015
Mortiboy MA	040714
Morton HJ	130214
Mullen DS	140415
Murison IA	140207
Murphy DR	310513
Mutch GJ	030513
Needham JA	080212
Newton JP	130611
Noel AA	310715
O'Callaghan JED	180613
O'Connor DA *MBE*	180211
O'Ehring AJ	141009
O'Kane JP	180512
Osborne SM	140815
Owen M	010414
Owens MD	290313
Padley RP	070510
Palmer DJ	180613
Palmer MNH	180613
Parnell GS	030511
Parr SA	150610
Parsons HJ	161013
Parton MT	180510
Pattison S	150509
Pearce RJ	150610
Pearson D *PgDip GCGI EngTech MInstRE*	050914
Peebles AC	060712
Pelton DK	140213
Pennington ALM	090211
Peters DJ	130214
Phillpott RD	030910
Phipps PA	080212
Pick AD	160410
Pickering PJ	130214
Pickett SA	121010
Plater TM	311213
Pollock M	171012
Prentice RM	110410
Prevett KJ	080515
Price GJ	030511
Pryce BR	300811
Quinn GR	150213
Regan JA	120612
Reilly DA	160609
Rizzuti F	110210
Robb DJS	150610
Roberts JG	121010
Robinson GA	171214
Robinson RAH	170614
Robinson S	080612
Robinson SP	080515
Robinson WD	050914
Ross D	050413
Rosser DJ	120612
Rouse DM	311213
Ruddy LA	060614
Rutherford IW	270209
Ryder PRD	010711
Sanger AJ *MBE*	030409
Scott TP	171012
Seymour D	260609
Sharpe CS	260914
Sharrock RG	120612
Simmonds PM	120609
Simpson M *LCGI ILM*	140510
Simpson SA	130214
Small JC	170614
Smart CJ	141009
Smith AJ	171012
Smith BRJ	141009
Smith CJ	150610
Smith DN	160710
Smith JL	050713
Smith JN	020813
Smith SP	170611
Snook DC *BEng MInstRE*	180613
Snow PR	130611
Somerville ID	290814
Southall BR	140213
Spreadborough J	160710
Stafford CG	110610
Stein JA	140213
Stevens MJ *MEng*	170614
Stickland BO	300614
Stockbridge GJ	311213
Stockley BJ	310713
Stott WT	170614
Strachan AI	090211
Stretton BC	120612
Stringer TS	170614
Suddaby MC	290116
Sullivan M	170614
Swarbrick C	170614
Taylor JS *BEng (Hons) IEng MIET GCGI*	040411
Taylor MW	120908
Tebbs GR	040411
Teesdale MR	030614
Tether JJ	120713
Thapa J	021015
Thomas JG	290814
Thomas JS	020514
Thomas MJ *MBE*	270309
Thompson AK *MEng*	140213
Thompson KAW	050413
Thompson MJ	170415
Thorne MR	140213
Till JS	010509
Tillman MA	100415
Tomaszewski NA	130814
Tomsett GC	140213
Tongs THJ	130214

Toogood OJ	171012
Turner PA	010515
Van Bruggen RC	110204
Van Der Merwe JA *MInstRE*	220610
Van Lochem SJ	180613
Vandenberg RL	170614
Waddington DML	130814
Waite TC	140213
Wakelin DJ	100715
Walker JK	110512
Walkworth JL	121010
Waller JF	121010
Ward AL	180613
Ward LR *BA (Hons)*	171012
Wardman JS	010414
Warren DAC	090211
Webb JM	140213
Wentworth RG	130214
West J	311213
West RAJ	130611
Wharram CJL	130611
Wheeler AT *IEng MIET*	190413
Whitbread AJE	130608
White ACI	010814
White BA	180613
Whitehouse AL	030415
Whittaker AE	130214
Wiggins P	020412
Wilkinson JH	161013
Wilkinson KS	130411
Williams DP	140613
Williams SC	080212
Wilson LA	090211
Woods BNR	170614
Wright AJ	130611
Wyatt JW	120612
Wyatt LN	140213
Yates M	220711
Young JM	120612

Lieutenants

Adams CM	130414
Aitken CJM	100814
Ankers ME	130414
Barrett AJS	141214
Barton TJ	151213
Bass JW	130414
Beaumont HC *BSc*	140413
Beeching HB	110813
Bergman DJ	141214
Bigwood CG	140413
Boiling TP	110813
Booty CA	110813
Boyle JP	140413
Bracey DW	110813
Bradford AH	141214
Breslin RC	100814
Broadfoot AS	100814
Burbidge JD *BEng*	140413
Butler C	100814
Cannons S	141214
Cavanagh AM	110813
Clafton KT	151213
Clegg WL	141214
Conlon JN	141214
Cork RH	130414
Crombie JMA	151213
Cross F	130414
Cummings LR	151213
Curry JC	141214
Davies MW	140413
Dennehy MCT	141214
Doyle TJ	100814
Eabry JR	140413
Ekberg JC	140413
Evans SC	130414
Fergus RL	140413
Finnie MJ	141214
Forrester MJ	100814
Fountain LT	141214
French DA	110813
Frew AH	140413
Frost S	140413
Garfield LJ	130414
George DC	140413
Gill JJW *BSc(Hons)*	140413
Gillan MJ	140413
Haley CA	141214
Hamilton RG	110813
Hams LW	110813
Harris MJ	130414
Harvey R	140413
Heather MA	100814
Higgins AK	130414
Holman EO	141214
Holmes AJ	110813
Holmes JN	110813
Howard CL	151213
Ingram RC	110813
Irvine AJH	151213
Irvine ED	151213
Jarvis CES	100814
Johnson RA *BSc PGCE*	110813
Jukes KL	151213
Kamble SA	151213
Knebel MJ	140413
Knoop LP	110813
Leafe CD	130414
Lewis OJ	140413
Linklater GW	151213
Lister JM	110813
Lock JJ	140413
Longstone S	141214
Marris CJ	140413
Marshall AJM	100814
Martyniuk AP	140413
Masson RJ	110813
McLeod M	130414
Mistry JJ	100814
Motion A	130414
Murrow JM	110813
Oliver J	110813
Osment AH	100814
Oxley RHC	110813
Parker LD	130414
Parry R	100814
Paske AD	100814
Peters CE	100814
Piper SE	130414
Porteous D	140413
Posner AJ	100813
Pugh GE	141214
Redding TS	140413
Richardson RB	110813
Rickard AJ	130414
Ruddy ECC	141214
Rushton AJ	301113
Siggs AN	151213
Sim GTJ	140413
Smales JM	130414
Sorabjee JPO	110813
Spearing AS	160608
Stables EJ	140413
Stevens-Fisher JL	151213

Sunley CA	110813
Sutherland PF	110813
Swanwick CJ	100814
Thackwray RC *BEng*	110813
Thorp SJ	130414
Tomlinson JM	151213
Varndell JP	151213
West MJ	141214
Weston SJ	151213
Whiston AJ	151213
Williams MO	140413
Willis AR	141214
Willis RS	060714
Wink GDD	151213
Woods HJ	100814
Wray JWK	100814

2nd Lieutenants

Aiton M	090814
Amies DK	080815
Anderson FC	120414
Baird CT	050114
Bakovljev AN	120414
Barnard CW	110415
Blair CR	050114
Borland E	121215
Bossom CLS	120414
Bristow KR	120414
Bromley GL	090814
Brown JE	050114
Brown WD	120414
Brunstrom T	120414
Buglass AJ	050114
Butler A	121215
Butwell R	080815
Campbell IA	110415
Carter JFB	080815
Casson BCM	050114
Clarke HG	121215
Clayton L	121215
Coles H	121215
Corcos M	131214
Corrie EL	080815
Dale AC	090814
Davis J	110415
Dixon JWS	080815
Dunford P	080815
Dunton GF	110415
Edwards TJM	121215
Ellett JR	090814
Ferrier WRL	120414
Fisher SR	110415
Fletcher AT	121215
Fletcher OJ	121215
Frankland RJ	120414
Garnett JGS	120414
Gay EM	120414
Gibbs DAC	110415
Gibson GHS	110415
Gittins KB	090814
Glazebrook JS	110415
Glover JA	090814
Gordon SDR	090814
Griffith WT	110415
Groom DJ	120414
Grylls JRH	090814
Hancock KE	080815
Hankin MJ	120414
Hardern L	110415
Harvey CJL	080815
Hayes CA	121215
Hesketh A	050114
Hitch RJ	050114
Hughes OA	090814
Jenkins HP	080815
Jochimsen JM	080815
Jones DH	121215
Jones TV	050114
Keal RC	090814
Key BDE	050114
Kidd IJ	080815
Kington AP	120414
Kuhnke MBD	120414
Kumar SN	110415
Lacey SD	090814
Learmond SD	010913
Ledsom BR	120414
Lethbridge JW	080815
Lindblom RAL	050114
Lloyd DJ	080815
Martin HCL	050114
McCrow TL	050114
McElroy PA	080815
McNaughton TC	110415
Meryon DE	050513
Milton AC *MPharm*	121215
Milton TO	080815
Moore CTR	050114
Mowforth JCJ	121215
Myatt LP	090814
Newman MC	080815
Norfield JO	050114
Owles DJ	080815
Palmer RPB	110415
Pritchard Smith SP	050114
Pullen GM	121215
Purcell A	120414
Quarton FM	110415
Quinton OR	080815
Rigby J	121215
Robertson JM	110415
Ruggles EL *MEng*	080913
Seeds JC	090814
Smart EW	121215
Smith AC *BA(Hons)*	190913
Smith KA	090814
Smith-Cooper RJ	050114
Szczyglowska JM	080815
Tasker RB	080815
Taylor OW	050114
Thaibsyah MJ	050114
Thomas MA	121215
Toms NR	090814
Turner BJ	121215
Wadsworth SE	110415
Ward SR	090814
Warne JW	090814
Warren VL	110415
Warrillow JAA	090814
Warwick HL	050513
Webber PR	050114
Wensley ER	080815
Whitby RE	050114
Whitehead TB	110415
Wingfield WJ	090814
Woodward MT	080815

ROYAL CORPS OF SIGNALS

The figure of Mercury holding a Caduceus in the left hand, the right hand aloft poised with the left foot on a globe all silver, above the globe a scroll inscribed CERTA CITO and below on each side six laurel leaves all gold, the whole ensigned with The Crown in gold

Regimental Marches

Quick March .... The Royal Signals March – Begone Dull Care
Slow March .... HRH The Princess Royal

Agents .... Lloyds Bank plc Cox's & King's Branch
Regimental Headquarters .... Griffin House, Blandford Camp, Blandford Forum, Dorset DT11 8RH
(Tel: 01258 482081 Mil: 94371 2081
Email: SOINC-DCOS-RHQ-RegtSec@mod.uk)

Alliances

Canadian Armed Forces .... Communications and Electronic Branch
Australian Military Forces .... Royal Australian Corps of Signals
New Zealand Army .... Royal New Zealand Corps of Signals
Indian Army .... Corps of Signals
Pakistan Army .... Corps of Signals
Sri Lanka Army .... Sri Lanka Signals Corps
Malaysian Army .... Royal Signals Regiment
Zambia Army .... Zambia Corps of Signals

Afiliated Regiments

Queen's Gurkha Signals

Colonel in Chief .... *HRH The Princess Royal KG KT GCVO QSO*

Royal Signals Corps Council

Master of Signals .... Lt Gen Nicholas A W Pope *CBE* 060314

Colonels Commandant .... Brig (Retd) J E Richardson *MBE* 100511
Brig (Retd) E M (Ted) Flint 010711
Brig (Retd) David A Hargreaves 230313
Brig (Retd) Michael Lithgow *CBE* 011013
Maj Gen John Crackett *CB TD VR* 010814
Maj Gen Ivan Hooper 010615

Corps Colonoel .... Col Simon Hutchinson *MBE ADC*

Lieutenant Colonels

Adams MWG	300606
Allen TJS *OBE*	300607
Anderson W	300612
Baker ND	300615
Bever MR	300609
Billingham MG *CEng*	300603
Bolam K	250415
Bradshaw IJ	300602
Brookes MC	300610
Bruce NC	300614
Buchanan IA *MSc CEng MIET*	300606
Bunce JRC	300602
Byfield RN	300615
Cathro AD	300608
Clee EF	210813
Coatsworth NR *MBE*	290412
Cook CD	300615
Cooper CN *MBE*	300614
Cooper TC	300608
Corkery AEA	300612
Cornell MC	300611
Courage OTB	300614
Craig RJ *MBE*	300615
Crane TP	150514
Dagless JW	300615
Dallyn EA *MBE*	300612
Davis EA	300600
Day PJ *MBE*	090714
Deans P	300610
Downes TJ	300612
Duckworth JB	300613
Eaton MA	300609
Emmerson KE	300613
Favager IG	300608
Fawcett AR	300613
Fayers MJ	300615
Fowkes LE	300612
France SO	300608
Fraser JH	300611
Gibson RS	300611
Giles RP	300602

Gillespie ST	300613
Gray AJ	300614
Gunning JS	300612
Hale PJ	300614
Hargreaves SVD	300614
Healey RJ *OBE*	300604
Hill T	300609
Hudson AP *MBE*	300600
Hunter IN	300605
Ingram GB	300612
Irwin G	300614
Jenkins HA	300605
Johnston GWA	300315
Keech M *BEM*	090112
Keen N	300601
Keilty SC *MBE*	310708
Kennedy JA *MSc MA psc(j)*	300612
Knight JR *MBE* Bsc(Hons) *CEng*	300612
Lamb GB	300615
Lapslie RW	300602
Leigh SA	300699
Lenthall GH	300611
Lucas AG	300613
Meadowcroft SN *BEM*	300614
Morton MJ	300615
Mould AJ	300613
Muir PRD *MBE*	300614
Mulholland RA *MBA*	300608
Owen KA	300614
Percival AE	300608
Pye RJ	130415
Raleigh DS *BSc MSc CEng*	300605
Ratcliffe CJ	300613
Renfrey SR	300605
Richardson SY	300613
Ruddock MW	300615
Scott A	060114
Scott HJ *MBE*	300614
Scott SG	300615
Sharkey DM	300609
Short SJ	300614
Smith AJ	300613
Solomons MA	300615
Somerville DW *MBE*	300602
Stanton IP	300610
Stephenson P	300606
Stevens NS	300607
Stoker GJ *MBE*	200315
Stokoe NM *OBE*	300612
Stoter DM	300613
Toze JE	300614
Turner J	300609
Walker WA	300614
Whimpenny DI	300602
Whitaker DA	110313
Whittley SW	300613
Wilson RA	300615
Woodley A	080815
Yardley NGC	300613

Majors

Ahsan I	310712
Alderson B	300900
Alexander CS	310705
Allen DR	310711
Anderson CJP	310714
Andrews P	310712
Armstrong LE	310712
Arthurton AB	310706
Ashton DJ	310707
Asplen PC	310714
Aylward AC	310708
Balfour JS	310707
Ballard EF	310712
Balsdon A	050607
Barber JC	310708
Barker KA	310706
Barratt M	310709
Barry AJ	310709
Beard BKN	310710
Bell JE	310713
Bell RA	310710
Bennett SR	310709
Bentley MS	310714
Biddulph CN	310707
Biggs AOH	310710
Birchall HL	310704
Boyden JV	310715
Brown AP	310703
Brown MA	310715
Brown RM	300901
Brunton PJ	310707
Bryan BH	310705
Bryan RW	310704
Buck PA	310703
Budding CS	310711
Budding J	310713
Burdge ACE	310710
Burdus A	310713
Burman KNL	310709
Burnett DS	310713
Byfield EA	310707
Cade JJ	310715
Cairns HC	310708
Calland SL	310712
Cameron E	310713
Campbell AS	310712
Cardwell WJ	310710
Carey J	310715
Carpenter PM	310713
Cauldwell JT	310709
Caveen JR	310711
Chamberlain DA	300412
Chatman J	310710
Church SC	310712
Clarke D	310714
Clay NS	310714
Clayton RL	310714
Clifford SL	310710
Cowie MJ	310709
Cox MJ	310713
Crossing L	310714
Darke GP	310710
Darlington RJ	310709
Davenport BP	310708
Davies CEJ	310709
Davies RB	310715
Davis L	310714
Davis MW	310707
Dawson JF	310714
Day RHC	310714
Devenish S	310712
Dick A	310711
Dinnis OR *MSc MBA CEng MIET*	310708
Dixon CM	310709
Dorrington GM *BSc*	310714
Duff MC *MSc*	310713
Dunn GLM	310713
Dunwoody KM	310714
Dyer RS	310713
Easterbrook M	310715
Eastman MR	310715

Edkins KJ	310711
Elliott IL	310715
Ellis JE	310710
Endean GP *MSc*	310711
Farragher DP	310707
Fielder JA	310713
Fielding DK	310715
Finnie OS	310704
Fisher N	310709
Flather MR	310711
Fogarty C	310711
Ford OJ *MSc*	310710
Foster RJ	310714
Fraser JC	310705
Freestone VJ	310712
Frost HR	310710
Galey DG	310713
Garrett AHT	310704
George NL	310713
Glover AB	310715
Gray SLR	310713
Greaves GA	310712
Greenwood EJ	110811
Grice KJ	310707
Grierson MJ	310706
Haines JZ	310714
Hammond RP	310715
Harrington JHN	300901
Harris MW	310707
Harris RJT	310713
Harrison TI	310715
Hartley CP	300900
Hawkins JKR	310709
Hay PA	310713
Heaton JC *MSc CEng MIET CITP MBCS*	310711
Higgins A *MBE*	310709
Hill CM	310711
Hoare JEG	310713
Hodges AC	310712
Hodgkins TSJ	310715
Hodgkinson PA	310711
Holbrook WR	310705
Holden M	310713
Holloway MD	310714
Hooker JW	310712
Howarth BDD	310704
Howell-Walmsley J	310706
Hume GD *MBE*	310711
Hutton ASF *BEng(Hons) MSc*	310707
Inglis G	300999
Irwin SE	310708
Jacques-Grey RS	310709
Jardine CL	310708
Jeffery BK	310710
Jones JS *BEng (Hons) MSc CEng CMgr*	310707
Jones M	310710
Keith FS	310712
Kelly AR	310715
Kelly L	310710
Kirk IJ	310712
Knott CR	310714
Lambeth JD	190508
Lappin TJ	310715
Larsen KA	310710
Lawson AJ	310708
Leathem AJ	310712
Lewin CJ	310706
Lewis AH	310711
Limbrey RJ	310711
Lish DA	310713
Littlefield SE	310714
Lockwood SM	310708
Long JC	310713
Long MD	310715
Longmuir DB	310712
Lowe RA	310712
Lyons JA *MBA MSc*	310706
Lyons JF	310715
MacPherson SJ	310711
Maddison VE	310707
Malcolm J	310708
Mallett MR	310714
Mannings SR	300998
Marcham DJ	310715
Matthews LS	310713
Mayne JN	310707
McCorry MC	310709
McCreath W *MSc CEng MIET*	310707
McGrail L	310714
McMillan JP	310713
McNelis MJ	310712
Meehan PS	310710
Mhango P	310715
Moody CSE	310714
Moody RA *BEng (Hons)*	310711
Moran T	310709
Morris NJ	310704
Mortimore EA	310709
Mulligan CP	310714
Murphy DM	310715
Murray MP	140814
Northridge CM	310715
O'Neill D	310715
O'Hara MJ	310715
Oldridge KL	310714
Oliver-Abell GJ *MSc MA*	310705
Oosterveen GMT	310711
Orr DR *BSc(Hons) MSc CEng*	310707
Overton KP	310714
Pace R	310714
Parkinson AJ	310708
Peers IJ	310713
Phillips DG	310714
Piears IR	310714
Plested RF	310710
Pollitt NJ	310715
Potter L	310713
Price BB	310712
Pryce-Jones NJ	310711
Psaila BL	310708
Purdy NCW *GCGI*	310715
Quinsey RC	310707
Raynor CJ	310715
Rea AD	310714
Reid FJ	310706
Reid J	310715
Reynolds NJA	310714
Rice SJ	310715
Richardson DG	310709
Roberts EL	310708
Robinson D	160813
Robinson T	310715
Rose PA	040907
Rose RJJ	300997
Ross AG	300996
Rouse M	310708
Ruxton SA	310714
Sargeant AL	310715
Sayner GE	310715
Scaife IJ	310713
Scaife KS	210607
Scott A	310708

Scott CR	190608
Senneck A	310708
Shakespeare AD	310705
Sideras M	310709
Simmons KJ	310709
Skimming DG	310708
Skinner TW	310714
Smart JL *BSc(Arch) MA psc(j)*	300997
Smith CD	310715
Smith DJ	310715
Smith LF	310710
Smith SM	310710
Snelgrove JA	310715
Spencer DP	310709
Stanger GA	310713
Stannard AD *MA(Cantab) MSci CMgr MCMI*	310710
Steven S	310507
Stillie JR	310710
Stockell PE	310711
Stowell PF *MBE*	310709
Sutcliffe PA	310709
Swift EM	310709
Taylor DR	310715
Taylor NJ	310715
Taylor NL	310708
Taylor WP	310710
Tedby FG	310714
Thewlis MB	310715
Thomas EM	310715
Thomas GAD	310715
Thompson AR	010707
Thompson IG	310713
Tinnion J	310715
Tonks PRG	310711
Tremelling MJ *MSc*	310715
Trengove NJ	220615
Tudhope RG	310715
Vickers ES	310715
Walsh JP *MSc BSc*	310715
Walton TJC	310711
Watson EK	310711
Watt JAM	310714
West MA	310708
Wettenhall PC	310707
White AM *F.InstLM*	300900
White BG	310704
White PR	310711
White ZK *MBE*	310712
Whitworth DC	310715
Wilford MD	310714
Williams PA	310709
Wilson JC	280509
Wilson SJ	310714
Witt JL	310709
Wood TO	300900
Wootten CJH	310707
Wright JTD	310707
Wright PS	310713
Yarroll CM	310710

Captains

Adams ETT	120612
Aldred TE	080212
Alger JJ	020409
Allen EJ	171210
Archambeau IM	110815
Ashman G	110210
Avery RM	080713
Ayres HR	090211
Bailes SP	010514
Bailey MP	220413
Bailey RJ	240815
Banting GN	140415
Barker AR	010609
Barker SL	040313
Barrett NJ	111011
Baynes GA	110815
Bennett MA	171012
Bensaid CAE	130214
Berry PR	050813
Bilney KJ	121010
Blezard GP	060415
Blyth JP	030708
Bonner RL	101011
Boughen D *MBE*	130712
Box LD	020411
Brent DGW	140415
Brind LS	140415
Brooker KJ	160511
Brown BJ	171012
Bryant MA	311212
Buckley PA	110507
Budden SM	140415
Buescher CVE *MA (Hons) MRes MLitt*	170614
Butler NJ	290615
Campbell G *MBE*	140709
Campbell LP	140213
Campbell RF	020409
Carr RM	010813
Cave AR	120612
Christie GL	050811
Collier CP	121010
Collier CR	140415
Collins DR	060809
Collins TM	161211
Conway LM	121010
Cook DW *BSc MSc MCGI*	050813
Cooper RA	120713
Cotterill ASH	180613
Coutts DG	080212
Crane LT	171012
Crawley PR	120811
Creese L	130208
Cummings DB	140415
Cutting SRK	181215
Dale JR	151215
Darby M	010714
Darling CRM	311213
Davidson CM	090211
Davies G	160609
Dawes CE	140415
Dodson JL	140415
Donoghue TN	170815
Dowd C	290914
Downing GEF	130214
Draper TA	140412
Drysdale RAR	280314
Duckering MP	090614
Dunbar DW	110610
Dunbavand MI	150713
Dunster SJ	171214
East KP	220413
Easton WP	270913
Eaton BL	110815
Eaton T	140415
Edge D	010514
Edkins DJ	010615
Edworthy BJ	130214
Eldridge EA	130214
Facey L	140415
Fairclough AP	311212
Farley-Thompson MJ	210412

Fatchett CD	290413
Fawcett IM	010710
Fensom AC	060309
Ferguson CB	130513
Flanagan AC	290615
Flannery IR	020606
Flavelle N	121010
Fleming S	220509
Ford JP	200114
Fowler IS	080914
Franks AB	140415
Fraser AH	280414
French JC *BA(Hons)*	180613
French MK	200614
Gauntlett MS	180613
Gavin DM	101011
Gibbons SSO	100513
Goodman MB	130214
Gordon CJ	140415
Gormley PM	080212
Goslin CP	120209
Graham PJ	180411
Graham TP	140412
Greener RJ	140213
Greenwood P	090710
Gronn JP	220413
Gunn DL *BSc(Hons) IEng MIET*	150914
Gutierrez EA	161013
Harrison TS	121010
Harryman JA	120811
Haughton SWT	161013
Haussauer CWP	250913
Hawke GAK	311213
Hetherington KA	260914
Heynes RD	020412
Hick TRJ	311212
Hickmott CG	140415
Higgins WT	110815
Hill MG	070909
Hill MJ	120112
Hill NA	040515
Hitch EL	030709
Hollingsworth MS	200614
Hopkins A	161013
Houlbrooke A	140213
Howie JT	110210
Howley TW	140213
Hudson KG *BSc(Hons)*	190911
Hutchings AJ	130214
Hynes AH	171012
Icke DK	290411
Ingham AP	030611
Ingold JSA	110815
Irons D	110815
Janvier DA	260811
Jefferson NM	300410
Jenkinson PA	060712
Jeyes A	160410
Johnston BL	151215
Joiner MW	160410
Jones CG	101011
Jones GC	170709
Jones TEB	121010
Joseph HL	140415
Jukes BA	161013
Kandola SS	151215
Karumba CM	150610
Kearney MT	280314
Keddie NS	140415
Keenan SJ	160414
Kerr KE	080212
King SR	120211
Lama C	130214
Lamb K	130715
Lamont DM	180313
Lane MJ	070414
Lang RA	190514
Langan K	040515
Lawrence SJC	251113
Leach PA	060707
Leary J	180613
Leigh JD	140213
Lenehan DJ	200614
Lester PD	020413
Levens MER	140415
Levick PJ	230511
Little WJ	040515
Loots JH	311212
Lorains J	120612
Luke RJB	140414
Maas GJ	200614
MacAulay CI	110210
MacDonald TW	260914
Malortie DHS	311212
Mapplebeck S	200614
Marsden S	130214
Mason JAH	140415
Mason LJ	200707
Mason PJ	040515
Mattacola MS	280510
McArthur GM	030815
McBean AP	020710
McCaskill SC	060715
McDonald M	200110
McDonnell DM	060715
McEvoy JS	171012
McGachy G	020408
McGrane AJ *GCGI*	140211
McGrath CM	161013
McGraw CJ	200614
McGregor NA	270509
McLelland JD	200614
McMullan MR	010312
McNeillie SD	311212
McNelis CG	141009
Mears DJ	010615
Meite RL	090211
Merchant GW	101011
Middleton GE	170408
Miller AJ	110509
Miller RM	310713
Mitchell AT	161013
Mitchell NJ *MBE*	010511
Mitchell SA	171012
Monk RS	131008
Moore EA	270309
Morris AD	010615
Morris SE	110210
Morris WJF	070510
Murray HSE	080212
Murray RS	070915
Naughton BJA	101011
Nichols NA	110210
Nicklin HH	150610
Noone DJ	110815
Nowosielski MJJ	250313
Osabwa PO	101011
O'Toole SJ	280613
Owen G	140213
Owens JM	200614
Pain CD	220711
Painter RK	311212
Palmer B	100408

Parkinson RLL	191214
Parr MR	200412
Parsons JGJ	140415
Pearson S	181113
Perfect JR	151215
Perkins NRM	120612
Pierson SJ	121010
Porter J *BSc*	220508
Powell GN	181215
Ramsden HS	160414
Randall DG	010615
Read K	191208
Roberts AA	080313
Roberts EL	140213
Roberts JE	310713
Roberts PJ	311213
Robinson K	060707
Rodway AJ	060412
Rose MS	171012
Ross MLM	270710
Rowland PC	171214
Rudd RD	080615
Samuel JR	010415
Scarrott W	010414
Scott KJ	090211
Shale EA	121010
Shaw ID	080615
Sillito JJ	110210
Simpson BL	280314
Simpson RT	140513
Smith SA	200614
Smith SJ	080212
South MG	060415
Southan SJ	050514
Stokoe GA	020412
Stone BM	291104
Stradling PJ	151215
Stubbs PJ	090206
Swatridge BL	260914
Taylor PMG	180613
Tee CA	130611
Thewlis A	311213
Thomas JG	080212
Thomas JH	110815
Thompson JC	180613
Thompson RM	110210
Thorburn BJ	280314
Tope DE	120612
Tucker S	150610
Turner AB	140213
Urey CWA	110815
Vanandel TC	240709
Wade RN	010615
Walczak AJ	120612
Walker ADM	170614
Wall AMF	310713
Wall D	240312
Wall RM	101011
Wallace G	310510
Wallis DJ	080313
Walsh V	150615
Watson PM	170613
Watts AM	180609
Watts SM	090410
Whinton OS	140213
Wilson Ramsay ME	121010
Winkles G	121010
Woodall TG	010615
Woodman MK	080214
Woollan BAM	080212
Woolley GJ *MBE*	010914
Wray MJ	151215
Wyldes ME	030611
Yaxley LH	140213
Yendell MCD	290711

Lieutenants

Andrew ZL	120415
Athow-Frost BC	090815
Atkinson NF	120415
Ayling N	131215
Balfour AJ	131215
Baxter DK	130414
Blee JT	130414
Booth AE	140413
Boyes AD	131215
Brookmier ZM	130414
Buttery AFG	090815
Cantell MJ	100814
Cauldwell BJ	131215
Chapman JR	131215
Ciborowski D	141214
Clarke NCA	090815
Davies MR	110813
Dorling CC	100814
Dornan JK	120415
Fraser JG	140413
Gammond CD	130414
Gillespie JR	141214
Green AE	131215
Griffiths RJ	151213
Heslop-Charman BA	131215
Hodder JP	100814
Hodgson SJ	100814
Homer AS	120415
Hoyland SL	120415
Hurst LR	120415
Jackson AT	130414
Jones HV	130414
Kane A	130414
Kuizinas LS	141214
Landon RG	120415
Limbrick PS	130414
Lockwood GJ	120415
Lumby MR	100814
MacAulay KA	141214
Mahoney MV	130414
Malan PDM	110813
Mason JS	141214
McCabe MS	100814
McKenna PA	120415
Miller OR	130414
Miskelly SJ	100814
Moffat PE	100814
Murphy JR	130414
Orme AD	130414
O'Sullivan KD	130414
Painter HC	130414
Parsons LA	100814
Patterson MR	141214
Robins CA	141214
Robinson LV	140413
Rose JA	141214
Seager JA	090815
Seaton DW	190414
Spowage BA	120415
Stevens NL	090815
Sumner CP	141214
Tabor TS	090815
Tarbox DC	100814
Thompson HW	090815
Thorogood WJ	130414
Tippett TJ	141214
Walker PF	100814

Willden JAG	100814
Wood LE	100814
Woulfe JM	130414

2nd Lieutenants

Allan-Mclean JT	120414
Ambrose JC	090814
Annable R	121215
Bennett LA	080815
Bunnett L	121215
Carter JCB	080815
Clark JG	080815
Clarke JW	090814
Cooke J	090814
Davis-Merry TR	080815
Drummond FAH	080815
Eveleigh AJ	121215
Flewitt AG	090814
Franklin OM	110415
Gallagher JR	090814
Goldsbury PK	080815
Griffith HL	080815
Hadfield K	121215
Hawkins R	121215
Hedouin D	090814
Henderson CA	110415
Heuston ME	080815
Illing RJ	110415
James OJS	110415
Keegan DW	110415
Kerrigan PJ	131214
Lovatt SJ	121215
MacLachlan DW	110415
Marchant JCK	080815
Miller AP	110415
Mitchell JAM	080815
Mould JR	121215
Nicholls A	121215
Perry GW	080815
Reid J	121215
Salero BS	121215
Sanderson AE	080815
Scott SA	090814
Shapiro MA	121215
Shortland LR	121215
Shrubb MO	131214
Stuart-Hill BJ	090814
Tonks GHM	110415
Whiting J	121215
Yaxley TJ	080815
Younge DPR	121215

ARMY AIR CORPS

A laurel wreath surmounted by The Crown; within the wreath, an eagle

An eagle within a circle inscribed ARMY AIR CORPS within the Union Wreath surmounted by The Crown. In the first corner the badge of the Glider Pilot Regiment. In the second and third corners the AAC monogram and in the fourth corner the badge of the Royal Artillery.

Normandy Landing. Pegasus Bridge, Merville Battery, Arnhem 1944, Rhine, Southern France, North West Europe 1944 – 1945, Landing in Sicily, Sicily 1943, Falkland Islands 1982, Wadi Al Batin, Gulf 1991, Al Basrah, Iraq 2003.

Regimental Marches

Quick March .... Recce Flight
Slow March.. The Thievish Magpie

Agents.. Royal Bank of Scotland plc, Holt's Farnborough Branch, Laurie House, Victoria Road, Farnborough, Hants GU14 2HJ
Corps Depot.. Army Aviation Centre, Middle Wallop, Stockbridge, Hants, SO20 8DY (Tel: 01264 784 272)
Regimental Headquarters...................... HQ Army Air Corps, Middle Wallop, Stockbridge, Hants, SO20 8DY (Tel: 01264 784 514 Email: AACHQ-RHQ-AsstRegtSec@mod.uk)

Corps Affiliations

Australian Military Forces..................... Australian Army Aviation Corps
Royal Navy .... HMS Ocean (L12) - Royal Navy
Other .... Salisbury Cathedral
The Honourable Company of Air Pilots
The Worshipful Company of Merchant Taylors

Colonel in Chief..................................... FM *HRH The Prince of* Wales *KG KT GCB OM AK QSO ADC(P)*.....................060292
Colonel Commandant............................ Gen *Sir* Adrian J Bradshaw *KCB OBE*...010709
Deputy Colonel Commandant .... Lt Gen (Retd) *Sir* Gary Coward *KBE CB*..010312

Lieutenant Colonels

Ackrill MJD	300614
Amlot DCJ	300613
Armstrong EK	311213
Ball RDH	300615
Banks NA	300609
Birkett AAR	300608
Bisset CA *MBE*	300612
Boreham GD	010116
Brown MJ	300615
Butterworth EJ	300614
Canham JH	110715
Cook JP *OBE*	300611
Cook PM	300609
Cubbin MA	300600
De Labilliere SDD	300615
Gilks AM *MBE*	300614
Godfrey AD	300613
Goodman AJ	300610
Haig AJR	300606
Hayhurst PM	300613
Houlton AV	300608
Hutchinson WNE	300609
Logan PDO	300610
Lyon RR	300614
Martin PD	090215
Mason SD	300613
Mawer RJ	300615
Melling RI	300615
Melville JL	300605
Neville MJ	300613
Olney RA	300611
Owen GL	300609
Probert M	120115
Rundle GM	300613
Senior JS	300615
Seymour RJ	300613
Shaw B	300608
Smith ID *MA*	300609
Spink GE	300604
Stein RGJ	300615
Stocker AD	300614
Tabrah A *MSc FCMI MRAeS*	300614
Tedman PT	300612
Trower DKP *MA MSc BSc(Hons) psc(j)*	300610
Weetman J *MBE*	050514
Willman AH	300611

Majors

Alesbury RPL	310712
Anderson HAP	310714
Anderson K	310715
Andrew DS	310714
Andrews CA	310711
Archer R MC	310715
Ashley RN	310708
Backhouse RWA	310713
Bambridge AP	310709
Barlow MR	310714
Barr SP *BSc*	310708
Barton NP *DFC*	310709
Bennett RJ	310714
Biggers SJ	310706

Brining SNG	310704
Brunwin TLG	310715
Burchell GAJ	310712
Burgess SF	220411
Burton CL	310715
Button PD	310703
Calvert NS	310705
Cammack JA	310713
Campbell CJ	170803
Campbell ES	310714
Campbell TP	310711
Cane OWS	310704
Challans IP	310711
Chivers MA	310703
Clements DS	310712
Cramphorn A *ATT ICAS (Dip) BSc(Hons)*	310715
Curphey DJ	181006
Curry CD	310705
Davidson AJ	310715
Deakin GJ	040906
Deegan PM	310715
Donovan JM	310702
Dufton RJ	310709
Eagles CJ	310714
English NG	310709
Farrimond PG	310711
Foran MD	310709
Fowler BS	310715
France WHP	310715
Gillson CE	310714
Goodacre DA	310707
Goodier PC	310714
Goodley HV	310715
Gough S *MBE*	310707
Graham SP	021205
Green MA	310715
Green RJ	310710
Harbottle EM	310710
Harris AW	310713
Harrison MM	310714
Hayward HM	310710
Hearn CC	310706
Hennessy DKR	310712
Hillman CPG	310710
Hindley RJW	300992
Hitch MD	310715
Hoare LG	310713
Howard-Higgins CMG *MA(Hons)*	310702
Hughes SW	310714
Jackson RJ	310714
Jenkins AR	011010
Jenkins G	310715
Johnson NA	100812
Johnston GE	140815
Jones BE	310715
Jones SJP *AFC*	310713
Kane DM	310715
King APJ	310715
Lambert D *MBE*	310715
Law HCE	190308
Leach-Thomas D	310712
Lee JL	310708
Leighton APC	310707
Lowe JP	310709
Loy KP	310712
Lyons JW	310713
Mack AWD	310707
Maddison KI	310708
Malpas JT	310715
Martin SJ	310703
McBride TD	300999
McCaighy AJ	310715
McCollum R	310714
McKenna AN *MBE*	310712
McManus JW	310714
Mead LA	310715
Miles RS	310713
Mills DP *MBA*	310715
Mitchell A	310711
Monnington CEA	310714
Moore TR	310708
Morrison A	310709
Morton-Race JP	310713
Murray RJ	310715
Murrell JR *MEng cfs tp*	310708
Newsam K *MEng*	310714
Nicholson LAH *DFC*	180710
Noy OE	310714
Paden EL	191214
Painter MD	310715
Pannett JGA	310709
Pearce SJ	310712
Peters IJS	300605
Pimm MJ	310713
Pittaway TWJ *MBE*	310709
Pope SFD *BSc(Hons) MA*	310713
Porter JR	310715
Pugh NM	310714
Raikes HR	310715
Ramsay CM	310715
Reesby LR	310713
Rickers AL	130514
Ricketts ME	310712
Rivett AB	310713
Roberts JJR	310711
Robertson JC	310714
Sams DJ *MBE*	310711
Scott CWD	310707
Sharpe ND	310714
Shillito BP	310714
Short DGA	310712
Shorter DA	310712
Simcock RJ	310713
Smit RA	310711
Somerville JAG	310713
Southall GJ	310715
Stead OJ	310710
Stewart-Davis JG *MCGI*	010409
Strong DJ	310710
Stuart ER	310715
Thomas BW	310715
Thompson AJ	310714
Thompson NF	300996
Thwaites JM	160108
Tracy RH	300987
Tymon JP	310712
Vaughan AP *phi cfs*	310705
Ward GP	310711
Warner AD	310712
Watson RIG *BSc MSc*	310712
Webb RP	310711
Whatnell PA	310715
Wheeler PRD	310702
White AD	310713
Whitfield RMP *cfs*	010503
Williams AC	310705
Wilsey SRW	310710
Wood MA	190704
Woodhouse LP	310714
Zipfell AJ *BSc*	310714

Captains

Anderson M	080413
Anstey RT *MEng*	080212
Aslett MC	020309
Bancroft A	070414
Bannister TN	080212
Barber CCJ	130214
Bernard LP	171012
Bishop ST	260914
Blackmore SH	101011
Blois J	140412
Bosher GM	171012
Bowles JM *BA(Hons)*	160615
Bramley RWS	121010
Briggs BWR	310712
Browning JK	060508
Bush PC	070408
Cambrook JD	141009
Campbell-Davis A	161013
Carter R	160209
Charlton SS	151215
Cherry JJ	060409
Clement J	060411
Clive HPD	080211
Cranfield EA	130611
Dargavel PRJ	060410
Davenport TM	180613
Davison DI	311212
Dix GB	040515
Doncaster JA	130906
Durrell RES	151215
Eccles JR	020412
Edmondson DA	151215
Everett JMF	130214
Farrell L	180515
Field CJ	150610
Finch SA	010615
Fleming DP	060411
Floyd DA	311213
Forbes D	010715
Fowler BP	161013
Francis WJ	080212
French TK	180613
Gant TP	130810
Garner RI	160609
Gibbins OJ	310713
Girdler SM	060411
Gittoes RJ	140309
Grannell NA	140414
Gwilliam AJ	140412
Hackford T	140415
Hallums MP	070414
Hamblin MSE	121010
Hammond JA	020209
Hay CE	120612
Hayward L	060109
Hedley MCC	130411
Henley JW	160414
Hewitt SM	120209
Hill JC	140714
Hindmarch SA	010996
Howard AJ	150610
Howard SJ	120612
Howden GW	311212
Hyland DL	060411
Ibbotson MR	010213
Ison MD	080212
Jarrett SRJ	180613
Jewson JTN	311213
Johnson B	140213
Johnston TR	070414
Jones JW	140415
Jones RDW	030212
Jones RM	170614
Kaulback SE	161013
Keiderling RP	310713
Kendall NR	270315
Kennerley RB	140213
Kent MW	080413
Kinnear WC	130214
Kiy IJ	130214
Lean JC	100815
Ledwith TKE	130214
Lee BC	161211
Lee-Smith EE	121010
Lee-Smith JC	150610
Linegar JS	080413
Long JP	120612
Lonsdale RJ	110815
Lowrey JD	140415
Lyne MJE	130611
Macklin DAD	140213
Marsden E	311213
Marshall JW	101011
Marshall SA	060410
Martin AJ	311212
Mathers HR	060710
McClurey-Rutkiewicz SK	140415
McCrea RM	130214
Morton CM	070414
Murray RLT	151215
Murrell LD	040515
Musgrove TCJ	130814
Nacmanson NJ	160414
Nelson JM	140213
Nicol MMG	060410
O'Brien ND	010409
Pantoja EJ	110815
Parkes KJ	080413
Parkes PE	101011
Parmenter AM	310713
Pattinson MG	010715
Pearce SM	010715
Potts R	201009
Price DAH	161013
Price SR	060410
Robertson-Cowley AJ	260914
Robinson MP	311212
Rodgers AW *CMgr MCMI*	060410
Ross GJ	080413
Russell CW	110210
Shergold HL	171012
Simpson RGJ	110815
Smith DJ	060411
Smith DP	170614
Snell OJR	080212
Stack TL	080211
Steinberg PW	141009
Stephan MJ	020513
Sudworth CP	130610
Sweeney TD	090608
Taliku M	060410
Tant SC	191214
Thatcher SA	040510
Thornton MJ	210613
Torbett N	101011
Tovey SC	110515
Trayhurn JR	111209
Tyrrell TJM	130611
Vann JM	110815
Vickers CJ	020412
Walker CL	120612
Walkinshaw MR	040515
Waller GK	010611

Ward RM	171214
Watkinson IM	180613
Wight DM	010812
Wilson PJK	080211
Wilson YJ	070414
Zehner WZ	180613

Lieutenants

Adams MB	131210
Adcock MJ	090815
Bennett MKS	131215
Binding GA	140413
Bird NE	131215
Birrell NWG	130414
Brown LD	120415
Brownlow JD	090815
Bull JP	100814
Cole MA	120415
Collings ME	120415
Cray SL	141214
Creighton CF	120415
Doherty AJ	141214
Doyle MJ	131215
Duffus JAM	100814
Evans TJB	090815
Finch SE	151212
Fitz-Gerald CM	120415
Fuke CJ	141214
Gartside EB	131215
Gellender DE	141214
Gibson Fleming WR	140413
Gorwood EL	100814
Goss TM	120415
Granell JL	090815
Grundy EM	130414
Haddrill JH	131215
Hall TSR	131210
Hares RE	110813
Harrop JW	141214
Hartland CJ	120415
Hollyer DI	140413
Howell SJ *BSc*	131215
Hunt LRD	130414
Hurley LA	100814
Hyslop JD	120415
Jacka KP	090815
Johnson JCJ	140413
Johnston JT	100814
Jump SW	110813
Kiernan JA	100814
Levien RJW	100814
Lindley JP	130414
Lumb EJ	131215
MacBrayne SC	110813
MacLennan I	090815
Marshall MD	100814
Miller JS	130414
Moran LF	140413
Nijjar BS	131215
Pannell RA	130414
Pardoe AB	120415
Pollard AJW	130414
Rawsthorne JJ	130414
Richardson NJ	131215
South AR	110911
Steer DT	110813
Taggart SM	100814
Walker TA	090815
Wallace LDA	141214
Whyte RDR	090815

2nd Lieutenants

Baker WJ	110415
Bedford HJ	110415
Calder-Smith TGH	110415
Carter CJ	121215
Clamp WJ	110415
Coogan CJ	121215
Eaton HS	121215
Elliott OGU	080815
Fraser TI	121215
Hampson ST	121215
Hannah RA	110415
Hearnshaw W	110415
Hookham F	121215
Johnson LJ	080815
Johnstone M	121215
Lowe D	080815
Morgan TP	080815
Osborne SW	110415
Pizzoni MGE	080815
Plumb JS	121215
Roberts AL	121215
Selby TP	110415
Ward AP	110415

INTELLIGENCE CORPS

A Union rose within two branches of laurel surmounted by a crown; below the laurel a scroll inscribed INTELLIGENCE CORPS

Manui Dat Cognitio Vires

Regimental Marches

Quick March .... "The Rose and the Laurel"
Slow March.. "Trumpet Tune (and Ayre)"

Agents.. Holts Branch, The Royal Bank of Scotland plc
Regimental Headquarters...................... Chicksands, Shefford, Bedfordshire SG17 5PR
(Tel: 01462 752340/01 Fax: 01462 752374)
Email: intcorpshq-icc-corpssec@mod.uk

Alliances

Canadian Armed Forces......................... Canadian Forces Intelligence Branch
Australian Military Forces..................... The Australian Intelligence Corps

Colonel in Chief.................................... FM *HRH The Prince Philip Duke of* Edinburgh *KG KT OM GBE ONZ QSO AK GCL CC CMM ADC(P)*

Colonel Commandant........................... Maj Gen Jim R Hockenhull *OBE*...190714
Deputy Colonel Commandant .... Brig (Retd) Ewan R Duncan *OBE*...010114

Lieutenant Colonels

Barrow AG	300606
Bavin MA	300612
Bowman APR	300614
Brown JE	300612
Cadman MA	300613
Clarke MF	300607
Cox AT	300615
Emmett MG	300615
Evans GJ	300614
Fairweather NL	300614
Farrag SM	040714
Galbraith FE	300612
Green MA	300614
Haden NJ	300615
Hetherington AE	300613
Janes AC	300613
Jones DGS	300607
Jones MH *MBE*	300613
Lomax D	300613
Malone VAJ	300607
Markham LE	050115
Marks SJJ	300613
O'Driscoll TE	300609
Peebles ME	300611
Pugh-Cook RM	300608
Thewlis-Smith ND	300615
Thomas SJ	300609
Tomlyn MTH	300610
Williams SR *MA PCGE MCGI*	300604
Winter AJ	300613
Wreford PRF	300605

Majors

Alloway DG	310713
Attree AN	310715
Bailey RS *LLB(Hons)*	310714
Barber AI	310710
Barber K	310715
Barnes SE	310714
Barnett GN	310713
Barnett HV	310715
Bellringer DR	310715
Bentley MJ	310709
Bowman D	310709
Boxer CAH	310711
Bright RP	310714
Bromage AH *BSc MCMI*	310708
Buchan F	310714
Bunney TJH	310705
Butler JA *MA*	310714
Churm P	310707
Clifford GDH	310704
Cloke RJT	310709
Connelly JO *BEM*	310709
Cook AG	310710
Cottrell JA	300996
Curling RK	310711
Davidson AM	310708
Dee JAC	310710
Dennison PL	310715
Dhillon PS	310714
Diamond R	310708
Dixon AJH	310715
Dobson CG	310712
Doidge AS	310715
Duke C	310709
Duncan DR	310709
Farrier W	310715
Feeney RP	310715
Flavell S	100812
Friskney CP	310709
Givens RI	310712
Gomez A	310715
Green AL	310709
Groome TJ	310715
Haseldine AJ	310704
Hawker M	300999
Hawkins AEC	310711
Hetherington JAJ	310710
Holl JD	310706

Holmes GJ	310715
Hooker PS	310706
Howarth HM	310709
James J	310706
Jenkins CJ	310706
Kajzer-Hughes GP	310713
Logan IJ	310711
Loosemore MJ	310713
MacIntyre DI	310708
MacLeod JM	310712
Marchant AB *BSc*	310709
Mason CN	310713
Mawdsley RJ	310715
McCarthy CF	310715
Moth AS	310707
Murray CJ	310708
Nettleship M	310712
Oladjins MD	310714
Oldershaw JA	310715
Owen AR	280807
Parke-Robinson FS	310705
Parsons AJ	310714
Pepper MEH	310711
Porter GR	310708
Puxley SP	310708
Riley WN	310714
Roberts SJ	310712
Seton-Sykes CA	310712
Shepherd AJF	310714
Shindler AM	310715
Speedman RJ	310712
Stabler DC	310712
Stables AP	310711
Stephens BL *QGM*	310715
Tate K *MBE*	310712
Tosh WM	310706
Tyler AJ	310713
Vallor JC	310714
Verret IK	310710
Weatherstone IRG	310712
Whewell AR	310715
Wood JM	310715
Woodhead MG	310710
Wotton PJ	280904

Captains

Balsom BJ	090211
Bance-Smith YH	070911
Banks HE	141009
Beard AP	121010
Bell RL	101011
Berry J	050414
Bracken AJ	090808
Brandling-Harris LV	200614
Brazier JM	120612
Buchan J	010411
Burge ERA	130214
Chmiel JS	110815
Churchman MJ	161013
Clark SM	090211
Clarke CD	011014
Connaughton MA	110110
Cook JME	171214
Cooper CR	100710
Cooper LRE	180613
Coulthard KN	110815
Cowling GR	150210
Crawford LM	010415
Crisp AGT	170614
Davies AP	150610
Dawkins HWA	130214
Dawson HJ	040401
Denny-Morley J	110210
Digby KJ	310314
Dugdale A	130611
Dunn ML	190514
Dyson PMJ	141009
Edwards TP	101011
Eggett C	020414
Evans PJ	230511
Farber OEJ	171012
Featherstone MSR	020412
Fensome MP	140415
French ST	161013
Frere-Cook HLC	200614
Galatin CA	010415
Gill AW	310311
Gilliland JG	151215
Green JMT	130611
Greenwood JST	151215
Griffiths PS *MBE*	130415
Grujic L	140213
Hale CD	190410
Hamilton BP	130214
Harlen S	020412
Haslam-Greene HL	140213

Hayes SJR	140415
Higham TF	151215
Hilton MDA	141009
Hogan BP *MBE*	110411
Hunter-Choat SE	151215
Ingold CK	101011
Jakeway SM	020412
Jennings MF	080313
Johnstone-Burt TW	120612
Jones AD	170614
Jones AR	050413
Joyce CM	130611
Kinghan SJ	140213
Kirby RA	140415
Kitchin T *MBE*	050413
Liddell HRD	080212
Liddle DA	070514
Linscer A *MBE*	080609
Lowish C	270711
Lucas CE	080211
MacDonald ADD	120612
MacMaster JH	080212
Maddock RJ	
McCarthy SVA	130214
McColl RE	110815
McCormack DL	171012
McKenzie SJ	230511
Mellows AJ	151215
Menelaou AD	140213
Metherell B	030613
Moore LA	130609
Nathanson MW	121010
Newton BWH	130611
Nickerson C	040515
Noble HA	080212
Norris CR	090211
Oliver ND	171012
Partridge TR	101011
Paterson SC	170614
Reeves JE	010414
Robertson FCS	180613
Robinson JA	140213
Rouse J	110815
Rowlands RC	130214
Russ AJ	161013
Ryan PA	110411
Sawyer AP	151215
Scott ST	180613

Shutt BJ *BSc(Hons) MSc MLitt OT*	130214
Smith BA	180613
Squires TA	080212
Stacey RP	140415
Stanier JM	180613
Stead S	120410
Stephens YR	180613
Taylor HJG	151215
Taylor SK	060413
Thoburn GAH	080609
Thompson K *MA*	040411
Thorpe A	080212
Tilford NG	080615
Tugwell REA	151215
Unsworth LA	130214
Upham EDO	260514
Varcoe KA	120612
Walter HA	151215
Weston DR	130415

Lieutenants

Bennett SM	120415
Boughey JR	120415
Breeds MJE	140412
Cass AR	131215
Eadon-Rayner DW	141213
Ferrier AI	141213
French EP	100814
Gourevitch ASB	090815
Gunning J	131215
Heathcote DF	131215
Herbert LJ	090815
Hillier ZK	141213
Irving JMW	100814
Johnson MJ	120415
Jones LE	120415
Keating FDR	120415
Kinson TH	120415
Leyshon EL	090815
Mowbray RP	140413
Murtagh DJ	090815
O'Sullivan RD	130414
Pollard CJ	090815
Proctor MK	141213
Richardson MM	100814
Robson AR	090815
Rosen R	141213
Simmons B	141213
Stearn LR	120415
Studwell JG	130414
Tevlin FM	100814
Ward DG	100814
Weaver SL	120415
Wilcox BA	100814
Wilks PH	140412
Williams CD	141214

2nd Lieutenants

Beddall JM	131214
Beresford-Webb PR	121215
Chillery JJ	121215
Cross A	080815
Cutter B	110415
Duffield R	080815
Farrag JE	080815
Hares LA	121215
Harrison JJ	110415
Hine JD	110415
Holmes ZW	080815
Hughes ZS	121215
Lyle AB	080815
Mason-Johns ON	131214
Morizet DN	110415
Nicholson P	121215
Porter WD	110415
Stone NM	121215
Taylor CJ	110415
Tetstall ER	110415

ROYAL ARMY CHAPLAINS' DEPARTMENT

Upon a wreath of laurel and oak a Maltese Cross. In the centre a quatrefoil voided with a circle inscribed with the motto IN THIS SIGN CONQUER. The whole ensigned with The Crown

For Jewish Chaplains

Upon a wreath of laurel and oak a Star of David. In the centre of the Star, a circle containing a quatrefoil voided. The whole ensigned with The Crown.

Regimental March

Quick March .... Trumpet Voluntary
Slow March .... Trumpet Voluntary

Agents .... Holt's Branch, Royal Bank of Scotland plc, Lawrie House, Farnborough, Hants GU14 7NR

Royal Army Chaplain's Department .... Army Headquarters | MOD CHAPS (A), 2nd Floor, Zone 1, IDL 433, Ramillies Building, Marlborough Lines, Monxton Road, Andover SP11 8HJ (Tel: 01264 381865 Email: LF-CHAPSA-STAFF-CHAPLAIN-SO2@mod.uk)

Alliances

The Canadian Armed Forces .... Chaplains' Branch
Australian Military Forces .... The Royal Australian Army Chaplains' Department
New Zealand Army .... Royal New Zealand Chaplains' Department

Patron .... HER MAJESTY THE QUEEN

Church of England .... Archbishop of Canterbury's Episcopal Representative
The Deanery, Windsor Castle, Windsor, Berks SL4 1NJ

Jewish .... The Secretary, The Jewish Committee for H M Forces,
25 Enford Street, London, W1H 2DD

Methodist Church .... The Secretary of the Methodist Royal Navy, Army and Royal Air Force Board,
13 Park Road, St Dominic, Saltash, Cornwall, PL12 6TL

Presbyterian Churches:

Church of Scotland .... The Convener, Committee on Chaplains to H M Forces,
Faculties Office, University Office, Regent Walk, Aberdeen, AB24 3FX

Free Church of Scotland .... The Representative on the Interdenominational Advisory Committee,
Offices of the Free Church of Scotland, Edinburgh, EH1 2LS

Presbyterian Church in Ireland .... The Convener, Forces Committee,
Church House, Fisherwick Place, Belfast, BT1 6DW

Presbyterian Church of Wales .... The Representative on the Interdenominational Advisory Committee,
53 Richmond Road, Cardiff, CF2 3UP

Roman Catholic Church .... Roman Catholic Bishop of the Forces (RC)
Bishops Oak, 26 The Crescent, Farnborough Park, Farnborough,
Hants, GU14 7AS

United Navy, Army and Air Force Board comprising:

Baptist United Reformed Church .... The Secretary of the United Navy, Army and Air Force Board,
Bookham Baptist Church, Lower Road, Bookham, Leatherhead,
Surrey, KT23 4DH

Chaplains to the Forces (1st Class) ranking as Colonels

Cole TAR *Rev MA BD MTh*	300412
Eagles PA *Rev QHC CF*	270108
Evans IA *Rev*	160712
Langston CM *Rev*	300614
Totten AJ *Rev MBE*	300612

Chaplains to the Forces (2nd Class) ranking as Lieutenant Colonels

Abeledo BJA *Rev*	300612
Aldred PJ *Rev*	300614
Barrett DJ *Rev*	300614
Bosher PR *Rev Cert Ed (PCE) MTh*	300613
Fava MPD *Rev*	180909
Forster S *Rev*	140308
Gough JRB *Rev*	050508
MacPherson DJ *Rev*	300614
Maynard CA *Rev BA(Hons) MTh*	140909
McCormack PJ *Rev MBE*	060910
Moesel JS *Rev*	010710

Olliff R *Rev* 120410
Steele AC *Rev MBE* 300612
Stevenson IJ *Rev* 311213
Swinn SP *Rev* 300614
Whiting S *Rev MBE BA* 300612

Chaplains to the Forces (3rd Class) ranking as Majors

Adams DJ *Rev* 261110
Allen GD *Rev* 011006
Anderson DP *Rev* 220112
Barry KG *Rev* 131003
Bell CD *Rev* 260612
Bennett ASF *Rev* 230210
Bloxam-Rose SF *Rev MA PhD* 220211
Brown DG *Rev* 100111
Burley RD *Rev MA MPhil* 040607
Burrows PG *Rev BSc(Hons)* 120513
Callanan CD *Rev* 051014
Clarke JS *Rev* 230412
Collingwood GL *Rev (CE) BA MA DipMin* 231111
Colson IR *Rev BSc BTh DipRE MA* 120109
Conning DP *Rev BTh (gk)* 180814
Corrigan RD *Rev* 150913
Crees DP *Rev* 160215
Cumming DJ *Rev* 131003
Dalton AI *Rev* 220812
Daniel J *Rev* 220812
Downes RJ *Rev* 151214
Duncan JC *Rev* 290107
Dunwoody SJH *Rev* 100111
Evans HD *Rev* 100112
Farmer SJ *Rev* 030300
Farrell ND *Rev* 241114
Frail NR *Rev* 100712
Franklin SA *Rev* 181099
Gandiya LF *Rev* 150604
Gosnell N *Rev SRN BTh(Hons) MA(Ed) MA* 150604
Grant-Jones MD *Rev* 160215
Green PA *Rev* 040515
Groocock CJ *Rev* 080506
Haldon-Jones MV *Rev* 110996
Hall RAB *Rev* 290409
Hancock S *Rev* 290908
Hanrahan PJ *Rev* 260911
Henderson M *Rev* 210211
Hernandez DF *Rev* 310106
Humphryes GJ *Rev* 140113
Hyde JM *Rev* 240912
Ingham AW *Rev* 030907
Jackson AJ *Rev* 260911
Jamieson JG *Rev* 040515
Keith GMW *Rev CF* 160614
Kellock CN *Rev MA BD* 190813
King NR *Rev* 040515
King PWS *Rev* 250612
Kinsella NP *Rev* 040515
Latifa AM *Rev* 100111
Lodwick SH *Rev* 040607
Mackay SA *Rev* 070914
MacKenzie HM *Rev* 150913
MacKenzie SL *Rev* 150604
MacLeod CF *Rev* 260911
MacLeod RN *Rev* 060498
Mairara JR *Rev* 150913
McCaulay STJ *Rev* 200910
McCourt P *Rev* 150909
McDowell NG *Rev BA MAR* 141002
McWhirter J *Rev* 220812
Mentzel KD *Rev* 080902
Middlemiss D *Rev* 150913
Morgan DT *Rev* 150913
Oliver AT *Rev* 051014
Priest RM *Rev CF* 101000
Rendell HM *Rev BA MDiv MPhil(Oxon) PGCE* 120114
Richards SA *Rev* 220812
Richardson RJ *Rev* 200910
Roache A *Rev* 250612
Scott GJ *Rev BD PGCE* 041015
Sharkey S *Rev* 150913
Smith GC *Rev* 241212
Smith RM *Rev* 170209
Strachan AE *Rev RAChD* 180208
Thatcher SB *Rev* 041005
Thomason MP *Rev BA CF* 130212
Todd NS *Rev* 130212
Tome Da Silva CA *Rev BEd BTh LLB LLM* 130212
Turner SP *Rev* 051014
Vince DE *Rev* 241212
Vincent JL *Rev* 220909
White K *Rev BA MTh* 260911
Withers CM *Rev* 070914
Young SBK *Rev* 250612

Chaplains to the Forces (4th Class) ranking as Captains

Adolphe KJ *Rev (UB)* 270415
Archibald PB *Rev BSc BTh* 290413
Berry GT *Rev* 300412
Birnie RJ *Rev BTh(Hons) MA* 140408
Bradbury JRG *Rev* 300412
Caldwell JW *Rev (CE)* 140915
Chadwick MWA (CE) 011215
Coles MSR *Rev* 300412
Critchlow D *Rev (CE)* 140915
Dixon P *Rev (CE)* 140915
Gillham CA *Rev BN BA* 290413
Goodison MJ *Rev CF BSc(Hons) BD* 010712
Green B *Rev Dr* 290914
Groves MR *Rev B Div* 011012
Harding AB *Rev* 020511
Hiney TRC *Rev* 290914
Jones CWA *Rev* 300412
Jones KP *Rev* 020511
Linton GI *Rev BD* 280414
McConville G *Rev* 290914
McLay NJ *Rev BD BA* 071106
Middleton D *Rev PGDip GradDip MA FIDTA* 270610
Neiland PA *Rev* 011012
Pratt SS *Rev (CE)* 140912
Price IMR *Rev* 250211
Rogers IC *Rev* 300412
Smith P *Rev (RC)* 270415
Stokes CC *Rev* 020511
Thom DJ *Rev (CS)* 270415
Van Sittert P *Rev* 031011
Walters AL *Rev (M)* 140915
Wiley JJD *Rev (UB)* 140915
Wilson A *Rev* 290603
Wilson SG *Rev (CE)* 270415

THE ROYAL LOGISTIC CORPS

A gilt eight-pointed star forming the background, upon which, in gilt, is a laurel wreath Also in gilt, two crossed axes lie above the laurel wreath. Onto the axes is superimposed the Garter, in Oxford blue, bearing the Garter motto, in gilt, within which is centrally placed a shield bearing the arms of the Board of Ordnance. The shield sits on a field of scarlet enamel. A gilt Monarchal crown displaces the uppermost point of the Royal Star. Beneath the Garter is a scroll bearing the motto WE SUSTAIN

Regimental March

Quick March .... On Parade
Slow March .... Lion, Sword and Crown

Agents .... Holt's Branch, Royal Bank of Scotland plc, Lawrie House, Farnborough, Hants GU14 7NR
Regimental Headquarters .... RHQ The RLC, Dettingen House, Princess Royal Barracks, Deepcut, Camberley, Surrey, GU16 6RW
(Tel: 01252 833 593 Mil: 94214 5593 Fax: 94214 5375
Email: RLCRHQ-RegtSec-SO1@mod.uk)

Alliances

Australian Military Forces .... Royal Australian Corps of Transport
Royal Australian Army Ordnance Corps
Royal Australian Army Catering Corps
New Zealand Army .... Royal New Zealand Logistic Regiment
Indian Army .... Army Service Corps of India
Army Ordnance Corps of India
Pakistan Army .... Army Service Corps of Pakistan
Army Ordnance Corps of Pakistan
Sri Lanka Army .... The Sri Lanka Army Service Corps
The Sri Lanka Army Ordnance Corps
Malaysian Army .... The Malaysian Army Service Corps
The Malaysian Ordnance Corps
South African Defence Forces .... Personnel Service Corps of the South Africa National Defence Force
Canadian Armed Forces .... Canadian Forces Logistics Branch

Affiliated Regiment

The Queen's Own Gurkha Logistic Regiment

Colonel in Chief .... *HRH The Princess Royal KG KT GCVO QSO*
Deputy Colonels in Chief .... *HRH The Duke of* Gloucester *KG GCVO*
HRH The Duchess of Kent *GCVO*
The Master General of Logistics .... Lt Gen Mark W Poffley *OBE* 010612
Regimental Colonel .... Col Darren N Corrie *MBE ADC* 010814
Colonels Commandant .... Maj Gen (Retd) Malcolm D Wood *CBE* 050406
Maj Gen (Retd) Chris M Steirn *CBE* 050408
Maj Gen (Retd) David J Shouesmith 010608
Maj Gen (Retd) J S (Seumas) Kerr *CBE* 050409
Lt Gen Mark W Poffley *OBE* 150509
Brig (Retd) Chris J Murray *CBE* 010710
Maj Gen (Retd) Ian M Copeland *CB* 010411
Brig Duncan F Capps *CBE* 010914
Maj Gen Angus S J Fay 011114
Deputy Chief of the General Staff .... Lt Gen M W Poffley *OBE* (*late* RLC) 010415

Honorary Ordnance Officer
HM Tower of London .... Maj Gen (Retd) Malcolm D Wood *CBE* 050412
Honorary Catering Adviser .... Mr (Hon Maj Gen) David Morgan-Hewitt 020810

Regimental Secretary .... Lt Col S A Yafai *RLC*

Lieutenant Colonels

Allen D 300608
Allen PA 300615
Arnold PJ 300604
Asbee JRG 300611
Ashman DA 300612
Askew RAC 300610
Astley NI *MSc MBE* 300605
Atkins JW 300608
Baker R 280312
Barton NIM 300606
Barwick RG 150915
Bateman GA *MBE* 300603
Bayliss IR 300615
Beaumont PMK 300613
Beck EWT 300615
Berry SJ 300607
Biggs M *MBE* 230114
Blenkinsop NR *BA(Hons) MA MSc PGCE CMILT* 300611
Boswell DJ 010115
Bowler MC 300615
Brown MW 300613
Browne RJ 300615
Bunkle OG *psc(j)* 300612
Burgess JH 300608
Burgess TAW 300611
Caldwell SJ *psc(j)(Can) psc(j)(Ku)* 300606
Chestnutt JEA *MBA BSc(Hons)* 300613
Child CJS 300608
Claridge MK 300613
Clouston DS *MBE* 300610
Collins MA 300613
Comer MJ 300613
Conlan PD 300609
Cooper DML 300609
Cornell SA 300614
Courtier MS 300608
Coward EN 300607
Craig JRC 300608
Crew N 300615
Crossland TJ 300613
Dagless KJ 300614
Daley LJN 300610
Davidson WA 300613
Davies RG 300607
Davis MJ *GM* 300604
Dempsey MJC 300612
Devine BJ 300614
Donoghue SE 300611
Duncan AJ 300606
Duxbury BA 300608
Evanson-Goddard MA *OBE MA* 300612
Eze EC 300605
Finnigan DT 310313
Fisher DJ *MBE* 300615
Fletcher JS *Dip* 300614
Flint NGA 300614
Foreman SP 300613
Francis CJ *MBE* 300610
Frankland KL 300614
Galloway JW 300608
Galvin SD 310814
Gardiner AJ *MA RLC* 300608
Gascoigne RJ *BSc MDip MSc* 300607
Genko MR 300615
Gilbert JM 300612
Giles LM *BSc(Hons) GCGI MA psc(j) PGCE* 300611
Gliniecki M *QGM* 300605
Gosling DC 300613
Gould TR 300615
Hallett RG 300615
Hanson CI *BEng(Hons) Psc(j)(Aus)* 300615
Heath AN 300606
Heaton-Smith JB 300614
Henson CJ *QGM* 300610
Hesketh MJ 300613
Hing MJ 300614
Hirst SA 300610
Hoey AOG 300605
Hoff AP 300609
Holder PD *QCVS* 300610
Holman NF 300613
Howard BK *MA PGDip GCGI MIExpE MILM* 300614
Hughes DM 300608
Hughes GKM *OBE* 300606
Hutton-Fellowes E *BSc(Hons)* 300614
Illingworth PM 300612
Jenkins DE 300614
Jermy SP *GCGI ATO* 300613
Jones R *MBE MSc MiH LCG* 180315
Joynes NG *QGM* 300615
Kavanagh DG 300604
Keppel-Compton RT *RLC MA* 300607
Kerner JR *MA GCGI CMILT* 300609
Kerr J 280915
King PM 300610
King PR 300608
Leach JD 180613
Lillywhite AC *MBE* 300614
Lloyd MR *MBE* 200815
MacRory-Tinning SJ *MSc MA* 300609
Madams AM 300615
Maddison A 300612
Manson RI 300609
Marshall PA *MBE* 300606
Mason DM 300612
Maxwell DM 300613
McCormack TS 300613
McCrann JSD *MBE* 300612
McNair RWL 300607
Middleditch MJF *MBE QGM* 300614
Morton CM 300613
Moss AP *OBE* 300609
Moverley GM 300615
Nanovo VT 300611
Nixon AC 300604
Norreys SE 190614
Parker AJ *MBE* 300614
Pemberton-Pigott TJD 300611
Poole I 300609
Potter MJ 300612
Priest JSR *MBE* 300611
Ralfe PD 110515
Rawlinson MG 300611
Rea DM 300612
Read D 300615
Reehal PS *MBE* 300614
Reid D 221213
Reid VC *MBE* 300613
Reyland DA 300610
Rhodes JER 300613
Riddell CE 300607
Robinson LM 300605
Scannell MA 300614
Scattergood ID *MBE MC* 300609
Scott ZDC 300613
Shepherd NR 300608
Shilton AR 300603
Skinsley PM *BSc(Hons)* 300614

Skipper I *MA* 300608
Slight CJ 190915
Smalley CN 300614
Smith PD 311213
Smith PT 300613
Smith RC *OBE* 300610
Stannett PR *BA(Hons) MSc* 300607
Stephens AJ 121014
Stevenson SJ 300613
Stockdale A 300615
Stocks MD 300611
Stuart CP *MEng* 300613
Stuart MK 300615
Summersgill SA *MBE* 300614
Sunderland DRH *MSc* 300608
Sunderland JDV *BA(Hons) MA psc(j)* 300612
Symonds TJ 300613
Taylor MG *MBE* 300613
Tinlin SK 010114
Tonkins WRJ 300611
Vaughan GE 300611
Vickerman PM 300614
Wagstaff R 300613
Wakelin NJ 300613
Walker FMU 300611
Watkins SJR 300615
West JC 300615
Whitbread LF 300614
White SPR 300612
Wilkes NCB 300602
Williams PN 300609
Woodley CR *MBE* 160413
Yafai SA 310514
Zanchi AC 300612

Majors

Abel CM *LLM* 310714
Adams BJ 310709
Ainsworth EL 300605
Alexander CA 310708
Allen DM 310711
Allen GJ *MA CMgr MCMI CMILT MCIPR* 310711
Allen RJ 310715
Allford CM 310715
Amor RP *BSc(Hons)* 310712
Anderson LT *MBE* 310709
Anderson ND 310707
Ashton MA 310710
Aumonier B 260908
Austin DS 310712
Austin MR 310702
Austin VL 310714
Baker KH *MBE MSc CEng MIExpE* 300900
Barker SJ 310715
Barlow DL *BSc(Hons)* 310710
Barron R *BSc(Hons) MBA (Open)* 310705
Barry MR 310714
Bastin JD *GCGI MSc* 300999
Battersby DM *BSc(Hons)* 310704
Beauman KM *MBA CMILT MCMI* 310705
Beere JW *BA(Hons)* 310711
Bennett TE 310712
Berry NG 310714
Bhundia AS *BSc(Hons)* 310712
Birkby AM 310704
Birtle I 310711
Blunden EJ *BSc(Hons)* 310715
Booth I *MBE* 310709
Bowen CN 310706
Bowerbank S 310712
Bowman EML 310713
Bowsley MD 310715
Brassington JD 310707
Brewer GP 310712
Brewer PM 310712
Brock GS *MSc PG Dip* 300994
Brook OF 310712
Brown AMJ 310713
Brown DA 310709
Brown JL 310705
Brown JW *BSc(Hons)* 310711
Browne PNK 310715
Bruce IF 310709
Brudenell JK 310712
Burke KA 310708
Butler LJ 130208
Butterworth CP 310711
Calkin CD 310704
Callen-Organ PA 310705
Calvert PVE 300901
Camilleri SCP 310715
Campbell RJ 310715
Carter CA 310714
Cartwright-Terry JGF 310714
Chapman PJ 310711
Cheetham RS 310714
Chinnadurai RV 310712
Chohan MJ 310703
Clarke JA 310713
Clarke LA 310712
Clydesdale AN 300994
Colbourne MJ 310711
Coles SM 310715
Coningham JP 310714
Conyer RJ *MBE* 310712
Cook HF 310711
Cooke G 310703
Cooke SG 310709
Cooper GA 310705
Corbett JC 310715
Cornell A *BA(Hons)* 310710
Cornish PJ 310715
Coulson AJ 310713
Cox AA *LLB(Hons)* 310713
Cox IA 310714
Cox SJ 310709
Cripps NL 310713
Crompton VJ *MBE* 310711
Cross JF 310712
Cross SE 130704
Cugudda DA 310712
Culverwell FP 310715
Cusworth RS 310710
Dance LM 310714
Dangerfield FA *BEd(Hons)* 310712
Darke RJ *BSc* 310714
Davie AR *BSc(Hons)* 310705
Davies LA 310715
Davis LC 310715
Davis PE *MBE* 310712
Dean PR 300996
Dempsey DE 270412
Dermody JG 300901
Dickinson KL 310712
Dilkes B 310713
Dines SJ 310707
Docherty DW 310707
Dodgson KP 310703
Donoghue C 310704

Doughty KR	310709
Douglas-Evans B	310715
Dove SN	310714
Duddy DG	300999
Duggan AL	310712
Dunlop N	310711
Dunlop S *MA*	310710
Dyer CW	310711
Eason GDA	310715
Eaton PA *MBE*	310710
Eaton PD	180414
Edwards J	310708
Edwards R	310713
Egan RJ	310706
Eggett N	310708
Ekman BR *BComm*	310714
Elliott JE	310714
Emmerson RA *MBE*	310708
Enever M	310708
Evans ARJ	310710
Evans N	310708
Evans TR	310714
Falinski NM	310712
Faulkner JE *MBE*	310706
Fawsitt JC	310709
Ferguson D	310713
Ferguson SJ	310707
Field SJD	310706
Fisher SJ	310703
Flach JG	310712
Fleming JA	310706
Fletcher GP	310712
Foote MA *BA(Hons)*	310707
Ford AD	310710
Ford BH	310715
Forrest-Anderson JMW	310707
Fortune THN	310714
Foster DP	310715
Fox GS	310715
Frame JC	310714
Fraser AR	310709
Freeman ST	310709
Fry DBM	310713
Fulford C	040513
Futter RJ	310709
Gallagher JL	310710
Galloway A	310715
Gardner RJ *MBE*	310714
Gartside AP	310710
Gascoyne AJ *BSc(Hons)*	310705
Geary AJC	310709
Gilbert RC	310714
Gittins RE	300998
Goate PA	310714
Godderidge D	310703
Goodchild AV	310707
Gordon DRM	310714
Greaves DJ *BSc(Hons) MBA*	310712
Green EJ	310710
Green LA	310707
Griffiths A	310703
Griffiths CS *BSc(Hons)*	310713
Grimes R	310702
Groce DC *BA(Hons)*	310711
Habbershaw R	310715
Hadley JM	300901
Haigh K	310706
Haigh RM	310715
Hall DR	310709
Hall TA	310702
Hallsworth JS	310713
Hambley AR	310714
Hammett DM	310715
Hammond NJ	310713
Hampton-Stone C	310707
Hankins LP	310710
Hankinson BS *BSc*	310709
Hardway MT	310711
Harris MJ *LLB*	310715
Hayward LC	310714
Heakin EC	310712
Heather ASR	310709
Henderson M	310711
Hennigan GG	310711
Heppenstall NA *BA(Hons)*	310715
Heppinstall KA *BSc(Hons)*	310706
Herbert PA	310704
Hewins HL	310707
Hillis RJ	020404
Hoban J *BA(Hons)*	310707
Hodgson JR	310712
Hodgson S	310713
Holden DL	310715
Holland MA	100950
Honeyman AW	310712
Hook SR *MBE*	310711
Hopes DL	310709
Hopkinson ASJ	300999
Horn SC	310712
Horsman RD	310714
Horton-Slade N	310714
Howard D *MBE*	310711
Howell JG	310715
Hughes SJ	310713
Hull SC	310707
Hussey DP	310715
Hutcheon A	310715
Icely MR	310707
Iles GJ	310715
Ingram DJ	310712
Ireland AE	310715
Jenkins AJ *BA(Hons)*	310714
Jenkins G	310708
Jenkinson SF	310707
Jennings JC	310706
Jennings PJ	300995
Jilge KL	310713
John JW	310709
Johnson BD	310712
Johnson SL	310711
Jones MF	310714
Jones SW	310710
Jones TG	310713
Joy AN *QGM*	310708
Kavanagh PE *BEng(Hons)*	310715
Kaye RD	300995
Kemp SN	310706
Kendrick NM	310714
Kent CJE	310711
Kidd AM *BA(Hons)*	310715
Kingston PDF	310711
Krykunivsky NV *RLC*	310708
Lahorgue PA	310713
Lamb AGF *BSc(Hons)*	310713
Lambert MWA	310704
Landy JP	310714
Langridge SR	300998
Lappin AS *MILT*	300995
Lavery SJM	310715
Lawrence PI	310711
Lawson AI *BSc(Hons)*	310713
Le Grande SC	310706
Lear KW	310708
Leeper JFB	310704

Lees TJR	310713
Leng RA *BEng(Hons) GCGI*	310707
Lewis AG *MBE*	310702
Lewis ECC	310706
Lister AJ *BSc(Hons) CMILT*	310714
Little SJ	310702
Lloyd AJ	310712
Loader NT	310706
Lockett JF	310712
Long EF	310713
Long MC *QGM*	310710
Lowe DJ	310713
Luckett SP	310706
Lyons LJ	310713
Mann KJ	310715
Mansell AJ	310715
Manship PA	310713
Marshall JH	310706
Marshall R	040407
Mason GJN *MBE*	310711
Mason JE	310715
Masters AR	310705
Masters CL	310705
Mathias AH	310706
McBirnie DR	310712
McCord RJ	310709
McCroary JA	310711
McCullough HPM	310714
McCune PT	310709
McGuffog M	310714
McKinney IS	310715
McVey AGJ	300997
Meadows SW	310709
Meager AK	310708
Meiklejohn LJ	310714
Melia DA *BSc(Hons)*	310714
Mellor SL	310704
Menear C	310710
Miles JR	310711
Miller DT	310707
Miller MV *LLB(Hons)*	310710
Mitchell AG	310707
Monument JS	310713
Moore AJ	310709
Moreton JP	310712
Moreton MJ *BA(Hons)*	310705
Mortimer RT	310715
Moss CP	310712
Moss RJ	310706
Moxon CD	310704
Moy JSJ	310709
Mulhern S	310704
Mullins SJ	070403
Munce CG	310709
Mycroft A	310711
Nawaqaliva MW *CMILT*	310706
Neil GP	310707
Nelson EM	300900
Nicolle BB	310715
Nodder FD	300900
Nott DS *LLB(Hons) pi*	310708
Nulty JA	300995
Nyman OT	310714
O'Brien C *MSc(Hons)*	310711
O'Brien CM	310715
O'Flynn MJ	310715
Owers WEJ *MBE QGM*	310713
Palfrey BL	310714
Palmer B	310711
Parkes TD	310710
Parry-Belcher IC	310710
Parry-Belcher NJ *LLB(Hons) PGDip Dip*	310707
Partridge MA	310715
Pascoe PR	310714
Pass D	310715
Pattinson JR	310712
Paull J	310713
Pelan RK	310711
Pentland DC	310709
Perkins SP	310710
Perkins SV	310714
Pettitt AHN	310708
Phillips JE	310705
Philogene AGW	310715
Pibworth AJ	310703
Pickersgill DJ	310710
Pittaway MWJ	310714
Pitts CE	310710
Player MRH *BSc(Hons)*	310714
Pollock DS *BSc(Hons)*	310714
Pope EL	310706
Porter JG	310715
Potter NM *BSc*	310712
Preira CNR *MBE*	010809
Prendiville AJ	310708
Prescott NK	300900
Prtak DJ	310712
Pugh CC *BSc(Hons)*	310702
Pugh GG	310705
Racey D	310706
Ralling CFJ	310713
Ramsumair JS	310712
Rathbone JJ	310713
Rathbone JWF	310711
Rattenbury CJ	310705
Ravenscroft TP	310712
Reehal BR	310713
Rees-Gay ZE	310710
Rendall JD BA	310709
Renton GH	310710
Revell JP *BSc(Hons) MILT EMLog*	310703
Richardson AS	310712
Rickard LM	310705
Riddell KML	310709
Ridler AR	310709
Ritchie KA	310715
Ritchie PJ	310705
Roberts GA *BA(Hons) CGLI ato*	310709
Roberts NA	310711
Roberts SR	310710
Robertson SBW	310715
Rockall AC	310710
Rogerson PC	310704
Ronald CA	310713
Rondelli D	310713
Rosevink EB	310714
Ross MJ	310715
Ross PJ	310707
Rouse AR	310714
Ryder SJ	310714
Sanders DA	310712
Sanders RJ	300995
Saukuru TK *QGM*	310710
Saunders CB	310713
Saunders SAE *MSc*	310713
Sawyer BC	310710
Schofield RA	300999
Scott CJ	300995
Searle ALW	300997
Sedgwick EM	310711
Seers TM *MBE*	310715

Shaw TG 310712
Shepherd PF 310714
Shields AJ 100812
Skinner DE 310707
Slater TM 300901
Slatter AP 310714
Slaughter DR *MBE* 310715
Smallshaw MA 310709
Smith DA 310702
Smith NA *BA(Hons)* 310706
Smith RF *BEM CMILT* 310712
Sorungbe KAO 310703
Spicer AB 310702
Spurden A 020404
Stables W *MBE* 310708
Stainthorpe PE 310707
Stanford NJ *BSc(Hons) MSc MBA* 310706
Stanton NC *MBE* 310707
Statham NF 310715
Stephens AK 310704
Stevens DR 310712
Stewart LA 300901
Stewart MD 300901
Stileman EJ 310704
Stott M 310713
Straker KA 310708
Sugdon GR *MA(Oxon)* 310712
Summerell IG *MBA BSc(Hons) CILT* 310714
Sutherland SB *MBE* 310710
Swales AC *MBE MChem* 310712
Swan RJ 310713
Swift NA 310714
Symonds GE 310711
Symons J 310711
Symons MJ 310709
Tasker RR 310703
Taylor DS 310712
Taylor FJ 310713
Taylor K 310711
Taylor MWM 310715
Tennant MJ 310715
Theodorakakis HT *MBE BComm* 310711
Thewlis GM 310713
Thomas HC 310715
Thompson C 310706
Thompson MA 310715
Thomson ELS 310713
Thorpe AK *MBE* 310713
Throp KE 310711
Tickner M 300901
Tindale AP 310710
Topping A 310712
Townsend SN *BSc* 310709
Tyers MG 310715
Tyrrell IJ *CMILT BSc(Hons)* 310712
Urch MJS 300994
Vain JCH 310713
Valler ND 310715
Vann RAS 310715
Vernon SJ 310713
Vincent JR 310712
Violet CM 300900
Wade CR *BSc(Hons)* 310709
Walker DL 310712
Walker DMP 310711
Walker PA 310714
Wallace K 310705
Wallis TE 310713
Walsh CJ *TD* 310707
Warren DP 310706
Waters SL 310714
Watt PA *BSc(Hons) BA(Hons)* 310714
Weir MI *BSc* 310712
Wells MS 310711
West AF 310708
White MM 310710
Whitwam AA 310713
Whitworth C 310707
Wilcock CP 310715
Wilcox T *Dip* 310714
Willcocks RD 310708
Williams HG *MBE* 170813
Williams JN 310704
Williams RG 310709
Williams SA 310710
Wilmot A *MBE MSc(Hons)* 310714
Wilson KN *MBE* 310715
Winchester MR 310710
Wincott GM 310709
Windsor MG 310711
Winfield E 310711
Wise AGM 310714
Wolstenholme NDZ 310710
Wood CN 310715
Wyse WPP 300992
Yates CN 310709
Yates JBA 310709
Youngman D 310714

Captains

Abel RL 310713
Agius TL 090209
Aikman NT 010713
Alexander D *BEng(Hons)* 151215
Allen MR 050710
Allen RL *BA(Hons)* 140415
Allinson NR 050115
Anderson L *BEng(Hons)* 120209
Anderson PR *BSc(Hons) EMLog CMILT* 180213
Anderson RL 160412
Andrews ES 290609
Armitage TP 310713
Ashington-Pickett CE *MEng* 130214
Ashley LV 040711
Askey D *MSTA* 060410
Bagley JA 040411
Bagshaw SJ *BSc(Hons)* 101011
Baker RA 141207
Banks SP 140412
Barker JEG 030613
Barlow J 010413
Barlow JJ 130814
Barlow TP 160410
Barnes RJ 310713
Barnett RW 141009
Barr PW *BSc* 130611
Barrie AJ *BSc(Hons) Dip* 110815
Barringer JR 31/17/12
Barton MJ 070414
Bate RC *BSc(Hons) MBA* 130611
Beadle JLN *BSc(Hons)* 151215
Bedford PJ 180613
Begley JC 140415
Bell RC *BA(Hons)* 170614
Bennett GA 060409
Bevan TB 180613
Bill EMD 171214
Birchnall SP *Dip* 110213
Blake J 170614
Bodycomb MJ 010413

Bolger RP	161013
Boomer MA *BSc(Hons)*	160410
Boucher JP	150610
Boyce AJ	101011
Boyd DE	160414
Boyden CR	170614
Boyle WSD	070414
Bragg MP *MBE*	040411
Bransby DM	140213
Brazier AP	130411
Brodie SJ *BA(Hons)*	110815
Brown CL	070414
Brown LV *MBE*	121010
Brown MC	111012
Burgess DG	030815
Burston PA	060513
Butcher WR	101011
Butterworth A	131014
Byrne RR	150610
Cahill KJ *BA(Hons)*	140415
Calway AL	110512
Cameron JJ	120811
Campbell CJ	161013
Cant DS *BEng(Hons) GCGI*	130214
Carley SF	070414
Carlton JL	311213
Carpenter KJ	150310
Carter SJ *MA(Hons)*	140415
Cassidy LE	311213
Catherwood MS *DipHE*	100413
Cayless DMJ	110210
Champion ND	070414
Charlesworth RJ	130214
Christie D	161211
Clark OAM *BA(Hons)*	170614
Cockfield AD	311212
Coffield SA	250216
Cole A	050509
Collins-Lindsay SR	110612
Collishaw BJ	010208
Conlin MT	160609
Cook SR	161211
Cooke RG *BSc*	151215
Cornwell DP	120811
Corr HM	101013
Cousins CA	080212
Cowan BW *BA(Hons)*	161013
Cowen FH	311213
Crane RJ	060410
Crawford RM	070610
Creek TG	140415
Critchlow LJE	140415
Cussins PE *BA(Hons)*	130214
Dalby GE	070415
Dalglish RD *BA*	130214
Darrock L	130214
Darver FA	171210
Dassanaike YS	101011
Daulton J *BA(Hons)*	140415
Davidson SD	040814
Davies MJ	170613
Davies RA	170614
Davies WG	250311
Davis NFC	110210
Dawson JF	311212
Dean MP *BEng(Hons)*	130214
Dean MS	080212
Desai KKH *BEng(Hons)*	121010
Devlin RM	171012
Dewstowe MD	200415
Dickerson GR	180411
Dorsett PR	030815
Dray AL	160609
Dray JA *BSc(Hons)*	130214
Dunlop E	070414
Dunn SL *BSc(Hons)*	170614
Dunwell AM	160712
Eade HJ *BSc(Hons)*	130214
Easthill NJ	060514
Ebsworth LD	310713
Ede JAG	070714
Edwards AS *BSc(Hons)*	170614
Edwards C	110815
Ellis MW	200212
Elton MJ	120209
Evans CIR	140213
Evans NPW	110210
Evans RJ	070414
Evans Fry JCM	120612
Fearnfield MJ	171012
Fidell JP *QGM*	160609
Field H *MEng*	130214
Fielder C	310713
Fitzgerald TN	120612
Fleming DI *BA(Hons)*	110815
Foley KP	171012
Forknell ST	121010
Foster E	311213
Foster SG	311213
Fox SVC	180613
Francis A	070414
Francis RW	020412
Frankling JR	141009
Fraser DWL	130611
Freed CT *BSc(Hons)*	120612
Frost CP *BA(Hons)*	130214
Fuller WB	190813
Gagg JE *BSc(Hons)*	151215
Gajdus JR	110815
Gannon AJ	270913
Gates JO *BA(Hons)*	170614
Genari CR	140415
Ghaibi A	121010
Gibbs RAC	140415
Gibbs RK	171214
Gilbert DM	171012
Gilgar RP	180613
Glass AM	160609
Glover SA	160213
Godwin CJ *BA(Hons)*	140415
Gomersall NE	310713
Goodall TJ	310712
Goodchild JJ	050814
Goodfellow PJ *BEng(Hons)*	110815
Goodman ND	130608
Gordon AR *BSc(Hons)*	140415
Gradwell A	200812
Graham CP *BSc(Hons) Dip*	151206
Gray TL	160410
Green AJ	160414
Green C	310712
Green SL	131008
Greenhalgh JW	140412
Gresham KL *BSc(Hons)*	110815
Griffiths AJ *BSc(Hons)*	140415
Grinham RNJ	090409
Groome AE	140213
Gurung RJ *RLC*	180610
Hale MW	311212
Hands PJ	070414
Handy NF	070414
Hanley EJ	250211
Hanna AJ *Dip*	171214
Hardwick CZ *MA*	170614

Harkin LS	120115
Harold JT	110210
Harris JR	310713
Harris SM	140213
Harrison A	110210
Harrison AP	020812
Harrison BJ	310713
Harrison DL	131008
Hart J	161013
Hartle TA	311213
Hartley RJ	120209
Hayes M	060410
Hearth MJC	130411
Heavey DR	310713
Hegarty JW	060514
Hegarty NP	060410
Heinrich BT	310713
Hemsworth NA	131015
Henderson MR	171214
Herbert GP	060611
Heyworth CD	130208
Hildred LD *BEng(Hons)*	110815
Hill JJ	180411
Hill-Harding RA	110213
Hind AG	060410
Hindmarsh SJ	110210
Holdcroft GT *MSc*	151215
Hollins PC *BSc(Hons)*	130214
Holmes AJ	200611
Holt ZLK	160414
Homer NS	060409
Horan SWG	100314
Horner IM	260813
Howard MT *BArch(Hons)*	110815
Howard TRY	080212
Howes AJQ	080212
Howse JD	310713
Hughes AR	140412
Hughes SCR	310713
Hulme HR	161013
Humphreys JE *BA(Hons)*	170614
Hutton AK	170614
Ingham WG	121010
Ingleby GM	130611
Ingram SL	160410
Ingram SM *BA(Hons)*	110815
Irvine RD *BScSoc(Hons) BSc(Hons)*	130214
Isherwood TJ *BA(Hons)*	151215
Jarman DI	120612
Jean-Marie JA	311213
Johl JE	180613
Johnson SJ	020412
Johnstone CAD	060409
Jones DR	250113
Jones DRO	180515
Jones M	010809
Jones SA	200212
Jordan REV	110210
Jung WR *BEng(Hons)*	140415
Kearton AP	050115
Kedge JR	080212
Kelly RJ *BA(Hons)*	140415
Kemp GM *BSc(Hons)*	011013
Khepar NAS	161013
Kilburn JAW *BSc(Hons)*	130214
Kinahan JES	140415
King RI	070714
Kinsella AF	110815
Knott GR	130814
Kuhn JA	140415
Lambert RS *BSc(Hons)*	171012
Lane AW	040815
Langbridge RM *BSc(Hons)*	130214
Langridge JC	110509
Laverack MJ	010811
Lawrence AE	180613
Lee MJ	120710
Lees MH	110210
Lintvelt HAJ	311213
Lloyd PA	180613
Logie H *MSc*	161009
Long CP	100613
Lowe G	170411
Lowe J	020409
Lowry MC	090211
Lynn WJ	230215
Marples JC	170608
Marsden D	040213
Marshall R	040509
Martin AR	060409
Martin JA	010415
Mason DM	150610
Mathieson ND	140213
Matthews DS	300712
Matthews M *BSc(Hons)*	170614
Maxwell AG	310712
May JAH	171012
McBride JA	180613
McCarthy RC	110210
McCartney NA	140415
McCartney WJH	311212
McCletchie K	100212
McCormick OD	090107
McGarvey-Miles MA *BSc(Hons)*	110815
McGarvey-Miles OM *BSc(Hons)*	110815
McLaughlin IS	070414
McLean AJ	311213
McLeod G	130208
McLoughlin WF *BEng(Hons)*	110815
McNama CA	160414
McNaughton ML	130810
McNeill SD	060409
McSherry CS	060409
Meek AR	280414
Melly R	110210
Millan BR	110815
Millen GK	140415
Miller RG *BSc(Hons)*	090211
Milligan JM	010413
Milligan SJ	140415
Mitchell RG	170614
Mogg GD	060410
Moloney RO *BSc(Hons)*	010711
Monk CV	161013
Monks SD	271014
Morgan CR	130709
Morgans DT	280111
Mortimore AL	140213
Mulcahy CWJ *BSc(Hons)*	130214
Murphy MJ	040411
Murphy MJ	091011
Murphy TO *BSc(Hons)*	130214
Musselbrook T *BSc(Hons)*	140415
Naismith DFE *BA(Hons)*	140213
Nesfield WL	120612
Nicholas AJ	171210
Nicholson RD *BSc(Hons)*	130214
Nimigon TW *BA(Hons)*	170614
Norman AR	171012
Normanton JM	010808
North CD	120109

O'Donnell AJ	130611
Offord RK	110815
O'Leary FJ	310713
Oliver G	210909
Oliver TJ	130214
Orr MW	060409
Ottaway JPJ	310713
Paradine RT *BSc(Hons)*	171012
Parker SA	090412
Parkes JRM	080212
Parslow DC *BA(Hons)*	151215
Pasalk MMK	120612
Pearson-Burton SC	161013
Peat AO GM	020115
Pendlebury AA	110210
Petch JM *MEng(Hons)*	110815
Peters MJ	230209
Peterson CF *BSc(Hons)*	160609
Petherbridge AJ	180613
Phillips CA	010708
Polson EAF	140412
Pomfrett MFR	171012
Potter RE *BSc(Hons)*	140415
Powell LMM *MEng*	151215
Powell M	101011
Power GA	090409
Powers SI	030510
Prestwood RJH	151215
Pugh SJ	131008
Randell GP	171012
Rann JM	130415
Rayner TH *BA*	190710
Reehal JMJ	151215
Rees DH	070414
Revell JS	060410
Rheeder SN	071109
Rhodes JJ	161013
Richardson KA	171210
Ridgway JR	040411
Ridgway LA	010615
Ridley EM *BSc(Hons)*	170614
Ritchie TB	160609
Roberts K	290713
Robertson AI	020511
Robinson CE	090211
Robinson SA	140415
Robson DL	080212
Rodbard-Hedderwick PAG	310713
Ross WF	060410
Rossiter TM	310713
Rudge RAE	310713
Ruocco MJ *BSc(Hons)*	130214
Rusk DJ	040411
Rutt SW *BSc(Hons)*	110815
Sandle AJ	180612
Sands SJ	290713
Sanford JE MA(Hons)	121010
Scarfe BS *BA(Hons)*	130214
Scates AM *LLB(Hons) LLM MA*	161013
Schultz KA	090211
Scott CJ	090408
Scott DA	180411
Seddon LAA *BSc(Hons)*	130814
Selman L *BSc(Hons)*	161013
Shannon AJP *BA(Hons)*	090211
Shaw AD	130611
Shazell JN	070414
Shearan A	040411
Shelton GF *BSc(Hons)*	150610
Shepherd AG	311213
Shepherd LF	180613
Shortis SCK	150610
Sidebottom RK	180515
Slater DM	080212
Slatter JO	150610
Slaughter SE	310712
Smale JD *MA(Hons)*	171012
Smit D	140409
Smith BHR	140213
Smith DJ	150610
Somerville RA *MA(Hons)*	110815
Southwell D	270508
Spencer-Small SJ *BSc(Hons)*	130214
Spilsbury JB	161013
Spraggett MW	120612
Stahlmann AG *MEng(Hons)*	151215
Stanford TW *BScEcon(Hons)*	110815
Starling JN *BSc(Hons)*	130214
Stevenson SR	060409
Stilgoe OJ	140415
Stokes D	140415
Stratford A	130611
Stratford AC	310713
Stride TJ	120612
Strydom GWB	100109
Sturgeon RFD	310809
Sutton JC	090211
Swift CJ	020712
Tait ARP	161013
Talman JS	090812
Taylor CR	200513
Taylor CW	130208
Taylor GJ	300712
Taylor MC	120612
Tee SA	161013
Tester JJ	120612
Thackway AJ	150610
Thomas AE *BSc*	171012
Thompson A	080212
Thompson AM *BSc(Hons)*	151215
Thompson-Burt AR	140415
Todhunter P *BEng(Hons)*	130214
Town JT	311212
Travis HEH *BSc(Hons)*	140415
Trott JS	080212
Tucker TA	120612
Tudor MN	101011
Turner D	310713
Utley M	070414
Vannerley KL	310712
Verge EF *BSc(Hons)*	140415
Vidler P *BSc(Hons)*	151215
Visser ME	190413
Wakeham RS	141009
Walker L	080615
Wallace DJ	280708
Walter J	310713
Ward AL *BSc(Hons)*	110815
Ware JK	130810
Warren JP	130611
Waterston SOM *BSc(Hons)*	161013
Watson BJM	151215
Watson M	290615
Wealthall GWG	151215
Webster DRJ	310712
Weedall L *BSc(Hons)*	070512
Weeks JJ	140412
Welbourn JT	080313
Wells JA	160410
Wells LAJ	110210
Welsh HB *BEng(Hons)*	170614
Westlake G	070415
Whately-Smith JP *BA(Hons)*	151215
Whiteley CBJ	130611

Whitewick NG 140408
Wilczynski AC 310713
Wilde TK *BA(Hons)* 110210
Williams GA 171210
Williams GS 250213
Williams MGG 131015
Willis HE *BSc(Hons)* 090211
Willoughby MG *MCGI* 080210
Wilson AR 311212
Wilson JR 311213
Wilson-Page JA 140415
Winter JG 311213
Withers DM 140213
Wood BJ 020412
Woods CS BA 110815
Wooldridge JPM *BSc(Hons)* 140213
Wylie JA 010313
Yell BI 280213
Young DE 130611
Younger SC 020913
Ziemba JA 310713

Lieutenants

Abbott ML *BA(Hons)* 130414
Akers DA 131215
Asadipour Farsani B *MEng MRes* 131215
Ashmore AN *BSc(Hons)* 090810
Bennett HCM 131215
Beveridge FCS *BSc(Hons)* 130414
Biddulph CR 230611
Binskin-Barnes JRN *BSc(Hons)* 141214
Blackburn TA 131215
Blair FF *LLB(Hons)* 130414
Bleakman DM *BSc(Hons)* 141214
Boardley ME *BA(Hons)* 141214
Booth MR *BA(Hons)* 120415
Boyce JA *BSc(Hons)* 130414
Brewerton JW 131215
Broad JS *LLB(Hons) PGDip* 120415
Broom RA *BSc(Hons)* 120415
Caine JA *BEng* 151213
Campbell ACN 131215
Carlin JT *BSc(Hons)* 131214
Cassily M *BEng(Hons)* 100814
Chalmers C 151213
Charters RA *BSc(Hons)* 131210
Clarke GAL *BEng(Hons)* 120415
Cole A *BSc(Hons)* 100814
Coleman MJP *BA(Hons)* 100814
Cooke RE *BSc(Hons)* 100814
Corbett EJM *BEng(Hons)* 131215
Costin TG *MEng* 100814
Covington NJ *BA(Hons)* 100814
Crowley JP 131215
Currie JN 131215
Da Costa Nathanielsz J *BSc(Hons)* 100814
Darrington G 130414
Davies MR *BA(Hons)* 141214
Day TE *BSc(Hons)* 141214
Dixon HDM *BSc(Hons)* 090815
Douglas WJF *BA(Hons)* 100814
Doyle-Tanner JD 100814
Draper RJ *BEng(Hons)* 141214
Du Plessis E 130414
Dunbar RM 100814
Elliott AJ 131215
Field EL *BSc(Hons)* 090815
Field MJ 131215
Fisher JK 171212
Fisher LJE *BSc(Hons)* 120415
Forsyth DS *BEng(Hons)* 130414
Francis RGM 131215
Frost TCS *BA(Hons)* 120415
Furlong TM *BA(Hons)* 141214
Gates HS *MSc* 130414
Gibbs MP 131215
Gibson D 090815
Gourlay BP 131215
Graham CIM 131215
Guest JJ *BEng(Hons)* 100814
Gutzu AJ *BSc(Hons)* 130414
Hand NJ 120415
Hansmeyer JL 131215
Hardaker AR *BSc(Hons)* 100814
Harrison AP 120415
Harvey GT 120415
Head AJ 141214
Hobson AD *BSc(Hons)* 100814
Husband NHJ 090815
Hyndman AC *BSc(Hons)* 090815
James RD *BSc(Hons)* 090815
Jansen WH 151213
Jenner RS *BSc(Hons)* 100814
Jones SD 090815
Joyce TS 131215
Keable-Kinsella AH *MChem* 090815
Kennedy SS 130414
Krempel STH *BA(Hons)* 151213
Lee MD *BEng(Hons)* 090815
Lester Z 100814
Levens DR *BSc(Hons)* 120415
MacLaverty AS 120415
Manning AT *BEng(Hons)* 110813
Mayes JH *BEng(Hons)* 090815
McCurdy DJ 100814
McGarrity R 100814
McKeen J *BEng(Hons)* 120415
McLeod F *BSc(Hons)* 130414
Melhuish RAP *MA(Hons)* 090815
Mercer J 090815
Millard AZ 130414
Mitchell FJG 221014
Nelson KM 120415
Nicholls AKL 141214
Nugent AR *BSc(Hons)* 090815
Nutine MFR *BSc(Hons)* 011114
O'Connell FO 100814
Parsons BD *BSc(Hons)* 120415
Parsons CJC 090815
Patterson S *BSc(Hons) DIS* 130414
Pearson GF 131215
Pfleiderer CG 130414
Reeves MR *BA* 130414
Reynolds JWJ *BA(Hons)* 060514
Richardson AJ 141214
Rumble TJ *MEng* 090815
Sabha AOM *BSc(Hons)* 100814
Saddleton TG *MEng(Hons)* 100814
Salmon JL *BSc(Hons)* 141214
Smith BD *MA(Hons)* 120415
Smith DJ *BA(Hons)* 090815
Sorrell V *BSc(Hons)* 120415
Stearne HP 230314
Stephenson CD *BSc* 100814
Stevenson JC 140414
Stevenson-Coulshaw TWF *BSc(Hons)* 130415
Stockbridge AC *BA(Hons)* 090815
Subba Row NC 090815
Thomas GN *BSc(Hons)* 120415
Todd OJ *BA(Hons)* 141214
Travers NET 100814

Tuck AAD *BA*	090815
Turner GR *BSc(Hons)*	141214
Wardell BA	131215
Wathen JGI	131215
Whitby KG *BSc(Hons)*	141214
Williams BM *BSc(Hons)*	141214
Wills J *BA(Hons)*	141214
Wilson DAW	100814
Wood JM *BA(Hons)*	110813
Wright JM *BSc*	100814
Wright MME *BA(Hons)*	110813

2nd Lieutenants

Adamson SE	110415
Akbareian-Clarke TC	121215
Ardley JA	121215
Beddoe JL	131214
Birch SA	080815
Brown NJ	121215
Buchanan TWS	080815
Carpenter S	110415
Carter JM	110415
Clancy S	110415
Coe AS	121215
Cole ML	121215
Dales M	110415
Edwards L	131214
Ellis AC	080815
Everard RA	110415
Garner GH	121215
Harrop J	110415
Hiam JS	110415
Howard GR	110415
Hurst S	110415
Kirkham S	080815
Krarup SG	110415
Lavender CWM	110415
Nelson A	110415
Newman TG	080815
Orrell TP	121215
Pawley CHW	110415
Richards TMA	110415
Rickwood A	121215
Roberts GL	080815
Rough A	110415
Sainsbury DJ	131214
Sayer R	121215
Sergeant AJ	080815
Seymour WXR	110415
Shelton P	121215
Smith RD	110415
Stapylton-Boyce MWP	080815
Suff HAJ	080815
Tams RS	080815
Taylor DT	121215
Tester LR	121215
Thompson LM	080815
Tookey DRL	110415
Tran J	080815
Turner SW	121215
Walker MP	110415
Walters BJ	120414
Wardell S	110415
Wilson BA	080815
Young ZM	080815

ROYAL ARMY MEDICAL CORPS

The Rod of Aesculapius with a Serpent entwined in silver surrounded by a wreath of laurels and surmounted by a Crown in gold. Thereunder a scroll inscribed IN ARDUIS FIDELIS in silver.

Regimental Marches

Quick March .... Here's a Health unto His Majesty
Slow March .... Her Bright Smile Haunts Me Still

Agents .... Holts Branch, Royal Bank of Scotland plc, Lawrie House, Farnborough, Hants, GU14 7NR
Corps Headquarters .... RHQ RAMC, HQ Army Medical Services, Slim Road, Camberley GU15 4NP (Tel: 01276 412751 Fax: 01276 412793 Email: rhq_ams@hotmail.com)

Alliances

Canadian Armed Forces .... Medical Branch
Australian Military Forces .... Royal Australian Army Medical Corps
New Zealand Army .... Royal New Zealand Army Medical Corps
South African .... National Defence Force
South African Military Health Service
Pakistan Army .... Army Medical Corps
Sri Lanka Army .... Sri Lanka Army Medical Corps
Zambia Army .... Zambia Army Medical Service

Colonel in Chief .... *HRH The Duke of* Gloucester *KG GCVO*
Master General .... Lt Gen (Retd) Louis P Lillywhite *CB MBE* 010117
Colonels Commandant .... Brig (Retd) Peter J Fabricius *QHP* 010114
Col (Retd) Mark V Pemberton 010116
Col (Retd) Clifford Dieppe 010316

AMS Corps Colonel .... Col Ashleigh Boreham

Lieutenant Colonels

Baxter JBM	300612
Blocke AD	300611
Caruana DM	300615
Chadwick RN	300610
Connolly MJ *Pg Dip GCGI MA FCMI MIHM*	300613
Crew TA *MBE*	300613
Day AJ *OStJ MSc MBA MIHM*	300613
De Rouffignac P	300610
Gadd RDM *MBA(LS) CMgr FCMI AMIHM(S) FIC*	300608
Haddock M	300607
Hall SA	010914
Harold AJ	300615
Hepburn MJ	300615
Heywood JW	300608
Jeffery RGF	300609
Johnson AG	300613
Jones DA *BEM*	010113
Liddington RA	010412
McCluskey AJ	300606
McQueeney S	300615
Meredith AG	300613
Millett CH	300609
Millsop AKG *Bsc(Hons) PGDip FCMI psc(j)(GE) psc(j)*	300612
Moorhouse VH	300615
Nadin SJ	300614
Nicholson M	010115
O'Callaghan TI	250914
Patrick K	020611
Payne MP *BEM*	201115
Pope S	300615
Redman SEJ	300606
Reynolds P	300609
Romanovitch APG	300613
Ryan MA	300608
Shorrock AC	300607
Smyth HS	300615
Southwood TJ	300612
Steele TP	300607
Taylor NA	311214
Thomas GD	300605
Tracey SR	300608
Tynan MP	300609
Williams EF	300609
Williams SL	300609
Wills M	300609
Wilson DAJ	300615
Woodward DI	300612
Worthington PC	300614
Yates A *MA*	300606

Majors

A'Lee JA	310713
Alexander SA	310713
Allenby-Dilley OJ	310715
Armon LE	310713
Ashelby JM	310713
Baguley NG	010212
Barclay JG	310708
Barnett M	310711
Betts DC *BA(Hons)*	310714
Bodle DJ	310713

Bonser CD *MSc PgDip SpDipEM CMIOSH* 310715
Borton D 190308
Brown JHG *MSc BSc(Hons) MCSP HCPC* 310709
Bunn SJ 310714
Burgess-Gould KS 300901
Cameron A 310715
Campbell ID 310711
Candlish GG *psc(j)* 300901
Carter JS 310709
Chacksfield CP 310714
Clarke EJT 310713
Clarke FD 310713
Clarke TP 310710
Cobb GL 310715
Conrad SJ 310708
Cornish LM 310713
Daly AS 310707
Davidson BG 310713
Davies MBP 310715
Davies NAD 310715
Dawson C 310715
Dembry RB 310702
Desborough P 310712
Dickens CD 310713
Dobson MJ 310713
Dower CN 310708
Edwards MJ 310704
Eversfield SJ 310712
Fawcett JR *MBE* 310712
Fawcett R 310715
Ferreira J 310714
Fidell KJ *MSc MCSP* 310702
Findlay ALM 310709
Firth RC 300900
Fisher JA 310713
Fitchett GA 310706
Foulger AP 310707
Frankland TJ 310712
Galpin TWG 310710
Gamble L 310715
Garwood M 310714
Gibbs JTJ 310711
Gibson CW 310710
Gibson JB 310713
Goodwin NJ 310711
Gordon BP 020514
Greener JHD 310712
Gurung B 310713
Gurung S 310714
Hall LJ 310713
Harley RTC 310713
Hart MA 310715
Harvey M 310713
Harvey MJ 310715
Hawling DA 310709
Hayes GJ 310714
Hayes GPV 310715
Hayhurst DJ 310714
Heagerty RDH 310709
Hempsey S 310713
Henderson DD 310709
Hinton RP 310715
Hinton-West AF *BSc MIHM* 310704
Holland AJ 310708
Holton PA 310714
Horton SVG *BSc(Hons)* 310709
Hunter M 310709
Irvine SJ 310703
Jacques CRF 310711
Jenkins ME 310715
Jerrard MD 310709
Johnson SS 310714
Jolly R 310708
Keeling AT *OBE* 310711
Keenan LTJ 310712
Kemp CA 310712
Kemp NJ 310712
Keys GP 310710
Le Feuvre PA *MBE* 310708
Leighton PW *MBE MSc* 310709
Leonard JRL 310715
Lewis AM *MBE* 310709
Light EA 310708
Lilleyman EG 310714
Lord JP 310715
Lucas-Hartley LK 310715
MacDonald SI 310714
Madders O 310710
Masling CH 310708
McGuffie KE 310712
McIntosh KW *MBA* 310715
McKinnie CB 310714
McKinnie FL 310714
McVey TM 310714
Moldrik CJ *MSc* 310712
Moore GW 310706
Morris AS 310709
Morris JNC 310715
Morris OF 310715
Oakes MN 310708
O'Brien RF 310713
Owen MJ 310709
Patel P 310714
Penhallow R 310715
Porter JE 310712
Preshaw JA 310714
Pywell AJ 310712
Rae E 100812
Rai Y 310711
Rawlinson TP 310709
Rennie PEJ *MSc* 310710
Robertson I *MSc MPH DLSHTM* 310705
Robinson EJ 310710
Rush N 310714
Salt JM MA 310711
Sanderson KL 310713
Sandle PJ 310708
Scott PJI 310707
Semakula FM 310715
Short FC 310709
Simmons PS 310706
Smith S *MBE* 310714
Snape MD 300707
Stammers HJ *PGDip SEM BSc(Hons) BA(Hons)* 310714
Steele S 310713
Stevens AL 310713
Stevens KA 310715
Taylor AJ 310712
Taylor CD 310714
Taylor MI 310706
Thompson PCD 310715
Thorne ADG 310713
Toop SL 310713
Van Rooyen HJM 310714
Vickerstaff AL 310713
Vincent AJ 310713
Wade A 310710
Wakeham AD 310711
Wallace R 310714
Ward JWS 310713

Wareham AP	310712
Warner A *PG Dip*	310710
Watson CE	310712
Watson JG	310707
Whelan SD *BSc(Hons) MCIEH*	310715
Wignall SJ	310712
Williams DC	310708
Williams S	310712
Williams SJ	310707
Winfield JIB *BSc(Hons) MIHM MCMI*	310707
Wise RG	310714
Wood CJ	310715
Woods JG	310712
Woolsey TS	310707
Wright DC	300707
Yates PAJ	310715
Young SJ	310712

Captains

Ashby TP	020811
Atkinson RF	140213
Austin DR	010413
Bairstow DC	131207
Balchin WEA	010410
Bale TJ	110815
Bamford NW	010413
Barnes WG	050514
Beckett JJ	010413
Bidd GR	170614
Biggin FM	010214
Birch ORA	290512
Bourne GE	010412
Brabin M	020415
Bradshaw TE	150413
Brannigan AJ	150610
Brass CJ	191004
Breed MJ *BSc(Hons) MSc*	210412
Bridges PN	020409
Bristow PK	020415
Britland O	140415
Britton HE	020415
Broughton JR	140415
Brown GWP	160410
Bullivant GP	250412
Bundy CN	161013
Butler PRJ	121010
Campbell Ricketts WMN	130611
Clarke AP	080212
Clarke MP	140511
Collins BGE	080212
Collins MH	120612
Crosby CJ	020415
Crothers REJ	141009
D'Abreu-Hayling SA	280113
Dalziel S	290414
D'Ardenne SA	310713
Davies ML	010412
Dimmer AE	140415
Doe TWF	130214
Doyle AL	010411
Duff SJ	010211
Eagan JH	030212
Efstratiou TJ	111209
Ferry RG	311010
Fitchett CA	150712
Forbes KE	010812
Forbes MR	111209
Fox RJB	161013
Freegard DL	121010
Game AJ	010413
Geeson SY	030211
Gillies EA	060415
Gold MJ	010410
Gordon MJ	181215
Gordon VJA	010514
Green AW	140415
Greene A	021012
Grindrod JN	010410
Hales JK	010411
Hall DJ	010412
Hannan R	251215
Harris D	020415
Hatch R	160614
Hawthorn DI	091111
Heaton RL	010913
Hivey ER *MRPharmS*	270710
Hobbs LM *BSc(Hons) MCSP*	070112
Houston WEF	161013
Howley SD	020415
Impey DA	010410
Islam M	141009
Jenkins WF	311212
Johnston DMP	170609
Jones CD	121010
Jones NP	110815
Kerr ADJ	161013
Kidd RG	010412
Kilpatrick GN	180613
Kinvig PD	010410
Knox LE	020215
Langman MG	010414
Law K	021012
Lawson EJ	071112
Lines AM	020415
Magee TE	191214
Mahoney TW	311212
Marshall HL	030209
Mathews RD	010410
McCubbin RA	140213
McFarlane C	020415
McGowan PA	130411
McTaggart DA	030212
Meeke RE *MPharm*	300711
Miles ALP	100611
Miles C	140415
Moger GJ	030511
Molyneux PM	010211
Montana R	010410
Moorhouse ID	020409
Morgan AS	010412
Morgan-Jones SR	010410
Morris DF	161013
Nicholson CLK	020415
O'Keefe JM	010411
Oliver SL	140415
Pallett SJC	060814
Parker VC	150610
Patel PJ	150313
Paterson M	050313
Paveley TT	310713
Pearson FA	161013
Peart JM	070913
Peters WF	311213
Phillips LA	210114
Pote CG	020412
Precious DA	060112
Prescott JP	151211
Pye AJ	061011
Pye D	181215
Pyne AJ	121010
Radcliffe EJ	280110
Rai S	120508
Ramshaw VM	130410

Reeve SR	020415
Reilly AJ	170614
Reynolds AN	020409
Richardson LI	010412
Rieder JJM	170614
Riley MJ	311213
Riley MR	030811
Robinson AL *MSc BSc(Hons)*	010410
Robinson SA	171012
Rook AR	021013
Rowland AE	290811
Saveker RA *MBChB DMCC DipABRSM*	010812
Scott AM	171213
Silvester SJ	050314
Sleeman SW	310712
Stagg EA	010211
Stein DG	010414
Stephenson G	010410
Stevens EC	170608
Stockton MP	151215
Stoddart JJ	171012
Stringer MSB	130214
Strivens TM	191214
Swannick JT	140213
Talbot S	151215
Taylor ED	021012
Taylor FME	221113
Tibbitts CHS	180613
Torrens-Spence K	120612
Truscott ST	160412
Turner JL	190511
Unsworth DJ	140415
Upham CM	090113
Valentine C	010211
Wady AB	170614
Wattam LW	121010
Watts DAS	140213
Willcox CJ	180613
Williams SE	021012
Williamson TS	030212
Willis DM *BSc(Hons) PGCE FHEA*	010914
Willoughby KM	030314
Woodward M	120111
Wright SJ	180613
Wyllie WG	010414
Young SE	110810

Lieutenants

Casey TP	141214
Casterton CAM	090815
Croton MJ *BA(Hons) ACMI*	130414
Culley JPA	130414
Dench AJ	130414
Froehlich GF	141214
Gant JR	120415
Hair AS	090815
Harcourt TDL	130414
Hardy DD	110813
Humphrey JP	141214
Johnston CM	251011
Lee CJ	100814
MacArthur IT	120415
March JJ	131215
McFarlane RA	141214
Mitchell EJ	130414
Morris C	130414
Oliver MJ	090815
Phillips VL	120415
Rye KF	200412
Scrafton LJ	280614
Simmons SAL	131215
Skillman RR	131215
Stone ER	090815
Taylor ER	131215
Taylor RR	120415
Toye BTG	120415
Troeller M	100814
Wainscot AJ	011211
Winstanley RJW	100814

2nd Lieutenants

Beirne SFA	080815
Blacklock J	111215
Exelby EJ	110415
Greenacre JS	121215
Palmer EE	260715
Park CL	270514
Sharp RKN	261214
Stanners GM	080815
Stokes CA	010811

Medical Officers (RAMC MO)

Lieutenant Colonels

Abraham-Igwe CU *MSc FRCS*	300613
Adams SA	020210
Anakwe REB	300615
Appleyard T	300611
Ardley CN	300613
Baden JM	170309
Bailey MS	300610
Baker AK	300605
Banfield GK	010803
Barratt JA	300605
Bartels OJM	300612
Bennett NJ *FRCS(Plast)*	010202
Bourne SC	300609
Bowley DMG *MBBS FRCS (Eng) FRCS (Gen Surg)*	010804
Burrow DJ *MRCGP MRCS(Ed) MBBS BSc(Hons)*	300615
Bushby AJR	010804
Butler M	300609
Capanni PD	300606
Clack JD	300614
Combes JG	311207
Cubison TCS	010807
Curry IP	010802
Davies ML *BSc(Hons) MBBCh FRCS MD*	300614
Davies MS *FRCA MBBS BSc (Hons) RNMH*	300610
Davis PR	010905
Dufty NE	300615
Edwards DP	010802
Eke AJ	010890
Everest AJ	300608
Finch PJC	071000
Fordham GT	300611
Foster MA *BSc MB ChB DMCC FRCS(Plast)*	300614
Glover NM	300609
Goldie CE	300610
Greasley LA	300608
Griffiths DE	300615
Griffiths GW *MSc FRCGP DRCOG*	250803
Gurney I	300613
Haldane AG *BSc MBBS*	300615
Harrigan MJ	050900

Haworth KJ *MB ChB BSc MSc MRCGP MFOM* 300605
Hayman JJ 300607
Heppell PSJ *MBChB FRCSEd(Plast)* 300608
Hill JJ 300608
Hinsley DE 300609
Hobbs CM 010800
Hodgson CL *MB ChB MRCGP DCH* 311213
Hooper TJ 300615
Horne ST 300613
Howe GB 160899
Hunt PAF 300614
Jacks AS *BSc MBBS FRCOPHTH* 010802
Jackson SMS *MBBS MSc MFOM MRCGP DrCOG DMCC* 300614
Jeffery SLA 010804
Johnston AM 300610
Kane GG 020403
Khan KN *MB ChB* 300608
Le Clerc SP 300613
Leigh-Howarth M 010200
Lewin JH 230808
Lowes T 300607
MacKenzie N 190602
Maytham GD 300614
McKinnon KA 300615
McLennan JV 300610
McNee PAJ 300613
Meyer CER 300613
Moor PS 300610
Moore AJ 300614
Mountain AJC 300611
Nicholson KR *MSc MBChB MRCP* 300615
Nicholson-Roberts TC 300611
Nordmann GR 300610
Okpala NCE 300615
Orr LE *FRCSorl DM PhD* 010807
Park CL 300614
Patil-Mead ML 300615
Phillip RD 091210
Pynn HJ 300615
Ramalingam T 010809
Reavley PDA 300611
Richards PR 190604
Roberts LJ *MBE* 311213
Rooms MA *BM DAvMed(UK) MFOM PGCMedEd* 010802
Roughton SA *MBBS DFSRH MRCGP DIMC MSc* 010803
Rowlands TK 300610
Sands AM 300614
Singer DMF *MB ChB MSc MRCGP FRCS DIP CS* 300608
Smith MR 300611
Thornhill RJ 300612
Thorpe MA 300606
Tredget AD 300611
Walters PL 300609
Ward NJ 300610
Webster BB 300615
Weir MJS *MB ChB MRCGP* 300605
Williams JR 300615
Williamson KP 300614
Woghiren ORE 300610
Woodhouse JIJ *MBBS DTM&H MRCGP MSc RAMC* 220805
Woods DR 010804
Woods KL 300613
Woolley T 300608
Wright CR 300613
York SP 170909

Majors

Ahmad TK 040809
Allan RJB 060808
Ambler WCN 050814
Anderson JR 010812
Aslam SA 020805
Atkinson FW 060813
Atun AR 040804
Bahadur S 010806
Bailey KGH *DMCC DRCOphth DOccMed MRCGP* 070807
Baird Clarke CD *MBBS BMedSci MSc* 120505
Ballard MS *FRCR MBBS RAMC* 040809
Barker T 040808
Barlow AR 060813
Barnes TEL *MBChB* 050814
Barratt JW *MBBS DMCC* 050814
Bauld RA 050814
Baxter DLJ 310710
Beech ZKM 010210
Beresford-Jones PG 100911
Berry JEA 180909
Bettison EL 030813
Billings AK *BSc MBChB mRCGP* 020811
Biswas JS *MBBS MRCP(Lond)* 020810
Blanch RJ *BSc(Hons) MBChB(Hons) MRCSEd* 020810
Blankenstein TN 060813
Blethyn KL 060813
Booker RJ *MCEM MRCGP Dip.IMC RCS Edin* 020810
Booker TEF 040809
Boyd MC 010811
Boylan MD *MBBCh FCEM DipIMC DipRTM RAMC* 050808
Breeze J *MRCS MFDS* 200704
Briard RJ 020805
Brown CMS 020810
Brown KV 060808
Buck DOB 040815
Buckley AM 050814
Burns DS 290813
Buxton WP *MBBS* 050814
Caesar B 120407
Calder AA 310707
Callegari PE 010812
Cameron CL 020810
Cameron-Smith MB *MB BChir MRCGP* 070211
Campbell KP 010812
Campbell LJ 010813
Campbell MJ 141210
Chambers D 060808
Charlton JW 010812
Chatham-Zvelebil NM 060813
Chauhan R 040810
Chinery JP 040809
Christie AR 010812
Clarke S 010812
Clark-McKellar J 050814
Clay KA 020810
Claydon MA 060813
Coley EL 010812
Cooper DJ 020811
Coulson TL 040809
Coulter HSO 040815
Cox AT 010807
Cranley MR 010812
Dart RF 060808

Davey CMT 010812
Davies PG *FRCA* 010811
Davies RL 050814
Davison MA 120207
De Maria SL 010210
De Montes EM 010909
Denby NA 060813
Dennison NC 010812
Dhesi SS 010812
Dickinson AJ 010807
Docherty PW *MBChB FRCA* 040809
Draper J *MB ChB BaO MRCGP DRCOG* 061112
Duffield CAB 050814
Edwards DS 010207
Eisenstein NM *BM BCh MA (Oxon) MRCS* 060813
Evans BJ 010806
Evans IR 290813
Evans SL 060813
Fadden SJ 010812
Faerestrand NH 310712
Faulconer ER 020810
Fell TH 010813
Fernando MCD 040209
Fetherston CR 070807
Fieldhouse EAS 210108
Fletcher TE *MBE* 050809
Forde ME *MB ChB MRCGP MPH* 070503
Foster PL 060813
Fowler TR 050814
Frost EJ 020811
Gill JAK *MBBS MSc FRCA* 020810
Gillingham SJ 050814
Gittins P 020811
Goldsmith CR 040809
Gough MRC 020813
Gout SJ 010809
Granger CJ 040815
Grant J 130907
Granville-Chapman J *MBBS MRCS* 070807
Grundy-Wheeler HC 010812
Guest SN 020811
Gumbley AE 060213
Guthrie HC 120215
Hale PJ 060808
Hall AR 010812
Hall BGR 011111
Halliwell JPK 010813
Harrisson SE *MB BS FRCS (SN)* 010806
Hazlerigg ARA 050814
Herd MK 070807
Hicks AJ 020810
Hill NE 010806
Holdsworth DA 020811
Hollingsworth AC *MB ChB (Hons) MRCSEd* 020811
Howes R *MBChB DMCC* 050814
Hughes MJ 060812
Hume DC 050808
Hunt DM 020810
Hunt EJF 061112
Hutley EJ 020805
Ingold JM 020811
Irving AC *MB BCh MRCSEd DRCOG DCH MRCGP* 060813
Isherwood SC 010205
Isles MG 250912
Jacobus TEG 040809
Jago AS 050814
Jeevaratnam JA *BMBS BMedSci* 010812
Jeffery NP 010806
Jenkins DR *MBE MA (Oxon) BM BCh MRCP* 010812
Jeyanathan J 030811
Johnson SA 140208
Johnston JJ 020810
Johnstone TJ 060808
Jones CPL 020811
Julian MD 050814
Keene DD 010810
Kivell GE 060810
Knight KA 040815
Knott JJW *BM MRCGP DiMM RAMC* 050807
Konfortova CT 040809
Konig TC 020805
Kumar AJ 030813
Ladele AO 080810
Lamb LEM 060207
Lampl CFK 050814
Lawton GS 040804
Le Feuvre AJ 030204
Lee KJH 020811
Lentaigne JD 020811
Lewin IJS 060813
Lewis PJ 050803
Lewis SE 070807
Luke DP 020805
Lyne-Pirkis CHD 060813
Lyon JD 030811
MaCleod NJ *MBE* 040809
Marsden MER 050814
Martin NAJ *MBBS MD MSc DMCC FRCS(Plast)* 020805
Masters K 240115
Mathieson SP *MBBChMRCGP* 010812
Maund AG 110311
McBride OMB 020811
McIntosh EJ *MBChB DipIMC RCSEd* 020811
Mieville KE 010812
Millar-Brown AM 010812
Mitchell JL 060813
Monteiro De Barros JNJ 050814
Moore AC 060813
Morgan MJM 060813
Morris-Butler RJ 040815
Moy RJ 030810
Murphy DM 140110
Naumann DN 090312
Naumann LK 010812
Nelson A 050814
Nelson SC 050814
Newman J 010812
Owen SJ 020811
Page CLJ 190811
Page KMA *MBBS MRCGP* 030811
Papworth JEJ 300301
Park CK 060808
Parsons IT 040815
Pearkes TD 060813
Pearson J 010812
Pelham AT 050814
Phillips RE 050814
Phipps AV 071107
Poon H 020811
Pope CD *MBBS FRCA* 290806
Pretsell EMJ 050814
Pribul VC 020810
Quantick OJ 050814
Rainey OH 020810

Raitt S 020810
Ramakrishna S 010812
Ramasamy A 010206
Randall-Carrick JV 060813
Rao A 240706
Reed RC *BSc FRCA* 060808
Reynolds ND *MBBS BSc(Hons)* 060813
Richards SB 060813
Roberts CCS 010812
Robiati LA 050814
Rodger MP *BSc MBChB MSc MRCS* 010807
Roscoe D 040809
Round JA 060808
Royston CL 010806
Sanders GJ 060808
Sellon EA 010812
Sharpe DB *MB BS BSc(Hons) MCEM DIMC RAMC* 060813
Sharrock AE 020810
Sierens SG 060813
Simms MGN *MB ChB MRCGP PGDIP RCSEd MCEM* 020805
Singleton JAG 111111
Smith CA *MCEM DipIMC* 020810
Stacey MJ 020810
Stansfield TJ 070807
Staruch RMT 040815
Stewart MJ 060813
Steynberg SL 050814
Stuart AJ 270809
Tabner K 020811
Taylor B *MB ChB(Hons) BSc FRCA* 030811
Taylor CJ *BSc MBBS FRCS(Plast) RAMC* 070206
Taylor N 060813
Thiel MA 060813
Thomas RJ 050814
Thomas SH *BA(Hons) BM MRCGP* 040809
Thompson JR *MRCGP DipIMC RCSEd* 010811
Troth TD 040815
Trow CR 010812
Tunstall CL 020811
Vargha GR 010812
Walker ES 040815
Walker J 060808
Walker NM 020805
Wall CM *MB BCh* 030809
Wall WD 040809
Wedgwood JTA 040815
Weir AGA *MBChB BSc MRCSEd RAMC* 010812
Weiss VC 040812
Welsh SB 040815
Wheatley RJ 060207
Whitaker JKH 010213
White SH 020810
Wilde GD *BSc(Hons) MB ChB(Hons) MRCGP* 060808
Wilkinson KL 010812
Wilkinson PAH 050814
Willdridge DJ 010809
Williams A *BSc MBBS MRCP MD* 050803
Williams ET 020813
Williams KL 010812
Wood TA 040809
Woolley TGD 060813
Wordsworth MJJ *MA BM BCh DMCC MRCS* 050814
Wyldbore M *MBBS BSc(Hons) MRCA* 060808
Yates MD *BMBS MA BSc DFSRH DMCC MRCGP* 060813
Yim GH 050814
Zaffar SH 080301

Captains

Abbott C 010812
Adamson SG 030811
Akerman AJ 110911
Ayalew Y 030811
Barker SD *BSc* 010812
Baum LS 010812
Blenkinsop GC 030811
Blenkinsop PA 030811
Bonham CT 070813
Bremner SE 120407
Buckland-Hoby M 070813
Carslake HB 030811
Carter NJ 030811
Chandler HC *MBChB* 030811
Childerley R 030811
Clews-Jones AS 050815
Court MF 030811
De Burgh H 070813
Dickinson DJ 300910
Duncan PGA 170314
Dunnill SD 030811
Evans T 270912
Falconer-Hall TJK 050815
Farnworth A 010812
Farrell DJA 010812
Fenn TD 070813
Foster SA 050815
France KE 060814
Fudge DJ 070813
Galvin NPW *BMBS DMCC* 010812
Gough AM 010812
Graham GEA 070813
Hamer AT 030811
Handford CG 060814
Harring HM 010808
Hartley JA 060814
Hector JK 040815
Henderson HP 070813
Hindmarsh DG *MBChB* 030811
Howard M 270912
Jefferys SE 230113
Jenkins TF 291213
Johnson AA *MA (Cantab) MBBS DMCC* 030811
Kawai-Calderhead WG 050911
Kelleher MJ *MBChB DMCC* 030811
Kerans GW 010812
King GJ 070813
Kirwan-Izzo MV *MBChB DMCC* 030811
Lamb AH 010812
Lewis PEH 030811
MacLeod KE 070813
Maitland LMR 060814
Makin SL 030811
Malone MHC 011011
Mason AE 070813
Matuska H 070813
Mawson CR 050815
McAleer SR *MB ChB* 030811
McKane JLM 070813
McLachlan AP 030811
Miles JA 030811
Millington JM 040810

Milne GM	070813
Mitchell AA	040810
Navaratne LMB	030811
Nicholls AKS	010812
O'Brien MA	070813
Osborne LG	060814
O'Sullivan OLP	070813
Packer TW	070813
Pang AYL	030811
Paterson GN	070813
Pearson RL	070813
Quicke MC	070813
Quinn I	070813
Reader J	010812
Sanders LR	070813
Sawford HJ	050815
Shaw JA	270912
Shimmings MA	060814
Shirley JW	070813
Smedley VT	021012
Smith GD *MBBS DMCC Dip IMC RCS.Ed RAMC*	030811
Starkey K	030811
Stewart SK	030811
Strachan DL	050815
Sweeney CC	070813
Tallowin S	070813
Taylor HM	030811
Tollerfield JC	070813
Tucker VA	030811
Vijayakumar V	010812
Walls JS	070813
Welby-Everard PGE	070813
West MD	070813
Westwood KM	070813
Wetherill NCT *BM DMCC*	030811
Wilkins D	060814
Williams AMA	010812
Winstanley MC	070813
Wood CM *MbBCh DMCC*	030811
Wright KA	070813

Lieutenants

Allan RJC	280714
Anderson KP	010811
Coates RO	010812
Cohen HML	280714
Davies LG	010812
Elliott LJ	010812
Fryer CH	010812
Geddes TC	010812
Gillett RL	010812
Harris EJ	180714
Herron JBT	010812
Hodgetts JM	010812
Howard EF	010812
Kemeny CJ	010812
Matthews JH	010812
McClean C	010812
McVey JB	010812
Rickard LJ	010812
Ruddick CEC	110714
Severs EJ	010812
Theobald GO	010812
Webster S	280714
Wright AE	010812

2nd Lieutenants

Bainbridge AC	010813
Bertram IJ	010814
Davies RJ	010814
Deeming FD	010814
Downes GM	010813
Hastings B	010813
Johnstone AA	010813
Kyle EA	010813
Mackey JP	010813
McMillan KR	010813
Murphy RJ	010813
Pearson-Jones TW	010813
Pickering CD	010813
Roger AHA	010813
Sandhu AS	010813
Smith MJE	010813
Tweed JA	010812

CORPS OF ROYAL ELECTRICAL & MECHANICAL ENGINEERS

Upon a lightning flash, a horse forcene gorged with a coronet of four fleur-de-lys, a chain reflexed over its back and standing on a globe. Above, a crown upon a scroll bearing the letters REME

Arte et Marte

Regimental March

Quick March .... Lillibulero and Aupres de ma Blonde
Slow March .... Duchess of Kent

Agents .... Holt's Branch, Royal Bank of Scotland plc, Lawrie House, Farnborough, Hants GU14 7NR
Regimental Headquarters .... RHQ REME, MOD Lyneham, Lyneham, Chippenham SN15 4XX
(Tel: 01249 894520 Mil: 95481 4520 Email: REMERHQCorpsSec@mod.uk)

Alliances

Canadian Armed Forces .... The Electrical and Mechanical Engineers Branch of the Canadian Armed Forces
South African Defence Forces .... Technical Services Corps
Australian Military Forces .... The Corps of Royal Australian Electrical and Mechanical Engineers
Indian Army .... Corps of Electronics and Mechanical Engineers
Pakistan Army .... Corps of Electrical and Mechanical Engineers
Sri Lanka Army .... The Sri Lanka Electrical and Mechanical Engineers
Malaysian Armed Forces .... The Royal Malaysian Electrical and Mechanical Engineers

Colonel in Chief .... FM *HRH The Prince Philip Duke of* Edinburgh *KG KT OM GBE ONZ QSO AK GCL CC CMM ADC(P)*

Master General .... Lt Gen (Retd) A C Figgures *CB CBE (until 010417)* 010412
Lt Gen Paul W Jaques *CBE (from 010417)*
Colonels Commandant .... Lt Gen *Sir* Christopher M Deverell *KCB MBE (until 010716)* 011109
Lt Gen Patrick N Y M Sanders *CBE DSO (from 010716)*
Maj Gen (Retd) Stephen M Andrews *CBE* 010310
Maj Gen (Retd) K E Ferguson 010411
Lt Gen P W Jaques *CBE* 010312
Maj Gen (Retd) John M R Henderson *CB* 010614
Maj Gen Robert M B Nitsch *CBE* 010614
Brig (Retd) Martin J Boswell 011015
Maj Gen Mark J Gaunt *CEng FIMechE MRAeS* 010716

Corps Colonel .... Col D G Scott *ADC*
Corps Secretary .... Lt Col (Retd) M J Tizard *CEng FIET*

Lieutenant Colonels

Ackroyd CA *BSc CEng MIET* 300615
Anders-Brown DS 300615
Arnold MR *MSc MA CEng BEng pscj ae* 300614
Atkinson AS 300608
Bastone DC 300611
Batty DC 300611
Beck PJ *CEng* 300607
Brayshay DD 300615
Bridges SR *BEng MSc CEng MIET* 300615
Brierley PA 010116
Bryant AJ *CEng FIMechE* 300607
Burke BT *MBE* 300610
Camilleri PT 070515
Candlin SJ 280116
Case RH 300605
Casey SJB 300615
Champion DL *MSc BTech* 300606
Cooper RJ 300608
Cowen SD *BSc (Hons)* 280514
Coxon NJ 300607
Crichard G 300610
Cummings PA *BEng (Hons) CEng MIMechE* 300615
Cunningham A *CEng FIMechE* 300610
Cuthbert-Imrie BHP *CEng MIET aeo* 060114
Doyle ND 300613
Edwards MJ 300615
Eggett GJ *MSc CEng MIET(elec) MInstLM* 280514
Ellis JA 300607
Evans AI *BEng (Hons) CEng MIMechE ae* 300615
Faithfull-Davies EJ 300613
Fitzsimons BP 300609
Fletcher PL 300608
Forrest WW *MBE* 010115
Garbutt RM 300613
Gibb RM 300611
Gill LC 300612
Gillies TJ 300614
Hall DE 300615
Hall TA 300609
Heardman J *BEng MSc C Eng MIET* 300610
Hirst TD 300613
Hodgson T 310713

Houldsworth AP 300608
Howarth AJ *MBE CEng MIMechE* 300614
Howells SI *MBE* 010315
Hughes PB *BEng(Hons) MBA CEng FRAeS* 300614
Ireland CS 300615
Jeavons MD *MBE* 300613
Johnson PA *MSc MA BEng(Hons) CEng FIMechE* 300610
Johnston A *BSc(Hons) MA MSc CEng CMgr* 300612
Jones MB 300612
Judd JC 300601
Kerton MS 300614
King C 300613
Kitchener BCJ 311213
Kolczak R 300615
Leach MJ 300609
Learmonth MA 300612
Lewis A 300610
Loader PG 300611
Marie PS 300609
Marshall AC 300601
McArthur PJ 300612
McEvoy DJ 300614
McGready AH 300615
McMillan P 300611
McNally OP 300607
Moore NE *MBE* 300613
Nasse SE 300614
Nevin SG 300607
Owen PG 300614
Paris HVI 300608
Parkinson AJ 280914
Phillips CP 300613
Phillips IJ 300613
Prosser PD 300612
Quant GP *MBE* 030715
Rogers AJ 300612
Rosie LR 250914
Sharples NJP *BEng MSc CEng* 300610
Smith AM 300613
Smith SG *MBE* 300614
Somerville AM *MBE* 220115
Stace NK 300613
Stradins PJ *BEng MDA CEng MIET CMgr FCMI* 300610
Stratton-Brown TJ 300615
Sweeting C 300614
Teare AD *BSc(Eng) MSc CEng FIMechE* 300601
Thorne AR 300611
Thorpe RP 300603
Thursz JCM 300605
Torbet JD 300613
Treharne JS *BEng(Hons) MSc CEng MIEE* 300614
Wade MD *CEng MIMechE* 300614
Ware MJ 300612
Wells RW *QGM BEM* 271013
Welsh RP *BEng MA MSc CEng FIMechE* 300608
Williams RI 300615
Wilson PA 300609
Winthrop IS 300606
Young RJ 300607

Majors

Alexander MGD 310714
Algate MV 310712
Allinson SJ 310709
Allison TJ 310710
Anthistle JM 310715
Atkins AP *BSc MSc MBCS CITP CEng MIET* 310704
Atkinson ELC 310711
Ayres CD 310711
Baddeley CG 310713
Badham-Thornhill KF 310710
Bailey W 310711
Baker CD 310714
Baxter RJ 310705
Beaumont GA 310712
Beaumont K 310714
Beevor SCB 310713
Benson CG 310715
Bharat SJ *CEng IMechE* 310710
Biffen JW 310713
Bishop DS 310713
Bloomfield BR 310715
Blunn JD 310715
Booth GT 310714
Bosher D 310715
Bower DA 310715
Bradbury JG *MSc MBA CEng MIET* 310706
Bramwell PJ *BSc(Open)* 310714
Brankin AP 310713
Bremner A 310707
Brewer IC 310702
Brinkman C *CEng MIMechE* 310712
Britton MA 310714
Broadhurst GA 310711
Broster CN 310702
Buchanan DS 310714
Bunker DJ 310711
Burden WDH 310702
Burrell TC *BEng(Hons)* 310715
Burton G 310715
Bush D 310705
Calder R 310715
Cameron EC 310709
Carrotte PJ *CEng MIMechE* 310711
Carter RA 310713
Cary MP 310714
Chambers SP *BEng(Hons) CEng MIET* 310709
Chapman MD 310711
Cheek JCS *MBE MSc CEng MIMechE MCGI* 310706
Coles DAG 310710
Connolly G 310708
Cook WE 310715
Cooper SR 310715
Cope MD 310702
Copley-Smith SP 310707
Corsie GM *MSc BEng (Hons) IEng AEO* 310715
Cousins D 310714
Cowan R 310715
Craig AT 310709
Creed BB *MBE* 310710
Crilley GW 310715
Cush PA 310715
Davis MJ 310710
Dawson IS 310711
Dennis MH *MSc CEng MIMechE MCGI aeo* 310704
Denton PD 310706
Denton TM *CEng* 310711
Dickson ST *MEng IEng* 310715
Dove-Dixon JGA 310706
Dutton SP 310710
Dymow N 310710
Edwards GF 310713
Elliott AR 310708

Evans RA IEng *MIET* 310713
Fallowfield DJ 310710
Feek GJ 310710

Ferguson M *IEng MSOE MIRTE MCGLI* 310710
Finner D 310714
Foster LG *CEng BSc(Hons) MIET* 310709
Francis PA 310711
Fraser AN 310713
Fulford GP 310713
Fyfe RW *MSc BSc CEng MIET MCMI* 310708
Gardner MS 310712
Gaskin SH *MBE* 310710
Gentry RN 310715
Gisby RW 310714
Goode MA 310708
Gough AS 310715
Grainger AR 310713
Green TD 310714
Greensmith MT 310710
Greenwood NL 310710
Gregory MJ 310713
Hackney JJ 310713
Hampshire AJ 310706
Hanson J *MBE MSc* 310709
Harris DJ 130815
Hartman LJ *ae CEng MIMechE* 310707
Haslam DR 310709
Hayes CA 310713
Hayward JP 310707
Henry JW 310712
Hill JA 310715
Hill SMD *BEng(Hons) CEng MIET ae* 310706
Hobbs PJ 310713
Hollinger S 310715
Holmes SD 310714
Holmes TM 310706
Horn MB *BEng(Hons) CEng MIMechE* 310709
Horsefield B 310704
Houston BD 310713
Howard-Harwood MI 310704
Howard-Perry KM 280806
Huggins A 310712
Innes G *EngO* 310710

James RCJ 310709
Jenkins R 310712
Jenkins RD *IEng* 310715
Johnson J 310707
Johnston DW 310710
Jones BP 310708
Jones BS 310709
Jones MA 310713
Jones SD 310709
Keane MDR *IEng MSOE MIRTE* 310714
Kelly-Smith DL 310704
Kendall- Reid P *IEng* 310714
King AJ 310714
King IR 310715
Kirchel M *MBE* 310710
Lambert T 310709
Lamont BD *MBE* 310712
Larder RE 310712
Lavelle MD 310715
Leach MR 310709
Lees JR 310713
Leng JR 310713
Leslie DSA 310711
Lethbridge DP *MEng(Hons) CEng MIET ae* 310710
Letts SN 310712
Lewin MR *BEng(Hons) Msc CEng MIMechE* 310704
Lines PJ 310714
Lively JP 310711
Lock AR 310715
Lockwood JP 270412
Logie P 310711
Lovelock AA *BEng(Hons) CEng MIET AssocCIPD* 310711
Lowe A 310714
Lowen JD 310710
MacKenzie N 310713
Macklin RH 310711
Maitland CJ 310714
Maitland JM 310711
Mansfield SA 310714
Massey MPD 310713
Maw AW *MBE* 310709
McCarthy LDL *BSc(Hons) MSc CEng MIET FCMI* 310702
McDonald R 310708
McIntyre ND 310715

McKendrick KM 310714
McMeechan J 310715
Miles KJ 310708
Millar JM 310705
Miller MA 310707
Mitchell AP 300999
Moffat CHW 310707
Morgan OC *REME* 310710
Mullen J 310713
Murley JM 310714
Murphy BJ 310711
Myers SA 310704
Naivalurua RK *BSc IEng MIET* 310709
Naylor WM 310712
Nicholson MR 310715
Noke P 310714
Norman DL 300998
Norton ARA 310706
Oakes PS 310714
O'Connor SM 310711
Odling TR 310711
Oldnall RBS 310714
Oliver P 310712
Ord CK 310715
Patey MW *IEng* 310715
Peters RA *MBE BSc MBA CEng MIET* 310714
Piearce MP 310706
Platt AC 310714
Price HM *BEng(Hons) CEng MIMechE ae AEO* 310703
Rae IC 310715
Redfern KV 310715
Ritson G 310714
Rix JS *BEng(Hons) EngO* 310712
Roberts VJ 310711
Robertson AM 310708
Robertson JN 310712
Robertson S 310713
Rogers DA 310711
Rogers P 310709
Rogers SG 310712
Round-Turner PM 310713
Rouse IM 310713
Sampson JJ 310703
Sands IE 310709
Sands RM 310710
Saunders LR 300901

Sekhon TS 310712
Seth AKM 310711
Shearer MW 310711
Shenton RK *CEng BEng (Hons) MIET* 310709
Sibley JD 310713
Simpson DA 310712
Smith DJ 310709
Smith MT 310713
Smith NF 310712
Smithurst PA 310714
Soane GS 310714
Spencer MS *MBE* 310710
Steptoe DB 310707
Stokes JD 310715
Stuart APD 310704
Sullivan FK *CEng* 310708
Sutton MJ 310712
Symons MJ 310713
Tait KA 310715
Talbot A 310715
Tawlks DE 310714
Taylor BRG *MBE* 310710
Taylor PR 310704
Taylor RN 300900
Taylor SJ 300994
Tebbutt J 310715
Tilsley MW *MBE MIET IEng* 310713
Tinniswood A 310715
Todd RC 300994
Toland DC 310710
Trengove IR 310706
Tribe AD 310712
Turnbull A 310715
Turner TJP 310711
Turnock SP *CEng MIMechE BEng(Hons)* 310711
Walker AC *MSc IEng MIMechE AEO* 310715
Walker JW 310712
Wallace IS *BEng(Hons)* 310711
Wallace JVO 310710
Warrener ME 310714
Waterston DAJ 310714
Watson CJ *BEng(Hons)* 310715
Watt JF 310702
Watters EG *CEng MIMechE* 310705
Webb ALK 310712
White GAO 310712
White LK 310709
Whitehead NC 310712
Wigmore EJM 310712
Wilcox MA 310709
Williams JG 310710
Willison TA 310708
Willshire DF *MBA BSc IEng MIET MCMI* 140815
Wilson DI 310715
Wilson MC 300996
Wooldridge JT *QCVS* 310714
Wright SE 270412
Yarker AJ 310710
Yates N 300900

Captains

Aitken NGE 140415
Allan MGH 010813
Allcock ND *MBE* 260410
Allen AL 010513
Ashton RM *MEng* 090211
Axon KR 110815
Bage MT 260814
Bagshaw MS 080212
Bailey DJR *IEng MSOE MIRTE* 260814
Ball MW 130214
Bamber JS 140213
Barbieri DA 310810
Barnett LE 161013
Bartlett JC 030511
Bashforth RJE 180613
Bass SJ 310810
Bate RE 121010
Bell PI 240815
Billingham R 140415
Booth CT *IEng MIMechE* 171012
Bourton MT 180613
Boyd G 130611
Bradley ID 161013
Broad CM 080212
Brogan MW 260814
Brook RB 161013
Brooks C 110815
Brooks JG 161013
Brown AJ 140213
Bruce WM 240815
Burchell DS 120612
Burnard WK *MBE* 280812
Burrows S 160414
Campbell JLR 130214
Carter DJ 140213
Casey MJ 130611
Caswell PA 140213
Caswell-Treen GE 060514
Catchpole RL 311212
Chignell GS 050515
Clarke DC 260410
Clarkson MP 280812
Clench SJ 161013
Codd BJ 150813
Comber CGJ *MC* 010513
Connor SC 050515
Cooper DA 010909
Cornock PA 180613
Corrigan A 130214
Cotton MB 080811
Couldridge D 130309
Coward CB 110815
Coward CL 130611
Crowther HC 080212
Cummings RJ 250915
Dalrymple D 280812
Davidson AJM 080212
Deacon AR 140415
Desroches AG 240815
Devine A 310810
Dickson MP 130214
Donovan MA 060514
Douglas-Evans AM 170810
Douthwaite PG 140213
Down AJ MSc 200409
Duffield RG 170614
Dunlop GJ 130214
Dyer PJ 151215
Edgar KM 130214
Edwards DP 080212
Ellis WT 240815
Ewens JA 151215
Fielder CR 260814
Finch PG 050515
Fisher CW 080212
Flynn JP 080212
Fortune AG 050515
Foster AJ 030511
Foster MP 120612

Frampton M	050515
Francis R	170614
Friend SJL	130611
Frost ML	130214
Gadsby V	120612
Gogna SS	220607
Goodacre BJ	140415
Goose SP	010909
Grewal RS *BEng(Hons)*	010813
Griffiths B	110815
Griffiths GC	150413
Griffiths J	200409
Hall TK	030511
Hanks CJ	170815
Harris JF	110815
Haugvik C	260410
Hazel CM	110712
Hinson IT	010813
Hockley PC	130611
Horne DK	170613
Hosken J	280812
Hughes R	161013
Hughes RD	180613
Hughes SG	010909
Humphery TH	130214
Hurt DW	090211
Inman PJ *BEng(Hons) Mech Eng*	170614
Irvine DM	240815
Isaac TA	050515
Isitt PJ	150610
Jeffery MA	160609
Jessop HDL	180613
John SRL *MBE*	280812
Jones CW	090211
Jones SJ	060410
Jordan PS	300811
Kelly CL	300811
Kelly SGJ	310810
Kennedy RA	161013
Kenny JA	140415
Kent TR *BSc*	140213
Keogh MJ	140214
Kinghorn L	030511
Knudsen EP	130214
Lackenby RA	010909
Lamont SA	030511
Larsen OD	080212
Lawrence N	050515
Lee LD	280812
Lees HC	030511
Lewis RD	290413
Ling RJ	090211
Logie G BEng(Hons)	110210
Lovell MA	060514
Ludlow PA	130214
Machin KM *BEng(Hons)*	311212
Machin MD *BEng(Hons)*	110815
Madronal SL	060514
Manning AWA	080212
Marsden RS	171012
Marsh CP	280812
Mason MG *EngO IEng MCMI MCGI MSOE*	070512
Masterson SH	210408
Maxwell AS	140213
McBeath GRE *IEng MIRTE MSOE*	030511
McCann EG	080212
McCluskey TA *IEng AMRaeS*	300811
McDavid IV	300811
McDonald CJ	110815
McGlynn S	030511
McHugh JA	310810
McIver PJE	101011
McLean MHC *MEng*	140415
McMahon RA *MBE*	300811
Melia DM	101011
Metcalfe MD	151215
Millar RP	010813
Milne SJ	140415
Morgan LD	060514
Morris AH	050515
Morse HR	090211
Mortimore AC	260814
Muir DC	130214
Muirhead AD	140415
Murray AD	050515
Nel SD	100611
Nicholls MA	180613
Nicholson SCH	141009
Nugent NM	120612
Nyoni TG	121010
Oatley DJ	260814
O'Brien MPA *BEng(Hons)*	110210
O'Brien PL	140213
Odling AC	130214
Oldrid SL	060514
Onstenk JGH	140415
Owen TE	170614
Park A	170614
Peak MDB	110815
Peaple CO	010713
Perry RJ	261012
Phoenix S	110210
Platts SAG	180613
Pogson-Hughes-Emanuel R *BEng(Hons)*	300312
Postlethwaite CJ	080212
Proctor DS	300811
Pugh TWR	290612
Rawson JCQ	161013
Redburn C	240815
Reed JM	101011
Reynolds P	200409
Reynolds PG	200409
Ridley-Holloway JP	161013
Rimmer MJ	130214
Risdale DA	200409
Roberts GJ	090211
Roberts MB	110815
Robertson DR *BSc(Hons) IEng MIET*	260814
Robertson JT	140415
Robinson E	110815
Rodger IA	161013
Saunders MJ	150413
Schenk JR	141009
Scott JR	010909
Sewell JP	090211
Shaw BA	260410
Shrimpton EJ	040814
Skingsley ST *BEng(Hons)*	110815
Smith DL	050515
Smith GJ	260410
Smith GJ	280812
Smith IA	280812
Smith PM	151215
Spencer MP	180613
Springall JF	130214
Stewart CJ *REME MEng*	130611
Sugrue JC	010909
Surman KE	160609
Sykes SS *MBE*	240815

Thomas BR	060514
Thomas I	110210
Thompson SC	121010
Thomson A	060514
Topping AJ	140415
Turner HJA	140213
Twinn RG	010713
Vallance RJ	200409
Vance J	150612
Voss JVF	010909
Ward APJ	080212
Ward D *IEng*	260410
Ward KL	161013
Ward PW *IEng MIMechE*	080212
Watson MH	010513
Wells JP	130214
Whitehouse JM	050515
Wilding M	150413
Williams AC	161013
Williams DR	010909
Williams LW	151215
Wilson DJ	311213
Wilson LG	140213
Winterbourne HR	140213
Wood RK	120612
Wood SF	130214
Woodhouse DB *MEng(Hons)*	080212
Woods CJ	090211
Woods SR *BSc(Hons)*	121010
Woodward BJ	090810
Young PW	080212
Young RM	261012

Lieutenants

Allchin AR	131215
Angbo Y	141214
Arrowsmith JW	130414
Aubrey JD	100814
Barnes GR	141214
Barr LE	090815
Brownlie AS	090815
Cartwright OJ	100814
Chaytor DRG MEng	090815
Ciesielczuk RG	141214
Copeland GW	120415
Cornes CJ	100814
Coughlan JJ	131215
Crofts TA	120415
Daniels BAL	130414
Dougal SC	090815
Douglas DCR	141214
Duggan LSJ	090815
Dykes JC	090815
Edwards ME	130414
English JK	100814
Golding JM	090815
Granqvist-Ahmed SJJ	100814
Groom A	090815
Gunn TAA	100814
Hall CP	120415
Hall LA	100814
Harrison MF	090815
Harrison-Wolff AK	100814
Hodges AM	120415
Hodgkiss ID	151213
Hunjan JS	120415
Hunt DJ	151213
Jackson TW	130414
Jasper KL	100814
Jones CD	100814
Keenan J	100814
Lawrence JG	140413
Lawson JS	100814
Leakey SKL	100814
Lowe WJ	141214
Main GW	130414
Maloney SP	100814
Martin JRD	120415
McHutchon SG	100814
McNamee OP	140413
Middleton DN	110813
Milne CA	090815
Mumby CM	141214
Murphy RJ	120415
Nevin-Maguire CAB	120415
Oliver RJ	090815
Read BT	131215
Ritchie AJ	100814
Rudkin TL	140413
Sarsfield RW	120415
Shand AJ	130414
Starr AT	130414
Tankaria MF	120415
Thompson D	141214
Tooth SAJ *MEng*	090815
Turner-Piques JC *MEng(Hons)*	100814
Underwood LD	120415
Warburton AJ	131215
West AEL	100814
White CC	130414
Wilkinson BP	131215
Williams KJ *MSc(Hons)*	090815
Williamson J	090815
Wooster PR	120415
Wreathall SA	090815
Ziabek NJ	140413

2nd Lieutenants

Askins EL	080815
Churcher R	121215
Davidson RP	110415
Folley T	110415
Franklin MA	080815
Gordon GP	080815
Greening ML	121215
Griffiths J	080815
Gwynn-Jones J	080815
Hardman AK	080815
Hayward RWE	110415
Hinwood JT	080815
Holmes JC	121215
Lewis MD	121215
Marengo JT	080815
McAfee OJ	080815
Rowe J	080815
Sangan MI	080815
Shelmerdine-Hare RH	110415
Swingler EP	080815
Taylor IA	121215
Tovey JD	080815
Wallis PF	080815
Webber CS	110415
Whittaker G	080815

ADJUTANT GENERAL'S CORPS

A laurel wreath surmounted by a crown; within the wreath the Royal Crest. Beneath a scroll inscribed ANIMO ET FIDE in silver

Regimental March

Quick March .... Pride of Lions
Slow March... Greensleeves

Agents... Holt's Branch, Royal Bank of Scotland plc.
Regimental Headquarters...................... Worthy Down, Winchester, Hants SO21 2RG
(Tel: 01962 887 820) (Mil: ext 2820)

Colonel in Chief..................................... HER MAJESTY THE QUEEN
Deputy Colonels in Chief....................... *HRH The Duchess of* Gloucester *GCVO*
HRH The Duchess of Kent *GCVO*

Colonel Commandant .... Lt Gen James I Bashall *CBE*..310715
Assistant Colonel Commandant............ Maj Gen Robert M B Nitsch *CBE*..290615
Deputy Colonels Commandant.............. Lt Gen T P Evans *CB CBE DSO (until 130516)*..011013
Maj Gen Robert B Bruce *CBE DSO (from 130516)*
Maj Gen J R Chiswell *CBE MC (until 220716)*..010514
Maj Gen Ben J Bathurst *CBE (from 220716)*
Lt Gen Richard E Nugee *CVO CBE*..280215
Maj Gen Stuart R Skeates *CBE*..290615

Branches of the Adjutant General's Corps are as follows:

STAFF AND PERSONNEL SUPPORT BRANCH

On 6 April 1992

Royal Army Pay Corps Women's Royal Army Corps (less those transferred to other Arms and Services) And the Staff Clerks of the Royal Army Ordnance Corps Staff and Personnel Support Branch

On 1 April 1993

Regimental Clerks from all Arms and Services of the Army joined the Branch

PROVOST BRANCH

On 6 April 1992

Corps of Royal Military Police and Military Provost Staff Corps became: Provost Branch

On 4 March 1997

The Military Provost Guard Service joined the Branch

EDUCATIONAL AND TRAINING SERVICES BRANCH

On 6 April 1992

Royal Army Educational Corps became: Educational and Training Services Branch

ARMY LEGAL SERVICES BRANCH

On 6 April 1992

Army Legal Corps became: Army Legal Services Branch

A laurel wreath surmounted by a crown, within the wreath the Royal Crest. Beneath a scroll inscribed ANIMO ET FIDE in silver

STAFF AND PERSONNEL SUPPORT BRANCH

Antecedent Corps Marches

Quick March .... Imperial Echoes

Branch Headquarters............................ DSPS(A), Gould House, Worthy Down, Winchester, Hants SO21 2RG
(Tel: 01962 887228 Mil: 94271 2228) (Fax: 01962 887568)
Email: so2-exo@dspsa.mod.uk

Alliances

South African Defence Forces .... Finance Service Corps

Deputy Colonel Commandant................ Lt Gen T P Evans *CB CBE DSO (until 130516)*..011013
Maj Gen R B (Bob) Bruce *CBE DSO (from 130516)*

Lieutenant Colonels

Bagnall AE *MBE*	300612
Bennington RA	300613
Benwell NR	300605
Brain JJ *MBE*	300615
Brooks G *ACIB*	300614
Burton ST	300607
Carrell NC	300615
Castle-Smith SJ *MBE*	300608
Charge GB	300609
Cox MR	300612
Deasy S	300608
Evans P *MBE*	090413
Frost FE	300610
Graham K *OBE*	300613
Griffiths AD *OBE*	300613
Griffiths RC *MBE*	300613
Hadfield RE *BSc(Hons) MDA Chartered MCIPD*	300610
Hull CL	300610
James-Park EA *MBE*	300608
Large IG	300614
Leahy JM	010114
Lindsay-Smith MRM *MBE*	300611
Lockwood NH	300615
Malone DN	210615
Marshall DJ	020315
Martin KJ *BA(Hons)*	301205
Meldon P	300604
Moore PJ	300610
Nicholas PJ	300614
Pearson GM	300603
Robertson VC	300607
Robson T	300612
Rutherford DJ *MBA FCMA CGMA*	300614
Shephard SJ	300611
Vardy SM	300614
Watt DS *MBE FCMA*	300608
Whiting VJ	300615
Worsley TC	300607
Wright PWB	300614

Majors

Allardice SL	310710
Apps CS	310714
Ashman P	310707
Avenall JR	310709
Bailey D *Assoc CIPD*	310710
Barr BA	310713
Batchelor LM	310704
Bates S	310711
Berry TL	310715
Bevan CE *MSc ACMA CGMA*	070207
Bird KJ	310712
Bonnett CA	310713
Booty PS	310715
Brewster KA	310712
Briody M	310712
Brown DJ	310714
Bucknell ALM *BSc(Hons)*	310710
Bull FA	310710
Burke SJ	310713
Bye WPF	310702
Bythell JP	310710
Carcone PN	310712
Carrick D	310707
Chibiya C	310715
Circo SJ	310715
Clarke RJ	310710
Cleland RJ	310711
Coates AS	310715
Coleman VL	310715
Concannon JGP	310706
Cooke BJ	091006
Crossman R *BA(Hons)*	310711
Cugudda L	310714
Curtis IA	310711
Davis NJ	310715
Dennis HL	310708
Devereux KJL	310708
Dexter SE	310709
Doig JA	310713
Drapper NI	310713
Dunford AA *MBE BSc(Hons)*	310706
Dunlop SC	310709
Eagle PR *MBE*	310707
Ehlen GC *Dip*	310708
Ehlen S	310709
Elliott KM	310714
Fairs AJ	310709
Fallon JV	310706
Fowler JL	310715
Frank AS	310713
Fraser G	310709
Garnett P	310715
Gaywood J	310715
Gill A	310715
Gill PJ	310707
Ginn WF	310708
Goldsmith AMD	310709
Goldsmith EJ	310714
Gorman GS	310710
Graham M	310715
Grandison HJ	310715

Green PD *BA(Hons)* 310714
Greetham DM 310713
Gurung B 310712
Gurung K 310713
Harrington SC 310713
Hart CJP 310705
Haslett MJ 310714
Hawkins WD 310705
Hendrie G 310713
Hicks JD *MBE* 310715
Hill PA 310710
Howitson-Morley EL *MSc BEng(Hons)* 310709
Hutchinson SL 310713
Jones DM 310712
Kelly KA 310711
Kennedy MB 310712
Kennedy Y 310706
Killoran J 310708
Larner A 300999
Lawrence J 310712
Ledger DW 310705
Leeson C *MBA* 310711
Lewis R 310712
Long J 310715
Lowe AJ *BEM* 310704
Mack NM 310714
MacLeod HE 310711
Magowan AEM 310708
Mark-Richards MTA 310711
Marsh S 300997
Martin OT 310714
Maxwell CJ 310712
May SJ 300993
Mayo AVE 310710
McChlery HM 310714
McDonnell KC 310715
McInally JED 050101
McMillan EM 310714
McTaggart AM *ACMA CGMA BA(Hons)* 310709
Mhere DJM 310715
Millen G 310711
Moffat TM 310713
Morton C 310714
Mullen CS *MSc* 310709
Murray-Knight P 310714
Navarro De Paz RJ 310713
Omara JM 310709
O'Nions PM 310709
Pagett JA 310709
Peck DM *ACMA* 310708
Perera MP 310708
Petty JP 310714
Pottinger EN 310714
Powley-Williams AE 310714
Pritchard H 310709
Prowse TE 310711
Reynolds HK 310714
Richardson JI 310710
Richardson PG 010507
Richardson SHE 310710
Rourke JD 310712
Ryan MJ 310709
Sadler MB 310709
Salt AJ 310711
Sanders RE 310706
Saunders NR 310715
Sloan G 310715
Smith LC 310704
Smyth C 310709
Street MD 310711
Subba B 310715
Taylor TJ 310715
Thomas LM 310708
Thomas NM 310712
Thomson AK 310709
Tilbury TAG 310713
Topliss KA 310715
Turnbull NC *MSc* 310709
Wilkins IHR 310712
Wilkins QM 310703
Williams JJ 310712
Wilson AE 310715
Wilson T 310703
Wood DB 310712
Wright T 310710

Captains

Adcock JL 161013
Allen KI 140512
Anderson GWJ 121215
Asong A 161013
Avis SM 070915
Ayre MJ 131214
Ayre RP 310713
Baker KE 050911
Barnard SJ 060910
Bates SS 131110
Bayards JJ 310713
Beaney M 101011
Beck J 070513
Birrell MR 100111
Boardman JP 090211
Bond SM 200410
Boyes DW 040510
Brannigan CG 090211
Brown P 121215
Brown PJ 140512
Buckenham BD 090211
Callaghan ME 130411
Callender SJ 161013
Campbell PJ 121215
Carney KM 141213
Caruso A 090913
Clare RM 080914
Clark NA 280212
Clemens TM 110515
Coles DS 030912
Compson Bem ME 070915
Coole T 120514
Cousins MJ 240809
Cowie EA 131214
Crawshaw MGW 110815
Creak JB 070513
Cuff MA 140213
Dawson PR 110515
Denton RM 090112
Dixon PE 050911
Docherty PG 101011
Dolby JS 110815
Donaghue JL 080914
Dowdell JE 171012
Duce C 060910
Edmonds GN 080914
Eves PP *MBE* 120514
Ferguson S 110515
Fidler NS 151212
Foster S 121215
Fowler-Robinson GL 141009
Francis GJ 050109
Franklin JM 240809
Gillard CA 110815
Gray PA 030912

Green BS	131214
Greenwood SAF	130611
Gurung MB	020409
Gurung S	070915
Gurung T	010809
Gutierrez DV	121010
Hall AM	090112
Hall JEC	161013
Harman VE	101011
Harrison JAJ	110815
Hartley JO	130611
Hatton MC	160414
Hemmingway G	040510
Henning CD	110815
Henry JL	170614
Hern DL	100111
Hinton N	040510
Hockram ST	040510
Hodgson WP	080212
Horton L *MBE*	070915
Howlett JM	121215
Hurst D	170614
Innes SW	140910
Johnson LJ	120514
Jones MA	130912
Jones SE	260812
Kellie TJ	070915
Khan WS	050811
Knowles KL	161211
Lackenby HA	110815
Lester RA	050911
Lewis SW	140213
Lidgley HM	150414
Limbu K	070915
Lynch J	121215
MacNeill GL	101011
Magin C	090913
Magness S	080914
Mallett GA	060910
Marx MA	070214
McAfee HG	280408
McDonald IH	311213
McEvoy TA	121010
McGregor BD *MBE*	070108
McGrory AJ	140415
McLaughlin S	100111
McLean S	121215
McManus G	280408
Milligan KA	140415
Mole NA	311213
Murphy DD	080313
Nelson EJ	171012
Noble MFP	280910
O'Connell DJ	070513
Osei Kuffour F	151215
O'Shea S	040613
Peake BA	130611
Peck NJ	140415
Peel SJ	170614
Petley-Jones TR	080212
Pidgeon DR	090211
Plant AK	130214
Plant SJ	060910
Price JW	070513
Riasat ZB	030511
Rignall AH	161214
Roberts NJ	090913
Robinson JP	280408
Robinson PA	070915
Robinson PJ	110210
Rockett MJ	101011
Roe RM	130611
Russell P	151212
Rutterford AJ	110515
Salkeld IR	171214
Sapsford SW	311213
Scott IC	151212
Shakya J	090913
Sherief A	150610
Shianti ED	091006
Smith GL	110210
Sorrell JR	080212
Spencer CSP	151212
Stalker CL	100314
Stevenson DP	110515
Stockham BT	101013
Tatters K	131214
Taylor BN	110515
Taylor CK	040110
Taylor CM	080914
Templeton EL	230713
Thompson SL	130814
Tomlinson GM	151212
Towl MI	070915
Wakeman JP	151215
Ward R	110515
Whitecross DJ	110815
Whitehouse KJ	110515
Wilkinson RT	121215
Wilkinson SA	270409
Williams J	060910
Willson DC	311213
Wilson KA	141213
Wilson LMC	200614
Wiltshire LM	080212
Wink GR	170614
Wiseman RW	110515
Wooster ADA	140415
Young JI	121215

Lieutenants

Adcock SP	130414
Ashton SM	120415
Bolton JA	141214
Branchett T	090815
Brown M	120415
Coombes DWE	141213
Coulson G	100814
Crunkhorn ED	141213
Cryer RJ *BA(Hons)*	100814
Dawes SE	151213
Disney WL	120415
Exley EM	130414
Fewster DHF	130414
Foster PL	100814
Gurung S	110813
Hart DPO	100814
Haworth AJ	130414
Heayes JM	100814
Humphreys EL	090815
Hurst VM	100814
Pearson AC	120415
Price HE	110813
Rasbash JHP	141214
Reid KL	120415
Stewart MI	130414
Walker DM	141213
Watson JSA	110813
Wealsby LE	090815
Williams DM	120415

2nd Lieutenants

Bennett TD	121215
Bertram L	080815
Boyd JC	080815
Cooke JS	110415
Derham WR	080815
Eltringham KJ	080815
Gorman ER	080815
Gorman KJ	080815
Graham R	110415
McLaren AP	090814
Myers AR	131214
Rai A	080815
Richardson SR	110415
Smith RA	131214
Wragg JP	110415

PROVOST BRANCH

Adjutant-General's Corps (Royal Military Police) (AGC (RMP))
Adjutant-General's Corps (Military Provost Staff) (AGC (MPS))

RMP: Within a laurel wreath, the Royal Cypher with Crown above. Beneath, a scroll inscribed "ROYAL MILITARY POLICE".

MPS: The Royal Cypher ensigned with the Crown and thereunder a scroll inscribed "MILITARY PROVOST STAFF CORPS" all gold.

MPGS: The Royal Cypher ensigned with the Crown and thereunder a scroll inscribed "MILITARY PROVOST GUARD SERVICE" in gold, the whole surmounting crossed Government keys in silver.

Antecedent Corps Marches

Quick Marches.. The Watch Tower (RMP)
The New Colonial (MPS)
Steadfast and True (MPGS)

Branch Headquarters............................ Headquarters Provost Marshal (Army), Ramillies Building, (IDL 431), Marlborough Lines, Monxton Road, Andover, Hampshire, SP11 8HJ

Alliances

Canadian Armed Forces......................... Canadian Forces Security Branch
Australian Military Forces..................... The Royal Australian Corps of Military Police
New Zealand Army................................ Royal New Zealand Military Police
Pakistan Army.. Corps of Military Police (Pakistan)
Sri Lanka Army...................................... The Sri Lanka Corps of Military Police
Malaysian Armed Forces....................... Malaysian Military Police

Deputy-Colonel Commandant (Provost).. Maj Gen J R Chiswell *CBE MC (until 220716)*..010514
Maj Gen B J Bathurst *CBE (from 220716)*
Director: The Provost Marshal (Army)... Brig R W Warren *MBE (until Jul 16)*..111012
Brig David S Neal *(from Jul 16)*
Regimental Secretary (RMP)................. Col (Retd) J T Green *OBE*

ROYAL MILITARY POLICE

Lieutenant Colonels

Forsythe BL *MBE*	300612
Gartland DM	300610
Hagues PH	050913
Hipkins JRD	300614
John M	300614
Jordan AP *MSc MA MLitt psc(j)*	300610
Logan G	300614
Malin K *BSc(Hons) MIExpE*	300602
McAllister JD	300614
McNeill D	010215
McNeill VE *MBE*	300615
Meredith S	300611
Parke-Robinson JM	300615
Roylance EK	300613
Warren IS *pscj(Can) MIfl*	300607
Waterworth CA *MBE*	300613
Wilson SS	300608
Young TJ *MA BSc(Hons) ARCS*	300612

Majors

Aaron DK	310714
Alecock JR	310707
Archer RM	310714
Ballantyne SA *MBE*	310712
Barter SC	310709
Bass CG	310713
Bass RA	310710
Baysting DL	310704
Beeforth CJ	310713
Bevan MJ	310713
Blackmore TR	310715
Bowen LA	310707
Boyd MA	310714
Brooks TE	310713
Brunt REJ	310713
Cann MR	310705
Charvat JPI	310702
Cox MA	310712
Cresswell DD	310710
Davies KS	310715
Dray DJ *MBE*	310705
Floyd PJ	310714
Gale L	310709
Gledhill-Wallace BA	310710
Graham-Smith JA	310713
Grant RJ	310715
Gray BJ	310715
Greaves BT	310708
Grogan AJ	310705
Hacker PAL	310708
Hall MC *MSc*	310710

Harvey J	310710
Hornsby L	310710
Innes SA	310712
Kay JB	310708
Love DJ	310715
Miller KL	310707
Mitchell LM	310715
Murray-Ross Z	310711
Nealon AD	310702
O'Leary EMP	091008
Parmenter RJ	310714
Penman MT	310715
Phillips RL	310712
Ramsay AJ	310715
Ringrose LA	310712
Robinson-Kirk C	310715
Robson CML	310714
Rotchell KP	310711
Sangster G	310708
Schutte RPC	310715
Scott D	310710
Scott KW	310705
Shapland M	310714
Sheather MJM	310711
Smith KA	310711
Staples DJ	310714
Stearman DR *MSc*	310712
Stitson TA	310712
Tamplin DN *BSc(Hons) MCGI*	310711
Thomson JW	310713
Waldren-Ward RL	310709
Waller WJ	310711
Walters GM	310708
Ward GC	030407
Welch SL *LLB(Hons)*	310711
White MK	310715
Wilkes ASJ	310712

Captains

Allen KJ	020414
Ashton GA	020415
Ashurst BB	151215
Atterton J	311213
Balmer R	180415
Banfield PA	110815
Bates AEM	140213
Bucknall TA	171214
Cameron-Smith BR	160609
Carter MJE	170614
Crossland PJ	131015
Derbyshire DJ	130214
Doherty SN	250213
Fawcett C	140415
Ferguson D	120612
Fraser ES	171214
Fulham LRL	170614
Geary KA	110815
Geldenhuys C	170309
Green AD	130214
Gurr NC	120713
Harding TN	110815
Hatch JS	310713
Hemmings KB	141009
Henson TAM	110815
Horgan SN	101011
Horsman DJ	120612
Ingham CJ	130214
Irvine GL	130611
John C	100114
Kay AJ	151215
Kendall TM	140213
Kimber SC	040411
Marsom NWD	110815
McCurdy RM	160609
McMahon SA	161013
Meredith SAM	140415
Miller CM LLB (Hons)	170614
Moorcroft DJ	171012
Moore A	171012
Mullaney PB	020412
Novak S	180613
Oakland DS	120612
O'Neill JR	140415
Painter SE	090211
Paterson PS	040411
Perkins AJB	151215
Price JM	130214
Reid P	020412
Robbins SJM	040110
Robinson-Brown L	080212
Rose JM	171214
Saunders AC	020415
Saunders DR	020412
Schofield G	020408
Simmons RL	161013
Southerton AJ	030409
Spanton TA	020414
Spencer MD	310713
Stanford BG	010413
Steele J	130410
Sumner LA	020415
Symes A	130611
Taylor NW	010110
Thomas IG	101011
Tickner SA	020410
Tracey DC	101011
Trueman LA	020414
Turnbull M	040515
Turner H	020415
Vogel CR	170614
Wedgwood-Jones V	270611
Whorlow SL	110815
Wilkinson CA	130411
Williams RV	101011
Williams SA	110815
Woods BS	311213
Wright JL	010413
Wright KL	040411

Lieutenants

Clifford JA	141214
Coombs DA	141214
Crawford CWA	141214
Keenan M	130414
Kerr AW	141214
Labbett C	120415
Langley DJA	120415
Lewis SJ	131215
Maclean TA	120415
Mclaughlin JD	131215
Nayagam MS	130414
Powell JW	100814
Reed RC	120415
Reid Milligan CE	120415
Rilling JW	120415
Skinner FT	120415
Smith MC	120415
Stribling JF	100814
Thomas J	100814
Thompson LN	130414
Thompson M	090815
Windley RW	131215
Worthington MA	130414

2nd Lieutenants

Bullous LA	121215
Fullwood NEM	110415
Fulwood NEM	110415
Goates EJF	110415
Miller KC	110415
Moffat JM	080815
Naylor JM	121215
Wicks JJ	110415
Workman CR	121215
Wright J	110415

MILITARY PROVOST STAFF

Major

Hutchinson JM	310714
Snook LC	310713

Captains

Cull RJ	210113
McMullan NG	020412
Reedman MC	010614
Wharton JD	010413

EDUCATIONAL AND TRAINING SERVICES BRANCH

A fluted flambeau of six flames there on a crown, and below the crown a scroll inscribed ETS.

Antecedent Corps Marches

Quick Marches .... Guadeamus Igitur (Let us Rejoice) and The Good Comrade

Branch Headquarters............................ Trenchard Lines, Upavon, Pewsey, Wilts SN9 6BE
(Email: AGCRHQ-Pers-ETS-SO3@mod.uk)

Alliances

Australian Military Forces .... The Royal Australian Army Educational Corps
New Zealand Army .... The Royal New Zealand Army Educational Corps

Deputy Colonel Commandant............... Maj Gen Stuart R Skeates *CBE* 290515

Lieutenant Colonels

Allen WAS	300614
Barltrop SW	300612
Browne AK	300609
Burgon JL *MA Ed PGCE(FE) BA(Hons)*	300614
Crome DJ	300609
Elms RE *MSc MA BSc(Hons) PGCE(PCET)*	300614
Farthing T	300612
Firth PM	300615
Foster JD	300613
George PM	300613
Hall IE	300607
Hayman ME *MSc*	300611
Hunter JF	300611
Ketterer MT	300615
Kinkaid P	300615
Lightfoot CMR	300610
MacDonald CK *OBE*	300610
Martin GA *MBE*	300615
Plant DJ *MBA MA MEd BA(Hons) PGCE*	300606
Pogson RKJ *BSc(Hons) MA*	300610
Reid AJA	300613
Sharp MPG	300610
Simpson HA *MA*	300604

Majors

Abu-Romia J	310715
Adams PJ	310714
Allen SR	310709
Amos GH	310709
Atkinson MJ	310702
Bagnold RA	310709
Baines NL *BA(Hons)*	310713
Bass N	310709
Bayne EAM	310715
Boag EA	310709
Boardman FH	310713
Brown CJ	310715
Burt AD	310708
Burton GI	310713
Butler MD	310714
Buttifant PJ	310710
Child KAB *MBE MSc BEd(Hons) PGCE(PCET)*	300901
Coates CJ	310711
Collett CAE	310714
Cooke KE	310714
Craig-Braddock L	310713
Crompton JH	310711
Cursons M	310708
Dowling FGG	310712
Duckitt KA	310711
Eade MJ	310715
Eade SA	310715
Edger RC	310708
Emmett CD	310708
Evans K	310709
Evans NE	310715
Fardy SJ	310714
Field VR	310708
Fowler JJ	310712
Frost AJ	300997
Fuller LE	310711
Gibb DM	300994
Hamilton CA	310712
Harding JKA	310710
Harrison RJ	310703
Hart C	310715
Harvey CE	310706
Hayakawa DP	310708
Holden BR *BA(Hons)*	310712
Howard CL	310713
Howarth FK	310709
Hurndall JML	310705
Igoe BJ *BSc*	310712
Iqbal F	310713
Janvier CE	310710
Johnson FA	310715
Kwakye PK	310713
Lamont RY	310712
Landragin FR	310707
Lewis NR	300994
Lynn DJ *MBE*	310714
MacPherson KJ	310715
Makuve M	310714
Martin CS	310711
Maycock C	110812
McGann PJ	310713
McNish NM	310715
Moss JD *MA BSc(Hons) PGCE*	310715
Oliver TK	310710
Oosterveen C	310711
Oosthuizen CG	310714
Painting JC	310710
Panayiotou JH	310713
Parker SK	310714
Perkowski AK *MSc*	310715

Powling SE *MBE*	310707
Rankin EL	310706
Roche LDT	310711
Seth VCB	310713
Sharp R	310714
Sheeran MJ	310714
Silva CE	310709
Sterling M	310709
Stokes BRJ	310710
Sturman NP	310715
Taffs J *MA PGCE BSc(Hons)*	310706
Tankaria-Clifford LA	310710
Taylor EC	310714
Taylor GJ	310705
Terblanche C	310707
Vosper AN	310715
Walker JJ	310712
Walsh CA	310715
Way CA	310710
Way NL	310712
Weddell ND *MBA MSc PGCE BSc(Hons)*	310715
Whysall GM	310712
Wilson MB	310713
Wood TCA	310709
Wright RJ	310715
Zingone CA	310715

Captains

Adams LK	110815
Anderton RM *MPhil*	180613
Ashton JRG	090211
Aslam LY	061115
Atkinson D	170614
Ayres DTL	171012
Baker MJ	080212
Barke IR	030511
Barnett GPS	040510
Bates NS	140415
Beacock DCL	161013
Bell DA LL.B	140213
Berry LDA	151215
Bird L	151215
Blacklock PR	170614
Brazier RA	130214
Brewington A	290413
Britton NT	170614
Bromley SW	090211
Brown ML *BA*	080512
Brown S	080512
Brown SW	171012
Burgess DM	151215
Byrne FM	110815
Chambers AS	140213
Clarke MT	110815
Connolly DR	170614
Constantine CL	040510
Cooper JP	161013
Cooper SD	161013
Crean RPD	140213
Darling EM	080212
Dickens J	151215
Doak RJ	130214
Donnelly DJ	080212
Doyle GS	130214
Eckersley SR	090211
Egas-Kitchener CR	140213
Evans VK	101011
Farnham RA	151215
Fowles RP *BSc(Hons) FdSc PGCE(PCET)*	161013
Fraser DRS *MA(Hons) PGCE (PCET)*	120612
French JS *MEng*	171012
Gardner JBT	090211
Giles RD	290413
Gosling VM	110815
Gwachiwa OM	130611
Hambly CM	140415
Heneghan SA *MEng PGCE (PCET)*	130214
Holligan KA	101011
James MW *BSc(Hons) PGCE*	171012
Jarvis MJ	050515
Jarvis RE	130611
Jones L	290413
Jopson RE	171012
Kinghan AB	180613
Kingston AS	011106
Kingston MR	141009
Lancaster GPJ	130214
Lawrie SR	170614
Mattock JJ	140415
Mayor SL	180613
McCallum SC	140415
McCartney B	280414
McClean RJ	030511
McDougall PD	050515
McGain-Harding DJ	040510
McLeish IA	080710
Mills RJ	080512
Milne FW	180613
Morgan G	180613
Mulholland KN	171012
Nelson KE	130611
Owen KM	280414
Patton CEJ	110815
Politowicz GS	140213
Poulton AV	170614
Rann LA	130611
Richards MD	180613
Rowley OT	110815
Russell JM	120612
Smith CA	080512
Smith ET MA	130611
Stonebridge-Smith GE	120612
Storey C	110815
Sutherland VG	240815
Tayler PJ	170614
Thompson DJ	101011
Wakenshaw LE	151215
Wallis PA	080512
Westerman CA	090211
Whitehead RC	110815
Wildman PC	171012
Willcox R	140415
Willcox-Jones AE	180613
Woolley LC	151215
Young AM	180613

Lieutenants

Baxter W	131215
Bell AD	090815
Bondar DN	090815
Collier TA	130414
Condron VJK	141214
Conlon J	120415
Dawson M	090815
Emery MC	120415
Fergusson Fripp JA	100814
Gannaway BS	120415
Hayton CCA	141214
Heavyside MJ	100814
Holderness AG	141214

Howe MLG	141214	Raw NL	100814	Flintoft JP	080815
Hughes DC	151213	Scott A	131215	Ford MJ	110415
Hyde TN	131215	Strange JWD	131215	Goodman PAG	121215
Johnston MA	100814	Walker SM	131215	Haigh LDB	110415
Keir JH	131215	Wearmouth AM	131215	Huntington JA	120414
Malekpour CD	100814	Williams HR	130414	Read JEG	080815
Manuel ST	130414			Rew FS	080815
Maymon VL	130414	*2nd Lieutenants*		Schroeder PD	080815
Meikle A	120415	Beardsell LM	121215	Simpson JRL	080815
Millwater EH	120415	Boyles DW	121215	Skinner KL	110415
Moran CS	120415	Chapman WA	080815	Sleeman JRJ	110415
Porter ORE	120415	Cliffe VA	080815	Steele M	121215
Rampton MC	100814	Daly SM	080815	Tiffin JPR	121215

ARMY LEGAL SERVICES BRANCH

The Figure of Justice superimposed upon Globe surmounted by the Royal Crest. Behind the Globe Crossed Swords with blades uppermost on a black ground within a circle inscribed JUSTITIA IN ARMIS. On a scroll below ARMY LEGAL CORPS

Antecedent Corps Marches

Quick Marches.. Scales of Justice
Branch Headquarters............................ Directorate of Army Legal Services, Ramillies, Marlborough Lines, Monxton Road, Andover, Hants, SP11 8JH

Alliances

Canadian Armed Forces......................... Canadian Forces Legal Branch
Australian Military Forces..................... The Australian Army Legal Corps

Deputy Colonel Commandant............... Lt Gen Richard E Nugee *CVO CBE* 280215

Lieutenant Colonels

Bartlett AT	130209
Bowen JL	300606
Bowman HE	130212
Braddick-Hughes CE	010207
Brown AC	130212
Child TCS	170214
Coombes GD	050305
Cowx CJ	240409
Culver MJ	290906
Dakers MB	130805
Davies GE	110910
Davies GR	110910
Davies PM	130212
England JC	170214
Finlayson AGW	130212
Fryatt AG	010713
Heron CP	170912
Larkin CPA *LLM*	160215
Madge CO	150215
McDonnell S	010207
Moreland NF	250904
Mynors HRB	170214
Nooney S	230913
Peters WJS	200910
Phillips DW	200309
Phillips VL	170214
Read RJ	300613
Siddique BM	270211

Majors

Adair CD	310714
Agnew JF	310714
Beazley SJM	310710
Brogan PB	220210
Brookes JL	140209
Bryson FV	310715
Burnett JA	140211
Campbell LJ	080212
Carmichael JAM	310711
Churchyard AC	190207
Clarke RA	310715
Collie MJ	310715
Cotton DJ	140211
Crowther AM	310715
Dangerfield NW	310712
Davies TRL	220210
Davies WB	310713
Edwards JL	140211
Elliott SF	310713
Ellis HG	140211
Farquhar AC	230913
Giles H	310711
Grant E	170208
Gray BA	290410
Halward R	310714
Harris JB	140611
Hayler BAM	310715
Jones L	310112
Keery NW	310714
Maddocks JH	190109
Maher JL	080212
Nurse AVP	310709
Olsen-Ling SE	310713
Oram P	310714
Roberts AL	310709
Thomas JE	230913
Watson S	310715
Whiting EE	310714
Whittaker DJ	310711
Wills A	310715

Captains

Blessley CJ	150113
Bond A	150113
Brooke S	150915
Brown JE	140114
Burchett RJH	150915
Davies L	130115
Dutton T	150915
Evans AO	170913
Eveleigh JR	170912
Eyre RL	140114
Fearnfield L	130115
Fox-Leonard M	150113
Heyward W	150915
Holland RAH	160112
Jarvis AA	170912
Keddie JLC	170111
Kevan LM	170913
La Barre JD	140114
Law GJ	140114
Lowry JJ	150914
Markham P	130115
Mcdermott JE	160112
Naughton JP	160112
Rennet F	170912
Sleeman G	160112
Storr C	160112
Thackery E	160112
Warburton S	150915

ROYAL ARMY VETERINARY CORPS

The Figure of Chiron in silver within a wreath of laurel thereunder a scroll inscribed ROYAL ARMY VETERINARY CORPS the whole ensigned with The Crown all gold

Regimental Marches

Quick March .... Regimental March of The Royal Army Veterinary Corps
(An arrangement based around "A-Hunting We Will Go")
Slow March... "Golden Spurs"

Agents.. Holts Branch, Royal Bank of Scotland plc, Lawrie House, Farnborough, Hants, GU14 7NR
Corps Headquarters.............................. RHQ Royal Army Veterinary Corps, Headquarters Army Medical Services, Robertson House, Slim Road, Camberley, Surrey, GU15 4NP
(Tel: 01276 412749 Mil: 94261 2749 Email: regtsecravc@hotmail.co.uk)

Alliances

Pakistan Army....................................... Pakistan Remounts, Veterinary and Farm Corps

Colonel in Chief.................................... *HRH The Princess Royal KG KT GCVO QSO*
Colonel Commandant........................... Lt Gen *Sir* James R Everard *KCB CBE (until 010317)* 010412
Brig C R V (Roly) Walker *DSO (from 010317)*
Chief Veterinary Officer........................ Col Neil C Smith *QHVS* 011114

RAVC

Lieutenant Colonels

Morrison MCE	300609
Pope RC *OBE*	300611

Majors

Hanson MK	191105
Hart RP	310713
Housby Skeggs NJ	071113
Kemp JN	310708
Leavis SJ	310709
O'Flynn AMJ	010907
Robinson MR	140903
Rose IRB	170305
Rowlinson JR	310715
Thompson MJ *MBE*	310712
Tootal DAC *BSc BVSc MSc (Res)*	081112

Captains

Barr SJ	151009
Bullard CJ	050911
Cooke N	281111
Harvey GCD	031012
Hyslop AC	300611
Jones SR	010412
McRink DJ *BVMedSci BVM BVS MRCVS RAVC*	021013
Quigley WR *MBE*	300613
Rowlinson JR	020409
Whiting CA	020810

RAVC (VO)

Lieutenant Colonels

Bowerman MR	300610
Hemming TS	300610

Majors

Budge CLS	081112
Curnick RS	010903
Gillies JS	010114
Hart RL	010914
Moran IE	010802

Captains

Church HL	020810
Fineman TA *BVetMed MRCVS*	020810
Jude EC	020810

RAVC (VSO)

Majors

Hart RP	310713
Leavis SJ	310709

Captains

Franks PA	010411
Gibbs MS	010411

SMALL ARMS SCHOOL CORPS

1853 School of Musketry
In 1919 renamed Small Arms School
In 1929 renamed Small Arms School Corps

A Vickers Machine Gun facing right, sights down, thereon a pair of crossed rifles with bayonets fixed, The Cown within the angle formed by the rifles above the machine gun; the whole within a laurel wreath; on the wreath scrolls inscribed on the left side SMALL on the bottom ARMS and on the right side SCHOOL

Regimental March

Quick March .... March of the Bowmen

Agents.. Lloyds TSB
Regimental Headquarters...................... Headquarters Small Arms School Corps, Land Warfare Centre, Warminster, Wilts BA12 0DJ
(Tel: 01985 222612 Mil: 94381 2612 Fax: 01985 222211
Email: DINF-SASC-CLK-E2@mod.uk / LF-Cap-Cbt-SASC-Adjt@mod.uk
Website: www.army.mod.uk/sasc)

Colonel in Chief..................................... *HRH The Duke of* York *KG GCVO ADC(P)*
Colonel Commandant............................ Lt Gen Patrick N Y M Sanders *CBE DSO*..240314

Lieutenant Colonels

Riddell AA	310705
Sandison KAR	010314

Majors

Anderson KJ *MBE*	310709
Buffey E	310713
Cleminson AJ	310707
Hanson SR	310711
Harverson E	310712
Hirst ND	310713
James SP	310715
Kyle AG	020407
Liddell KW	310710
MacMahon KNC	310715
Marr W	300608
Redding PA	310707
Ronan MA	270206
Rose CM	310708
Skinner G	310707
Watson RW	310713

Captains

Byrne TJ	030413
Christoforou-Hazelwood J	080612
Dobbs GJ	240415
Douglas M	030414
Dunn SM	070414
Galloway D	030415
Hawkyard JR	130415
Jenkins L	020411
Lynch MP	010410
Lynch RC	160407
Milton DD	020411
Moyle AJ	290713
Palmer GW	020412
Renton A	020411
Robinson M	100613
Smith GR	160614
West ML	070714
Wright GM	010410

ROYAL ARMY DENTAL CORPS

Within a laurel wreath a dragon's head and sword; beneath a scroll bearing the motto EX DENTIBUS ENSIS. The whole ensigned with The Crown

Regimental Marches

Quick March .... "Green Facings"

Agents.. Holts Branch, Royal Bank of Scotland plc, Lawrie House, Farnborough, Hants, GU14 7NR

Corps Headquarters.............................. RADC RHQ, Robertson House, Slim Road, Camberley, Surrey, GU15 4NP (Tel: 01276 412753 Fax: 01276 412793 Email: rhq_radc@hotmail.com)

Alliances

Australian Military Forces..................... The Royal Australian Army Dental Corps
New Zealand Army .... The Royal New Zealand Dental Corps

Colonel in Chief.................................... *HRH The Duchess of* Gloucester *GCVO*..170600
Colonels Commandant........................... Brig (Retd) Iain A Pretsell..010113
Col (Retd) J Q (Quentin) Anderson 010515
Honorary Colonel Commandant........... Col Peter D Jackson *QHDS TD* 010707

RADC

Lieutenant Colonel

Sutton G 300614

Majors

Covell ME *OStJ Pg Dip MHSC CMgr* 310707
Wiles PA 310713

Captain

Bassi VS 280912
Dale PA 010413
Marriott T 190513
Watson RJ 281214

RADC (DO)

Lieutenant Colonels

Case AC BChD LDS RCS (Eng) 030801
Coleman H *BDS BMSc MJDF* 300613
Curtis G 300908
Davies TJ *MJDF RCS(Eng)* 131204
Dufty JR *MClinDent BChD MFGDP MFDS MCGI* 300611
Harmer SG 311214
Jess JAM 300615
McDicken IN 300612
Murphy EF 051205
Palin BJ *BDS MJDF RCS (Eng) MCGI* 311213
Thomas AK 020607
Willey DA *BDS* 300608

Majors

Abu-Mughaisib MA 020708
Alesbury NR 310714
Ansell MJ 010801
Armer ASA 010807
Armstrong SJ 300114
Bartlett EM 280615
Beales LS 160713
Brown VL 181214
Burn SD 140711
Butler R 210708
Cheema R 180707
Clarke ID 190613
Crockard PA 270607
Cross BWM 040707
Cunningham FE 280714
Dando MJ 090708
Davies JD 081014
Davis AS 090709
Dobie SJ 040711
Dransfield KJ 011110
Drinkel TR BDS MJDF 250615
Edwards DC 220311
Field PR 250608
Francis JP 050706
Friend MJW BMSc (Hons) BDS (Hons) MFGDPUK 090806
Gibbs NGB 170607
Gracey CJ *BChD (Hons) MFDS RCS Ed* 031011
Gurung S 190710
Harper CJ 240714
Hattersley GJ 010708
James SH 110707
Jordan NP *BDS MFGDP* 030805
King M 300604
Kolanko JA 170613
Konarzewski TE 210711
Leckey RL *BDS MJDF* 180613
Lindsay RK 150707
McGrath CE 290714
McLean AP *BDS MFGDP(UK) MFDS RCS(Eng)* 160706
Moxon OM *BDS (Bris) MJDF RCS (Eng)* 190613
Nowak MJS *BDS MFGDP(UK)* 120705
O'Neill JE *MJDF* 040707
Padgett GK 180615
Parton LS 010812
Payne AJ 030708
Phillips AJ 010812
Porter SN *BDS MFGDP* 210609
Price RP 090709
Ramsey RA *MSc BDS MFDS MFGDP(UK) MSurgD* 180706

Scott JJ	010812
Slim WFF *BSc BDS MFDSRCS*	160703
Smith KE	200711
Smith R *BSc BDS MJDF RCS MFDS RCSPG*	240714
Smith RJR	190709
Stapleton BE	231009
Twamley M	270607
Tyrrell SV	180615
Usmani R	150707
Valler LM	010801
Welborn FL *BDS MFDS RCS(EDIN)*	180615
Wilson JJ	011110
Winship CE	011111
Woodward DJ *BDS*	120707
Woodward-Court AD	280609
Wright PJ	180614

Captains

Beaven APR *BDS*	170712
Blyth KA	090714
Curtis A	180712
Durkan CJ	200811
Esmaili SS	270712
Glauch CM	280611
Lloyd SJ	010914
McCammon A	310810
Porter KJR	080612
Roper KJ	120612
Shaw DJ *BDS MJDF RCS (Eng)*	280611
Walker HNJ *BDS (Newc) MJDF RCS (Eng)*	080611
Walters SL	290611
Winfield EAJ *BDS MJDF*	180612

2nd Lieutenants

Cheesbrough GA	010812
Summers EB	010812
Warmington RE	010814

ROYAL ARMY PHYSICAL TRAINING CORPS

Crossed swords surmounted by a crown

Regimental March

Quick March .... Regimental March of The Army Physical Training Corps
("Be Fit" words from "Land and Sea Tales" by Rudyard Kipling)

Agents.. Holt's Farnborough Branch
Regimental Headquarters....................... Headquarters RAPTC, Mackenzie Building, Fox Lines, Queens Ave, Aldershot, Hampshire GU11 2LB
(Tel: 01252 787145 Fax: 01252 787160
Email: raptchq-reg-sec@mod.uk)

Colonel Commandant............................. Lt Gen James I Bashall *CBE* 010312
Commandant... Brig John P S Donnelly *CBE (untl Dec 16)* ....Oct 12
Brig Paul Cain *QHS (from Dec 16)*

Assistant Commandant........................... Lt Col (SMAA) T P Scarr *RAPTC*

Lieutenant Colonels

Appleby P	010115
Davis SAJ	120514
Dupree BJ	190813
McDonald KM	121014

Majors

Black RD	310707
Collinson SD	310712
Darby JJ	310714
Deed CJ	310713
Ecott JE	310715
Field GM	110812
Gilbey R	310712
Groves RA	310715
Hendrickson GC *MBE*	310712
Hughes JPA	310714
Humes AM	310715
Lewis MJ	310709
McGregor PA	310714
Phillips IM	310710
Scarr TP	310709
Sinclair SD	310715
Stoddart BJ	310714
Taylor AJ	310708
Warwick M	310715
Whitaker RC	310713
Young RM	310712

Captains

Bareham IJN	150713
Barnett A	060409
Chappell SA	020614
Clark AA	160813
Crompton LJ	010614
Davison LJ	140915
Doree T	300512
Douglas SP	120911
Dunne EM	010615
Galley MW	010814
Gresty MS	210708
Hames CM	160715
Horner MR	140514
Irving S	190711
James L	010814
Logan G	310713
Lundie R	010609
Murdoch J	020413
Neville LC	020209
Oakes CM	210613
O'Shea NJ	010609
Pacter WR	190711
Reese BV	160715
Reid R	180509
Roberts CM	060812
Roberts RJ	140915
Saunders PC	150713
Sawyer LR	010514
Semple S	110612
Webster GJ	010815
Williams DE	190711
Wilson MF	300415
Windard RC	070414
Yates JA	270212
Young WJ	070613

GENERAL SERVICE CORPS

Lieutenants

Purvis DJ	270314

Officer Cadets

Ahmed N	050115
Beresford H	070914
Bettison LE	050115
Bolton CL	070914
Bourke D	050115
Buckley HG	050115
Carew SA	050115
Carr HB	040514
Chase L	040514
Cornell JW	050114
Coussins T	050115
Duckworth BF	050115
Dunford TE	070914
Errington KI	050115
Gale KL	050115
Hardman SL	070914
Harrower J	050115
Harvey AL	050115
Hind EJM	050115
Ives PJ	050115
Jones FTW	050115
Langford-Archer TP	050115
Lowe JN	050115
Loy AHS	050115
Morgan HH	070914
Munday JD	040514
Newman TAW	050115
Nicholls S	050115
Nicoll J	050115
Noyce PJ	050115
Parks NL	070914
Platts AJ	070914
Rundle M	050115
Runkee CS	040514
Sandys-Renton PLS	070914
Shepherd NVF	050115
Smail Woodford A	070914
Stone CA	070914
Telford M	050115
Thompson GM	050115
Thorn OR	060512
Tilley MR	050115
Upton BCW	070914
Whitmore G	070914

QUEEN ALEXANDRA'S ROYAL ARMY NURSING CORPS

The Cypher of HM the Late Queen Alexandra combined with the Dannebrog, the whole within a laurel wreath inscribed with the Corps motto SUB CRUCE CANDIDA surmounted by a Crown. On the lower portion of the wreath a scroll inscribed QARANC.

Regimental Marches

Quick March .... "Grey and Scarlet"

Agents... Holts Branch, Royal Bank of Scotland plc, Lawrie House, Farnborough, Hants, GU14 7NR
Corps Headquarters.............................. Headquarters Army Medical Services, Slim Road, Camberley, Surrey, GU15 4NP (Tel: 01276 412754) (Fax: 01276 412793) Email: regtsecqaranc@hotmail.com

Alliances

Australian Military Forces..................... Royal Australian Army Nursing Corps
New Zealand Army .... Royal New Zeand Nursing Corps

Colonel in Chief.................................... *HRH The Countess of* Wessex
Colonels Commandant.......................... Lt Col (Retd) Sue J Bush *RRC*..010511

Director Army Nursing Services and Matron-in-Chief (Army).................... Col David Bates *ARRC QHN (until Jul 16)*
Col Karen Irvine *RRC QHN (from Jul 16)*
(post renamed *Chief Nursing Officer Army*)

Lieutenant Colonels

Adam LS	300607
Beatty SM *ARRC*	300613
Bernthal EMM *PhD BSc(Hons) Dip NS RM RGN*	311215
Charlton AM	300612
Cumming JE	101011
D'Arcy JP	300615
Davies TJ *MBE MA*	300609
Dutton CM *MBE*	311215
Farmer AEB	300613
Findlay S	300610
Grieves TJ *RRC RGN*	300612
Hall GS	300613
Jackson PM	300614
Kenward G *BSc(Hons) MSc*	300611
Le Quelenec BT	300614
Manson PJ *MSc PGDip Dip(HE) RGN*	300614
Marshall CS	300613
McCourt AL *OBE ARRC*	300611
Penney TD	300614
Phillips-Harvey J	300608
Philpott AE *RGN/ DIP (HE) AMIHM (Sen)*	300608
Winder HS	300613

Majors

Anderson-McIntosh AJ	310711
Anderson-McIntosh MJ	310715
Bailey J	310708
Bassindale MEM	310713
Beaumont JL	310714
Beedie G	310715
Bell JC	310708
Berski MSA	310710
Birkby C *ARRC*	310709
Blair SPR	310706
Blake L	310710
Buck JA	310713
Buckingham TA	310715
Burden BL	310713
Byers R	310713
Carter C	310713
Champion LM	310713
Chitembwe A	310714
Clark J *ARRC*	220903
Cobb SJ	310712
Conley CI	310715
Cook KS	280913
Corkish NF	310713
Crane AL	310707
Cripps AMC	310711
Daive FL	310710
Dalby-Welsh KM	310708
Davies I *BSc(Hons)*	310708
Dawson-Couper ZJ	310715
Dewa A	310710
Dodd J	310709
Doyle CF *ARRC Dip He Dip SM RMN CMHN*	220609
Fertout MB *Msc BN(Hons) RN(MH) Cert Mgmt*	310712
Fletcher DJ *MBE*	310707
Gaal LR	310708
Game A	310714
Good RD	310709
Griffin TV	310709
Harley PE	310714
Harris ZC	310710
Harvey DL	310714
Hawkins SB *BSc(Hons)*	310710
Hazzard I	010707
Hill DA *BSc(Hons)*	311200
Hines SE	220105
Hobbs AP	310712
Hodge M	310707
Hughes AG	310715
Hulley EJ	310708
Hunter GK	310712
Illingworth DJ	310714

Jacques T 310715
Jamieson KD 310707
Jenkins DJ 310707
Jerram-Mason K 310713
Jezard SE 310715
Jordan CD 310708
Kagoda EK 310713
Kelly RA 310707
Kennedy PA 310710
Kenworthy LK 310712
Lankester FM 310708
Lethbridge CL 310710
Lewis DG *SCPHN* 310713
Lewis KD 310714
Lindstrom C *ARRC* 310710
Lintonbon LJ 170203
Lyall GD 310713
MacAulay IM 310708
Mackie IM 310710
MacLennan B 310713
Mallin RC 310711
Maloney MC 310712
Manley AJ 310710
Marriott NP 310714
Marston DL 310711
Martin G 121204
McFadden-Newman KJ *ARRC* 310711
McKay AT 310708
Michael GL *BSc(Hons) Dip N RMN RGN* 310705
Mitchell PB 310710
Morgan EJ 310708
Morris NJ 310710
Neale CE 310715
Neilson PK 310710
Niven MG 310713
O'Grady DP 310711
Pealin KJ 310709
Pearce PM 310715
Pozzi-Gurung HO 310709
Reed MJ 310715
Reidy P *RGN DIPN BSc (Hons) MScHP* 310706
Ricketts LM 310710
Ritchie JA 310710
Ritsperis D 271200
Robinson AJ 310710
Roden ML 310709
Rothwell SMJ *BSc PCert Mgmt RGN DipHSW MCGI* 310706
Royal PM 310712
Russell SJ 310712
Scripps HJ *BSc(Hons)* 310707
Shuck SW 310706
Southern C 310712
Spencer SD 310714
Stansfield CM 310713
Stockbridge KJ 310708
Templeman KM 310710
Thom SK 310715
Thomas J 310712
Thompson ZCJ 310714
Topott JMK 310710
Towler HP 310710
Tristham PE 251002
Trower CM 310710
Truscott R *ARRC* 310708
Vedere MF 310712
Vincent CC 310709
Vincent HN 310711
Viveash SG *RGN RN CHILD MSc BSc(Hons)* 310706
Watkins K 310709
Whelan CN 310711
Whittle GL 310710
Wincup P 310707
Wink PJ 310708
Winters J 310710
Woodall D 310712
Wright KM 061015
Yardley RG 310711
Yarker JM 310715

Captains

Avis CE 010910
Black RMG 260107
Browne EA 150610
Bulleid VA 101012
Carmichael ZL 140809
Carter BS 270709
Chambers JD 120714
Charlesworth AL 010411
Clark JI 010911
Collins MI 280513
Cook ME 260113
Cooper JT 060608
Crabtree GH 030711
Croft FJ 010610
Dedman MP 061009
Devlin JE 240508
Devonport L 151212
Dews JM 090312
Dews RD 021011
Dick M 021011
Dove RE 231110
Duckett CM 280111
Evans K 160712
Ferguson GP 190310
Freeth AG 280112
Haggarty SJL 301106
Holmstrom HL 130214
Hutchinson AL 020714
James HM 011009
Johnson AAC 300814
Jones HFI *ARRC* 150413
Jordan LS 210305
Keenan HE 121010
Krause JWM 280114
Lea SJG 090410
McArthur KMD 171012
McClenaghan JS 141013
McFarland SJ 010210
McGarry SFS 201109
McLeod AC 030214
McPhee GJ *ARRC* 210510
Millar AA 110712
Minchin PF 090211
Morris AED 190912
Moss LC 010910
Murphy NLS 210414
Newey A 161007
Palmer BR 030214
Pelling HJ 140213
Perrin EJ 110414
Petersen RJM 300814
Pollard CA 090211
Powell EJ 260113
Rawden MP 120313
Reed CLM 230413
Saunderson-Browne L 280115
Sewell DW 210214
Shaw SC 150609
Simms PM 051009
Simpson LJ 120313

Sloss HA	290412
Sutch JA	220914
Toole DS	190611
Turton SE	140312
Wallace HK	100911
Wilson PE	110712

Lieutenants

Archbold L	150413
Banks JJ *BSc RN(MH)*	050911
Charnley A	170412
Done JC	270914
Hain JH	270914
Hibberd AV	210614
Hildred KBH	011211
Keenan JA	310712
Kemp NL	170412
Llewellyn MLP	011012
MacDonald AD	110412
Miura AS	260711
Moll RL	040913
Nichol RA	080113
Potter J	280115
Raba R	130814
Rankin LMM *Bsc*	121011
Roberts SJ	190411
Scott ARC	131112
Smith RE	200212
Watson L	190411

2nd Lieutenants

Fisher NM	010812
McGuire JA	010814
Probert GLC	070615
Wolfe NL	010114

CORPS OF ARMY MUSIC

A laurel wreath surmounted by a crown, within the wreath a lyre. Beneath the lyre a scroll inscribed CORPS OF ARMY MUSIC. Either side of the lyre a scroll inscribed NULLI SECUNDUS

Regimental March

Quick March .... 'Come Landlord Fill the Flowing Bowl' & 'The Minstrel Boy' arr Burton

Agents.. Holt's Branch, Royal Bank of Scotland plc, Lawrie House,
Farnborough, Hants GU14 7NR
Regimental Headquarters...................... Kneller Hall, Twickenham, Middlesex, TW2 7DU
(Tel: 020 8744 8652) (Fax: 020 8744 8668)
Email: corpssec@hq.dcamus.mod.uk Website: www.army.mod.uk/music

Alliances

Australian Military Forces..................... The Australian Army Band Corps

Colonel-in-Chief .... *HRH The Countess of* Wessex *GCVO*...010907
Colonel Commandant............................ Lt Gen T P Evans *CB CBE DSO (late LI) (until 130716)*.....................................010113
Maj Gen Paul A E Nanson *CBE (from 130716)*
Director.. Col Barry W Jenkins *(Late RA)* .... Jan 12
Prinicipal Director of Music (Army) ..... Lt Col D L Wolfendale *BA (Mus) LRSM ALCM*... Oct 15

Majors	
Aldridge MD *BMus (Hons) LRSM LTCL*	310714
Barringer DA	310714
Davies KL	030105
Griffiths J *BA(Mus) LRSM*	310713
Hallett C	310715
Haw SN *MBE Grad Dip Mus BA MMus*	310711
Johnson IM *BA(Hons)*	310714
Miller B	220302
Norley PW *MA BA LRSM LDBBA CNCB MCGI*	310712
Roberts KFN *MMus FLCM LRSM psm*	310707
Sale L *BA LRSM*	030409
Smith ME	310715
Stredwick P	310706
Wolfendale DL *BA (Mus) LRSM ALCM*	310710
Yates VL	310711

Captains	
Adams AR	290107
Bennett GW	020413
Bywater CM	080809
Collis-Smith PA	010911
Frost EE	250512
Gurung B	150914
Halliday SJ	020408
Hammond DB *MBA MA BMus (Hons) FRSM PGCE*	171108
Marshall JR	130910
Matthews J	050109
Milne JHF	020414
O'Neill SA	060715
Petritz-Watts L	200614
Riley SP	020409
Skipper N ALCM	010713
Teggarty J *MMus BMus (Hons) LRSM LTCL*	010315
Williams AD *MMus MCGI BMus (Hons) ALCM*	050710

Lieutenant	
Wheeler BM	141214

2nd Lieutenant	
Waters BM	110415

RETIRED OFFICERS

Listing officers who have retired between 1st Match 2015 - 1st March 2016 and the date of their retirement.

Lieutenant Generals

Berragan GW KBE CB (Late RA)	201115
Mayall SV KBE CB (Late QDG)	290715

Major Generals

Burley SA CB MBE ((Late RE))	150715
Conway MD CB (Late AGC (ALS))	120116
Cowan JM DSO OBE (Late BW)	190915
Eeles NH CBE (Late RA)	251115
Henderson JMR CB FIMechE FCILT (Late REME)	180715
Weighill RPM CBE (Late RA)	120116

Brigadiers

Allison PJ (Late RTR)	270715
Bibby GK CBE (Late COLDM GDS)	170515
Boyd PSW MBE (Late RE)	231115
Brittain JR (Late REME)	191215
Brown AR (Late REME)	121215
Brown ED MBE (Late RGBW)	010815
Claydon CJ MBE MA (Late AAC)	060815
Davies NR CBE MC (Late PARA)	270116
Deakin SF OBE (Late PWRR)	240715
Dodson MP MBE (Late HLDRS)	120315
Dunn ML (Late RLC)	030815
Forster-Knight EO CBE (Late AGC (RMP))	021115
Lowder GE *MBE (Late SCOTS)*	100216
Maddan DJH (Late GREN GDS)	290915
McCall BW (Late REME)	041115
Milligan MAL (Late RA)	270615
Morris GS CBE (Late AGC (ETS))	220915
Napier PML OBE MA MSc (Late R WELSH)	261015
O'Hanlon MPJ (Late R IRISH)	040915
Stopford JRH (Late IG)	021215
Watts TJP OBE (Late R SIGNALS)	280216
Young NM QHDS MBA BDS FDS FFGDP MGDS (Late RADC)	130415

Colonels

Alexander IC OBE (Late RLC)	290915
Allen AA MBE (Late REME)	130815
Amberton I (Late RADC)	070415
Arundell RG (Late RIFLES)	020515
Ash JP (Late RLC)	030715
Barber FPA *Rev* VG CF QHC (Late RAChD)	171215
Barsby NI (Late RLC)	300515
Bates D ARRC QHN (Late QARANC)	280216
Bennett KL (Late AGC (ETS))	250815
Brambell DJ BSc CEng FICE MInstRE psc(j) (Late RE)	040116
Byrne NJ (Late RLC)	020515
Carrington SM (Late RLC)	020315
Chafer KI OBE (Late AAC)	201015
Clapp RN (Late R SIGNALS)	081015
Court ML (Late REME)	081015
Cowen SH ADC (Late RHG/D)	300915
Cuthbert AC (Late QRH)	211015
Denny JW MBE (Late RRF)	140216
Doran MJ (Late Rifles)	030415
Duncan AD (Late REME)	230915
Eadie PA (Late AAC)	071015
Eggleton SIJ (Late INT CORPS)	020915
Ewens AJ (Late REME)	270715
Gillespie PN (Late RAMC)	020515
Green BJW (Late RTR)	280515
Harrington DR (Late RA)	010815
Harris IVK (Late R IRISH)	230315
Harris SPF OBE (Late RE)	041215
Hazel JME OBE (Late INT CORPS)	021115
Hearn G OBE (Late R SIGNALS)	050815
Herring RJ CBE (Late RLC)	301115
Howard AG (Late RE)	241015
Hughes DE (Late RHG/D)	030715
Hurley SJ BDS MFGDP(UK) MSc MA psc(j) (Late RADC)	181015
Jackson AG MBE (Late RE)	290815
James SG (Late RA)	080715
Jefferies RA MBE (Late LANCS)	160715
Jordan SK (Late RLC)	100415
Kilpatrick SPB OBE (Late PWRR)	081215
Llewellyn MP OBE FRGS GCGI psc (Late R SIGNALS)	011015
Loudon AJ MBE (Late R IRISH)	040915
Lowder GE MBE ((Late SCOTS))	100216
Marshall SW FCMI (Late AAC)	030315
Martin JM (Late 9/12L)	210715
Mathie RA (Late RLC)	010715
McComb SAF (Late RADC)	150216

McIlroy JD (Late RE)	021015
Morgan-Jones DJ MBE KHS (Late RAMC)	081015
Morphet AN (Late R SIGNALS)	210515
Nichol HW (Late INT CORPS)	270216
Padgett S OBE (Late YORKS)	291015
Paterson CSK (Late R SIGNALS)	010315
Powell JRJ OBE MSc (Late PWRR)	210615
Redmond MG OBE (Late RA)	221015
Ringrose MC BEng MSc MA CEng FIMechE MAPM (Late REME)	010615
Schute JCC OBE (Late RGJ)	020915
Simpson NJ (Late AGC (ALS))	090415
Skeat CNR ADC (Late RE)	280915
Smailes MIT (Late RDG)	070116
Snedden SE (Late INT CORPS)	180915
Stuart JD (Late SG)	310815
Stythe JN (Late AGC (ALS))	211015
Swann DJL CBE (Late QRH)	021015
Taylor AP (Late RE)	270116
Thackway CSE MBE (Late RE)	161115
Thornton NPS (Late RIFLES)	030315
Tinsley I (Late RA)	090116
Vickers RPH (Late SCOTS DG)	240815
Vincent MAF MBE BSc MSc MBCS MIExpE (Late RA)	280815
Vosper JAL BSc (Hons) MSc MDS CEng CITP (Late R SIGNALS)	020715
Wilkinson GP CBE (Late RA)	031215
Wilman CJ (Late RE)	020116
Wilman JG (Late RE)	130915
Winchester RA (Late RA)	241015
Winkworth SA (Late RE)	310315
Wise PA (Late REME)	020715

Lieutenant Colonels

Adams EJ MBE (Late PARA)	100815
Aitken AR (Late R SIGNALS)	180415
Aldington DJ (Late RAMC)	020915
Argyle GW (Late RLC)	220415
Baines JJ (Late AGC(SPS))	021115
Baker H (Late RAMC)	250615
Ball DC BSc MSc (Late R SIGNALS)	010915
Barker M CEng FIMechE (Late REME)	290915
Barr AMM (Late QARANC)	270815
Barrett JM MBE (Late PARA)	270116
Barter DJ (Late RE)	070915
Bartle-Jones G (Late WG)	050515
Bayliss M (Late RA)	140715
Beadle DM (Late RADC)	140216
Binnie DP (Late REME)	120915
Birrell AM MSc BSc(Hons) FIMechE (Late REME)	280116
Blewitt GR (Late R WELSH)	040216
Blondel G (Late R SIGNALS)	010415
Blower IA MBE (Late R SIGNALS)	061015
Boanas ET (Late IG)	021215
Britton SJ (Late PARA)	011015
Brooks SJ (Late AGC(ETS))	240815
Burton-Doe MMT FCMA CGMA (Late AGC(SPS))	060116
Busby WR (Late RLC)	210615
Calder NG MC (Late SCOTS)	020715
Cameron AHM MBE (Late RA)	220815
Campbell PB (Late AAC)	091215
Cannon SB (Late REME)	230715
Cassidy PA BEM (Late AGC(RMP))	230715
Chambers M BSc(Eng)(Hons) MSc CEng FIMech (Late REME)	110415
Charlesworth JR OBE (Late RTR)	311215
Charlwood NDB (Late R ANGLIAN)	131015
Charnick A CMCIEH Grad IOSH (Late RAMC)	280315
Christian MR *Rev* FRSA CF (Late RAChD)	180415
Clarke JR (Late REME)	080415
Coates EG (Late RRF)	200116
Cooper DA OBE (Late PARA)	010515
Costen MD MBE (Late PARA)	020415
Coutts GML (Late RE)	020615
Crick PE MSc CEng MICE MInstRE (Late RE)	170715
Crosbie P (Late QARANC)	110415
Cushnir JHM (Late SCOTS DG)	020915
Danvers CHD MA (Late KRH)	030515
Davies BE (Late RE)	040815
Davies GH (Late RTR)	110815
Davies MA MBE (Late RL)	280715
Dixey CR (Late RLC)	290915
Donaldson KDM (Late RTR)	030415
Dorney RM (Late GREN GDS)	130515
Dreelan ICJ (Late AGC(ALS))	080415
Duggan DJ (Late R SIGNALS)	230116
Earnshaw JJ (Late RE)	210415
Edwards GW MBE (Late RIFLES)	100715
Ellis TB (Late AGC(ETS))	160315
Eyre JP (Late RHG/D)	160515
Finnegan AP RMN RGN PhD MSC BN DIPAMS (Late QARANC)	010116
Fisher JC MBE (Late RHG/D)	080615
Fitzgerald D (Late MERCIAN)	210415

Foucar AC (Late RIFLES) 300415
Fox ASK MBE (Late RE) 130515
Fraser CWW (Late RLC) 290815
Garner JP (Late RAMC) 081215
Gibbs KM (Late AGC(ETS)) 040915
Glover EF (Late AGC(ALS)) 280515
Grace EC (Late RA) 010216
Gray RV MBE (Late RIFLES) 270715
Greaves JJ MBE (Late RE) 170315
Hanson PJ (Late AGC(ALS)) 220915
Harper IG MBA MA MA MSC DipM PgDip FIHM (Late RAMC) 250315
Hartley JC (Late INT CORPS) 090216
Hawkes LJ (Late R SIGNALS) 020116
Hazell T (Late AGC(ETS)) 040515
Heap B MBE (Late RE) 081015
Hennessy EP (Late RAMC) 011115
Hicks GEJ DSO MBE (Late PARA) 140615
Hopla RW (Late CAMUS) 250715
Howard RN (Late RLC) 070815
Howell BL (Late RA) 180216
Hunter IPL (Late RAMC) 230315
Iffland DM (Late RA) 130415
Ingleton G (Late RA) 280915
Jacobs CM (Late RA) 190315
Janes JRE (Late R SIGNALS) 271015
Jenkins A (Late R SIGNALS) 010515
John T (Late RRF) 070615
Kendrick P (Late R SIGNALS) 150915
Khan M (Late RAMC) 110915
Large AJ OBE (Late R SIGNALS) 260415
Larsen AA (Late RE) 080415
Law DJ MBE (Late RA) 121215
Lawson MS MBE (Late AGC(SPS)) 060415
Le Feuvre JE MBE (Late RA) 230415
Lennox BM (Late RE) 231115
Levett-Scrivener MJ MBE (Late RE) 011015
Levine JLJ MBE psc(n) ais MCBS CITP MAPM (Late GREN GDS) 061015
Lindsay Obe WR OBE (Late LG) 290815
MacAulay DG (Late R SIGNALS) 100615
Maple GP (Late RA) 100615
Marinos ACE (Late R ANGLIAN) 090116
McAlister IR MBE (Late SCOTS) 110715
McComb AWT OBE (Late R SIGNALS) 020715
McCreedy N (Late R SIGNALS) 060815
Merceron DJ *Rev* (Late RAChD) 140515
Mills SCD OBE (Late RIFLES) 060815
Morgan NP MBE (Late CAMUS) 181215
Morris WA (Late RA) 210116
Morrison AM (Late AGC(ALS)) 020915
Mortlock CJ (Late RE) 210815
Neal DH (Late PWRR) 140615
Newson PG (Late INT CORPS) 030116
Nicholas MA MBE (Late R ANGLIAN) 030216
Northover BA (Late AGC(ETS)) 010415
O'Hara DG (Late AGC(SPS)) 110415
Osborne DGS (Late AAC) 050415
Osment PA (Late R SIGNALS) 100515
Overton VJ (Late GREN GDS) 300515
Page RM MBE (Late RE) 080915
Paris D (Late REME) 100915
Parker AG (Late RLC) 211115
Parker AG OBE (Late RE) 271015
Parks PT MBE (Late RA) 151215
Parr RL MBE (Late RLC) 150915
Parry AJ (Late RLC) 050615
Parsons IM BSc MSc CEng FIMechE (Late REME) 100216
Pattison NK (Late REME) 290915
Pearce AM (Late RE) 061115
Perrey AD (Late INT CORPS) 151215
Pettet GF MBE (Late RLC) 090415
Pigg AG MBE (Late YORKS) 080515
Pim RGB (Late WG) 030915
Poole TP (Late RE) 150615
Powell SJ O St J FInstLM (Late RAMC) 140315
Price PK (Late RE) 250415
Price-Jones TL (Late AGC(SPS)) 011015
Redwood DA (Late AAC) 070415
Reid RJS MBE TD (Late RAMC) 260415
Reid Obe PA OBE (Late AGC(SPS)) 110216
Richardson JA (Late RIFLES) 110415
Rimmer MJG (Late RA) 020515
Robinson EG (Late RE) 110116
Robinson PD (Late RA) 010515
Rodger IG (Late R SIGNALS) 011015
Roskelly JK (Late RLC) 160815
Roughton NH (Late RA) 011115
Rushworth AJ (Late RE) 020815
Russell NA (Late AGC(SPS)) 010216
Russell SJ (Late INT CORPS) 201115
Sanderson CJH (Late RLC) 060715
Sawtell RF (Late YORKS) 090815
Scott-Masson PABG (Late LD) 260915
Sherburn A (Late RA) 151015
Simpson JP (Late RLC) 061015

Smith CP (Late R SIGNALS) 260315
Smith NCRG (Late RE) 131115
Smith NP (Late RAMC) 110415
Somerville PD (Late REME) 260415
Southam NJ (Late INT CORPS) 190615
Stevens DA OBE (Late RLC) 010815
Stewart G (Late RAMC) 030415
Stewart AT (Late SCOTS DG) 060116
Stibbe GGE OBE (Late LG) 081215
Strangways RG (Late INT CORPS) 120615
Stratford-Wright KP (Late RE) 150915
Talbot-New GE (Late QARANC) 190815
Tarmey NT (Late RAMC) 010216
Taylor AW (Late RAMC) 090216
Taylor JE (Late AAC) 020715
Terrett EPG (Late AAC) 031015
Tester JE MBE (Late INT CORPS) 071015
Thomas GOR (Late RAMC) 021015
Tilley MN MBE CEng FCIBSE (Late RE) 031015
Tonkins RM (Late RE) 061214
Troughton JBM (Late AAC) 070515
Urquhart RK (Late RAMC) 010515
Vevers GM (Late SCOTS) 030815
Vincent DG MBE (Late R ANGLIAN) 190615
Wallis G (Late PARA) 250315
Walsh AD CMgr FCMI FInstLM P Log psc(j) (Late RLC) 170415
Walton MR (Late RA) 020615
Watt JN (Late YORKS) 240915
Wenham MH (Late R ANGLIAN) 180415
Whelan MG (Late AAC) 020715
White DW BSc CEng MIET MCGI (Late REME) 050915
Wiley AGC (Late AAC) 070315
Wilson JM (Late RLC) 301015
Woodman TGW MBE (Late RLC) 040715
Woolnough P (Late REME) 080415
Worrell DIC (Late REME) 111215
Worsley AEH MBE (Late RIFLES) 041015
Young MEJ (Late RA) 030515

Majors

Abbott S (Late PARA) 031215
Adams G (Late AGC(ALS)) 030915
Airey PJD (Late RA) 050915
Alhaji SD (Late RAPTC) 030415
Anderson CR (Late R SIGNALS) 040415
Aspin MD (Late RLC) 201015
Badger J (Late AGC(SPS)) 011015
Bailey DW (Late RE) 090116
Banks AM FRGS GCGI (Late AGC(RMP)) 171015
Barclay JG (Late RA) 010316
Barton C (Late RE) 010415
Beaumont P (Late RE) 070515
Beighton TP (Late R ANGLIAN) 161015
Bennett HJ (Late RAMC) 180515
Bettinson GF (Late RA) 150815
Blinco WH (Late RRF) 240415
Boissard AMJ BAplSc psc abq (Late QDG) 250315
Booth RGK (Late CAMUS) 090116
Bowers IRO MBE (Late RLC) 140415
Bramble NA (Late RAMC) 180615
Briscoe GH MBE (Late LANCS) 011215
Broadhurst I (Late RLC) 070415
Broughton SC (Late WG) 300715
Bruxner TM (Late RIFLES) 030615
Buckley S (Late R SIGNALS) 110415
Burridge RD (Late RE) 011115
Bushby ARP (Late AAC) 160515
Button CL (Late RA) 311015
Caie CE (Late R SIGNALS) 020415
Callaghan RP (Late RA) 290615
Camozzi GR (Late LANCS) 080815
Campbell MJ (Late AGC(ETS)) 090116
Carling CM (Late REME) 020315
Carstairs J (Late AAC) 051215
Carter RE (Late RLC) 281015
Chamberlain DF (Late AGC(ETS)) 090116
Chow CLG (Late RAMC) 050815
Clamp M (Late PARA) 181115
Clare CJ (Late QARANC) 091215
Clark KA (Late QARANC) 080415
Clement AR (Late RLC) 280715
Clifford RL MBE FCMI (Late R SIGNALS) 130216
Collins M (Late RLC) 250315
Collins MA (Late RE) 130216
Connolly D *Rev* (Late RAChD) 210415
Conway SL (Late RLC) 210515
Cook DJ MBE (Late MERCIAN) 081015
Cooke G (Late RLC) 180415
Costigane A (Late QARANC) 181215
Crowther HN (Late SASC) 200315
Curran QS (Late REME) 130415
D'Apice CMJ (Late COLDM GDS) 230915
Davey MS (Late INT CORPS) 211015
Davidson E (Late INT CORPS) 010715
Davies M (Late RE) 190415

Davies MS (Late AGC(ALS)) 010515
Dawson RM (Late AAC) 010316
Day MS CGMA ACMA (Late AGC(SPS)) 020815
Dent GJ (Late RE) 160415
Dickinson AK (Late RAMC) 100715
Doyle PGA (Late RA) 190915
Driver JM nMRCGP PG (cert) SEM (Late RAMC) 060815
Drummond I (Late RE) 010515
Duncan AM (Late R SIGNALS) 060515
Dunn NS (Late SCOTS) 090116
Eade AJ (Late RE) 010116
Eardley WGP (Late RAMC) 141015
Eastman TAH (Late WG) 251015
Emmett NJ (Late AAC) 010415
Eskell MR (Late RE) 160815
Everett MD (Late RL) 020615
Eves MP (Late REME) 020515
Eyre-Brook MG (Late RL) 090116
Faull JE MBA MIET IEng (Late REME) 161215
Field KR (Late RA) 290615
Fillipich GK (Late INT CORPS) 031215
Fisher AK (Late RLC) 180715
Flett JJ (Late REME) 200715
Ford SM MBE (Late AGC(ETS)) 311015
Francis NA (Late RE) 090116
Francis PB (Late AGC(ETS)) 260315
Freeman-Griffith DJA (Late RA) 260715
Galle N (Late RLC) 180615
Gardiner RC (Late QARANC) 230415
Gee M (Late RA) 010315
Gibbs JA (Late RAMC) 290315
Gibson JK (Late RA) 150715
Giemza-Pipe JC (Late RA) 310116
Gittins P (Late INT CORPS) 120915
Godfrey DR (Late AAC) 130915
Goodwin RA MBE (Late MERCIAN) 030615
Gordon IA MBE (Late RLC) 281015
Gospel KD (Late RLC) 150415
Graham DPA MSc BSc ato (Late RLC) 200715
Gray AGR (Late RA) 021015
Griffiths NJ (Late R SIGNALS) 211215
Griffiths PG (Late R SIGNALS) 030515
Grist PD (Late INT CORPS) 210815
Gurung H (Late QG SIGNALS) 080715
Halford DC (Late AGC(ETS)) 121015
Hall JC (Late RLC) 281215
Hamilton AS (Late RLC) 020515
Hammond RC (Late QRH) 011215
Hanlon AC MBBS MRCGP (Late RAMC) 080715
Hansford RC (Late MERCIAN) 061015
Hardman RD (Late RAMC) 050216
Hare ACR (Late AAC) 020515
Harrison LA (Late YORKS) 201015
Harrison MJ MBE (Late AGC(RMP)) 020815
Harrod SC (Late SASC) 060615
Harvey ANT (Late AGC(SPS)) 010815
Hastie CE (Late AAC) 010316
Hawkins TW (Late SCOTS) 270815
Hayes KM (Late RAMC) 051115
Hayward JD (Late RE) 010815
Healing HMP (Late AAC) 050116
Heaven MD (Late PARA) 090116
Hemming DA (Late RE) 010515
Herbert DJ (Late REME) 120615
Higgins S (Late RAPTC) 140915
Hinchliffe JP (Late YORKS) 071015
Hinnell PS (Late RRF) 260815
Hobbs MAB (Late RLC) 080216
Hodges SC (Late RAMC) 170415
Hodgson DA MBE MDA BSc(Hons) MIET (Late REME) 050415
Hollas F (Late AGC(ETS)) 090116
Holliday SH (Late REME) 100815
Hood MA MSc (Late RLC) 011115
Horne BS (Late RL) 290615
Howard RM (Late RLC) 290615
Hughes D (Late R SIGNALS) 270915
Hughes HM (Late R SIGNALS) 020415
Humphreys DJ (Late RE) 160515
Huxley JCF (Late R IRISH) 100815
Ing SJF (Late R SIGNALS) 070415
Inglis W (Late RAMC) 010715
Iswariah AD (Late RE) 210815
Jack IH (Late REME) 010915
Jackson SD BSc(Hons) (Late RLC) 080415
Jamieson RA (Late RLC) 080515
Jardine FD (Late REME) 311015
Johnson JI (Late QARANC) 180615
Jones CC BEng (Hons) CEng MIMechE (Late REME) 110415
Jones NA (Late AGC(ETS)) 010515
Jones RL (Late AAC) 010515
Jones RM (Late PWRR) 110615
Kamara CSD (Late R SIGNALS) 280515
Kell CJ (Late R SIGNALS) 240216
Kempster AJ (Late AGC(ETS)) 031015

Kenyon RA (Late REME)	160415
Kerr JEB MBE (Late SCOTS)	280815
Kerrigan MJ (Late PARA)	080815
Khadka MInstLM (Late QOGLR)	220216
Kibble LJ (Late RHG/D)	220515
King AD (Late AGC(SPS))	120415
King OGH (Late LD)	030415
Kingston DV *Rev* (Late RAChD)	140815
Knox D (Late AAC)	240915
Kyte PD (Late RIFLES)	300915
Ladner KF (Late RLC)	010415
Lambert LJ (Late RE)	090116
Lawrence MS (Late REME)	180415
Laws HH (Late AAC)	030315
Lawson AJ (Late RLC)	100216
Lelliott JP (Late RLC)	060815
Leverton LL (Late RE)	020515
Lewis PH (Late AAC)	270915
Liddell J (Late QARANC)	120915
Limbu (Late QOGLR)	030915
Linton TD (Late RAMC)	050815
Lithgow Smith KM (Late RAMC)	090915
Lloyd LA (Late AGC(ALS))	311015
Long VL (Late AGC(RMP))	040815
Lusi PJ (Late RE)	230915
MaCartney AT (Late RLC)	020915
Mack CD (Late RDG)	011115
Mackie SAP BSc(Hons) (Late REME)	020216
MacNeil IH (Late RA)	010116
Magee CG (Late RLC)	090515
Maguire FAT (Late RAMC)	010915
Mancini A (Late RA)	060116
Mann BJ (Late REME)	021115
Marsh NS (Late RE)	080815
Martin PM (Late R ANGLIAN)	130615
Martin JE AICSI (Late AGC(SPS))	011115
Mason AN (Late AGC(ETS))	210915
Maxwell W (Late R IRISH)	191015
McCarthy M MBE (Late RRF)	010715
McDermott TR DSO (Late RTR)	180915
McGhee SM (Late RE)	230915
McGinley CG (Late R SIGNALS)	210715
McKenzie SE (Late REME)	020216
McLearnon BJ (Late RLC)	150815
McNeil RJ (Late PARA)	050915
Miller CWS (Late R SIGNALS)	110615
Miller MA (Late R SIGNALS)	140116
Morrissey PL (Late QDG)	290216
Moyle SA (Late RLC)	150915
Murdy R (Late RAMC)	250315
Murray JJ (Late AGC(RMP))	090116
Nash LP (Late AGC(SPS))	020915
Naylor G (Late PARA)	190216
Newman DR (Late RAMC)	270415
Nuttall DJ (Late RA)	171115
O'Kane FJ (Late RL)	200615
O'Rourke AR (Late RA)	231015
Paramore A (Late RLC)	050315
Parr VA (Late RAMC)	020415
Paterson AK (Late RLC)	251215
Patrick PG (Late RLC)	150515
Pelan AJ (Late RLC)	080515
Pendlenton RM (Late AGC(ETS))	100515
Pietrzak HA (Late RE)	280715
Piggott GR MBE (Late COLDM GDS)	130915
Pike TW (Late RGR)	030116
Pluck R *Rev* (Late RAChD)	030515
Plummer RJ (Late IG)	071115
Poole KLW (Late RLC)	300915
Posgate IT (Late RIFLES)	030116
Prowse JS (Late SCOTS)	130915
Pusey JA (Late AAC)	020815
Rai I (Late RIFLES)	130915
Ramsay PD (Late REME)	010316
Randell PN (Late R SIGNALS)	140415
Rawdon-Smith HJ (Late INT CORPS)	180615
Razzell IG (Late RAMC)	260815
Read DG (Late AGC(SPS))	210915
Renshaw J (Late R SIGNALS)	250715
Reynolds ME *Rev* (Late RAChD)	010415
Reynolds SJ BEng CEng MSc MIMechE (Late REME)	090216
Richardson AH (Late REME)	200715
Richardson EM (Late RADC)	010415
Riley MW (Late AGC(SPS))	270815
Rimmington RK MBE (Late RLC)	111015
Roberts MJ (Late QRH)	131215
Robins CR (Late AGC(RMP))	201115
Robinson N (Late AGC(ALS))	280815
Robinson SD (Late AAC)	050915
Russell RA (Late RAMC)	010116
Scott CD (Late RA)	160915
Seargent RJ (Late AGC(SPS))	170216
Seys AAD (Late QDG)	130915
Shahi D (Late RGR)	311215
Sharland S (Late QARANC)	011115

Sharpe SD (Late RE)	020915
Sheerin JG QGM (Late PARA)	060915
Shepherd HR (Late AGC(RMP))	060315
Skene RJM (Late SCOTS DG)	031215
Sloane-Mather RJ RGN BSC HONS DIP HE MEd PGCert (Late QARANC)	160216
Smith BJ (Late AAC)	130815
Smith R (Late SCOTS)	130116
Smyth SR (Late RA)	240216
Snell KB CEng (Late REME)	050915
Sowerby GM (Late REME)	010315
Suddaby MJ (Late SCOTS)	031015
Swannell MJ (Late RA)	010515
Sweny DMH (Late PWRR)	260915
Taft DJR (Late R SIGNALS)	011115
Talbot JD (Late INT CORPS)	130116
Taylor BJ (Late AGC(ALS))	010116
Taylor CA (Late RRF)	010515
Taylor K (Late R WELSH)	050915
Thomas G (Late RLC)	310815
Thompson JI (Late RE)	190915
Thompson MR (Late REME)	080915
Tippett MD (Late QARANC)	280315
Todd EMC (Late INT CORPS)	121215
Torrington NSR MSc (Late RLC)	010515
Trehane G (Late QARANC)	080315
Treliving ERG (Late RTR)	010915
Triska DL BSc MBBS (Late RAMC)	020116
Tye C (Late AGC(SPS))	170615
Vallor M (Late AGC(ALS))	041115
Van Cutsem NPG (Late LG)	180315
Vobe RN (Late REME)	010815
Wadham SN (Late REME)	250515
Walsh CA (Late AGC(SPS))	011015
Watson ARW (Late SCOTS)	061015
Watters KJ (Late RAMC)	310315
Watterson RH (Late CAMUS)	100216
Welstead JG (Late RA)	031015
Whitaker C (Late INT CORPS)	050915
Wilcock MP (Late AAC)	010515
Wilkinson S MSc (Late RLC)	310315
Williams AM (Late RE)	260915
Williamson MAN MBE (Late SCOTS)	110415
Wills GMA (Late R SIGNALS)	201015
Wilman PC (Late CAMUS)	260415
Winks A (Late AGC(SPS))	171015
Wire AM (Late RAMC)	150216
Woods CBB (Late RE)	011015
Worsley NJ (Late RA)	121015
Wright DTN (Late QARANC)	020915
Wright N (Late RADC)	010116
Wymer RJ (Late R SIGNALS)	280515
Wyse DJ (Late RE)	281115
Young DA (Late RLC)	070815

Captains

Abbott WJ (Late RE)	240415
Ackerman LC (Late RA)	160915
Addison RC (Late RLC)	140415
Alexander FJG (Late REME)	130515
Allen HG (Late RAMC)	010815
Amos HAH (Late LD)	070415
Arnold ER (Late LANCS)	171015
Arrowsmith CT (Late RDG)	120815
Atkins CA (Late AGC(SPS))	270415
Baldwin BJ (Late WG)	070415
Barker AP (Late YORKS)	150815
Barker SA (Late RLC)	080915
Barnard JS (Late REME)	211015
Bartlett MJ (Late RIFLES)	170715
Bartrum NOH (Late RL)	031015
Bashir A (Late RRF)	310116
Batchelor R (Late PARA)	300815
Beacom MA (Late REME)	220216
Bell FW (Late RE)	140415
Blake GJN (Late AAC)	160415
Borup MH (Late LANCS)	020515
Boulton DE (Late RE)	141215
Boulton SJ (Late AGC(RMP))	161015
Bowman SA (Late YORKS)	010315
Braddock DM (Late RA)	010715
Bridger PD (Late YORKS)	031017
Brierley JWS (Late MERCIAN)	120615
Broomhead NA (Late REME)	081215
Brown IR MBE (Late INT CORPS)	011115
Buchanan RAM (Late RIFLES)	220515
Budge RH (Late GREN GDS)	170315
Bull DN (Late RA)	180915
Bull JCJ (Late INT CORPS)	110915
Bullock RG (Late RA)	150116
Burney PJ QGM (Late RIFLES)	140515
Burrows CA (Late PARA)	070815
Bush DS MBE (Late AAC)	221115
Butcher CC (Late RA)	300415
Butler-Reid BDN (Late RAMC)	050815
Carter JR (Late YORKS)	120715

Castello JDD (Late RTR)	040915
Chapman SL (Late RE)	110116
Cilliers JM (Late RAMC)	020615
Clapham GS (Late R SIGNALS)	010815
Clarke N (Late REME)	140415
Clarke SP MPharm (Late RAMC)	171015
Claxton MS (Late R SIGNALS)	290415
Climpson JS (Late R SIGNALS)	090815
Clough P (Late RRF)	020715
Coates RA (Late PWRR)	011015
Cockburn J (Late RA)	010915
Conetta A (Late RE)	281015
Corrigan TF (Late AAC)	130216
Coxon DP (Late AGC(RMP))	010815
Craig DGA (Late RE)	070116
Crofts MS (Late RTR)	270116
Crookshank AK (Late RDG)	020515
Crowe JA (Late R SIGNALS)	110515
Croxford S (Late LANCS)	111215
Cryer ME (Late REME)	130116
Dalley CL (Late RLC)	220116
Dalzel-Job MJI (Late SG)	240615
Dalziel CEB (Late SCOTS)	020915
Davey KB (Late RE)	080515
Davies AB (Late AGC(ALS))	270216
Davies DI (Late AGC(SPS))	231215
Davies PM (Late RAMC)	240615
Davis SG (Late RLC)	271115
Day LA (Late RE)	100116
Denlegh-Maxwell TNM (Late YORKS)	060515
Deppe NK (Late RE)	050715
Dix SJ (Late QRL)	010515
Dixon JS (Late RA)	120515
Douglas MRT (Late PARA)	210116
Dovey ET (Late AAC)	230415
Downes MJ (Late RLC)	030615
Du Boulay SACH (Late SCOTS)	151215
Du Plessis J (Late LG)	181215
Duncalfe TM (Late R ANGLIAN)	290116
Eamer DJ IEng MIET MCGI (Late REME)	021015
East JA (Late COLDM GDS)	190515
Easton JF (Late RA)	290515
Eid GF (Late RRF)	050915
Elder CJ (Late RLC)	151215
Ellis CJ BSc(Hons) (Late RLC)	151215
Estabrook JK (Late RLC)	010715
Evans PD (Late R WELSH)	300615
Evans RCT (Late AGC(RMP))	151215
Evoy CG (Late RLC)	041115
Fallon SG (Late RLC)	101115
Fielden RP (Late RA)	060615
Fisher CD (Late RL)	030715
Fitzpatrick LAJ (Late MERCIAN)	290815
Fleetwood DA (Late 9/12L)	070415
Floyd AE (Late IG)	020415
Ford MJ (Late RLC)	251015
Fry KR (Late INT CORPS)	090515
Fry WA (Late RL)	250915
Furmidge-Owen A (Late SASC)	280915
Garratt AJR (Late SCOTS)	030615
Gill RK (Late RLC)	110515
Goldsmith DJ MBE (Late RRF)	020715
Gordon JA (Late INT CORPS)	100615
Graham-Watson FN (Late IG)	040415
Grant RF (Late SCOTS)	100415
Graybrook RH (Late RE)	010515
Green AG (Late SASC)	160315
Green JD (Late R IRISH)	190315
Green RAC (Late AGC(RMP))	140415
Greenfield MT MBBS BSc(Hons) DMCC (Late RAMC)	280715
Grinling RJG (Late SCOTS DG)	170715
Gurung B (Late QOGLR)	110515
Gurung H (Late RAMC)	011015
Gurung M (Late QGE)	010515
Gurung P (Late RGR)	200715
Hackett EJD (Late INT CORPS)	030315
Hall DJ (Late RE)	020715
Hall WA MC (Late RA)	010515
Hamilton AJ (Late IG)	230415
Handley RH (Late RA)	301115
Harland SJ BSc(Hons) (Late RLC)	140715
Harman HL (Late RLC)	300116
Harris AM (Late AGC(ALS))	130515
Harris PHG (Late 9/12L)	250415
Harrison JL (Late AGC(RMP))	290415
Hassard EA (Late RIFLES)	290815
Hayes KJ (Late RL)	031015
Heaney SJ (Late REME)	230116
Hickey DJP (Late RA)	071115
Hills RWJ (Late RHG/D)	010315
Hinchliffe R (Late RAMC)	310515
Hiorns T (Late RE)	210915
Holcroft OJC (Late GREN GDS)	040315
Holland JE (Late AAC)	120515
Homer RC (Late RLC)	090715

Howard KJ BA(Hons) MSc (Late RLC)	031115	McPhun AC (Late R SIGNALS)	140415
Howe TSL (Late RE)	220915	Middleton CW (Late MERCIAN)	010515
Hudson RL (Late RLC)	010915	Millar RM (Late 9/12L)	010515
Hunter RI (Late RLC)	011015	Millard JDR (Late REME)	240315
Hutchinson SJ (Late R SIGNALS)	310116	Millns CE (Late RADC)	010116
Inglis IE (Late RLC)	260315	Milne SJ (Late R SIGNALS)	130815
James BD (Late SCOTS)	020315	Moffat CF (Late REME)	141215
James NA (Late INT CORPS)	060415	Moore RJ (Late INT CORPS)	010315
Jammes HJA (Late COLDM GDS)	170415	Moore Dutton DP BSc(Hons) (Late RE)	300815
Jarrett-Kerr WE (Late RE)	121215	Morgan-Evans RO (Late R WELSH)	161115
Jenkins WHR (Late IG)	180715	Morris JDC (Late AGC(ETS))	080715
Johns GI (Late RE)	080315	Mousley N (Late QARANC)	291015
Johnson CC (Late RAMC)	030915	Munns PJ (Late PWRR)	050815
Johnson DM HNDip (Late RLC)	140415	Myers KT (Late REME)	040715
Jones BN (Late RLC)	040615	Needs AG (Late INT CORPS)	120715
Jones NV (Late RLC)	030415	New VR (Late AGC(ETS))	151215
Jones OR (Late SG)	200915	Newton TR (Late RTR)	310315
Kelly JWW (Late SCOTS DG)	050415	Nightingale JW (Late RTR)	290415
Kendall JJ (Late RAMC)	010515	Nightingale HMR (Late RE)	301015
Kendall RTA (Late RIFLES)	210315	Nolan PS (Late RE)	130116
Kinch KJB (Late RAMC)	010415	Norman JR (Late AGC(ALS))	031015
Kingston MA (Late AAC)	010415	Oakshett NJ (Late AGC(ETS))	281115
Kufluk-Thackery PGM (Late RA)	010915	Old EL (Late AGC(ETS))	140415
Kuku FAOO (Late GREN GDS)	140615	Oliver JR (Late RE)	300915
Kynaston VA (Late RAMC)	010415	Oliver K (Late R SIGNALS)	011115
Lane RG BSc(Hons) (Late RLC)	181015	Ottaway MKT (Late RLC)	011215
Larkin JM (Late RTR)	050116	Parsons AV (Late REME)	230415
Laye JK (Late R SIGNALS)	171115	Patel BB LLB OMT (Late RE)	230116
Leach KJ (Late AGC(SPS))	150116	Pates NJ (Late AGC(ETS))	150815
Leach AG (Late AAC)	111115	Pemberton OC (Late COLDM GDS)	020415
Leong ZA (Late PARA)	011015	Perks AD (Late RE)	191215
Lloyd George FO (Late WG)	240216	Piggott JPF (Late AAC)	280915
Lock WD (Late PARA)	120915	Pike AJ (Late AGC(RMP))	021115
Locke DC (Late RE)	010415	Pincombe MJ (Late RAMC)	180915
Lockwood DM (Late SCOTS DG)	010715	Piper N (Late RE)	281015
Lohman LA (Late RLC)	111015	Pitman SA BA(Hons) (Late RLC)	180415
Lowe RJ (Late RE)	280315	Pitt FJM (Late AGC(ETS))	290415
Lowis SAC (Late LANCS)	011115	Platt TW (Late RA)	020415
MacDermot TP (Late IG)	310515	Pope JRM (Late IG)	111215
MacDonald LJ (Late RA)	110515	Posthumus N (Late AAC)	240116
Martin REA (Late RIFLES)	140415	Powell GM (Late QDG)	060615
Matthews BP (Late R SIGNALS)	010615	Powell JRH (Late RLC)	101215
McAdam EMK (Late PARA)	190116	Prier T (Late RLC)	310815
McBride RN (Late QDG)	200515	Pun Y (Late QGE)	200415
McClement AP BSc(Hons) (Late RLC)	151215	Queening JRL (Late RTR)	230615
McDonald DJ (Late RA)	160216	Quince JE (Late R ANGLIAN)	110715
McGuffie AJ (Late SCOTS)	010715	Ramsay GDJ (Late SCOTS)	260315
McKenzie S (Late R SIGNALS)	020915	Ravenscoft AJ (Late R SIGNALS)	300415

Rawdon-Mogg JCT (Late RHG/D)	201115
Rees BJ (Late RA)	120415
Riminton J (Late RA)	180615
Roberts C (Late AAC)	141215
Roberts FHB (Late SCOTS DG)	010515
Robertson NS (Late SG)	150415
Robins LA (Late RE)	210415
Robinson JM (Late RE)	090116
Robinson SC (Late RE)	160415
Roka K (Late RGR)	200715
Romaniuk MJC (Late RE)	140216
Rous WJ (Late AAC)	160415
Russell T (Late AGC(ETS))	130315
Sandey MCH (Late SCOTS)	121215
Saunders H (Late RA)	060315
Saville JEM (Late AGC(ETS))	110815
Scott-Barrett JH (Late SG)	300815
Secker JS (Late RLC)	050315
Smith CAK (Late RAMC)	130715
Stewart DB (Late RLC)	131115
Stewart ID (Late AGC(RMP))	220915
Stewart SA MBE (Late RDG)	310815
Stoddart R (Late SCOTS)	280815
Stott P (Late AGC(RMP))	150815
Streetley N (Late R SIGNALS)	140915
Swaby MS (Late RA)	021015
Swann CM (Late R SIGNALS)	140415
Swift DJ (Late REME)	310715
Talbot CTD (Late RHG/D)	010515
Taylor DB (Late RE)	180216
Taylor MP (Late R SIGNALS)	181115
Taylor RW (Late RLC)	230715
Thomas NS MBE (Late AGC(SPS))	010815
Thompson WF (Late RAMC)	070315
Thorne JM (Late R SIGNALS)	040116
Thornton GB (Late RA)	020216
Tibbetts GR (Late R SIGNALS)	201015
Tomlin S (Late PWRR)	180915
Tommony CL (Late REME)	300415
Tuffin AT (Late RIFLES)	110715
Turner DJ (Late R SIGNALS)	131015
Twyman LG (Late LD)	130815
Van Dijk L (Late REME)	121015
Vaughan JP (Late LD)	140315
Vinall-Hough GN (Late RE)	171215
Vosper GEC (Late MERCIAN)	080515
Walker SA (Late RRF)	060116
Walker TA (Late PARA)	080815
Waller JM (Late INT CORPS)	230815
Walters MD PhD (Late CAMUS)	230216
Westlake SL (Late PARA)	220815
Whitehouse DJ (Late RAVC)	011115
Whitten EC (Late LD)	180615
Whittingham LT (Late QRL)	010515
Wilkinson TM (Late RAMC)	160915
Williams WP (Late AGC(SPS))	090116
Williamson-Green SC (Late QARANC)	121115
Willis MA (Late RIFLES)	050116
Wilson JP (Late COLDM GDS)	080815
Wilson SJ (Late RE)	170915
Winder H (Late RAMC)	191215
Winstanley PP (Late RIFLES)	180315
Worthington AJ (Late AAC)	150615
Wright AK (Late PARA)	020515
Wright FJ (Late WG)	110915
Yates HL (Late RE)	210615
Young SJ (Late YORKS)	290216

Lieutenants

Bosch NR (Late RE)	090216
Davies TP BA(Hons) (Late RLC)	151015
Evans RE (Late INT CORPS)	140415
Farrell ZS (Late REME)	040415
Floyd SE (Late AGC(SPS))	151215
Gittins J (Late R WELSH)	110815
Haley EL (Late R SIGNALS)	100615
Hogg GM (Late RAMC)	100915
Jarvis-Smith LE (Late INT CORPS)	110815
Leonard SE (Late RE)	151215
Long MJC (Late AGC(SPS))	140415
McCullough CLD (Late RA)	180315
Over DJH (Late SCOTS)	290415
Rose CER (Late AGC(SPS))	140415
Thompson AK (Late AGC(ETS))	180915
Waters NHD (Late RIFLES)	110815

DEATHS NAMED LIST

Listing deaths of officers in the regular army between 1st April 15 - 31st March 2016 and their date of death

Lieutenant Colonel

Dyer Jonathan F (Late PWRR)	190815

Major

Rudsdale Nigel P (Late RE)	190815

Captains

Bartle Thomas O (Late AGC(RMP))	310116
Feeney James A (Late R Welsh)	150515
Rajendran Imayavaramban (Late RAMC)	300715

SECTION IV

(as at 1st March 2016)

SENIOR OFFICER LIST (AR)

SENIOR OFFICERS OF THE ARMY RESERVE

MAJOR GENERALS

Brooks-Ward SH *CVO OBE TD VR (Late RY) Deputy Commander Field Army* 301015

Crackett J *CB TD VR (Late R SIGNALS) Assistant Chief of the Defence Staff (Reserves and Cadets)* 010413

Lalor SFN *CB TD VR (Late HAC) Assistant Chief of the Defence Staff (Reserves and Cadets)*........................010307

Munro RTI *CBE TD VR (Late PARA) Assistant Chief of the Defence Staff (Reserves and Cadets)*..............260912

Smith GS *CB QVRM TD VR DL (Late RGJ)*...............290310

BRIGADIERS

Beacom NC *QVRM TD (Late R SIGNALS)* 010109

Bell SMJ *QVRM TD (Late CHESHIRE)* 140909

Bruce of Crionaich AAB *OBE ADC DL (Late GEN LIST)* 120115

Coull CA *ADC (Late SCOTS)*...................................... 011214

D'Inverno JG *QVRM TD (Late RHF)*.......................... 240706

Evans SP *CBE (Late RLC)* 030112

Gilbert PH *TD (Late RAMC)* 010414

Harvey CJ *OBE QVRM TD (Late REME) Assistant Commander Force Troops Command*..................010115

Mooney JP *QVRM TD ADC (Late LONDONS)* 010312

O'Brien TN *CBE TD DL (Late RLC)* 010207

O'Leary WJ *TD DL (Late REME)* 030112

Potter SJ *QVRM TD (Late R SIGNALS)* 070113

Robertson HJ *QVRM TD (Late R SIGNALS)*............... 190313

COLONELS

Adkins IC *(Late REME)* 160413

Akinkunmi AA *(Late RAMC)* 010413

Astbury NRW *(Late RY)* 141014

Atkinson DC *QVRM TD (Late REME)* 010109

Barnes AF *(Late RLC)* 281005

Barnes JR *(Late RLC)* 300694

Bennett SW *(Late RLC)* 270910

Black AJ *TD (Late RAMC)* 010210

Black WC *BDS MGDS RCSEd FFGDP(UK) (Late RADC)* 300606

Bruce-Smith KJ *TD (Late R SIGNALS)* 130596

Campbell CH *TD (Late SCOTS)*...................................... 240308

Cheshire NR *(Late INT CORPS)* 010713

Coles EMC *TD (Late QARANC)* 090113

Cooper AJ *QVRM TD (Late R MON RE(M))* 010712

Davies K *MBE RRC TD (Late QARANC)* 210808

Davis JE *OBE QVRM TD DL (Late QARANC)*................ 300403

Deahl MP *TD (Late RAMC)*... 310503

Dixon SG TD *(Late RLC)* 300412

Easton NP *QVRM TD (Late LONDONS)*.......................... 231000

Edwards CW *OBE TD (Late R SIGNALS)*........................ 290710

Elvidge RD *TD BSc MRICS (Late RE)* 010407

Evans GA *(Late RAMC)* 090112

Fox RJ *(Late RLC)* 170109

Frampton Hobbs RJD *(Late R Wx Y)*............................... 010313

Garrett SC *TD (Late HAC)*.. 140807

Gibbs GK *(Late RE)* 300604

Goble TJL *(Late AAC)* 160207

Graham SJM *(Late QOY)*.. 241011

Grant H *(Late SCOTS)*.. 011010

Green MFT *TD (Late RWR)*.. 310707

Guinness DEM *MBE (Late RY)* 090614

Guzkowska MAJ *QVRM TD (Late INT CORPS)*............ 050905

Hopkins DE *(Late GH)*.. 040105

Hopper SJ *(Late RRF)* 120813

Hughes JG *(Late YORKS)* 210111

Jackson PD TD *(Late RADC)* 141107

Jackson RG *TD* (Late RAMC)* 310707

Jenkins TP *OBE TD (Late PWRR)*.................................... 011214

Jones OC *TD (Late QARANC)*.. 070313

Kinloch JAB *TD (Late RA)* 010804

Kumik PC *TD (Late REME)* 010411

Langley GE *TD (Late RE)* 010309
Lankester CM *TD (Late R SIGNALS)* 010914
Lewis PJ *(Late QOY)* 060907
Limb MS *OBE TD (Late RLC)* 051205
Lodge MA JP *MA (Late YORKS)* 230707
Long PM *(Late R Wx Y)* 220714
Lyttle JOM *MBE TD (Late R IRISH)* 170614
Matthews VJG *OBE (Late RIFLES)* 010313
McArthur DJ *OBE TD (Late QARANC)* 310109
McDowell SE *TD (Late QARANC)* 010408
Medway NB *TD (Late QARANC)* 250615
Middleton D *MBE TD (Late RA)* 011011
Mogg DK *TD (Late PWRR)* 190113
Moles IGD *OBE QVRM TD MB BCH MRCGP (Late RAMC)* 090106
Murphy RST *TD (Late HAC)* 070109
Neilson RF *(Late RAMC)* 280811
Overton MAJ *TD (Late LONDONS)* 100614
Partridge WMJ *TD (Late RA)* 011298
Platt AA *(Late RLC)* 010112
Rayson SW *(Late RLC)* 080813
Redgate TCW *TD (Late RE)* 301109
Rew DA *TD (Late RAMC)* 160708
Ridout CEA *(Late QARANC)* 010406
Robinson MJ *(Late RLC)* 010703
Rolland IA *(Late REME)* 010713
Salmon AJ *TD (Late RE)* 010405
Sanders DA *TD (Late RLC)* 010407
Seal TJ *TD DL (Late RLC)* 121211
Sharma SK *(Late RAMC)* 180808
Sheridan MC *(Late RAMC)* 300713
Singh HJ *MBE TD (Late QARANC)* 011014
Smyth AMG *QVRM TD MSc (Late RE)* 031011
Straughan G *OBE TD (Late RRF)* 010208
Sykes JP *(Late RLC)* 010308
Telford DM *TD (Late QARANC)* 150113
Townend CJ *RRC (Late RAMC)* 011112
Trow K *TD (Late QARANC)* 090311
Walbridge PJ *(Late QARANC)* 240811
Walton ACD *(Late WM)* 300405
Whitton ADC *(Late RAMC)* 140904
Willmott PN *OBE TD (Late R SIGNALS)* 010206
Wilson JLN *(Late SCOTS)* 010706
Wood AC *TD (Late RE)* 011113

ARMY RESERVE

ROYAL MONMOUTHSHIRE ROYAL ENGINEERS (MILITIA)

The Prince of Wales Plume, Coronet and Motto ICH DIEN, surmounted by a crown, on either side of the Plume the letters Rand E, below a scroll inscribed ROYAL MONMOUTHSHIRE

Regimental Headquarters: Monmouth Castle, Monmouth NP25 3BS,

Royal Honorary Colonel........................ *HRH The Duke of* Gloucester *KG GCVO*..110677
Honorary Colonels................................. Maj Gen (Retd) R R (Dickie) Davis *CB CBE*..011214
Capt (Retd) Ken M Soar (Jersey Field Squadron)...011214

Lieutenant Colonels

Browning MC	160608
Pritchard AC *TD*	260914
Washington D	010904

Majors

Beaumont CM	030299
Bloomer JG	071209
Brown NY	130415
Davies D	131011
Owen GS	121007
Phillips DG	010414
Smith JWG TD	241098
Spratley NK	010811

Captains

Anderson AP	120913
Batchelor PJ	080310
Bell D	091101
Carr D	011004
Field DAR	210708
Forster ACT	180909
Harmes AP	080212
Hein ACS	131008
Jones DA	010407
Little SJ	061111
Norgrove SC	011012
Pates CA	270611
Steadman C	080310
Stockman GI	111014
Trescothick-Martin JR	141110
Tuckett HM	270312
Watson ED	080310
Williams DR	050607

Lieutenants

Busby NJ	210313
Davies GR	170706
Lavin P	010411
Pinel FL	160511
Powell GD	010513
Wisbey JL	101012

2nd Lieutenants

Falconer JL	130813
Hankinson AE	290713
Lelliott RS	280713

THE HONOURABLE ARTILLERY COMPANY

Artillery

An old fashioned cannon with a scroll above inscribed HAC
and a scroll below inscribed ARMA PACIS FULCRA;
the whole surmounted by St Edward's Crown

Infantry

A grenade with monogram HAC on the ball
"South Africa 1900-02"

The Great War: 3 Infantry Battalions and 7 Batteries of Artillery - **Ypres 1915-17, Somme 1916, 18,** Ancre Heights, **Ancre 1916, Arras 1917, 1918,** Scarpe 1917, 18, Arleux, Bullecourt, Pilckem, Polygon Wood, Broodseinde, Poelcappelle, **Passchendaele,** Amiens, Albert 1918, Bapaume 1918, Drocourt-Queant, Hindenburg Line, Epehy, St Quentin Canal, Cambrai 1918, Selle, Sambre, **France and Flancers 1914-18,** Piave, **Vittorio Veneto,** Italy 1917-18, Rafah, Egypt 191517, **Gaza,** El Mughar, **Jerusalem,** Jordan, Megiddo, Sharon, Damascus, Palestine 1917-18, Aden

The Second World War: Bourgebus Ridge, Antwerp, Le Havre, Rhine, North-West Europe 1944-45, Knightsbridge, El Alamein, El Hamma, Sbiba, Thaia, Tunis, North Africa 1941-43, Sicily 1943, Cassino II, Coriane, Senio, Italy 1944-45

Regimental Marches

Quick... March British Grenadiers
Slow .... March Duke of York
Canter... Bonnie Dundee
Trot... The Keel Row
Walk .... Duchess of Kent

Regimental Headquarters...................... Finsbury Barracks, City Road, London EC1Y 2BQ
(Tel: 020 7382 1543)

Alliances

South African Defence Forces .... Transvaal Horse Artillery

Captain General.................................... HER MAJESTY THE QUEEN
Royal Honorary Colonel........................ *HRH Prince* Michael *of Kent GCVO*..310112
Colonel Commandant .... Gen *Sir* Richard L Barrons *KCB CBE* 140513
Regimental Colonel................................ Col *The Hon* Mark A F Vincent *MBE (late* RA)..010315

Lieutenant Colonels

Barnes SM	010214
Bate AGE *BSc (Hons)*	010214
Caie ADC *TD*	270903
Doherty JW	150912

Majors

Bobjerg-Jensen PC	010805
Burgess RDB	020402
Chorley JP	080609
Daniel DL	031111
Dommett MN	071199
Gabb AHS	061200
Goodinson JB	201004
Grove WH	
Jakeman RB	210612
Keeson RGC	231113
King MD	030610
Longbottom JR *MBE*	110308
Marment CV	020102
Ormond-King CJS	020700
Reader SWL	030609
Russell MNG	060599
Small AN	030609

Captains

Allnutt HVE	010711
Brady GME	101111
Brett J	010913
Champness JC *BA(Hons)*	010714
Cobb GR	011108
Collins M	200111
Cooper AM *BA(Hons)*	091206
Cruickshank AL	280115
Gates DCS	010714
Hall GM	010913
Horwood PG *BVETMED*	220207
Johnson DJ	010711
Lakin D	201009
MacTaggart IM	170213
McAulay CMJ	100811
Scott JPR	160915
Selley BJ	161293
Smiddy FO	160915
Sola DJP	010711
Waddell RA	130606

Lieutenants

Bedford S	021013
Bromfield JAB	280115
Burbeck ME	270405

Edge NGA	270715
Jackson PT	021012
Jassal VA	060110
Kaye LG	020714
Lloyd Jones C	100400
Moore JA *BEng(Hons)*	280913
Perkins RT	290913
Ring JSH	300309
Sawell NG	170213
Sutton B	180215
Westlake JRG	021012

2nd Lieutenants

Bhardwaj AC	060413
O'Connor GP	010812
Stradis A *MSc BA*	270713
Wade CR	140813
Wharton GJC	280913

YEOMANRY OF THE ROYAL ARMOURED CORPS

Light Cavalry Army Reserve regiment

Bases: London, Croydon, Windosr, Nottingham, Leicester, Dudley and Telford

Colonel Commandant Yeomanry .... Lt Col (Retd) *The Rt Hon the Lord* de Mauley *TD*...............................010611

The origins of the Yeomanry Regiments now included in the Royal Armoured Corps are as follows:

ROYAL YEOMANRY

The Sherwood Rangers Yeomanry
The Leicestershire and Derbyshire (Prince Albert's Own) Yeomanry
Kent and County of London Yeomanry (Sharpshooters)
Inns of Court and City Yeomanry
Westminster Dragoons (2nd County of London Yeomanry)
The Shropshire Yeomanry
Staffordshire, Warwickshire, Worcestershire Yeomanry

ROYAL WESSEX YEOMANRY

The Royal Wiltshire Yeomanry (Prince of Wales's Own)
The Royal Gloucestershire Hussars
Royal Devon Yeomanry
The Dorset Yeomanry

QUEEN'S OWN YEOMANRY

The Queen's Own-Yorkshire Yeomanry
The Duke of Lancaster's Own Yeomanry
The Cheshire Yeomanry (Earl of Chester's)
The Northumberland Hussars

SCOTTISH AND NORTH IRISH YEOMANRY

The Ayrshire Yeomanry (Earl of Carrick's Own)
North Irish Horse
The Fife and Forfar Yeomanry / Scottish Horse

THE ROYAL YEOMANRY

Regimental March

Quick March .... The Farmer's Boy

Locations and Affiliations

RHQ .... Fulham House, Fulham High Street, London SW6 3JS (Tel: 0207 384 4201 Email: RY-CS-PSAO@mod.uk)

C&S (Westminster Dragoons) Squadron .... Fulham

A (Sherwood Rangers Yeomanry) Squadron .... Nottingham

B (Warwickshire & Worcestershire Yeomanry) Squadron... Dudley

C (Kent & Sharpshooters Yeomanry) Squadron .... Croydon

D (Shropshire Yeomanry) .... Telford

E (Leicestershire & Derbyshire Yeomanry) Squadron .... Leicester

The (Inns of Court and City Yeomanry) Band....... London

3 Troop, C (Kent and Sharpshooters Yeomanry) Squadron .... Windsor

Role Affiliations

Regiments .... 1st The Queen's Dragoon Guards

Honorary Colonels

Royal Honorary Colonel .... *HRH Princess* Alexandra *The Hon Lady* Ogilvy *KG GCVO*................100402
Honorary Colonel .... Lt Gen *Sir* Barney W B White-Spunner *KCB CBE*..............................161010
Commanding Officer .... Lt Col C J MacEvilly

Lieutenant Colonels

MacEvilly CJ *LLB LLM Barrister*	300315
McMenemy SJ	010115

Majors

Alderson AB	010603
Bragg TWH	141110
Edwards MS	300995
Falshaw R	030610
Field CED	250413
Franklin AJ	280111
Gaddum THM	010409
Harrison GN *TD*	011106
Hodson M	010101
Howell TD	031111
Marsh RD *TD*	200396
Marshall EJH	171198
Mason MI	030610
Mason RCS	300905
Nall RGA *TD*	200903
Shaw IS *BSc(Aero) AMRAeS RAF*	141113
Villar JG *TD*	200602
Webb MT	010714

Captains

Barron NP	150708
Beattie JHL	280505
Chadwick CJ	251014
Critien ADS	010813
Critien GJG	060812
Davey PM	210410
Elliott CJ	150506
Faldo SC	121010
Fincham MJC	010111
Fischer DE	280909
Frith KW	011102
Graham JWR	010908
Hallsworth SJ	160410
Harris JR	090710
Hodgkinson MW	010411
Jenkins AD	161208
Key ORM	271012
Longmore HAE	250707
Masterton TJF	120705
Mawby WH	100914
McKenzie TAC	130812
McMullen SD	020409
Monk IWJ	150610
Mulligan OP	261209
Ross P	010407
Rotheram CA	010409
Ruck Keene DNJ	110210
Sparrow PB	010410
Tilbrook JR	010803
Tomlin G	150704
Trinick CJ	030408
Turner GR	011103
Tyler AJ	100512
Von Barloewen DW	131212
Warburton T	100910
Ward JL	010506
Whitehead MGB	270710
Wythe WR	250513

Lieutenants		*2nd Lieutenants*		**Role Affliations**	
Buxton RA	171014	Billingham JR	270914	**QDG**	
Greenway RTC	021014	Hebblewhite LMD	121112	*Captain*	
Skipper A	011111	Higton NA	171009	James SG	200506
Vakil AB	010811	Jones EDD	141012		
		Long JG	280913		
		Saunders MS	160713		
		Sherburne RT	280713		
		Tew AJ	280913		

THE ROYAL WESSEX YEOMANRY

Regimental March

Quick March .... God Bless the Prince of Wales

Locations and Affiliations

RHQ .... The Armour Centre, Allenby Barracks, Bovington, Dorset BH20 6JA
(Tel: 01929 402024 Email: RWXY-RHQ-ADJT@mod.uk)

A (Dorset Yeomanry) Squadron .... Allenby Barracks, Bovington, Dorset
B (Royal Wiltshire Yeomanry) Squadron .... Old Sarum House, Salisbury, Wiltshire
C (Royal Gloucestershire Hussars) Squadron .... Cirencester (with a detachment at Donnington, Telford, Shropshire)
D (Royal Devon Yeomanry) Squadron .... Barnstaple and Exeter
Y (Royal Wiltshire Yeomanry) Squadron .... Swindon, Wiltshire

Role Affiliations

Regiments .... The Queen's Royal Hussars
The King's Royal Hussars
The Royal Tank Regiment

Royal Navy .... HMS Portland
HMS Enterprise

Honorary Colonels

Royal Honorary Colonel .... HRH The Earl of Wessex *KG GCVO ADC(P)*
Honorary Colonel .... Lt Col (Retd) *The Rt Hon the Lord* de Mauley *TD* 010715
Commanding Officer .... Lt Col J Godfrey

Lieutenant Colonels

Rothwell MJR	010105
Utting DW *LLM*	011202
Wildish JD	250910

Majors

Baker NL	240102
Bathurst AES	130203
Caldwell BH	010509
Chafer SN	010415
Dalley JM	040111
Dalzell MW	030610
Dinan MJ *TD*	021006
Fowle CS TD	120201
Gentle EF	311012
Jones TR	010614
Lea JJ	010608
Morgan JDH *TD*	151200
Morgan RM	011211
Morley J	041210
O'Neil Roe GCB	170310
Payne JRW *TD*	010904
Phillips AMG	010604
Speers CJL	140111
White RP	220513

Captains

Arkell GJ	290711
Arkell JP	120209
Campbell RW	161213
Chamberlin MJ	220407
Collinson AP	010109
Coventry CC	080215
Crump JT	170704
Dorey EL	010804
Ebbern EH	010213
Feaver SR	140514
Frampton Hobbs EC	031194
Frankland TEF	140811
Gausden RA	130709
Gooch TR	140413
Griffiths IT	160305
Hanbury-Bateman PW	190107
Heelis RAP	120301
Hickey BJ	040906
Hodges EDL	310711
Hood GJF	021013
Jerabek WA	051009
Kayll JM	131008
Kemp-Gee HA	010410
Knight TS	230613
Lindsay LF	070202
Martin NJG	221108
Meyer JJB	200711
Mitchell PJ	220907
Ogglesby JM	010708
Plumridge MS	020910
Rawdon-Mogg CJD	190310
Rickard T	010407
Roe GB	010111
Selby Bennett AC	271008
Trott MR	230604
Troughton DM	020408
Verdon TO	020801
Vere Nicoll HA	010711
Warwick DRM	170608
Whetter RS	140500
White DJ	190613

Lieutenants

Endsor DT	270911
Gracey TJF	010905

2nd Lieutenant

Connors KP	030813

Role Affliations

KRH

Majors

Banks TC	010410

QRH

Lieutenant Colonel

Bromley Gardner CAJ	300600

Major

Thorman JP *TD*	080200

Captain

Oliver JN	071211

RTR

Captain

Proctor CC	120209

THE ROYAL MERCIAN AND LANCASTRIAN YEOMANRY

A Mercian Eagle topped by a Saxon Crown superimposed upon a Lancastrian Rose below the Duke of Lancaster's Coronet

This regiment is being disbanded as part of the national reorganisation of the armed forces. Command of its squadrons will be handed over to The Royal Yeomanry and The Queen's Own Yeomany.

Regimental Marches

Quick March .... The Light of Foot
Slow March .... Scipio

Locations and Affiliations

RHQ .... Redford Barracks, Colinton Road, Edinburgh EH13 0PP
(Tel: 0131 310 5341 Email: SNIY-RHQ-ROSO@mod.uk)

Squadrons relocated.

Colonel in Chief and Honorary Colonels

Colonel in Chief .... HER MAJESTY THE QUEEN
Honorary Colonel .... Maj Gen (Retd) A P Farquhar *CBE DL* 010408

Lieutenant Colonels

Acton FS *MSc*	210408
Brooke JP	151111
Curtis WG *TD*	020407

Majors

Collis RWN	170407
McEwan MD	060702
Morris PC	260410
Shute JAC	010110
Swayne DA *TD*	010196

Captains

Aspinall JF	090204
Bowker BR *MCMI MIfL Cert Ed*	010407
Edwards AS	180208
Hamilton-Russell MJG	300309

Lieutenants

Bowden RE	180909

THE QUEEN'S OWN YEOMANRY

A fox on a scroll inscribed QUEEN'S OWN YEOMANRY

Regimental March

Quick March .... D'ye Ken John Peel

Locations and Affiliations

Regimental Headquarters and
Command & Support (C & S) Squadron .... Fenham Barracks, Barrack Road, Newcastle upon Tyne NE2 4NP
(Tel: 01912 393 133 Website: www.army.mod.uk/QOY)

A The Queen's Own-Yorkshire Yeomanry Squadron .... York
B The Duke of Lancaster's Own Yeomanry Squadron .... Wigan
C The Cheshire Yeomanry (Earl of Chester's) Squadron, ... Chester
D The Northumberland Hussars Squadron .... Newcastle upon Tyne

Role Affiliations

Regiments .... The Light Dragoons

Honorary Colonels

Royal Honorary Colonel.. FM *HRH The Prince of* Wales *KG KT GCB OM AK QSO ADC(P)*..170600
Honorary Colonel .... Maj Gen (Retd) David J Rutherford-Jones *CB*.....................................010914

Lieutenant Colonels	
Burdon-Cooper RA	120914
Costello SWD *TD*	270614
Fairfax TP *TD MSc BSc (Hons)*	010705
Ledsham CJ *TD VR*	221110

Majors	
Bankes WNW	280313
Barker TCA *MICG MILM*	140207
Boyle RML	310704
Hartshorne RG	131105
Hutchinson MC	010403
Hutton GH	071114
Kyle JW	120311
Mortimer D	260106
Murray SA *TD LLB (Hons) DIP LP*	010902
Norton HPD	191108
O'Riordan PD	011114
Pennett MT	230509
Potter NWE	200608
Smart SB	310113
Valentine P	080212

Captains	
Armstrong RM	261113
Bridle SE	281014
Burns AQ	011106
Cockburn R	280309
Dawber SE	071211
Dunlea-Jones R	301006
Earle RWN	011111
Eastham J	010212
Findlay IR	010304
Geddes AC	010706
Jobes A	070510
Mallin AJ	050110
McFarlane A	020409
McGearey A	231013
Miller GG	060205
Miller TC	210514
Siddell AJ	180109
Weir DRW	
Yates RP	230309
Zank DT	120903

Lieutenants	
Eaton JAJ	100511
Gray CJ	300712
Greenwell MJ	080205
Hemphill JA	011211
Hewitt AM	031011
Norman JD	260905
Ramsay SD	011011
Roberts CPC	260312
Windslow CA	011111

2nd Lieutenants	
Coolican JM	290912
Cruttenden RJB	171012
Howard KM	270913
Mellis NJS	270913
Sikora DA	040813
Spearing WJ	060914

THE SCOTTISH AND NORTH IRISH YEOMANRY

A wolf's head superimposed on crossed lances.

The Army's newest Army Reserve regiment in the Light Cavalry role, entering the Army's Order of Battle on 31 October 2014. Created out of the restructuring of the Yeomanry regiments.
The regiment is formed from the RHQ of the Royal Mercian and Lancastrian Yeomanry and three squadrons of the Queen's Own Yeomany: A (Ayrshire Yeomanry) Squadron, B (North Irish Horse) Squadron, C (Fife and Forfar Yeomanry) Squadron. A new HQ (Lothian and Borders Horse) E squadron will is in Edinburgh.

Regimental March

Quick March .... Garryowen
Slow March .... Garb of Old Gaul

Locations and Affiliations

Regimental Headquarters and
Command & Support (C & S) Squadron .... Redford Barracks, Colinton Road, Edinburgh, EH13 0PP
(Tel: 0131 310 5341 SNIY-RHQ-ROSO@mod.uk)
E (Lothians and Border Yeomanry) Squadron ...... Edinburgh
A (Ayrshire (Earl of Carrick's Own) Yeomanry)
Squadron .... Ayr
B (North Irish Horse) Squadron .... Belfast
C (Fife and Forfar / Scottish Horse) Squadron ..... Cupar

Role Affiliations .... The Royal Scots Dragoon Guards

Colonel in Chief and Honorary Colonels

Colonel in Chief .... *TBC*
Honorary Colonel .... Dr Melfort Andrew Campbell *OBE* 241114
Commanding Officer .... Lt Col James Campbell-Barnard *MBE*
Squadron Leaders .... Maj Mark Gannon (North Irish Hourse Squadron)

Majors

Gannon M	
Grant CS	011015
Montgomery SJ *BSc(Hons)*	150506

Captain

Goodbody RE

2nd Lieutenant

Howlett WJW	071009

Role Affiliations

SCOTS DG

Lieutenant Colonel

Allen DAJ	300609

Major

Kahn DJ	070114

Captains

Cochlan G	151104
Crawford JWP	201014

ROYAL ARMOURED CORPS

GENERAL LIST - OFFICERS NOT LISTED ELSEWHERE

RAC SUB BRANCHES

HCAV - Royal Horse Guards and 1st Dragoons (RHG/D)

Major

Goodman MC *BSc* 040213

Queens Royal Lancers (QRL)

Lieutenant Colonel

Purbrick TJG 011103

ROYAL REGIMENT OF ARTILLERY

Regimental Headquarters: Artillery House, Royal Artillery Barracks, Larkhill, Salisbury, Wiltshire SP4 8QT
(Tel: 01980 845528 Fax: 01980 845210 Email: RARHQ-RegtSec@mod.uk)

Colonel Commandant .... Gen *Sir* Richard Barrons *KCB CBE* 140513

Honorary Colonels

101 Regt RA (AR) .... Col (Retd) W T Gracie *TD (ACF) (until 010416)* 010410
Col David R Harrington *(from 010416)*
103 Regt RA (AR) .... Maj Gen S R Skeates *CBE (until 010416)* 150212
Brig W J F (Bill) Kingdon *(from 010416)*
104 Regt RA (AR) .... Lt Col (Retd) D G Clarke *OBE TD* 210413
105 Regt RA (AR) .... Col (Retd) Jim A B Kinloch *TD* 010712
106 Regt RA (AR) .... Lt Gen Richard E Nugee *CVO CBE* 010615
RA National Reserve HQ .... Brig (Retd) David J Greenwood 011213

Lieutenant Colonels

Allen JC TD	041014
Barrington Brown C *TD MA MBA g tacsc*	120402
Bates PN *OBE*	300605
Cleverly JS *TD*	010315
Evans HM *TD*	050909
Fisher JR	300907
Forbes AJG	271008
Forbes LM	091213
Frank AR	011102
Haigh PA *TD BEng (Hons) AMI MECH E*	310812
Halliday SJR *TD*	011210
Hitchman SC *TD*	010203
Horner RH *MBE*	091103
Humphrey DA *TD*	010611
Morris TH	050899
Nield SH *MBE TD*	201010
Ross ILJ *TD*	010707
Russell ALV	230603
Servaes J	050408
Towers JM	301107
Ward FN	010614
Woellwarth NH	011214

Majors

Arundel TJ	020108
Auckland-Lewis JC	080200
Bader BS *BSc (Hons) PGCE PGDip AES FRPSH*	310314
Bailie IA	010599
Ball AE	310705
Belcourt PL	160401
Bertram DG	120115
Brooks KMT	191199
Brown AW	011006
Brown DP	010413
Butcher CS	300996
Byers LS *TD*	011101
Clark CR *MCMI MCGI*	021290
Cobb-Smith CSG	240408
Collins PJ	011008
Cookes HN TD	210103
Corrigan JJ	150107
Cowell-Smith PE	050291
Crosby A TD	190500
Cunningham JED	310712
Davies SHL	300991
Dwyer SA	270410
Estick SJ *BSc (Hons) PgDip MCMI*	310708
Evans RD	060514
Eve RR	300993
Every AJ *TD*	090101
Faux W	310502
Fox T	240108
Friel RM	010614
Gilbert HF	041108
Gledhill A	110714
Glencairn-Campbell CD	070115
Grant SG	310705
Gray JJM *TD*	160601
Gray SA	310710
Gray SJ	300994
Greaves DM	090711
Gregory K	220909
Gwizdala JPA *BA*	300698
Hacon AN	021190
Halliday WSJ	210504
Hampson PT	020994
Haslam PW *TD*	140601
Hatton P *TD*	010304
Hedges GA	010408
Hemstock NT	010506
Hewitt EJ	310706
Higgins JRC *TD*	010498
Hilton KA *TD*	011001
Horne ADE	310703
Horton DC *TD*	300995
Ibbs DPM	040512
Jackson SD *BSc(Hons) MSc*	010614
Jones P	300901
Joslyn MA	300195
Kavanagh WP	010714
Kenyon JPA	180314
Kershaw PJ	230413
King RA	010206
Kirkwood SA *TD*	010600
Larkham PP	010807
Leadbeater RJ *TD*	190303
Logan KS	300989
Lonsdale ID *TD*	070595
Lynch DJ	200404
Mabbott J	310707
MacFarlane AJ	010506
Maher CM	010107
McMillan KJ	030513
Merrylees AG	010604
Metcalfe RS	300995
Morgan SJ	010102
Morrison AW	310707
Morrison MW	141207
Muntz SGA	300993
Murday JPM	060197
Murray WG	010907

Norman ML	310707
O'Connor MJ *TD*	251093
Parker EM	010910
Patchell LP *BSc(Hons) PhD*	010712
Pender JA	220112
Pennett TW *TD*	011200
Power JL	050115
Rafferty AC	300993
Ralph FA	010311
Reade T	010510
Ritchie PG	111014
Roberts AP	190706
Robson BR	231013
Salloway PC	060795
Samosa S	051110
Sargent NP	310704
Scoins KA	081210
Searle JP	010908
Sim HD *TD*	110903
Simpson NH *TD*	120100
Sivyer IF	040512
Skillman DJ	191087
Sloan AST	010805
Smallwood AM	101012
Smiles N	140913
Smith RV *TD*	010603
Spain HA	250116
Sparks JN *TD*	010300
Sweet TJ	300986
Symmons JE	151107
Tancock SC	140107
Taxis CL	211010
Thurley MR	050905
Valenzia MD	300991
Vallack PA *TD*	010601
Waldron-Lynch T	010411
Wallace WSI	010413
Walters RC	011006
Ware RE	300995
Wheeler CI	150107
Williams JP	040213
Wilson IA *TD*	310795
Winton PD *TD*	170906

Captains

Auty JB	140503
Baddeley CS	130606
Bazley AJ	010304
Blackborough G	231109
Boardman DJQ	011004
Brown NJ	180412
Buckley DM	300905
Butcher SRA	011207
Collins LJ	221010
Coney AM	150113
Cook NR *TD*	011203
Cooper RJ	020108
Copley AG	160101
Crawford MC	011107
Crisp SW	070214
Cullen GP	070600
Cutts CE	021208
Dandy LM	010814
De Silva Jayasingh RDP	020601
Delf JP	170603
Dempster JW	190507
Dickie NT	010813
Eden ATE	050605
Fenwick DJ	090710
Fletcher SC	010813
Frost BM	230309
Frost JP	020907
Gallier JAM *BSc(Hons)*	010809
German PM	120312
Gibson JM	310308
Gillies FR	161011
Groves RG	100309
Gunson JPA	260712
Hall DM	220410
Hancock CJ	050607
Harris PD	150309
Herbert MA	181007
Hughes NA	010410
Loader ATR	230613
Luce SA	010711
Lumley AJ	260210
Mackay RJ	260310
Mason PE	010407
McAughtrie RAJ	230614
McBride R	020311
McDonald CA	230108
McEwen EL	161012
Meadows D	150914
Metcalfe AJ	010605
Morrell AH	130813
Nwaonu MC	121214
Oliver SLJ *MBE*	060409
Parrott TA	041001
Paterson D	191108
Patterson PF	010409
Perkins WA	291006
Phillips S	081008
Pinnell LJ	010102
Pudsey-Dawson CE	070114
Scott CD	010812
Scott NA	290308
Smith KN	030708
Sowton PB	130709
Thomas CJ	110607
Townend MSM	170807
Turner WTR	241007
Vickers M	110314
Wallace HAR	241207
Wheale JP	130600
Williams TOL	150910
Willington AD	241007
Wilmont RJ *MBE*	250106
Wood CK	080313
Young SP	160309

Lieutenants

Aylward RM	070508
Bastow PG	010811
Bird TS	280915
Campbell AM	010813
Carey DJ	040111
Clark W	070312
Harris TF	021111
O'Byrne CS	280714
Parker WAN	021013
Rees DM	010813
Wilkinson RS	051111
Williams A	030709

2nd Lieutenants

Brett AJ	280713
Broad JDA	220514
Clark-Majerus NA	270914
Coomber CE	031011
Harrison AJ	300907
Heydenrych DW	290309
Moore DMT	270713
Reid NE	290913

CORPS OF ROYAL ENGINEERS

Regimental Headquarters: Brompton Barracks, Chatham, Kent ME4 4UG
(Tel: 94661-2121 Email: corps.secretary@rhqre.co.uk)

Royal Honorary Colonels	*HRH The Duke of* Gloucester *KG GCVO*	110677

Honorary Colonels

21 Engineer Regt AR	Lt Gen (Retd) Robin V Brims *CB CBE DSO DL*	010315
71 Engineer Regt AR	Vacant	
75 Engineer Regt AR	Col N D O Williams *TD JP DL (until 060317)*	
	Col Alastair J Cooper *QVRM TD VR (from 060317)*	
101 Engineer Regt (Expolsive Ordnance Disposal) AR	Mr Julian Miles Holland *OBE DL*	010211
131 Independent Commando Squadron RE AR	Gen *Sir* Gordon K Messenger *KCB DSO* OBE ADC(RM)*	230111
135 Geographic Squadron RE AR	Dr Vanessa Vivian Lawrence *CB*	010809
Jersey Field Squadron RE (Militia)	Capt (Retd) Ken M Soar	011214
170 Engineer Group AR	Brig (Retd) C M Sexton *(until 010516)*	011011
	Mr Steve J Morriss *(from 010516)*	
Engineer and Logistic Staff Corps RE AR	Maj Gen Richard J Semple *CBE*	040315

Lieutenant Colonels

Adams SJ	030615
Bell AT *QVRM TD*	020508
Blades J *TD*	280714
Brown JP	271014
Bulmer MHK	010414
Castle JW *MBE MSc*	011211
Dick T	010709
Fisk PA	290806
Graham DW *TD*	020810
Gray D	010311
Hann M *MBE TD*	011004
Hill AP	010711
Hislop AR	300611
Lancaster JM *TD*	010212
Lewis R TD	060514
Matthews SRS	010311
Rudd AR TD	010214
Ryan AJG	010811
Smith AC *CEng*	050115
Smith TFS	010304
Snelling BG *TD*	010606
Somers RM *TD*	010402
Spencer SM	290514
Taylor JJ	010609
Walker H	280997
Walters PR	010415
Wilson JM *TD*	100111

Majors

Allardice D *BSc(Hons) MRICS ICIOB*	010513
Anderson WG *TD FRICS FInstLM MInstRE*	120192
Baldwin E	071002
Barclay DJ *TD BSc(Hons) MBCS*	150105
Bint R	010108
Cairns PS	111098
Calderwood CL	310707
Callingham PJ	220908
Carroll JJ	290908
Carter MP *BSc(Hons) MRICS*	310305
Charles JE	291191
Chick JA	211089
Chisholm ART *BEng (Hons) CEng MICE MInstRE*	010912
Cobbett G	010809
Copland EP	210712
Craig AG	010809
Curtis GM	300507
Davis PG *QVRM*	060606
Donnelly CT	160213
Douglas AS	241206
Down KH *TD*	010191
Dunford LJ	101114
Edmondson C *TD*	010603
Eytle MG	310708
Finch FR *IEng MIET MInstRE MBIFM*	010415
Fox GM	010810
Freemantle PR	011206
Godsall-Stanton PJM	300996
Gray PA	090209
Green AS *MBE MSC CEng MIMechE*	310707
Greenhalgh LC	010712
Grogutt E	010604
Hainge CM	270900
Hall D	230811
Hay LAW	231014
Hayhurst RA *BEng (Hons) MSc CEng MICE*	310709
Heffer MJ	010809
Helme PM	310705
Hemmens RE	010401
Heyes SM	010404
Holman JN *MA TD*	200606
Hudson DP	150812
Hughes KA	040213
Hutchinson SR	240804
James K *MBE JP*	010812
James MP	010409
Kehoe AG	121113
Kennedy RJ	200513
Keogh DP	300907
Lakey G	310708
Lavin GJ	010815

Leslie SA	241002
Lindow MP	010413
Lucas JD	010499
MacLeod JA	180996
Makinde DB *TD*	210909
Manning JG	201009
Martin DA	150506
McKnight PWE *BSc(Hons)*	150605
McLean AJ	010495
McNee M	010410
Mockridge NC	010810
Murray CF	010808
Myers DS	010500
Nathanail CP	010702
Nixon AP *MBE*	120214
Oldcorn DT	211010
Oliver MG	010203
Peden EA *TD*	211010
Pirozzolo MG	261197
Prescott AG	011107
Pugh MC	051196
Queen GT *TD CEng MIAgrE MICE MInstRE*	070100
Rae JAM *TD*	010405
Rawdon-Mogg AM	050714
Robinson D	010498
Roden PA	010601
Russell BM	020412
Sage JW	300988
Salmon PFE *TD*	150302
Shallcross ADM	310707
Short MTJ *MBE*	310705
Smith LM *TD*	300690
Smyth JD	061213
Steel G *BEng CEng MIMechE*	010513
Stewart JD	080502
Stewart ZE	010606
Turvey OG	010406
Webb LES *TD*	260698
White DA	121014
Wilcock CM *BSc (Hons) CEng MIStructE MICE*	260811
Willmott D	010108

Captains

Adams KW	250106
Affleck MP	060409
Archer NJ	140708
Barron SC	040212
Barton NP	010414
Bennett T	170413
Betts MA	170409
Bezdel SJ	181213
Bill DG	210210
Binns MW	171108
Bond AJ	250414
Bowes-Lyon AS	070114
Brocklebank ST	010908
Brown KR	070202
Bunting IA	100308
Burgess JSJ *BSc (Hons) BVSC MRCVS*	220707
Christmas LJ	010413
Chu A	011114
Clarke AS	210202
Clough ML	131208
Cook DJ	010411
Coulson CJ	190515
Courtnage MJ	210306
Cringle DP	190507
Crooks SC	010407
Cully DJ	010612
Douthwaite JP	161011
Drysdale S	311005
Dudley OS	101007
Dunn GA	050505
Dutton EJ	020412
Edmondson PK	140912
Fairlie ML	070912
Falconer RM	220813
Fitzpatrick MJ	260510
Franklin GS	070510
French RMT	161007
Gibson P	010901
Giles SP	190208
Goodwin AJ	300711
Goodwin BJ	191113
Goodwin CE	170112
Gough MH	100713
Graham C	040514
Green CW	220614
Gwilliam GRW	181096
Haagensen KM	150610
Hall PJ	141012
Hall SJ	020212
Hamilton AL	101007
Hammond IL	010908
Handley R *TD*	251098
Harvey CD	210614
Hassain JSH	061210
Heathcote JA	100511
Henshelwood RM	310311
Herd DG	251209
Hollas MR	080395
Hoyle RL	251106
Irving LD	130611
James IS *OBE*	051085
Jaxon N	010908
Jeffery TC	010803
Jones CI	240214
Judge CP	101011
Julian JEP *BA GCGI MCIPS EngTech MInst RE*	130208
Kennedy MRJ *QGM*	131214
Lake AJ	160113
Lamont PR	020408
Leach RA	310807
Loader K	010411
Machray RJ	170413
Manwaring AM	170613
Martell CE	300713
Martin-Bowtell G	220310
Mavin I	230108
Mitchell PC	010906
Morley P	170413
Mukhtar EA	110713
Neave MJ	010214
Nunn CC	130214
Olbrechts I	010411
Parks CI	011110
Pitts NC	110304
Pritchard MA	190914
Raeper NAJ	091114
Rigg PM	090215
Schioler T	070912
Sharp HJ	161007
Sharpe EJK	090905
Sleeman MA	190307
Smart AD	180709
Smedley HE	111010
Soliman N	120612
Solly JM	270811
Somodi JT	090211
Speight G	010704

Stevenson NR	011207
Sutcliffe IJF	141207
Taylor IP	071210
Theakstone TM	010407
Thomas LT	170413
Thompson F	010111
Thompson JC	010412
Thompson JW	080703
Thompson PA	140810
Thorpe AN	170608
Timmermann JP	181105
Tully NE	300606
Watson JGT	010907
Williams JG	290308
Wright PW	190914
Zalewski RG	040408

Lieutenants

Brew-Graves SH	260710
Clutterbuck RO	010415
Doocey PA	310308
Flight TJ	
Hanking-Evans GA	020506
Hine DC	210912
Jackman SI	010315
Jones LS	130114
Larcombe JR	011014
Lihou DO	261113
Loughrey M	180213
Lowe MS	290713
Mahony RA	010103
Paul CT	310711
Pearson MRH	021012
Potts SM	021012
Robertson SC	010812
Small LE	051213
Thorburn NMA	021013
Walker I	251012
Wilkins RW	140914
Williams G	010806
Wood DV	260711
Wynne-Roberts MC	120115

2nd Lieutenants

Appleby JA	010914
Arbuthnot KR	010814
Atkins CHE	290913
Borland MA	040813
Coates JA MEng MIET	061014
Dale CE	270914
Earl VJD	101212
Gardner CJ	031010
Gibson RDM	280908
Glass JA	150614
Hill AJ	270913
Hounsome DF	290912
Long S	310115
Mitchell DR	130413
Murphy JJ	061012
Ollerenshaw RJ	270713
Stubbs RV	160212
Trounce RB	270909
Truscott TD	010804

Officer Cadets

Antenbring BJ	010914
Ball JD	010611
Bolton BR	030913
Briggs PM	200910
Brown KNM	100914
Burchell RE	030913
Carle JA	240114
Coe JE	280812
Creedy JH	200910
Dalton SP	010914
Darney B	280812
Devine MS	010611
Drake CBR	010914
D'Souza JJ	280812
Easingwood BR	280812
Edgar CEM	040913
Emanuel B	030913
Frake MR	280812
Garrard MJD	010611
Gask J	280812
Gaskins-Rogers RW	030913
Graff AS	280812
Harris JFO	010914
Hobrough C	010914
Irving HD	040913
Jones AW	010611
Kavanagh GP	040913
Kenzie CF	290714
Kilsby KGS	030913
Madley JL	061113
Mangan MR	010611
Mcfadden CH	010914
Mcgeoch TM	010914
Moore GW	100914
Mortlock CA	140909
Nicholl WG	040913
Noble KB	030913
Nuttall EA	030913
Palfrey JK	280812
Patel PN	030913
Phillips-Mahon SA	040913
Rainford IR	280812
Robertshaw AJ	280812
Royle M	040913
Rushby TM	030913
Salisbury RJ	010914
Sapsford CJ	010914
Selka AWH	010611
Smith BC	280812
Solway JJ	010611
Spencer JM	010611
Stokes R	100914
Tizick A	040913
Tognarelli LMJ	280812
Twitchett KA	040913
West SL	030913
Wilkinson S	030913
Wilson JF	280812
Wilson LS	040913
Woodward SM	040913

Engineer and Logitistic Staff Corps (ELS)

Major

Duckworth SO *OBE DL*	011015

ROYAL CORPS OF SIGNALS

Regimental Headquarters: Griffin House, Blandford Camp, Blandford Forum, Dorset DT11 8RH
(Tel: 01258 482081 Mil: 94371 2081 Email: SOINC-DCOS-RHQ-RegtSec@mod.uk)

Honorary Colonels

32 Signal Regt AR	Col (Retd) A C C Lapsley *QVRM TD DL (until 180417)*	210708
	The Rt Hon Ruth E Davidson *MSP (from 180417)*	
37 Signal Regt AR	Maj Gen John Crackett *CB TD VR*	011111
39 Signal Regt AR	Mr William Varley Fell *CMG*	011215
71 Signal Regt AR	Col (Retd) S P Foakes *TD DL (until 010217)*	161012
	Col (Retd) Ray K Wilkinson *QVRM TD VR (from 010217)*	
63 (SAS) Signal Squadron AR	N/D	
81 Signal Sqn AR	Mr L W Stone *(until 010716)*	
	Mr Mark Hughes *(from 010716)*	
254 Signal Sqn AR	Brig (Retd) Roger A Hood *QVRM TD DL*	010117
Joint Service Signal Unit AR	ACM *Sir* Stuart Peach *KCB CBE ADC DL(RAF)*	081010
Colonel Commandant	Brig Hugh J Robertson *QVRM TD (AR)*	010515

Lieutenant Colonels

Bailey JD	010214
Barrass JA	211011
Bell K *MBE*	100910
Burgess SJ	150116
Cairns DS *QVRM TD*	160112
Chappell JA *MBA MSc*	010713
Connelly V	010213
Cosgrove M *MBE*	011211
Crilly AF	030406
Douglas DG	010308
Ellis JK	241014
Fraser-Brenchley MR *BA(Hons) MA TD*	180606
Haggerty BS *TD LLB (Hons) (Open)*	120814
Hellard SM *B Eng(Hons)*	010113
Kendall JR	010909
Lamb AT	100308
Lovett RJ	010613
Manley JI	010109
Mears AJ	050903
Oldfield AJ	170611
Picton JM	170113
Quinn AJ *TD*	011211
Rankin SWG	010615
Russell JA	011213
Sheriff VJ	060913
Smith MPN	041113
Smith SA	010709
Streete SL *MBE TD*	120905
Tremaine J	230914
Villiers P	221015
Walker NA *MSc sq ais*	040914
Walker SR	070408
Whitmore AC *BSc (Hons) ais MBCS FCMI*	300601

Majors

Ahern JP *TD*	011294
Allen M	120511
Atkinson MGP *TD*	080200
Baker MA *TD*	010895
Ballantyne A	010401
Barber GW	300900
Bertram L	010214
Bowden RJ *TD CMIOSH*	121098
Bowdler AP	090115
Bowes JB	011106
Browning JC *CEng MIET*	231014
Bumby SH	130114
Cahill MS	250413
Campbell AR	310707
Carr WK	010801
Cherry S	260913
Church AA	010409
Clout SH *TD*	010407
Cockburn AN *BSc (Hons) MBCS*	110610
Croager PM	260914
Curtis-Rouse MF	011010
Davidson IA *BSc MBA MCGI FIRM PMP*	150808
Dods DM *LLB Dip LP TD*	200204
Downing AL	130710
Erskine S	290615
Fensome JT	010507
Fernand LT	010811
Fitzpatrick RA	010908
Flanagan KM	120497
Fowler-Smith PH *TD*	130102
Francis KM	010410
Geddes JF *TD*	060292
Gordon D	010400
Grimwood RJ	300999
Hannan NK *BSc(Hons)*	121012
Harris JW	180912
Hawes AD	130909
Hilton JC	020896
Howe DM	010203
Hubbard JS	010807
Humphries KS	130209
Hunt SC	130904
Irvine DG	080715
Jephcote HM	280710
Jones PA	121012
Jones RM	080912
Keppler ADP	010413
Kerr KW *MCMI MCGI LCGI*	310710
Knight AG	010605
Lankester TJR *TD*	300998
Larkam DW	091090
Lenton RB *TD*	131098
Longcake MJ	270710
Lovett CLR	020608
Mason GR	020914
Mayell LM	200710
McBride SPG *TD*	030614

McCartney RD	260615
McClean JC	010493
McGiveron PJ	170807
McHenery SG	081111
McKenzie-Bell MS	010105
McNaught JG	111013
McVey T *QVRM*	010407
Mell PG	021112
Merrick D	010810
Metcalfe KL *TD*	010303
Mitcham PJ	011210
Montgomery CJ	010106
Morris AW	220213
Moseley CR *TD*	010407
Munson DG	010892
Nixon RG	111013
O'Neill KJ	261011
Orr AD	131013
Orr-Cooper SJ *TD*	010401
Osei-Agyemang S *MSc BSc CISM MBCS MIET*	021012
Palfrey RJ	240614
Palmer SP *TD*	011096
Parkes NG *TD*	050396
Paterson R	050711
Pearson JD *TD*	230902
Pemble MWA *BEng MIET FBCS FICAF CEng*	011106
Poulson JW	061113
Powell AJ	250205
Price KM	080414
Prince DA	160100
Pringle JE *MSc MIIA MBIM*	010803
Pun S	310509
Pyman JF *TD*	300894
Quincey CD	020614
Reid NP	010401
Richardson CL	010406
Rodenhurst PR	011106
Rogers PS	080109
Rowson SA	010105
Rustidge KS	010701
Ruthven WP	301205
Scott JD	071011
Smith PH	251195
Stammers R *BSc(Hons)*	110610
Stevenson G	250613
Stowell HE	121007
Titheridge DA *TD*	080101
Trevelion SL	090413
Turnbull M	130505
Ukpai PO	011013
Vardy DJ	110501
Ward TJ	100909
White AL	010906
Wilson DJH	300907
Woodroffe AJ *CEng BSc (Hons) MBCS CITP MINST*	010307
Wrate KV	010412
Wurr GR *BA Cert Ed*	030402

Captains

Allan RM	010211
Alleyne GDM	220811
Anderson RC	130810
Anderson RO	261006
Appleby L	180214
Armstrong KAG	130611
Ashton HM	010410
Barrie W	120309
Bartlett LM	060409
Baxter HL	180310
Blake CB *MSc BSc CFE CISSP CISM*	260104
Brindley CWH	241293
Brookes MP	070912
Brown JAG *BSc*	210709
Browne GD	211014
Brumfitt A	230408
Burki AK	171210
Cherry C	240310
Cheung DS	020710
Chisholm JC	011012
Coffey DJ *BSc MIET MCMI*	231110
Cooke SE	040213
Cooper KN	070113
Corrigan KS	090210
Crilly MS	190214
Cuff JA	140105
Davies-Walters K	080212
Dobson AD	080115
Donson G *MSc BA(Hons)*	201103
Dorrian-Clark BK	160911
Drennan AS	010303
Duff LJ	011212
Durtnal SJ	010409
Dyer HM	010810
Edmunds DF *TD*	090312
Evans HGP	220607
Fallon RM	041111
Farmer SA	120809
Fletcher DW	270315
Frame IA	010810
Freeman BD	071014
Gaffney MR	170114
Garner P	080407
Gaw GP *BSc MSc VR*	220704
Ghavalas B	200206
Gould E	250908
Green AJW	220614
Gurung R	280504
Hanna MD	010412
Harrison AS *MCIM*	180705
Hatton PJ *MBE*	190313
Hennis SC	131008
Hollins JME	160609
Holt EJ	310114
Hood RJ	091007
Hosseinian B	270315
Howell-Walmsley CH	151002
Hunsdale JP	240611
Hunter B	220613
Hunter NL *BSc IEng MIET*	200206
Jelfs CR	071105
Johnson LL	130810
Jones LGA	031212
Jordan LA	150714
Kinnoch JS	170714
Kitson JA	161007
Knight PA	310301
Kong CA	261012
Lawrie HL	010909
Leonards MJ	021213
Lithgow SM	060212
Lynn SRH	011113
Mackay I	010613
Manickavasagan R	310507
Masters DJ	020710
McGowan IL	040712
McIntyre DM	250611
Mee KH	010410
Milford TW *BA (Music) LRSM LLCM*	310305
Milligan CE	180310

Mitchell PG	220612
Monk DR	020611
Moran AM	010407
Morrissey TG *MBE*	270106
Neill NJ	010206
Nevill VA	160412
Noakes TM	221200
North OR *BSc(Hons) MIEE*	200206
O'Regan VJ	200913
Oxley MJ	010412
Pearson JJ	170914
Pearson OW	050811
Peskett CS *MBCS CITP*	201106
Peters AR	160412
Poussa M	031012
Puddicombe ER	310115
Pun U	210901
Reeves J *BSc (Hons) PgDip MIET MCMI MCGI*	160614
Rigby DJV	050312
Roberts T	210613
Roy H	040106
Rutherford R	210503
Saunders AEJ	160203
Saunders DM	160212
Settle A	010303
Sewell L	101005
Sharman AM	261010
Sherchan R	120706
Shipp TW	031212
Singers BM	230108
Smith GC	011004
Smith RH	010412
Stanhope MA	140105
Stokes J	020710
Stubley DJ	180705
Summers MP	200312
Taffs AJ	120315
Topps GJ	090414
Tucker CS	110512
Turner AJ	
Vince AW	230115
Ward MA	010407
Washbrook AL	010711
Webb S	290710
Whiteley PC	100706
Whitmore WL *BSc(Hons)*	260914
Wire AM	240611
Wood JR	160914
Wood KM *BSc(Hons)*	010202
Wyatt AJ	220811
Young AK	060307

Lieutenants

Allen JJ	300707
Bolt HA	270710
Buckingham DM	210915
Carter DS	011201
Davis CR	300913
Fulton SL	011005
Gostling JWJ	010812
Jolley MA	030409
Mitchell SI	290506
Morris AJA	280715
Perkins EW	150114
Skidmore HM	260914

2nd Lieutenants

Atkinson CE	010814
Jell A	050814
Levison SF *BA(Hons)*	130313
MacDonald DM	021011
MacInnes NI	290914
McHardy G	130514
Osment MA	030813
Pickett LC	151012

Officer Cadets

Allen CJM	200910
Auden MT	010611
Banfield GW	030913
Bartlett AG	010914
Batts SE	010611
Bodger SJ	140909
Body J	030913
Bridgman HJ	010914
Brown LEB	010914
Carpenter LM	010914
Close NA	030913
Cripps JR	010611
Cubbin HSJ	030913
Daulby TS	010914
Dickson L	010914
Doyle HM	280812
Drew SP	010914
Drummond-Hay EJ	280812
Elford DJ	010914
Fox LJ	280812
Griffiths SN	010611
Hathway ND	280812
Heath AJN	030913
Hoban DJ	010914
Holdsworth CE	010611
Horswill E	010611
Horvath JB	280812
Ironmonger EL	051011
Jones I	030913
Kirkpatrick LD	140909
Mangham PC	030913
Marsden H	010914
Narey PE	010611
Parker OJ	030913
Parkinson BS	030913
Pickles CE	010611
Piercy WT	280812
Potts AI	010914
Potts MTJ	280812
Sayers RE	030913
Taylor BM	010914
Taylor SJ	030913
Thomas RSC	030913
Trippier JL	280812
Wallis JA	100914
Walsha MJ	020711
White DP	280812
Wilkinson MJ	280812
Williams JS	030913
Wilson HJ	030913
Yates WAG	030913

THE SCOTTISH DIVISION

52nd LOWLAND REGIMENT
6th (AR) BATTALION, ROYAL REGIMENT OF SCOTLAND

Upon a Saltire, a Thistle within a circlet inscribed NEMO ME IMPUNE LACESSIT

Regimental Headquarters: Walcheren Barracks, 122 Hotspur Street, Glasgow G20 8LQ

Regimental March

Quick March .... Scotland the Brave

Honorary Colonel .... Brig Charlie A Coull *ADC* 010116

51st HIGHLAND REGIMENT
7th (AR) BATTALION, ROYAL REGIMENT OF SCOTLAND

Regimental Headquarters: Queen's Barracks, 131 Dunke1d Road, Perth PHI 5BT

Honorary Colonel .... Brig (Retd) *The Hon* Hughie B H E Monro *CBE* 220914

Lieutenant Colonels

Campbell J	300605
Carroll PJ	310508
Chelsea ECT	010807
Davies CMM *MBE TD*	011208
Davies R	011215
Doyle R	160703
McElhinney JR	011114
Stimpson DG	040711

Majors

Allan JMT	100604
Anderson JL *TD*	160201
Anderson JR	051113
Austin WJ	281197
Barker RJ	100605
Bristow JDM	300102
Bunce IM	240715
Cameron AM	230108
Cameron RN	130215
Campbell AI	110511
Cockerill H *TD*	150906
Crosbie PWA	031114
Davidson JM *TD*	280994
Donald J	161111
Edwards MA	310502
Fairrie AH	100301
Greening PEK	010110
Henderson JB *MBE*	040810
Hendry-Adams IA	280409
Howard MJ	210703
Jackson JA	011113
Langdale JSL	010805
Lee WG *QVRM TD*	270295
MacLean-Bristol CB	011000
MacLellan JC *TD sq(v) MCIBS Dip CRM*	050201
Maxwell JG *TD*	040789
McInally A	110708
McLeod G *MBE TD*	010888
McSorley D	080904
Milroy CJA *TD*	010190
Ogilvie MP	010602
Ord NE	160805
Orr IA *MBE*	101293
Reilly JA	010310
Rorie PA	050902
Rose A	010714
Sheldon JCP	010714
Sutherland KG *TD*	010403
Tait KM	210997
Vicca MJ *TD MA (Hons) GCGI MCMI*	211002
Williams AM	120100

Captains

Bracher JR	130611
Burnett GAF	290413
Cannon HDC	011209
Doughty RCW	281014
Fisher DJ *DipSP&C MCMI*	051209
Greene KRP	120203
Harley SD	310101
Hayler BV	101210
Hume KA	010900
Keen AW	010509
Knox A	080204
MacDonald MM *TD*	011203
MacLeod CI	120811
Marginson WD	151206
McIntosh G	010407
McNally MJ	220711
Menzies SR	190906
Ross IWG	020408
Scott KA	010215
Stevens M	120412
Stewart AW	090510
Stuart MRH	010315
Syfret ER	050714
Telfer KD	230108
Valentine JA	010811
Wallace AW	010810
Wheatley NA	200205

Lieutenants		*2nd Lieutenants*	
Durrant BTG	031012	Anderson BJ	160114
Forrester MR	011013	Bisset AJ	270913
Mill GAN	280708	Daley AD	040813
Thornton MJ	290913	Nicol KJ	270909
Walker RA		Orr MR	270913
Weir MD	300913		

THE GUARD'S DIVISION

THE LONDON REGIMENT

HQ Company Battersea, The London Regiment, 27 St John's Hill, Battersea, London SWII ITT
(Tel: 020 7801 2519 Fax: 020 7801 2544 Email: LondonsROSWO@mod.uk)

Honorary Colonel .... *HRH The Earl of* Wessex *KG GCVO ADC(P)* 010511

Deputy Honorary Colonels .... Col David K Mogg *TD* 011113
Brig Alastair B R Bruce of Crionaich *OBE ADC DL* 011014
Col Nigel P Easton *QVRM TD* 010705
Maj Gen (Retd) *Sir* Sebastian Roberts *KCVO OBE* 010712

Regimental Lieutenant Colonel .... Col Marc A J M Overton *TD* 010515
Honorary Regimental Colonel .... *The Rt Hon Lord* Robertson of Port Ellen *KT GCMG PC*
(A Company (London Scottish)) 011200

Lieutenant Colonels

Carter DL	161115
Clements RMS *TD MSc*	010715
Griffin MSJ *TD*	011111
Hill RJ	011112
Ludlow MWH	011205
Smart TA	160513
Torbica M *MBE TD*	081212

Majors

Black RL	091000
Bowman JR	240913
Buchanan IAB	070209
Celm R	230408
Cheese LA	010912
Durcan JDM	030614
Green CDS	031212
Lincoln PM	230405
Lundy SMP	310703
McEwing JG	141298
Morgan GM	180598
Newell CE	180407
Rankin-Hunt D *LVO MBE TD*	150789
Storey NJ	140114
Strickland GMH	030610
Swanston JC	010611
Swayne JAC	260110
Wirgman RR	140199

Captains

Balfour PAP	030606
Barklem JR	130713
Brown RA	150501
Coulton DT	281109
Craster HM	010713
Denman RM	071210
D'Inverno JM	011112
Elms JL	150205
Gilmore CMB	100312
Hill RA	300806
Insall NHS	190614
Jacobs B	270609
Jones MR	250513
Lewis AP	271113
Miller JH	041104
Paul EC	050312
Percival C *TD*	191005
Price RJ	200708
Weston PJ	130411
Wickman AP	090209

Lieutenants

Allchurch MNS	130307
Croft TA	090612
Markeson OJ	310312

2nd Lieutenants

Biety-Eggert CMJ	030813
Burns ARCP	040813
Butler M	210114
Clarke WD	030813
Rose HA	161010
Scarsbrook KJ	270713

THE QUEEN'S DIVISION

3rd BATTALION
THE PRINCESS OF WALES'S ROYAL REGIMENT

Regimental Headquarters: Leros TA Centre, Sturry Road, Canterbury, Kent CTI IHR

Honorary Colonel ....Mr John Gordon Cluff *DL* 010510

Lieutenant Colonels

Cocker AJ	011214
Ladd JAP *TD*	011108
Neame MQ *TD*	010203
Windmill SM	010301

Majors

Butlin MJ *TD*	010408
Craig JP	130199
Dwyer BJ	070710
Francke GR	310705
Hall IL	020212
Harris AK	190309
Hurman MJ	090890
Kemp ID	030191
Laws JM	270914
Long G *MBE*	051110
MacAlpine-Downie CR *TD*	010405
Mott RO	310706
Peckham NM	030512
Redfern JA	190291
Reynolds JK	310797
Sparks JR *TD*	110308
Stanley SJ	221108
Sutton B	010213
Sutton NC	210103

Captains

Ardley S	261004
Barker SA *BSc(Hons) MSc (Oxon)*	160113
Barker TJ	260507
Chalk AM	060114
Cottrell PA	260390
Cuthbertson EC	130606
Douglas NA	080809
Fieldsend LD	140708
Keers AJ	010799
Lewis DPM *BA(Hons) PGCE*	030911
Reed DC	061113
Richmond D	260411
Scott RF	130711
Slegg JG	220212
Stroud C	160806
Titchener JA	250108
Walsh GSA	120811

Lieutenants

Bayley RM *BSc(Hons) MIET*	240312
Bowdidge CL	280714
Boxall BL	040111
Laybourne RJ	310712
Rogers CP	250711
Sodhi MS	290309

2nd Lieutenants

Barry H	111013
McGeoghan JA	270914
Yardy LD	270713

3rd BATTALION
THE ROYAL ANGLIAN REGIMENT

Regimental Headquarters: The Keep, Gibraltar Barracks, BURY ST EDMUNDS, Suffolk IP33 3RN
(Tel: 01284 752394 Fax: 01284 752026 Email: RHQRANGLIAN-ChfClk@mod.uk)

Honorary Colonel.................................. Maj Gen (Retd) Simon L Porter *CBE*..................................051014

Lieutenant Colonels

Spiers KE	160913
Sutherland NJ	220413

Majors

Bevin MJ	010908
Chilvers P	121102
Coulson AJW	150810
Dickson AG	051110
Irwin-Parker TJ	010608
Rushmere GJ	010412
Scott LJC	010908
Shaw GB	140999
Swallow CW *MBE*	310708
Tuke RSP	010408
Tusa JHA *TD*	010597

Captains

Brazier MD	270407
Cay P	260214
Davies AS	090908
Dunn JJ	110614
Finbow CE	010212
Fowler RJ	290608
Granell JR	040214
Hale SC *MBE*	310309
Hart MV	050312
Horner AJ	011108
Hudson PCH	010108
Little RAB	210510
MacLeod H	280514
Matts EA	300910
Purse RW	171214
Speechley AG	280514
Swift AG	140608
Thomas GR	160311
Waterfield GH	170115

Lieutenants

Davies NS	280514

2nd Lieutenants

Forsyth KA	290913
Strain AEN	270713

5th BATTALION
ROYAL REGIMENT OF FUSILIERS

Regimental Headquarters: HM Tower of London, Tower Hill, London EC3N 4AB
(Tel: 0203 166 6909 Fax: 0203 166 6920 Email: INFHQ-QUEENS-RRF-RegtSecAsst@mod.uk)

Honorary Colonel .... *Lord* James William Eustace Percy 010810

Lieutenant Colonels

Banks IC *TD*	011207
McDermott RP	280209

Majors

Blaney P	071011
Coatsworth SJ	310701
Crook KN	260614
Fairbairn SR	170704
Ferguson GRW *FPWI MRIN*	230890
Hill MG *TD*	010805
Hunter JH	010706
McGuire I	060512
Murphy GA	310706

Captains

Evans CJ	240214
Hall CJ	180100
Jones GB	010499
Lodge DP	080908
Marcon JR	270113
Richardson PM	130814
Smith DE	281113

2nd Lieutenants

Aynsley-Smyth DF	280913
Charlesworth WAJ	030813

Officer Cadets

Davison C	020313

THE KING'S DIVISION

4th BATTALION, THE DUKE OF LANCASTER'S REGIMENT

Regimental Headquarters: Kimberley Barracks, Deepdale Road, Preston PR1 6QB

Honorary Colonel ....Mr M J (Jeremy) Gorick *DL* 151013

Lieutenant Colonels

Hughes RG *QVRM TD*	081006
Lighten JG	160911

Majors

Bartlett GJP	010902
Bridge MR *TD*	010502
Cook DJ	121113
Davies P	010714
Derby AJ	091104
English RM *TD*	151193
Hayes PK	010407
Keighley MH	210408
Kennon NT	241011
Lydiate MS	110714
Quegan PE *QVRM TD*	010999
Sinclair RD	010413
Smethurst CR *MSc Chartered MCIPD*	080689
Thornton AJ	011010
Turner AJ	130796
Turner GS *BA(Hons)*	110714
Williamson JG *TD*	050396
Wright GR	300988

Captains

Banks GT	220607
Bowden-Williams MK	080414
Cashen JA	010407
Fearnley GL	010911
Haldenby P	010609
Holsgrove AJS	010812
McMinn A	010407
Moor TEA	020713
Oakes RA *MC*	070202
O'Brien CJ	190114
Smirthwaite JN	011012

Lieutenants

Nutter SM	260214
Seddon MWR	080413
Yiannakis NVC	260506

4th BATTALION, THE YORKSHIRE REGIMENT

Regimental Headquarters: Worsley Barracks, Fulford Road, York, YO10 4EB
(Tel: 01904 668062 Email: 4yorks-bhq-2ic@mod.uk)

Honorary Colonel .... Col (Retd) George A Kilburn *MBE*..010614

Lieutenant Colonels

Davies PA *TD*	010208
Moss S	021013
Scott CMG *MBA MIoD*	010600
Yates M	180814

Majors

Albon K	010902
Allen AH	041013
Atkinson RG *TD*	171099
Barker JRL	011105
Cooper AR	130207
Cripps RG	311009
Dodd JR	090307
Hindmarch SP	071011
Hoggarth PA *TD*	010801
Howard CE *TD*	010406
Hunt JM	260911
Hunter MK *TD*	010902
Hutchinson KG	160509
Radford AM *TD*	020395
Schofield DM	120714
Sneyd IR	121013
Watson MR *TD*	010404

Captains

Barton PB	010106
Baxter DW	011111
Clegg GE	030300
Dawson PN	021211
Donaldson PJ	020412
Hall MP	150710
Johnson SA	021211
Jones S	200509
Nancolas AS	171205
Sinnott MS	010413
Thompson D	150710

Lieutenants

Kerr R	240914
Sage-Passant L	021011
Willey DJ	131109

2nd Lieutenants

Cottrill TP	270713
Dower SJ	270713
Shine D	121011
Shuttlewood CB	141012
Taylor FC	260915
Vachha DA	040813

THE PRINCE OF WALES'S DIVISION

4th BATTALION, MERCIAN REGIMENT

Regimental Headquarters: The Mercian Regiment, Heath Avenue, Lichfield, Staffordshire WS14 9TJ
(Tel: 01453 434390 Email: RHQMERCIAN-AOWelfare@mod.uk)

Honorary Colonel ....Brig Simon M J Bell *QVRM TD*..010612

Lieutenant Colonels	
Clare P	301115
Mulholland LM	011015
Turner NH	010899
Walkley PJ	080907
Yardley IJL	010905

Majors	
Anning SP	310710
Barnbrook RSJ *MCGI*	310703
Bond IA	130713
Brothwood PJ	210999
Bullard PJC	020403
Carpenter-Balmer TRA	071011
Clarke NL	151092
Collie MD *TD BA(Hons)*	010698
Comery AP	120714
Cooper AP	310702
Crowe GJ	300900
Green JE	310706
Johnson PJ *QVRM*	010312
Longley-Brown GJH	211195
Owen PFR	081008
Purslow PW	281199
Richardson J	090104
Rusby MR *OBE*	101288
Seager APH	040706
Wadland AJA	150602
Watters CR	140110
Yardley AJG	080101

Captains	
Atherton DL	171213
Cupples ST	181213
Elms JB *MBE*	020409
Forbes MVO	220812
Heath N	290904
Jones RH	010906
Karim PD	010909
Koniarski KM	160609
Lam JKM	310108
Reeves CB	181109
Rossiter DA	010410
Storey C	160609
Watts LP *BA*	111114
Whittle RI	111114
Wibberley CR	140998
Wignall AJ	010810
Young FE	030308

Lieutenants	
Cornell PW *LLB*	260911
Dean JA	071008
Highet PD	010414
Jones MA	290914
Rawji DJ	310712

2nd Lieutenants	
Fadipe CO	010811
Moulding SL	270713
Needham CJ	280713
Sansom SJ	170613

3rd BATTALION THE ROYAL WELSH

Regimental Headquarters: Maindy Barracks, Cardiff CF14 3YE
(Tel: 029 20781202 Fax: 029 20641281
Email: RHQRWELSH-RegtlSec@mod.uk / RHQRWELSH-AsstRegtlSec1@mod.uk)

Honorary Colonel .... Brig (Retd) Russ N Wardle *OBE* 050714

Lieutenant Colonels

Norrington-Davies PJ *psc*	250299

Majors

Buckley JW *TD*	241101
Burton D	121007
Daniels P *MBE*	270313
Evans DL	270313
Gay NS	010794
Gumm IR *TD*	291002
Hills SMA	040213
Howells G	311090
Hughes SMM	300989
Hurst J	010208
Johnson RD	310705
Jones AR	010306
Laing MA	300999
Mann NG *TD*	011095
Moses JC	070304
Powell MS	080804
Ray PA	010208
Thomas JA *TD*	020589
Williams DA *TD*	010999

Captains

Evans MR	010710
Greaney CN	020409
Hartwell A	280111
Hudson B	010309
Hughes GR	280115
Hughes ME	010413
Jones MG	010308
Pascoe DM	090200
Rickard RJ	010202
Russell JAA	091003
Steele JE	310312
Williams D	010808

Lieutenants

Butcher GA	300908
Fisher-Jones JD	011111
Priddy D	260711

2nd Lieutenants

Bacon WJ	121013
Bowles-Farthing SR	061012
Edwards G	270914
Harris JM	010311

6th/7th BATTALIONS THE ROYAL RIFLES

6th Battalion HQ: Wyvern Barracks, Exeter, Devon EX2 6AR
(Tel: 01392 492 510)

7th Battalion HQ: Brock Barracks, Oxford Road, Reading, Berks RG30 1HW
(Tel: 0118 953 0239 Email 7RIFLES-ROSO@mod.uk)

Royal Colonel, 6th Battalion.................. *HRH The Duke of* Gloucester *KG GCVO*
Royal Colonel, 7th Battalion.................. *HRH The Duchess of* Gloucester *GCVO*

Deputy Colonels....................................Col Simon C Chapman *TD (AR)*..010614

RIFLES

Lieutenant Colonels

Cummings JR	010707
Gaskin PH	010712
Gordon CDS	010812
Greenwood HJ	011205
Griffin DR	010404
Harper TJ	011208
Malloch JC	250110
Maxwell-Batten DM	010115
Skliros JM *TD*	010211
Wilkinson SE *TD*	011005

Majors

Ainsworth PHP	010597
Ayling KS *TD*	030896
Blackburn KF *TD*	010697
Baker HJ *TD*	010704
Baker JM	080612
Bartlett SW *QVRM TD*	010714
Blake MP	100806
Blanchard GKG *TD*	291094
Bolton JA	010812
Broderstad ERC	190302
Bull PH	010814
Clark PR	310702
Conroy WF *TD*	021286
Coulon MD	220690
Davis LB	270711
Dicks MJ	151208
Eldridge JW	101210
Evans JA	230615
Fitter AJ	150411
Freer SJ	010709
Fyfe AAJ	101210
Gill MP	091007
Gomes LL	221110
Harrison RDF	030603
Hayward-Smith SP	270711
Higgins DN	061213
Hrycak MJ	230615
Inglis-Jones JA	010105
Jeffries DS	010512
Ladds RWE	010402
Laverick MA	051110
Lloyd MJ	010604
Long RLH *TD*	071093
Lowe SFW *TD*	230405
Lupton RA	010105
Martin TB	201112
McCullough RJ	120312
McMillan RG	200114
Milner KG	010191
Nicholls JM	310707
Penhale JP	260905
Peniston-Bird TB	280111
Perriton NAJ	010615
Prudent AL	280908
Quertier J	011206
Ridge C *TD*	260403
Roberts AJE	120211
Roberts AM *TD*	010205
Roberts BLG	310703
Robson WH	240205
Rock RM	141201
Ryan P	
Saunders TJJ *MBE*	301090
Shackleton JF	010506
Sharpe WM	210702
Smith TR	070813
Smyth PR *MBE*	010410
Spalton RJ	310707
Stewart RJ	141011
Sturrock CGF	010198
Sutherland AG *TD*	160312
Sykes CR	290710
Watson MP	181010
Weatherley IR	280908
Willis CJ *MBE*	050498
Wilson-Hutton-Stott TH	010710
Wort JC *TD*	241190

Captains

Bevan OA	190909
Black AD	010807
Clare BJ	170709
Ellis MM	260812
Ellwood TM	281109
Featherstone MD *BScEcon(Hons)*	080212
Firth BJ	290109
Flexman JBJ	191213
Freeman TG	140308
Holgate ST	091007
Hood TJ	220208
Hope PA	150510
Horsman N	271107
Howard NDM	
Kaye GT	220111
Ledger AP	051298
Lippiett OJW	140511
Longman S	030407
Morris PC	010410
Neads AS	051114
Nichols J	170511
Pascoe WJA	230414
Phipps AW	010698
Pooley AT	230414
Price RJ	150409
Ryder JC	250209
Sainsbury DM	111207

Salisbury DM	030407
Salisbury M	310706
Sanandres O	010414
Santer JM	110911
Sladden RJ	010909
Stevenson DG	241012
Tarry KGJ	010112
Taylor NS	010112
Timmermann TP	260807
Towers RT	110314
Vandaele-Kennedy RA	200998
Vannerley SEV	101210
Warren SD	200804
Watmore SP	140412
Willing EJD	170509
Woods DW	131008

Lieutenants

Ahluwalia R	300914
Banfield AJ	091113
Bowdidge LMP	031012
Cowap T D	041211
Franklin PD	161013
Godwin WB	010806
Marson AL	130214
Peckham JB	310312
Start PC	200112
Stuart M	120215

2nd Lieutenants

Burns AJ	121013
Kent MJ	300912
Ogden TJ	030813
Slack TR	280913
Smith IJ	021114
Tin GN	090910

Officer Cadet

Braycotton DT	020713

RIFLE VOL

Lieutenant Colonel

Evans TG	010707

Major

Allen TH	010402

Captains

Freeman DJ	120212
Pigot GDH	070114
Seefeldt SA	110510

2nd BATTALION ROYAL IRISH REGIMENT

(Formerly The Royal Irish Rangers (AR))

Company and Battalion HQ: 147 Charles Street, Portadown, PORTADOWN, Co Armagh, BT62 4BD
(Tel: 028 9226 0042 or 028 9226 0043 Email: 2RIRISH-BHQ-RRMT-OC@mod.uk)

Honorary Colonel..................................Col Hubert K McAllister *OBE TD*..010614

Lieutenant Colonels

Agnew RWR	011010
Cassells SM *MBE QVRM*	010216
Hudson M	200513
Middleton DG	300612

Majors

Anderson KM	120704
Baillie P	170892
Baxter SCR	010710
Bland JRC	310707
Campbell R	030705
Given LWG	160307
Gray CD	300998
Hanna DG	010799
Harbison AS	310706
Hetherington S	010397
Johnston TA	030803
Johnston WG	010707
Johnstone DA	010406
Latus GR	010713
Lawther RS	101096
Livingstone MW	140599
Mahood GR	010412
McFarland TG	011004
McGrory SM *BA (Hons) MA MA MBA psc(j)*	010799
Middlemas T	090104
Nickels WT	011112
Rea EJW *BSc(Hons)*	140514
Shilliday MA *TD*	310802
Stevenson P	010996
Strain GL	011208

Captains

Anthony DJ	130611
Campbell CC	110510
Gaspar ASL	180613
Graham RD *BSc (Hons)*	010305
Jenkins SW	010108
Knox JNT	040414
Mackean SCR *BSc*	160590
McQuitty I	300412
Monteith AR	010108
Morrow JJ	010305
O'Callaghan BP	010609
Turner CHM	010210
Waller G	010407
Young JS	010305

Lieutenants

Abbott SR	031011
Baker MA	101212
Cahoon J	270909
Edwards AS	140510
James SM *BSc (Hons)*	230907
Scott RT	260404

2nd Lieutenants

Beattie SMP	020814
Colwell CJ	270914
Glass CT	020814
Maybin SI	020814
Richmond NJW	270914
Smyth J	270714

4th BATTALION THE PARACHUTE REGIMENT

Regimental Headquarters: Merville Barracks, Circular Road South, Colchester, Essex. CO2 7UT
(Tel: 01206 817082 Email: secretary.pra@btconnect.com)

HQ Company .... Leeds (Battalion HQ), Thornbury Barracks, Pudsey, Leeds LS28 8HH
A Company (Scotland)........................... Glasgow (Finnieston), Edinburgh (Lanark Road)
B Company (Southern England)............ Central London (White City), Croydon (Mitcham Road)
C Company (Northern England)............ Leeds (Pudsey), Liverpool (St Hellens), Newcastle Upon Tyne (Heburn)
D Company (Midlands) .... Nottingham, Rugby

Honorary Colonel.................................. Lt Col (Retd) John D Handford *OBE* 300915
Commanding Officer............................. Lt Col G Timms *MC* 2013

Lieutenant Colonels		*Captains*		*2nd Lieutenants*	
Evason PC *MBE TD*	010401	Carr C	110314	Gilbert M	210613
French HG *TD*	310305	Dieppe JF	260913	Gleizes LR	300907
Jordan WM *TD*	020407	Dunn CF	230309	Jones TH	080411
MacAulay DA	300309	Edwards SMR	011212	Loasby AC	021011
Southall DTL	010811	Ford GJ	050514	Wilson AJK	290912
		Harper DE	221114	Wood CA	290912
Majors		Hurrell MS	100308		
Brown RH	310396	Krause-Harder Calthorpe DL	121210		
Crowther NM	101009	Lamming SD *QVRM*	091007		
Greatrex JH	120714	Patton JT	230309		
Humphrey PRM	010799	Phillips SM	011001		
Lord DJ	011006	Pratt B	010413		
Merrylees JW *TD*	010600	Rowell AWF	160412		
Newcombe S	170407	Sergeant AJ	011212		
Nicholls RJ	010705	Stewart AW	230309		
Spandler MJ	310713	Tovey JS *MBE*	241107		
Sweeney RA	231014	Williams ST	150212		
Turner CE	290714	Wilson IS	170609		
Wilson RPP	030609	Wood LJ	130406		
Winter GQ	281010				

INFANTRY

(OFFICERS NOT LISTED ELSEWHERE)

Coldstream Guards

Major

Webber WB	300900

Grenadier Guards

Captains

Nicholas DMN	101208

Scots Guards

Captains

Milligan IF	121113

Welsh Guards

Captains

Plewa AJ *MBE*	090405

Royal Gurkha Rifles

Captains

Gurung D	090115

General List

Majors

Poe AD	010493

Captains

Smith OI	010410

2nd Lieutenants

McIntosh CJ	020814

Officer Cadet

Tait RLG	121014

ARMY AIR CORPS

Regimental Headquarters: Middle Wallop, Stockbridge, Hants, SO20 8DY
(Tel: 01264 784 514 Email: AACHQ-RHQ-AsstRegtSec@mod.uk)

6 REGIMENT ARMY AIR CORPS

675 Sqn AAC.. Taunton and Yeovil
677 Sqn AAC.. Bury St Edmunds, Norwich and Ipswich
678 Sqn AAC.. Milton Keynes and Luton
679 Sqn AAC.. Portsmouth and Middle Wallop

Honorary Colonel.................................. Lt Col *The Viscount* Edward C Chelsea *DL*..040116

Lieutenant Colonels	
Butler CLS	300607
Coburn MA	200314
Newcourt AFM	011009
Majors	
Barbone AW *MBE*	300992
Baxter MR	021095
Bennett W	230510
Dean PJ	150914
Ferraro JA	010212
Gell DA	081006
Humphreys B *MBE*	240414
Johnston DD	130603
Kitson PS	120314
Le Gresley EM	010809
Manzur AW *cfs*	300514
McDonnell JMP	010414
McGee DR	010414
Milnes JAJ	251114
Nettleton PTJ	190914
Peake TN	010705
Pillai GDE	210103
Reynolds SA *BSc(Hons)*	120405
Ridgley GC	010910
Roberts MSE	240614
Stott IJ	010414
Tench NF	170414
Terry MC	300993
Webber J	120312
Wharmby NC	300900
Captains	
Archer AK	060114
Barnes AD	010506
Bartle PP *MSM MCGI*	081014
Brennan MJ	080304
Bull KJ *MPhys (Oxon) MRAeS*	250914
Cameron IA	030307
Clements JS	150405
Dundas R	170706
Firth PM	130214
Gerskowitch CJ	060214
Hallas CS *MBE*	010414
Holden RE	240377
Jones T	010804
Mayhead JN	090914
McLeman KE	191009
Merrett JPD	150414
Peacock G	011009
Thompson JQW	310712
Wilkinson PR	141114
Lieutenants	
Constable TS	260411
Saha NP	121112
2nd Lieutenants	
Cognolato D	280913

ROYAL ARMY CHAPLAINS' DEPARTMENT

Army Headquarters | MOD CHAPS (A), 2nd Floor, Zone 1, IDL 433, Ramillies Building, Marlborough Lines, Monxton Road, Andover SP11 8HJ (Tel: 01264 381865 Email: ArmyCG-StaffChapSO2@mod.uk)

Chaplains to the Forces (2nd Class ranking as Lieutenant Colonels)

Robertshaw JS *Rev* 011214
Sutton JJE *Rev QVRM TD* 200814
Winfield FJL *Rev* 051015

Chaplains to the Forces (3rd Class ranking as Majors)

Adams RR *Rev BD Hons Dip PS CCRS CF* 011010
Banbury DP *Rev* 280610
Blackwood KT Rev 091115
Blakey SA *Rev* 310883
Blewett TJ *Rev* 190601
Butler CS *Rev MBE* 150215
Chester M *Rev* 250895
Cobain AR *Rev* 140114
Ewbank MR *Rev* 210109
Fieldhouse Byrne G *Rev* 131112
Freeman KF *Rev* 170600
Gamble IR *Rev MBE* 070206
Gorringe EGA *TD CE Rev* 020315
Grafton RP *Rev* 210812
Graham TKD *Rev BSc (Hons) BTh OblSB* 011210
Hall RJ *Rev MBE CF* 070108
Hope CH *Rev* 031101
Hopkins P *Rev* 010715
Hull DA *Rev* 080915
Jennings JP *Rev* 151099
Kinsey L *Rev QVRM TD* 050298
Livingstone R *Rev* 240510
Lynch FJ *Rev* 200611
MacDonald RIT *Rev* 170215
Nelson JF *Rev* 060796
Newman JEM *Rev* 120110
Patterson PW *Rev* 060812
Powell SW *Rev* 141215
Pyke BJ *Rev* 141015
Richardson LL *Rev* 171207
Rowe C *Rev* 220914
Rowlands MH *Rev* 220405
Rowlands SD *Rev* 130211
Sanders RD *Rev* 090714
Spain M *Rev* 250116
Turnbull PF *Rev* 301115
Van Den Bergh VM *Rev* 080511
Whalley JP *Rev* 210108
White AJ *Rev* 280915
Whitehead PC *Rev* 081101

Chaplains to the Forces (4th Class ranking as Captains)

Aagaard AR *Rev* 180615
Bezerra Speeks MW *Rev* 170510
Birch GJ *Rev BTEC HND BA (Hons)* 080713
Birchnall TR *Rev* 250515
Donald ME *Rev* 101212
Durbin J Rev 011215
Edwards SD Rev 120115
Flowers TA *Rev* 010914
Game AJ *Rev* 010615
Haviland AMJ *Rev* 170915
Hill DR *Rev* 270709
Hitchiner EA *Rev* 120115
Hullyer P *Rev MA FRSA* 300812
Jepson J *Rev BA (Hons) MA* 260813
Johnstone MW *Rev* 130214
Jones JG *Rev* 130715
Kinch CD *Rev* 160810
Lowe JD *Rev DIP TH ACII CF* 090712
Lowe SJ *Rev* 060715
Norton BJ *Rev MTh BTh (Hons) Dip MA* 080713
O'Hagan SM *Rev* 200415
Reilly DMJ *Rev* 200712
Robinson PA *Rev MBA PgDip HND* 080713
Smith CD *Rev* 110415
Stone PJM *Rev* 230614
Trundle C *Rev* 140214
Wadsworth JA *Rev* 030815
Watson RJ *Rev* 070415
Wheelhouse BC *Rev* 261110
Wilson D *Rev* 011215

ARMY CADET FORCE ADULT VOLUNTEERS

Chaplains to the Forces (3rd Class ranking as Majors)

Bearn HH *Rev* 010606
Broddle CST *Rev* 121114
Bryson TM *Rev* 010612
Coe MJC *Rev* 131009
Howitt IR *Rev* 010615
Hurd AJ *Rev* 011214
Kerr P *Rev* 010711
Knights Johnson NA *Rev* 101212
Pell C *Rev* 280514
Stewart FMC *Rev* 101108
Williams N *Rev* 290310

Chaplains to the Forces (4th Class ranking as Captains)

Beer KL *Rev* 180714
Begg RJ *Rev MA(Hons) BD(Hons)* 301013
Bloor A *Rev* 270614
Boyd SA *Rev* 220210
Carmichael TA *Rev* 180714
Cloake DM *Rev* 261110
Deehan DJ *Rev* 170613
Dicks SM *Rev* 101212
Dietz MPR *Rev* 050215
Dow KA *Rev* 290413
Fanning PN *Rev TD BA BD CertEd* 270613
Fish M *Rev* 070312
Hamilton WG *Rev BA(Hons)* 300715
Hassan BJ *Rev* 281114
Jackson R *Rev* 041012
Johnstone DG *Rev* 210212
Kirkwood AR *Rev* 260810
Leggett NWM *Rev BA* 161012
Logan DDJ *Rev BD MA* 131212
MacKenzie C *Rev* 240311
Malam SM *Rev* 170815
Massey PDS *Rev* 291111
McCulloch AJR *Rev MA BD* 121112

McLaren W *Rev MA BD* 111111
Moriarty JA *Rev MA* 260514
Newman MS *Rev* 280514
Newnes SW *Rev* 150715
Parkinson RD *Rev* 060409
Perera GA *Rev* 171212
Phillips TL *Rev* 220415
Plant T *Rev* 280514
Powell *Rev* SW 141209
Quirey E *Rev* 290911
Selemani E *Rev* 030511
Sharpe LR *Rev* 180714
Sumsion PH *Rev BSc BA MA* 281011
Taylor SJ *Rev BSc* 281113
Theakston SM *Rev* 031212
Thomas SC *Rev* 170615
Tisdale MB *Rev* 010710
Volland MJ *Rev* 250213
West ERG *Rev* 030611
Whitley B *Rev* 040510
Wilson FA *Rev BD* 260713
Wright TC *Rev* 110815

THE ROYAL LOGISTIC CORPS

Regimental Headquarters: Dettingen House, The Princess Royal Barracks, Deepcut, Camberley, Surrey, GU16 6RW
(Tel: 01252 833 593 Fax: 01252 833 375 Email: RegtSec@rhqtherlc.org.uk)

Regiments .... 2 Operational Support Group, 150 Regiment, 151 Regiment, 152 (North Irish) Regiment, 154 (Scottish) Regiment, 156 Regiment 157 (Welsh) Regiment, 158 Regiment, 159 Regiment, 162 Regiment 165 Port and Maritime Regiment, 167 Catering Support Regiment 383 Commando Petroleum Troop, 384 Commando Petroleum Troop

Honorary Colonels

150 Transport Regiment .... Mr Stephen Thomas Larard 300914
151 Transport Regiment .... Brig Allan B McLeod (*late* RLC) 010115
152 (North Irish) Transport Regiment. Mr Robert W L Scott *OBE* 010513
154 (Scottish) Regiment .... *The Rt Hon* Adam P Ingram *PC* 010813
156 Transport Regiment .... Brig Tom N O'Brien *CBE TD DL* 050412
157 (Welsh) Transport Regiment .... Col Steve P W Lawton 010116
158 Transport Regiment .... Col (Retd) Mark C H Underhill *OBE* 011113
159 Supply Regiment .... Brig (Retd) Mark L Dunn 010214
162 Regiment .... Brig (Retd) Chris J Murray *CBE* 050405
165 Port & Maritime Regiment .... Brig (Retd) Tony Dalby-Welsh 011015
167 Catering Support Regiment......... ACM *Sir* Stuart Peach *GBE KCB ADC DL(RAF)* 010316

Honorary Catering Adviser to the Army . Mr David Morgan-Hewitt 020810

Honorary Ordnance Officer
Tower of London .... Maj Gen (Retd) Malcolm D Wood *CBE* 050412

Colonel Commandant .... Brig (Retd) Maurice J Sheen *CBE QVRM TD (AR)* 050408

Lieutenant Colonels

Allen JP	010909
Blake RT	011106
Braine SMA *MBE*	060115
Brooks D *TD*	010707
Browne NP	010504
Cattermull JA	010811
Coombes NA *TD*	010510
Cross KA	140314
Devonshire RM	260914
Falcon AH	010808
Gaudoin JP	010410
Gordon FM	250314
Harris ME	241107
Hinton A	010815
Hughes ML *BA(Hons) MA*	010912
Hurley IM *MBE*	010407
Jurd ND	170612
King EJ *TD*	010401
Lee ACS	050110
Lewis PJ	211011
Lydon JJ	310815
Macdougall NSI *TD*	010407
Owen CL	150103
Pitt LJ *OBE TD DL*	120999
Reeve DW	010413
Siebenaller M *TD FRGS FinstLM AFRIN MCGI*	010410
Smith TD	310514
Stanford GF *TD*	010499
Stone P	300609
Stonehouse SA *TD*	010410
Wilkinson AJ	220413
Wilkinson GH *MA*	290512

Majors

Aitken AM	011106
Andrew FC	170709
Aspin DL	300813
Atkinson TR	140505
Baker PW	130185
Baxter JC	310707
Beaumont BDN	310707
Bell PM	030511
Bevan NP	310706
Billings PR	151112
Bilsbarrow GD	230113
Bilton RW	010401
Boles RF	010405
Bolter NJ *BSc(Hons) CMILT GCGI*	041013
Booker RM	250891
Bouttell CD	250404
Bowdler NR	250715
Bradshaw CL	260514
Bratcher CA	021204
Briggs AD	310708
Broomfield TN	180910
Bryan HJ	110204
Burnan JI	010407
Byron MN	150915
Cameron HC	120208
Casey ME	270111
Cave JO *TD*	010404
Chambers K *TD*	010496
Chapman CM	010403
Clark AC	301299
Collier GL	121101
Collinson MNJ	010497
Cope LA	011015
Corkerton TAG	240410
Cotter SJ	231010
Croxford DJ	300991
Curtis C *TD*	010405
Dade R	300992

Davies CP 270311
Deck MD *MBE QVRM* 010413
Doherty PJ 080200
Drennan HW *BSc(Hons) FInstLM* 120610
Dyos MB 010411
Edwards HR 120607
Egan SB *TD* 010405
Emms M 170912
Evans DJ 210907
Evanson-Goddard LF 010413
Falinski SJ 151206
Flint RM 200206
Forbes A *TD* 280200
Fox DG 120905
Francey PD 310303
Fraser RG 230807
Fraser WG *MBE* 030993
Gane TI 271014
Gifford AP *TD* 190704
Goodwin IRC 010412
Gore TS 170913
Gotobed PM *TD* 060404
Gregory SA *BA(Hons)* 291114
Grimwood EJ 110308
Hall FJ *TD* 251104
Hamilton AR 220714
Hardy GW 010413
Harris GPR 310702
Harrison PA 010401
Herraghty D 181011
Hike CL 010412
Hill CA *MBE* 010405
Hill KAK *TD* 290101
Hope TW *MBE* 010409
Houston PB 011000
Hughes WE 080112
Igoe A 100112
Jacobs RR *TD* 310303
Johnston PAK 040515
Jolly M 280810
Jones RS 300991
Jones W *MBE TD* 010404
Joyner SM *TD* 011091
Keenan I *BEM* 010405
Key RL 010410
Kilby RB *TD* 010497
Knight DM 090614
Larard MFW *TD* 040608
Lawrence T 080410
Layton ME 010504
Lester AH 010408
Lewis RG 150915
Liddle TS 010495
Louis DJ *TD* 010497
MacDonald IM 101014
MaGinniss CH 010988
McCormack DM 020998
McDonnell IM 010498
McLeod RA 310711
Messervy SM *TD* 011201
Midgley SA 010413
Millen DAJ 090489
Moore HN 010408
Morfitt SJ 260604
Morris WG 220306
Mossop A 050607
Nicholas WHM *TD* 010403
Nicholson AC 060213
Noble DD 161095
O'Connell P 260600
Paget DW 010408
Parkyn RG *MBE* 150915
Paton RA *AE* 090311
Pinchard PG 090401
Pollitt-Lye S 010412
Pope MC 010405
Roberts CA *MSc DipHE* 310703
Roberts IR 150701
Roche KM 010409
Sainsbury DJ *TDACIB* 170700
Seggie BW *EdD MEd FCIPD FIfL FCMI IEng* 011106
Sinclair PJ 300992
Smith HC 090504
Steed TB 311013
Stewart JC 010806
Sutton RJ 011010
Taylor DT 310705
Teague R 010714
Thomas HAD *TD* 280505
Tremelling RT 111014
Turkington WJ *TD* 010403
Tween KN 010198
Urquhart DS *MBE TD* 021197
Wallace GA 120607
Walsh MW 011096
Walsh P 010798
Ward PJC 051209
Watt JC *TD* 210806
Watt RF 210806
Wells DRS 010406
Whitfield JR *MBE* 010607
Winton H 210614
Woodman S 010407
Young IA 061205
Young P *TD* 010406
Zaman M 310708

Captains

Ainscough PJ 010911
Alldritt L 061015
Arnold AA 010413
Balchin AC 200614
Bayly WH 100710
Billings MHD *LCGI* 110210
Blanchard AE *MBE* 200306
Blues KHS 261009
Booton JA 101210
Brown PK 131207
Bryan SM 120506
Bryant PA 010413
Burgess DG 150103
Byers GA TD 021200
Carnegie-Brown AG 080714
Chamberlain AS 010412
Clayson NR 211114
Conroy JR 010712
Conway LA 271106
Cooney AM 011006
Cooney IM 210410
Court EF 110215
Cowling MN *MBE* 110714
Davidson AK 040511
Debono-Evans MA 010411
Drew KPP 010407
Dzierozynski RT 020604
Eldred LE 070310
Evans DJ 010407
Farrar R 010410
Ferris SL 060106
Finnigan C 270412
Forsyth W 010499
Framingham M 010302

Garbuja M	070607
Geddes RR *MCGI MILT*	070408
Glasby LP	080507
Goffredi SJ	010410
Guy DJ	010407
Hawkins TMD	081003
Henry A	161108
Herlihy PM	170908
How KMH *BSc MBChB*	010807
Howdle - Rowe DJ	050811
Jackson WR	310804
Jenkin DR	130709
Jones GJ	040704
Kelly L	230312
Kent RA	041108
Kill NR	210912
Kirk AS	170911
Lord A	140510
MacKenzie RB *BSc*	130208
Mander BH	011111
Mantell PDK *TD BA*	240202
Marshall J	100710
Marshall S	130814
Masson AA	141207
Mather JC	281013
Mathieson SC	150105
Mayes CE	251113
McAulay E	271208
McCarthy KJ	020402
McLeod EPC	220607
Miller GE	010815
Mitchener PJ	010409
Moloney JR	310706
Monk DJ	170209
Morgan DH	241106
Morton AG	131008
Nevitt J *LLM MSc CMIOSH*	010407
Oak WSW	170608
Oliver J	170297
Ord C	010410
Page G	130208
Parry SWD	240614
Pearce A	131008
Peltor AM	010912
Porterfield SC	081113
Pountney ND	120804
Price JR *TD*	010388
Rai P	020708
Rai S	040605
Rai S	060212
Reed SJ	010407
Roe M	070207
Sage R	010511
Sapwell CJ	010409
Scammell J	010813
Scarr WA	111109
Senior P	020409
Sheeran NC	100710
Skinner VJ	091112
Smith KG	010407
Smith NC	300709
Soutar I *TD*	010497
Spafford PA	110709
Speak TW	020904
Squire TJ	030310
Stanfield B	280512
Stone J	151206
Tang AP	010407
Thapa D	030209
Thomas CEM	170608
Tomkins M	101107
Urey PA	210610
Van Lier ML	010412
Vaughan KG	080503
Ward NL	061008
Weston RC	010412
Whiston DS	281007
Wicks JR	010704
Willett CJ	010409
Williams D	010507
Williams KJ	160309
Withers RG	190998
Wotherspoon RW	130411
Wright AP *MBE*	130410
Wright DG	190308

Lieutenants

Abbott SEE	011011
Berry N *BA PGDip*	011012
Bolton EC	260710
Cann RJ	280914
Chittock S	021012
Christopher TJ	030815
Craig BE	300903
Cranston TA	010812
Crisp JA	191012
Dickinson JP	290913
Gibson LS	300613
Gray JA	030800
Holder EJ	011013
Hurley SB	260113
Jackson CL	130413
Kallaway WLB	290909
Kirby LI	300913
Magee AN	010515
McBride SP	110709
Parr MF	180913
Patel SV	060910
Smith MRS	290709
Sykes SN	021012
Taylor SA	280713
Williams AJB	021012
Wolfe AJ	031011

2nd Lieutenants

Ashton DC	021011
Crilly SJ	010815
Landells DJ	280713
Robinson PJ	010811

Officer Cadets

Aspinall PG	030913
Barr JWJ	010914
Beukes D	030913
Billington GEP	030913
Brandy DJ	030913
Burns H	100914
Casey HD	010611
Collins NG	200910
Cradock BM	010914
Dabbs AL	030913
Davies TJ	030913
Fox JA	010914
Franklin HE	280812
Gardner GJ	030913
Garner MP	010914
Gilford NES	200910
Griffin NL	140909
Hastings JSG	280812
Hawkins KM	010914
Hook TA	010611
Jackson PJ	240914
Janes RG	280812
Jellis JM	280812

Jones TW	140909
Jutsum KJ	040913
Kenny SA	280812
Kirkham H	280812
Lane MR	010914
Law EL	191011
Mallett DPD	030913
Martin SM	280812
McIlveen SG	280812
Measey OM	010914
Morris JAR	040913
Morris PDJ	030913
Morris RL	010914
Mottley LRG	030913
Newbold HA	270914
Nonas AJ	010914
Oldfield LJ	010914
Oxborough RC	280812
Oxnam BL	010914
Puddicombe AC	010611
Raw HJ	010914
Redding CA	010914
Rees-Doherty NC	010914
Roberts JA	010914
Royle JC	280812
Scott KG	030913
Shenfield JK	030913
Smith KC	040913
Sorabjee QS	280812
Stokes TAM	010611
Suffolk HF	010914
Suffolk OW	030913
Tansley EJ	030913
Thompson CEW	010611
Thompson EJD	010914
Turner JA	280812
Vann CR	030913
Vernon HM	030913
Webb KJ	030913
Williamson BLG	280812
Wright FK	030913
Wyndham-Smith SJ	280812

ARMY CADET FORCE ADULT VOLUNTEER

Lieutenant

O'Flanagan AF *MBE*	080410

ROYAL ARMY MEDICAL CORPS

Regimental Headquarters: HQ Army Medical Services, Slim Road, Camberley GU15 4NP
(Tel: 01276 412751 Fax: 01276 412793 Email: rhq_ams@hotmail.com)

Honorary Colonels

144 Parachute Medical Sqn AR	Brig (Retd) Alastair H McG MacMillan *DL*	011012
201 (Northern) Field Hospital AR	Mr Alan Foster	010512
202 (Midlands) Field Hospital AR	Dr Jonathan Mark Porter	010414
203 (Welsh) Field Hospital AR	Dr Peter John Carter *OBE*	110511
204 (North Irish) Field Hospital AR	Prof Martin E J Bradley	010911
205 (Scottish) Field Hospital AR	Mr Ian W R Anderson	010612
207 (Manchester) Field Hospital AR	Prof Anthony D Redmond *OBE*	010414
208 (Liverpool) Field Hospital AR	Prof John Edward Earis	010815
212 (Yorkshire) Field Hospital AR	*Sir* Andrew J Cash *OBE*	011108
225 (Scottish) Medical Regiment AR	Brig (Retd) Alistair H McG MacMillan *DL*	010214
243 (Wessex) Field Hospital AR	Dr Michael Alan Seeley	150514
253 (North Irish) Medical Regiment AR	Prof Hugh P McKenna	011107
254 (East of Englnad) Medical Regiment AR	Miss Jane L McCue	011016
306 Hospital Support Medical Regiment AR	*Sir* David Nicholson *KCB CBE (until 010716)*	010911
	Mrs Gemma K Wright *(from 010716)*	
335 Medical Evacuation Regiment AR	Prof Kathleen McCourt *CBE*	010113

Colonel Commandant .... Col (Retd) Heidi A Doughty *OBE TD DL (AR)* 010114

Lieutenant Colonels

Benn AL	110515
Bingham GM	141014
Cameron EA *MSc DLSHTM BA (Hons) DipM*	300609
Fasham DG	010413
Jackson AJS	080513
Judge MS	280214
Lawrence SB	141014
Moore AJL *MBE TD*	240707
Pearson JE	100908
Pearson RB *BPHARM.MRPHARMS MBA(OU)*	010313
Simpson I *MBE*	300609
Taylor AJ	010808
Thomis SP *TD BPharm MRPharmS MCPP BM BS*	011203
Ward G	311012
Ward L	310315

Majors

Banfield JHA	100112
Barker AP	101012
Battey FJ	011011
Beattie HM	171009
Bellew EM	010712
Bramwell-Walsh CL	171009
Burns LP	021206
Campbell M	240608
Carey T *TD SQ(V)*	010401
Carmichael IA	011115
Carr EJ	010414
Castle SA	261111
Chan JLC	061015
Cockcroft MG	241110
Cote NB	100614
Crozet CP	081108
Cruickshanks DR *TD*	010400
Dear KL	230910
Egan O	311213
Evans JN	300405
Fitton SE	310315
Fletcher JM	260698
Gallagher VE	310704
Geddes L	180910
Green PK	020804
Greenhow FW *MBE*	310708
Guilfoyle EA	170214
Hall BA	010311
Haran KM *TD*	280494
Harris AVL	270809
Harrop M	011099
Hewitt J	280410
Horn JC	150613
Howley LJ	041004
Hurley PA	010401
Keenan GP	310711
Kirkpatrick PI	290704
Knight R *BSc MIHM*	310706
Lambirth SJ	140706
Marsh AJ	061015
Martin GA	121113
Martin JM	240911
Mathieson A	140902
Mayo MJ	010613
McAuliffe IC	010907
McConnell GM	-
McFarlane AD	010703
Melley CR *BSc*	011007
Millarvie AJ	100908
Mitchell CK	011002
Moore DM	100614
Morton JP	270811
Murray R	231014
Neilson SKN *TD*	171009
Nelson P *TD*	140997
Newman P	010415
Orange SJ	030309
Ozanne RM	101012
Packer JE	100112
Paterson S	300111
Percival BI	281109
Phillips JC	301111
Phillips S	271114
Proctor PS *TD*	010506

Raetschus SD	011015
Read EM	110505
Riley WA	040904
Robinson NJ	081213
Ross AD	010713
Rowland CP	021009
Saunders VC *BSc(Hons) MCSP*	271111
Savage SJ	310505
Schofield SC	310709
Shaw SJ	121210
Smith AJ	031115
Smith AR	201113
Smith M	011215
Smith Straney TA	010808
Smyth CR	310709
Sperrin MW	170210
St John-Green CJ *TD*	101197
Summers RH	291006
Thompson JM	310709
Thorman W	010110
Walton JJ	110214
Warnock FR	150209
Watkins AJ	100112
Weddell R	010715
Willis DL *TD*	090600
Wills RA	300997
Windas WR	011101
Wright MA	011015
Yates J	300988

Captains

Anderson FE *BA(Hons)*	250810
Andrews RC	010408
Bacon GM	020310
Bell JR	010406
Black GH	010407
Brownlow GS	010207
Burke-Jones J	010506
Cairns D	150312
Cairns GC	151214
Carroll AG	210807
Cole GJ	010411
Conway GT	131110
Court MW	130208
Cuffe DJ	300513
Dewar SG	240607
Dickson NL	051115
Dobbing FMM *MA BSc (Hons) RGN RM RSCN RHV*	011005
Drummond JV	050815
Ducat RDC	191007
Eckersley GF	080412
Farrell AT	040314
Forsythe JR	010506
Francis LR	161111
Gardner YA	150910
Greenwood IG	010406
Groves D	050909
Hainsworth CG	310709
Hall AJ	010407
Hamilton S	011085
Heal GD	220900
Hesse KL	070715
Hill GAF	191111
Hodges KJ	300905
Horner CE	171110
Hoube S	020715
Hunter JM	010207
Hunter SM	191108
Ingleston MJ	121010
Janaway AS	190505
Jarvis DM	301108
Jensen ARN	020405
Johnson JD	020415
Joyce BJ	301014
Khan AU	130912
Kirby BC	110204
Launders HM	180910
Lazenby P	010403
Lester KC	030298
Lewis CG	170310
Lilley AL	260913
McInnes TM	100608
Milburn LK	131004
Moore AF	240607
Morgan RL	050815
Ofori AKO	090804
Oldham LA	290308
Orchard DG	011113
Orr K	281112
Peasley MG	131113
Porter EEB *BSc(Hons)*	261111
Pottie CR AE	210112
Pritchard LE	010414
Rawcliffe PR	161012
Rees DBJ	300407
Richardson WD	020612
Riddell GE	260710
Robins JMW	050614
Ross-Thriepland S *MEng*	051115
Scott A	180213
Searson DJ	020211
Sharma J	071112
Smith SH	280110
Thomas PP	140511
Thornley K	031108
Trump MT	010707
Walker DJ	171107
Watson HW	050703
Watson J	310510
Watson NJ	090211
Webber RWS	010312
Welch MD	251114
Whitgift JZ	050815
Williams P	161208
Wills CE	190611
Winter PF	111213
Wolfe I	160407
Wong AKC	050815
Wynne MG	150910

Lieutenants

Baxter SE	100215
Beastall HC	010811
Bellia GF	051114
Catton AB	280714
Chandi HK	230313
Cheema D	260113
Church RH	100711
Cozens SJL	251114
Curl-Roper T	300713
Edwards PK	250310
Everiss DJ	240914
Ferraby DH	050415
Flint RCS	250614
Gething DJ	011108
Glover ML	281006
Hards M	010614
Hindocha A	220713
Hockenhull R	281014
Hucks AM	141115
Karsten ECL	010414

Kerai C	150514
Liggett H	180215
McKenna CER	190215
O'Mahony KJ	290714
Park CL	260113
Peters JW	180314
Price-Thomas EJ	250614
Reynolds SJ	260715
Searle RW	010410
Smith KB	280714
Sunder AK	271012
Usher NAD	300595
Willis MJ	010614
Wu K	270715
Wynell-Mayow WM	250715
Yates SEG	270715

2nd Lieutenants

Adams RDF	011013
Anderson-Knight HE	010216
Atugba ITJ	270713
Byrom ISJ	171114
Chase S	041114
Claireaux HA	260215
Cranmer EJ	121011
Crooks RJ	070913
Earle-Wright BJ	181104
Goodman BP	130115
Harris KO	230514
Hutchinson J	140515
Lambert ANH	050715
Marshall MRG	171114
Menzies A	091214
Murray MP	220613
Richardson KET	020315
Riddoch FI	270713
Smith RG	260915
Stewart RA	141114
Thompson DC	011212
Thompson E	270715
Weale RD	130115
Wood JAM	040215
Wrigley SJ	280914

Officer Cadets

Costley DJF	010411
Domeracki KA	231012
Harper FJ	010115
Heslop KE	141012
Murphy HL	191011

MEDICAL OFFICERS (RAMC MO)

Lieutenant Colonels

Allagoa BN	260606
Arul GS	141014
Bailey DJW	280711
Banerjee B *QVRM DL MBBS FRCSED*	010406
Barrell JP	141014
Bennett JDC	131198
Brady S	010408
Brice A	040216
Brooks AJ *OBE*	160108
Brown AL	100615
Bruce ASW *TD*	111209
Buxton N	041004
Campbell BE	010705
Cardwell ME *TD*	260707
Cloke DJ *BSc MBBS (Hons) FRCS(Tr & Orth)*	291110
Clough DGF	011002
Cordell NJ	060204
Curphey ARG	141014
Dennis ST *BM MRCS(Ed) FRCR*	050215
Dunbar JAT	081111
Fair SM	311012
Gibbons CT	061015
Gilliam AD	081111
Gilpin DA	141014
Hammond JS	291110
Hands CAH	140896
Hawes RS	040216
Hawes SJ	311012
Hettiaratchy SP	050215
Jansen JO	050215
Kay JL *BSc MBChB DRCOG MRCGP*	010899
Kennedy DWG	010906
Keoghane SR	011105
Livingstone CCA	081111
Loudon MA	010407
MacMillan AIM *QHS*	010408
Marshall CA	011008
Marshall SG	311012
Mason CM	070110
Mathewson KG	300604
Maxwell WB	081111
McAuley J *MB ChB MRCA MFAEM DipIMC DRCO*	010703
McCullough NP	141014
McFadzean WA	220603
McKenna JG	260707
Miller JE	261108
Moore NR	311012
Morrison PA	050215
Nguyen PTL *BMS BM BS*	141014
Patch DWM	081111
Phillips SL *TD*	011102
Reaveley MD	050215
Roberts MJ	060303
Robinson ADT *TD*	010297
Salisbury J *TD*	131113
Sawdy RJ	141014
Shieff CL *QVRM TD*	080300
Shorten WWJ *TD*	010703
Speers AG	050215
Spillane KM	010406
Stewart A	260707
Sunderland GT	010902
Varghese J	050215
Ward G	011299
Westerduin FP	141014
Wilson DI	011109
Woolgar JD	080513
Wright KD	141014

Majors

Attwood LA	211109
Austin GR	110301
Badh CS	290108
Balupuri S	250602
Beaven AW *MBChB MRCS*	010912
Bissett R	160902
Bolton JA *MBBS MRCGP RAMC*	161111
Bull JG	150310
Canty MJ	010116
Carneiro ADC	010209
Chan SSC	210103
Clitheroe EC	210312
Conybeare A	100810

Crockett AJB 010116
Cupitt MJ 201102
Davies W 210312
Dawes RJ 040708
Dresner MR 270705
Driver DJ 210814
Durrant HJ 061015
Eardley KS 010604
Evans EJ 010116
Farmery JSP 280312
Fawcett RJ 210312
Fendius A *MBBS* 211109
Fitzgerald LF *MBBS BSc(Hons) MCSP* 061015
Frew NC 010801
Gilmour AA 010116
Glynn GMA 010405
Gokhale R 010606
Henson VL 160107
Heycock RW 271111
Holbrook J 170304
Holland TS 061015
Hoyle AL *BSc(Hons) MBBS MRCPCH* 150613
Johnson CJD 260607
Johnson CM *MBBS FRCA FFICM* 010116
Johnson SM 280309
Jones A 170711
Kan SM 010405
Kan YM 200808
Kavanagh MJ 020895
Keenan ACM 091011
Kerr GR *MBBS FRCS(ED) FRCS* 010604
Knights RM 251209
Lamparelli MJ 030215
Ley SGD 090715
Lightfoot TC 160113
Lynch MRJ 290600
Mackay HE 150910
MacKenzie Ross RV 270706
Malinovski V 261111
Mann DV 170903
Marra IC 010116
Mayne JS 010116
McCrory C 260906
McNeill LWJ 291001
Morgan PN 010111
Morrison JJ 301110
Nagra I 070807
Nathwani RV 230910
Newton KF *MBCHB MRCS* 010116
Newton Ede MP 010808
Nicholson S 010812
O'Sullivan FE 110409
Page PRJ *MBBS MRCSEd* 280911
Pall D 210709
Parker RJ 270908
Paterson CA 101106
Pawar M 011211
Pettigrew LH 090206
Philip JN *DDA MBBS MRCS Ed FFD(OSOM)* 010116
Randalls PB 011203
Reed WS 140201
Rignall AW 120613
Robinson SJ 040406
Rushambuza RPM 110910
Rushbrook JL 010116
Russell P 100112
Sanderson CH 290802
Sapre B 150910
Saunders JH 010116
Schofield JD 230910
Shaw SM 061015
Shearer RD 040815
Shemar SJJ 180910
Sheppard TJ 270113
Shields RSD 280106
Smith IM 050909
Sommerville IKM 181194
Standring P *MBChB DCH FRCPCH* 170903
Stevens GA 010107
Stewart RW 010116
Sudheer SP 010411
Surgey AW 121210
Sutcliffe N 270302
Taylor DM 130405
Taylor SR 170909
Tellam SM 221003
Turner A 271004
Unwin TAE *MBBS MRCGP* 010892
Veitch JD 010116
Vithayathil KJ 200409
Walker C 060808
Walker CPR 021299
Watson KLM 010511
White RJ *MBChB MRCGP DRCOG DFFP* 040806
Williams GA 150504
Williams P 201109

Captains

Adamson L 070209
Allison CAG 060808
Armstrong CM 010812
Arthur RMA 101211
Attwood JM 030811
Baillie A 151210
Balogun-Ojuri BT 011014
Beaton CD 270810
Bew DP 260902
Bottomley TE 060814
Boyd JKF Dr 010109
Brown V 060814
Carden R 010812
Case TL 070813
Catley JM 050413
Chadwick AN 070813
Chapman LA 280706
Charnell AM 070813
Chavali M 080708
Clements MH 210809
Cohen L 131014
Colclough JA 020806
Connell TJ 011013
Cooper DE 060814
Cooper KL 010812
Cromey-Hawke SM 060814
Cross AM 010807
De Belder FR 070813
De Rosa A 050809
Dholakia S 170811
Dickenson EJ 040810
Dinsdale JA 200409
Dixon CJ 040810
Dolan RD 030811
Eckersley TM 040110
Ekpa JEA 141208
Ellington MC 060814
Elliott K 100512
Emmett SR 310110
Franks R 230512

Freshwater IL	150211	Meek DJ	010812	Spence MC	010113
Gamble EME	270309	Mella SL	300114	Squire EL	110911
Gilmore JH	201014	Mellor EK	010407	Stalker AJ	040810
Gladman EJA	070813	Monk AP	310306	Stevens WJ	270814
Gordon JB	020914	Morley JL	300409	Summers BA	010812
Goroszeniuk DZ	010309	Muir CP	090711	Tannassee TO	040810
Greek AI	160704	Murdoch I	010611	Taylor REB *MBBS MCEM*	280708
Haden MH	010311	Nathan Z	151112	Teasdale A	010812
Haldane CEF	090712	Ng OCT	060808	Thomas CLG	060814
Haslett AG	010812	Ogden K	040810	Tipping M	121208
Heslop LM	010801	Ohringer G	070813	Todd A	031012
Heylings JM	010313	Osborne MP	070813	Todd AR	010812
Hitchin SP	050809	Paranna V	231107	Turner LJ	151114
Horwood JP	290705	Patel JA	080511	Turner SJ	050809
Hughes AH	010407	Paxton WJ	281014	Van Breda PG	050309
Hurry R	120204	Pells GM	060814	Van Zyl B	060814
Hurst SA	080710	Poh CK	010812	Vint H	190610
I'Anson CD	210914	Pye DM	090711	Watson PB	030811
Jarvie DJ	020806	Rahman SM	060814	Webster MA	060814
Jephcote SL	010812	Ralhan V	070813	Weir S	060814
Johnston CJC	030310	Read DJ	120612	Wetten A	030811
Jones GP	011009	Rees DM	010611	Whelton C	271212
Karim L	101114	Reeves KA	020410	Whittam AM	030811
Kilner JA	010812	Riddell RNJ	040311	Wijesuriya JD	041209
Lawrence M	270711	Ritson AJ	020612	Wilson GT	070813
Leaver CJ	050808	Robertson LC	130108	Wong C	010206
Lerman DA	010907	Ross MJ	070813	Worsley AS	260112
Lumley A	080609	Rossi J	030811	Wright HE	040811
Lyons MWH	130210	Russell TAT	070813	Yates AT	030811
Malik NS	030811	Rutherford-Davies J	270905		
Marshall S	141014	Ryan NAJ	310312	*Lieutenants*	
Martin G	010312	Scrafton DK	010812	Chaudhry S	060902
Mathers JD	030806	Shah AA	280914	Lazarova L	270711
McKenzie EM	151207	Shah N	070813		
McMaster A	070813	Sheel ARG	040810		
McQueen SG	050809	Skinner EJ	010213		

CORPS OF ROYAL ELECTRICAL AND MECHANICAL ENGINEERS

Regimental Headquarters: MOD Lyneham, Lyneham, Chippenham SN15 9HB
(Tel: 01249 894520 Mil: 95481 4520 Email: REMERHQCorpsSec@mod.uk)

Honorary Colonels

101 Battalion (Wrexham)................... Col (Retd) John Charlesworth *TD* 011113
102 Battalion (Newton Aycliffe)........ Col (Retd) J R M Hackett *CBE (until 010716)* 070610
Mr John Greaves *(from 010716)*
103 Battalion (Crawley)..................... Brig W J (Bill) O'Leary QVRM *TD DL* 140914
104 Battalion (Northampton)............. Maj Gen (Retd) Tim N Tyler *CB* 150509
105 Battalion (Bristol)....................... Maj Gen (Retd) John M R Henderson *CB* 010215
106 Battalian (East Kilbride)............. Mr John Alexander Campbell 011015

Corps Colonel..Col Ian Adkins *(until Apr 16)*
Col Mark Simpson *TD VR (from Apr 16)*

Lieutenant Colonels

Agathangelou L	011011
Ashdown PR	160110
Black A	131210
Cooper GL *TD*	130114
Harris DJ	011113
Hearty KP *QVRM*	010505
Jackson DM	270814
Merriott HK *TD*	011108
Murdoch CJ	300603
Quinn LE *BEng MSc PhD CEng MIET*	011108
Shewry PA	010914
Simpson MA *TD VR*	110416
Tessem-Cotton E *BEng (Hons) CEng MIET ACIBSE*	050115
Wheelans CN	010112
Williams LT *TD*	011211

Majors

Attlee JR *TD*	280498
Balsillie AF	011214
Barham EMH	240903
Basey KA	010306
Bates CJ	040304
Bradley PP *ae ee gw*	020993
Brotherston M *QVRM*	011107
Brown CPT	300115
Callaway KA *MBEng RICS*	010510
Clubley SM	250312
Coward DM *IEng MSOE MIRTE*	280602
Crawford THW	010405
Currie HM	011108
England C	120503
Forde SL	211107
Gilfillan AE	150612
Goodfellow GC	010706
Goodman D	101105
Greenslade SP	010604
Hardy CS	010214
Izzard WJ	061213
Johnson WR	010404
Lee NH	010116
Linehan PJ	110313
Malpass CJ	190410
McEntee NP *TD*	011203
McLean JM	270410
Moorhouse DJ *CEng IMechE*	300993
Moreman S *TD*	160198
Morgan CN	141009
Moyo PA	010205
Neil AW	010314
Oakes MC *MSc C Eng FIMechE MCIPD FRGS*	181213
Pallett BC	010408
Prince CW	010405
Rees PG	011007
Reynolds JK	310706
Richards J	011214
Roberts HM	280111
Russell PJ	100115
Salisbury CS	080200
Shaw G	120304
Sim M	010809
Spence P	141002
Spencer A	241114
Stacey CB	010515
Stuart PM	081293
White SR	080200
Wilson ED	010108

Captains

Bailey JAA	100308
Bruton LA	010313
Casey RF	261196
Chamberlain ETJ	010407
Dawson GJ	160112
Draper J	230407
Eynon MW	170409
Falconer E	230213
Falkous KJ *MEng*	120612
Field ES	130214
Fox JP	311011
Glass PB	070211
Green NC	170111
Griffiths MFR	010407
Gurung L	300608
Gurung S	011007
Hardy D	141209
Harrison CS	070613
Harrison PS *BSc (Hons) SRCh MChS*	140710
Head CD	210708
Hunt AT	260610
Irwin LL	150210
Keenan NB	130115
Langham SJR	120203
Lee JJ	130415
Lillie TI	130613
Lovelock-Jeffels NS	150811
MacDonald AKM	011210

McShane TO	130606
Morton RLS	310313
Murphy EM	040405
Murphy M	010407
O'Mahony MA	230315
O'Rourke M	050510
Patey GJ	190710
Stevens RG	010407
Stone KJ	010703
Thomas M	290407
Tomsett DJP	110601
Tribelnig SA	270612
Turner PR	130212
Wilson KJ	230209

Lieutenants

Blackman SEL	020604
Guilfoyle SL	200913
Higgs SJ	270909
Nixon S	280714
Roberts PRJ	290709
Tasker HS	010812

2nd Lieutenants

Bowers GK	091110
Emery DL	020814
Lawson T	270713
Lewis GD	280713
Smith MJK *MEng*	050513

Officer Cadets

Baker EJ	030913
Balfour WAM	030913
Bass DHR	010914
Beckett JA	010611
Brown AJ	280812
Bullock BJM	280812
Butler ME	010914
Carrott T	280812
Chapman JA	280812
Clarke EC	030913
Cleland VGC	010914
Collicott J	010611
Corrigan AB	280812
Courtney SJB	200910
Cox LA	040913
Craig NGF	030913
Craven JA	010911
Crawford LG	280812
Crosby M	040913
Davidson LE	200910
Dyer Z	030913
Eyre PDE	030913
Foster TE	200910
Fudge SE	010914
Gadd MPA	200910
Garrard MR	010611
Golding JC	040913
Grant ED	280812
Hamlin P	280812
Hodgkinson JPB	030913
Horsburgh D	040913
Houze JAR	030913
Hurst SJ	200910
Hutt ST	280812
James WA	010914
Jardim AP	010914
Jellard SCJ	280812
Johnson GG	010611
Johnson ST	040913
Keene FJA	010914
Kempa TG	010914
Kirkham H	280812
Lebeter LG	280812
Luxton AJ	010914
MacFadden H	010914
Marriott MJ	010914
Marshall LD	100914
McBroom C	280812
McEntee NJ	280812
Moore TE	030913
Oliver J	030913
Parker AN	030913
Parker F	280812
Perrin JLM	010914
Pettit CE	030913
Pickerill AH	010611
Rhodes PSG	010611
Rutledge DJC	280812
Shaw J	030913
Sochon FPB	010914
Thompson-Darch RA	010914
Thorne BJ	010914
Turner RE	100914
Virumbrales-Bell R	010914
Walter RM	010611
Wardell ZA	010914
Williams LT	030913
Wright H	010611
Wyse SG	280812
Yates J	280812

ADJUTANT GENERAL'S CORPS

Regimental Headquarters: Worthy Down, Winchester, Hants SO21 2RG
(Tel: 01962 887 820 Mil: ext 2820)

(STAFF AND PERSONNEL SUPPORT BRANCH)

Lieutenant Colonels

Barr-Jones LI	020614
McKinney-Bennett EA	010808
Wilde LM	010408

Majors

Bargrove MJ	011006
Boardman SP	310109
Bowen PF	300997
Bowes AR *TD*	091195
Breach IA	300998
Davis JA *MBE BEd FCIS PGDip*	170290
Eve CY	110308
Flynn PL	310507
Fryer P	011102
Garner GK *TD*	090794
Gordon MH	260110
Green DM *TD*	010602
Hackett TE	080115
Harnby GR	150699
Harrington KJ	011214
Henderson LJ	310706
Hudson CD	310702
Jacobsen FME *TD*	010198
Lodge D	310704
Marchant-Wincott AC	210109
Morgan Monk LR	051009
Pegg MJ	210808
Senter PAD	061213
Simons DJ	310712
Thomas JC	311001
Thompson JL	011095
Vere-Whiting JJ	060306
Winchester AR	300992

Captains

Aitchison IJ	150106
Barclay TAC	011101
Blythe PF	-
Bryson MS	010407
Halpin GE	221013
Harries MH	020804
Heffernan JP *BEM*	100912
Houlton J	010413
Humberstone KE	150510
Johnson PF	010707
Kell JW	060611
Madden MA	250306
McNab J	020713
Norman CR	100608
Salt AJ	010804
Snell AJ	150600
Spilsbury EL	100807
Stevens TL	220113
Stredwick XYZ	040205
Vaggers MJ	141109
Wakefield JA	150693
Winrow D	160510

ADJUTANT GENERAL'S CORPS

(EDUCATION AND TRAINING SERVICES BRANCH)

Lieutenant Colonels

Duke MA	210115
Hanlan CG	300606
Knell KE	300608
Mack AR	300605
Walker SD *TD*	011104

Majors

Baxter KI	310714
Bergman ST	010808
Bielecki S *PhD TD*	011204
Broadbent RJR	010403
Brown CC	190309
Gardner FR	010706
Gracey AJ *BA (Hons) MA PGCE FInstLM*	310707
Green PP	300901
Greenwood NR	300996
Hamlin J	300505
Harris SJ	301289
Hoban DM *ACGI MEng CEng MICE*	310706
Holman MS	010893
Jennings JR	150115
Lambert SJ	300990
Matson TJ	091114
McQuade KL	310703
Midgley CJ	310708
Murphy DD	310706
Parkes JR	031208
Pope NS	290978
Preston RS	190914
Prudhoe KH	011112
Pullman S	121013
Sheldon J	310702
Spencer V	310706
Tognarelli WG	300991
Twentyman NG	300992
Whitehead JR	020699
Yare GG	300709

Captains

Ali K	130994
Booth NA	310702
Brown E	190613
Browne CHG	220415
Chinn TSG	130512
Close JS	130208
Dowling CJ	231206
Ellson JF	250811
Ferguson CMH	160609
Garner A	120110
Gibson AM	070706
James OE	241207
Lee RG	270913
McGoran HJ	290709
O'Callaghan CT	021105

Pearsall MD *BA(Hons) PGCE*	010815	Whitlam CE	010711	*Lieutenants*	
Robinson AM	190189	Woolsey CR	120914	Hunt M	140412
Sharman-Davies K	270913	Wright M	150309	Klymchuk IS	021012
Soley AW	301109				
Whishaw KL	081214				

ADJUTANT GENERAL'S CORPS
(PROVOST MARSHAL (ARMY))
ROYAL MILITARY POLICE (AR)

Honorary Colonel..Mr Simon D'Olier Duckworth *OBE DL*..010315

Lieutenant Colonels		*Captains*		Roberts JMP	261012
Black G	120911	Bradbury MP	080507	Sparkes KA	280306
Bradley DR	011213	Cook TD	110508	Spurling GL	010794
Holden RJM	011208	Cooke DP	010813	Thompson PI	300714
Ward DJ	011114	Crosbie AJ	130614	Van Straaten ME	160614
		D'Arcy G	070906	White PW	080209
Majors		Deeming GR	180912		
Atkinson PA	031208	Gerrard TN	131208	*Lieutenants*	
Bealey DG	310502	Gordon JR	300412	Ebbern NJ	280909
Bolwell SJ	011209	Hallam CSM *TD*	260491	Ellis PJD	230614
Bray NJ	141210	Hardy M	121006	Harratt L	300912
Davies B	040213	Horrocks LA	070806	Lake MA	020904
Ellson JV *TD*	071008	Jessop SM	010407	Livesey FE	180609
Payne NW *TD*	230301	Kyriakou FS *MBE*	250412	Wilson A	290914
Wood SM	191000	Moran FB	230504		
Wray P	160114	Nash A	080613	*2nd Lieutenants*	
		Orme CP	090211	Bate J	140714

ADJUTANT GENERAL'S CORPS
(PROVOST MARSHAL (ARMY))
MILITARY PROVOST STAFF (AR))

Captains	
Guildford CL	030214
Read RB	010710

ADJUTANT GENERAL'S CORPS
(ARMY LEGAL SERVICES)

Majors		Hobbs JE	101208	*Captains*	
Barkley AR	101208	London JFJ *LLM LLB*	101208	Fouracre AMG	010406
Bashir N	100206	Moss AM	101208	Hyland D *LLB (Hons) MBA*	081207
Burger R	101208	Roscoe MSW *BA (Hons) PgDL Barrister*	060813		
Burns SH	100206				
Eyton-Jones JA	250493				

ROYAL ARMY VETERINARY CORPS

Regimental Headquarters: Headquarters Army Medical Services, Robertson House,
Slim Road, Camberley, Surrey, GU15 4NP (Tel: 01276 412749 Mil: 94261 2749 Email: regtsecravc@hotmail.co.uk)

Honorary Colonel Commandant............ Col Neil C Smith *QHVS* 011114

Lieutenant Colonels

Huey RJ *TD*	010210

Majors

Heeley AM *BVSC*	171009
Lockhart RL *BVM&S MRCVS*	171009
Simpson MJ *BVM&S MRCVS*	171009
Tannahill VJ	010715
Whittle CSJ *BVSC MRCVS*	061108

Captains

Armstrong ELR	010709
Morgan ER *VETMB MRCVS*	050997
Nathwani LJ *BVETMED MRCVS BSc(Hons)*	170805

SMALL ARMS SCHOOL CORPS

Regimental Headquarters: Land Warfare Centre, Warminster, Wilts BA12 0DJ
(Tel: 01985 222612 Mil: 94381 2612 Fax: 01985 222211
Email: DINF-SASC-CLK-E2@mod.uk / LF-Cap-Cbt-SASC-Adjt@mod.uk Website: www.army.mod.uk/sasc)

Majors

Adams CS	040806
Atkinson A	191006
Bissett RJ	011006
Hastie RG	010604
McClelland AE	300901
O'Connor JP *BA(Hons) Bus Stud (Open)*	310711
Sayers R	200502

ROYAL ARMY DENTAL CORPS

Regimental Headquarters: Robertson House, Slim Road, Camberley, Surrey, GU15 4NP
(Tel: 01276 412753 Fax: 01276 412793 Email: rhq_radc@hotmail.com)

RADC (DO)

Lieutenant Colonels

Crutchley RJ	081111
Hebburn-Heath SP	080796
Maceachen WRJ *TD*	020407
Revington PJD	010206
Tyrer GL *TD*	010503

Majors

Dickson RDB *TD BDS MPhil*	201094
Heath NDC	271004
Hedderly Brind BJ	010405
Hitchcock KM	230605
Jaffery RM	010708
Martin K	061015
McIntyre IT	110902
Soszko JJB	040196
Tully JR	220700

Captain

Grant SWJ	270710

RADC

Lieutenant

Yadev NP	071213

INTELLIGENCE CORPS

Regimental Headquarters: Chicksands, Shefford, Bedfordshire SG17 5PR
(Tel: 01462 752340/01 Fax: 01462 752374 Email: intcorpshq-icc-corpssec@mod.uk)

Honorary Colonels

3 Military Intelligence Bttn (HQ London)	Mr Paul D J Rimmer	160711
5 Military Intelligence Bttn (HQ Edinburgh)	Maj Gen (Retd) Andrew D Mackay *CBE*	010615
7 Military Intelligence Bttn (HQ Manchester)	Mr Conrad Stuart Prince *CB*	010315
Specialist Group Military Intelligence (HQ Bristol)	Mr Christopher Nigel Donnelly *CMG TD*	010515
Media Operations Group	Gen *Sir* Nicholas Carter *KCB CBE DSO ADC Gen*	010112

Lieutenant Colonels

Abercrombie LA	300710
Allen DM	010410
Brittan RB	280108
Clarke BS	040413
Dowle JA *TD*	130115
Evans T	220513
Harrison MG *TD*	151008
Lindsay GJ	101212
Pendlebury-Green J	011211
Sedgwick AF	230215
Stanley PA	010906

Majors

Bennington AL	010712
Blandford T *BA ACA MCMI*	171014
Briggs L	030314
Cain WJ	010811
Coulson JM	010412
Coulson SG	261113
Curran A *BSc MRes PhD LCGI*	220415
East AJ	040298
Fensome PE	010900
Godfrey AM	291013
Gregory E	080502
Gustafson KC *PhD*	041013
Haskell SL	010103
Huntley DM	011211
Idziaszczyk M	010408
Ingram RJ	011006
Jenkins PJL	010413
Kennedy SD *BA TD*	290702
King RJ	270406
Lewis MH	070113
MacMillan NR	010810
McCracken IH	040106
Miller SN	010899
Mottram PB	190905
Mullin C	160606
Officer RL	041214
O'Keefe KF *TD*	010709
Orr DW	030314
Perry TD	010312
Roberts JP	010109
Rofe SR	121112
Saunders AG	110303
Strachan NA *TD*	010102
Thompson J	210704
Townsend JPC	310306
Tugendhat TGJ *MBE*	010110
Walker IJ	311012
Weale AJ	080200
Whitney AK	011001
Wilson A	070807
Wright S *MA(Hons)*	100498
Yates PP	300613

Captains

Anderson EF	160714
Arnold-Forster J	250114
Bailey CR	010414
Bailey LMA	150911
Bailey PG	100714
Beaumont LMA	040913
Belton AJ	010110
Blackadder JA	040406
Blatchford CR	010203
Bonner WE	130611
Burns ISD	041008
Butland H *BSc*	070607
Carter HJ	020215
Church ROS	090715
Clague RG	180613
Cleary JP	010908
Coates MS	161007
Cook AE	250114
Cork JM	030909
Crawford EJ *MA(Hons) CA*	010309
Cronin-Nowakowski S	011098
Cross CIJ	010408
Currie IS	100714
Dalton JM	010594
Danvers JFW	071112
Earl SA	310312
Economou ME	160714
El-Sherbiny T	071112
Eppleston JJ	080212
Evans DT	010310
Farquharson GM	040409
Farquharson IM	011100
Ferry K	060607
Fletcher TJ	290711
Gallagher AE	300508
Gribbin JL	010209
Hall JN	130407
Hamilton JC	311006
Harrison KS	031214
Heayberd RE	090715
Hersee SE	041007
Hewson GPD	071112
Hills PDM	121214
Holloway PJ	270307
Hoogesteger NMJ	160714
Ince AM	010412
Kent CR	100714
Kent MP	100714
Kneale V	071112
Landon TG	010814
Lavery V	010412
Lee AN	090715
Leech JA	071112

Lindblom AC	280209
Littlewood RS	080504
Lovegrove PM	160906
Lynch PJ	071112
Lyne LJ	030311
Main AS	180112
Marques BG	100714
Martin MP	010410
Mason DE	120209
Masters DR	110607
Matthews NGA	050406
McLoughlin TA *MSc CMgr FCMI*	240212
Mitchell DAG	010412
Morfill AD	120612
Morgan DR	131008
Morrison RI	101011
Mountford TMP *OBE*	010495
Murphy ME	071112
O'Sullivan TRH	270209
Owen PD	280203
Owen RK	040913
Oxley R	030813
Parry PA	020409
Pawlowski CP *MBE*	100205
Prowse SI *MBE MSc BSc(Hons)*	121002
Riddell M	260410
Roberts NH	010111
Roberts NJ	190511
Schlanker JD	010911
Shackel C	050401
Sivell-Muller M	151004
Smith GA	161010
Smith GV	120808
Smith LM	190511
Stanhope D *BSc(Hons) PGCE*	290106
Stanley AR	300900
Staunton-Lambert DP	230109
Teare JCJ	030310
Tomlyn IM	140604
Torp-Petersen ND	160609
Turner MJ	041209
Walker-Cousins JTM	020806
Waring MPJ	131008
Williams KAR	030713

Lieutenants

Bailey HK	280915
Black SA	280915
Bramwell MJ	280915
Gerrard TG	280114
Goodhind WR	280915
Heawood C	300915
Hetheridge GP	190613
Hoddinott CS	030815
Littledale J	260711
Mooney EP	300915
Moss EA	030412
Nason AA	280915
Orr DD	011215
Paxton DM	270715
Phipps LG	270715
Porter RD	250706
Sanghera A	210112
Toase C	030815
Whittle DAH	010811
Wills OD	010811

2nd Lieutenants

Baird JJJ	280914
Boyd LE	040813
Cogdell-Brooke L	280913
Dawes TE	031010
Hastie EW	280914
Henshall A	021010
Howell CE	270713
Kimble HJ	280908
Livingstone IG	110714
Logan IA	191011
McDonald JP	010713
McVicker-Orringe S	260915
Nestius-Brown AM	280914
Newbould TJ	030813
Roddis HE	030813
Scobie GAH	010815
Selfridge NC	280913
Selman M	010815
Stewart RWK	020814
Whelan TEA	250814
Whiteley M	020814

ROYAL ARMY PHYSICAL TRAINING CORPS

Regimental Headquarters: Mackenzie Building, Fox Lines, Queens Ave, Aldershot, Hampshire GU11 2LB
(Tel: 01252 787145 Fax: 01252 787160 Email: raptchq-reg-sec@mod.uk)

Major

Dolan JC 090304

QUEEN ALEXANDRA'S ROYAL ARMY NURSING CORPS

Regimental Headquarters Army Medical Services, Slim Road, Camberley, Surrey, GU15 4NP
(Tel: 01276 412754 Fax: 01276 412793 Email: regtsecqaranc@hotmail.com)

Colonels Commandant.......................... Col Jane E Davis *OBE QVRM TD DL (AR)* 010514

Lieutenant Colonels

Allen NH *TD*	011212
Allen WJ	311012
Andrews ME	160113
Armstrong D *TD*	060303
Ball HC	290915
Beesley PA	141014
Byers AEM *TD*	301115
Clarke CJ	141014
Cook PD	010112
Cooke J	260116
Davies S	101213
Durrant MRK *TD*	010196
Evans CAH *TD*	060114
Gallacher SWF	020810
Goodman A	100507
Haddock DL	241015
Horsburgh CG	041103
Inglis DL *TD*	101210
Jackson AL	010212
Kane MJ	010112
Laverick-Stovin SH	120315
Leatham MW *TD*	011109
Lingard J *ARRC TD*	170210
Maiden VR	261108
McCormick C	290814
McGhee SJA	290811
McGrath AP	010813
McGrath MJ *TD*	010509
O'Callaghan SKJ	301212
Richter M *RGN*	010410
Saunders MJ	110216
Siddle RG *TD*	280404
Stearn DSJ	090115
Tysall HL	090112
Verow KJ	010605
Watkins KS *QVRM TD*	130314
Whittaker C *RRC TD*	010103
Worrall JA	141014

Majors

Ainscough JM	280394
Allwood DM	310708
Anderson MA	030806
Baigent LJ	121210
Banks PJ	171009
Barrett D	250301
Bateman LJ	311009
Beaumont JM	140514
Beckwith AL *BSc(Hons) RM*	130412
Bennett KM	061015
Blakemore SA	190315
Blase RG	121113
Bloomfield CA	161111
Bond AC	040602
Bowes-Crick EJ	061015
Bradley IEC	310710
Brehany J	030806
Brownsell MD	310708
Buenaventura JC	040411
Bunyan SJ	010815
Burt DK	100112
Cadman M *ARRC*	310709
Cameron FAM	290695
Capstick DM *RGN*	220799
Carpenter D	180910
Carr E	030806
Cartwright EA *TD*	110895
Cefferty MR *TD*	230491
Chapman R	030806
Clarkson PJ	261111
Colley JE	070593
Crabb RR	200214
Creagh MP	061015
Crossey VJ	310707
Dagless EJ	260809
Darragh E *TD*	140894
Davies ES	230808
Davies LA	230808
Davies-Tuthill AJ	170711
Dickson GE	200214
Donald ID	011212
Downey G	310709
Dutt R	310709
Dutton MM	030806
Eastwood-Dunwell C *RMN RGN*	171009
Ellis HJ	180910
Evans JL *TD*	251103
Fisher AJ	100210
Fitzpatrick BC	030806
Forbes KJ	310708
Fraser JM *TD*	230804
Gallimore J	020911
Galluccio P	010604
Garland SE	250909
Gill CJC	300909
Gilpin JRD	200214
Gittins CG	120907
Godfrey JA	150613
Godfrey NP	310708
Goff SB	081211
Goldsmith P	060410
Gregor NK	310708
Hadfield JAD	011113
Hagerty AJ	010405
Hall JA *TD*	161294
Hamilton DE	161015
Harrison S	210312
Harrison WJ	010809
Hayward SJ	300809
Heath RS	250909
Heddington DR	161015
Hignett WA	250909
Hill S	090315
Hird JA	150613
Holloway DG	261111
Hooper D	311297
Hulme A	071299
Hynam G	010610
Instrell RL	140613
Jacek BR	010402
James S	270312
Jamieson WDC *TD*	070501
Johnson SR	160197

Jones S 070405
Jones V 310506
Kelly JC *RGN RM DIPHSM MA HRM LLB(Hons)* 020701
Kendrick MI *BSc(Hons) RGN* 010806
Kidd SP 011107
Levett TM 080610
Lewis SJ *TD* 010699
Lim TCU 310709
Maddison T 230414
Malby AD *TD* 200301
Malcolm PB 080711
Marshall RB 310710
Maund LJ 080711
McIntosh HJ 220709
McKenna A 200810
McLaughlin KM 150209
McLeod MC 101012
McMahon RM 061015
McMillan OM 200214
Mezciems AL *RM* 240298
Micklewright S 161110
Montgomery JM 310708
Moore KH 150910
Morgan IT *TD* 230695
Morrison KM 100915
Moss DJ 310709
Myles G 310709
Nicholls AD 130510
Nixon EM *TD* 170295
Odams SET 040213
O'Hanlon JM 030806
Oldham SM *TD* 190796
Oliveira KP *BSc (Hons) RGN RM* 140613
O'Neill MB 150209
Orpen MA *TD* 180100
Parnell CM 200806
Parry A 310709
Pashley JA 101204
Peel RH *BSc(Hons) RGN RM* 171009
Pelgrom M 310708
Pennant SB 020302
Phillips CAJ *BSc (Hons) NP PG Dip Ed* 310707
Poyner JM 081213
Price AEC 171009
Price SL 030806
Price VK 050910
Pullen JD *RGN RM RHV MA* 140613
Quigg S 030806
Remmett-Booth HJ 150597
Rice NC 180809
Rice-Thomson MP 210312
Richardson Y 310709
Rowley AJ 081213
Saunders JA 011107
Scott A 011113
Semple M 150209
Shaw SJ 080711
Shuttleworth IR 011210
Siddle L *TD* 030806
Simpson-Hayes GC 011015
Skellon SF 280410
Skelton DL 061015
Sleight SR 180910
Smith AG 210408
Smith ET *TD* 211096
Smith KR 311009
Smyth GS 240413
Spencer IH 030806
Steen J *TD* 171194
Stubbs AJ 261111
Sullivan EJP 280709
Taberner A *TD* 010195
Taberner L 010809
Tams Gregg JS 150209
Taylor DM 030806
Teague-Hellon EM 061015
Thomas DJ 260510
Thompson KL 310708
Tibbles AM *TD* 190999
Tierney LE 310709
Tisshaw C 010412
Turner JEP 121210
Vogan EM 150209
Waddell R 101012
Walker L 240911
Walsh MP 290310
Wardle MS 011013
Warren RV 030806
Watkins K 030806
Watt RH 030909
Wilson DA 150209
Woodcock PP *TD MBA RGN BSc (Hons) CERTED FE* 261111
Worsley DJ 111295

Captains

Adams SJ 170411
Aitchison JA 010408
Almond SG 180303
Andrews A 110912
Aretz D 180599
Armstrong AM 040405
Baker TA 010704
Berry CS 260213
Beynon LC 201108
Bird JSE 280312
Blay AJ 161005
Bliss C 151107
Bond RM 111211
Boxley DJ 310305
Brownsword NT 310306
Byatt L 030309
Calver S 250197
Carter P 070911
Casey EL 290309
Chambers JW 140406
Chambers RI 310308
Chapman CL 050909
Collins SJ 270711
Cook JA 011297
Cowan I 071104
Cross SK 010408
Crossley AK 010407
Crow ZA 240706
Cvancara J 061214
Davey LJ 190801
Davies DL 221009
Davies JE *RGN SEN* 030603
Deoroop M 120203
Easton P 260511
Farrell KM 010312
Feeney TR 121293
Fitzgerald G 140403
Forbes N 230311
Frederick CE 070598
Gallagher NP 270300
Garbett RS *BSc (Hons) MSc BN RGN* 310307
Garratty S 140302
Geddes DJ 110701
Gilmore K 280901
Godfrey R 110303
Grafton DJ 090807

Gregg A	170310
Grew FM	270711
Griffin KG	310310
Hall DD	040307
Hamblin T	041109
Hargreaves JE	081202
Harlett-Joy CM	230501
Harris EM	040498
Harrison LM	210312
Hawkings DW	260113
Hayward KM	230414
Heath T	280709
Hill CA	140900
Holland RL	310303
Holliday M	070502
Howard VJ	290805
Hoyle ADC	050909
Hughes MP	261200
Hughes PT	290709
Jamieson DM	220701
Johnson-Cole WKO	040605
Johnston SM	010710
Jordan JE	230311
Kelly PD	010408
Kitchiner NJ	140509
Kyzer KE	110996
Lamport CP	150108
Landells A	310709
Lane BJ	310303
Legge AJ	090902
Lewis M	140509
MacLean S	190902
Mallett JM *BSc(Hons) DipHE*	081113
McAuley R	170914
McCormack MJ	100210
McDermott TF	180110
McIntosh LC	011212
McKay NP	011210
McLaughlin CE	301106
McMaster H	150910
Messenger P	171202
Miller M	100213
Molloy J	220604
Moore MM	040799
Morgan JA	111207
Morrisey CS	090709
Moss RL	070312
Murray D	030611
Nolan JP	011208
O'Donnell M	130109
Okon IEE	081000
O'Neill B	010408
Ongoma CM	300507
Parry NMR	010408
Poole DC	240399
Preece FS	270702
Rapur HE	220901
Reynolds RJ	160913
Richards M	261297
Ridpath MA	120603
Robertson AC	070305
Royle AP	230299
Ruddy CD	260511
Shamsaee WE	270113
Smales JI	150398
Smith L	210312
Smith MJ	280709
Spoors GM	010306
Sprake A	091214
Starmer ZC	101004
Staziker J	090412
Steele TM	080103
Summers PA	220105
Tabbinor P	010410
Tansey PE	010409
Thomas-Garwood PU	021102
Tupper DL	041111
Wilcox DG	011210
Williamson A	010408
Wilson AJ	020906
Wilson K	190503
Wilson SJ	181110
Yourston DJ	020610

Lieutenants

Barrington A	030914
Camilleri AL	230309
George AL	270713
Gray KC	260814
Langlands FA	090313
Loftus JJ	010907
Reid SJ	021011
Talbot CJ	120811
Williams M	100405

Officer Cadet

Welch KA	231010

UNIVERSITY OFFICERS TRAINING CORPS (UOTC)

Royal Honorary Colonels

City of Edinburgh Universities OTC	HRH The Princess Royal *KG KT GCVO QSO*	210715
University of London OTC	HRH The Princess Royal *KG KT GCVO QSO*	210489

Honorary Colonels

Aberdeen Unniversity OTC	Mr Andrew Edward Hanning Bradford	010911
Birmingham Univeristy OTC	Brig (Retd) Mark P Banham *MBE*	300914
Bristol Univeristy OTC	Gen (Retd)*Sir* Mike Jackson *GCB CBE DSO DL (until 010816)*	010511
	Maj Gen Ranald T I Munro *CBE TD VR (from 010816)*	
Cambridge University OTC	Gen (Retd) *Sir* Peter Wall *GCB CBE DL FREng*	230213
East Midlands Universities OTC	Vacant	
City of Edinburgh Universities OTC	Maj Gen (Retd) Mike L Riddell-Webster *CBE DSO*	010814
Exeter University OTC	Maj Gen Chris L Tickell *CBE*	010815
Glasgow and Strathclyde Universities OTC	Col (Retd) Allan C C Lapsley *QVRM TD DL*	010310
Leeds Univeristy OTC	Vacant	
Liverpool University OTC	Prof Nigel P Weatherill	010713
University of London OTC	Lt Gen James I Bashall *CBE*	010215
Manchester and Salford Universities OTC	Lt Gen Patrick N Y M Sanders *CBE DSO*	010413
Northumbrian Universities OTC	Maj Gen Greg S Smith *CB QVRM TD DL*	011113
Oxford University OTC	Maj Gen (Retd) J M Cowan *CBE DSO (until 180217)*	010413
	Lt Gen Mark A P Carleton-Smith *CBE (from 180217)*	
Queen's Univeristy OTC	Col Iain G D Moles *OBE QVRM TD*	020415
University of Sheffield OTC	Mr Neil A MacDonald	011214
Southampton University OTC	Maj Gen Robert M B Nitsch *CBE*	131014
Tayforth Universities OTC	Maj Gen (Retd) Kevin D Abraham *CB*	010613
Univeristy of Wales OTC	Brig (Retd) Iain D Cholerton *CBE*	230308

UOTC UNITS

Aberdeen	Roy Strathdee Building, 152 Don Street, Aberdeen AB24 1XQ (Tel: 01224 483861 Email: aberdeenuotc@btconnect.com)
Belfast	Tyrone House, 83 Malone Road, Belfast, County Antrim, BT9 6SJ
Birmingham	Montgomery House, Stoney Lane, Birmingham B12 8AT (Tel: 0121 449 3741 Email: bhamuotc@globalnet.co.uk)
Bristol	Artillery Grounds, Whiteladies Road, Bristol BS8 2LG (Tel: 0117 973 3533 Email: Bristolotc-raowo@mod.uk Website: www.bristoluotc.mod.uk)
Cambridge	TA Centre, Coldham's Lane, Cambridge CB1 3HS (Tel: 01223 247818 Email: cuotc@cuotc.army.mod.uk Website: www.cam.ac.uk/CambUniv/Societies/cuotc)
East Midlands	TA Centre, Broadgate, Beeston, Nottingham NG9 2HF (Tel: 0115 968 3820 Email: emuotc@btconnect.com)
Edinburgh	Duke of Edinburgh House, 301 Colinton Road, Edinburgh EH13 0LA (Tel: 0131 310 5443 Email: ceuotc-adj@tanet.mod.uk Website: www.ceuotc.info)
Exeter	Acland Buildings, Wyvern Barracks, Exeter EX2 6AR (Tel: 01392 492452 Email: exeteruotc-adjt@tanet.mod.uk)
Glasgow and Strathclyde	95 University Place, Glasgow G12 8SU (Tel: 0141 339 6611 Email: Glasgowotc-ChiefClerk@mod.uk)

Leeds .... Carlton Barracks, Carlton Gate, Leeds LS7 1HE
(Tel: 01904 668624 Email: luotc@btconnect.com)

Liverpool.. Crawford Hall, Mather Avenue, Liverpool L18 6HF
(Tel: 0151 729 2031 Email: liverpooluotc-chclk@tanet.mod.uk)

London .... Yeomanry House, Handel Street, London WC1N 1NP
(Tel: 0207 414 3890 Email: adjutant@ulotc.co.uk
Website: www.ulotc.co.uk)

Manchester and Salford .... University Barracks, Boundry Lane, Manchester M15 6DH
(Tel: 0161 228 2185 Email: msuotc@tiscali.co.uk)

Northumbrian... St Cuthberts Keep, Holland Drive, Newcastle-Upon-Tyne NE2 4LD
(Tel: 0191 239 5328 Email: northumbrian2@btconnect.com)

Oxford .... Falklands House, Oxpens Road, Oxford OX1 1RX
(Tel: 01865 242488 Email: OxfordOTC-Adjt@mod.uk)

Sheffield .... Somme Barracks, Glossop Road, Sheffield S10 2HU
(Tel: 0114 252 6310 Email: Sheffielduotc-chclk@tanet.mod.uk)

Southampton .... 32 Carlton Place, Southampton SO15 2DX
(Tel: 02380 332211 Email: UOTCSouthampton-hq-admin@mod.uk)

Tayforth .... 16 Park Wynd, Dundee DD1 5HG
(Tel: 01382 225981 Email: tayforthotc-adjt@mod.uk)

Wales UOTC

Headquarters Wales UOTC, Maindy Barracks, Whitchurch Road, Cardiff CF14 3YE
(Tel: 02920 726183 Email: WalesOTC-RAOWO@mod.uk)

Wales (Aberystwyth)......................... TA Centre, Park Avenue Aberystwyth SY23 1PG

Wales (Bangor)................................. The Barracks, Llanberis Road, Caernarfon LL56 2DD

Wales (Swansea) .... John Chard VC House, Glamorgan Street, Swansea SA1 3SY

Wales (Wrexham).............................. Hightown Barracks, Wrexham LL13 8RD

UOTC A

2nd Lieutenants

Anderson-Bickley EGW	210814
Bamford JC	071014
Barnhurst H	231010
Buck DC	020814
Cockle NAF	020814
Colthup TE	121013
Gladwin RN	030813
Gleizes HL	211012
Harrison OJK	121013
Hunter HFL	121013
King E	121013
Knight RCG	290913
Moore KJM	061012
Munnings JA	121013
Paul OJ	290712
Porter CG	020814
Pulger-Frame MM	161014
Raleigh AM	060914
Reed JS	020814
Ryder M	231010
Sharp E	231010
Szczyglowski CP	281011

UOTC B

2nd Lieutenants

Arnold DL	270713
Bagshaw MT	141012
Bryan AJ	290912
Capper CSG	171012
Carn ANR	021011
Farrow TA	270713
Green RR	301012
Hastings DG	141012
Kittler AK	131010
Murray R	020814
Newman NCC	161013
Pearce EM	121013
Shackleton JGJ	211012
Swarbrick RJ	131013
Taylor SC	121112
Warner JTJ	191011
Wheeler WF	121112
Wyn-Jones GL	151012

GENERAL SERVICE LIST

Lieutenant Colonel

Blakey WD 040116

Majors

Duff HM *TD* 051201
Harrison TGS 040204
Heywood LM 040213
Pitt RM 140714
Wawn CJN *TD* 110997

Captains

Grant MJ 010410
Grayson MPM *MVO VR* 221101
Greenwell JP 050403
MacIsaac W *MBE QVRM* 20612
Stacey SNJ 200402

Lieutenants

Barton DS 241114
Davison S 101213
Halawi HB 031214
McCarthy CJ 241114

2nd Lieutenants

Beek CA 040813
Bennett M 141012
Brown AJ 280914
Clancy A 280914
Conlon T 260915
Cumberlidge MD 121113
Floodpage A 151012
Hancock M 260915
Haydon MW 030813
Hopkin BC 070614
Houston WAV 131004
Janzen-Morris AB 260915
Jarvis GH 290712
Jenkins AAD 111013
Keays CT 101211
Maxwell CJ 111013
McCreadie WAL 061013
Morrison AJ 290707
Mosey HT 221014
Mrozicki A 211011
Nicol A 190612
O'Dell TF 061013
Plunket ODC 091013
Pooley RS 241012
Powderham S 121011
Reid RL 031012
Sharman G 290912
Tankard JM 141012
Taylor EH 190215
Turner RC 290915
Washington-Smith TG 091013
Webb-Bowen JG 021011
Wilkinson LM 021011
Wiltshire AJ 290912
Zhao J 030813

Officer Cadets

Huck LJ 120214
Jerstice MA 141014
Page VS 010914
Parsons STW 240215
Power R 131013
Sutcliffe JA 200115
Williams B 091214
Young FD 091013

SECTION B
COMBINED CADET FORCE

Captain General... HER MAJESTY THE QUEEN

There are over 260 CCF contingents based in both state and independent schools and colleges throughout the UK.

Lieutenants	
Abbott JM	290411
Adams K	060205
Adamson J	050703
Adcock DP	220302
Adcroft H	010900
Aggrey ME	220715
Ahrens SL	091015
Albon S	310805
Alexander A	280314
Allan SC	010315
Allen-Mirehouse LFJ	121214
Amirthananthar A	200515
Amos SJ	140415
Anderson BJ	060707
Anglim B	010900
Appleton GC	020915
Archer MJ	140611
Armitage DR	140212
Armon M	060304
Ashford MD	280409
Ashlee-McCrae N	010903
Ashworth I	180110
Atherton A	010900
Atkins AS	080513
Atkins WLM	170711
Atkinson JB	070712
Austin E	210907
Auty TS	110509
Ayres R	010900
Badham E	010900
Bage I	010900
Bain J	091100
Bain W	051204
Baker S	271005
Ball N	010909
Ballard J	231205
Balmbra M	010900
Balmer J	101013
Bancroft R	180409
Banerjee R	010713
Banwell MJ	010812
Barber A	010900
Barker AGA	010110
Barker JP	231110
Barlow LE	010815
Barlow PM	221002
Barmby D	011210
Barnard C	010911
Barnard J	250210
Barnard K	010900
Barnes JA	040211
Barr I	191204
Barr JTM	011012
Barrett N	010900
Barrow C	020911
Barton LE	121112
Bassett P	010903
Bates MJ	030309
Batten A	010900
Bayley T	090203
Beasant DJ	010312
Beasley GC	260614
Beckett G	010900
Beggs A	030412
Belfield SMF	230112
Bennett AS	110213
Berrow A	010900
Berry M	231100
Bicknell E	171007
Billington JS	261101
Binnie S	270208
Birkill TA	020911
Birmingham C	081113
Bishop D	010900
Bishop H	160106
Black FS	051211
Black S	010913
Blackburn HT	111210
Blackford MS	220991
Blackwood I	300900
Blattner R	010409
Bleakley JJ	060607
Bloxham CE	091109
Bohl M	160105
Bolderow S	161104
Bond MD	190116
Bosher S	180102
Brandt D	010503
Brennan M	210201
Bridle DWA	220114
Brightman C	010900
Brighton AJ	010907
Brinkworth R	010315
Brister P	010900
Bromfield JG *MBE*	010900
Brooker PA	090614
Brooks J	010900
Brown A	140113
Brown A	010900
Brown GL	230911
Brown M	010900
Brown P	190311
Brown PL	081212
Bryant G	131205
Buchanan M	010900
Buckner M	300911
Budd J	010900
Bullion R	190301
Bunn A	270311
Burford VE	010410
Burnett E	090706
Burns R	010900
Burns SI	260811
Burrell S	050611
Burt D	010900
Burton C	050903
Burton G	010913
Butt P	010104
Butt R	100210
Buxton O	281113
Camm J	200401
Campbell A	240301

Campbell CH	010409
Campbell G	110313
Campbell IAN	080313
Campbell-Thomas J	281103
Campion AJ	060114
Cannell J	081005
Cannon BJ	080914
Capjon BA	300913
Capper L	111204
Cardwell CEM	010307
Carmichael C	010900
Carmichael CM	290707
Carr NJ	010901
Carson D	010901
Carter M	200301
Carus A	270507
Cavaglieri N	170706
Cawley G	070304
Chadwick DA	010913
Chadwick W	140109
Chamen P	160307
Channing D	140502
Chapman DK	070115
Chapple D	101205
Charania A	061009
Charlton MA	011011
Charnock F	010900
Chatterjee R	151007
Chauhan H	120209
Cheadle SJ	180515
Cheney TA	280613
Cherry C	010900
Chivers LL	280311
Christie J	051110
Christmas MR	010406
Christy IM	051007
Clarke R	010900
Clarke R	251104
Clarke S	010900
Clayton M	240805
Clewlow M	010900
Cliff B	010612
Clift JW	300807
Clingain ESR	050216
Clinton T	010513
Cluley DR	091212
Coakes AR	010509
Coates E	050312
Cockerill EA	010701
Coe S	170311
Coker M	310302
Cole D	010900
Coleman J	200215
Colgate CC	010414
Collins T	010900
Coltart KC	101009
Commander MJL	100209
Conway R	250612
Cooley N	061004
Coomber RC	060713
Cooper C	031203
Cooper CR	050707
Cooper D	010900
Cooper NA	130713
Coppard RJ	250215
Copson G	060511
Corbet S	190705
Corthine R	010913
Cousins SL	300913
Coyne LJ	011006
Craggs DG	270506
Craig Membrey A	120514
Crane J	011004
Crick PJ	010900
Crookes J	010900
Crossland L	011008
Crutchley M	010900
Culley DP	010900
Cumine SG	220511
Cunningham C	010501
Cunningham JE *MBE*	040712
Currie ALA	210313
Curwood SJ	010900
Dareve KD	120315
Darvill C	061207
Davenport K	010900
David N	010900
Davidson RL	030108
Davies A	150507
Davies CL	010310
Davies G	010900
Davies I	100102
Davies R	090106
Davies SA	240114
Davies SA	010900
Davis J	081104
Daws W	301115
Dawson C	010900
Dawson G	010900
Dawson K	111011
Day J	010900
De Gale JS	301111
De Silva RLN	190515
Dean C	010900
Denning M	201002
Derrick HPI	240216
Dewar D	010900
Dexter RGA	101007
Dick NG	220914
Digby M	240206
Diggins S	040505
Dobney F	010915
Dobson D	010704
Donaldson SJ	250509
Dovey T	211107
Doyle G	131001
Drake DE	221008
Draper GE	031007
Draper H	010900
Drinkall D	010412
Drinkall F	040204
Driver J	011000
Duckworth WR	240209
Dudin J	010900
Dudley MAJ	130412
Duff CJ	010106
Duggan DJ	250216
Dummett M	011014
Duncalf HJ	041013
Dunlop PD	151110
Dunlop R	280202
Dutoit P	101101
Dyer B	280803
Dyer C	101207
Dziemianko A	270107
Eades EJ	010414
East J	110604
Eastham J	151213
Eaton C	010900
Eaves KE	010913
Eckton AR	190710
Eglin D	290106
Eldridge CJ	191109
Ellen SK	051010

Emerson SW	130998
Eustace C	300905
Evans D	180604
Evans DR	230813
Evans N	090209
Evans T	010408
Evanson R	010101
Everitt K	010900
Eversfield P	060404
Ewing AD	111007
Faiers R	050312
Fairclough SC	201109
Fairwood HW	100113
Falzon A	100210
Fanneran H	030608
Farley S	090302
Farmer CJ	011014
Farnan MG	260612
Farnworth P	010900
Fawcett J *BA(Hons) MA*	060606
Featherstone JJ	101003
Ferguson JF	140714
Fernandez P	020204
Finn A	160310
Finn P	150906
Fischbacher N	010302
Fisher M	240115
Fitzwater R	010900
Flanders J	251005
Fleming ZK	280614
Fletcher-Campbell C	010900
Flower NC	-
Floyd RM	270615
Follows MR	220114
Foot L	160514
Forbes MP	010105
Forey J	071008
Foster MW	010501
Francis JC	211209
Francis N	260512
Franks M	010900
Friling SM	020310
Froy C	211001
Fuller K	010900
Gaffney P	060214
Gallagher GM	230411
Galley P	030811
Gallier NP	010510
Garden D	010900
Gareh M	010900
Garfirth S	010501
Garley SR	291015
Garthwaite MD	030211
Gartside J	141112
Garvey J	131100
Garvie AC	161210
Gates SB	010900
George A	250107
Gibb JW	110414
Gilbert O	120514
Gildea JAR	221106
Gill E	010900
Gill K	121014
Gillespie J	010900
Gilliland A	010900
Gilmour E	010900
Glynethomas P	281103
Goddard HE	050815
Godding CL	121112
Godfrey DJ	120110
Godfrey MH	240501
Golden PJ	220110
Gooch TA	030409
Goodall AJ	230709
Gordon TA	250411
Gormley EA	011010
Gott P	010900
Graham J	310812
Graham RP	310111
Grainger E	150113
Grant A	220408
Grant A	240112
Grantham IC	040715
Gray A	181110
Gray HR	210411
Greenwood AM	200116
Greenwood JM	120216
Greer DB	070410
Grime J	011005
Groom C	010900
Gunn JR	300415
Gunnill J	141006
Hall AW	070912
Hall C	270903
Hall VAM	190912
Halleron MAM	010314
Hambleton M	240607
Hamid M	010900
Hamlett R	210214
Hampshire M	010900
Hanna RL	070708
Hannah A	010900
Hardy GW	110515
Harkness SM	010413
Harmes J	010102
Harper RA	111010
Harrison M	061211
Harrison SE	300414
Harriss F	010900
Harrup P	050704
Hart CA	010107
Hart JE	010513
Hart M	010900
Hart SE	120203
Hartley D	190116
Harvey H	060603
Harwood PA	080112
Hastie K	171207
Hastings R	010900
Haswell MD	040313
Hatchell CE	070115
Hawkes MH	010213
Hawkins MGS	010900
Hawkins MSF	050310
Hawley A	291110
Hayday T	010900
Haynes F	190116
Hayter KP	131009
Hayward G	010900
Hayward JE	171106
Haywood SP	010111
Heap L	210306
Heard S	090711
Hebdon AL	230514
Hegarty JJ	081012
Hempsall C	291107
Henderson CS	211113
Hendy AW	270614
Henvey FJ	101106
Hewitson J	010112
Hiddleston R	250806
Higginbottom D	190602
Higgins D	061203
Highway PJ	060512

Hill GR	010215
Hill MS	251011
Hills S	010407
Hitching RM	121107
Hobday I	120506
Hoey KJ	110609
Hogben G	170103
Holdaway J	210411
Holder A	010504
Holding A	311011
Holding RA	011112
Holdsworth M	220210
Holloway R	160513
Holmes S	010510
Holmstrom M	120703
Holmstrom W	010900
Hone M	010900
Hooker R	010900
Hopcroft AJ	200215
Hopkins PM	161003
Horley P	060915
Hoskin A	140305
Howard SM	230410
Howarth J	021205
Howe CL	230508
Howe R	120209
Howl PJ	011213
Howman S	071102
Howson DM	191215
Hudson A	070507
Hudson S	010900
Hughes GJ	010712
Hughes J	010404
Hullis S	220113
Hunt AW	020415
Hunt LJ	300615
Hurst E	011007
Hurst JE	130912
Hurst P	010900
Husband WCR	011011
Hutchings A	240215
Huxter AN	010412
Huxter CE	090212
Huxter E	010900
Hynard PA	010410
Igolen-Robi C	010900
Imeson JS	010900
Ingram C	100915
Irvine P	190201
Irwin AH	120214
Jackson C	060511
Jackson CE	220216
Jackson CP	150612
Jackson DA	251013
James FC	010908
James R	030811
James S	030811
Jarvis RCM	290107
Jefferis TJ	141006
Jenkins AJ	220912
Jennings C	010900
Jennings G *QVRM*	291108
Jennings M	081107
Jephcote SJ	011015
Jervis O	201203
Johns P	010900
Johnson J	020213
Johnston R	010913
Jolley P	010900
Jones A	091212
Jones AR	160610
Jones CJ	140504
Jones M	010901
Jones M	070702
Jones RJ	011211
Jones SM	250412
Jowett JR	211112
Joyce R	190907
Kaye EA	190610
Kellett RJ	150910
Kelly HJ	041011
Kelso IAO	080409
Kelson SJ	280514
Kempton R	300808
Kendrick R	080405
Kenyon S	010900
Kiff GM	141009
Kiggell J	150613
Kiggell L	010903
Kilsby J	160203
King E	160513
King E	010508
King P	010900
King TG	230810
Kingston AG	060812
Kirk FM	300409
Kirkham BW	120509
Klempner D	200201
Kovacevic Z	030710
Kupfer T	260510
Kyte NJ	070709
Lacey J	010406
Lacey R	010900
Lagdon D	201015
Lamb M	021210
Lamb MJ	010414
Land W	010900
Lane RG	080213
Law M	231205
Law S	010900
Lawrence IJ	010314
Lawson SK	200312
Lawton P	240216
Laycock PA	041213
Le Poidevin RC	101012
Leach AD	070113
Leak JM	200407
Leat MWJ	110310
Leaver PC	170415
Ledson D	030709
Lee A	221101
Lee C	010900
Lee MR	091015
Lee MS	010409
Lee N	020609
Lehmann D	010912
Leonard N	010602
Leonard R	010900
Lewis KE	240106
Lewis M	250703
Liberman TJ	040413
Liggins C	310314
Lilley JK	010190
Lindsay RAJ	191112
Ling TC	120212
Linnell NK	220115
Llewellyn T	180612
Lloyd DC	111211
Lloyd TM	181110
Lloyd-Williams M	010900
Lock G	010900
Lockhart RJ	270614
Lodge DR	010214
Lonsdale P	010900

Luckett D	060809	McCullough JE	010910	Nagle G	010900
Lydford PM	011112	McDonagh T	160905	Neale PM	251104
Lyon AE	250609	McDowell R	210305	Newbury DT	150609
Lythgoe C	020702	McEwen CES	070314	Newman ME	241012
MacAulay SA	010215	McFaul SR	200312	Newton J	080515
MacCarthy SK	300909	McGee AJ	140415	Newton P	010900
MacDowel B	120108	McGowan IV	100113	Nichols MCD	180213
Mace GM	010607	McGowan M	080607	Nicol R	090607
Machin R	141006	McGregor AR	010811	Nighy DJ	290309
MacKay CR	030216	McIntosh L	010612	Noble A	010900
MackIntosh N	010101	McKee L	280810	Noble P	010907
MacLeod N	010900	McKie I	010900	Norman MM	180811
Maitland M	010900	McKinnon JM	101207	Norrington A	060809
Malcolm E	191003	McNab TR	100214	Norris JL	080912
Marcandonatos RJ	201106	McNaught WM	150615	North A	161213
March-Shawcross EG	121213	McQuitty SMF	170905	Novis TWG	130510
Markos JS	290514	Medley MI	050815	Nugent CJ	011214
Marrett R	010900	Megit D	051202	Nunn AM	300912
Marshall J	281114	Megit R	170901	Nuthall DE	141114
Marshall N	190815	Menneer R	010900	O'Brien OR	311013
Marshall TTA	020915	Merrick A	280709	O'Bryan JM	010798
Martin LJ	160309	Messenger PJ	010313	O'Connell MB	041013
Martin NW	310811	Migallo NP	120907	O'Connor PI	230514
Martin P	130304	Mildinhall SJ	280114	O'Donoghue M	090605
Martin PHS	130111	Millar R	010404	Ogden L	010900
Martin PJ	300613	Millbery G	050205	Ogg R	270112
Massie E	190108	Miller T	010900	Oliver FLF	160513
Master-Jewitt G	030912	Millward O	260614	Ollerenshaw MJ	250314
Masters M	270903	Milton P	151008	O'Neill J	180802
Matheson LJ	061211	Moir C	010900	O'Ram EM	281014
Mathewson A	141207	Molloy M	311004	Othen AD	190507
Matthews E	010900	Money JD	040311	Ottewell HV	240512
Matthews K	190513	Monk PCT *TD*	010406	Overend A	010900
Maund A	010900	Monument L	280408	Owen I	170604
Maund C	010900	Moon N	170501	Owen J	010900
Maxfield R	121005	Moore MC	160710	Owen M	090609
May RE	161009	Morgan D	261007	Owen M	160812
Mayhew D	010116	Morrell C	310302	Page DJ	090911
Mazur P	270214	Morris DN	180216	Page N	240403
McAdam C	010900	Mortimer HJ	151009	Painter H	091008
McAlinden RS	080108	Morton N	250306	Palma SC	281114
McAnuff P	071115	Motteram E	011001	Palmer CH	011113
McAulay H	310502	Mould JS	160615	Palmer S	020606
McCahon W	010900	Moxham AW	011011	Pardoe R	160608
McCall IA	261109	Muirhead A	050313	Patch S	080202
McCallum C	010900	Mulkerrins A	010900	Patchett J	151002
McCallum K	010900	Murphy DJ *MA*	150415	Patel H	010913
McCaughey K	090605	Myers-Allen M	010900	Patrick A	010900

Patterson IG	301114	Pullen DJ	011104	Rowe D	010900
Paul KD	201211	Quentin AD	010907	Rowlands R	061114
Payne C	220295	Radojcic S	010900	Ruffle S	151110
Payne S	090303	Randle RL	050310	Rush MJ	120412
Peacock AG	111215	Rankin TH	050611	Russ J	061008
Peake M	050405	Rathbone EM	010911	Rutter GE	030789
Peall M	010900	Rattray WAR	180313	Ryall R	010900
Pemberton OC	160615	Rawlings A	111205	Ryan C	260612
Penfold A	010900	Read PJ	011211	Rylance R	010110
Penny R	010900	Reardon D	091207	Rylands TG	121112
Penny RJ	130910	Reed AB	081014	Sadiq H	030915
Perera OJN	041015	Reeves M	101204	Salih SP	300809
Perks IJ	010411	Reid C	010901	Salmon R	011202
Pervin S	191209	Reid KE	010213	Sammons RA	260312
Phillimore DC	220116	Relph RG	290110	San Jose CA	011210
Phillips G	230307	Reynolds A	011212	Sanderson AJ	010412
Picken RD	230114	Richardson H	010900	Sansom DRL	170608
Pickett D	010900	Richardson TI	100715	Sapsford J	010907
Piper I	010900	Richmond D	010900	Saunderson S	010900
Pitt J	010900	Rickard L	240201	Savage A	010900
Plum LF	071011	Ricketts J	140702	Saxton MJ	240411
Pollard AM	060314	Riding J	081202	Sayell CR	010308
Pollard J	130105	Ridley DW	090713	Sayers TRH	011015
Ponter WT	150104	Ridley NC	010111	Scaife M	091208
Pooley J	010404	Rigby MHN	230515	Scarll A	201002
Pope WK	050312	Roache AM	010911	Schofield M	140515
Potter G	010900	Roberts H	171002	Schofield SJ	031007
Potter P	081203	Roberts M	180315	Scoble G	010907
Poustie J	010900	Robertson LM	240314	Scorer N	301110
Powell G	121201	Robinson CS	270409	Scott JS	171111
Powell JB	111209	Robinson D	010900	Scourfield M	210312
Powell MJ	070710	Robinson NP	200114	Scrowston A	041011
Powell R	031003	Robson AJ	160611	Seaman J	010900
Powell S	241109	Robson REP	040315	Sebastian PW	170414
Preston DF	270311	Rodenhurst RJ	220111	Seccombe G	010810
Price B	010902	Rodger G	200206	Sefton AH	120609
Price D	300306	Roebuck JA	010714	Shakespeare I	220104
Price J	010900	Rogers K	070308	Shaw A	290106
Price J	310805	Rogers PS	240111	Shaw GR	050313
Price V	010900	Rondel C	221010	Shaw SJ	120607
Pring AW	221015	Rose BES	230510	Sheldon CM	220914
Pringle A	160709	Rose LM	150613	Sheldrick B	180902
Prior M	270912	Ross ACP	290311	Shephard P	010900
Pritchard L	010900	Ross ADM	230514	Sheppard K	010900
Proudlove SL	231110	Rothnie N	010900	Shield D	010900
Pryde C	010900	Rothwell PN	070808	Shield MG	020610
Pugh M	081111	Rouan J	170615	Shields D	010900
Pugh S	021209	Rouse NH	260614	Shilling SA	020611

Shindler KJ	310116
Shooter DC	111009
Short A	010900
Short SM	150103
Simkins M	170602
Simper O	080208
Simper W	140607
Simpson D	210998
Simpson JR	041012
Skeate M	191100
Skinner M	010900
Slemen M	010900
Smiddy SC	290906
Smith AF	111108
Smith BR	110506
Smith C	010900
Smith H	150704
Smith KA *MBE*	010900
Smith L	220914
Smith L	010900
Smith M	010900
Smith SA	170502
Sowah L	010905
Spawforth G	010900
Spedding I	010900
Spivey B	210306
Spracklin C	010402
Standen CM	270613
Standley CT	190613
Stanforth J	210503
Stanley JM	010211
Stapleton P	010900
Starkey L	200812
Staves J	010406
Stead G	020112
Stead M	010901
Stephens P	010900
Stephens R	010900
Stevens M	050205
Stevens S	010908
Stewart C	010900
Stimpson PSH	170414
Stockton R	010900
Stowell G	010900
Strecker K	021205
Stumbles P	031000
Sturt PD	110210
Suchy HJ	051012
Sudding CJ	081009
Summers SJ	221110
Sunner CF	040208
Swales R	070603
Swallow AM	021015
Swift EMH	100915
Swinburne D	280601
Switzer R	240606
Sykes AM	141209
Sykes K	010900
Symes C	160301
Tabb L	170908
Tanner J	060910
Taylor D	010900
Taylor RC	030911
Tebay DE	171013
Temple SL	161009
Tennant N	101215
Terry CJ	040111
Terry SJ	171209
Tester IJ	231009
Tetlow G	240508
Thomas A	010910
Thomas EJ	010915
Thompson MJ	050112
Thomson AF	080209
Thorn N	010900
Tidy S	310810
Ting RE	180911
Todd BJ	010900
Toley R	010900
Tomalin D	010908
Tomaszewski N	010900
Topham N	010900
Tovey LJ	070315
Townley DM	110111
Treharne A	010403
Tremewan S	010900
Trimby C	010115
Trott R	010900
Tuck MA	040714
Turnbull DU	070111
Twigg J	010900
Tynan E	110112
Urquhart IAN	010910
Vasa A	010911
Vaughan R	100306
Vintner AR	311204
Vodden H	010900
Vokes M	010903
Vyse JS	040912
Wadsworth JC	010912
Waghorn PR	010406
Walden J	010900
Waldron RD	200414
Walker W	310113
Wallace A	010900
Wallace D	010900
Waller R	010900
Ward B	060308
Waring N	010900
Warren MR	051010
Warren RM	100702
Waters J	200106
Waters JI	041011
Watkins DJ	281113
Watling H	310113
Watson EL	011110
Watt DJ	210116
Webb TA	250308
Welsby I	011010
Welsh W	240103
West J	110708
West MT	051209
Whatley JM	220113
White A	100109
White AJ	011013
White JRC *TD*	040214
White NL	110201
Whitehead DJ	050911
Whitehouse D	010900
Whitmore R	230613
Whittaker NM	010714
Wilcockson M	010900
Wilkinson A	010900
Wilkinson LJ	240612
Williams E	150603
Williams ID	291014
Williams J	041204
Williams P	161005
Williams SEL	310314
Willmore A	020806
Wills RJ	011112
Wilson GL	240715
Wilson PA	210111
Winkley CH	090215

Winter SJ	180305
Witts JC	090114
Wood AJ	110710
Wood J	081208
Wood R	161205
Woodall NJ	010404
Woodall S	010900
Woodcock MJ	301015
Woodhams F	030912
Woodhams J	030912
Woodsmith N	010900
Woolcott D	010900
Workman A	080615
Worrall T	151006
Wright CDP	050710
Wright E	270102
Wright G	150606
Wright R	040905
Wynell-Mayow LJ	050912
Wynn A	180601
Yetman M	240611
Young SAH	010900

2nd Lieutenants

Abbott G	100912
Aiano SGG	030409
Alderson LJ	121110
Alexander A	080514
Al-Khamiri SM	090414
Allard JM	280612
Allcock SJ	310108
Alston CE	160514
Andersen P	131213
Anderson T	071015
Andrews JW	250715
Andrews L	051112
Ashfield AD	111113
Ashman MA	101215
Atkin AB	010415
Atkinson HL	291013
Baddeley MM	211013
Baird WDJ	070115
Barfield V	220115
Barker M	010707
Barnett J	270110
Barrett N	211014
Bartlett DS	120614
Batchelder G	230511
Bates BD	040714
Bates CP	010914
Beard A	040505
Beaumont AM	141113
Beber RK	150910
Bedworth MI	100614
Beggs D	111213
Belding S	260115
Bell M	300615
Bell PMF	250915
Ben-Cheikh DC	040216
Bish HFC	170215
Bishop DJ	080210
Blackford DS	100915
Blair S	140512
Blamires DI	011108
Blay SV	011215
Boak SJ	160514
Boast EA	210611
Bolton PA	290915
Bowes A	111209
Bowyer-Bower TAS	200312
Boyle ZK	060511
Brady SI	290311
Breheney SD	060214
Brewis D	250610
Bridgeman CJ	220311
Brien KB	280406
Brock WG	250112
Broughton C	040215
Brown BR	091109
Brown PW	190310
Brown SA	210715
Bumford M	070414
Burke A	190412
Burke DE	151113
Burnside J	180216
Bustin T	251006
Cade MA	230216
Cahill CJJ	170506
Cain CJ	110214
Caine JA	110313
Calder AE	220909
Callow PA	010714
Cann ACG	191214
Carey HEM	120314
Carey JR	230915
Carter JR	290915
Caulfield AR	120214
Cavill AJ	280114
Chamberlain WL	270415
Chambers E	280514
Champ JK	230216
Chandler VP	121113
Chisholm CJ	170314
Christmas GW	270315
Clark AP	180613
Clark S	100913
Clarke DC	171212
Clarke J	300715
Clarke RGD	120314
Clarke TJ	230215
Claxton WR	101215
Clifford N	120313
Cochrane J	021213
Cockburn G	010113
Cole B	300909
Cole J	210709
Collie AE	220909
Collingwood MSJ	080414
Collinson PJ	-
Cookson RKA	060612
Cooper F	181214
Coopper N	051110
Cowie PJ	020713
Cowlard MG	160615
Cox SD	121113
Coyle EM	221014
Cradock A	220915
Cram FM	280309
Crane LE	170614
Crichton LEA	220212
Croker NJ	011013
Crossley AM	190412
Crowther A	010900
Darbyshire S	110214
Davidson IC	030714
Davidson JA	240915
Davies T	261114
Davis CTN	041212
Davis L	300615
Dawkins HJ	101215
Dawson G	231009
Dawson J	121214
Deakes K	210705
Dedynski ML	051115

Denholm CD	130614	Gick E	240305	Henshaw V	021109
Derbridge NP	050213	Gisby JE	010915	Herriott SA	031011
Dickson RA	240216	Glass HCA	110615	Hewson CE	201213
Dienn ER	070214	Goddard AH	131211	Hibbert IP	030414
Dixon PD	111115	Goldhawk M	031213	Higgins GC	220915
Donaldson C	080714	Goldsmith RW	131210	Higginson NAC	060214
Douglas GE	290615	Goodall DS	070414	Hill LJC	280514
Dowding MS	280314	Goodfellow CJ	120212	Hillyard N	220116
Duckham M	050215	Gordon L	230914	Hinxman HS	071015
Duffield JDJ	250215	Graham DBA	181209	Hockley JP	100915
Duffin RP	300915	Graham FM	070515	Hodgson JE	010414
Durrant TC	220908	Grant M	220505	Hoey E	130906
Eardley D	300615	Gray L	070214	Holden C	011215
Eccleston J	030314	Gray MW	140114	Holden HMA	080514
Echeverry V	050309	Green CE	010714	Holdsworth TE	091015
Egglestone CA	090913	Green I	080114	Holmes CAA	230216
Eloho-Emmanuel HE	070115	Green M	270213	Holmes MJ	040315
Emmens WF	210116	Greenland F	111213	Holt JL	131112
Ermgassen F	111114	Griffiths S	021205	Horner RM	280114
Fairbrother MJ	070115	Grimes PJ	300615	Hou TJ	230914
Fairnington EJ	240915	Grimshaw JR	210513	Hough JA	020712
Faja ZR	291014	Gurnhill S	140603	Houlden TLM	090614
Farr HE	090415	Haldane H	190412	Howard-Murphy A	030210
Fathers DJ	020216	Halley CD	250615	Howell AC	030714
Ferris EV	300910	Hamilton HEM	240807	Howlett A	180613
Field GC	121212	Hammond SS	021213	Hughes MJ	101215
Fielden AJ	210116	Hampson SC	070515	Hunter R	170305
Finn CF	260108	Hannah RM	120314	Innes JD	260614
Fisher R	160710	Hannavy K	241115	Isherwood MA	021013
Fisk C	210905	Hardman SF	260614	Jago CH	020309
Flavell KM	190614	Hardyman MKJ	270409	Jeffrey MKW	250614
Fletcher RJ	031214	Hargreaves MG	070515	Jennings EA	310712
Follett RND	041012	Harley DHP	080315	Jheeta HS	070515
Forbes AN	231215	Harmon S	010207	John M	140715
Ford HE	040315	Harper KL	170216	Johns RL	140915
Freeman MP	120314	Harrison EG	120608	Johnson LA	131112
Frigieri-Williams N	040116	Harrison J	280114	Johnson TJ	260314
Frost A	240913	Hart LE	100915	Johnston	260315
Fryer AK	220508	Hartill EA	250412	Jones J	100315
Galvin TPC	260914	Hawkins DRO	250609	Jones RL	150116
Gannarelli CMS	230914	Hawkins GKF	230509	Judd WM	140813
Garner-Richardson JR	181114	Hayes ST	101013	Kelly K	020211
Garrison WA	240415	Haynes D	121113	Kempster RC	121113
Garside EA	060614	Hayward J	280212	Kenney K	181214
Gausinet S	121115	Head SJ	011012	Kettle L	030402
Gent LJ	230415	Hearn JL	251115	Keys RH	091112
Gibbon L	011215	Hebberd B	130515	Knight LF	220512
Gibbs WH	181115	Henderson-Sowerby MA	71114	Knight P	010414

Knowler SA	100913	Megaw N	200415	Perkins JMJ	270215
Kumar D	050514	Mellows RE	100216	Perkins LA	010411
Kyle K	070115	Meredith CR	210509	Pettitt SJ	150514
Lacy B	190505	Midgley J	280705	Phelps LC	291014
Lait DJ	171109	Miller AJ	150413	Phillips C	171214
Lamarra JA	020712	Mitchard JJ	280909	Phillips HB	260614
Lane BMW	240512	Mitchell KA	090614	Philpott SE	020311
Larvin CM	150515	Mobbs G	300906	Pilkington M	101213
Last C	200415	Moffett PT	130215	Platts A	011015
Latham D	130715	Mollison HJ	260914	Porter SD	041115
Laurie ER	260510	Monk FS	260713	Potts KE	230115
Lawless MJ	070115	Moon CJ	130910	Powell EJ	091012
Lawrence SE	230415	Moorby TE	181111	Powell MI	021115
Le Lacheur TC	020915	Moore K	010900	Powell SL	190813
Le Sauvage RG	270215	Moreton ML	230216	Powell Y	021203
Leiper JBN	220409	Morris E	180314	Poynter P	100308
Lemoine PS	200411	Morris EM	150415	Preece DT	030714
Letts B	130515	Mott DW	100611	Prescott ESJ	011215
Lewis HE	150208	Muir PS	280415	Preston M	130515
Liddell-Grainger SV	270612	Mulligan CP	241108	Quigley RH	200410
Long DJ	180314	Murphy MC	020614	Randall KJ	280715
Lumley-Wood PM	240713	Murray EP	041013	Reay CE	290915
Lymn SG	121208	Nathanson H	010808	Rees CJ	250715
MacGregor KF	131014	Noble J	111214	Rees YJ	070414
Mackay AA	070115	Northover AJ	300615	Reeves AJL	250915
Mackay PJ	090414	Nutting SJ	101215	Reeves CE	270115
Magee REC	141209	O'Connor V	130715	Reeves I	200415
Main CA	200312	Offord V	070515	Regan SM	010415
Malone NG	260614	Oliver J	200415	Renwick SW	100315
Manning NJ	300615	Onyenuchie RA	020713	Reynolds SP	110914
Mansfield CJ	021013	O'Toole TC	100107	Rice OC	140915
Mason J	140906	Papadopoulou C	200415	Richards IJ	250715
Massey CM	071014	Park DJ	240915	Richardson GM	091210
Masters G	310103	Parker NC	260614	Rigley JC	160514
Matthews HE	290915	Parkinson J	081210	Robbie SS	230915
Matthews P	120314	Parsons JR	250614	Robert FP	270115
Matthews SE	081014	Pasha R	210915	Robertson RS	090215
Maughan JJ	091214	Pass J	140912	Robinson M	090414
Mayberry C	230211	Patel SM	080315	Robinson MA	040315
McCafferty JA	300714	Paterson J	060515	Robinson SM	050411
McCandless P	230712	Paull JM	070115	Robinson VA	010213
McCormack N	210212	Paynter DJW	110313	Rock PB	051015
Mcgarvey JC	020414	Pearson CG	181114	Rodgers AK	180215
McGuire S	280215	Pearson JV	040412	Rogers S	300311
McIntyre G	011102	Peil LB	250715	Ross AH	300115
McKnight HR	170112	Peppiatt J	080611	Rosser PA	071112
McNaughton J	020713	Percival JC	120214	Rosslyn-Smith J	260312
McWhirter AG	030712	Perkins D	090513	Rowe GWG	180615

Rowlands DP	101013
Rowley DJ	130313
Ruprai JK	290915
Rushton PJ	160514
Russell DS	190110
Samways DM	181215
Sanderson LA	040315
Sandford A	250304
Scally R	300915
Schultz AL	160215
Scott HM	070910
Scott KE	110914
Sears SM	300615
Selby-Bennetts M	080115
Semple RJ	240915
Senior LIA	230914
Shah TF	121113
Shannon WS	240610
Sheldrick SE	080410
Shelley J	290413
Shelley JJ	290115
Shields JA	250613
Shinkwin JJ	280514
Simkins FJ	140912
Simmons E	241114
Simmons H	050814
Singfield RA	060510
Smart BE	101215
Smith BD	160216
Smith EJ	181114
Solomon JM	120908
Sooklal H	291014
Soord-Gurney OAJ	090315
Spight SJ	260314
Sritharan K	280514
Srodzinski LD	010714
Staight CA	180314
Stanford GEO	010914
Steel K	131114
Stewart RH	070408
Stirling DL	260216
Storey JR	110913
Stremes JT	291008
Struthers IP	240611
Stubbings DG	051015
Sudbury IA	240513
Suenson Taylor HK	150514
Sullivan NS	111215
Summerfield AD	230713
Sutcliffe A	010900
Swinchin-Rew GJ	220915
Syms MP	011215
Tachauer GJ	131212
Tan XH	230914
Tarn RJ	300915
Taylor BD	150312
Taylor C	250610
Taylor EG	300713
Taylor GJ	200513
Taylor KL	051015
Taylor MM	141112
Taylor SA	131211
Taylor TJ	180211
Tester PS	091214
Thomas J	010900
Thomas JE	051015
Thomas SP	200314
Thompson EG	150514
Thompson GW	030714
Titchen JEP	020813
Toner H	300715
Townend B	011215
Tricker BG	171215
Trigg JL	010316
Tudge K	060411
Turner MCE	171213
Unthank DRJ	121114
Vanstone DLL	260614
Varney AL	290915
Venables T	061215
Vernon CRG	050216
Wade AM	140113
Wakeling C	120215
Walker A	200906
Walker SLJ	010915
Wantling AR	300414
Ward R	200415
Warren MJ	160514
Watson L	310315
Watson P	101215
Webb S	240512
Wedgwood-Day TJ	110107
Weighill JA	070115
Wells AJ	040216
Wells MF	300615
Whale D	030811
Wheelhouse DJ	011215
Whillis EJ	020615
Whitehead A	200415
Whitehead JT	010414
Whitesmith SA	141215
Whittaker JS	291014
Wilkinson G	010900
Williams JE	010216
Williams R	071015
Williams RM	011113
Williamson V	121112
Willis RS	210809
Wilson AM	010115
Wilson JPA	091115
Wilson MA	010216
Wood CK	011215
Wood G	010402
Wood NS	250912
Woodhouse J	271115
Woodling R	051005
Woolcott J	111011
Woolley PG	060715
Wright A	160104
Wright C	030703
Wyllie W	240415
Yarwood AMV	011114

ARMY CADET FORCE

Colonel in Chief......FM *HRH The Prince* Philip *Duke of* Edinburgh *KG KT OM GBE ONZ QSO AK GCL CC CMM ADC(P)*

1st Battalion The Highlanders ACF
HRFCA Sub Office, Gordonville Road, Inverness, Inverness-Shire IV2 4SU
(Tel: 01463 231829 Email:hi-1hldrs-ao@rfca.org.uk)

Honorary Colonel......Col Carolyn Caddick
Commandant......Col Iain Cassidy
Deputy Commandant (Adults)......Lt Col Mike MacDonald
Chief Executive Officer......Maj Jim Stout
Caithness Company Commander......Maj S Mezals
Inverness Company Commander......Maj K Reid
Western Isles Company Commander......Maj N MacLeod
Moray Company Commander......Maj C Higgins
Ross Company Commander......Maj G MacDonald
Battalion Training Officer......Maj Martin Whyte

1st (Northern Ireland) Battalion ACF
CEO (1), 35 Manse Road, Carryduff, BELFAST BT8 8DA
(Tel: 028 9081 5221 Email:ni-1bn-ceo@rfca.org.uk)

Honorary Colonel......Dr Angela Josepha Garvey
Cadet Commandant......Col Paul Shepherd *OBE*

2nd Battalion The Highlanders ACF
2nd Battalion The Highlanders Army Cadet Force, Rocksley Drive, Boddam, Aberdeenshire AB42 3BA
(Tel:01779 481011 Email:hi-2hldrs-ao@rfca.org.uk)

Honorary Colonel......Brig C S Grant *OBE*......020112
Commandant......Col Scott Dunn

2nd (Northern Ireland) Battalion ACF
35 Manse Road, Carryduff, Belfast BT8 8DA
(Tel: 028 9081 5223 Email: NI-2BN-ao2@rfca.org.uk)

Honorary Colonel......Air Commodore H Smyth *OBE DFC ADC*
Commandant......Col Keith Dowell
Deputy Commandant......Lt Col Andrew Anderson

Angus and Dundee Battalion ACF
Angus and Dundee Battalion ACF, Barry Buddon CTC, By Carnoustie DD7 7RY
(Tel: 01382 533349 Email:ao@adcadets.co.uk)

Honorary Colonel......Assistant Chief Constable Derek Penman......011213
Commandant......Col Martin Passmore
Deputy Commandant......Lt Col George Smith

Argyll And Sutherland Highlanders Battalion ACF
Argyll And Sutherland Highlanders Battalion ACF, Hartfield House, Bonhill Road, Dumbarton G82 2DG
(Tel: 01389 763 451 Email:hi-ash-ao2@rfca.org.uk)

Honorary Colonel......Col A K M Miller *CBE*......010811
Commandant......Col Niall Archibald
Deputy Commandant (West)......Lt Col Gillian Moncur *MBE*
Deputy Commandant (East)......Lt Col Darren Hughes
Cadet Executive Officer......Maj Philip Fulton
Training Maj......Maj David Blair

Bedfordshire & Hertfordshire ACF
Army Reserve Centre, 28 St Andrew Street, Hertford SG14 1JA
(Tel: 01992 582423 Email: Beds&hertspro@armymail.mod.uk)

Honorary Colonel......Mr Richard Hugh Beazley *DL*......190814
Commandant......Col Chris Sharwood-Smith

Black Watch Battalion ACF

Black Watch Battalion ACF, Queens Barracks, 131 Dunkeld Road, Perth PH1 5BT
(Tel:01738 626571 Email:hi-bw-ao@rfca.org.uk)

Honorary Colonel..Rev Prof Norman Walker Drummond *CBE FRSE* 010814
Commandant..Col James M K Erskine *MBE*
Deputy Commandant ....Lt Col Craig Hubbock
Training Officer..Maj S Rae
Cadet Executive Officer ....Maj A C M Potter

Buckinghamshire ACF

Army Reserves Centre, Viney House, Oxford Road, Aylesbury, Bucks HP19 8RN
(Tel: 01296 744553 Email: se-buc-cao@rfca.org.uk)

Honorary Colonel..Mrs Amanda Nicholson *DL* 010114
Cadet Commandant ....Col K S Grover
Deputy Commandant ....Vacancy
County Training Officer..Maj M Yearwood
Cadet Executive Officer ....Maj S Tresidder

Cambridgeshire ACF

Cambridgeshire Army Cadet Force, County Headquarters, Denny End Road, Waterbeach, Cambridge CB25 9QU
(Tel: 01223 862949 Fax: 01223 441830 Email: ea-camceo@rfca.org.uk)

Honorary Colonel..*Sir* Hugh Duberly *KCVO CBE*
Cadet Commandant ....Col M Knight *MBE*
Deputy Commandant ....Lt Col Cox
Cadet Executive Officer ....Maj Geoff Hammond
1 Company Commander ....Maj Cattermole
2 Company Commander ....Maj Swan
3 Company Commander ....Maj Morris

Cheshire ACF

Cheshire Army Cadet Force HQ, Fox Barracks, Liverpool Road, Chester CH2 4BU
(Tel: 01244 390252 Email: nw-che-ao1@rfca.org.uk)

Honorary Colonel..Mr T.D Briggs *MBE*
Commandant..Col R J Ayres
Deputy Commandant ....Lt Col A Mottram
County Training Officer..Maj T Fish
Cadet Executive Officer ....Maj N J Carpenter
Normandy Company Commander..........................Maj P Price
Messines Company Commander............................Maj L Bebbington
Somme Company Commander...............................Capt J Storey
Pathfinder Company Commander..........................Capt A Smith

City And County Of Bristol ACF

County Headquarters, City & County of Bristol ACF, Army Reserve Centre,
Ashmead Road, Keynsham, Bristol BS31 1SX
(Tel: 0117 9863344 Fax: 0117 9860345 Email: wx-bri-ao2@rfca.org.uk)

Honorary Colonel..Brig Steve P Hodder 020212
Commandant..Col Hector Stamboulieh
Deputy Commandant ....Lt Col Barry Angus
County Training Officer..Maj Jon Beake
Officer Commanding 'C' Company........................Maj Stephen Scull

Cleveland ACF

HQ Cleveland ACF, Army Reserve Centre, Stockton Road, Middlesbrough TS5 4AD
(Tel: 01642 242414 Email: countyhq@clevelandacf.co.uk)

Honorary Colonel..Mr Alasdair MacConachie *OBE DL* 010710
County Commandant ....Col A K Laker
Deputy County Commandant.................................Lt Col J Dauncey

Cornwall ACF

Cornwall ACF HQ (The Rifles), 7 Castle Canyke Road, Bodmin, Cornwall PL31 1DX
(Tel: 01208 73183 Fax: 01208 74468 Email: wx-cor-ao1@rfca.org,uk)

Honorary Colonel..........Col L Donnithorne..........010915
County Commandant..........Col J M Coia *TD*
Deputy Commandant..........Lt Col Paul Deakin
County Training Officer..........Maj David Holman
Cadet Executive Officer..........Maj S Wilkinson *MSc*
Inkerman Company OC..........Capt M Ambrose
Gibraltar Company OC..........Maj S Edwards
Lucknow Company OC..........Capt Demelza Stevenson

Cumbria ACF

Ypres Block, The Castle, Carlisle CA3 8UR
(Tel: 01228 516223 Email: nw-cmb-ao2@rfca.org.uk)

Honorary Colonel..........Mrs Susan Odling Villiers-Smith..........011014
Commandant..........Col A Steven
Deputy Commandant - Adult Training..........Lt Col A Richmond
Cadet Executive Officer..........Maj S Matthews

Cyprus ACF

(established 2017)
Episkopi and Troodos Station ACF Headquarters, E Block, Episkopi, BFPO 53
(Tel: 00357 25963593 Fax: 00357 25962147
Email: BFC-EPI-Stn-Cdr@mod.uk Email: BFC-Epi-Stn-ArmyCadetForce@mod.uk)

Derbyshire ACF

Derbyshire ACF, Army Reserve Centre, Sinfin Lane, Derby DE24 9GL
(Tel: 01332 772025 Email: em-der-ao1@rfca.org.uk)

Honorary Colonel..........Lt Col D J Elsam *MBE*..........171114
Commandant..........Col Chris Young
Deputy Commandant..........Lt Col Chris Doyle

Devon ACF

(Tel: 01392 256251 Email: wx-dev-ao@rfca.org.uk)

Honorary Colonel..........Brig S D Young *CBE DL*..........010810
County Commandant..........Col A R Fulford
Deputy Commandant Personnel..........Lt Col S Nicholson
Deputy Commandant Training..........Lt Col I MacLeod *OBE*
Cadet Executive Officer..........Maj S Estick
County Training Officer Military..........Maj MJ McColm

Dorset ACF

Dorset Army Cadet Force Headquarters, Poundbury Road, Dorchester, Dorset DT1 1SZ
(Tel: 01305 263954 Email: wx-dor-ao@rfca.org.uk)

Honorary Colonel..........Maj Gen J S Kerr *CBE*..........010413
County Commandant..........Col Darren Jeffries
Deputy Commandant..........Lt Col Steve Williams
Cadet Executive Officer..........Maj Dave Abbott
County Training Officer..........Maj Andy Garrett

Durham ACF

HQ Durham ACF, TA Centre, Picktree Lane, Chester le Street, County Durham DH3 3SR
(Tel: 0191 3498660 Email: ne-dur-ao@rfca.org.uk)

Honorary Colonel..........Col W T Gracie *TD*..........010815
County Commandant..........Col Brian Kitching
Deputy Commandant (2IC)..........Lieut Colonel Malcolm Scott
Deputy Commandant (Training)..........Vacant
County Training Officer..........Maj Neil Foster

Essex ACF
Army Reserve Centre, Springfield Lyons, Colchester Road, Chelmsford, Essex CM2 5TA
(Tel: 01245 462302 Email: ea-ess-info@rfca.org.uk)

Honorary Colonel ....Col C A F Thomas *TD DL*
Commandant ....Col I R MacDonald
Deputy Commandant ....Lt Col Ian Coffin

Glasgow And Lanarkshire Battalion ACF
Glasgow & Lanarkshire Battalion Army Cadet Force, HQ & WETC Dechmont,
Gilbertfield Road, Cambuslang, Glasgow G72 8YP
(Tel: 0141 641 0858 Email: lo-gl-ao1@rfca.org.uk)

Commandant ....Col Alex McNamee
Deputy Commandant ....Lt Col Derek Coulter
Cadet Executive Officer ....Maj Colin McCormack
Battalion Training Officer....................Capt Christopher Peacock
A Company Commander....................Maj Henry Canavan
B Company Commander....................Maj Walter Kerr
C Company Commander....................Maj Alec Stirling *MBE*
D Company Commander....................Maj Donna Laird

Gloucestershire ACF
The Cadet Centre, Arle Road, Cheltenham GL51 8JU
(Tel: 01242 700063 Email:wx-glo-ao@rfca.org.uk)

Honorary Colonel ....Maj Gen *Sir* Evelyn Webb-Carter *KCVO OBE DL*....................010112
County Commandant ....Col Paul Saunders
Deputy Commandant ....Lt Col John Cave
Chief Executive Officer ....Maj Alec Masson

Greater London (City Of London And North East Sector) ACF
Sector Headquarters, City of London & North East Sector Army Cadets,
Army Reserve Centre, 900 Lea Bridge Road, Walthamstow, London E17 9DW
(Tel: 020 8988 0320 Email: cityandnelondonacf@rfca.org.uk)

Honorary Colonel ....Mr John Dominic Reid *OBE*....................010415

Greater London (South East Sector) ACF
Cadet Training Center, Wat Tyler Road, Blackheath SE3 OQZ
(Tel: 020 8692 4066 (option 2) Email: gl-se-aol@rfca.mod.uk)

Honorary Colonel ....Mr Shaun Bailey 010414
Sector Commandant....................Col Simon Ettinghausen *TD*
Deputy Commandant ....Lt Col Chris Booth
Training Maj ....Maj Paul Harrison
Officer Commanding 7 Company....................Maj Simon Johnson
Officer Commanding 9 Company....................Maj Paul Morris
Officer Commanding 10 Company....................Maj Nigel Warren

Greater London (South West Sector) ACF
27 St Johns Hill, Battersea SW11 1TT
(Tel: 020 7924 3229 Email: gl-sw-ao1@rfca.org.uk)

Honorary Colonel ....Brig J P Mooney *QVRM TD* 310814
County Commandant ....Col Colin Jones
Deputy Commandant ....Vacant
Cadet Executive Officer ....Maj Dave Groom
Adult Training Officer....................Maj Mark Purse

Greater Manchester ACF
Greater Manchester Army Cadet Force, The Colonel Mary Creagh Training Centre,
Spenleach Lane, Hawkshaw, Bury BL8 4JJ
(Tel: 01204 512600 Email: nw-gm-nwhqao@rfca.org.uk)

Honorary Colonel ....Warren James Smith
Commandant....................Col Mike Glover
Deputy Commandant ....Lt Col Paul Irvine
Cadet Executive Officer ....Maj Tom Cornmell

Hampshire And Isle Of Wight ACF
Newburgh House, Newburgh Street, Winchester, Hampshire SO23 8UY
(Tel: 01962 865711 x100 Email: se-hiw-cao@rfca.org.uk)

Honorary Colonel..Amanda Nicholson
County Commandant...Col Andy Dawes
Deputy Commandant (County 2 I C)....................Lt Col Mark Thomsett
Deputy Commandant...Lt Col Rodger Mills
Deputy Commandant...Lt Col Conrad Wilson
Cadet Executive Officer..Maj Tom Meggison

Hereford And Worcester ACF
Suvla Barracks, Army Reserve Centre, Harold Street, Hereford HR1 2QX
(Tel: 01432 359917 Email: wm-hw-ceo@rfca.org.uk)

Honorary Colonel..Brig Martin Vine *OBE*..040809
Commandant..Col Andy Taylor
Deputy Commandant...Lt Col Andrew Booton

Humberside And South Yorkshire ACF
Cadet Training Centre, Driffield Camp, Driffield, East Yorkshire YO25 9HD
(Tel: 01377 253548 Fax: 01377 241024 Email: yh-hsy-ao1@rfca.org.uk)

Honorary Colonel..Chief Constable Timothy S Hollis *CBE QPM*......................................310712
Commandant..Col N Wilkinson
Deputy Commandant (Personnel & Admin)..........Lt Col F T Owen
Deputy Commandant (Training)............................Lt Col M Cruddas
Cadet Executive Officer..Maj T Atkinson
County Training Officer..Maj J M Britchford
County Adult Development Officer........................Maj D Buckley

Isle Of Man ACF
Isle of Man Army Cadet Force, HQ & Training Centre, Tromode Road, Douglas, Isle of Man IM2 5PA
(Tel: 01624 671210 Email: nw-iom-ao@rfca.org.uk)

Honorary Colonel..Maj C F Wilson..010511
Commandant..Maj Dean Johnson
Deputy Commandant...Acting Capt Kevin Farrington
Cadet Executive Officer..Capt Steve Champion

Kent ACF
Kent ACF, Yeomanry House, Boxley Road, Maidstone, Kent ME14 2AR
(Tel: 01622 750328 Email: ceokent-se@rfca.org.uk)

Honorary Colonel..Col WMJ Partridge *TD DL*...011012
Commandant..Col Chris Gilbert

Lancashire ACF
HQ Lancashire ACF, Fullwood Barracks, Watling Street, Preston, Lancs PR2 8AA
(Tel: 01772 717078 Email: nw-lan-ao1@rfca.org.uk)

Honorary Colonel..Lt Col *The Hon* R C Assheton *TD DL*...010113
Commandant..Col Neil Jurd
Deputy Commandant (SO1 Adult).........................Lt Col Norman Mustard
Deputy Commandant (SO1 Cadets).......................Lt Col Gareth Wright
Cadet Executive Officer..Maj Tony Armstrong
Normany Company Commander............................Maj Nicola Jones
Egypt Company Commander................................Maj Patricia McParlan
Salerno Company Commander..............................Maj Joanne Eccles
Wingate Company Commander............................Capt Alex Saunders

Leicestershire, Northamptonshire And Rutland ACF

Leicestershire, Northamptonshire & Rutland Army Cadet Force, County Headquarters,
Tigers Road, South Wigston, Leicester LE18 4WS
(Tel: 0116 2779701 Email: em-lnr-ao@rfca.org.uk)

Honorary Colonel....................Mr Richard Everard *OBE DL*
Commandant....................Col Michael Coleman
Deputy Commandant (Training & Admin)....................Lt Col Mandy Davanna
Deputy Commandant (Leics)....................Lt Col Sean Smales
Deputy Commandant (Northants)....................Lt Col Anthony Turner
Cadet Executive Officer....................Maj Richard Breeze
Area Commander - A Company....................Capt Lee Dorey
Area Commander - B Squadron....................Maj Colin Wells
Area Commander - C Company....................Maj Tim Chappel
Area Commander - D Company....................Maj Lesley Deacon
Area Commander - E Company....................Capt Paul Davanna
Area Commander - F Squadron....................Maj Alex Calver

Lincolnshire ACF

Lincolnshire ACF, County Cadet Headquarters, Sobraon Barracks, Lincoln LN1 3PY
(Tel: 01522 528109 Fax: 01522 528118)

Honorary Colonel....................Mr Toby Edward Drake Dennis....................050514
Honorary Colonel....................Col G W C Newmarch
County Commandant....................Col J A Field *MBE*
Deputy Commandant (Military)....................Lt Col T Bird
Deputy Commandant (Support)....................Lt Col Thompson
Cadet Executive Officer....................Maj D Mullock

Lothian And Borders Battalion ACF

Lothian & Borders Battalion Army Cadet Force, Drumshoreland House, Broxburn, West Lothian EH52 5PD
(Tel: 01506 856698 Email: lo-lb-ao2@rfca.org.uk)

Honorary Colonel....................Mr Gavin Stott....................010714
Commandant....................Col E Marshall
Deputy Commandant -Burma, Alma & Minden.....Lt Col D Balfour
Deputy Commandant -Rhine, Tangier & Kohima..Lt Col J Tonner
Cadet Executive Officer....................Maj N Thorne
Battalion *Training Officer*....................Maj John Murdoch

Merseyside ACF

St Georges ACF Centre, Altcar Training Camp, Hightown, Merseyside L38 7JD
(Tel: 01519 292069 Email: nw-mer-ao1@rfca.org.uk)

Honorary Colonel....................Dame Lorna Muirhead
Commandant....................Col Ian Holmes

Middlesex And North West London ACF

Middlesex & NW London ACF, Princess Louise House, 190 Hammersmith Road,
Hammersmith, London W6 7DJ
(Tel: 020 8563 9842 Email: gl-mxnw-ceo@rfca.mod.uk)

Honorary Colonel....................Lt Col M G A (Adrain) Drage *OBE*....................011209
Sector *Commandant*....................Col Mark Hodson *TD*

Norfolk ACF

Norfolk Army Cadet Force, Cadet Centre, Norwich Street, Dereham, Norfolk NR19 1AD
(Tel: 01362 694515 Email: ea-norao1@rfca.org.uk)

Honorary Colonel....................Lt Gen Jacko Page
Commandant....................Col Clem Maginniss

Northumbria ACF

Northumbria Army Cadet Force, Fox Barracks, High Pit Road, Cramlington, Northumberland NE23 6RA
(Tel: 01670 732 323 Email: ne-nor-ceo@rfca.org.uk)

Honorary Colonel....................John Stevens, Baron Stevens of Kirkwhelpington
Commandant....................Col David Middleton *MBE TD*

Nottinghamshire ACF

Nottinghamshire ACF, 120 Swiney Way, Toton, Nottingham NG9 6QX
(Tel: 01159 837645 Tel: 01159 837642 Email: em-not-ao@rfca.org.uk)

Honorary Colonel....Mrs Nicola June Weston *DL*....011215
Commandant....Col Alan Burt
Deputy Commandant - Military Training....Lt Col M. McGuire
Deputy Commandant - Non Military Training....Lt Col Neil Atherton
County Training Officer....Maj Andy Webster
Cadet Executive Officer....Maj P Hill

Orkney Independent Cadet Battery ACF

Orkney Independent Battery (RA) Lovat Scouts, Army reserve Centre, Kirkwall, Orkney
(Tel: 01463 231829 Email: ao@1highlanders.co.uk)

Honorary Colonel....Maj Malcolm R S MacRea
Commandant....Maj Andrew Barton

Oxfordshire ACF

Oxfordshire (The Rifles) ACF, Brotheridge House, Arncott Wood Road, Upper Arncott, Bicester, Oxon OX25 1AB
(Tel: 01869 259681 Email: se-oxf-cao@rfca.org.uk)

Honorary Colonel....Brig R A Draper *CVO OBE*....010710
Honorary Colonel....Maj Gen D J Shouesmith
County Commandant....Col D Bowyer
Deputy Commandant....Lt Col A Holder
County Training Maj (Core)....Maj N Baigent
County Training Maj (Enrichment)....Maj S Oxford
Cadet Executive Officer....Maj G Arnold
County Quartermaster....Maj S Foster
OC Calais Company....Maj L Dynan
OC Nivelle Company....Maj P Rodwell
OC Quebec Company....Maj G Cook
OC Somme Company....Maj P Williams

Royal County Of Berkshire ACF

Brock Barracks, Oxford Road, Reading RG30 1HW
(Tel: 01189 023541 Email: se-ber-ceo@rfca.org.uk)

Honorary Colonel....Brig Peter Walker *OBE*....201013
Commandant....Col Evan Brown

Shetland Independent Cadet Battery ACF

Fort Charlotte, Market Street, Lerwick
(Tel: 01779 481011 Email: ao@2highlanders.co.uk)

Honorary Colonel....Maj John Taylor *QGM*....010610
Commandant....Maj Andrew Barton

Shropshire ACF

HQ Shropshire ACF, Copthorne Barracks, Copthorne Road, Shrewsbury, Shropshire SY3 8LZ
(Tel: 01743 231779 Fax: 01743 359861 Email: Info.shropshireacf@rfca.org.uk)

Honorary Colonel....*Sir* A E H Heber-Percy *KCVO KSU*
County Commandant....Col Newbrook
Deputy Commandant....Lt Col Phillips
Cadet Executive Officer....Maj Coleman
Somme Company Commander....Capt Miller
Lucknow Company Commander....Capt Broster
Peninsula Company Commander....Capt Nicholls

Somerset ACF

Jellalabad House, 14 Mount Street, Taunton, Somerset TA1 3QE
(Tel: 01823 284486 Email: wx-som-ao@rfca.org.uk)

Honorary Colonel....Brig Nick P Knudsen....010315
Commandant....Col Stephen Bartlett *QVRM TD*
Deputy Commandant G1....Lt Col Rupert Elliott
Deputy Commandant G7....Lt Col Andy Axten

Staffordshire & West Midlands (North Sector) ACF
Building 115, Beacon Barracks, Stafford ST18 0AQ
(Tel: 01785 257804 Fax: 01785 248730 Email: info.staffsacf@rfca.org.uk)

Honorary Colonel..Mr Michael George Frewer
Commandant..Col Rick Logan

Suffolk ACF
Suffolk ACF, TA Centre, Yarmouth Road, Ipswich, Suffolk IP1 4BH
(Tel: 01473 252562 Email: ea-sufao1@rfca.org.uk Email: ea-sufao2@rfca.org.uk)

Honorary Colonel..Lt Col M J Beard..010914
Commandant..Col G W French *TD*
Deputy Commandant...Lt Col A T Smith
Cadet Executive Officer...Maj K J Humphrey
County Training Officer...Maj J J Preston
OC A company (Bury St Edmund's).......................Maj R Simpkin
OC B Company (Lowestoft)..................................Maj G Haldenby
OC C Company (Ipswich).....................................Maj M Abbott

Surrey (Princess of Wales's Royal Regiment Battalion) ACF
(Tel: 01483 425372 Email: se-sur-chq@rfca.org.uk)

Honorary Colonel..Brig Paul A D Evans *OBE*..011109
Commandant..Lt Col John R C White *TD*
Cadet Executive Officer...Maj Ian Wadley

Sussex ACF
Highcroft House, 198 Dyke Rd, Brighton BN1 5AS
(Tel: 01273 552222 Email: se-sx-cao1@rfca.org.uk)

Honorary Colonel..John Moore-Bick *CBE DL*
County Commandant...Col David Steel
Deputy Commandant...Lt Col James Morris
Cadet Executive Officer..Maj Peter Kelly
County Training Officer..Maj Sarah Earley
Adult *Training Officer*...Maj Sarah Earley
Padre...Revd (Maj) George Butterworth

Warwickshire And West Midlands (South Sector) ACF
Warwickshire ACF, Tennal Grange, Tennal Road, Harborne, Birmingham B32 2HX
(Tel: 01214 277758 Email: wm-wss-ao1@rfca.org.uk)

Honorary Colonel..Maj Michael D Collie *TD*..011211
County Commandant...Col Nigel Sarling
Deputy Commandant...Lt Col Richard Gale *TD*
Cadet Executive Officer..Maj Steve Huyton
County Training Maj...Maj Delroy Tucker

West Lowland Battalion ACF
The West Lowland Battalion Army Cadet Force, Fusilier House, Seaforth Road, Ayr KA8 9HX
(Tel: 01292 264612 Email: lo-wl-ao1@rfca.org.uk)

Honorary Colonel..Dr Blythe Duff..010213
Battalion *Commandant*..Col Padraig Wellington
Deputy Commandant (South)................................Lt Col Graham Dempsey
Deputy Commandant (North)................................Lt Col Alan Middleton *MBE*
Cadet Executive Officer...Maj Ian MacKenzie
Training Maj..Maj Rab Mackie
Company Commanders
Balaclava Training Group..................................Maj Kevin Wallace
Kohima Training Group.....................................Capt Daniel Clissett
Inkerman Training Group..................................Maj Robert Mackie
Minden Training Group.....................................Capt Tom Hudson

Wiltshire ACF

Headquarters Wiltshire Army Cadets, Le Marchant Barracks, Franklyn Road, Devizes, Wiltshire SN10 2FE
(Tel: 01380 724114 Email: wx-wil-ceo@rfca.org.uk)

Honorary Colonel....Lt Gen Sir Roderick Cordy-Simpson *KBE CB DL*....010615
County Commandant....Col Mark Nash
Deputy *County Commandant*....Lt Col Roman Bartoszewski
County Training Maj....Maj Peter White
Cadet Executive Officer....Maj Sarah Rawlings
OC A Company....Maj Lee Bampfield
OC B Company....Maj Amanda Calaz
OC C Company....Maj Rey Brown
OC D Company....Maj Adam Reavill

Yorkshire (North And West) ACF

Yorkshire (N&W) Army Cadet Force, The Cadet Training Centre, Building 107,
Queen Elizabeth Barracks, Strensall, York YO32 5SB
(Tel: 01904 490529 Email: yh-ynw-ceo@rfca.org.uk)

Honorary Colonel....Mr David James Selka....120711
Commandant....Col Malcolm Render
Deputy Commandant (North)....Lt Col M Bell
Deputy Commandant (West)....Lt Col S Emmerson
Deputy Commandant (Training)....Lt Col H Gell

ARMY CADETS WALES

Honorary Colonel Cadets (Wales)....Mr Alan Edward Peterson....010216

Clwyd And Gwynedd ACF

Clwyd & Gwynedd ACF HQ, Kinmel Park Camp, Bodelwyddan, Denbighshire LL18 5TY
(Tel: 01745 583794 Email: wa-cg-ao1@rfca.org.uk)

Commandant....Col L T Williams *TD VR*
Deputy Commandant - Cadet Training....Lt Col M Prangnell
Deputy Commandant - Adult Training....Lt Col M L Craven
Training Officer....Maj G E Hughes
Cadet Executive Officer....Maj Bernie Pagent

Dyfed And Glamorgan ACF

(Tel: 01656 657593 Email: dyfedandglamorganacf@rfca.org.uk)

Honorary Colonel....Brig R N Wardle *OBE*....010713
Commandant....Col Brian Westlake-Toms
Deputy Commandant....Lt Col Debra Harding
Deputy Commandant....Lt Col Manny Manfred
County Training Officer....Maj Richard Holder
Cadet Executive Officer....Lt Col Kevin Smith

Gwent And Powys ACF

Gwent and Powys Army Cadet Force, Robert Jones VC House,
Cwrt-y-Gollen Training Camp, Crickhowell, Powys NP8 1TH
(Tel: 01873 813756 Email: gwentandpowysacf@rfca.org.uk)

Honorary Colonel....Brig R H T Aiyken *CBE DL*
Commandant....Col Rob Hughes
Deputy Commandant....Lt Col T Sturges
Cadet Executive Officer....Maj Derek Munro

Lieutenants

Abbott D	100613
Abbott MR	300309
Abbs MJ	011211
Abel SD	020216
Acquah V	140715
Adams K	220705
Adams R	101013
Adams W	010900
Adcock CSL	311011
Adcock N	201202
Air S	200702
Aitken A	150307
Akester A	200312
Alexander G	070206
Alfer PA	130611
Alladice PM	011112
Allen A	011102
Allen J	180911
Allen R	281015
Allington MI	040313
Allington R	010911
Alway G	010900
Ambrose MAR	151111
Ambrose R	111205
Anderson M	190914
Anderson PR	220910
Anderson SA	011013
Anderson VE	010310
Andrews W	130305
Angel AN	251109
Angus B	180103
Angus CSI	160615
Annis J	151105
Ansell DJ	160615
Ansell L	011109
Anstey D	010404
Anstey SC	041202
Archibald L	080212
Archibald NA	041080
Armstrong NJ	031111
Armstrong T	220914
Arnold J	311012
Arrowsmith B	070810
Ashburn JL	160615
Ashford GR	010900
Ashley J	041011
Ashton RE	010900
Asplen MJ	111205
Aston J	240112
Atherton N	010900
Atkin PA	010216
Atkins P	010110
Atkinson I	190508
Averill DM	140615
Avison B	010900
Axten A	010607
Aylard C	010514
Ayres AH	010913
Ayres W	141012
Bacon AC	010504
Badruddin P	010900
Bagge GJ	101210
Baggs A	010711
Baigent N	220506
Bailey NA	120505
Baker M	010913
Balfour D	010705
Ball A	010900
Ball KH	040901
Bampfield LA	120611
Banyard IM	050215
Barkat J	240212
Barkat JE	150915
Barker KL	150915
Barlow P	010900
Barlow W	010900
Barnes AR	010900
Barnshaw G	010404
Barritt R	070807
Barton AP	220508
Bartoszewski R	010900
Batin MV	011006
Batin SEC	140715
Batsford J	011104
Batty B	200911
Bauer T	010103
Baxendale JV	220508
Bazeley DW	011205
Beadle MD	181011
Beake J	150111
Beale C	080311
Beale HM	010914
Bebbington L	181012
Bees C	010810
Bees M	010302
Beetson B	290306
Beirne A	020502
Bell M	301101
Bell R	090613
Bellingham IT	031014
Bennett NM	220814
Bennett T	190403
Benson D	030612
Bentham D	010900
Berriman DM	220311
Berry A	020702
Berry NR	180810
Bettany SP	010900
Betts K	080311
Betty SA	011104
Beverley Z	080312
Bex A	040712
Biddulph SP	170914
Bilsland J	200607
Binks REC	230403
Bird M	150101
Bird T	180703
Bishop L	010900
Bizzell NOL	010615
Blackburn M	070710
Blackmore JB	010812
Blackwood HMA *MBE*	290914
Blair D	091004
Blair S	050215
Blake ARW	011013
Bloom MG	300513
Bloor K	010402
Boden MJ *TD*	130113
Bogan S	010102
Bone A	010900
Booth C	150508
Booton AW	020710
Boraston M	161002
Boucher PG	140415
Boulton AL	100609
Bowbrick TJ	110612
Bowers-Tolley M	010900
Bowes LA	141014
Bowkett L	291106
Bowler N	281014
Bowles JA	010101
Bowyer DG	010214
Boyce E	210505

Boyd DA	170315
Boyne PJ	070710
Bradburn RJ	070410
Bradbury IM	010900
Bradshaw PM	011207
Brady A	010411
Bramble I	010498
Branch D	201106
Branch ID	040111
Brant P	010900
Brazil A	050711
Breeze RD	010986
Brennan-Raymond SM	200208
Brewster A	271102
Brian S	021206
Bridge CS	140811
Bridgeman M	010900
Bridgeman S	090204
Bridges GC	130215
Britchford J	010900
Britton G	010101
Brocklehurst J	080313
Brogden JP	050711
Brooke SM	051010
Brookhouse VA	280607
Brooks D	061014
Brooks S	210305
Brooks S	060606
Brooks VL	101213
Broom P	120106
Broome P	041208
Broster GT	100413
Brough D	010611
Brough L	171010
Brough LJ	021013
Brown A	170305
Brown A	130502
Brown D	011011
Brown DB	220311
Brown E	030308
Brown J	010602
Brown J	010900
Brown M	210302
Brown R	170306
Brownlee P	291013
Brownlie J	220508
Bruce J	010900
Bruce JM	120311
Brunetti AN	010306
Bryant MP *MBE*	010900
Bryant P	030713
Buck D	010900
Buckell G	051010
Buckley DJ	210798
Budryk K	010900
Bull RG	111003
Bunce P	010801
Bunney J	290109
Burberry D	010310
Burbidge BD	010609
Burge DJ	271015
Burnham AJ	170315
Burns GG	060909
Burns J	010900
Burns R	130501
Burns W	011200
Burrell-Taylor V	010900
Burrows MD	070810
Burt A	010900
Burt LF	010900
Burtenshaw EL	010612
Burton AJ	050805
Burton JD	271015
Bush T	031210
Bustin-Mulkern AT	120614
Butler B	010900
Butler PJ	210914
Butterworth G	111005
Caddy SF	121107
Caiger J	010900
Cairns N	010908
Calaz M	280109
Callaghan SP	260213
Calton T	020103
Calver AD	070312
Cameron A	290312
Cameron RA	221112
Campbell A	070212
Campbell C	220111
Campbell C	010712
Campbell MN	101109
Campbell-Charters C	070210
Campbell-Henry M	160814
Canavan H	080101
Carey N	051203
Carmichael E	021102
Carpenter NJ	210702
Carr AD	220112
Carr M	010809
Carr P	010402
Carrington K	111205
Carruthers RJ *OBE TD*	010900
Carruthers SH	011010
Carter HC	280712
Carter JM	271010
Cartwright RA	110615
Caskey T	081013
Cassidy D	230108
Cassidy ISJ	220312
Catchpole BO	021100
Caufield T	260802
Cave MB	080311
Cawrey D	200810
Chakrabarti H	010900
Chalfont M	010900
Champion S	080401
Chandler L	010202
Chapman A	250403
Chapman J	250505
Chapman SC *TD MB ChB DipRACOG FFPM CDir*	120213
Chappell TW	200807
Charles S	011009
Charleton IJ	110313
Charlton M	160902
Cheeseman PT	061010
Chipp D	100615
Chivers WT	111012
Choonara A	010706
Christian PA *OBE*	010401
Christophers G	010900
Churcher P	310102
Cicconi MLG	290608
Civil MA	271113
Clare N	070212
Clare-Brown K	011205
Clark AP	030709
Clark DL	010900
Clark EJ	070714
Clark M	290604
Clark SL	160614

Clarke J	190410	Cox NL	301009	Davis Hall H	101013
Clarke M	031208	Cox T	010202	Davison B	021209
Clarke PL	140503	Craig BR	080311	Davison M	010710
Clarke S	210910	Craig JR	011013	Davison S	270711
Clement DM	270707	Crammond IG	071112	Dawes A	010900
Clissett D	110413	Crammond K	161109	Dawes H	290607
Cload J	030203	Cray MPA	010807	Dawkins V	220404
Cochrane BT	271013	Creek KJ	100212	Dawson EC	091006
Coffin I	010900	Cresswell A	070602	Day B	010900
Coia JM	141210	Crimes JM	021209	Deacon LE	160712
Colbridge TA	271015	Croft M	210116	Deakin P	010601
Cole DM	010412	Croney S	260605	Dean S	010109
Cole KIC	060410	Croniken SM	040712	Deane TL	111115
Coleman D	010900	Cross P	080203	Deans S	181004
Coleman D	260407	Crouch K	051203	Death S	311205
Coleman J	011209	Crowe KD	110912	Decarteret G	010900
Coles V	070814	Crowhurst C	010900	Dee K	100811
Colhoun MS	110313	Crowley CJ	231013	Deegan RE	180507
Collett J	010900	Crowther G	010900	Deeley A	171206
Collier T	060204	Cruddas M	010802	Dempsey G	010900
Collinge M	251114	Cubbon B	271015	Denison AI *OBE*	010900
Connell KJ	070702	Curley JE	160615	Dent HE	140713
Connelly L	040703	Curran P	010701	Dent K	290606
Connor D	150415	Currie R	190302	Dent R	150708
Connor KA	200315	Curry A	010900	Dey RSR	251114
Connor KJ	011008	Curtis E	200607	Dick LM	190912
Coogan EC	010714	Curtis P	160901	Dickson R	041011
Cook A	100103	Dadley J	011014	Dine CT	100413
Cook G	041208	Daley EM	011210	Disney M	010900
Cooke T	070603	Daley J	090209	Diss R	030813
Cooney B	010900	Dalton DR	200910	Dixon L	190404
Cooper C	031212	Daniel E	300401	Dixon P	010908
Cooper G	170114	Daniels J	010900	Dixon T	010406
Cooper JH	190411	D'Arcy CM	171115	Doak D	310509
Cooper NH	190913	Darroch J	110206	Doak ED	110910
Cooper P	191001	Dauncey J	061200	Dobb AM	291013
Cooper TI	020914	Davanna MJ	010900	Dodds L	070212
Coppard R	050913	Davidson AS	051009	Donal SP	010514
Corner LJ	180712	Davie M	110609	Donaldson AM *MBE*	071013
Cornforth A	081209	Davies A	210312	Donegan SP	170310
Cornish G	110801	Davies CW	271015	Donnell S	270602
Cornmell T	010900	Davies E	240704	Donnelly DJ	280606
Cornock MA	010216	Davies J	010102	Donnithorne L	010900
Costello K	261104	Davies M	270305	Dorey LJ	140912
Coull CB	010900	Davies S	010804	Douglas K	010900
Coulter CAE	130813	Davies T	250301	Downing WL	250709
Coulter D	010900	Davis R	040711	Downs C	210203
Cox L	310102	Davis RE	030215	Dowson AS	070415

Doyle CB	010900
Doyle M	060510
Drain JJ	271013
Drain S	010409
Draper P	011014
Drinkwater S	010310
Drury R	210411
Duffy M	070910
Duke PB	271015
Dunbar K	131005
Dunlop T	171014
Dunn C	010513
Dunn S	130502
Durban AE	060408
Durrand AB	150312
Du-Tracy GS	140714
Dutton JA	201204
Dyas IP	210711
Dynan LT	110413
Eames P	180911
Earl DN	010406
Earley SL	010309
Eccles J	010411
Edgar L	031100
Edgar M	011001
Edgerton C	201107
Edward DE	041011
Edwards A	220114
Edwards C	210312
Edwards G	171115
Edwards KP	310703
Edwards S	010813
Edwards SJ	010204
Edwards SS	030315
Egre DJH	010712
Elderton A	010909
Eldridge LM	251114
Elliot AC	170315
Elliott P	011209
Elliott R	010900
Ellis PN	140713
Ellis SL	010406
Ellison S	170615
Ellwood CG	010609
Elmer SP	261115
Elmstrom SA	241010
Elshaw M	010611
Epworth J	241014
Erskine JMK	020779
Etherington P	170315
Etherington R	191205
Evans D	280102
Evans DL	220607
Evans L	020216
Evans MA	290414
Evans PM	170314
Evans RE	010900
Evans S	120314
Ewart M	210900
Fabian M	010900
Fanthorpe S	180504
Farmer JR *TD*	010510
Farmer PJ	200211
Farmer T	260606
Farrington K	041200
Farrington KA	180913
Fay D	280404
Feeney A	010309
Fell JA	090501
Fellows G	010900
Fellows MJD	161006
Ferguson I	010900
Ferguson SG	290414
Ferris M	130501
Field JA	110481
Fielding D	161005
Finlayson B	031014
Fish AR	210910
Fisher A	010900
Fisher BA	150614
Fisher K	251007
Fisher WR	181213
Fitzpatrick I	160911
Fitzsimons T	111003
Flamson I	280601
Flanagan MD	271014
Flanagan S	010900
Fleming ES	010215
Flodman M	271113
Flood FJ	150106
Flood SD	010214
Flower D	010907
Flynn M	011213
Fogerty J	010900
Forder G	210310
Forrester CFT	230808
Fortune AP	020216
Forward BJ	311012
Foster C	010900
Foster N	260606
Foster NW	151209
Foster SJ	160814
Fram P	010102
Frampton SW	050711
Francis AJ	130602
Franklin J	300401
Fraser SB *MBE*	120201
Freebody M	140804
Freeman N	010900
French GW	011008
Frew J	190109
Frost RAJ	220110
Frost S	010900
Fry A	010900
Fulford AR *OBE*	220202
Fullard N	060714
Fullard R R	080211
Fuller DI *OBE*	010402
Fulton PF	030214
Gaffney A	010900
Galbraith F	080215
Gale R	011103
Galeitzke K	241005
Gallacher WP *FCMI FInstLM MCGI MIFL QTLS*	011013
Gallifant K	210808
Gamble DA	270709
Gann TJH	171115
Gannon AA	220216
Garden A	290412
Gardner S	070814
Gardner VL	011013
Gardner S S	230413
Garman G	010900
Garratt SE	280411
Garrett AR	010999
Gatter K	011209
Gaughan MS	010900
Geernaert-Davies M	260501
Gell H	010900
Gentle D	010900
Gerrard BG	011107
Gerrard J	011214
Gerrish MH *MBE*	010214

Getling F	010714	Grover K	010900	Hawkins J	160701
Geyser A	210705	Groves AE	010909	Hawkins W	180507
Gibb MS	141014	Groves J	111003	Hawley S	300999
Gibbons C	170502	Groves P	111002	Hay A	171101
Gibson C	140515	Gubby M	110607	Hay DP	010406
Gibson K	010108	Guest RJ	010104	Hayes D	010900
Gilbert C	011209	Guild J	010900	Hayes S	171105
Gilbert IR	070711	Gullidge P	190702	Hayter T	011000
Giles DR	170706	Gurung B	220905	Hazel JFT	141114
Gill AS	010406	Gurung K	070710	Heald KJ	010900
Gill D	061104	Gurung M	070306	Hearth J	221102
Gillespie D	090714	Guy K	280106	Heffernan AKP	050115
Gillespie E	091005	Hackett L	281014	Heggie J	301108
Ginty M	210908	Hadley P	280211	Heil CL	140715
Girvan JR	110515	Haldenby G	041204	Henderson L	010900
Glass M	070101	Hall C	020810	Hendry A	130604
Glaysher MA	200210	Hall C	030215	Henwood EC	010406
Glover A	251102	Hall C	030215	Hepburn G	220912
Glover MJ	101211	Hall M	050408	Heron G	010900
Goalby G	020210	Hall TLG	080114	Hewitt D	110413
Godfrey A	241010	Hallett J	061210	Hexter RA	160615
Goodwin R	010900	Hallum RG	170605	Heyl S	180301
Goodwin RAC	011009	Hames A	010900	Hickey DP	010900
Gordon CA	101007	Hamilton K	070401	Hickie DM	051004
Gotts P	010707	Hammond D	120812	Hicks TP	050314
Gough AM	200406	Hammond GR	310812	Higgins CCM	080211
Grace PJ	160615	Hammond P	180602	Hill B	030514
Grady E	220405	Harding D	030301	Hill D	010111
Grainger D	010900	Harding JM	220310	Hill K	010900
Gray A	121104	Hardman K	250512	Hill SP	220513
Gray ST	101007	Harman HG	310511	Hillman GI	160412
Greaves S	091094	Harper L	210504	Hillman L	041011
Greenlee J	010900	Harriman S	301013	Hilton B	010203
Greenley SC	220907	Harris B	010610	Hilton PJ *TD*	150178
Greenslade C	030312	Harris C	160309	Hinch NJ	210808
Greenslade LG	230311	Harris MJ	010514	Hiorns J	131006
Greenwood AH	100513	Harris-Deans GP	110615	Hirons AA	080211
Greenwood TM	290406	Harrison C	280410	Hoare MJ	110607
Gregory J	260209	Harrison P	120401	Hoare S	010412
Gregson AJ	180315	Harrison R	100801	Hoban WM	190415
Grey M	010102	Hart J	060713	Hobbs DL	220114
Grey R	260209	Hart PM	200514	Hobbs MA	180702
Griffiths M	140611	Harte JA	010900	Hobbs NW	290414
Griffiths R	291005	Harvey KL	110210	Hodder S	160310
Grogan JA	010810	Hassan AN	170909	Hodgin EL	261013
Groom C	010900	Hatch HA	230113	Holder ER *TD*	080914
Groom DT	040214	Haughey M	070814	Holder R	010901
Groom O	190101	Haughie S	010306	Holland AP	031110

Holland L	010900	Ives K	230108	Jones S	310511
Holland R	271294	Jack J	230510	Jones SP	090411
Holloway TW	010309	Jackson B	260215	Jones T	070714
Holman D	040702	Jackson JC	010412	Joseph A	010202
Holman J	030314	Jackson M	011014	Joynes G	010900
Holmes CD	061011	Jackson MJ	100109	Jump E	161208
Holmes I	010409	Jackson P	110805	Jupp G	101205
Holmes KW	010900	Jackson S	180301	Kane DJ	271005
Honeybell MA	060710	Jacques AK	010113	Karran SE	010406
Hood NR	220311	James M	010402	Karunaratne N	010904
Hooley M	010900	James RE	111107	Kavanagh B	010406
Hooper PL	090705	Jamieson S	010205	Keating AD	191012
Hope PM	010900	Jammes RR	150409	Keating G	200406
Hopkinson SD	251114	Jardine A	230712	Keaveney RA	010314
Hopper DM	111109	Jeanes P	010900	Kell JM	010714
Horton B	010900	Jeans A	010702	Kelly JL	010406
House LC	150915	Jefferies P	010900	Kelly PB	270899
Howard C	120602	Jenner SL	060710	Kelly RS	200911
Howarth-Hynes A	070603	Jennings IF	010514	Kelly SF	010900
Howell LP	140415	Jobson K	230403	Kendall SR	060710
Howes SJ	170310	John R	010900	Kennerley L	220207
Howse AJ	040306	John SE	040907	Kenny R	201101
Hubbuck C	010900	Johnson DW	200613	Kerr A	010714
Hubbuck PD	110113	Johnson JA	170310	Kerr WF	100312
Hudson TL	300511	Johnson M	050406	Ketteringham A	260605
Hughes A	240706	Johnson P	010110	Keys A	010302
Hughes D	080104	Johnson RN	010414	Kiff T	120903
Hughes G	210514	Johnson SW	071105	Kimber G	231110
Hughes P	010900	Johnson V	140715	King MA	130715
Hughes R	010201	Johnson VF	150415	King N	071107
Hull D	210305	Johnston J	170606	Kinsey P	110703
Hume B	010900	Johnston L	010601	Kirby D	051207
Humphrey KJ	011114	Jon D	011111	Kirk CM	010911
Hunter C *TD*	010802	Jones A	020388	Kirkpatrick TW	010106
Hunter D	010113	Jones A	011004	Kitchen J	010107
Hurwood RS	010501	Jones C	200911	Kitchen VHL	011009
Hutchinson C	011100	Jones C	271102	Kitching B	010900
Hutton C	151003	Jones D	161204	Kitching J	271102
Hutton M	060703	Jones DA	150915	Kitching M	100914
Huyton S	010414	Jones DM	210113	Knight K	150415
Hyde J	010102	Jones G	210604	Knight M	010214
Hyde P	010900	Jones I	151209	Knowles P	160316
Hyslop E	050405	Jones M	010900	Knox C	080805
Iddiols G	170314	Jones M	080903	Knutton K	010900
Iddon K	270305	Jones MC	270114	Konstantinious D	210208
Inseal N	010502	Jones NM	111107	Kornicki EB	110313
Ireson R	010900	Jones P	120903	Kyle IH *TD LM JP*	110411
Irons BAR	171115	Jones R	190101	Lake J	070312

Laker A	010900
Lally C	010900
Lamb W	220207
Lambert L	010900
Lambert R	010109
Lane R	010810
Lang JA	010900
Langham J	120505
Lankshear D	271113
Lannon E	010414
Lawler JT	150115
Lawrence J	010900
Lawrence JD	011014
Lawrence P	011112
Lawrence TJ	150915
Lawton GH	120810
Leafe M	301108
Leather T	010900
Leckey A	200612
Ledger CP	070510
Ledger MA	180301
Ledlie P	141014
Lee A	051010
Lee F	010900
Lee IR	270712
Lee JA	210312
Lee JE	170909
Lehman M	011109
Lemerle A	151004
Lengden M	010900
Leonard R	300301
Lester AJ	100303
Levell VG	020509
Levitt PE	171115
Lewis KR	110807
Lillicrap DT	010900
Lilly GP	011210
Limbert K	161015
Lincoln PT	131100
Line CJ	011007
Linford DI	020216
Lister B	010107
Liu S	010313
Lloyd A	221102
Lloyd N	171115
Lobar P	031200
Lockhart R	010900
Lockyer NJ	030714

Lodge D	070209
Lodge JM *TD*	020478
Lofts S	151014
Logan RP	010310
Lomas IC	010900
Lomas J	010308
Lomas PA	210207
Long AZ	140415
Long G	180702
Longden R	010102
Longmuir T	010900
Longworth AJ	200412
Loram RL	270612
Lorimer KM	300407
Louden RD	301012
Lucas B	010900
Luckhurst P	310102
Luscombe NR	100705
Luti CL	030708
Lynch G	010900
Lynch P	210404
Lynch-Blosse R	010900
Lyons SJ	130711
MacBean M	031200
MacDonald G	150714
MacDonald I	010900
MacDonald M	270909
MacDonald P	100103
MacDonald R	010900
MacFadyen P	010900
Machin I	010905
Mack TD	160615
MacKenzie I	010900
MacKenzie K	230209
Mackie RJI	070710
MacLeod ID *OBE*	010900
MacLeod N	010900
MacNab SA	220910
Maddox AH	-
Madeley S	051010
Magill A	010910
Magor V	010900
Maher AB	240311
Major IW	041012
Mallinson DB	030215
Manchee TA	010216
Manley T	180290
Mann CJ	171115

Mansfield CS	180913
Marley N	011104
Marren S	010900
Marriott AW	061010
Marshall E	180206
Marshall E	011200
Marshall KE	011113
Marsland I	210312
Martin D	010900
Martin G	010900
Martin JA	010900
Martin R	200215
Martin R	071101
Martin S	060202
Martin T	310515
Martin VR	190411
Mason E	010900
Mason I	161012
Mason N	241008
Massam D	140503
Massey C	200514
Masson A	150904
Masson K	080616
Masters GR	011014
Mather D	010306
Mathers PS	251114
Matthews R	111204
Matthews S	010213
Matthews SD	011111
Matthews SD	011001
Matyear P	020405
Maung H	010703
Maung HLA	-
Mauran G	070211
Mawe G	050892
Mawe G	010908
Maxwell R	011210
Mayall DWJ	250807
Mayberry J	010900
Mayes WJ	181011
McAleese T	010900
McAllister EJ	010712
McAllister T	010900
McAndrews MW	010214
McBratney BJ	-
McBride B	010110
McCall JIM	230713
McCammond SJ	240511

McCarthy S	120608
McClay S	020412
McCleery CJ	290914
McCleery D	010900
McCluskey M	010401
McColm MJ	010900
McConnell J	161005
McCutcheon TP	020708
McDermott JJ	220513
McDowall DG	011211
McFadyen DYA	011101
McGee EJ	180812
McGerty J	010900
McGlen SD	020414
McGough P	010104
McGuire M	120305
McIntyre AL	041209
McIntyre JA	160809
McIntyre R	141000
McKelvie D	011009
McKenna C	310714
McKenna SA	141210
McKeown JL	210312
McLean J	290106
McLean N	081102
McLeod L	260106
McMahon P	050109
McMullan P	051012
McNamee A	010900
McNaney T	010900
McNulty D	181004
McPike W	221006
McSherry PJ	271006
McTaggart SL	081208
McVay AC	110412
McVean A	051010
McWilliams A	010705
Meads JRP	090209
Meares K	050301
Meares PS	010501
Medhurst ML	251114
Medhurst MW	051010
Medler RC	200514
Meggison T	010808
Methven CJ	010900
Methven SE	120503
Meyers SA	140303
Mezals A	290109
Mezals S	210707
Middleton AD	010913
Milburn S	010713
Millar A	070209
Miller C	050505
Miller D	050505
Miller J	200911
Milligan T	010813
Mills ME	250209
Mills PI	221008
Mills R	260702
Milne C	070604
Mitchell A	090605
Molloy BJ	171114
Moncur GF *MBE*	021081
Monk AS	160615
Moody D	040314
Mooney PI	170314
Moore J	030912
Moore JRM	150705
Moore M	111002
Moore RH	011013
Morgan AE	171010
Morgan D	060203
Morgan PJ	230414
Morris A	011209
Morris A	010101
Morris BL	170909
Morris P	151003
Morris RE	251015
Morris W	011000
Morris W	011110
Morrison D	120207
Morrison G	010900
Morrissey BA	011112
Morton T	200214
Mottram A	271009
Moynham A	010900
Moynham SA	311012
Mulligan GT	020216
Mullis M	010900
Mullock DC	010810
Mumby I	011201
Munro DJ	130502
Munro N	210302
Murdoch H	170915
Murdoch J	061104
Murdoch N	220302
Murfin RW	010603
Murray P	010900
Murray R	011105
Murrin JM	080506
Mustard N	310513
Myers A	040905
Myers KM	050411
Mytton E	010602
Nash LP	010216
Nason J	110806
Naylor P	241012
Neal G	010110
Nelson M	010900
Neville MR	010900
Newbrook G	010900
Newbury G	020702
Newens C	061103
Newman CG	150512
Newman J	090116
Newman M	010900
Newton G	171200
Newton SL	010715
Nicholas N	120304
Nicholls CP	010714
Nicholson K	090611
Nicholson S	010900
Nilsson O	010900
Nisbet J	160913
Noble K	010102
Nolan M	280607
Norman C	140602
Norman R	010900
Norman SL	230513
Norris D	210306
Notice A	010900
Nugent T	090403
Oakley S	030614
Oakley S	160802
O'Brien K	110703
O'Brien NF	081205
O'Connor SM	010715
O'Donoghue M	170713
O'Meara P	010900
O'Neill HB	010900
O'Regan D	020216
Osborn D	020714
Osborn JP *MBE*	300914
Osborne MC	120210

Ostacchini SR	010405	Pollock RDM	010403	Reardon C	010111
Outram D	280302	Porritt A	180109	Reavill ASJ	170111
Oweh PT	220513	Porter DJ	010608	Reavley C	010900
Owen FT	210404	Potter ACM	011013	Redgrave G	010307
Owen MB	011013	Potter M	290609	Reditt J	260102
Oxford S	310109	Potts G	040909	Reece T	030301
Packer IR	141014	Povey C	210507	Rees J	020216
Pagent B	010900	Power JC *QVRM TD*	010402	Rees MJ	141011
Palfreyman R	010900	Poxon I	150814	Rees NGD	271015
Palmer DEO	141114	Prangnell M	220506	Reid K	080615
Palmer SR	171115	Preece SE	230512	Reid M	010900
Pannell J	011014	Prendergast DI	051207	Reilly JI	010115
Panter AD	070508	Prescott G	280703	Reilly JI	010115
Parker KL	200911	Preston J	120402	Render M	010900
Parker P	231096	Price A	050405	Rex TE	240910
Parkin D	131104	Price G	200908	Reynolds J	280603
Parkin J	010414	Price JJ	160615	Rhind S	110703
Parr T	280605	Price K	011201	Richards A	310109
Parry A	010213	Price M	010900	Richards C	270402
Passmore M	010801	Price PT	220513	Richards G	010900
Paterson C	061104	Price S	030712	Richardson A	300903
Paterson F	010900	Priest PD	270611	Richardson E	170705
Paton CC	270509	Pritchard PH	010900	Richardson J	170315
Paton K	010407	Probert N	080703	Richardson P	010900
Patton N	140412	Protheroe JL	070212	Richardson WP	070404
Pearce C	170306	Pryor SE	010614	Riches J	300101
Pearce RC	281014	Pugh A	251113	Richmond A	010900
Peddie G	041204	Pugh P	010900	Richter J	010900
Peel J	070213	Purse J	010900	Ricketts M	110509
Peers A	010502	Purvis P	300109	Ridgment K	290513
Pellett A	190401	Quelcuti C	290513	Ridings E	010900
Penny R	011101	Quicke RN	011208	Ridley M	010900
Peploe AJ	010906	Quinlan K	010304	Rigley AJ	311011
Peplow JA	210514	Quirk N	011005	Riley C	010900
Pepper M	291113	Radcliffe A	151014	Ring MJ	020713
Peterson JM	081003	Rae G	240403	Rippon N	180702
Petrie AG	020311	Rae S	220209	Risbey CR	151009
Petrie JL	290312	Raffell KJ	241014	Roach JA	270712
Pettinger N	011008	Rafique-Fayez H	021011	Roach M	010900
Phillips EF	171012	Ralph JK	200309	Robb A	010900
Phillips P	011014	Ramsey S	011101	Robb PM	160615
Philpott A	010210	Ranson LCA	250908	Roberton M	210209
Pickering JW	150401	Rapado R	180603	Roberts CL	010904
Pickering K	010901	Raper PA	010412	Roberts CT	120314
Pickin C	010900	Raven GD	141014	Roberts D	010900
Pilcher K	111205	Rayner CJ	171115	Roberts ME	060710
Pilling L	111200	Rayson T	010612	Robertson D	160615
Pirie N	010900	Read JF	130310	Robertson I	010900

Robertson J	080101
Robertson R	010900
Robinson D	011208
Robinson DJ *MBE*	010214
Robinson J	010900
Robinson M	090910
Robinson PL	011013
Robinson T	010900
Robson CA *MBE*	010713
Robson MA	310707
Rodgers B	010900
Rodwell P	300409
Roe P	250304
Rogers V	010900
Rolfe MJ	010207
Romani RD	220513
Ronner S	070814
Row P	020511
Rowley AJR	071107
Royle WS	180909
Ruddick R	140413
Ruffels JA	140715
Rusbridger DJ	010110
Rushby D	010900
Rutherford D	291113
Rutherford RG	060308
Ryan CA	220511
Ryan J	010900
Ryan M	010900
Sackree IM	010107
Saint S	050103
Sarling N	010503
Saunders D	010900
Saunders D	050204
Saunders PL	010913
Saunders WJ	230511
Saw DJ	070213
Sawyer CL	021111
Sayers MP	280915
Saywell A	010900
Scales T	131100
Scammell E	170714
Scard CM	221013
Scollick M	180401
Scott CA	130513
Scott KM	010900
Scott M	010900
Scott M	010900
Scott RS	011114
Scott W	010401
Scull S	010900
Sealy CM	271015
Seddon D	111008
Sellers GJ	010713
Selvester D	010900
Shaikh AH	031012
Shallow MA	220910
Sharkey A	010901
Sharwood-Smith C	010900
Shaw JR	011105
Shaw WCL	311010
Shawley D	230605
Shayle K	011201
Shearer J	011209
Shepherd A	050314
Shepherd PH *OBE TD MSc FHEA MCGI*	011007
Sheppard RM	051112
Shergill KS	170315
Sherratt GD	061010
Shucksmith M	261104
Sidorowicz C	010900
Simmonds R	010306
Simpkin RD	221009
Simpson JL	240114
Singh Z	171012
Skelton M	201106
Slater D	011011
Slater P	010900
Sleator K	010914
Smail H	190205
Smales S	110807
Small M	010900
Smalley DG	310116
Smillie P	010102
Smith A	010900
Smith A	190904
Smith A	010900
Smith A	010900
Smith AG	020609
Smith D	010614
Smith D	130912
Smith D	250310
Smith DS	010906
Smith G	060301
Smith G	071103
Smith I	190301
Smith I	010900
Smith KN	010900
Smith M	241000
Smith M	010900
Smith R	010900
Smith SA	170615
Smith SM	140915
Smith V	010911
Snead D	180210
Snead EC	240109
Sofley T	160714
Sokolowski E	010900
Somers S	011100
Sowerby CR	281014
Spence CE	010511
Spence M	010900
Spencer SR	220311
Spencer SW	100210
Spilsbury S	101104
Spivey R	070606
Spowage AF *MBE*	010900
Spring CS	160914
Squire DC	010900
Squirrell J	050807
Staincliffe JD	030713
Stamboulieh H	010900
Stanwick JK	231110
Starbuck CW	040501
Stark HE	200404
Stebbings N	190404
Stebbings R	100210
Stebbings S	060204
Steed A	010101
Steele D	011006
Steven AT	010112
Stevenson D	070613
Stewart CG	281014
Stewart IR	170615
Stirling A *MBE*	010900
Stobbart P	010909
Stockford JV	221015
Stone D	271007
Stone L	170909
Stone P	010900
Stoneman LA	030513
Stopford-Pickering JP	171115
Stordy MT	230113

Storey J	180315	Threader I	230107	Vines LJ	031012
Stout JD	220207	Till J	050411	Wadley IW	100511
Stout K	010102	Timney MJ	030907	Wake Z	011109
Stringer A	220114	Tisshaw CC	011013	Wakefield K	240706
Stuart I	120704	Todd A	011208	Wakelin DB	010514
Stuart PE	231111	Tonner JA	190706	Walding MA	141014
Studd ME	050411	Tooey GVB	140415	Wales J	121106
Sturcbecher JJ	190910	Tooze P	010900	Walker DR	100210
Sturges TM	080302	Torrance JP	250212	Walker K	010115
Summers J	180610	Toseland AR	100413	Walker N	020502
Sutherland RJH *MBE TD*	010314	Tough C	150106	Walker W	301108
Swales P	010312	Townell SM	310714	Wallace K	300406
Swan B	070115	Toy DJ	050411	Wallen R	011209
Swan D	151104	Toye JWA	010213	Wallen R	010214
Swan D	100413	Toze AP	021111	Wallis RCJ	030613
Swann S	010900	Tranter P	290102	Walters KR	080211
Swanney AJ	011015	Travers I	171200	Walton ID	150702
Sykes B	010900	Treeby I	260408	Walton RA	051207
Tasker D	140812	Tresidder SJ	010913	Ward NB	171115
Tatler TR	151214	Trevena N	021206	Ward NF	261104
Taverner K	070814	Tromans KS	250308	Ward PA	271013
Taylor AS	010112	Troughton T	060213	Ward S	210713
Taylor D	021006	Troy DC	230309	Ward SM	181009
Taylor DC	311012	Truby DC	010406	Ward SMB	100510
Taylor DM	250209	Trunks A	010900	Ward-Davies W	060213
Taylor FIE	140714	Truscott J	010900	Wardman A	010411
Taylor GJ	200912	Tucker DJK	030614	Ware M	080710
Taylor J	160307	Tucker G	010701	Warnock MV	010502
Taylor M	010611	Tucker TK	110413	Warren MR	300695
Taylor PK	010900	Tuhey KMF	040910	Warren N	080807
Taylor S	010900	Turkington ER	010212	Warren SJ	220312
Taylor S	010900	Turnbull A	171105	Warren SM	010909
Tearney C	011001	Turner AW	120306	Warwick I	211111
Theakstone A	111001	Turner IC	171115	Waterson AT	221004
Theobald WRJ	261015	Turner PJ	030215	Wathey R	060410
Thomas R	010900	Turner S	141212	Watkins S	010900
Thompson C	050501	Twidale K	011010	Watson DJ	070213
Thompson M	121104	Twigg D	220114	Watson G	010900
Thompson NW	040712	Twyman S	190401	Watson G	010610
Thompson T	010900	Tyrer I	010909	Watson N	160615
Thomsett M	010914	Tyson J	251112	Watson N	200208
Thomson M	221006	Tyson-Woodcock P	010900	Watson PA	310706
Thomson R	181209	Van Oppen J	140415	Watson SL	090612
Thorne AM	010900	Van-Falier A	010900	Watt S	150912
Thorne N	010304	Vernon JA	011015	Watts J	010900
Thornley P	181001	Verrinder C	261110	Watts N	231114
Thorpe E	010209	Vile P	010900	Waugh JF	240512
Thorpe RS	170315	Vincent MK	010408	Way C	260605

Webb G	140402
Webb MG	100510
Webber FN	090404
Webber MA	080589
Webster A	110210
Webster A	201006
Weedon M	230108
Weir MS	
Welburn S	011013
Welch D	160615
Welch K	301009
Wells CA	231110
Wells HT	010407
Wells RD	230311
Wenlock P	010105
West J	010900
West R	010900
Westbrook MS	110608
Westlake R	151211
Westlake-Toms B	010904
Westmore D	070210
Westwood DN	011210
Whatley J	261103
Whatley M	131004
Whiffin JP	241009
Whitbread P	010403
White B	010900
White C	310102
White J	010913
White NC	261111
White P	260602
White SPJ	280812
Whitelock SP	010315
Whitmore B	201106
Whittaker P	010900
Whyte M	020209
Whyte MC	050615
Wiggins AW	041109
Wignall G	110413
Wilding GK	231105
Wilkinson NW	011112
Wilkinson S	290713
Williams C	180606
Williams CJ	100501
Williams D	120608
Williams DT	010900
Williams DW	010610
Williams HM	130807
Williams JC	200514
Williams MA	100414
Williams ML	150207
Williams N	010900
Williams O	010402
Williams P	070312
Williams S	281114
Williams V	080814
Wills OS	100714
Wilson C	010900
Wilson GP	051213
Wilson J	220203
Wilson JS *OBE*	010900
Wilson K	010714
Wilson KN	111212
Wilson N	261104
Wilson R	010410
Wilson T	190301
Wilson TS	160310
Windle J	301013
Winsor DM	120608
Wiseman G	010504
Wood CJM *TD*	010501
Wood G	101207
Wood JF	010213
Wood L	230511
Wood L	130511
Wood NAP	111203
Wood R	010206
Woodruff A	010714
Woods A	010900
Woods K	081205
Wookey CS	271113
Wooley R	050806
Wootton MJ	010900
Wray CA	071013
Wright CF	120609
Wright S	260602
Wynn S	191207
Yarr G	250107
Yates M	200607
Yates P	010104
Yearwood MJ	090909
Yerbury RA	250514
Young BR *MBE*	010406
Young CI	010900
Young FS	020216
Young ME	040712
Young MJ	010900
Young SG	250613
Young T	231110
Young-Hotz S	210506
Ziemelis PS	110210

2nd Lieutenants

Acheson DW	010615
Adams DA	021114
Adams RJ	210914
Adams TG	130915
Aitken AJ	120715
Akam CH	140615
Allen CM	150315
Allen GN	221115
Allen S	011114
Amara-Carnell M	130915
Anderson AD	180609
Anderton PT	160613
Andrews AS	150315
Aran DCL	110514
Arundell RJ	130414
Atherton GB	200513
Baker DJC	010806
Ball HCA	161111
Bambury KA	221115
Barr DS	230512
Beard L	010515
Beckham ML	221115
Bell TM	170913
Bennett DJ	130414
Bilboe CW	090413
Billinge A	011013
Bird CL	270408
Blackwood AJG	041013
Blair D	221115
Blamire GC	221115
Blenkinship M	011114
Bloy NJ	020215
Bonner CEM	140615
Boulton SRW	231115
Bowyer M	010215
Bradbury HB	010811
Brady LP	011115
Brinsley AM	250112
Brookes AL	140615
Brown AW	010409
Brown SW	140915

Buchhierl EA	011115	Feltham PR	021114	Horn IA	120515
Callender CES	300116	Ferrari A	200513	Howieson R	010415
Campbell R	160709	Fletcher RJ	110208	Huck JP	221115
Carter SR	010214	Ford-Hunter RJ	021115	Hudson T	150213
Casey DCR	221115	Forster CF	160614	Hugill R	010215
Chapman PR	220914	Fraser SP	151209	Hutchings PE	010215
Chinnook SC	020215	Fuller KD	010215	Ironside S	130714
Clayton MJ	160809	Galloway R	281013	Jackson-Lyall S	221115
Coburn GE	170613	Gardner A	140615	James K	100309
Cocker S	030214	Geddes AJ	010515	Jardine K	310812
Connor AC	140714	Geraghty PA	121015	Jeffries KLM	011115
Cook AGP	010112	Gibbings SRL	120313	Jerdan D	011112
Cook JK	100515	Gilbert AJ	140615	Johnston KE	020215
Cook RA	190415	Golding PA	150315	Jones CM	010115
Cooper M	310713	Goldsmith DJ	200215	Jones T	150904
Corcoran IN	030412	Goodband RJH	260310	Kelly PJ	160314
Cottrell JP	150315	Gooder GA	011010	Kenworthy JL	120715
Cowan SV	170313	Gowland S	140615	Keyte AJ	140615
Coward MIE	220215	Gray LJ	020214	Keyte CF	011115
Craven ML	060408	Green A	050216	Kirk M	010412
Cumming DJ	221115	Green JE	060611	Knox VE	140414
Dane MA	011013	Green S	190511	Lambert BJ	200315
Darby SA	121113	Greenway WPC	150913	Lambert DP	130915
Davies HL	031110	Griffiths DA	200310	Lamming HL	130714
Davies-Cooke PB	011109	Grisdale B	220216	Laurence-Young P	120715
Davison P	310116	Hall A	010107	Layer B	020713
Dawson C	021114	Hambly C	090511	Lazell JRA	220215
Denton CGC	140713	Hames MAN	220815	Leaman MJ	190415
Dhillon JS	221115	Hargrave CF	150615	Lecras WAE	010915
Dixon DR	220215	Harris DE	151012	Lehmann KL	310116
Dixon GL	230713	Harrison WS	150615	Lennon D	070814
Dods KS	221115	Harrow SJ	120313	Lingard AJ	221115
Dreyfus C	310116	Hartley-Smith MR	210914	Lister SM	310116
Dynan J	220215	Harvey JC	120715	Lloyd CT	281011
Easterbrook M	170915	Hastings DW	011115	Lockett B	150315
Edgar SJ	140615	Hatch RM	261112	Long A	041209
Edwards JH	011115	Hathaway SN	010802	Lovegrove W	150614
Egginton ED	011115	Hay L	120209	Lowther ID	040211
Elie D	240403	Hayward JG	150315	Lund AJ	231115
Ellis SEA	020215	Hearst L	230914	MacFarlane T	011115
Ellison W	010106	Heisel PK	130212	MacFarquhar LMW	011115
Elrick BJ	011106	Henderson R	050314	Maddock P	140714
Emery A	130515	Henry J	140615	Major DAJ	220215
Etherington RJ	160314	Henwood LC	220215	Mapletoft GB	130915
Evans DJ	130915	Hill SE	140615	Marshallsay KJ	030810
Eyre SJ	031114	Holt C	020214	Martin AL	150315
Felix S	220215	Hone J	220215	Martin TR	150315
Fell EL	010412	Hordle J	241006	McAleer CP	040313

McCluskie SA	130915	Redfern L	120715	Thomas D	120715
McDowell GL	160314	Richards L	110213	Thompson SA	190415
McGonnell A	170613	Richardson GM	011115	Thornton AC	110911
McGowan PD	010712	Riding S	010216	Thornton KP	010409
McIntosh SJ	010515	Roberts HR	140615	Tidy TI	130414
McKenzie SG	180615	Robinson BC	050216	Tobin KM	130714
McKinney P	170313	Ross P	200415	Toseland CM	010508
McQuaid AJ	020214	Rowlands S	010310	Trunks ZJ	120715
Metcalf EL	011115	Ryalls KD	220215	Tweed GS	130915
Milburn G	210914	Salmon LA	150315	Twyman A	050216
Miller JTC	011115	Sammons K	241013	Urquhart LL	140413
Miniss B	031114	Sanders MS	130414	Uttley KR	011109
Moody JA	110514	Saunders GAR	130915	Varley DJ	080113
Moore B	171113	Scott CR	140615	Vernon J	011014
Mulvey BG	221115	Seddon NL	160315	Vickers DNF	051213
Munro RA	170414	Seekings MD	150614	Waldron MC	011111
Neale PA	150614	Sharpe ME	150614	Watkinson HR	160912
Neil M	011109	Shaw SCK	210216	Webster MR	110514
Nevell E	130715	Shepherd EI	050313	Wernham CA	120715
Newman L	160708	Shergold SE	160314	West S	021115
Nijjar H H	240914	Short FCL	200315	Whitehouse B	041212
Noble CKM	180609	Shorter YC	220711	Whitfield M	010414
Norman SLW	180111	Simons J	060309	Williams K	200315
Norman SM	140414	Singleton D	271013	Williams S	261012
Norris OWJ	010215	Slater HL	220216	Williams WS	221115
Nuttall D	010904	Smalley GR	310116	Wing R	220512
O'Dell AMV	011115	Smedley JP	150913	Wood JR	310116
O'Loughlin LD	160715	Smith BA	010216	Wood SE	230415
Oliver W	120715	Smith DE	221115	Woodruff NJ	011014
Olszewski P	021114	Smith E	180615	Worden MJ	210914
Parrot AE	271013	Smith MC	210216	Worgan RO	120715
Parry N	221115	Sperring TJ	140615	Wright SC	130715
Patton WS	190415	Squires V	110514	Yerli B	011114
Peacock CW	150113	Stewart MRG	190415	Zengeni TLT	031114
Peak JW	170715	Stewart R	011110		
Pengelly JJ	130915	Stonebridge-Smith A	120715		
Pentecost P	131004	Streets JS	221115		
Perkins SE	010709	Sullivan B	200815		
Pileci KJ	140714	Sutherland HCJ	010515		
Piling A	031114	Swash S	190415		
Platt D	011115	Talbot-New GEJ	111215		
Pollard C	100515	Taylor GM	010215		
Porter BMW	140615	Taylor-Rudd PS	131114		
Preece RJ	010216	Thomas GJ	130915		
Prior CM	200310	Thomas JR	170715		
Prior JE	310713	Thomas K	280813		
Radley J	260914	Thomas NMG	110212		
Reading N	130915	Thomas W	040413		

RESERVE FORCES & CADETS ASSOCIATIONS (RFCAs)

THE COUNCIL OF RESERVE FORCES & CADETS ASSOCIATIONS (CRFCA)

Holderness House, 51-61 Clifton Street, London EC2A 4EY
Tel: 020 7426 8350 Email: co-info@rfca.mod.uk

(correct for year: 2015/2016)

President................................ *The Rt Hon The Lord* de Mauley *TD*

Chairman............................... Lt Gen (Retd) Robin V Brims *CB CBE DSO DL*

Board Chairman.................... Capt I M Robinson *OBE RD RNR*

Vice-Chairmen....................... *Army*......Maj Gen S F N Lalor *CB TD VR*

Marine...Brig T H Lang

Navy......Capt N R V Dorman *RD ADC RNR*

Air..........Air Cdre I Stewart

Council Secretariat

Chief Exectuive......................AVM (Retd) Paul Douglas Luker *CB OBE AFC DL (until 29/09/16)*
Maj Gen James Gordon *CB CBE (from 30/09/16)*

Chief of Staff..........................Brig M P Banham *MBE*

Director Cadets & Youth........Cdr G R Bushell

Director Volunteer Estates.....Mr S Blissitt *MSc*

Director Engagement.............Ms F L Thomas *MSc MBA*

Secretary Pension Scheme.....Mr I Scarfe

The 13 Reserve Forces' and Cadets' Associations (RFCAs) are Crown Agencies, established by Act of Parliament under the Reserve Forces Act 1996. Each one is a separate, independent and autonomous Tri-Service corporate body with a function to support the Reserve Forces and Cadets.

Each of the RFCAs are represented on the CRFCA by its chairman.

Board Members...................... Maj Gen Greg S Smith *CB QVRM TD*.................................(Chairman East Anglia RFCA)

Col R M L Colville *TD DL*..(Chairman East Midlands RFCA)

Col M A J M Overton *TD*...(Chairman Greater London RFCA)

Col Allan C C Lapsley *QVRM TD ADC DL*.........................(Chairman Lowland RFCA)

Col N D O Williams *TD JP DL*...(Chairman North West & Isle of Man RFCA)

Col H K McAllister *OBE TD DL*...(Chairman Northern Ireland RFCA)

Lt Gen R V Brims *CB CBE DSO DL*....................................(Chairman North of England RFCA)

Col W M J Partridge *TD DL*..(Chairman South East RFCA)

Col K Davies *MBE RRC TD D*L
(from 2017 Capt Brian Thorne *RD RNR)*.........................(Chairman Wales RFCA)

Col O J H Chamberlain *QVRM TD* DL*..............................(Chairman Wessex RFCA)

Col *The Hon* P S Seccombe *TD*...(Chairman West Midland RFCA)

Brig D A Hargreaves..(Chairman Yorkshire & The Humber RFCA)

EAST ANGLIA

President

Mrs Helen Nellis *BA (Hons) MA Barrister*
(HM Lord-Lieutenant of Bedfordshire)
(as of 2017)

Chairman

Maj Gen Greg S Smith *CB QVRM TD*

Chief Executive

Col (Retd) Ray Wilkinson *QVRM TD VR*

Deputy Chief Executive

Lt Col Jackie Allan *QVRM TD VR*

Head of Estate Services

Mr Jonathan Lewis

Head of Business Services

Mr Nick Stephens

Association address

250 Springfield Road,
Chelmsford, Essex CM2 6BU
Tel: 01245 244800
DFTS: 94660 4800
Fax: 01245 492398
DFTS Fax: 94660 4823
Email: ea-offman@rfca.mod.uk
Website: www.earfca.org.uk

EAST MIDLANDS

President

Dame Lady Jeniffer Gretton DCVO JP
(HM Lord-Lieutenant of Leicestershire)

Chairman

Col (Retd) Murray L Colville *TD DL*

Chief Executive

Gp Capt (Retd) Nick D Sharpe

Deputy Chief Executive

Lt Col (Retd) Simon Worsley

Association address

Army Reserve Centre, Triumph Road,
Nottingham NG7 2GG
Tel: 0115 924 8610
DFTS: 94451 5610
Fax: 0115 924 8629
Email: em-comms@rfca.mod.uk
Website: eastmidlandsrfca.co.uk

GREATER LONDON

President

Sir David Brewer *KG CMG CVO JP*
(HM Lord-Lieutenant of Greater London)

Chairman

Col E G Cameron *TD DL*

Chief Executive

Col (Retd) Hugh M Purcell *OBE DL*

Chief of Staff and
Head of Youth, Cadets and
Community Engagement

Lt Cdr A Pringle *MRAeS MCMI MCGI*

City Secretary

Lt Col Peter L d'A Willis

Association address

Fulham House, 87 Fulham High Street,
London SW6 3JS
Tel: 020 7384 4640
Fax: 020 7384 4662
DFTS: 94624 4640
Email: gl-offrec@rfca.mod.uk
Website: www.glrfca.org

HIGHLANDS

President

R Adm M Gregory *OBE*
(HM Lord-Lieutenant of Dunbartonshire)

Chairman

Capt N R V Dorman *RD ADC RNR*

Vice-Chairmam (army)

Col J A B Kinloch *TD*

Chief Executive

Brig (Retd) M P Dodson *MBE*

Deputy Chief Executive

Mr Andrew Macnaughton

Association address:

Seathwood,
365 Perth Road, Dundee DD2 1LX
Tel: 01382 668283
Fax: 01382 566442
Email: hi-admin@rfca.org.uk
Website: www.hrfca.co.uk

LOWLANDS

President

Guy Clark
(HM Lord-Lieutenant of Renfrewshire)

Chairman

Col Allan C C Lapsley *QVRM TD ADC DL*

Chief Executive

Col (Retd) Robbie D Gibson *MBE*

Deputy Chief Executive

Col (Retd) Tom C Mathew

Association address

Lowland House,
60 Avenuepark Street, Glasgow G20 8LW
Tel: 0141 945 4951
DFTS: 94535 2014
Fax: 0141 945 4869
Email: lo-offman@lo.rfca.mod.uk
Website: www.lowlandrfca.org.uk

NORTH WEST OF ENGLAND AND ISLE OF MAN

President

Mr Warren Smith
(HM Lord-Lieutenant of Greater Manchester)

Chairman

Col N D O Williams *TD JP DL*

Chief Executive

Col Mark Underhill *OBE*

Deputy Chief Executive

Col Alex Barnes

Association address

Alexandra Court,
28 Alexandra Drive, Liverpool L17 8YE
Tel: 0151 727 4552
DFTS: 94552 8164
Email: nw-info@rfca.mod.uk
Website: www.nwrfca.org.uk

NORTHERN IRELAND

President

Col D Desmond *CBE*
(HM Lord-Lieutenant for the County of Londonderry)

Chairman

Col H K McAllister *OBE TD DL*

Chief Executive

Col Johnny W Rollins *MBE*

Deputy Chief Executive

Lt Col A D Sykes *MBE QGM BEM*

Association contact

Tel: 028 9066 5706
Fax: 028 9066 2809
Email: ni-info@rfca.org.uk
Website: www.reservesandcadetsni.org.uk

NORTH OF ENGLAND

President

Mrs Sue Snowdon
(HM Lord-Lieutenant of County Durham)

Vice President

Mrs Susan Margaret Winfield *OBE DL*
(HM Lord-Lieutenant of Tyne and Wear)

Chairman

Lt Gen R V Brims *CB CBE DSO DL*

Chief Executive

Brig Paul J A Baker *OBE*

Deputy Chief Executive

Lt Col Iain Clyde

Association address

53 Old Elvet,
Durham DH1 3JJ
Tel: 0191 383 6250
Fax: 0191 384 0918
Email: ne-comms@rfca.mod.uk
Website: www.rfca-ne.org.uk

SOUTH EAST

President

Mr N J Atkinson
(HM Lord-Lieutenant for Hampshire)

Chairman

Col W M J Partridge *TD DL*

Chief Executive

Col (Retd) Patrick T Crowley *MA*

Deputy Chief Executive West

Grp Capt (Retd) Keith Lane *RAF*

Deputy Chief Executive East

Lt Col P G B Ellis *QGM**

Association address

Seely House, Shoe Lane,
Aldershot, Hants GU11 2HJ
Tel: 0115 924 8610
Fax: 01252 357620
Email: se-offao1@rfca.org.uk
Website: www.serfca.org

WALES

President

The Hon Dame Shân Legge-Bourke *DCVO*
(HM Lord-Lieutenant of Powys)

Chairman

Capt Brian Thorne *RD RNR*

Chief Executive

Col Nick R Beard *TD DL*

Deputy Chief Executive

Lt Col Stephen S MM Hughes *MSc BSc(Econ)*

Association address

Maindy Barracks,
Cardiff CF14 3YE
Tel: 02920 375747
Email: wa-marketingasst@wa.rfca.mod.uk
Website: http://wales-rfca.org

WESSEX

President

Dame Jane Trotter *OBE DBE*
(HM Lord-Lieutenant of Gloucestershire)

Vice Presidents

Mrs Anne Maw
(HM Lord-Lieutenant of Somerset)

Mr David Fursden
(HM Lord-Lieutenant of Devon)

Chairman

Col Oliver J H Chamberlain *QVRM TD* DL*

Chief Executive

Brig Steve Hodder

Deputy Chief Executive

Lt Col P G Adams *AFC*
(not confirmed)

Association address

Mount House, Mount Street,
Taunton, Somerset TA1 3QE
Tel: 01823 250103
Email: wx-comms@rfca.mod.uk
Website: www.wessex-rfca.org.uk

WEST MIDLANDS

President

Mr Ian Dudson *CBE*
(HM Lord-Lieutenant of Staffordshire)

Chairman

Col *The Hon* P S Seccombe *TD*

Chief Executive
Col T F L Weeks *OBE*

Deputy Chief Executive and Director of Cadets and Youth

Maj M Young

Association address

Tennal Grange, Tennal Road,
Harborne, Birmingham B32 2HX
Tel: 0121 427 5221
Fax: 0121 427 8380
Email: wm-info@rfca.mod.uk
Website: www.wmrfca.org

YORKSHIRE AND THE HUMBER

President

Dame Dr Ingrid M Roscoe DCVO BA PhD FSA
(HM Lord Lieutenant of West Yorkshire)

Vice President

Mr Barry Dodd *CBE*
(HM Lord-Lieutenant of North Yorkshire)

Chairman

Brig D A Hargreaves

Chief Executive

Col (Retd) C E M Snagge

Deputy Chief Executive

Lt Col (Retd) Jeremy D Bleasdale

Association address

20 St George's Place,
York YO24 1DS
Tel: 01904 623081
Email: yh-info@rfca.mod.uk
Website: www.rfca-yorkshire.org.uk

THE COMBINED CADET FORCE ASSOCIATION (CCFA)

Holderness House, 51 – 61 Clifton Street, London, EC2A 4DW
(Tel: 0207 426 8370 Email: PA-GENSEC@armycadets.com Website: combinedcadetforce.org.uk)

CCFA Council (2017)

Capt General.. HER MAJESTY THE QUEEN

President .... VAdm P Hudson *CB CBE*
Vice Presidents
Royal Navy... R Adm BNB Williams *CBE*
Army.. Maj Gen M J Rutledge *CB OBE*
RAF.. AVM M J Routledge *CB*

Chairman .... AVM N D A Maddox *CBE*
Vice Chairman.. Lt Col M Hampshire
Hon Treasurer.. Miss Julia Hodgson

Representing the Ministry of Defence.................... Mr D Haigh
Representing Flag Officer Sea Training................ Lt R I Armstrong *RM*
Representing GOC Regional Command................ Brig M P Lowe *MBE*
Representing Commandant
Air Cadet Organisation.................................... Wg Cmd M Larwood-Hughes
Representing the Council of RFCAs...................... Maj Gen J H Gordon *CBE CB*
Representing the Headmasters' and
Headmistresses' Conference and the
Independent Schools Council........................... Mr M Mortimer
Representing the Association ofSchool and
College Leaders and the National
Association of Headteachers............................ Mrs J Taylor
Representing the National
Rifle Association and the Council
for Cadet Rifle Shooting.................................... Maj Gen I C Dale *CBE*
Chief Executive ....Col (Retd) Murdo N S Urquhart *OBE*

THE ARMY CADET FORCE ASSOCIATION (ACFA)

Holderness House, 51 – 61 Clifton Street, London, EC2A 4DW
(Tel: 0207 426 8377 Fax: 0207 426 8378
Email: marketing@armycadets.com Website: www.armycadets.com)

ACFA Board (2017)

Patron.. HER MAJESTY THE QUEEN

Member... FM *HRH The Prince* Philip *Duke of* Edinburgh *KG KT OM GBE ONZ QSO AK GCL CC CMM ADC(P)*

President .... Lt Gen A J N Graham *CB CBE*
Vice-President.. Maj Gen (Retd) M D Wood *CBE*
Chairman .... Maj Gen D McDowall *CBE*
Vice-Chariman .... Col D I Fuller *OBE MNM DL*
Chairman Finance Committee............... Col J A Fogerty
Hon Treasurer.. Mr A Goodwin

Chief Executive ....Col (Retd) Murdo N S Uruquhart *OBE*
Executive Officer to Chief Executive......Martin Meek
Director Finance, Operations &
Training (DFOT)..............................Mr Richard Walton
Executive Assistant to DFOT................Simon Woolridge

RETIRED AR OFFICERS

Listing officers who have retired between 1st Match 2015 - 1st March 2016 and the date of their retirement.

Brigadiers

Sutcliffe RWH OBE TD (Late RY)	110515

Colonels

Carey-Harris J TD QHN (Late QARANC)	100415
Cran AAW (Late REME)	010815
Lapsley ACC QVRM TD DL (Late R SIGNALS)	150615

Lieutenant Colonels

Allan JA QVRM TD (Late INT CORPS)	300915
Donaldson AM MBE (Late R IRISH)	250215
Evans AT OBE MSc CEng MIEE psc+ dis tem (Late R SIGNALS)	011115
Finch MJ (Late R SIGNALS)	050115
Hann TG TD (Late MERCIAN)	160216
Hunter Td EM TD (Late QARANC)	270116
Jowsey CJ TD (Late RLC)	201214
Metcalfe S QVRM TD (Late RE)	310116
Tomczyk AJ (Late SCOTS)	240216
Topham CME (Late RIFLES)	030915
Webb MJ (Late QARANC)	310116
Wong AL TD (Late R WELSH)	171015

Majors

Aston JL Rev (Late RAChD)	310515
Brown TA (Late QARANC)	250315
Clarke RS (Late RLC)	301115
Crockett IM (Late R SIGNALS)	010315
Deegan A *Rev* (Late RAChD)	310815
Denning PM (Late R SIGNALS)	210115
Dowling JW CMgr CEng MCIPD MIET MCMI (Late REME)	100315
Dunne M *Rev* (Late RAChD)	170216
Fountaine IHF CEng FIET (Late REME)	210715
Fraley DM TD (Late R SIGNALS)	271115
Fry HM RMN (Late QARANC)	010116
Gough AJE (Late RA)	010215
Green DN TD (Late QARANC)	160415
Hallows JM *Rev* (Late RAChD)	181015
Hills PL *Rev* (Late RAChD)	170115
Holmes Td CM TD (Late RLC)	010815
John MP MBE (Late RLC)	010615
Kelsall JI (Late QARANC)	020615
Kennedy A (Late R SIGNALS)	010915
Lewis VDS (Late RAMC)	231115
Llewellin WO TD (Late RLC)	010415
McDade AR (Late R IRISH)	290814
Milgate DJ (Late HAC)	010215
Morris CP TD (Late RLC)	301115
Nisbet KR TD (Late RLC)	191214
Peyton SS (Late LANCS)	280714
Raleigh S (Late RAMC)	311215
Rawson T (Late REME)	310315
Richardson T (Late RLC)	211215
Riley J (Late R SIGNALS)	191015
Scott Galli AP (Late R SIGNALS)	171215
Sirr K (Late R SIGNALS)	071015
Smith MD (Late RAMC)	040216
Stonebridge JM TD (Late RF)	281014
Szabo CLW (Late REME)	090515
Underwood JS TD (Late RLC)	010415
Underwood TJ (Late RE)	040315
Wallace AR (Late RLC)	290216
Weeks RBL (Late REME)	010316
White Td J (Late RLC)	230815
Wiggell JF (Late RLC)	191214
Wilson H (Late QARANC)	160415

Captains

Donkersley EF (Late QARANC)	020615
Ball J *Rev* (Late RAChD)	010115
Bandy GW (Late QARANC)	250315
Barrowcliffe AR (Late RAMC)	070515
Bowerman AM *Rev* (Late RAChD)	150715
Catto AG (Late RY)	031115
De Wilde OT (Late REME)	051215
Gutteridge SCD (Late RLC)	050216
Hall PE (Late R SIGNALS)	010116
Hall PE (Late RE)	010116
Koss RA TD (Late AGC (ETS))	270815
Masheter PG (Late R SIGNALS)	210115
Mckeown DI (Late QARANC)	160415
Mermagen CG (Late REME)	010815
Mills D *Rev* (Late RAChD)	010116
Moss JE (Late INT CORPS)	260615
Ong EJ (Late R SIGNALS)	310514
Perry MC *Rev* (Late RAChD)	010915

Samways PJ (Late R SIGNALS)	070216
Wright RE (Late R SIGNALS)	280815

Lieutenants

Simpson NJR (Late R MON RE(M))	160115

AMENDMENTS TO ARMY LIST ENTRY

The personnel data in this edition of the Army List has been sourced from the Ministry of Defence Supplements of The London Gazette and compiled to produce a dataset of personnel as of 1st March 2016. Every effort has been made to make this edition as accurate as possible. It is possible that some detail will be incorrect as promotions, awards, etc. promulgated prior to this date may not have been included in the supplements. The Editor regrets any inaccuracy and difficulties this may cause, and will endeavour to ensure that corrections appear in the next edition.

If you notice any errors or omissions in this edition please contact the editor at Dandy Booksellers Ltd. The corrections will be published in the next edition.

Readers who wish to comment on this edition of the Army List are invited to write to:

Miss C R Hooper
The Editor of the Army List
Dandy Booksellers Ltd
Units 3 & 4, 31-33 Priory Park Road
London NW6 7UP

Telephone: +44 (0)20 7624 2993
Fax: +44 (0)20 7624 5049
Email: enquiries@dandybooksellers.com
Website: www.dandybooksellers.com

ROYAL INDEX

SUBJECT INDEX

A

B

C

D

F

G

H

I

J

M

N

O

P

Q

R

S

U

W

PERSONNEL INDEX

Index of personnel listed in sections III and IV

(For appointments where the holder is either not currrently a serving officer in the regular army or army reserve or if their name can not be confirmed against their service number please view the relevant corps/regiment entry)

A

30238589 Aagaard AR, 327
24789797 Aaron DK, 259
25166202 Abayomi S, 197
562458 Abbott C, 246
N029468U Abbott D, 372
30165007 Abbott G, 359
30104101 Abbott JM, 352
30158737 Abbott ML, 238
562706 Abbott MR, 372
514157 Abbott RJ, 204
24540886 Abbott S, 279
W1061948 Abbott SEE, 331
30119636 Abbott SR, 323
30104316 Abbott WJ, 282
557710 Abbs MJ, 372
560805 Abel CM, 231
C37543 Abel RL, 234
30020657 Abel SD, 372
549744 Abeledo BJA, 227
549336 Abercrombie LA, 343
513289 Abraham CM, 38, 108
517809 Abraham KD, 349
559813 Abraham-Igwe CU, 243
30032469 Abu-Mughaisib MA, 268
25227684 Abu-Romia J, 262
25195959 Acheson DW, 383
30020174 Ackerman LC, 282
547283 Ackrill MJ, 220
547244 Ackroyd CA, 248
561514 Ackroyd P, 197
525327 Acornley JD, 110
30036457 Acquah V, 372
25219144 Acton BJP, 197
529721 Acton FS, 299
552293 Adair CD, 265
537719 Adam LS, 272
534936 Adam SR, 110
565857 Adams AJM, 169
566408 Adams AR, 275
554251 Adams BJ, 231
548838 Adams CB, 205
30040058 Adams CM, 211
549386 Adams CS, 342
30154592 Adams DA, 383
560606 Adams DJ, 228
557962 Adams EJ, 277
30067572 Adams ETT, 216
30063562 Adams G, 279
520589 Adams JS, 110
559997 Adams K, 352
562452 Adams K, 372
565148 Adams KW, 306
30040463 Adams LK, 263
30128126 Adams MB, 223
563526 Adams MD, 177
531605 Adams MS, 110
531832 Adams MWG, 213
521592 Adams OJ, 110
554252 Adams PJ, 262
536971 Adams R, 372
30139397 Adams RDF, 335
30192812 Adams RJ, 383
562636 Adams RR, 327
537021 Adams SA, 243
538227 Adams SJ, 305
565410 Adams SJ, 347
C29205 Adams TG, 383
548805 Adams W, 372
551234 Adamson GK, 153
556267 Adamson J, 352
30177453 Adamson JG, 185
30148931 Adamson L, 336
557360 Adamson RAG, 153
30195854 Adamson SE, 239
30030394 Adamson SG, 246
25019473 Adamson WF, 199
C31084 Adcock CSL, 372
24213722 Adcock DP, 352
25181515 Adcock JL, 256
30136565 Adcock MJ, 223
555028 Adcock N, 372
25181514 Adcock SP, 257
498359 Adcroft H, 352
25218895 Addison RC, 282
30143131 Addison-Black MQ, 185
527071 Addley GN, 110
526983 Adkins IC, 289, 338
25132687 Adolphe KJ, 228
24764329 Affleck MP, 306
551662 Agathangelou L, 338
24837820 Aggrey ME, 352
565195 Agius TL, 234
558664 Agnew JF, 265
558849 Agnew RJ, 174
30033253 Agnew RWR, 323
509382 Ahern JP, 308
30159369 Ahluwalia R, 322
557863 Ahmad TK, 244
30182784 Ahmed N, 271
565196 Ahmed SI, 205
30203564 Ahrens SL, 352
558642 Ahsan I, 214
30098051 Aiano SGG, 359
25004706 Aikman NT, 234
550611 Ainley J, 204
523211 Ainscough JM, 346
24826190 Ainscough PJ, 330
30015531 Ainsworth CM, 197
547086 Ainsworth EL, 231
30163701 Ainsworth LEJ, 170
518848 Ainsworth PHP, 321
556277 Air S, 372
562074 Airey PJD, 279
557732 Aitchison A, 153
561544 Aitchison IJ, 340
561147 Aitchison JA, 347
563719 Aitken A, 372
528845 Aitken AJ, 48, 108, 153
C36011 Aitken AJ, 383
548328 Aitken AM, 329
543908 Aitken AR, 277
30137064 Aitken ARC, 191
30088936 Aitken CJM, 211
30134864 Aitken NGE, 251
25213417 Aitken RES, 132
30178964 Aiton M, 212
30195698 Akam CH, 383
30098609 Akbareian-Clarke TC, 239
548730 Akerman AJ, 246
30204014 Akers DA, 238
C32245 Akester A, 372
544024 Akinkunmi AA, 289
549308 Albon K, 318
560671 Albon S, 352
558643 Alder JJ, 197
30085810 Alder MTH, 154
24772448 Alderman JP, 145
540407 Alderson AB, 295
527718 Alderson B, 214
25039360 Alderson EJ, 197
30140292 Alderson LJ, 359
538289 Aldington DJ, 277
550478 Aldred PJ, 227
25235087 Aldred TE, 216
559508 Aldridge JW, 148
24753818 Aldridge MD, 275
565586 Ale D, 188
560130 Ale P, 187
548125 Alecock JR, 259
24590201 A'Lee JA, 240
531909 Alers-Hankey RR, 110
561325 Alesbury NR, 268
559003 Alesbury RPL, 220
30122428 Alexander A, 352
30215097 Alexander A, 359
551728 Alexander CA, 231
546483 Alexander CS, 214
Alexander D, 50
30148937 Alexander D, 234
563870 Alexander FJG, 282
507357 Alexander G, 372
510272 Alexander IC, 276
565035 Alexander MGD, 249
24631913 Alexander SA, 240

B

544870 Baker ND, 213
527914 Baker NL, 297
525269 Baker PHS, 110
502353 Baker PW, 329
519136 Baker R, 196
550891 Baker R, 230
557662 Baker RA, 234
30076622 Baker RIJ, 202
563108 Baker S, 352
559434 Baker TA, 347
30208439 Baker WJ, 223
30153861 Bakovljev AN, 212
25195707 Balch BL, 182
560160 Balchin AC, 330
25062219 Balchin WEA, 242
25220938 Baldry CB, 208
24823463 Baldwin BJ, 282
519627 Baldwin BL, 181
529120 Baldwin E, 305
30159629 Baldwin JTI, 191
562078 Baldwinson BM, 197
24904010 Bale JBD, 199
25187107 Bale TJ, 242
30201344 Bales R, 203
30187458 Balfour AJ, 218
545766 Balfour D, 372
544872 Balfour JS, 214
558652 Balfour PAP, 313
30201407 Balfour WAM, 339
524261 Balgarnie AD, 204
546443 Ball A, 372
517245 Ball AE, 303
551660 Ball DC, 277
30038900 Ball DJ, 199
554456 Ball HC, 346
W1064026 Ball HCA, 383
565581 Ball J, 392
30146766 Ball JD, 307
545297 Ball KH, 372
30028274 Ball MW, 251
30135260 Ball N, 352
551241 Ball RDH, 220
558544 Ballans A, 204
538888 Ballantyne A, 308
30138976 Ballantyne GC, 154
558654 Ballantyne SA, 259
555380 Ballard EF, 214
561743 Ballard J, 352
562712 Ballard JF, 174
551929 Ballard MS, 244
565660 Ballard-Whyte LO, 127
523313 Balls JB, 174
515294 Balls PJA, 190
540966 Balmbra M, 352
24385743 Balmer J, 352
25011529 Balmer R, 260
30222116 Balogun-Ojuri BT, 336
555503 Balsdon A, 214
531811 Balsillie AF, 338
30024044 Balsom BJ, 225
30041362 Balupuri S, 335
560161 Bam DSR, 132
25210969 Bamber JS, 251
30071964 Bambrick OJC, 172
559222 Bambridge AP, 220
30171159 Bambury KA, 383
30223039 Bamford JC, 350
25011719 Bamford NW, 242
30053643 Bampfield LA, 372
562314 Banbury DP, 327
W0836550 Bance-Smith YH, 225
25028460 Bancroft A, 222
565107 Bancroft R, 352
552607 Bandy GW, 392
537102 Banerjee B, 335
30124526 Banerjee R, 352
30122252 Banfield AJ, 322
529100 Banfield GK, 243
30201409 Banfield GW, 310
560589 Banfield JHA, 333
30039545 Banfield PA, 260
508135 Banham MP, 349, 386
551122 Bankes WNW, 300
541570 Banks AM, 279
555842 Banks GT, 317
W1052659 Banks HE, 225
528429 Banks IC, 316
H8600252 Banks JJ, 274
530465 Banks NA, 220
544554 Banks PJ, 346
25220808 Banks SP, 234
550618 Banks TC, 298
539534 Bannister KL, 132
25185289 Bannister TN, 222
30087929 Banting GN, 216
530944 Banton SJ, 41, 110
515929 Banwell MJ, 352
30108907 Banyard IM, 372
539355 Barber A, 352
561388 Barber AI, 224
25232291 Barber CCJ, 222
533225 Barber FPA, 276
539164 Barber GW, 308
552302 Barber JC, 214
24779376 Barber K, 224
24906338 Barbieri DA, 251
514047 Barbone AW, 326
538705 Barclay DJ, 305
24710664 Barclay DS, 135
557163 Barclay JG, 240
557781 Barclay JG, 279
24658636 Barclay RM, 208
551530 Barclay TAC, 340
30168453 Barcroft HWL, 125
24737184 Bard MJ, 175
24900934 Bareham IJN, 270
30231151 Barfield V, 359
30134569 Barge PJ, 199
546395 Bargrove MJ, 340
545917 Barham EMH, 338
C26814 Barkat J, 372
C33490 Barkat JE, 372
24951591 Barke IR, 263
557373 Barker AGA, 352
553527 Barker AP, 333
24673841 Barker AP, 282
24853109 Barker AR, 216
526491 Barker CH, 196
24839034 Barker JEG, 234
30061364 Barker JP, 352
561193 Barker JRL, 318
30045289 Barker JW, 159
540370 Barker KA, 214
C25628 Barker KL, 372
30044726 Barker M, 359
504425 Barker M, 277
565306 Barker NS, 206
552098 Barker RJ, 311
30052403 Barker SA, 314
25172782 Barker SA, 282
30052284 Barker SD, 246
565207 Barker SJ, 231
24869772 Barker SL, 216
550406 Barker T, 244
551620 Barker TCA, 300
557679 Barker TJ, 314
30024103 Barker TR, 139
30077666 Barkes BR, 137
30040979 Barklem JR, 313
556204 Barkley AR, 341
549964 Barley ND, 159
564349 Barlow AR, 244
556609 Barlow DL, 231
W1031257 Barlow J, 234
30069267 Barlow JJ, 234
30199185 Barlow LE, 352
24791166 Barlow MR, 220
534267 Barlow P, 372
541377 Barlow PM, 352
562713 Barlow TP, 234
524867 Barlow W, 372
544276 Barltrop SW, 262
30079244 Barmby D, 352
502647 Barnard C, 352
551243 Barnard CJ, 206
30116695 Barnard CW, 212
533875 Barnard J, 352
25230360 Barnard JS, 282
540917 Barnard K, 352
513840 Barnard S, 110
24840493 Barnard SJ, 256
536171 Barnbrook RSJ, 319
549357 Barnes AD, 326
520230 Barnes AF, 289
548331 Barnes AR, 372
30141672 Barnes G, 142
30088949 Barnes GR, 253
30146723 Barnes JA, 352
30012297 Barnes JB, 118
488385 Barnes JR, 289
30056890 Barnes M, 182
30040091 Barnes MV, 133
25210971 Barnes NDW, 208
30068918 Barnes RJ, 234
24794977 Barnes SE, 224
536015 Barnes SM, 292
564222 Barnes TEL, 244
L8445029 Barnes WG, 242
24756516 Barnett A, 270

24877899 Bodycomb MJ, 234
539590 Bogan S, 372
30060479 Boggs JA, 172
30108619 Bogie EM, 200
563400 Bohl M, 352
30055865 Boiling TP, 211
551246 Boissard AMJ, 279
559725 Bolam K, 213
544285 Bolam W, 196
30138083 Boland KR, 139
563145 Bolderow S, 352
530272 Boles RF, 329
30128232 Bolger RP, 235
30137514 Bolitho TA, 142
25216391 Bolt HA, 310
541763 Bolter NJ, 329
30201421 Bolton BR, 307
30173063 Bolton CL, 271
30044434 Bolton EC, 331
W1060477 Bolton JA, 257
543375 Bolton JA, 321
558458 Bolton JA, 335
30245285 Bolton PA, 359
517250 Bolton RB, 196
554513 Bolwell SJ, 341
30187250 Bond A, 265
543136 Bond AC, 346
25233437 Bond AJ, 306
547099 Bond GS, 206
560647 Bond IA, 319
30196884 Bond MD, 352
543703 Bond PLC, 124
30038997 Bond RE, 117
562727 Bond RM, 347
25148887 Bond SM, 256
30192261 Bond WRR, 155
30184249 Bondar DN, 263
542488 Bone A, 372
24700158 Bone AJ, 208
W1061879 Bonella SM, 202
30120088 Bonham CT, 246
C28986 Bonner CEM, 383
565220 Bonner MPN, 138
W1058827 Bonner RL, 216
30035350 Bonner WE, 343
560168 Bonnett CA, 255
25015197 Bonser CD, 241
553766 Booker RJ, 244
505641 Booker RM, 329
554207 Booker TEF, 244
562721 Boomer MA, 235
565674 Boorman TD, 206
30043270 Boote CR, 185
30143150 Booth AE, 218
30075017 Booth AJ, 200
30042312 Booth C, 177
537022 Booth C, 372
30045703 Booth CT, 251
563544 Booth GT, 249
559094 Booth I, 231
30190407 Booth MR, 238
544286 Booth NA, 340
564889 Booth RGK, 279
564498 Booth SH, 200
30116605 Booth ST, 162
544879 Booton AW, 372
565890 Booton JA, 330
30039634 Booty CA, 211
564499 Booty PS, 255
555771 Boraston M, 372
539541 Boreham AC, 110, 240
559221 Boreham GD, 220
30072146 Boreham WJC, 169
30219382 Borland E, 212
30115447 Borland MA, 307
25231719 Borley JS, 172
25233399 Borley MC, 208
524265 Borneman CA, 110
30121059 Borthwick JA, 169
24683939 Borthwick PP, 154
552855 Borton D, 241
530858 Borton NRM, 108
30036718 Borup MH, 282
25133797 Borwick AM, 159
548857 Boryer CR, 184
25208539 Bosch NR, 285
24725518 Bosher D, 249
25197886 Bosher DJ, 172
25154680 Bosher GM, 222
545695 Bosher PR, 227
557248 Bosher S, 352
30137377 Bossom CLS, 212
30064453 Bossom TDA, 191
25185759 Bostock AH, 208
520037 Bostock SE, 169
562990 Boswell DJ, 230
510284 Boswell MJ, 248
25214469 Botha CM, 208
531920 Botsford MWL, 124
541468 Botterill EBJ, 197
30216440 Bottomley TE, 336
25228845 Boucher JP, 235
30075879 Boucher PG, 372
30212630 Boucher WJC, 203
560169 Boudet-Fenouillet SN, 174
25002006 Boughen D, 216
30180744 Boughey JR, 226
30028310 Bougourd TR, 208
C30296 Boulton AL, 372
25168313 Boulton DE, 282
24772686 Boulton SJ, 282
30025808 Boulton SRW, 383
30212804 Bourke D, 271
560824 Bourne AJ, 174
529718 Bourne AJP, 108
25021955 Bourne GE, 242
542260 Bourne SC, 243
25186208 Bourton MT, 251
562730 Boutle JJ, 200
553092 Bouttell CD, 329
559381 Bowbrick TJ, 372
P052800E Bowden CMA, 181
558668 Bowden HCR, 172
30136981 Bowden JR, 160
W1058777 Bowden RE, 299
522146 Bowden RJ, 308
563889 Bowden-Williams MK, 317
544881 Bowder JMH, 47, 110
30159188 Bowdidge CL, 314
30110991 Bowdidge LMP, 322
557040 Bowdler AP, 308
554852 Bowdler NR, 329
24713091 Bowen AF, 148
543256 Bowen CN, 231
25213496 Bowen JE, 181
545846 Bowen JL, 265
551247 Bowen LA, 259
516559 Bowen PF, 340
24797890 Bowen S, 169
24648689 Bowen W, 206
24824112 Bower DA, 249
520598 Bower MW, 171
562991 Bowerbank S, 231
30178084 Bowerman AM, 392
544853 Bowerman MR, 266
25016334 Bowerman V, 190
30139756 Bowers GK, 339
538925 Bowers IRO, 279
535509 Bowers-Tolley M, 372
C93550 Bowes A, 359
542403 Bowes AR, 340
546861 Bowes JB, 308
30105661 Bowes LA, 372
30115034 Bowes-Crick EJ, 346
559524 Bowes-Lyon AS, 306
562609 Bowie ADG, 132
24381573 Bowker BR, 299
563208 Bowkett L, 372
30043276 Bowkett WH, 162
545684 Bowler MC, 230
C36796 Bowler N, 372
25233734 Bowler NR, 154
549328 Bowles JA, 372
D8703387 Bowles JM, 222
30183203 Bowles-Farthing SR, 320
527609 Bowley DMG, 243
542656 Bowman APR, 224
559338 Bowman D, 224
562732 Bowman EML, 231
552973 Bowman HE, 265
562919 Bowman JR, 313
529460 Bowman KP, 196
25197514 Bowman SA, 282
30211540 Bowman-Shaw RAR, 144
529717 Bowron JH, 110
565675 Bowsley MD, 231
513713 Bowyer DG, 372
C37779 Bowyer M, 384
30173391 Bowyer-Bower TAS, 359
24831609 Box LD, 216
25232426 Boxall BL, 314
550625 Boxall GJ, 204
25165780 Boxall PJ, 190
548734 Boxer CAH, 224
556530 Boxley DJ, 347
25200177 Boyce AJ, 235
564101 Boyce E, 372
30152223 Boyce JA, 238
550626 Boyce TD, 206

C37912	Boyd DA, 373
30122140	Boyd DE, 235
25166044	Boyd G, 251
542657	Boyd GJ, 162
539198	Boyd J, 110
30197802	Boyd JC, 258
30088527	Boyd JKF, 336
30161156	Boyd LE, 344
563545	Boyd MA, 259
561492	Boyd MC, 244
516500	Boyd PSW, 276
527091	Boyd RJ, 110
30122469	Boyd SA, 327
25211969	Boyden CR, 235
562733	Boyden JV, 214
30068818	Boyd-Thomas WE, 118
30193890	Boyes AD, 218
24748220	Boyes DW, 256
556149	Boylan MD, 244
30133068	Boyle JP, 211
542658	Boyle RML, 300
543108	Boyle SC, 177
25022608	Boyle WSD, 235
30190509	Boyle ZK, 359
30222103	Boyles DW, 264
C25721	Boyne PJ, 373
30089882	Boyt HBH, 117
24688763	Boyter BA, 206
25013815	Brabin M, 242
30037178	Bracey DW, 211
30046900	Bracher JR, 311
558669	Bracken AJ, 225
30044868	Brackley J, 200
C35462	Bradburn RJ, 373
30156876	Bradbury HB, 383
528280	Bradbury IM, 373
552247	Bradbury JG, 249
30173437	Bradbury JRG, 228
30030017	Bradbury MP, 341
547400	Braddick-Hughes CE, 265
24745929	Braddock DM, 282
	Bradford AEH, 349
30076907	Bradford AH, 211
30046339	Bradford C, 127
559890	Bradley DR, 341
25230355	Bradley ID, 251
548408	Bradley IEC, 346
	Bradley MEJ, 333
24707728	Bradley NJ, 179
494274	Bradley PP, 338
30132562	Bradley SL, 200
546415	Bradley SN, 204
508707	Bradshaw AJ, 57, 106, 220
544702	Bradshaw CL, 329
516561	Bradshaw IJ, 213
563126	Bradshaw PM, 373
Q1037028	Bradshaw TE, 242
561830	Brady A, 373
30139378	Brady CR, 200
25166310	Brady GME, 292
C36147	Brady LP, 383
561348	Brady S, 335
30148132	Brady SI, 359
25022417	Bragg MP, 235
545295	Bragg TWH, 295
30121586	Bragger JEJ, 144
25165793	Brain DHG, 208
548146	Brain JJ, 255
533455	Braine SMA, 329
30088940	Braithwaite CR, 182
553186	Braithwaite JRO, 190
277408	Bramall of Bushfield E, 106
25005612	Bramall RM, 200
523153	Brambell DJ, 276
503379	Bramble I, 373
560744	Bramble NA, 279
526336	Bramble WJF, 107
30160581	Brame DWR, 202
30015570	Bramley RWS, 222
30078477	Bramson AE, 208
30155340	Bramwell MJ, 344
565040	Bramwell PJ, 249
560714	Bramwell-Walsh CL, 333
563149	Branch D, 373
561382	Branch ID, 373
30144634	Branchett T, 257
513439	Brand AG, 110
25202419	Brand DR, 208
30097281	Brandling-Harris LV, 225
554535	Brandt D, 352
30201419	Brandy DJ, 331
24757104	Brankin AP, 249
25202428	Brannigan AJ, 242
30011011	Brannigan CG, 256
30179354	Brannon NMR, 175
25182998	Bransby DM, 235
511767	Brant P, 373
30222359	Brash TR, 191
549472	Brass CJ, 242
549969	Brassington JD, 231
538314	Bratcher CA, 329
561726	Bray NJ, 341
555368	Bray PRG, 190
30009169	Braycotton DT, 322
548137	Brayshay DD, 248
564504	Brazier AP, 235
30082370	Brazier JM, 225
565596	Brazier MD, 315
24698148	Brazier PE, 206
566114	Brazier RA, 263
30116420	Brazier WPH, 127
C16962	Brazil A, 373
560825	Breach A, 172
539364	Breach IA, 340
515939	Brealey B, 196
30043624	Brearley GW, 135
30136894	Brecht EM, 182
563506	Bredin RJ, 164
D214691R	Breed MJ, 242
25215651	Breeds MJE, 226
564903	Breen NH, 174
547028	Breeze J, 244
525627	Breeze RD, 373
544707	Brehany J, 346
30210362	Breheney SD, 359
547867	Bremner A, 249
544290	Bremner AJ, 206
552707	Bremner SE, 246
24844501	Brennan KT, 200
553693	Brennan M, 352
561332	Brennan MJ, 326
555379	Brennan MO, 181
24710880	Brennan WC, 138
565478	Brennan-Raymond SM, 373
25170780	Brent DGW, 216
W1061978	Breslin HK, 200
30074133	Breslin RC, 211
30046907	Brett AJ, 208
30134582	Brett AJ, 304
W1056768	Brett F, 208
25186748	Brett J, 292
545505	Brett MW, 197
24908659	Brettle DR, 147
562992	Brewer GP, 231
537391	Brewer IC, 249
559527	Brewer PM, 231
30137604	Brewerton JW, 238
25194817	Brew-Graves SH, 307
W1034703	Brewington A, 263
30132073	Brewis D, 359
554844	Brewster A, 373
556327	Brewster KA, 255
563177	Brian S, 373
543916	Briant MI, 197
546354	Briard RJ, 244
557096	Brice A, 335
520113	Bricknell MCM, 52, 107
C37860	Bridge CS, 373
540373	Bridge EL, 196
24748969	Bridge MD, 182
538424	Bridge MR, 317
520463	Bridge STW, 110
30152134	Bridgeman CJ, 359
527409	Bridgeman M, 373
558271	Bridgeman S, 373
30023266	Bridger PD, 282
30148281	Bridges GC, 373
25126195	Bridges NM, 139
24656288	Bridges PN, 242
527779	Bridges SR, 248
30222467	Bridgman HJ, 310
25043834	Bridle DWA, 352
553149	Bridle NP, 153
562927	Bridle OW, 153
25196500	Bridle SE, 300
565962	Brien KB, 359
30113331	Brierley JWS, 282
554410	Brierley PA, 248
24937124	Briers AP, 200
551275	Briggs AD, 329
25183238	Briggs BWR, 222
561314	Briggs L, 343
30135406	Briggs PM, 307
557388	Briggs SI, 197
531923	Briggs TA, 138
24809321	Bright RP, 224
479180	Brightman C, 352
25147767	Brighton AJ, 352
560826	Brigstocke DMO, 197

30149545	Brimacombe JG, 200
490334	Brims RV, 305, 386
30140762	Brind LS, 216
25242771	Brindley CR, 172
30028735	Brindley CWH, 309
543259	Brining SNG, 221
557390	Brinkman C, 249
559172	Brinkworth R, 352
545230	Brinn JD, 144
30172833	Brinsley AM, 383
564293	Briody M, 255
561699	Briscoe GH, 279
513022	Brister P, 352
539403	Bristow JDM, 311
30115605	Bristow KR, 212
25038116	Bristow PK, 242
537900	Britchford J, 373
25232664	Britland O, 242
515941	Brittain JR, 276
530171	Brittan RB, 343
GR 7074	Britto EM, 193
25213646	Britton AJ, 208
542044	Britton AM, 138
542881	Britton G, 373
Q1036214	Britton HE, 242
562736	Britton MA, 249
30117963	Britton NT, 263
556621	Britton PNB, 197
545202	Britton SJ, 277
24700664	Brixton KG, 208
25210926	Broad CM, 251
30149547	Broad JDA, 304
30152612	Broad JS, 238
548554	Broadbent CMB, 153
558089	Broadbent DM, 162
526800	Broadbent RJR, 340
30088943	Broadfoot AS, 211
557598	Broadfoot C, 196
561246	Broadhurst GA, 249
557391	Broadhurst I, 279
30138013	Broadhurst SJ, 175
522343	Brock GS, 231
30175916	Brock WG, 359
24382427	Brocklebank ST, 306
556328	Brocklehurst GR, 153
C30308	Brocklehurst J, 373
557392	Brocklesby ME, 197
531420	Brockman EGS, 196
536169	Broddle CST, 327
539230	Broderstad ERC, 321
525584	Brodey AC, 132
30075686	Brodie SJ, 235
30171988	Broe IHM, 202
25010013	Brogan MW, 251
561504	Brogan PB, 265
C35510	Brogden JP, 373
545231	Bromage AH, 224
30100327	Bromfield JAB, 292
497781	Bromfield JG, 352
507413	Bromley Gardner CAJ, 298
30014230	Bromley GL, 212
30037667	Bromley SW, 263
552319	Brook OF, 231
30108728	Brook RB, 251
526936	Brooke JP, 299
30239062	Brooke S, 265
C30428	Brooke SM, 373
24911703	Brooker KJ, 216
24742660	Brooker PA, 352
30168816	Brookes AL, 383
546860	Brookes JL, 265
537392	Brookes MC, 213
25239809	Brookes MP, 309
24812284	Brookfield M, 208
555381	Brookfield RA, 153
564210	Brookhouse VA, 373
529463	Brooking JG, 128
30057019	Brookmier ZM, 218
552091	Brooks AJ, 335
24778523	Brooks AM, 169
25025840	Brooks C, 251
530377	Brooks D, 329
30050760	Brooks D, 373
8700230V	Brooks DT, 128
529888	Brooks G, 255
513668	Brooks J, 352
25098303	Brooks JG, 251
511819	Brooks KMT, 303
551250	Brooks NCR, 197
555831	Brooks PJ, 204
551251	Brooks S, 159
560121	Brooks S, 373
562422	Brooks S, 373
550711	Brooks SJ, 277
560278	Brooks TE, 259
30117318	Brooks VL, 373
528732	Brooks-Ward SH, 41, 289
24879593	Broom AN, 208
512154	Broom P, 373
30182150	Broom RA, 238
563216	Broome P, 373
556554	Broomfield DN, 164
25147884	Broomfield SM, 164
550953	Broomfield TN, 329
24725321	Broomhead NA, 282
539404	Broster CN, 249
C26844	Broster GT, 373
554825	Brotherston M, 338
551252	Brotherton AC, 197
561796	Brotherton BH, 126
536435	Brothwood PJ, 319
C35463	Brough D, 373
C23541	Brough L, 373
30073142	Brough LJ, 373
30233948	Broughton C, 359
544882	Broughton CL, 141
30143787	Broughton JR, 242
554028	Broughton SC, 279
30117842	Broumley Young C, 154
532360	Brown A, 373
545724	Brown A, 352
561986	Brown A, 373
562360	Brown A, 352
W1055640	Brown AA, 208
552956	Brown AC, 265
551253	Brown AD, 204
25213452	Brown AJ, 251
25196928	Brown AJ, 351
30179360	Brown AJ, 339
560439	Brown AL, 335
562312	Brown AMJ, 231
520602	Brown ANR, 128
541577	Brown AP, 214
511820	Brown AR, 276
30017698	Brown AS, 185
559161	Brown AW, 303
30110755	Brown AW, 383
30015372	Brown BJ, 216
C12543	Brown BR, 359
545319	Brown CC, 340
560172	Brown CDT, 206
565227	Brown CJ, 262
W0817718	Brown CL, 235
556706	Brown CMS, 244
549971	Brown CPT, 338
512578	Brown CTB, 177
556094	Brown D, 206
562037	Brown D, 373
557793	Brown DA, 231
25116692	Brown DB, 190
30060957	Brown DB, 373
30114602	Brown DD, 175
563163	Brown DG, 228
W0821109	Brown DJ, 255
561308	Brown DP, 303
566018	Brown E, 340
548384	Brown E, 373
25197712	Brown EC, 208
508148	Brown ED, 276
560173	Brown GA, 174
P044442B	Brown GL, 352
563078	Brown GWP, 242
548140	Brown IC, 204
24854013	Brown IR, 282
24867908	Brown J, 146
499972	Brown J, 373
551938	Brown J, 373
30106702	Brown JAG, 309
30118058	Brown JE, 144
30136978	Brown JE, 212
30204864	Brown JE, 265
544291	Brown JE, 224
30041471	Brown JF, 191
550561	Brown JHG, 241
549475	Brown JL, 231
538076	Brown JP, 305
558670	Brown JW, 231
30222190	Brown KNM, 307
550732	Brown KR, 306
551900	Brown KV, 244
30188682	Brown LD, 223
30222466	Brown LEB, 310
30014939	Brown LV, 235
30050575	Brown M, 257
509475	Brown M, 352
553972	Brown M, 373
24821978	Brown MA, 214
30014929	Brown MC, 235
24648581	Brown MJ, 206

545928 Brown MJ, 220
25016373 Brown ML, 263
30056551 Brown MW, 230
30218749 Brown NJ, 239
557396 Brown NJ, 174
541472 Brown NJ, 304
562737 Brown NY, 291
547284 Brown OCC, 164
24903930 Brown P, 256
30091261 Brown P, 352
25009338 Brown PJ, 256
24664176 Brown PK, 330
30142177 Brown PL, 352
530054 Brown PLO, 204
30126421 Brown PW, 359
561919 Brown R, 373
556015 Brown RA, 313
538417 Brown RC, 110
524062 Brown RH, 324
539462 Brown RM, 214
24781124 Brown S, 263
30244092 Brown SA, 359
542302 Brown SC, 204
30085366 Brown SW, 263
30202906 Brown SW, 383
558557 Brown TA, 392
25200154 Brown TJC, 190
25233454 Brown TM, 190
30216459 Brown V, 336
30135966 Brown VL, 268
30191860 Brown WD, 212
25213718 Brown WH, 180
542303 Browne AK, 262
N029820T Browne CHG, 340
W1057175 Browne EA, 273
534926 Browne JR, 164
25165866 Browne GD, 309
522625 Browne NP, 329
560828 Browne PNK, 231
547872 Browne RJ, 230
534926 Browne SJR, 42, 110
552305 Browning JC, 308
24856543 Browning JK, 222
537932 Browning MC, 291
536331 Browning SC, 204
25212472 Brownjohn PA, 154
30121475 Brownlee P, 373
30123258 Brownlie AS, 253
565980 Brownlie J, 373
30043066 Brownlow GS, 334
30191833 Brownlow JD, 223
560430 Brownsell MD, 346
557937 Brownsword NT, 347
526272 Browse SJ, 110
539633 Bruce ASW, 335
554670 Bruce IF, 231
522882 Bruce J, 373
30063990 Bruce JM, 373
536605 Bruce NC, 213
509493 Bruce of Crionaich AAB, 289, 313
525834 Bruce RB, 37, 107, 153, 254, 255
25003283 Bruce WM, 251
499134 Bruce-Smith KJ, 289
560829 Brudenell JK, 231
562356 Brumfitt A, 309
531986 Brumwell AA, 197
Brunei HM The Sultan, 25
Brunei HRH Prince Mohammed, 25
562172 Brunetti AN, 373
30114613 Brunsdon MJ, 165
30179108 Brunstrom T, 212
564017 Brunt REJ, 259
548866 Brunton PJ, 214
24648516 Brunton S, 208
25229140 Brunwin TLG, 221
30132145 Bruton DJ, 208
W0819321 Bruton LA, 338
559532 Bruxner TM, 279
30182973 Bryan AJ, 350
543641 Bryan BH, 214
544574 Bryan HJ, 329
30192493 Bryan PLG, 202
550634 Bryan REG, 190
536606 Bryan RW, 214
565140 Bryan SM, 330
30037926 Bryant AD, 162
527781 Bryant AJ, 248
510135 Bryant DG, 110
561745 Bryant G, 352
520603 Bryant JD, 39, 110
538926 Bryant JEF, 190
25213617 Bryant MA, 216
485283 Bryant MP, 373
538630 Bryant OJH, 174
30130449 Bryant P, 373
30104654 Bryant PA, 330
30148204 Bryning JD, 182
30103983 Bryson FV, 265
30038987 Bryson MS, 340
30023978 Bryson TM, 327
Buccleuch and Queensbury, Duke of, 153
562090 Buchan F, 224
30095645 Buchan J, 225
30076891 Buchan SA, 154
563894 Buchanan DS, 249
25213421 Buchanan GAC, 154
517406 Buchanan IA, 213
526274 Buchanan IAB, 313
563548 Buchanan JJ, 206
526984 Buchanan M, 352
L8703982 Buchanan RAM, 282
30138023 Buchanan TWS, 239
558812 Buchan-Smith KMA, 190
30186817 Buchhierl EA, 384
537815 Buck D, 373
30185968 Buck DC, 350
564221 Buck DOB, 244
563147 Buck JA, 272
544085 Buck PA, 214
539464 Buck VW, 110
C33981 Buckell G, 373
25185342 Buckenham BD, 256
24651039 Buckingham DM, 310
Q1018429 Buckingham TA, 272
564713 Buckland-Hoby M, 246
564980 Buckley AM, 244
546079 Buckley DJ, 373
30067251 Buckley DM, 304
30160528 Buckley HG, 271
24792595 Buckley JJ, 208
25197445 Buckley JW, 185
531300 Buckley JW, 320
30132938 Buckley MJ, 159
24651060 Buckley PA, 216
24722105 Buckley S, 279
25242772 Buckley SP, 208
30166127 Bucknall HCC, 144
505211 Bucknall J, 144
30076951 Bucknall JC, 144
30124698 Bucknall TA, 260
553342 Bucknell ALM, 255
30070016 Buckner M, 352
547874 Buczacki JNE, 132
30055864 Budd BJR, 202
549106 Budd J, 352
552152 Budd NJM, 197
30133464 Budden SM, 216
561772 Budding CS, 214
565452 Budding J, 214
30012041 Budge AHM, 142
25231720 Budge AW, 148
566021 Budge CLS, 266
566100 Budge RH, 282
520193 Budryk K, 373
559106 Buenaventura JC, 346
30135537 Buescher CVE, 216
24686794 Buff DE, 182
561804 Buffey E, 267
30116019 Buglass AJ, 212
24688968 Buglass MA, 206
30146027 Buitenhuis J, 182
30091505 Bull DN, 282
562068 Bull FA, 255
24809980 Bull J, 146
30042313 Bull JCJ, 282
30175687 Bull JG, 335
30082282 Bull JP, 223
564506 Bull KJ, 326
552930 Bull PH, 321
557039 Bull RG, 373
532069 Bull SH, 190
30154794 Bullard CJ, 266
531001 Bullard MJA, 110
559859 Bullard PJC, 319
30041100 Bulleid VA, 273
30184076 Bullen AFH, 154
30058890 Bullen OJD, 159
551669 Bullion R, 352
25037059 Bullivant GP, 242
25232433 Bullock AS, 139
30179351 Bullock BJM, 339
563519 Bullock FM, 208
549973 Bullock RG, 282
30195922 Bullous LA, 261
25143227 Bulmer CM, 197

501573 Coulon MD, 321
560846 Coulson AJ, 231
555923 Coulson AJW, 315
30154559 Coulson CJ, 306
25206623 Coulson G, 257
560391 Coulson IT, 197
553060 Coulson JM, 343
0091495X Coulson SG, 343
548736 Coulson TL, 244
30112832 Coulson WSJ, 180
C33842 Coulter CAE, 374
536900 Coulter D, 374
509226 Coulter DG, 20, 37, 62, 107
566037 Coulter HSO, 244
30055867 Coulthard KN, 225
25158579 Coulton DT, 313
549490 Courage OTB, 213
Q1055540 Court EF, 330
561047 Court MF, 246
518090 Court ML, 276
563562 Court MW, 334
30161057 Court TH, 191
518614 Courtier MS, 230
562026 Courtnage MJ, 306
30011201 Courtney JL, 182
30155505 Courtney RG, 175
30123288 Courtney SJB, 339
555408 Cousen JS, 190
W1054827 Cousins CA, 235
565041 Cousins D, 249
P056504S Cousins MJ, 256
30175798 Cousins SL, 353
30219521 Coussins T, 271
30045640 Coutts DG, 216
515198 Coutts GML, 277
25110147 Coutts JN, 175
554864 Covell ME, 268
25186186 Coventry CC, 297
30157112 Covington NJ, 238
30122208 Cowan BW, 235
554942 Cowan I, 347
517898 Cowan JM, 153, 276, 349
24743453 Cowan R, 249
30035687 Cowan SV, 384
30027061 Cowap T D, 322
565248 Coward BIH, 190
30028250 Coward CB, 251
W1056862 Coward CL, 251
534061 Coward DM, 338
516581 Coward EN, 230
497393 Coward G, 220
C30968 Coward MIE, 384
30174492 Cowell De Gruchy W, 135
545525 Cowell PMJ, 171
499772 Cowell-Smith PE, 303
30081966 Cowen FH, 235
30042635 Cowen JP, 125
547235 Cowen SD, 248
512588 Cowen SH, 276
546286 Cowey NJ, 138
25019282 Cowie EA, 256
30077848 Cowie JP, 133
559918 Cowie MJ, 214
30210519 Cowie PJ, 359
24853930 Cowlard MG, 359
24896697 Cowling GR, 225
565141 Cowling MN, 330
545649 Cowx CJ, 265
556342 Cox AA, 231
545417 Cox AD, 174
542190 Cox AT, 224
550407 Cox AT, 244
565697 Cox BN, 179
564785 Cox IA, 231
30080117 Cox J, 162
555766 Cox L, 374
30201432 Cox LA, 339
547113 Cox LB, 206
562112 Cox MA, 259
562113 Cox MJ, 214
552853 Cox MR, 255
W1058235 Cox NL, 374
30137947 Cox OG, 202
551264 Cox PM, 131
30162049 Cox SD, 359
550033 Cox SJ, 231
30121454 Cox ST, 162
514093 Cox T, 374
25242773 Coxon DP, 283
516582 Coxon NJ, 248
30073472 Coyle EM, 359
G900799M Coyne LJ, 353
30227471 Cozens SJL, 334
553830 Crabb RR, 346
30115453 Crabtree GH, 273
511139 Crackett J, 33, 213, 289, 308
538895 Cradden LPB, 181
30245329 Cradock A, 359
30222195 Cradock BM, 331
534567 Craft DA, 111
520823 Craggs DG, 353
24913723 Crago SP, 209
548832 Craig AG, 305
555409 Craig AT, 249
556923 Craig BE, 331
C37784 Craig BR, 374
25149215 Craig DGA, 283
555108 Craig GG, 126
30209316 Craig Harvey C, 147
523347 Craig JP, 314
C35093 Craig JR, 374
523348 Craig JRC, 230
30149464 Craig Membrey A, 353
30201670 Craig NGF, 339
538947 Craig RJ, 213
30080123 Craig WA, 178
554168 Craig-Braddock L, 262
517260 Craig-Harvey CA, 147
30096996 Cram FM, 359
30113065 Crammond IG, 374
30113730 Crammond K, 374
565699 Cramphorn A, 221
522082 Cran AAW, 392
549802 Crane AL, 272
560115 Crane J, 353
30221668 Crane LE, 359
30095701 Crane LT, 216
24554839 Crane RJ, 235
552212 Crane TP, 213
30047752 Cranfield EA, 222
563037 Cranley MR, 244
30162765 Cranmer EJ, 335
25205057 Cranston TA, 331
25213649 Craster HM, 313
25232280 Craven CA, 146
30169843 Craven JA, 339
550648 Craven JFA, 197
C28145 Craven ML, 384
30114335 Crawford CWA, 260
24852422 Crawford D, 200
556547 Crawford EJ, 343
524115 Crawford J, 111
25234107 Crawford JWP, 301
30179353 Crawford LG, 339
24846777 Crawford LM, 225
560090 Crawford MC, 304
545234 Crawford RH, 198
24750325 Crawford RM, 235
548101 Crawford THW, 338
540670 Crawley AJ, 159
565251 Crawley PR, 216
30148958 Crawshaw MGW, 256
543047 Cray MPA, 374
30127150 Cray SL, 223
563766 Creagh MP, 346
24888978 Creak JB, 256
30098381 Crean RPD, 263
525037 Creasey SJ, 111
30080261 Creed AWN, 191
556344 Creed BB, 249
30123289 Creedy JH, 307
30082979 Creek KJ, 374
30054398 Creek TG, 235
562407 Crees DP, 228
563561 Creese L, 216
30178515 Creighton CF, 223
556247 Cresswell A, 374
556650 Cresswell DD, 259
565075 Cresswell IM, 206
546222 Cresswell JP, 196
24692692 Cresswell NP, 174
551747 Crew N, 230
551127 Crew TA, 240
545207 Crewe-Read NO, 177
522356 Crichard G, 248
30130763 Crichton ATM, 172
W1056745 Crichton LEA, 359
536227 Crick PE, 277
547520 Crick PJ, 353
565700 Crilley GW, 249
549125 Crilly AF, 308
541645 Crilly MS, 309
30234896 Crilly SJ, 331
24801381 Crimes JM, 374
24822119 Crimmins DJ, 177
24568018 Cringle DP, 306
534305 Cripps AMC, 272

D

542231 Davies C, 174
30011036 Davies CA, 190
544305 Davies CD, 159
555119 Davies CEJ, 214
25220800 Davies CJP, 148
30081169 Davies CL, 353
518380 Davies CMM, 311
562411 Davies CP, 330
30129996 Davies CW, 374
25233864 Davies D, 198
557853 Davies D, 291
30077146 Davies DA, 162
24842829 Davies DE, 177
24884859 Davies DI, 283
30163585 Davies DL, 347
558922 Davies E, 374
560607 Davies ES, 346
565707 Davies G, 216
532288 Davies G, 353
549068 Davies GE, 265
30119500 Davies GG, 177
522588 Davies GH, 277
547896 Davies GM, 177
549983 Davies GN, 190
550198 Davies GR, 265
559954 Davies GR, 291
30139219 Davies HL, 384
557266 Davies I, 272
553039 Davies I, 353
518440 Davies J, 374
30102626 Davies JD, 268
555718 Davies JE, 347
30065746 Davies JGP, 177
540744 Davies JP, 184
550219 Davies JR, 131
519551 Davies K, 289, 386
562937 Davies KL, 275
24745475 Davies KS, 259
30226453 Davies L, 265
560852 Davies LA, 231
554828 Davies LA, 346
30186960 Davies LG, 247
24759268 Davies LK, 177
560139 Davies M, 374
548888 Davies M, 279
552258 Davies MA, 277
25099512 Davies MBP, 241
25004986 Davies MJ, 235
24714817 Davies ML, 242
25004328 Davies ML, 200
543147 Davies ML, 243
24848779 Davies MP, 138
30055871 Davies MR, 238
30173209 Davies MR, 218
542259 Davies MS, 243
563173 Davies MS, 280
30143676 Davies MW, 211
562121 Davies NAD, 241
510308 Davies NR, 276
566439 Davies NS, 315
30113713 Davies OJ, 202
559724 Davies P, 317
532697 Davies PA, 318
30015513 Davies PEB, 209
559498 Davies PG, 245
552972 Davies PM, 265
566589 Davies PM, 283
24753303 Davies R, 200
30209625 Davies R, 311
563322 Davies R, 353
W1059933 Davies RA, 235
24803525 Davies RB, 214
559557 Davies RD, 177
539411 Davies RG, 230
30015649 Davies RJ, 247
563513 Davies RL, 245
560793 Davies S, 346
C34266 Davies S, 374
30168528 Davies SA, 353
544182 Davies SA, 353
518882 Davies SHL, 303
549500 Davies SM, 190
30015588 Davies SP, 209
25228829 Davies SR, 172
549720 Davies SW, 205
30138273 Davies T, 359
551678 Davies T, 374
532763 Davies TJ, 268
543421 Davies TJ, 272
30201437 Davies TJ, 331
547897 Davies TMD, 198
30165307 Davies TP, 285
558061 Davies TRL, 265
25212919 Davies TWW, 169
30123476 Davies W, 336
25143920 Davies WB, 265
25196496 Davies WG, 235
541259 Davies WHL, 124
30186581 Davies WRV, 137
30022011 Davies-Cooke PB, 384
547635 Davies-Tuthill AJ, 346
W1057914 Davies-Walters K, 309
25233155 Davis AR, 200
558487 Davis AS, 268
25186103 Davis BJ, 179
30146126 Davis CR, 310
30217588 Davis CTJ, 191
558694 Davis CTN, 359
517821 Davis EA, 213
C37170 Davis Hall H, 374
30192926 Davis J, 212
559787 Davis J, 353
512973 Davis JA, 340
513136 Davis JE, 289, 346
25199930 Davis JET, 132
25214759 Davis JR, 175
24756999 Davis L, 214
30240411 Davis L, 359
565177 Davis LB, 321
W1055606 Davis LC, 231
24788120 Davis MAC, 200
529483 Davis MJ, 230
556500 Davis MJ, 249
551271 Davis MT, 174
547686 Davis MW, 214
25174514 Davis NFC, 235
565255 Davis NJ, 255
24719007 Davis PE, 231
559051 Davis PG, 305
560778 Davis PR, 243
C36618 Davis R, 374
514841 Davis RR, 204, 291
30047062 Davis RE, 374
555737 Davis SAJ, 270
24795309 Davis SG, 283
30202489 Davis-Merry TR, 219
C36410 Davison B, 374
30031120 Davison C, 316
25242774 Davison DI, 222
25232059 Davison HL, 139
25009387 Davison LJ, 270
548387 Davison M, 374
546438 Davison MA, 245
30193639 Davison P, 384
563246 Davison RH, 169
24681980 Davison S, 351
554245 Davison S, 374
25214045 Daw TE, 202
24669283 Dawber SE, 300
539743 Dawes A, 374
539412 Dawes APL, 111
30140669 Dawes CE, 216
536392 Dawes EJM, 111
566236 Dawes H, 374
30049647 Dawes RJ, 336
30077179 Dawes SE, 257
30075798 Dawes TE, 344
30254208 Dawkins HJ, 359
30040511 Dawkins HWA, 225
560059 Dawkins V, 374
30133352 Dawnay NM, 190
564901 Daws W, 353
559305 Dawson C, 241
30176363 Dawson C, 384
534723 Dawson C, 353
554233 Dawson EC, 374
30122446 Dawson G, 359
501426 Dawson G, 353
555688 Dawson GBJ, 206
24739066 Dawson GJ, 338
2653849L Dawson HJ, 225
563041 Dawson IS, 249
30231252 Dawson J, 359
30164718 Dawson JC, 127
30011672 Dawson JF, 235
562154 Dawson JF, 214
566373 Dawson K, 148
548348 Dawson K, 353
30197879 Dawson M, 263
24955183 Dawson PN, 318
24897464 Dawson PR, 256
566369 Dawson RM, 280
Q0823505 Dawson-Couper ZJ, 272
554869 Day AJ, 240
546699 Day B, 374
540026 Day CB, 198
535116 Day CG, 196
536973 Day J, 353
24884646 Day LA, 283

30163674 Etherington P, 375
561742 Etherington R, 375
30105908 Etherington RJ, 384
30195322 Etienne S, 203
561427 Eustace C, 354
545948 Evans AI, 248
25232325 Evans AO, 265
557429 Evans ARJ, 232
495162 Evans AT, 392
553038 Evans BJ, 245
531209 Evans CAH, 346
30068835 Evans CIR, 235
30147576 Evans CJ, 129
25232817 Evans CJ, 316
553239 Evans D, 375
558465 Evans D, 354
548781 Evans DJ, 330
564768 Evans DJ, 330
30036684 Evans DJ, 384
30109396 Evans DKH, 144
553915 Evans DL, 320
24722827 Evans DL, 375
24905678 Evans DO, 191
517823 Evans DR, 354
563923 Evans DT, 343
564103 Evans EJ, 336
30071493 Evans Fry JCM, 235
542071 Evans GA, 289
545949 Evans GJ, 224
566604 Evans GJ, 182
562920 Evans HD, 228
562139 Evans HGP, 309
525104 Evans HM, 303
521620 Evans HS, 162
541451 Evans IA, 111, 227
562691 Evans IR, 245
554659 Evans JA, 321
24819859 Evans JE, 209
540778 Evans JL, 346
525284 Evans JN, 333
25231908 Evans JNG, 182
556719 Evans K, 262
Q1049176 Evans K, 273
30157393 Evans L, 375
559898 Evans LG, 198
25023525 Evans MA, 375
30040085 Evans MB, 160
544319 Evans MH, 111
24590386 Evans MR, 320
553266 Evans N, 232
566614 Evans N, 354
W1056284 Evans NE, 262
25147945 Evans NPW, 235
545662 Evans P, 255
559571 Evans PC, 132
565713 Evans PD, 283
24817803 Evans PJ, 225
30211327 Evans PJS, 203
24891091 Evans PM, 375
558574 Evans RA, 250
30137173 Evans RAL, 191
25196519 Evans RCE, 185
25230457 Evans RCT, 283
544320 Evans RD, 303
497122 Evans RE, 375
30015383 Evans RE, 285
25025208 Evans RJ, 235
563211 Evans S, 375
30166385 Evans SC, 211
564777 Evans SL, 245
546979 Evans SP, 289
30172370 Evans T, 246
540631 Evans T, 343
488893 Evans T, 354
30146028 Evans TAG, 148
527119 Evans TG, 322
30115231 Evans TJB, 223
511527 Evans TP, 49, 59, 106, 189, 254, 255, 275
563080 Evans TR, 232
30193783 Evans TWJ, 148
W1056928 Evans VK, 263
503015 Evanson R, 354
545293 Evanson-Goddard LF, 330
537773 Evanson-Goddard MA, 230
522654 Evason PC, 324
541197 Eve CY, 340
520636 Eve RR, 303
30123225 Eveleigh AJ, 219
30178059 Eveleigh JR, 265
515968 Everard JR, 30, 41, 106, 120, 173, 266
30163974 Everard JWS, 137
30165080 Everard RA, 239
533690 Everest AJ, 243
30041085 Everett JMF, 222
24780125 Everett MA, 206
542318 Everett MD, 280
30015368 Everett SW, 180
25063929 Everiss DJ, 334
550251 Everitt K, 354
558058 Eversfield P, 354
563199 Eversfield SJ, 241
30120348 Evershed RM, 182
25197046 Everson BF, 162
547498 Every AJ, 303
551759 Eves MP, 280
24773153 Eves PP, 256
550665 Evetts RS, 118
25210918 Evitts GO, 209
551278 Evoy CG, 283
551427 Ewart M, 375
534978 Ewart-Brookes G, 111
557016 Ewbank MR, 327
24862167 Ewen MA, 182
527885 Ewens AJ, 276
30055873 Ewens JA, 251
30041339 Ewing AD, 354
30141691 Ewing CD, 139
528409 Ewing MJF, 153
30196225 Exelby EJ, 243
25213932 Exelby TL, 209
30040534 Exley EM, 257
558133 Exton T, 172
24788396 Eynon MW, 338
548552 Eyre CA, 206
532077 Eyre JP, 277
30201450 Eyre PDE, 339
W1054860 Eyre RL, 265
30202826 Eyre SJ, 384
553268 Eyre-Brook MG, 280
550666 Eytle MG, 305
531389 Eyton-Jones JA, 341
532102 Eze EC, 230
25227130 Eze KLA, 198

F

530291 Fabian M, 375
519605 Fabricius PJ, 240
533118 Facer JM, 111
30070147 Facey L, 216
566035 Fadden SJ, 245
30076117 Fadipe CO, 319
561541 Faerestrand NH, 245
24805308 Fagin PA, 147
30131525 Faiers R, 354
551727 Fair SM, 335
30214089 Fairbairn SR, 316
30241092 Fairbrother MJ, 360
30048893 Fairclough AP, 216
30127504 Fairclough SC, 354
30138067 Faire JRG, 118
525364 Fairfax TP, 300
25156388 Fairhall GS, 162
W1059351 Fairlie ML, 306
30245015 Fairnington EJ, 360
557916 Fairnington SJ, 206
525864 Fairrie AH, 311
559290 Fairs AJ, 255
549510 Fairweather NL, 224
30143257 Fairwood HW, 354
530959 Faithfull BJT, 172
548498 Faithfull-Davies EJ, 248
30227457 Faja ZR, 360
548174 Fake IC, 138
523499 Falcon AH, 329
25040302 Falconer A, 154
30153634 Falconer DC, 154
557432 Falconer DM, 162
W1059697 Falconer E, 338
529304 Falconer GP, 111
30137473 Falconer JL, 291
25110103 Falconer RM, 306
30114666 Falconer-Hall TJK, 246
W1052812 Faldo SC, 295
551761 Falinski NM, 232
544322 Falinski SJ, 330
25212884 Falkous KJ, 338
548904 Fallon JV, 255
30125707 Fallon OG, 209
559119 Fallon RM, 309
25009857 Fallon SG, 283
556672 Fallowfield DJ, 250
537972 Fallows AM, 111
547760 Falshaw R, 295
558353 Falzon A, 354
565643 Fanneran H, 354
536319 Fanning PN, 327

G

501598 Gallier NP, 354
C11270 Gallifant K, 375
552807 Gallimore J, 346
25004792 Gallimore PT, 209
562149 Galloway A, 232
24815174 Galloway D, 267
531984 Galloway JW, 230
C93768 Galloway R, 384
548797 Galluccio P, 346
556868 Galpin TWG, 241
24710926 Galvin AJ, 117
25234696 Galvin NPW, 246
554680 Galvin SD, 230
30222552 Galvin TPC, 360
30126175 Gambarini PN, 144
30046297 Gamble DA, 375
30112826 Gamble EME, 337
553036 Gamble IR, 327
30043223 Gamble JC, 180
565719 Gamble L, 241
522375 Gamble MJ, 43, 108
Q1018667 Game A, 272
25000403 Game AJ, 242
W0807866 Game AJ, 327
554191 Gammon JG, 162
525787 Gammon MCB, 196
30157542 Gammond CD, 218
555445 Gamp NJ, 198
549828 Gandiya LF, 228
546918 Gane TI, 330
C35812 Gann TJH, 375
30238914 Gannarelli CMS, 360
30190265 Gannaway BS, 263
24359324 Gannon AA, 375
30064610 Gannon AJ, 235
Gannon M, 301
25212493 Gant DJ, 182
30113763 Gant JR, 243
563586 Gant TP, 222
556359 Ganuszko PJ, 198
25240392 Garbett RS, 347
563685 Garbuja M, 331
21168458 Garbuja Pun N, 187
535986 Garbutt RM, 248
24590862 Garcia M, 206
C26577 Garden A, 375
514315 Garden D, 354
534982 Gardiner AJ, 230
24824597 Gardiner J, 127
30061485 Gardiner M, 209
562338 Gardiner RC, 280
30194236 Gardner A, 384
24773219 Gardner AC, 118
30139061 Gardner CF, 155
24823193 Gardner CH, 169
30115832 Gardner CJ, 307
520518 Gardner FH, 33, 108
519796 Gardner FR, 340
30201446 Gardner GJ, 331
522808 Gardner JA, 169
25186073 Gardner JBT, 263
561252 Gardner MS, 250
30215239 Gardner RJ, 133
562782 Gardner RJ, 232
566247 Gardner S, 375
C35348 Gardner SS, 375
30217127 Gardner TP, 185
30111435 Gardner VL, 375
565065 Gardner YA, 334
30064444 Gardner-Clarke HH, 185
543546 Gareh M, 354
W1057348 Garfield LJ, 211
547445 Garfirth S, 354
561703 Gargan FJ, 181
30010953 Garland NS, 125
24803617 Garland RW, 209
553782 Garland SE, 346
30206005 Garley SR, 354
521772 Garman G, 375
30068930 Garmory JP, 200
552534 Garmory SJ, 153
563102 Garner A, 340
542688 Garner AS, 171
532027 Garner DC, 205
30141467 Garner GH, 239
517188 Garner GK, 340
24688340 Garner J, 209
536047 Garner JP, 278
30222469 Garner MP, 331
30068919 Garner MR, 164
565559 Garner P, 309
565720 Garner RI, 222
30040367 Garner-Richardson JR, 360
30038962 Garnett BJ, 169
30116226 Garnett JGS, 212
565721 Garnett P, 255
24775289 Garrard CS, 206
30146788 Garrard MJD, 307
30163433 Garrard MR, 339
30133122 Garratt AJR, 283
30062938 Garratt SE, 375
561282 Garratty S, 347
540678 Garrett AHT, 215
553281 Garrett AR, 174
30054045 Garrett AR, 375
511016 Garrett SC, 289
25012095 Garrick W, 154
30238772 Garrison WA, 360
548910 Garrow AA, 205
30014959 Garside EA, 360
30083736 Garthwaite MD, 354
563589 Garthwaite RM, 206
534983 Gartland DM, 259
562649 Garton JAL, 142
557436 Gartside AP, 232
30137500 Gartside EB, 223
30188124 Gartside J, 354
526695 Garvey J, 354
24722187 Garvie AC, 354
24896031 Garwood M, 241
24888225 Gascoigne J, 200
522842 Gascoigne RJ, 230
547128 Gascoyne AJ, 232
24713624 Gascoyne DC, 200
529502 Gaselee JDA, 117
518792 Gash AS, 138
565476 Gask G, 141
30180039 Gask J, 307
25213157 Gaskell SPA, 209
517410 Gaskin PH, 321
556479 Gaskin SH, 250
30201447 Gaskins-Rogers RW, 307
30104818 Gaspar ASL, 323
543290 Gatenby GD, 174
25213029 Gates DCS, 292
30164669 Gates HS, 238
30137993 Gates JO, 235
544026 Gates SB, 354
513585 Gatter K, 375
563734 Gauci APM, 206
537158 Gaudoin JP, 329
551001 Gaughan MS, 375
563434 Gaunt M, 141
520645 Gaunt MJ, 37, 107, 248
30088931 Gauntlett MS, 217
24735785 Gausden RA, 297
30250373 Gausinet S, 360
560878 Gavin CC, 177
W1056813 Gavin DM, 217
552558 Gaw GP, 309
544326 Gawthorpe AS, 162
30054462 Gay EM, 212
519498 Gay NS, 320
25210960 Gayfer RA, 172
549521 Gayner JRH, 190
562784 Gaywood J, 255
550681 Geary AJC, 232
W1052639 Geary KA, 260
30115446 Geaves H, 137
561741 Geddes AC, 300
30191069 Geddes AJ, 384
554887 Geddes DJ, 347
30064439 Geddes JF, 191
508649 Geddes JF, 308
562326 Geddes L, 333
24688201 Geddes RR, 331
30138784 Geddes TC, 247
525865 Gedney FG, 37, 108
553702 Gee M, 280
543291 Gee NM, 196
30165381 Geering SJG, 202
551854 Geernaert-Davies M, 375
W0807364 Geeson SY, 242
562150 Geldenhuys C, 260
548641 Gell DA, 326
539112 Gell H, 375
30112041 Gellender DE, 223
30046395 Genari CR, 235
30007201 Genillard AE, 185
547916 Genko MR, 230
549522 Gent C, 196
30237042 Gent LJ, 360
30028239 Gent ZC, 209
537709 Gentle D, 375
546269 Gentle EF, 297
24743505 Gentles PL, 198
25165756 Gentry RN, 250
563418 George A, 354
Q1062294 George AL, 348

H

521638 Hart AM, 179
W1054711 Hart C, 262
24751190 Hart CA, 354
549273 Hart CJP, 256
30152683 Hart DPO, 257
30049508 Hart J, 236
C29212 Hart J, 376
30150346 Hart JE, 354
30254318 Hart LE, 360
489041 Hart M, 354
P047598N Hart MA, 241
25212576 Hart MV, 315
30028301 Hart NSG, 200
30030166 Hart PM, 376
W1056858 Hart RL, 266
24844363 Hart RP, 266
551293 Hart RP, 197
546892 Hart SE, 354
552162 Hart SJ, 206
550252 Harte JA, 376
30179315 Hartill EA, 360
528255 Hartington K, 112
30168554 Hartland CJ, 223
25214104 Hartle TA, 236
534996 Hartley CP, 215
30174631 Hartley D, 354
558726 Hartley JA, 246
534584 Hartley JC, 278
30061410 Hartley JEC, 191
535117 Hartley JI, 190
30031006 Hartley JO, 257
565741 Hartley PSA, 139
565280 Hartley RJ, 236
30212970 Hartley-Smith MR, 384
546820 Hartman LJ, 250
546953 Hartshorne RG, 300
30095838 Hartwell A, 320
24854115 Harvard JS, 200
565492 Harverson E, 267
24711015 Harvey AE, 198
30197919 Harvey AL, 271
24722613 Harvey ANT, 280
25232835 Harvey CD, 306
550672 Harvey CE, 262
528070 Harvey CJ, 289
30146813 Harvey CJL, 212
30046868 Harvey DL, 272
559484 Harvey DM, 153
30102330 Harvey GCD, 266
30180446 Harvey GT, 238
556855 Harvey H, 354
557235 Harvey J, 260
C30878 Harvey JC, 384
30118260 Harvey JN, 202
C35971 Harvey KL, 376
564742 Harvey M, 241
25154720 Harvey MJ, 241
30066282 Harvey R, 211
562164 Harvey S, 198
24617985 Harvey TG, 200
30175880 Harwood PA, 354
546523 Haseldine AJ, 224
306130E Haskell SL, 343
563953 Haskell TDE, 198
548932 Haslam DR, 250
527902 Haslam PW, 303
30047186 Haslam-Greene HL, 225
30160406 Haslett AG, 337
564952 Haslett MJ, 256
30015438 Hassain JSH, 306
30128364 Hassall ML, 209
C31058 Hassan AN, 376
30227513 Hassan BJ, 327
25185595 Hassard EA, 283
533990 Hassell AC, 112
563187 Hastie CE, 280
30151271 Hastie EW, 344
565161 Hastie K, 354
547411 Hastie RG, 342
560387 Hastings AE, 206
30207734 Hastings B, 247
30185182 Hastings DG, 350
30200814 Hastings DW, 384
544913 Hastings ID, 190
30180798 Hastings JSG, 331
25131918 Hastings MLW, 209
502968 Hastings R, 354
553303 Haswell MD, 354
30058708 Hatch HA, 376
25204531 Hatch JS, 260
W148012K Hatch R, 242
30188076 Hatch RM, 384
30196349 Hatchell CE, 354
537431 Hatcher GP, 205
30116510 Hatchley KJ, 135
25058256 Hathaway SN, 384
30015472 Hathaway-White JJ, 142
30180071 Hathway ND, 310
556139 Hattersley GJ, 268
24779536 Hatton CS, 132
30123877 Hatton MC, 257
528333 Hatton P, 303
564433 Hatton PJ, 309
C35246 Haughey M, 376
549740 Haughie JJ, 153
529210 Haughie S, 376
24830292 Haughton GJ, 142
30118900 Haughton SWT, 217
24826098 Haugvik C, 252
25212138 Haussauer CWP, 217
565281 Havelock AJ, 153
30244091 Haviland AMJ, 327
563864 Haw SN, 275
545966 Hawes AD, 308
560009 Hawes BT, 164
553596 Hawes RS, 335
30094838 Hawes SJ, 335
30068920 Hawke GAK, 217
30150789 Hawke LW, 154
25015694 Hawke SP, 200
565282 Hawken SJ, 209
534585 Hawker M, 224
30036717 Hawkes JM, 209
538975 Hawkes LJ, 278
547317 Hawkes MH, 354
30172181 Hawkes-Rossi WD, 202
30144522 Hawkesworth JPT, 200
564728 Hawkings DW, 348
559140 Hawkins AE, 206
557864 Hawkins AEC, 224
550235 Hawkins BJ, 206
30105430 Hawkins DRO, 360
30107826 Hawkins GKF, 360
558826 Hawkins HM, 206
542949 Hawkins J, 376
550692 Hawkins JKR, 215
548197 Hawkins JW, 206
30222201 Hawkins KM, 331
501494 Hawkins MGS, 354
566216 Hawkins MSF, 354
30217522 Hawkins R, 219
548198 Hawkins RB, 205
550142 Hawkins SB, 272
546524 Hawkins TMD, 331
553206 Hawkins TW, 280
564252 Hawkins W, 376
538823 Hawkins WD, 256
24809939 Hawkyard JR, 267
30086273 Hawley A, 354
540952 Hawley S, 376
552390 Hawling DA, 241
30161660 Haworth AJ, 257
C041962X Haworth KJ, 244
532088 Haws DJ, 198
30011680 Hawthorn DI, 242
Hawtin ML, 124
549878 Hay A, 376
S8703657 Hay CE, 222
546452 Hay DP, 376
518119 Hay DW, 112
547139 Hay JC, 135
C35138 Hay L, 384
545967 Hay LAW, 305
564434 Hay PA, 215
559590 Hay RJ, 198
558153 Hay SI, 198
559591 Hayakawa DP, 262
557461 Hayakawa MJ, 206
553752 Hayday T, 354
30184690 Haydon MW, 351
30184253 Hayes CA, 212
562226 Hayes CA, 250
543631 Hayes D, 376
8701707P Hayes DL, 198
24678135 Hayes GJ, 241
563955 Hayes GPV, 241
24775546 Hayes KJ, 283
556151 Hayes KM, 280
24792973 Hayes M, 236
25019673 Hayes MJ, 200
534689 Hayes PK, 317
561470 Hayes S, 376
25186569 Hayes SJR, 225
558154 Hayes SR, 174
30203207 Hayes ST, 360
564886 Hayhurst DJ, 241
537658 Hayhurst PM, 220
548934 Hayhurst RA, 305
534997 Hayhurst RM, 112

30081649 Hayler BAM, 265
560726 Hayler BV, 311
540263 Hayman JJ, 244
544336 Hayman ME, 262
30206137 Haynes D, 360
30196891 Haynes F, 354
C30648 Hayter KP, 354
541938 Hayter T, 376
30074387 Hayton CCA, 263
560231 Hayton MC, 153
528107 Hayward G, 354
556796 Hayward HM, 221
30171501 Hayward J, 360
550694 Hayward JD, 280
563144 Hayward JE, 354
24683729 Hayward JG, 384
547140 Hayward JP, 250
516377 Hayward JR, 145
Q1052299 Hayward KM, 348
24862659 Hayward L, 222
565283 Hayward LC, 232
566259 Hayward MA, 169
550695 Hayward ME, 126
30201893 Hayward RWE, 253
553242 Hayward SJ, 346
564102 Hayward-Smith SP, 321
548936 Haywood GA, 181
30065216 Haywood SP, 354
24823034 Hayzen-Smith SM, 200
25023579 Hazel CM, 252
30229481 Hazel JFT, 376
523124 Hazel JME, 276
552724 Hazell T, 278
556977 Hazlerigg ARA, 245
25183922 Hazlett MJ, 180
5208843W Hazzard I, 272
30179039 Head AJ, 238
555465 Head CA, 162
30067016 Head CD, 338
30091635 Head JM, 200
538701 Head RA, 112
30045220 Head SJ, 360
30174972 Heads DJ, 160
558512 Heagerty RDH, 241
564794 Heakin EC, 232
528889 Heal ERB, 39, 112
548088 Heal GD, 334
30125815 Heal JWA, 191
541555 Heald KJ, 376
520661 Healey RJ, 214
558155 Healing HMP, 280
25198859 Healy NTH, 200
25197097 Heaney SJ, 283
556004 Heap B, 278
565931 Heap L, 354
25070766 Heard S, 354
541820 Heardman J, 248
551989 Hearn CC, 221
518901 Hearn G, 276
30252447 Hearn JL, 360
25233526 Hearn TR, 209
566090 Hearne TG, 164
30078598 Hearnshaw W, 223
C35024 Hearst L, 384
554836 Hearth J, 376
564559 Hearth MJC, 236
545824 Hearty KP, 338
30201452 Heath AJN, 310
530091 Heath AL, 198
521641 Heath AN, 230
522606 Heath GC, 112
30119406 Heath JG, 129
560798 Heath N, 319
30186168 Heath NDC, 342
553780 Heath RS, 346
525169 Heath SG, 112
561727 Heath T, 348
30195025 Heathcote DF, 226
564933 Heathcote JA, 306
554294 Heather ASR, 232
30089134 Heather MA, 211
540043 Heatlie RJ, 112
25199041 Heaton AJ, 209
559930 Heaton JC, 215
30042452 Heaton RL, 242
536730 Heaton-Smith JB, 230
553305 Heaven MD, 280
30050470 Heavey DR, 236
30169805 Heavyside MJ, 263
30115288 Heawood C, 344
30058597 Heayberd RE, 343
30055889 Heayes JM, 257
556700 Hebard KM, 206
30239016 Hebberd B, 360
24826924 Hebblethwaite DM, 209
30185295 Hebblewhite LMD, 296
513049 Hebburn-Heath SP, 342
30175894 Hebdon AL, 354
548200 Heckles A, 198
30030395 Hector JK, 246
558639 Hedderly Brind BJ, 342
552392 Hedderwick RSJ, 153
30141240 Heddington DR, 346
554295 Hedgeley NF, 206
548938 Hedges GA, 303
24905955 Hedges NJ, 191
564560 Hedley MCC, 222
559594 Hedley MJI, 162
30123241 Hedouin D, 219
554528 Heeley AM, 342
543855 Heelis RAP, 297
525736 Heffer MJ, 305
C93951 Heffernan AKP, 376
30048876 Heffernan JP, 340
30038567 Hegarty JJ, 354
24867529 Hegarty JW, 236
24882123 Hegarty NP, 236
566594 Heggie J, 376
W1062744 Heil CL, 376
564562 Hein ACS, 291
30037226 Heinrich BT, 236
30171194 Heisel PK, 384
563300 Hellard SM, 308
30218618 Heller L, 170
555172 Hellier AMS, 184
30111545 Hellmers BL, 200
548939 Helme PM, 305
30060475 Helmrich CA, 200
555174 Helsby MC, 190
24879700 Hembery DD, 206
528890 Hemesley EJ, 169
534587 Hemmens RE, 305
542197 Hemming DA, 280
548121 Hemming TS, 266
25221728 Hemmings KB, 260
24781857 Hemmingway G, 257
542633 Hemns SM, 206
30041216 Hemphill JA, 300
564926 Hempsall C, 354
555175 Hempsey S, 241
545409 Hemstock NT, 303
W1058212 Hemsworth NA, 236
30123242 Henderson CA, 219
30206559 Henderson CS, 354
557146 Henderson DD, 241
557465 Henderson GA, 153
25233293 Henderson HP, 246
545425 Henderson JB, 311
515771 Henderson JMR, 248, 276, 338
506187 Henderson L, 376
548142 Henderson LJ, 340
563232 Henderson M, 228
563001 Henderson M, 232
25211099 Henderson MR, 236
554296 Henderson NDR, 198
30166911 Henderson R, 384
30227120 Henderson-Sowerby MA, 360
563507 Hendrickson GC, 270
562166 Hendrie G, 256
25222891 Hendriksen TR, 142
560549 Hendry A, 376
559087 Hendry DJ, 181
555176 Hendry MD, 206
30028742 Hendry-Adams IA, 311
30177858 Hendy AW, 354
25237537 Heneghan SA, 263
30119915 Henley JW, 222
560233 Hennessy DKR, 221
549670 Hennessy EP, 278
559595 Hennigan GG, 232
30146030 Henning CD, 257
530669 Henning JDR, 112
30202838 Hennings-Haahr GH, 129
564660 Hennis SC, 309
30163753 Henriques PJQ, 191
24648228 Henry A, 331
30195487 Henry J, 384
W1055114 Henry JL, 257
563045 Henry JW, 250
566325 Henry WC, 198
30114995 Henshall A, 344
30122092 Henshaw V, 360
25110256 Henshelwood RM, 306
529516 Henson CJ, 230
30210509 Henson CNG, 133
562795 Henson GA, 206
25033856 Henson SM, 209
30139689 Henson TAM, 260

560122 Hull D, 377
30110929 Hull DA, 327
551303 Hull SC, 232
558478 Hulley EJ, 272
30191447 Hullis S, 355
30177516 Hullyer P, 327
530484 Hulme A, 346
555191 Hulme CA, 207
30078940 Hulme HR, 236
W1054396 Humberstone KE, 340
528187 Hume B, 377
553979 Hume DC, 245
559928 Hume GD, 215
543849 Hume KA, 311
24851727 Humes AM, 270
30122255 Humphery TH, 252
517712 Humphrey DA, 303
24794859 Humphrey GW, 200
30050576 Humphrey JP, 243
546721 Humphrey KJ, 377
526107 Humphrey PRM, 324
522387 Humphrey SL, 37, 108
30082877 Humphreys AR, 133
30137201 Humphreys B, 165
555141 Humphreys B, 326
566405 Humphreys DJ, 280
30180693 Humphreys EL, 257
547936 Humphreys JA, 180
30137927 Humphreys JE, 236
560706 Humphries KS, 308
565012 Humphries R, 190
548954 Humphris SL, 171
562653 Humphryes GJ, 228
30014017 Hunjan JS, 253
Q8446699 Hunsdale JP, 309
24903757 Hunt AS, 209
564398 Hunt AT, 338
30194718 Hunt AW, 355
555939 Hunt C, 197
30055896 Hunt DJ, 253
550549 Hunt DM, 245
30065271 Hunt EJF, 245
25231929 Hunt IJ, 209
526797 Hunt JCA, 139
549359 Hunt JM, 318
25193151 Hunt LJ, 202
562657 Hunt LJ, 355
30045013 Hunt LRD, 223
30144805 Hunt M, 341
24780024 Hunt NDA, 198
546715 Hunt PAF, 244
24830639 Hunt RJ, 191
550948 Hunt SC, 308
556390 Hunt SDW, 207
557325 Hunt SJ, 160
558461 Hunt WTH, 181
24735750 Hunter B, 309
512760 Hunter C, 377
527136 Hunter CW, 205
547755 Hunter D, 377
549545 Hunter DK, 207
562176 Hunter ER, 159
25185633 Hunter FG, 160
557703 Hunter GK, 272
30202736 Hunter HFL, 350
520668 Hunter IN, 214
552919 Hunter IPL, 278
537770 Hunter JF, 262
537990 Hunter JH, 316
30044259 Hunter JM, 334
557147 Hunter M, 241
541093 Hunter MK, 318
565534 Hunter NL, 309
532232 Hunter NW, 112
563736 Hunter R, 360
30037704 Hunter RI, 284
24687908 Hunter SM, 334
528444 Hunter Td EM, 392
30198604 Hunter TWC, 185
24743151 Hunter WG, 153
566118 Hunter-Choat SE, 225
30076935 Hunt-Grubbe RB, 118
30192901 Huntington JA, 264
30071461 Huntley DM, 343
30193645 Hurd AJ, 327
503842 Hurley IM, 329
30115520 Hurley LA, 223
544128 Hurley PA, 333
30130306 Hurley SB, 331
525042 Hurley SJ, 276
511032 Hurman MJ, 314
548214 Hurndall JML, 262
24931746 Hurrell MS, 324
547937 Hurry R, 337
25213886 Hursey GPJ, 191
30124711 Hurst D, 257
564698 Hurst E, 355
549067 Hurst J, 320
30134999 Hurst JE, 355
30114723 Hurst LR, 218
543676 Hurst P, 355
25008851 Hurst PA, 209
30118579 Hurst S, 239
30191156 Hurst SA, 337
30123244 Hurst SJ, 339
30080095 Hurst VM, 257
D208848N Hursthouse PM, 181
25197721 Hurt DW, 252
509011 Hurwood RS, 377
551304 Husband AJ, 190
30184600 Husband NHJ, 238
539529 Husband WCR, 355
25154738 Hussey DP, 232
24774315 Hutcheon A, 232
30161685 Hutcheson LG, 162
G901165D Hutchings A, 355
25212889 Hutchings AJ, 217
T8287451 Hutchings PE, 384
535008 Hutchings ST, 47, 112
30187325 Hutchinson AL, 273
541828 Hutchinson C, 377
30237196 Hutchinson J, 335
24721111 Hutchinson JM, 261
558070 Hutchinson KG, 318
532167 Hutchinson MC, 300
565295 Hutchinson RAM, 198
524317 Hutchinson SG, 19, 112, 213
24792648 Hutchinson SJ, 284
563961 Hutchinson SL, 256
527968 Hutchinson SR, 305
524755 Hutchinson WNE, 220
552464 Hutchison G, 180
529524 Hutchison TMO, 145
528896 Huthwaite CS, 197
549179 Hutley EJ, 245
30180043 Hutt ST, 339
30074279 Hutt TWJ, 209
544524 Hutton AGS, 153
30028270 Hutton AK, 236
542717 Hutton ASF, 215
557272 Hutton C, 377
561748 Hutton GH, 300
543437 Hutton M, 377
25232822 Hutton TWJ, 148
541954 Hutton-Fellowes E, 230
566024 Huxley JCF, 280
565754 Huxter AN, 355
30086414 Huxter CE, 355
501892 Huxter E, 355
541722 Huyton S, 377
525382 Hyams TD, 38, 108
531972 Hyde J, 377
30033197 Hyde JM, 228
558001 Hyde NI, 207
25020031 Hyde P, 191
519554 Hyde P, 377
30115426 Hyde TN, 264
30055809 Hyland D, 341
24766608 Hyland DL, 222
537438 Hyland GMS, 179
555999 Hynam G, 346
24803396 Hynard PA, 355
30054047 Hyndman AC, 238
C900690F Hynes AH, 217
30115285 Hynes AMP, 180
30187126 Hyslop AC, 266
560125 Hyslop E, 377
30048890 Hyslop HDG, 200
30114839 Hyslop JD, 223

I

30225745 I'Anson CD, 337
25187593 Ibbotson MR, 222
552278 Ibbs DPM, 303
554685 Icely MR, 232
24869297 Icke DK, 217
C13124 Iddiols G, 377
560136 Iddon K, 377
565183 Iddon TJ, 198
518632 Idziaszczyk M, 343
512624 Iffland DM, 278
559318 Igoe A, 330
565069 Igoe BJ, 262
549734 Igolen-Robi C, 355
25221742 Iles GJ, 232
536494 Ilic N, 112
25232167 Illing RA, 154
30113521 Illing RJ, 219

J

K

564582 Kayll JM, 297
21168280 Kc D, 186
30112785 Keable-Kinsella AH, 238
30179048 Keal RC, 212
24781180 Keane MDR, 250
30121062 Kearney MT, 217
564583 Kearse GW, 131
30037181 Kearse PG, 182
24906380 Kearton AP, 236
C35551 Keating AD, 377
30180264 Keating FDR, 226
562409 Keating G, 377
541129 Keating MR, 112
30031235 Keating PFB, 191
C37431 Keaveney RA, 377
30167590 Keays CT, 351
30142079 Keddie JLC, 265
W1055825 Keddie NS, 217
30046874 Kedge JR, 236
551184 Keech M, 214
30172160 Keegan DW, 219
24723165 Keeley JA, 141
563204 Keeling AT, 241
550331 Keen AW, 311
510896 Keen N, 214
561980 Keenan ACM, 336
555199 Keenan GP, 333
W1062427 Keenan HE, 273
554143 Keenan I, 330
30055854 Keenan J, 253
30153014 Keenan JA, 274
564816 Keenan LTJ, 241
30168813 Keenan M, 260
8701487V Keenan NB, 338
30121068 Keenan SJ, 217
564331 Keene DD, 245
30222205 Keene FJA, 339
543169 Keers AJ, 314
30046828 Keery NW, 265
566559 Keeson RGC, 292
555695 Kehoe AG, 305
30083107 Kehoe JAC, 209
25216672 Keiderling RP, 222
537166 Keighley MH, 317
557401 Keilty SC, 214
30079293 Keir JH, 264
24692462 Keir S, 198
553323 Keith FS, 215
C041975P Keith GMW, 228
30088504 Keith OS, 160
541130 Kell CJ, 280
C35808 Kell JM, 377
24697548 Kell JW, 340
30138164 Kellard WAO, 133
25219064 Kelleher MJ, 246
30073062 Kellett RJ, 355
25230341 Kellgren-Parker L, 209
25036846 Kellie TJ, 257
2634370R Kellock CN, 228
25220825 Kelly AR, 215
24905983 Kelly BL, 160
24796203 Kelly CL, 252
520747 Kelly DA, 112
30158620 Kelly HJ, 355
564584 Kelly JAG, 207
533722 Kelly JC, 347
494109 Kelly JL, 377
30012321 Kelly JWW, 284
30005637 Kelly K, 360
556732 Kelly KA, 256
556692 Kelly L, 215
561637 Kelly L, 331
528550 Kelly MJ, 112
556399 Kelly NA, 174
523302 Kelly PB, 377
560093 Kelly PD, 348
25213062 Kelly PJ, 384
554740 Kelly RA, 273
30141653 Kelly RJ, 236
C34572 Kelly RS, 377
556489 Kelly SA, 162
546370 Kelly SF, 377
24797971 Kelly SGJ, 252
24773186 Kelly WJ, 129
30149733 Kelly WR, 154
540621 Kelly-Smith DL, 250
563771 Kelsall JI, 392
C35643 Kelso IAO, 355
30216057 Kelson SJ, 355
2649815P Kemeny CJ, 247
559615 Kemp CA, 241
546537 Kemp EMC, 198
W1064015 Kemp GM, 236
510173 Kemp ID, 314
554927 Kemp JN, 266
562554 Kemp NJ, 241
W147345W Kemp NL, 274
548963 Kemp SN, 232
25234600 Kemp WJ, 131
30222206 Kempa TG, 339
25202414 Kemp-Gee HA, 297
561411 Kempster AJ, 280
30207735 Kempster RC, 360
565502 Kempton R, 355
25225709 Kendall BM, 144
D231959Q Kendall JJ, 284
544643 Kendall JR, 308
C041794V Kendall NR, 222
24794798 Kendall- Reid P, 250
30011657 Kendall RTA, 284
C36013 Kendall SR, 377
30099279 Kendall TM, 260
534160 Kendrick MI, 347
564404 Kendrick NM, 232
549446 Kendrick P, 278
564124 Kendrick R, 355
552022 Kennedy A, 392
532164 Kennedy AP, 112
548704 Kennedy CC, 198
25166011 Kennedy DP, 162
540553 Kennedy DWG, 335
534013 Kennedy JA, 214
550018 Kennedy JA, 171
559291 Kennedy MB, 256
565765 Kennedy MRJ, 306
24904400 Kennedy NA, 209
561441 Kennedy PA, 273
25198782 Kennedy PS, 209
25231564 Kennedy RA, 252
24854509 Kennedy RJ, 135
558983 Kennedy RJ, 305
527041 Kennedy SD, 343
30131572 Kennedy SE, 202
30151119 Kennedy SS, 238
30015378 Kennedy TP, 201
545940 Kennedy Y, 256
565028 Kennerley L, 377
30080873 Kennerley RB, 222
30230026 Kenney K, 360
561277 Kennon NT, 317
566211 Kennon SJA, 191
544929 Kenny DB, 179
30076268 Kenny JA, 252
24805016 Kenny N, 198
552850 Kenny R, 377
30180053 Kenny SA, 332
565461 Kent AG, 177
560255 Kent CJE, 232
25200378 Kent CR, 343
30161588 Kent MJ, 322
25213259 Kent MP, 343
24830603 Kent MW, 222
559399 Kent RA, 331
30098327 Kent TR, 252
546652 Kenward G, 272
24685196 Kenworthy JL, 384
X027002H Kenworthy LK, 273
561739 Kenyon JPA, 303
528292 Kenyon MP, 112
550462 Kenyon RA, 281
542567 Kenyon S, 355
30185778 Kenzie CF, 307
547723 Keogh DP, 305
25242728 Keogh MJ, 252
543380 Keoghane SR, 335
532084 Keppel-Compton RT, 230
560608 Keppler ADP, 308
30201343 Keracher SL, 202
30215049 Kerai C, 335
25214108 Kerans GW, 246
559897 Kerbey AJ, 198
532541 Kerner JR, 230
518138 Kernohan DA, 197
C36753 Kerr A, 377
523925 Kerr AD, 112
30123575 Kerr ADJ, 242
30188707 Kerr AG, 129
24697166 Kerr AJ, 209
30087548 Kerr AW, 260
24721556 Kerr C, 198
549550 Kerr GJ, 207
521169 Kerr GR, 336
545213 Kerr J, 207
561215 Kerr J, 230
532204 Kerr JR, 112
495356 Kerr JS, 229
30054601 Kerr KE, 217
557928 Kerr KW, 308
563171 Kerr L, 145

554903 Kerr JEB, 281
560912 Kerr MD, 153
535194 Kerr P, 327
30141476 Kerr R, 318
30177152 Kerr WF, 377
563971 Kerrigan MJ, 281
30080884 Kerrigan PJ, 219
521654 Kerry-Williams CP, 198
25232848 Kersey ARD, 175
566299 Kershaw PJ, 303
30046878 Kershaw SE, 146
543372 Kerton MS, 249
21169294 Kerung B, 185
24738313 Kesterton SA, 172
554662 Ketterer MT, 262
560603 Ketteringham A, 377
558463 Kettle L, 360
533084 Kettler CCR, 197
30197482 Kevan LM, 265
30201974 Key BDE, 212
25213745 Key ORM, 295
537046 Key RL, 330
527670 Keys A, 377
561449 Keys GP, 241
30186460 Keys RH, 360
30186416 Keyte AJ, 384
C37135 Keyte CF, 384
545763 Khadka, 281
560392 Khamcha T, 187
30101819 Khan AU, 334
541946 Khan KN, 244
536777 Khan M, 278
25221744 Khan WS, 257
21168197 Khanal AK, 209
21168756 Khapung Limbu K, 186
21168634 Khatri CB, 188
21168601 Khatri Chhetri D, 185
30042885 Khepar NAS, 236
21168294 Khokaja Pun D, 187
561401 Kibble LJ, 281
555488 Kibble TJ, 162
565807 Kidd AM, 232
30204218 Kidd IJ, 212
24903643 Kidd RG, 242
553923 Kidd SP, 347
25242725 Kiddie FPG, 209
30124523 Kiernan JA, 223
559618 Kierstead CS, 132
30047180 Kiff GM, 355
556895 Kiff T, 377
543582 Kiggell J, 355
529531 Kiggell L, 355
497450 Kilburn GA, 318
30028283 Kilburn JAW, 236
531907 Kilby RB, 330
24774411 Kill NR, 331
24759583 Killick SJ, 181
556254 Killoran J, 256
30034586 Kilner JA, 337
30112798 Kilpatrick GN, 242
30170183 Kilpatrick SA, 202
512947 Kilpatrick SPB, 276
555918 Kilsby J, 355
30201470 Kilsby KGS, 307
532177 Kimber AE, 112
C17001 Kimber G, 377
24876362 Kimber SC, 260
24772596 Kimberlin GC, 175
W1061984 Kimble HJ, 344
30141650 Kinahan JES, 236
30132751 Kinch CD, 327
30084579 Kinch KJB, 284
564292 King AD, 281
558753 King AJ, 250
525655 King AN, 112
556684 King APJ, 221
540624 King C, 249
565304 King CL, 190
30204217 King E, 350
564765 King E, 355
30160420 King E, 355
515922 King EJ, 329
566122 King GJ, 246
559621 King GR, 159
24779781 King IR, 250
547026 King M, 268
C37532 King MA, 377
562283 King MD, 292
25215371 King MS, 162
564846 King N, 377
544540 King NCY, 190
30105865 King NR, 228
551310 King OGH, 281
527716 King P, 355
525798 King PM, 230
518140 King PR, 230
565415 King PWS, 228
541933 King RA, 303
30090315 King RAF, 160
24898012 King RI, 236
540341 King RJ, 343
30188591 King SR, 165
565384 King SR, 217
30105461 King TG, 355
511508 Kingdon WJF, 108, 303
555490 King-Evans RE, 141
30112362 Kinghan AB, 263
30092369 Kinghan SJ, 225
W0817482 Kinghorn L, 252
514582 Kingsberry TL, 112
547949 Kingsbury OJ, 181
545989 Kingsford JNJ, 135
30062197 Kingston AG, 355
25007670 Kingston AS, 263
541043 Kingston DV, 281
24397067 Kingston MA, 284
554449 Kingston MEW, 117
W0837133 Kingston MR, 263
557496 Kingston PDF, 232
25179734 Kington AP, 212
548964 Kinkaid P, 262
522176 Kinloch JAB, 289, 303
30021387 Kinnear WC, 222
25106341 Kinnoch JS, 309
30156867 Kinsella AF, 236
30105088 Kinsella NP, 228
509530 Kinsey L, 327
558505 Kinsey P, 377
30177579 Kinson TH, 226
25012941 Kinvig PD, 242
521057 Kippen IR, 162
553021 Kirby BC, 334
564947 Kirby D, 377
30087429 Kirby LI, 331
560258 Kirby R, 198
30132995 Kirby RA, 225
559376 Kirby SRJ, 198
561258 Kirchel M, 250
564896 Kirk AS, 331
30051276 Kirk CM, 377
30098929 Kirk FM, 355
558754 Kirk IJ, 215
30173372 Kirk M, 384
30148200 Kirkham AJ, 180
30100678 Kirkham BW, 355
30180034 Kirkham H, 339
30180054 Kirkham H, 332
30146859 Kirkham S, 239
30148076 Kirkham TW, 135
556553 Kirkin AE, 207
563192 Kirkman S, 128
564762 Kirkpatrick LD, 201
30089209 Kirkpatrick LD, 310
552094 Kirkpatrick PI, 333
545679 Kirkpatrick TW, 377
30134370 Kirkwood AR, 327
544773 Kirkwood SA, 303
560132 Kirmond JL, 205
30046886 Kirwan-Izzo MV, 246
562971 Kitchen J, 377
565545 Kitchen VHL, 377
550463 Kitchener BCJ, 249
24875044 Kitchin T, 225
30150686 Kitchiner NJ, 348
532677 Kitching B, 377
554899 Kitching J, 377
C30971 Kitching M, 377
560399 Kitching MR, 117
548966 Kitching REC, 145
534014 Kite BDA, 112
562811 Kitson JA, 309
542995 Kitson JF, 190
533781 Kitson PS, 326
30137139 Kittler AK, 350
542723 Kivell GE, 245
30128864 Kiy IJ, 222
25233958 Kjellgren JAF, 117
551522 Klempner D, 355
W1056984 Klymchuk IS, 341
513903 Knaggs CPH, 112
W1039788 Kneale V, 343
W1049022 Knebel MJ, 211
527308 Knell KE, 340
557912 Knight AG, 308
561526 Knight CJ, 132
24700700 Knight DM, 330
30200601 Knight JJ, 147
557677 Knight JR, 214
30117953 Knight K, 377

L

30080328 Liddle DA, 225
506479 Liddle TS, 330
30123922 Lidgley HM, 257
30232997 Liggett H, 335
30119918 Liggins C, 355
553148 Light EA, 241
544542 Light GC, 147
534499 Lighten JG, 317
531624 Lightfoot CMR, 262
30220192 Lightfoot TC, 336
25233307 Lihou DO, 307
25220809 Liladhar N, 170
Q1062549 Lilley AL, 334
30049588 Lilley BR, 201
533902 Lilley JK, 355
563625 Lilleyman EG, 241
558757 Lilleyman TC, 207
511354 Lillicrap DT, 378
24656854 Lillie MM, 127
30011666 Lillie TI, 338
30147107 Lilly GP, 378
538004 Lillywhite AC, 230
486287 Lillywhite LP, 240
555041 Lim TCU, 347
530332 Limb MS, 290
25058458 Limbert K, 378
548772 Limbrey RJ, 215
30042240 Limbrick PS, 218
561909 Limbu, 281
21168291 Limbu K, 185
21169269 Limbu K, 257
21169296 Limbu Khim C, 209
21168231 Limbu S, 185
21168223 Limbu T, 185
566212 Linares JC, 209
24707101 Lincoln KA, 174
543611 Lincoln PM, 313
550997 Lincoln PT, 378
559008 Lindblom AC, 344
30207009 Lindblom RAL, 212
30157113 Lindley JP, 223
24862924 Lindley N, 191
554622 Lindow MP, 306
520764 Lindsay GJ, 343
536682 Lindsay LF, 297
549089 Lindsay Obe WR, 278
30138077 Lindsay RAJ, 355
525878 Lindsay RH, 145
553713 Lindsay RK, 268
542997 Lindsay RRE, 153
25003572 Lindsay TM, 154
550995 Lindsay-Smith MRM, 255
555042 Lindstrom C, 273
30040742 Line CJ, 378
25034392 Linegar JS, 222
30029963 Linehan PJ, 338
24935013 Lines AM, 242
565316 Lines PJ, 250
30117448 Linford DI, 378
30014672 Ling RJ, 252
30123148 Ling TC, 355
25142885 Lingard AJ, 384
538247 Lingard J, 346
30082694 Linklater GW, 211
30231131 Linnell NK, 355
24841943 Linscer A, 225
557505 Linsdell JP, 198
30206310 Linton GI, 228
565959 Linton TD, 281
515820 Lintonbon LJ, 273
25218463 Lintvelt HAJ, 236
560268 Lipowski AG, 154
556985 Lippiett OJW, 321
555217 Lish DA, 215
24792105 Lishman G, 209
24688303 Lister AJ, 233
563423 Lister B, 378
25232852 Lister JA, 191
30079865 Lister JM, 211
30203740 Lister SM, 384
25234608 Litchfield REA, 201
504479 Lithgow M, 213
24756563 Lithgow SM, 309
552270 Lithgow Smith KM, 281
24865186 Litster W, 201
566228 Little OCS, 191
542730 Little PM, 112
562742 Little RAB, 315
540893 Little SJ, 233
556128 Little SJ, 291
25001495 Little WJ, 217
30044435 Littledale J, 344
24651696 Littlefield SE, 215
24802002 Littler PWJ, 198
546993 Littlewood RS, 344
30023544 Liu S, 378
2649951T Lively JP, 250
W1053805 Livesey FE, 341
529958 Livesey GM, 205
561636 Livingstone CCA, 335
528221 Livingstone GR, 112
30183074 Livingstone IG, 344
30038112 Livingstone MW, 323
561802 Livingstone R, 139
30128016 Livingstone R, 327
511303 Llewellin WO, 392
W1057120 Llewellyn MLP, 274
511347 Llewellyn MP, 276
539001 Llewellyn N, 112
30178229 Llewellyn T, 355
543958 Llewelyn JA, 207
555219 Llewelyn-Usher HS, 148
554788 Lloyd A, 378
564800 Lloyd AJ, 233
24759763 Lloyd Butler A, 201
30114748 Lloyd CJM, 175
30097535 Lloyd CT, 384
30121051 Lloyd DC, 355
30137322 Lloyd DJ, 212
30043240 Lloyd George FO, 284
557506 Lloyd HT, 124
554321 Lloyd Jones C, 293
30018423 Lloyd LA, 281
550580 Lloyd MJ, 321
554689 Lloyd MR, 230
C22173 Lloyd N, 378
559628 Lloyd NR, 184
30087683 Lloyd PA, 236
560971 Lloyd SJ, 269
30081610 Lloyd TM, 355
30054740 Lloyd-Davies GW, 209
525879 Lloyd-Jones RH, 112
25185752 Lloyd-Jukes T, 139
532870 Lloyd-Williams M, 355
24694084 Loader ATR, 304
24544178 Loader K, 306
552746 Loader NT, 233
539002 Loader PG, 249
30115439 Loasby AC, 324
534540 Lobar P, 378
25120656 Lock AR, 250
536521 Lock G, 355
552096 Lock GWJ, 144
30143103 Lock JJ, 211
531016 Lock NJ, 112
30015554 Lock WD, 284
551790 Locke AN, 169
25230335 Locke DC, 284
557627 Locke QS, 209
C25761 Lockett B, 384
560917 Lockett JF, 233
30178446 Lockey HJN, 160
527147 Lockhart CA, 48, 118
543056 Lockhart R, 378
30177849 Lockhart RJ, 355
563317 Lockhart RL, 342
21169154 Locksam K, 185
563628 Lockwood AG, 169
25008847 Lockwood DM, 284
30180259 Lockwood GJ, 218
565053 Lockwood JP, 250
541661 Lockwood NH, 255
557460 Lockwood SM, 215
30062904 Lockyer NJ, 378
540474 Lodge D, 340
557814 Lodge D, 378
544940 Lodge DP, 316
539299 Lodge DR, 355
500901 Lodge JM, 378
518634 Lodge MA, 290
30118314 Lodwick GW, 209
553028 Lodwick SH, 228
550439 Lofts S, 378
564098 Loftus JJ, 348
548683 Logan DC, 198
30188697 Logan DDJ, 327
25005231 Logan G, 270
550037 Logan G, 259
30163552 Logan IA, 344
5208751G Logan IJ, 225
524328 Logan ISC, 112
505052 Logan KS, 303
529005 Logan PDO, 220
545743 Logan RP, 378
25154751 Logie G, 252
W0819567 Logie H, 236
555220 Logie P, 250
Q1047712 Lohman LA, 284
534253 Lomas IC, 378

30081958	Marsden E, 222
30055935	Marsden G, 164
30222213	Marsden H, 310
30147949	Marsden JP, 148
564778	Marsden MER, 245
24821041	Marsden MR, 210
W1061995	Marsden RS, 252
25087893	Marsden S, 217
539798	Marsden TGJ, 205
557830	Marsh AJ, 333
30011650	Marsh BJ, 210
24870436	Marsh CP, 252
30015359	Marsh DAN, 201
24700265	Marsh NS, 281
24865014	Marsh PE, 210
530718	Marsh RD, 295
551323	Marsh RG, 207
530113	Marsh S, 256
508215	Marshall AC, 249
30178438	Marshall AJM, 211
539290	Marshall CA, 335
541397	Marshall CJ, 207
543575	Marshall CS, 272
541665	Marshall D, 113
549279	Marshall DJ, 255
539591	Marshall E, 378
561836	Marshall E, 378
530190	Marshall EJH, 295
30115686	Marshall HL, 242
566336	Marshall J, 331
30191456	Marshall J, 356
551324	Marshall JH, 233
24818646	Marshall JR, 275
30035620	Marshall JW, 222
30078317	Marshall KE, 378
30222214	Marshall LD, 339
30168811	Marshall MAJ, 182
30169846	Marshall MD, 223
545792	Marshall MI, 171
30171708	Marshall MRG, 335
521664	Marshall N, 32, 107, 196
30096846	Marshall N, 356
25024130	Marshall P, 154
521665	Marshall PA, 230
24688268	Marshall R, 233
24840568	Marshall R, 236
548729	Marshall RB, 347
30222603	Marshall S, 337
564601	Marshall S, 331
24826851	Marshall SA, 222
520920	Marshall SG, 335
30188634	Marshall SJ, 172
508216	Marshall SW, 276
30138453	Marshall TTA, 356
30158735	Marshall TW, 191
C34616	Marshallsay KJ, 384
C35410	Marsland I, 378
25235141	Marsom NWD, 260
30051870	Marson AL, 322
557745	Marston DL, 273
30138985	Martel CGL, 125
566168	Martell CE, 306
25186725	Martin AJ, 222
30115305	Martin AL, 384
24844081	Martin AR, 236
561505	Martin CS, 262
528473	Martin D, 378
543453	Martin DA, 306
25091595	Martin EOG, 210
546646	Martin G, 273
30177920	Martin G, 337
513491	Martin G, 378
548237	Martin GA, 262
563096	Martin GA, 333
24870697	Martin GDH, 210
30186611	Martin HAT, 146
30201370	Martin HCL, 212
25009703	Martin JA, 236
533188	Martin JA, 378
552829	Martin JE, 281
30037117	Martin JFZ, 149
558556	Martin JM, 333
515736	Martin JM, 276
30089141	Martin JRD, 253
30175161	Martin K, 342
515555	Martin KJ, 255
30151733	Martin LAD, 170
537461	Martin LJ, 356
560054	Martin M, 197
30075620	Martin MJ, 201
24915778	Martin MP, 344
547502	Martin NAJ, 245
562216	Martin NJG, 297
30106101	Martin NW, 356
563636	Martin OT, 256
558005	Martin P, 356
550106	Martin PD, 220
25166841	Martin PHS, 356
556940	Martin PJ, 180
30175908	Martin PJ, 356
558184	Martin PM, 281
551157	Martin R, 378
C30771	Martin R, 378
25165885	Martin REA, 284
30113792	Martin RM, 154
30048887	Martin S, 201
546181	Martin S, 378
539004	Martin SJ, 221
30180055	Martin SM, 332
30043776	Martin T, 378
30037376	Martin TB, 321
30066618	Martin TR, 384
30149050	Martin VR, 378
564317	Martin-Bowtell G, 306
30127141	Martyniuk AP, 211
25234757	Marwaha JS, 201
30034188	Marx MA, 257
25166516	Masheder CD, 198
24690027	Masheter PG, 392
545997	Maskell AJ, 169
553344	Masling CH, 241
25197432	Mason AD, 210
30120095	Mason AE, 246
542634	Mason AJ, 205
545998	Mason AN, 281
30169759	Mason AR, 202
30150837	Mason CM, 335
562828	Mason CN, 225
565326	Mason DE, 344
25154755	Mason DM, 236
537462	Mason DM, 230
514674	Mason E, 378
558185	Mason GJN, 233
518637	Mason GR, 308
C29641	Mason I, 378
566208	Mason J, 361
30145763	Mason JAH, 217
24872064	Mason JE, 210
565616	Mason JE, 233
30171828	Mason JS, 218
520376	Mason KJS, 138
30011758	Mason LC, 201
24743235	Mason LJ, 217
24906171	Mason MG, 252
30091119	Mason MI, 295
566272	Mason N, 378
565503	Mason PE, 304
25013742	Mason PJ, 217
544213	Mason RCS, 295
537463	Mason SD, 220
30015367	Mason SM, 172
539005	Mason TN, 198
30109682	Mason-Johns ON, 226
558547	Massam D, 378
540697	Massetti SM, 205
30060498	Massey C, 378
25045767	Massey CM, 361
562217	Massey MPD, 250
30099732	Massey NS, 191
30164324	Massey PDS, 327
565156	Massie E, 356
540004	Masson A, 378
559125	Masson AA, 331
541666	Masson CP, 205
565935	Masson K, 378
30052509	Masson RJ, 211
24954267	Master-Jewitt G, 356
539609	Masters AR, 233
548152	Masters CL, 233
30130102	Masters DJ, 309
539007	Masters DR, 198
547051	Masters DR, 344
559977	Masters G, 361
548395	Masters GR, 378
30202743	Masters K, 245
559116	Masters M, 356
24775094	Masterson SH, 252
524339	Masterton TJF, 295
566655	Mather D, 378
24781416	Mather JC, 331
563784	Mather RB, 207
25231015	Mather SI, 201
25008918	Mathers AJ, 201
560925	Mathers ARC, 184
W1046799	Mathers HR, 222
561242	Mathers JD, 337
C33810	Mathers PS, 378
W1056692	Matheson AC, 201
562952	Matheson LJ, 356

24660401 Mathews RD, 242
565162 Mathewson A, 356
543021 Mathewson KG, 335
549569 Mathias AH, 233
509545 Mathie RA, 276
536773 Mathieson A, 333
562830 Mathieson ES, 172
30056670 Mathieson ND, 236
558332 Mathieson SC, 331
559176 Mathieson SP, 245
539121 Matson TJ, 340
24900230 Mattacola MS, 217
541418 Matten SD, 207
25185423 Matthews BCJ, 125
24877025 Matthews BP, 284
24865195 Matthews DM, 178
24912687 Matthews DS, 236
545904 Matthews E, 356
30245506 Matthews HE, 361
25010243 Matthews J, 275
529807 Matthews JA, 113
30115300 Matthews JH, 247
550029 Matthews JP, 177
C37330 Matthews K, 356
562831 Matthews LS, 215
30127158 Matthews M, 236
557513 Matthews NGA, 344
30132950 Matthews P, 361
559815 Matthews R, 378
Matthews RWC, 144
C36644 Matthews S, 378
532346 Matthews SD, 378
554914 Matthews SD, 378
30224781 Matthews SE, 361
533210 Matthews SRS, 305
511873 Matthews VJG, 290
30075355 Mattin JA, 165
25170844 Mattock JJ, 263
25197070 Matts EA, 315
30113711 Matuska H, 246
535024 Matyear P, 378
30236643 Maughan JJ, 361
30136326 Maughan JWP, 182
526606 Maund A, 356
30027846 Maund AG, 245
539516 Maund C, 356
545570 Maund GA, 169
559776 Maund LJ, 347
529741 Maundrell RT, 141
521159 Maung H, 378
521199 Maung HLA, 378
C36620 Mauran G, 378
24544119 Mavin I, 306
559462 Maw AW, 250
562219 Mawby EE, 128
30123894 Mawby EGK, 135
557514 Mawby WH, 295
539610 Mawdsley JCW, 197
25225858 Mawdsley RJ, 225
541870 Mawe G, 378
30079634 Mawe G, 378
544812 Mawer RJ, 220
30137686 Mawson CR, 246
30051499 Mawson JA, 118
561805 Maxfield R, 356
25228844 Maxwell AG, 236
25197719 Maxwell AS, 252
557515 Maxwell CJ, 256
30203490 Maxwell CJ, 351
30031234 Maxwell CNH, 191
539008 Maxwell DM, 230
510897 Maxwell JG, 311
30112388 Maxwell R, 378
512488 Maxwell W, 281
30022676 Maxwell WB, 335
30132987 Maxwell WJ, 172
541866 Maxwell-Batten DM, 321
30128053 Maxwell-Scott A, 146
25197769 May JAH, 236
30055930 May R, 202
30038592 May RE, 356
512645 May SJ, 256
558492 Mayall DWJ, 378
499545 Mayall SV, 124, 276
30150732 Mayberry C, 361
533923 Mayberry J, 378
516017 Maybery RL, 46, 113
30202403 Maybin SI, 323
566406 Maycock C, 262
563814 Mayell LM, 308
24851386 Mayers SC, 210
556418 Mayes AG, 207
Q1049531 Mayes CE, 331
30123310 Mayes JH, 238
551325 Mayes SOL, 207
30045217 Mayes WJ, 378
563906 Mayhead JN, 326
30062362 Mayhew D, 356
24772306 Mayland SA, 210
30041778 Maymon VL, 264
547720 Maynard CA, 227
25006142 Maynard RL, 201
549570 Mayne JN, 215
30046517 Mayne JS, 336
541237 Mayo AVE, 256
556117 Mayo MJ, 333
W1058398 Mayor SL, 263
552204 Maytham GD, 244
539921 Mazur P, 356
527255 McAdam C, 356
25147346 McAdam EMK, 284
535025 McAfee AJM, 138
24856252 McAfee HG, 257
30146864 McAfee OJ, 253
30171774 McAleer CP, 384
25214114 McAleer SR, 246
547646 McAleese T, 378
24716822 McAleney AG, 153
563800 McAlinden RS, 356
507491 McAlister IR, 278
532815 McAllister EJ, 378
503174 McAllister HJ, 323
554840 McAllister JD, 259
30174926 McAllister KRE, 117
535167 McAllister T, 378
25166665 McAndrew DJC, 178
C35079 McAndrews MW, 378
30205457 McAnuff P, 356
518405 McArthur DJ, 290
24933200 McArthur GM, 217
W1053973 McArthur KMD, 273
543373 Mcarthur PJ, 249
30044790 McArthur RJL, 201
565328 McAughtrie RAJ, 304
W1050388 McAulay CMJ, 292
563346 McAulay E, 331
544824 McAulay H, 356
30072090 McAulay L, 170
543022 McAuley J, 335
30161764 McAuley R, 348
24811671 McAuley WC, 153
561857 McAuliffe IC, 333
24884438 McBean AP, 217
24867276 McBeath GRE, 252
558765 McBirnie DR, 233
523771 McBratney BJ, 378
C30979 McBride B, 378
533904 McBride HGM, 113
W1058789 McBride JA, 236
563038 McBride OMB, 245
N980420N McBride R, 304
30128487 McBride RN, 284
30116984 McBride SP, 331
542413 McBride SPG, 308
527828 McBride TD, 221
30180044 McBroom C, 339
24721630 McBurney CA, 190
30089169 Mccabe MS, 218
30220602 McCafferty JA, 361
556750 McCaffery JM, 198
546552 McCaffrey PS, 197
498402 McCahon W, 356
564604 McCaighy AJ, 221
507027 McCall BW, 276
30047072 McCall IA, 356
C35959 McCall JIM, 378
515731 McCall PJ, 113
542738 McCallion SEJ, 207
543868 McCallum C, 356
24759933 McCallum JB, 146
561715 McCallum JD, 153
542894 McCallum K, 356
556419 McCallum RO, 198
30141981 McCallum SC, 263
30215982 McCammon A, 269
30148788 McCammond SJ, 378
30178853 McCandless P, 361
25092728 McCann EG, 252
W1061077 McCarthy CF, 225
30236288 McCarthy CJ, 351
25112628 McCarthy JEM, 191
548637 McCarthy KJ, 331
531989 McCarthy LDL, 250
553235 McCarthy M, 281
551085 McCarthy MP, 197
559900 McCarthy P, 177
25174543 McCarthy RC, 236
30207150 McCarthy RD, 202
565909 McCarthy S, 379

30168201 McGowan IV, 356
564142 McGowan M, 356
564606 McGowan PA, 242
C37274 McGowan PD, 385
554922 McGown GA, 153
24722984 McGrail L, 215
24786201 McGrane AJ, 182
25164076 McGrane AJ, 217
24688891 McGrath A, 207
560716 McGrath AP, 346
565603 McGrath CE, 268
560721 McGrath CM, 217
522020 McGrath MJ, 346
30157084 McGrath RC, 147
30123534 McGraw CJ, 217
544367 McGready AH, 249
509430 McGregor AR, 356
24678428 McGregor BD, 257
24651796 McGregor NA, 217
24700251 McGregor PA, 270
513503 McGregor RJA, 177
30017700 McGroarty M, 180
30148966 McGrory AJ, 257
551328 McGrory CF, 169
538740 McGrory SM, 323
24801730 McGuffie AJ, 284
555131 McGuffie KE, 241
24755450 McGuffog M, 233
30060975 McGuinness EJ, 202
547167 McGuire I, 316
30203121 McGuire JA, 274
561935 McGuire M, 379
30234106 McGuire S, 361
563987 McGuirk RP, 207
30138616 McHardy G, 310
564212 McHenery SG, 309
24781290 McHugh JA, 252
30155492 McHutchon SG, 253
514018 McIlroy JD, 277
30076781 McIlroy KB, 139
30180056 McIlveen SG, 332
548747 McIlwaine TLU, 131
559760 McInally A, 311
552982 McInally JED, 256
24595779 McInnes TM, 334
559872 McInroy C, 153
30176684 McIntosh CJ, 325
558276 McIntosh EJ, 245
566451 McIntosh G, 311
560044 McIntosh HJ, 347
24863056 McIntosh KW, 241
W0818908 McIntosh L, 356
562976 McIntosh LC, 348
30205294 McIntosh SJ, 385
30029823 McIntyre AL, 379
30029876 McIntyre DM, 309
559226 McIntyre G, 361
30147357 McIntyre IT, 342
C00804 McIntyre JA, 379
24678108 McIntyre ND, 250
551018 McIntyre R, 379
C35534 McIver PJE, 252
W1062110 McKane JLM, 246
546956 McKay AR, 141
551125 McKay AT, 273
McKay B, 184
552437 McKay GA, 207
547741 McKay J, 153
30089073 McKay NP, 348
541396 McKechnie ARI, 207
30080767 McKechnie MAJ, 125
30118481 McKee L, 356
30079334 McKeen J, 238
30047172 McKellar RW, 125
30119413 McKelvie D, 379
518280 McKend IG, 108
563638 McKendrick KM, 250
558632 McKenna A, 347
562984 McKenna AN, 221
30222504 McKenna C, 379
30232467 McKenna CER, 335
McKenna HP, 333
529658 McKenna JG, 335
30078655 McKenna PA, 218
558549 McKenna SA, 379
24679798 McKenny A, 169
30122013 McKenzie EM, 337
24762986 McKenzie S, 284
550004 McKenzie SE, 281
C33143 McKenzie SG, 385
25035926 McKenzie SJ, 225
25166650 McKenzie TAC, 295
555979 McKenzie-Bell MS, 309
532158 McKeown D, 113
559386 McKeown DI, 392
W1061950 McKeown JL, 379
543864 McKie I, 356
24688443 McKinney IS, 233
30079258 McKinney P, 385
531880 McKinney-Bennett EA, 340
562148 McKinnie CB, 241
564608 McKinnie FL, 241
564975 McKinnon JM, 356
544012 McKinnon KA, 244
30168332 McKnight HR, 361
563777 McKnight PWE, 306
30140779 McKone LM, 170
566388 McLachlan AP, 246
552439 McLannahan ATG, 174
30145445 McLaren AP, 258
30163051 McLaren W, 328
24707425 McLaren WMG, 154
24738284 McLaughlan P, 146
557735 McLaughlin CE, 348
24906952 McLaughlin IS, 236
30159980 McLaughlin JD, 260
561163 McLaughlin KM, 347
W1032217 McLaughlin S, 257
30083154 McLay MTW, 146
30177257 McLay NJ, 228
25213287 McLean AAI, 210
25185707 McLean AJ, 236
522723 McLean AJ, 306
553196 McLean AP, 268
30181210 McLean CWM, 144
563398 McLean J, 379
547294 McLean JM, 338
554624 McLean LJ, 207
W1064013 McLean MHC, 252
554786 McLean N, 379
25035846 McLean S, 257
557288 McLearnon BJ, 281
563639 McLeish IA, 263
556424 McLellan MG, 172
30132401 McLelland JD, 217
552440 McLeman JFS, 127
545250 McLeman KE, 326
552677 McLenaghan CJ, 207
25005823 McLennan C, 210
540850 McLennan JV, 244
522856 McLeod AB, 49, 108, 329
W1059042 McLeod AC, 273
537920 McLeod EPC, 331
30075487 McLeod F, 238
563640 McLeod G, 236
519827 McLeod G, 311
561755 McLeod L, 379
30027630 McLeod M, 211
558291 McLeod MC, 347
552222 McLeod RA, 330
526374 McLeod-Jones MI, 181
30150190 McLoughlin TA, 344
30055929 McLoughlin WF, 236
554327 McMahon AJ, 198
565781 McMahon IM, 182
30092086 McMahon P, 379
25021781 McMahon RA, 252
30134267 McMahon RM, 347
30124403 McMahon SA, 260
532010 McMahon SC, 108
30093383 McManners WJ, 137
24792271 McManus G, 257
24716578 McManus JW, 221
30057054 McMaster A, 337
560050 McMaster H, 348
24867137 McMeechan J, 250
556224 McMenemy SJ, 295
24906105 McMichael SA, 147
560948 McMillan EM, 256
559638 McMillan JP, 215
564997 McMillan KJ, 303
30137043 McMillan KR, 247
552190 McMillan OM, 347
547229 McMillan P, 249
30089497 McMillan RG, 321
565136 McMinn A, 317
545575 McMonagle LM, 205
30046091 McMullan AA, 182
24889550 McMullan MR, 217
24911274 McMullan NG, 261
30186835 McMullan P, 379
24710130 McMullen SD, 295
W0803468 McNab J, 340
30170210 McNab TR, 356
516310 McNair RWL, 230
24852864 McNally MJ, 311
543792 McNally OP, 249
30121066 McNama CA, 236
539070 McNamee A, 379

30082172 Middleton CW, 284
30178235 Middleton D, 228
522631 Middleton D, 42, 290
546555 Middleton DG, 323
30149457 Middleton DN, 253
24756404 Middleton GE, 217
25216058 Middleton HGV, 201
24831135 Middleton SE, 210
25234749 Middleton TPP, 175
550740 Midgley CJ, 340
564279 Midgley J, 361
532614 Midgley SA, 330
30178437 Miers JW, 191
561291 Mieville KE, 245
543238 Mifsud ND, 205
552824 Migallo NP, 356
25233862 Mikulskis OM, 181
25006441 Milburn G, 385
555240 Milburn LK, 334
30199397 Milburn S, 379
25218888 Mildinhall SJ, 356
D244238P Miles ALP, 242
25156310 Miles C, 242
30039536 Miles CL, 165
30030398 Miles JA, 246
544953 Miles JP, 138
557520 Miles JR, 233
552443 Miles KJ, 250
558768 Miles RS, 221
562031 Milford TW, 309
551172 Milgate DJ, 392
25185511 Mill GAN, 312
25235171 Millan BR, 236
554847 Millar A, 379
25193117 Millar AA, 273
25214589 Millar AJ, 210
548245 Millar ENS, 205
30158736 Millar JA, 185
30075557 Millar JJA, 201
546556 Millar JM, 250
561923 Millar R, 356
24710858 Millar RM, 284
24725902 Millar RP, 252
550034 Millar SD, 205
30181207 Millar SJ, 172
561158 Millar-Brown AM, 245
30156933 Millard AZ, 238
25231198 Millard JDR, 284
529547 Millard JR, 205
551603 Millarvie AJ, 333
549578 Millbank RG, 207
559978 Millbery G, 356
30014139 Millen CJ, 139
520562 Millen DAJ, 330
556255 Millen G, 256
30147952 Millen GK, 236
509555 Millen NCT, 128
30046869 Miller A, 170
24762232 Miller AJ, 217
30194572 Miller AJ, 361
30114340 Miller AP, 219
30155945 Miller AR, 191
557777 Miller B, 275
564258 Miller C, 379
30121813 Miller CA, 139
30127850 Miller CM, 260
508219 Miller CWS, 281
564079 Miller D, 379
24815733 Miller DG, 201
550035 Miller DT, 233
25001067 Miller GE, 331
561740 Miller GG, 300
565785 Miller HT, 207
24797915 Miller J, 180
C20544 Miller J, 379
510874 Miller JE, 335
563029 Miller JH, 313
30027195 Miller JJ, 210
30160583 Miller JS, 223
30082298 Miller JTC, 385
30207376 Miller KC, 261
552827 Miller KL, 260
30232138 Miller M, 348
554426 Miller MA, 250
565784 Miller MA, 281
548777 Miller MV, 233
24863744 Miller N, 162
30119432 Miller OR, 218
30010973 Miller RG, 236
30077128 Miller RM, 217
510040 Miller SN, 343
527833 Miller SSM, 118
529107 Miller T, 356
30113345 Miller TC, 300
549579 Miller TJ, 172
528651 Millett CH, 240
24786587 Milligan CE, 309
566605 Milligan IF, 325
24821132 Milligan JM, 236
30140855 Milligan KA, 257
507909 Milligan MAL, 276
30040945 Milligan SJ, 236
30200941 Milligan T, 379
565416 Millington JM, 246
W1062275 Millns CE, 284
25182004 Millns TD, 170
559642 Mills AJ, 162
516912 Mills AS, 113
522911 Mills D, 392
562835 Mills DP, 221
30156446 Mills EC, 202
566131 Mills FJC, 144
526379 Mills IP, 113
560293 Mills JPG, 190
C93290 Mills ME, 379
C21600 Mills PI, 379
554046 Mills R, 379
25005980 Mills RJ, 263
508101 Mills SCD, 278
540700 Millsop AKG, 240
30178283 Millward O, 356
30079340 Millwater EH, 264
558981 Milne C, 379
30090314 Milne CA, 253
30106725 Milne FW, 263
25232619 Milne GM, 247
24862388 Milne JHF, 275
562836 Milne MH, 162
25230333 Milne SJ, 252
24803767 Milne SJ, 284
515638 Milner KG, 321
8300769K Milnes JAJ, 326
517046 Milroy CJA, 311
30217903 Milton AC, 212
24841006 Milton DD, 267
30076451 Milton P, 356
24713476 Milton PD, 198
30146866 Milton TO, 212
30015362 Minards EJ, 133
560295 Minards WJ, 132
30017704 Minchin PF, 273
C36735 Miniss B, 385
536695 Minton GE, 159
30089164 Miskelly SJ, 218
525238 Mistlin A, 113
30076010 Mistry JJ, 211
559242 Mitcham PJ, 309
30114268 Mitchard JJ, 361
557522 Mitchell A, 221
561975 Mitchell A, 379
566184 Mitchell AA, 247
557065 Mitchell AG, 233
535991 Mitchell AP, 250
30066063 Mitchell AT, 217
24823615 Mitchell B, 175
558189 Mitchell CJ, 207
538990 Mitchell CK, 333
25233239 Mitchell DAG, 344
30074085 Mitchell DR, 307
30153520 Mitchell EJ, 243
30195968 Mitchell EW, 127
30153843 Mitchell FJG, 238
518158 Mitchell GI, 108
30169721 Mitchell HW, 182
30111554 Mitchell JAM, 219
30124733 Mitchell JE, 155
561542 Mitchell JL, 245
30216654 Mitchell KA, 361
561336 Mitchell LM, 260
24750388 Mitchell M, 210
24872977 Mitchell NJ, 217
551895 Mitchell PB, 273
563716 Mitchell PC, 306
512653 Mitchell PG, 113
30174986 Mitchell PG, 310
24735481 Mitchell PJ, 297
30133468 Mitchell RG, 236
W1059423 Mitchell SA, 217
564281 Mitchell SI, 310
561230 Mitchener PJ, 331
25015347 Mitchinson S, 162
24762294 Mitton R, 210
30058692 Miura AS, 274
30170094 Moag BG, 129
566209 Mobbs G, 361
555957 Mockridge NC, 306
549667 Moesel JS, 227
536337 Moffat AD, 113
565334 Moffat CF, 284

30215515	Moriarty JA, 328
30078465	Morizet DN, 226
25214770	Morley AC, 191
565790	Morley AM, 207
30127287	Morley J, 297
30128893	Morley JL, 337
25213084	Morley OJH, 144
30059912	Morley P, 306
506481	Morphet AN, 277
531505	Morphew RER, 179
558552	Morrell AH, 304
553756	Morrell C, 356
30074131	Morrell DJ, 178
24830594	Morrell DTP, 144
528083	Morris A, 379
532542	Morris A, 379
24866747	Morris AD, 217
Q1041203	Morris AED, 273
25021855	Morris AH, 252
30041538	Morris AJA, 310
558017	Morris AS, 241
517303	Morris AW, 309
C36320	Morris BL, 379
30153521	Morris C, 243
523687	Morris CP, 392
30147060	Morris CWJ, 129
30113476	Morris DF, 242
25028404	Morris DG, 210
30210977	Morris DN, 356
30215494	Morris E, 361
30238782	Morris EM, 361
553357	Morris GA, 139
519017	Morris GS, 276
30201497	Morris JAR, 332
30014978	Morris JDC, 284
563994	Morris JNC, 241
25203701	Morris LMJ, 170
542745	Morris NJ, 215
553881	Morris NJ, 273
25128643	Morris OF, 241
557562	Morris P, 379
561873	Morris PC, 299
564711	Morris PC, 321
30201504	Morris PDJ, 332
24618614	Morris RE, 379
530390	Morris RH, 113
25235225	Morris RJ, 201
30222220	Morris RL, 332
W1060940	Morris SE, 217
505313	Morris TH, 303
546558	Morris TPD, 164
547011	Morris W, 379
C93926	Morris W, 379
553720	Morris WA, 278
549114	Morris WG, 330
24848920	Morris WJF, 217
566396	Morris-Butler RJ, 245
30142850	Morrisey CS, 348
24853236	Morrison A, 210
559220	Morrison A, 221
25214656	Morrison AJ, 351
503623	Morrison AM, 278
548250	Morrison AW, 303
563484	Morrison D, 379
544841	Morrison G, 379
561979	Morrison JJ, 336
560502	Morrison KM, 347
531023	Morrison MCE, 266
553719	Morrison MW, 303
538913	Morrison PA, 335
25135058	Morrison RI, 344
	Morriss SJ, 305
C31273	Morrissey BA, 379
563646	Morrissey MP, 132
561800	Morrissey PL, 281
565181	Morrissey TG, 310
560475	Morrow JJ, 323
30115002	Morrow R, 202
25197716	Morse HR, 252
559757	Mort P, 181
30143084	Mortensen TFW, 146
25006566	Mortiboy MA, 210
25010044	Mortimer D, 201
548560	Mortimer D, 300
30166502	Mortimer DEJ, 201
563509	Mortimer HJ, 356
539770	Mortimer IS, 108
565337	Mortimer RT, 233
25005074	Mortimore AC, 252
30102783	Mortimore AL, 236
555263	Mortimore EA, 215
30089202	Mortlock CA, 307
550210	Mortlock CJ, 278
24462998	Morton AG, 331
564690	Morton C, 256
25029211	Morton CM, 222
544935	Morton CM, 230
30084409	Morton HJ, 210
561421	Morton JP, 333
547969	Morton MJ, 214
562058	Morton N, 356
548251	Morton NI, 198
566621	Morton RLS, 339
537516	Morton RS, 205
528175	Morton T, 379
555560	Morton-Race JP, 221
530521	Moseley CR, 309
558774	Moseley RJ, 139
545060	Moses JC, 320
30160322	Mosey HT, 351
546809	Moss AM, 341
529195	Moss AP, 230
558193	Moss CP, 233
551038	Moss DJ, 347
30082696	Moss EA, 344
24663166	Moss JD, 262
550525	Moss JE, 392
558252	Moss LC, 273
542057	Moss RG, 177
543321	Moss RJ, 233
562561	Moss RL, 348
532904	Moss S, 318
547508	Mossop A, 330
25231728	Mossop HEH, 125
25215525	Mossop JON, 131
25234755	Mossop TCH, 133
548606	Moth AS, 225
25201889	Motion A, 211
30175086	Mott DW, 361
559868	Mott NP, 148
539013	Mott RO, 314
506059	Motteram E, 356
30201506	Mottley LRG, 332
C35151	Mottram A, 379
547761	Mottram PB, 343
563995	Moukarzel NRK, 148
536321	Mould AJ, 214
30216807	Mould JR, 219
8423968	Mould JS, 356
30162711	Moulding SL, 319
536052	Mountain AJC, 244
30124666	Mountain TDE, 118
30124061	Mountford EG, 203
532011	Mountford TMP, 344
30032594	Mousley HJE, 202
Q1041150	Mousley N, 284
533094	Moverley GM, 230
30046888	Mowbray GA, 201
30146575	Mowbray RP, 226
30136468	Mowforth JCJ, 212
552446	Moxey PC, 164
543322	Moxham AW, 356
566404	Moxham PD, 207
30179973	Moxley J, 202
544374	Moxon CD, 233
565607	Moxon OM, 268
551334	Moy JSJ, 233
556908	Moy RJ, 245
24844265	Moyle AJ, 267
30174488	Moyle JD, 202
564803	Moyle SA, 281
30030417	Moynan FCB, 142
551712	Moynham A, 379
C37253	Moynham SA, 379
24738231	Moynihan J, 177
556142	Moyo PA, 338
30163028	Mrozicki A, 351
25024327	Muckle PS, 175
549583	Mudd MJ, 132
24753512	Mudd NI, 201
25233548	Muir CP, 337
30124667	Muir DC, 252
25144081	Muir GT, 180
563996	Muir GW, 153
546384	Muir PRD, 214
25018399	Muir PS, 361
555538	Muir RKS, 153
30169084	Muirhead A, 356
25200062	Muirhead AD, 252
24748646	Muirhead DC, 181
25230123	Mukhtar EA, 306
30028293	Mulcahy CWJ, 236
536896	Mulhern S, 233
W1058742	Mulholland KN, 263
538455	Mulholland LM, 319
530118	Mulholland RA, 214
30176625	Mulholland WA, 117
30010988	Mulira CWE, 147
562230	Mulira JJS, 174

N

O

560693 Owen I, 356
483426 Owen J, 356
538751 Owen KA, 214
W0823975 Owen KM, 263
24853598 Owen M, 210
518443 Owen M, 356
30129143 Owen M, 356
C27024 Owen MB, 380
557156 Owen MJ, 241
539328 Owen PD, 344
545217 Owen PFR, 319
546564 Owen PG, 249
W1056879 Owen RK, 344
559175 Owen SJ, 245
513544 Owen SP, 147
25230332 Owen TE, 252
24818212 Owens DM, 118
25234764 Owens JM, 217
24792620 Owens MD, 210
522002 Owers RC, 113
565143 Owers WEJ, 233
30143280 Owles DJ, 212
30180059 Oxborough RC, 332
561370 Oxford S, 380
25185820 Oxley MJ, 310
24769110 Oxley R, 344
W1062086 Oxley RHC, 211
24779541 Oxley SJ, 207
30222210 Oxnam BL, 332
558283 Ozanne RM, 333

P

24748765 Pace R, 215
554379 Pack AR, 199
551344 Pack DT, 184
25115699 Packer IR, 380
561681 Packer JE, 333
566134 Packer TW, 247
24830673 Pacter WR, 270
542503 Paden EL, 221
W1058575 Padgett GK, 268
509562 Padgett S, 277
30051995 Padgett TH, 135
24700474 Padley RP, 210
30117475 Pagden-Ratcliffe FAX, 117
524118 Page AG, 205
561160 Page CLJ, 245
513353 Page CST, 109
30079847 Page DJ, 356
563622 Page G, 331
558206 Page KA, 177
561280 Page KMA, 245
556001 Page N, 356
518166 Page NA, 113
558278 Page PRJ, 336
25031178 Page RG, 175
556014 Page RJ, 139
544964 Page RM, 278
30220920 Page VS, 351
531975 Pagent B, 380
546450 Paget DW, 330
549591 Pagett JA, 256
25125792 Pain CD, 217
30040410 Paine HDG, 125
566269 Painter H, 356
30166393 Painter HC, 218
556992 Painter MD, 221
30015612 Painter RK, 217
W1056618 Painter SE, 260
550780 Paintin EJ, 141
556450 Painting JC, 262
564623 Palastanga KV, 199
563656 Palfrey BL, 233
30180035 Palfrey JK, 307
549592 Palfrey RJ, 309
532348 Palfreyman R, 380
549880 Palin BJ, 268
30171559 Pall D, 336
551091 Pallett BC, 338
30155635 Pallett SJC, 242
30032026 Palma SC, 356
24803667 Palmer B, 217
551345 Palmer B, 233
30077207 Palmer BR, 273
541168 Palmer C, 197
543717 Palmer CH, 356
25210933 Palmer DEO, 380
25199480 Palmer DJ, 210
W1054033 Palmer EE, 243
560310 Palmer FN, 207
24797767 Palmer GW, 267
551801 Palmer JAE, 147
30057338 Palmer JFD, 182
549593 Palmer JGK, 197
533311 Palmer JV, 113
529552 Palmer M, 177
548258 Palmer MCA, 171
B8703878 Palmer MNH, 210
25214680 Palmer RPB, 212
558009 Palmer S, 356
527282 Palmer SP, 309
30094907 Palmer SR, 380
559654 Palmer TG, 199
24795343 Panayi AAT, 159
559655 Panayiotou JH, 262
25231732 Pang AYL, 247
534428 Pannell J, 380
30078548 Pannell RA, 223
550781 Pannett JGA, 221
30059790 Panter AD, 380
30145978 Pantoja EJ, 222
30236811 Papadopoulou C, 361
530125 Papenfus JR, 199
539092 Papworth JEJ, 245
30089438 Paradine RT, 237
511059 Paramore A, 281
30136012 Paranna V, 337
30180696 Pardoe AB, 223
565963 Pardoe R, 356
537473 Pardy DC, 113
30028599 Parfitt KD, 205
552450 Paris D, 278
527744 Paris HVI, 249
30044211 Park A, 252
554808 Park CK, 245
30199043 Park CL, 243
551046 Park CL, 244
30137248 Park CL, 335
30201399 Park DJ, 361
24870830 Park DWM, 154
24816913 Parke JG, 147
523955 Parker AG, 278
513925 Parker AG, 278
540061 Parker AJ, 230
30201503 Parker AN, 339
30141480 Parker B, 162
554797 Parker EM, 304
30180046 Parker F, 339
511892 Parker HJ, 205
30135974 Parker JCS, 201
30171566 Parker JRG, 133
C32790 Parker KL, 380
30075523 Parker LD, 211
30154324 Parker NC, 361
30201505 Parker OJ, 310
547418 Parker P, 380
517583 Parker PJ, 113
30046677 Parker RJ, 336
25018835 Parker SA, 237
564603 Parker SK, 262
W1039091 Parker VC, 242
C37703 Parker WAN, 304
551154 Parke-Robinson FS, 225
550801 Parke-Robinson JM, 259
557091 Parkes JR, 340
30057335 Parkes JRM, 237
24901216 Parkes KJ, 222
502220 Parkes NG, 309
543313 Parkes NM, 113
30047759 Parkes PE, 222
561218 Parkes TD, 233
30114644 Parkes TR, 142
528008 Parkhouse DAF, 113
558259 Parkin D, 380
556024 Parkin J, 380
548672 Parkinson AJ, 249
553367 Parkinson AJ, 215
30201507 Parkinson BS, 310
538095 Parkinson CEA, 197
30142170 Parkinson J, 361
25009737 Parkinson JW, 201
30045016 Parkinson RD, 328
524349 Parkinson RE, 109
W1058788 Parkinson RLL, 218
24968457 Parks CI, 306
30136649 Parks NL, 271
553093 Parks PT, 278
564003 Parkyn B, 124
561317 Parkyn RG, 330
P902692Y Parmenter AM, 222
563658 Parmenter RJ, 260
534152 Parnell CM, 347
24826148 Parnell GS, 210
30106747 Parr MF, 331
24853103 Parr MR, 218
536828 Parr RL, 278
25174554 Parr SA, 210
564414 Parr T, 380

Q

R

S

24553994 Smith AR, 334
25231406 Smith BA, 226
30090514 Smith BA, 385
30180037 Smith BC, 307
30040043 Smith BD, 238
30256821 Smith BD, 362
30104372 Smith BHR, 237
30127227 Smith BJ, 201
561367 Smith BJ, 282
25147712 Smith BR, 358
25221733 Smith BRJ, 210
549739 Smith C, 358
25043718 Smith CA, 263
556709 Smith CA, 246
8701684W Smith CAK, 285
25220799 Smith CD, 216
25032669 Smith CD, 327
549025 Smith CDW, 135
25229113 Smith CJ, 210
566138 Smith CJ, 182
550817 Smith CP, 279
547420 Smith D, 381
C29191 Smith D, 381
C36132 Smith D, 381
518957 Smith DA, 234
30017927 Smith DC, 175
558624 Smith DE, 316
30121943 Smith DE, 385
24878844 Smith DJ, 222
25174564 Smith DJ, 237
30194272 Smith DJ, 238
555583 Smith DJ, 251
566556 Smith DJ, 216
549026 Smith DK, 199
25028678 Smith DL, 252
24809845 Smith DN, 210
25198635 Smith DP, 222
505586 Smith DS, 381
30143800 Smith E, 385
30240806 Smith EJ, 362
555059 Smith ER, 199
30148557 Smith ES, 203
25182043 Smith ET, 263
526050 Smith ET, 347
556460 Smith EWM, 172
551525 Smith G, 381
557736 Smith G, 381
566095 Smith GA, 344
30030296 Smith GC, 228
562546 Smith GC, 310
25234833 Smith GD, 247
24725723 Smith GJ, 252
W0813555 Smith GJ, 252
W1052901 Smith GL, 257
25023361 Smith GR, 267
517219 Smith GS, 289, 349, 386
560776 Smith GV, 344
562568 Smith H, 358
30036134 Smith HC, 330
523838 Smith I, 381
551605 Smith I, 381
24678030 Smith IA, 252
539809 Smith ID, 220
30218004 Smith IJ, 322
550377 Smith IM, 336
555301 Smith JC, 159
556444 Smith JK, 136
24762078 Smith JL, 210
24738628 Smith JM, 201
24849552 Smith JN, 210
565098 Smith JR, 207
550818 Smith JRL, 135
511907 Smith JWG, 291
30082269 Smith KA, 212
566186 Smith KA, 260
526710 Smith KA, 358
30114088 Smith KB, 335
30201479 Smith KC, 332
561554 Smith KE, 269
564217 Smith KG, 331
24697460 Smith KN, 304
549933 Smith KN, 381
555780 Smith KP, 124
557134 Smith KR, 347
559356 Smith L, 348
510844 Smith L, 358
30184178 Smith L, 358
547146 Smith LC, 256
553408 Smith LF, 216
556808 Smith LJ, 199
512763 Smith LM, 306
W1056212 Smith LM, 344
30120061 Smith LP, 185
549955 Smith M, 334
504811 Smith M, 358
550951 Smith M, 381
551667 Smith M, 381
30106799 Smith MA, 172
536081 Smith MA, 199
30195307 Smith MC, 260
30048070 Smith MC, 385
557251 Smith MD, 392
24707871 Smith ME, 275
30018729 Smith MJ, 139
556555 Smith MJ, 207
563362 Smith MJ, 348
30201478 Smith MJE, 247
549616 Smith MJE, 208
30055910 Smith MJK, 339
547188 Smith MJT, 138
524375 Smith MJV, 114
543829 Smith MPN, 308
533745 Smith MR, 244
25216973 Smith MRS, 331
548702 Smith MT, 208
562876 Smith MT, 251
548014 Smith NA, 234
532214 Smith NC, 114, 266, 342
24540267 Smith NC, 331
510386 Smith NCRG, 279
30191121 Smith NE, 137
559469 Smith NF, 251
518187 Smith NP, 279
25147206 Smith OI, 325
30198209 Smith P, 228
25190366 Smith PA, 201
549155 Smith PD, 231
531543 Smith PG, 114
518507 Smith PH, 309
30153523 Smith PM, 252
539825 Smith PT, 231
24753793 Smith R, 282
P904468W Smith R, 269
503209 Smith R, 381
30050736 Smith RA, 258
562274 Smith RA, 154
537491 Smith RC, 231
30080478 Smith RD, 239
552833 Smith RD, 162
30067549 Smith RE, 274
561507 Smith RF, 234
25151002 Smith RG, 335
566329 Smith RH, 310
30172636 Smith RJ, 160
551368 Smith RJA, 128
559619 Smith RJR, 269
25008049 Smith RL, 201
25213495 Smith RM, 162
536513 Smith RM, 114
559479 Smith RM, 228
551369 Smith RP, 190
511517 Smith RR, 109
533127 Smith RV, 304
24670736 Smith S, 241
30043903 Smith SA, 218
543133 Smith SA, 308
533299 Smith SA, 358
30087923 Smith SA, 381
550819 Smith SG, 249
559223 Smith SH, 334
25210932 Smith SJ, 218
551370 Smith SM, 216
25019635 Smith SM, 381
24828277 Smith SP, 210
540343 Smith SR, 164
553016 Smith Straney TA, 334
546900 Smith TA, 148
527278 Smith TD, 329
530627 Smith TFS, 305
563750 Smith TR, 321
539749 Smith V, 381
30047393 Smith WM, 203
30148071 Smith-Cooper RJ, 212
516516 Smyth-Osborne EA, 38, 48, 107, 117, 118
24870993 Smithurst PA, 251
534168 Smyth AMG, 290
565369 Smyth BP, 175
551371 Smyth C, 256
C039826L Smyth CR, 334
30070493 Smyth GI, 180
30030407 Smyth GM, 201
562426 Smyth GS, 347
539207 Smyth HS, 240
30081132 Smyth J, 323
538039 Smyth JD, 306
0091548H Smyth PR, 321
565825 Smyth SR, 282
30040223 Smyth ZW, 155

558818 Stubbs PJ, 218
30080680 Stubbs RV, 307
564335 Stubley DJ, 310
30161061 Stuckes D, 146
C36912 Studd ME, 382
30170101 Studwell JG, 226
550591 Stumbles P, 358
30073100 Sturcbecher JJ, 382
530571 Sturgeon MJM, 114
24748309 Sturgeon RFD, 237
553689 Sturges TM, 382
25199934 Sturgess JP, 202
30091620 Sturley DT, 172
565374 Sturman NP, 263
536345 Sturrock AJW, 114
531306 Sturrock CGF, 321
25227129 Sturt PD, 358
544997 Stuthridge SR, 205
24839258 Styles JA, 133
497599 Stythe JN, 277
21168731 Subba B, 256
30128236 Subba Row NC, 238
30186819 Suchy HJ, 358
30205725 Sudbury IA, 362
25017778 Suddaby MC, 210
535058 Suddaby MJ, 282
538112 Sudding CJ, 358
30150002 Sudheer SP, 336
565420 Sudlow AM, 124
30055337 Sudlow JG, 118
30124668 Sudworth CP, 222
30215662 Suenson Taylor HK, 362
30051623 Suff HAJ, 239
30222231 Suffolk HF, 332
30201483 Suffolk OW, 332
554184 Sugdon GR, 234
24725668 Sugrue JC, 252
C32593 Sullivan B, 385
559113 Sullivan EJP, 347
551379 Sullivan FK, 251
30132279 Sullivan M, 210
30254593 Sullivan NS, 362
24726134 Summerell IG, 234
30198801 Summerfield AD, 362
25219065 Summers BA, 337
30137363 Summers EB, 269
30122119 Summers J, 382
25223871 Summers MP, 310
561151 Summers PA, 348
553888 Summers RH, 334
30141375 Summers SJ, 358
536166 Summersgill SA, 231
30169277 Sumner CP, 218
24898288 Sumner LA, 260
30161067 Sumsion PH, 328
30187963 Sunder AK, 335
535059 Sunderland DRH, 231
530409 Sunderland GT, 335
540724 Sunderland JDV, 231
30043793 Sunley CA, 212
30036138 Sunner CF, 358
562321 Surgey AW, 336
565831 Surman KE, 252
25208337 Sutch JA, 274
551684 Sutcliffe A, 362
557572 Sutcliffe IJF, 307
30231431 Sutcliffe JA, 351
30122369 Sutcliffe N, 336
559924 Sutcliffe PA, 216
509220 Sutcliffe RWH, 392
532800 Sutherland AG, 321
30124727 Sutherland HCJ, 385
25215581 Sutherland JGO, 191
532607 Sutherland KG, 311
541180 Sutherland NJ, 315
30114883 Sutherland PF, 212
550073 Sutherland RD, 199
527590 Sutherland RJH, 382
544118 Sutherland SB, 234
25161184 Sutherland VG, 263
544425 Sutthery EP, 162
553874 Sutton B, 293
558231 Sutton B, 314
551960 Sutton G, 268
30011684 Sutton JC, 237
538356 Sutton JJE, 327
560977 Sutton MJ, 251
517854 Sutton NC, 314
30205251 Sutton O, 160
556113 Sutton RJ, 330
25225717 Suzuki TA, 182
25197739 Swaby MS, 285
546587 Swain AW, 205
25004757 Swain LJ, 133
560978 Swales AC, 234
25211285 Swales HE, 160
566648 Swales P, 382
556091 Swales R, 358
W1058828 Swallow AM, 358
549630 Swallow CW, 315
30096850 Swan B, 382
561483 Swan D, 382
C27358 Swan D, 382
560979 Swan RJ, 234
557573 Swan-Ingrey LTY, 199
556468 Swann AC, 162
25219826 Swann CM, 285
514037 Swann DJL, 277
553414 Swann MA, 181
544561 Swann S, 382
543988 Swannell AD, 199
536735 Swannell MJ, 282
30193085 Swanney AJ, 382
30089404 Swannick JT, 243
30061687 Swanston JC, 313
30089180 Swanwick CJ, 212
W1064011 Swarbrick C, 210
25182127 Swarbrick DA, 182
30193950 Swarbrick RJ, 350
30177709 Swash S, 385
30137870 Swatridge BL, 218
520743 Swayne DA, 299
523425 Swayne JAC, 313
549631 Sweeney AK, 169
25232064 Sweeney CC, 247
24683321 Sweeney PJ, 170
24850474 Sweeney RA, 324
24757307 Sweeney TD, 222
558555 Sweet AM, 154
497528 Sweet TJ, 304
536736 Sweeting C, 249
30170896 Sweetman GE, 162
549632 Sweny DMH, 282
560541 Swift AG, 315
25023045 Swift CJ, 237
25174565 Swift DJ, 285
550483 Swift EM, 216
30041524 Swift EMH, 358
543074 Swift J, 114, 162
533656 Swift JFP, 37, 107, 177
560980 Swift NA, 234
532545 Swinburne D, 358
30245941 Swinchin-Rew GJ, 362
30195891 Swindells SFC, 191
30146933 Swingler EP, 253
30210998 Swinhoe A, 155
558384 Swinn SP, 228
529850 Swinyard LFM, 114
562391 Switzer R, 358
25186100 Syfret ER, 311
30052462 Sykes AM, 358
503611 Sykes B, 382
550484 Sykes CR, 321
526898 Sykes FC, 114
30067880 Sykes FL, 202
505526 Sykes JP, 290
535169 Sykes K, 358
533762 Sykes MP, 114
30136951 Sykes SN, 331
24868989 Sykes SS, 252
30024712 Symes A, 260
536833 Symes C, 358
543852 Symmons JE, 304
555509 Symonds GE, 234
551380 Symonds TJ, 231
559692 Symons J, 234
554185 Symons MJ, 251
554376 Symons MJ, 234
30251911 Syms MP, 362
532161 Szabo AN, 205
512833 Szabo CLW, 392
564661 Szczerbiuk A, 199
30139356 Szczyglowska JM, 212
30161062 Szczyglowski CP, 350
30039522 Szkoda JKT, 202
25015175 Szymanski DM, 170

T

549633 Taaffe KD, 177
561485 Tabb L, 358
564197 Tabbinor P, 348
531180 Taberner A, 347
558023 Taberner L, 347
559502 Tabner K, 246
30184371 Tabor TS, 218
535061 Tabrah A, 220
24901689 Tacey LA, 202
30190080 Tachauer GJ, 362

25143191 Taffs AJ, 310
547191 Taffs J, 263
562285 Taft DJR, 282
565832 Tagg OJ, 177
30090423 Taggart SM, 223
554159 Tai NRM, 114
538767 Tait A, 205
544531 Tait AG, 153
30124573 Tait ARP, 237
24759423 Tait D, 154
557731 Tait G, 154
30095061 Tait JR, 154
563672 Tait KA, 251
537827 Tait KM, 311
563698 Talbot A, 251
30156741 Talbot CJ, 348
25196611 Talbot CTD, 285
564859 Talbot JD, 282
30040261 Talbot S, 243
543351 Talbot-King PF, 199
544234 Talbot-New GE, 279, 385
516039 Talbot-Rice RH, 54, 107
24822773 Taliku M, 222
30080148 Tallowin S, 247
25155028 Talman JS, 237
21168295 Tamang B, 188
21168708 Tamang G, 188
21168148 Tamang H, 185
21168287 Tamang I, 188
21167317 Tamang P, 188
21168762 Tamang P, 186
555603 Tamplin DN, 260
549687 Tams Gregg JS, 347
30212207 Tams RS, 239
30237452 Tan XH, 362
548546 Tancock SC, 304
556470 Taneborne P, 128
554904 Tang AP, 331
30183699 Tankard JM, 351
30055906 Tankaria MF, 253
553525 Tankaria-Clifford LA, 263
W1052471 Tannahill VJ, 342
565164 Tannassee TO, 337
560351 Tanner DJ, 129
30066699 Tanner J, 358
564199 Tansey PE, 348
30201535 Tansley EJ, 332
30124669 Tant SC, 222
Tarsa MJ, 44
30055907 Tarbox DC, 218
531097 Targett BF, 114
548647 Tarmey NT, 279
30255739 Tarn RJ, 362
24783632 Tarry KGJ, 322
493947 Tasker D, 382
30111705 Tasker HS, 339
30216513 Tasker RB, 212
546589 Tasker RR, 234
24754995 Tate K, 225
24569525 Tatler TR, 382
W1041809 Tatters K, 257
563121 Taverner K, 382
562887 Tawlks DE, 251
520720 Taxis CL, 304
30069632 Tayler PJ, 263
548434 Taylor A, 114
555443 Taylor AJ, 270
564186 Taylor AJ, 241
533158 Taylor AJ, 333
562888 Taylor ALA, 199
30053612 Taylor AM, 202
24656244 Taylor AP, 139
509582 Taylor AP, 277
545602 Taylor AR, 199
500684 Taylor AS, 382
511913 Taylor AW, 279
24773599 Taylor B, 127
561793 Taylor B, 246
30171483 Taylor BD, 362
30063307 Taylor BJ, 282
30222232 Taylor BM, 310
24829496 Taylor BN, 257
25027818 Taylor BR, 147
548514 Taylor BRG, 251
30131765 Taylor C, 362
545000 Taylor CA, 282
24863257 Taylor CD, 241
25218593 Taylor CJ, 226
548576 Taylor CJ, 246
W1030085 Taylor CK, 257
25099736 Taylor CM, 257
25024660 Taylor CR, 237
563699 Taylor CW, 237
549716 Taylor D, 358
554235 Taylor D, 382
24887505 Taylor DB, 202
24866776 Taylor DB, 285
30073041 Taylor DC, 382
545120 Taylor DM, 336
550130 Taylor DM, 347
C93448 Taylor DM, 382
24722964 Taylor DR, 216
560352 Taylor DS, 234
25233833 Taylor DT, 239
545833 Taylor DT, 330
563664 Taylor EC, 263
30196484 Taylor ED, 243
30199072 Taylor EG, 362
30205447 Taylor EH, 351
30076634 Taylor ER, 243
556818 Taylor ET, 199
30222158 Taylor FC, 318
30219304 Taylor FIE, 382
562287 Taylor FJ, 234
30217933 Taylor FME, 243
543867 Taylor G, 197
25004988 Taylor GJ, 237
546047 Taylor GJ, 263
25232518 Taylor GJ, 362
30060886 Taylor GJ, 382
30094320 Taylor GM, 385
30080327 Taylor HJG, 226
30120144 Taylor HM, 172
566394 Taylor HM, 247
30013720 Taylor IA, 253
557609 Taylor IP, 307
30137439 Taylor J, 165
562368 Taylor J, 382
540400 Taylor JE, 279
532119 Taylor JJ, 305
30030392 Taylor JR, 142
24831815 Taylor JS, 210
540546 Taylor JW, 162
557574 Taylor K, 234
24707498 Taylor K, 282
30245457 Taylor KL, 362
30067451 Taylor M, 382
25186400 Taylor MC, 237
545601 Taylor MG, 231
549635 Taylor MI, 241
30186721 Taylor MM, 362
25002275 Taylor MP, 285
24789641 Taylor MW, 210
24648734 Taylor MWM, 234
562599 Taylor N, 246
540954 Taylor NA, 240
25174566 Taylor NJ, 216
25205303 Taylor NJ, 135
557758 Taylor NL, 216
24726584 Taylor NS, 322
W0807776 Taylor NW, 260
30192264 Taylor OW, 212
24899616 Taylor PA, 137
548558 Taylor PK, 382
30108065 Taylor PMG, 218
545001 Taylor PR, 251
540725 Taylor RC, 114
30031289 Taylor RC, 358
30033104 Taylor REB, 337
550319 Taylor RI, 199
528953 Taylor RM, 159
536278 Taylor RN, 251
30188230 Taylor RR, 243
30047878 Taylor RW, 285
25009960 Taylor S, 144
523976 Taylor S, 382
550100 Taylor S, 382
30153694 Taylor SA, 331
30166489 Taylor SA, 362
24876583 Taylor SB, 117
30185391 Taylor SC, 350
515461 Taylor SJ, 251
526586 Taylor SJ, 159
30201471 Taylor SJ, 310
30206316 Taylor SJ, 328
24907642 Taylor SK, 226
25233383 Taylor SL, 182
25212480 Taylor SR, 154
30175579 Taylor SR, 336
25205051 Taylor TDA, 162
531546 Taylor TDK, 199
565833 Taylor TJ, 256
30146947 Taylor TJ, 362
555302 Taylor WP, 216
25215657 Taylor-Dickson FWH, 133
30071373 Taylor-Rudd PS, 385
563018 Teague R, 330
562488 Teague-Hellon EM, 347
548292 Teale NA, 190

30146934 Thompson LM, 239
30166384 Thompson LN, 260
30128257 Thompson M, 260
560036 Thompson M, 382
24678949 Thompson MA, 234
24862421 Thompson MJ, 210
564748 Thompson MJ, 266
D977674Q Thompson MJ, 358
562291 Thompson MR, 282
511917 Thompson NF, 221
30083344 Thompson NW, 382
24802318 Thompson PA, 307
566588 Thompson PCD, 241
561229 Thompson PI, 341
24702243 Thompson PL, 172
515788 Thompson PRC, 197
30120204 Thompson RE, 142
25174568 Thompson RM, 218
30065272 Thompson S, 203
30100468 Thompson SA, 385
30011002 Thompson SC, 253
30087623 Thompson SL, 257
24869776 Thompson SN, 191
505439 Thompson T, 382
30057339 Thompson WF, 285
Q1043391 Thompson ZCJ, 273
30044432 Thompson-Burt AR, 237
30222234 Thompson-Darch RA, 339
559697 Thoms CF, 208
550602 Thomsett M, 382
527174 Thomsett SC, 114
25022293 Thomson A, 253
30023237 Thomson AF, 358
559293 Thomson AK, 256
556822 Thomson ELS, 234
30112278 Thomson HSC, 191
564739 Thomson JW, 260
30091697 Thomson LFS, 182
563027 Thomson M, 382
30123896 Thomson MJG, 202
527198 Thomson R, 382
531040 Thomson RJ, 109, 189
30123366 Thomson RL, 203
555307 Thomson SR, 199
30028306 Thorburn BJ, 218
30079254 Thorburn NMA, 307
25201730 Thorburn RWJ, 182
503948 Thorman JP, 298
539051 Thorman W, 334
509009 Thorn N, 358
30042694 Thorn OR, 271
560360 Thorne ADG, 241
556023 Thorne AM, 382
540729 Thorne AR, 249
25016753 Thorne BF, 202
30222235 Thorne BJ, 339
24797405 Thorne GI, 202
24792434 Thorne JM, 285
25198851 Thorne MR, 210
561199 Thorne N, 382
30068655 Thorne RLP, 131
525426 Thornhill MJ, 114
566309 Thornhill RJ, 244
555759 Thornley K, 334
527313 Thornley MT, 205
552675 Thornley P, 382
30173935 Thornton AC, 385
550957 Thornton AJ, 317
30155453 Thornton EH, 127
25214571 Thornton GB, 285
30030227 Thornton IJ, 160
30110756 Thornton KP, 385
30010970 Thornton MJ, 222
30160266 Thornton MJ, 312
533573 Thornton NPS, 277
30199774 Thornton RT, 203
561538 Thornton TG, 197
25232840 Thorogood MD, 170
25224980 Thorogood WJ, 218
30164250 Thorp SJ, 212
25198701 Thorpe A, 226
558822 Thorpe AK, 234
564049 Thorpe AN, 307
535698 Thorpe DM, 169
30092862 Thorpe E, 382
512370 Thorpe MA, 244
538655 Thorpe NB, 114
512961 Thorpe PJ, 114
513954 Thorpe RP, 249
C33618 Thorpe RS, 382
565928 Threader I, 382
556471 Throp KE, 234
529581 Thurgood AM, 114
543398 Thurley MR, 304
522874 Thurlow RD, 114
547195 Thurstan JHF, 144
528602 Thursz JCM, 249
562894 Thwaite MJ, 181
523906 Thwaites JM, 221
24882022 Tibbetts GR, 285
30106221 Tibbitts CHS, 243
30137816 Tibbitts GWS, 137
30172211 Tibble PD, 182
537094 Tibbles AM, 347
517325 Tickell CL, 38, 107, 204, 349
24830996 Tickle SJ, 170
24713549 Tickner DFW, 199
541099 Tickner M, 234
24818405 Tickner SA, 260
25026004 Tidman DG, 202
562371 Tidy S, 358
30055908 Tidy TI, 385
554232 Tierney LE, 347
30183882 Tiffin JPR, 264
30217493 Tigwell PJ, 203
551166 Tilbrook JR, 295
559700 Tilbury TAG, 256
25025042 Tilford NG, 226
C30412 Till J, 382
24705400 Till JS, 210
540069 Till TPO, 144
30161756 Tillard OJB, 146
30059900 Tilley JA, 202
518516 Tilley MN, 279
30219782 Tilley MR, 271
24896850 Tillman MA, 210
25140704 Tillotson S, 139
548516 Tilney AMA, 135
565061 Tilsley MW, 251
24875803 Timlett TJ, 182
557718 Timmermann JP, 307
562292 Timmermann TP, 322
539668 Timmis JRH, 114
539722 Timms G, 324
C20442 Timney MJ, 382
517593 Timothy JR, 114
24808085 Tims DF, 131
30079601 Tin GN, 322
561224 Tindale AP, 234
30141802 Ting RE, 358
531552 Tingey L, 114
548295 Tingey PJ, 169
527175 Tink JD, 153
554699 Tinlin SK, 231
24762364 Tinnion J, 216
24781393 Tinniswood A, 251
514423 Tinsley I, 277
546649 Tippett MD, 282
30175370 Tippett TJ, 218
30155727 Tipping M, 337
24841270 Tisbury SJ, 191
30130227 Tisdale MB, 328
561368 Tisshaw C, 347
519058 Tisshaw CC, 382
30199657 Titchen JEP, 362
555761 Titchener JA, 314
538189 Titheridge DA, 309
30221097 Titman BR, 119
545401 Tizard MJ, 248
30201765 Tizick A, 307
30192432 Toase C, 344
C36818 Tobin KM, 385
30046899 Tod WMC, 137
30209613 Todd A, 337
30051704 Todd A, 382
557578 Todd AP, 185
Q1062539 Todd AR, 337
513646 Todd BJ, 358
25128302 Todd EMC, 282
537219 Todd M, 114
564913 Todd NS, 228
25234901 Todd OJ, 238
525829 Todd RC, 251
W1065365 Todhunter P, 237
30180040 Tognarelli LMJ, 307
515573 Tognarelli WG, 340
558234 Toland DC, 251
547728 Toley R, 358
564389 Tollemache TAH, 144
30011954 Tollerfield JC, 247
559932 Tolley PK, 197
537530 Tomalin D, 358
522694 Tomaszewski N, 358
25219343 Tomaszewski NA, 210
531871 Tombleson P, 197
542415 Tomczyk AJ, 392
564482 Tome Da Silva CA, 228
530924 Tomes SC, 114

532324 Tomkins BJH, 190
W0802232 Tomkins M, 331
24627743 Tomkinson DM, 208
562432 Tomlin G, 295
549037 Tomlin NKG, 153
30016320 Tomlin S, 285
30022899 Tomlinson DM, 164
24862019 Tomlinson GM, 257
30155608 Tomlinson JM, 212
523907 Tomlinson RK, 205
30214619 Tomlyn IM, 344
548834 Tomlyn MTH, 224
24869729 Tommony CL, 285
30089198 Toms NR, 212
551920 Tomsett DJP, 339
25210952 Tomsett GC, 210
30242254 Toner H, 362
538122 Toney MA, 114
30015648 Tongs THJ, 210
512517 Tonkins RM, 279
540731 Tonkins WRJ, 231
30128237 Tonks GHM, 219
561785 Tonks PRG, 216
24867239 Tonner JA, 382
30130714 Tooey GVB, 382
561089 Toogood OJ, 211
30080449 Tookey DRL, 239
Q1045165 Toole DS, 274
509586 Toomey RHD, 41, 109
562293 Toop SL, 241
562348 Tootal DAC, 266
30089140 Tooth SAJ, 253
30155468 Tooze JP, 203
547550 Tooze P, 382
30080526 Tope DE, 218
510397 Topham CME, 392
30189947 Topham ME, 192
542964 Topham N, 358
24692404 Topliss KA, 256
554734 Topott JMK, 273
563020 Topping A, 234
30144912 Topping AJ, 253
30137446 Topping MG, 155
24831306 Topps GJ, 310
542375 Torbet JD, 249
25200558 Torbett N, 222
543083 Torbica M, 313
565838 Torp-Petersen ND, 344
30048258 Torrance JP, 382
30036715 Torrance JRE, 154
30053502 Torrens-Spence DJ, 129
30084711 Torrens-Spence JP, 129
30047762 Torrens-Spence K, 243
531991 Torrington NSR, 282
551502 Tortoishell D, 169
565378 Tory LHW, 129
C34820 Toseland AR, 382
30062930 Toseland CM, 385
547196 Tosh WM, 225
543625 Totten AJ, 114, 227
561647 Tough C, 382
30150571 Touton AM, 202
30138839 Tovey JD, 253
24666783 Tovey JS, 324
30192786 Tovey LJ, 358
25232727 Tovey MN, 165
25037511 Tovey SC, 222
518965 Tower WJ, 144
536376 Towers JM, 303
24650658 Towers RT, 322
561431 Towes RJW, 202
25070397 Towl MI, 257
558479 Towler HP, 273
25233246 Towler TJH, 154
30024117 Town JT, 237
542245 Townell SM, 382
546954 Townend AAR, 172
561720 Townend AH, 181
30251946 Townend B, 362
527607 Townend CJ, 290
552655 Townend MSM, 304
30145424 Townley DM, 358
556823 Townrow JN, 129
543357 Townsend JPC, 343
25237862 Townsend MS, 144
30080745 Townsend RC, 172
552502 Townsend SN, 234
C30503 Toy DJ, 382
30192262 Toye BTG, 243
30078049 Toye JWA, 382
C36003 Toze AP, 382
547198 Toze JE, 214
30112920 Tracey BRN, 142
30028955 Tracey DC, 260
30117088 Tracey JR, 165
546053 Tracey SR, 240
510870 Tracy RH, 221
30115298 Trafford D, 202
30146935 Tran J, 239
553872 Tranter P, 382
551153 Travers I, 382
518966 Travers MPM, 162
30150427 Travers NET, 238
24815403 Travis D, 175
W1058377 Travis HEH, 237
562294 Trayhurn JR, 222
30103200 Treasure CM, 154
25222249 Treasure GJ, 202
543487 Tredget AD, 244
565887 Treeby I, 382
557034 Treffry-Kingdom MJ, 208
551144 Trehane G, 282
25218850 Trehane JM, 175
G901151V Treharne A, 358
542796 Treharne JS, 249
562897 Treliving ERG, 282
30119038 Tremaine J, 308
565379 Tremelling MJ, 216
552181 Tremelling RT, 330
533881 Tremewan S, 358
545002 Trengove IR, 251
24742044 Trengove NJ, 216
562672 Trescothick-Martin JR, 291
24878001 Tresidder SJ, 382
564340 Trevelion SL, 309
563214 Trevena N, 382
25213505 Trevis RJ, 202
30120076 Trezise CH, 160
24869671 Triandafilou D, 175
559473 Tribe AD, 251
24916890 Tribelnig SA, 339
30252766 Tricker BG, 362
30256233 Trigg JL, 362
560713 Trimby C, 358
24710316 Trinick CJ, 295
30181030 Trippier JL, 310
566170 Triska DL, 282
542279 Tristham PE, 273
30125320 Troeller M, 243
30054684 Tromans KS, 382
566590 Troth TD, 246
30053197 Trott JS, 237
562468 Trott MR, 297
543193 Trott R, 358
24656436 Troughton DM, 297
518199 Troughton JBM, 279
C33186 Troughton T, 382
30040761 Trounce RB, 307
561310 Trow CR, 246
533728 Trow K, 290
562336 Trower CM, 273
541391 Trower DKP, 220
565905 Troy DC, 382
553561 Truby DC, 382
25037872 Trueman LA, 260
548296 Truett AJE, 181
559243 Trump MT, 334
30207246 Trundle C, 327
543060 Trunks A, 382
30148034 Trunks ZJ, 385
546621 Truscott J, 382
557268 Truscott R, 273
25026733 Truscott ST, 243
562533 Truscott TD, 307
30015601 Trypanis GAF, 131
30137792 Tuck AAD, 239
526194 Tuck JJH, 114
30178108 Tuck MA, 358
513958 Tucker AV, 114
24686790 Tucker CS, 310
562027 Tucker DJK, 382
538533 Tucker G, 382
559702 Tucker RJ, 172
25185533 Tucker S, 218
25172618 Tucker TA, 237
C36749 Tucker TK, 382
W1058849 Tucker VA, 247
24652046 Tuckett HM, 291
30148381 Tudge K, 362
25231516 Tudhope RG, 216
25198378 Tudor MN, 237
30011973 Tuffin AT, 285
560649 Tugendhat TGJ, 343
30027220 Tugwell REA, 226
495819 Tuhey KMF, 382
549041 Tuke RSP, 315
30058675 Tulett AG, 202
25199842 Tulloch WJL, 146
544161 Tully JR, 342

U

V

W

564053 Walker JWC, 208
25216883 Walker JWR, 180
C35031 Walker K, 382
25028808 Walker L, 237
564939 Walker L, 347
481887 Walker of Aldringham M, 106
24803124 Walker MA, 208
30087148 Walker MP, 239
562301 Walker MP, 208
545605 Walker MPM, 169
553816 Walker N, 382
520724 Walker NA, 308
547501 Walker NM, 246
564811 Walker PA, 234
537552 Walker PAJ, 115
30116617 Walker PF, 218
30113105 Walker RA, 312
24710364 Walker RD, 129
536834 Walker RG, 205
25194174 Walker RP, 178
564674 Walker SA, 285
538839 Walker SD, 340
W1056536 Walker SLJ, 362
30080454 Walker SM, 264
541865 Walker SR, 308
30139278 Walker TA, 223
30030385 Walker TA, 285
566326 Walker W, 358
566558 Walker W, 382
557382 Walker WA, 214
557132 Walker-Cousins JTM, 344
25204437 Walker-Mcclimens JS, 202
25035640 Walkinshaw MR, 222
560797 Walkley PJ, 319
30014914 Walkworth JL, 211
30015521 Wall AMF, 218
547084 Wall CM, 246
25182235 Wall D, 218
30014968 Wall DA, 178
497536 Wall P, 106, 349
25185550 Wall RM, 218
560153 Wall S, 159
554812 Wall WD, 246
549309 Wallace A, 358
501712 Wallace AR, 392
566250 Wallace AW, 311
518204 Wallace CP, 115
538882 Wallace D, 358
24726152 Wallace DJ, 237
24755398 Wallace G, 154
25128699 Wallace G, 218
562063 Wallace GA, 330
559706 Wallace HAR, 304
24710990 Wallace HK, 274
555316 Wallace IS, 251
565063 Wallace JVO, 251
546056 Wallace K, 234
562021 Wallace K, 382
30045673 Wallace LDA, 223
544817 Wallace PJ, 205
24755916 Wallace R, 241
25216103 Wallace RS, 191
559393 Wallace WSI, 304
505603 Wallen R, 382
549396 Wallen R, 382
24453633 Waller G, 323
25166448 Waller GK, 222
560988 Waller HD, 199
30011032 Waller JF, 211
25238427 Waller JM, 285
490174 Waller R, 358
555317 Waller WJ, 260
30170895 Walley JF, 203
25210924 Wallis DJ, 218
511082 Wallis G, 279
30222240 Wallis JA, 310
25056267 Wallis PA, 263
30123369 Wallis PF, 253
24870881 Wallis RCJ, 382
556829 Wallis TE, 234
25231736 Walls JS, 247
30138791 Walsh A, 155
535067 Walsh AD, 279
W1060201 Walsh CA, 263
561650 Walsh CA, 282
531454 Walsh CJ, 234
514837 Walsh CNP, 199
560394 Walsh EW, 208
565385 Walsh GSA, 314
30030390 Walsh JA, 160
24762984 Walsh JP, 216
30138507 Walsh JP, 202
560481 Walsh MP, 347
534319 Walsh MW, 330
5205030K Walsh P, 330
25032144 Walsh V, 218
549979 Walsh VJ, 208
30120799 Walsha MJ, 310
30109786 Walsh-Woolcott MJD, 135
30154977 Walter HA, 226
30072095 Walter J, 237
30146936 Walter RM, 339
30237019 Walters AL, 228
553221 Walters B, 162
30182404 Walters BJ, 239
553426 Walters GM, 260
555614 Walters JD, 199
25213294 Walters JM, 164
30037110 Walters KR, 382
24877302 Walters MD, 285
30022736 Walters ML, 162
543387 Walters PL, 244
30073076 Walters PR, 305
522067 Walters RC, 304
548517 Walters SJ, 127
30127074 Walters SL, 269
513059 Walton ACD, 290
546847 Walton ID, 382
30210714 Walton JJ, 334
508250 Walton MR, 279
564937 Walton RA, 382
30115028 Walton SAB, 139
559751 Walton SK, 169
559707 Walton TJC, 216
533200 Walton-Knight RJ, 109
563515 Walton-Prince SJ, 181
30037057 Walton-Rees LW, 129
30011053 Wane CM, 199
30214928 Wantling AR, 362
30077872 Warburton AJ, 253
30239013 Warburton S, 265
566298 Warburton T, 295
25242726 Ward AL, 211
30055904 Ward AL, 237
30190140 Ward AP, 223
25185586 Ward APJ, 253
565501 Ward B, 358
24678638 Ward D, 253
30120237 Ward DC, 162
30175931 Ward DG, 226
558503 Ward DJ, 341
536114 Ward FN, 303
524223 Ward G, 333
532666 Ward G, 335
24716757 Ward GC, 260
556475 Ward GP, 221
548632 Ward JL, 295
557583 Ward JWS, 241
W1064009 Ward KL, 253
549629 Ward L, 333
30076489 Ward LR, 211
24655007 Ward MA, 310
C35599 Ward NB, 382
559353 Ward NF, 382
541798 Ward NJ, 244
W0808145 Ward NL, 331
30078775 Ward PA, 162
24728083 Ward PA, 382
559071 Ward PJC, 330
25174573 Ward PW, 253
25004682 Ward R, 257
30236186 Ward R, 362
30133470 Ward RM, 223
557786 Ward S, 199
559982 Ward S, 382
549043 Ward SJA, 136
C33526 Ward SM, 382
C35632 Ward SMB, 382
30199265 Ward SR, 212
546868 Ward TJ, 309
W1062335 Wardall EL, 202
C29457 Ward-Davies W, 382
30194056 Wardell BA, 239
30202518 Wardell S, 239
30222241 Wardell ZA, 339
526428 Wardlaw R, 49, 107, 186
25222560 Wardle DP, 202
553748 Wardle MS, 347
504983 Wardle RN, 320
W1044654 Wardman A, 382
25040816 Wardman JS, 211
563705 Ware JK, 237
30132138 Ware M, 382
540816 Ware MJ, 249
527385 Ware RE, 304
565873 Wareham AP, 242
548306 Wareing AM, 181
542060 Warhurst CI, 205

556838 Wilde APT, 164
550844 Wilde BM, 174
552108 Wilde GD, 246
514338 Wilde LM, 340
W1048104 Wilde TK, 238
24879912 Wildey LD, 172
531271 Wilding GK, 383
25003568 Wilding M, 253
545713 Wildish JD, 297
521721 Wildish TCL, 115
30087453 Wildman PC, 263
564750 Wiles PA, 268
553512 Wiles RE, 136
553443 Wiles SP, 136
518548 Wiley AGC, 279
30131890 Wiley JJD, 228
24748241 Wilford MD, 216
555326 Wilkes ASJ, 260
516050 Wilkes NCB, 231
30039582 Wilkins D, 247
564288 Wilkins IHR, 256
538880 Wilkins QM, 256
24680232 Wilkins RW, 307
534756 Wilkinson A, 358
542383 Wilkinson AJ, 329
25186728 Wilkinson BJ, 191
30089143 Wilkinson BP, 253
564683 Wilkinson CA, 260
30168313 Wilkinson CJP, 155
25031510 Wilkinson D, 162
C28021 Wilkinson G, 362
25230124 Wilkinson GCH, 139
542935 Wilkinson GH, 329
528966 Wilkinson GP, 277
535125 Wilkinson HJP, 197
30118556 Wilkinson JH, 211
562924 Wilkinson KL, 246
564684 Wilkinson KS, 211
30130140 Wilkinson LJ, 358
30040666 Wilkinson LM, 351
30181033 Wilkinson MJ, 310
549860 Wilkinson MN, 135
543723 Wilkinson MR, 205
518720 Wilkinson NW, 383
564877 Wilkinson PAH, 246
25109765 Wilkinson PR, 326
502504 Wilkinson RK, 308
25131819 Wilkinson RS, 304
25019105 Wilkinson RT, 257
30202686 Wilkinson S, 307
562388 Wilkinson S, 383
547551 Wilkinson S, 282
W0815663 Wilkinson SA, 257
527656 Wilkinson SE, 321
24852628 Wilkinson SR, 202
30123251 Wilkinson TM, 285
507072 Wilks CL, 204
30077434 Wilks EP, 125
564060 Wilks NE, 208
30141405 Wilks PH, 226
552516 Willcocks RD, 234
30113449 Willcox CJ, 243
556840 Willcox EMG, 177
30038250 Willcox JJ, 133
W1061472 Willcox R, 263
W1058831 Willcox-Jones AE, 263
30089191 Willden JAG, 219
548775 Willdridge DJ, 246
559844 Willett CJ, 331
24844183 Willetts MA, 182
30195049 Willetts MJ, 178
543690 Willey DA, 268
25233377 Willey DJ, 318
30140638 Willey JS, 202
542182 Williams A, 246
560083 Williams A, 197
25203681 Williams A, 304
30000184 Williams AC, 253
539064 Williams AC, 221
25013955 Williams AD, 275
542130 Williams AD, 208
24929225 Williams AJB, 331
524510 Williams AM, 311
549650 Williams AM, 282
W1062421 Williams AMA, 247
518666 Williams AP, 109, 174
25234992 Williams B, 125
30222153 Williams B, 351
30155609 Williams BM, 239
Williams BNB, 391
562438 Williams C, 383
30142437 Williams CAG, 142
30140390 Williams CD, 226
551879 Williams CJ, 383
25201551 Williams CM, 162
24713597 Williams D, 320
30030321 Williams D, 331
565945 Williams D, 383
525953 Williams DA, 320
559748 Williams DC, 242
24877678 Williams DD, 202
24775604 Williams DE, 270
30018733 Williams DM, 257
24821690 Williams DP, 211
24840102 Williams DR, 253
565583 Williams DR, 291
461802 Williams DT, 383
30129977 Williams DW, 383
556120 Williams E, 358
547512 Williams EF, 240
563142 Williams ET, 246
24780344 Williams G, 199
562471 Williams G, 307
564061 Williams GA, 238
565401 Williams GA, 336
557589 Williams GG, 177
25025682 Williams GS, 238
24648991 Williams HG, 234
30037916 Williams HM, 383
25215062 Williams HR, 264
533168 Williams ID, 358
565846 Williams IR, 190
W1032431 Williams J, 257
561107 Williams J, 358
C33225 Williams JC, 383
30255001 Williams JE, 362
557590 Williams JG, 251
553430 Williams JG, 307
560377 Williams JJ, 256
536755 Williams JM, 138
545009 Williams JN, 234
558248 Williams JP, 304
552109 Williams JR, 244
30201384 Williams JS, 310
30196164 Williams K, 385
556842 Williams KAR, 344
30089145 Williams KJ, 253
24634821 Williams KJ, 331
561312 Williams KL, 246
525832 Williams LH, 115
30201381 Williams LT, 339
542271 Williams LT, 338
30130000 Williams LW, 253
562545 Williams M, 348
24683738 Williams MA, 383
511542 Williams MD, 115
25224790 Williams MGG, 238
563497 Williams ML, 383
25233946 Williams MO, 212
526598 Williams N, 383
561876 Williams N, 327
490686 Williams NDO, 305
550249 Williams O, 383
24690213 Williams P, 334
30141787 Williams P, 336
561305 Williams P, 358
C28475 Williams P, 383
559914 Williams PA, 216
25215909 Williams PAN, 129
552518 Williams PJ, 118
534624 Williams PN, 231
30011301 Williams PT, 202
30250418 Williams R, 362
549051 Williams RAD, 154
30120387 Williams RG, 172
554392 Williams RG, 234
550845 Williams RI, 249
30208674 Williams RM, 362
30056326 Williams RV, 260
563255 Williams S, 242
549901 Williams S, 383
30191705 Williams S, 385
30047046 Williams SA, 260
552519 Williams SA, 234
30060532 Williams SC, 211
532042 Williams SC, 115
30193379 Williams SE, 243
30174665 Williams SEL, 358
550846 Williams SJ, 242
561801 Williams SJ, 139
540471 Williams SL, 240
520727 Williams SR, 224
557592 Williams ST, 324
30169849 Williams TC, 178
562532 Williams TJ, 175
565584 Williams TOL, 304
565946 Williams V, 383
30130215 Williams WP, 285
30189554 Williams WS, 385

30138185 Winship CE, 269
565934 Winsor DM, 383
25199844 Winstanley CER, 191
30043091 Winstanley MC, 247
25185680 Winstanley PP, 285
518982 Winstanley RD, 141
30166468 Winstanley RJW, 243
547210 Winter AJ, 224
548065 Winter GQ, 324
30197985 Winter JD, 203
30063982 Winter JG, 238
30023362 Winter PF, 334
563810 Winter SJ, 359
25210946 Winterbourne HR, 253
25213239 Winterman CM, 164
555799 Winters J, 273
30109805 Winters MB, 139
520538 Winthrop IS, 249
30076237 Winton H, 330
538547 Winton PD, 304
30150809 Wire AM, 310
564881 Wire AM, 282
524419 Wirgman RR, 313
25232414 Wisbey JL, 291
564687 Wise AGM, 234
531993 Wise PA, 277
558836 Wise RG, 242
30077028 Wise SA, 203
558524 Wiseman G, 383
24775236 Wiseman RW, 257
545194 Witcombe ND, 205
24844201 Witham MA, 135
556486 Witherell AN, 169
30106263 Withers CM, 228
C041811B Withers DM, 238
542427 Withers RG, 331
25213862 Withey ER, 185
562309 Witko MJ, 208
555587 Witt JL, 216
30175081 Witts JC, 359
550925 Woellwarth NH, 303
554085 Woghiren ORE, 244
30085556 Wolf AP, 203
30075704 Wolfe AJ, 331
550852 Wolfe AP, 164
24561347 Wolfe I, 334
30184512 Wolfe NL, 274
562421 Wolfendale DL, 275
544444 Wolfenden GR, 172
555633 Wolstenholme NDZ, 234
25212585 Wong AKC, 334
532656 Wong AL, 392
552695 Wong C, 337
557682 Wood AA, 190
539969 Wood AC, 290
W1059948 Wood AF, 202
30024502 Wood AJ, 139
515445 Wood AJ, 359
533872 Wood AW, 199
24791591 Wood BJ, 238
30160457 Wood CA, 324
556989 Wood CJ, 242
499934 Wood CJM, 383
564259 Wood CK, 304
30251947 Wood CK, 362
562310 Wood CM, 154
W1058766 Wood CM, 247
559719 Wood CN, 234
560787 Wood DB, 256
24795148 Wood DG, 199
25215669 Wood DJ, 202
30077322 Wood DP, 182
25219534 Wood DV, 307
30199596 Wood EFW, 129
30146102 Wood EH, 131
557683 Wood G, 383
C08070 Wood G, 362
539067 Wood GM, 199
554886 Wood J, 359
30136676 Wood JAM, 335
503974 Wood JF, 383
563713 Wood JFC, 208
25190827 Wood JM, 225
30116427 Wood JM, 239
30146295 Wood JM, 203
C039530A Wood JR, 310
30224981 Wood JR, 385
547606 Wood K, 153
557687 Wood KM, 310
30152614 Wood L, 383
C35071 Wood L, 383
30089188 Wood LE, 219
564688 Wood LJ, 324
561378 Wood MA, 221
495263 Wood MD, 229, 329, 391
24789760 Wood MAJ, 159
551397 Wood MW, 197
558361 Wood NAP, 383
540739 Wood NI, 169
531927 Wood NMB, 172
30181938 Wood NS, 362
561437 Wood R, 359
562379 Wood R, 383
25210973 Wood RK, 253
30146023 Wood SE, 385
W1061776 Wood SF, 253
528795 Wood SM, 341
24713599 Wood TA, 199
553769 Wood TA, 246
555329 Wood TCA, 263
519147 Wood TM, 197
532043 Wood TO, 216
561440 Woodall D, 273
532068 Woodall NJ, 359
547447 Woodall S, 359
25028155 Woodall TG, 218
30161195 Woodbridge TG, 144
30178359 Woodcock MJ, 359
540410 Woodcock PP, 347
533577 Wooddisse RW, 43, 50, 109
563714 Woodfine JR, 177
524400 Woodham JM, 109
559721 Woodhams EW, 199
512771 Woodhams F, 359
514698 Woodhams J, 359
30025128 Woodhams NGB, 127
25231139 Woodhart JGH, 125
556849 Woodhead MG, 225
30047761 Woodhouse DB, 253
30254575 Woodhouse J, 362
530261 Woodhouse JIJ, 244
24722724 Woodhouse LP, 221
533523 Woodhouse S, 115
24688118 Woodings SJ, 208
557708 Woodley A, 214
549159 Woodley CR, 231
565454 Woodling R, 362
25210936 Woodman MK, 218
543417 Woodman S, 330
508258 Woodman TGW, 279
559232 Woodroffe AJ, 309
C26481 Woodruff A, 383
C37220 Woodruff NJ, 385
545888 Woods A, 383
25230320 Woods BNR, 211
30109791 Woods BS, 260
550675 Woods CBB, 282
W1055652 Woods CJ, 253
30113938 Woods CS, 238
546249 Woods DL, 205
528026 Woods DR, 244
564689 Woods DW, 322
30055899 Woods HJ, 212
559722 Woods JG, 242
561630 Woods K, 383
547793 Woods KL, 244
30153983 Woods MBR, 202
532761 Woods PD, 197
25166166 Woods SR, 253
25163476 Woodsend JK, 202
520832 Woodsmith N, 359
30028251 Woodward BJ, 253
555634 Woodward CM, 175
542809 Woodward DI, 240
553710 Woodward DJ, 269
24906524 Woodward M, 243
556487 Woodward MHJ, 132
30146944 Woodward MT, 212
527186 Woodward RJR, 138
30201490 Woodward SM, 307
558486 Woodward-Court AD, 269
30105896 Wookey CS, 383
520793 Woolcott D, 359
30160792 Woolcott J, 362
25234995 Wooldridge JP, 202
30101191 Wooldridge JPM, 238
562311 Wooldridge JT, 251
562549 Wooley R, 383
30015545 Woolf BF, 117
30022105 Woolgar JD, 335
536757 Woolgar NRE, 132
25210920 Woollan BAM, 218
30166880 Woolland FCL, 125
25028485 Woolley GJ, 218
30153526 Woolley LC, 263
530156 Woolley MMR, 132
25035978 Woolley PG, 362
551152 Woolley T, 244

Z